THE NEW DIRECT MARKETING

How to Implement a Profit-Driven Database Marketing Strategy

THE NEW DIRECT MARKETING

How to Implement a Profit-Driven Database Marketing Strategy

THIRD EDITION

DAVID SHEPARD ASSOCIATES, INC.

WITH INDIVIDUAL CONTRIBUTIONS BY
RAJEEV BATRA, PH.D.
RICHARD DEERE
ANDREW DEUTCH
ROBERT KENDRICK
GEORGE ORME
BRUCE RATNER, PH.D.
RUSS REMPALA
DHIRAJ SHARMA, PH.D.
DAVID SHEPARD

Boston, Massachusetts   Burr Ridge, Illinois
Dubuque, Iowa   Madison, Wisconsin   New York, New York
San Francisco, California   St. Louis, Missouri

Library of Congress Cataloging-in-Publication Data

The new direct marketing :   how to implement a profit-driven database
    marketing strategy / David Shepard Associates, Inc.; with
    individual contributions by Rajeev Batra . . . [et al.]. — 3rd ed.
        p.   cm.
    Includes index.
    ISBN 0-07-058056-1
    1. Direct marketing—Data processing.   2. Database marketing.
    3. Database management.   4. Direct marketing—Statistical methods.
    5. Internet marketing.   I. Batra, Rajeev.   II. David Shepard
    Associates.
    HF5415.126.N48   1998
    658.8′4—dc21   98-30382
                                                                          CIP

McGraw-Hill

A Division of The **McGraw·Hill** *Companies*

         5 6 7 8 9   BKM BKM   0 9 8 7 6 5 4 3

ISBN 0-07-058056-1

The sponsoring editor for this book was *Stephen Isaacs,* the editing supervisor was *John
M. Morriss,* and the production supervisor was *Suzanne W. B. Rapcavage.* It was set in
Times Roman by Progressive Information Technologies.

CONTENTS

Chapter Four

Sources and Uses of Marketing Data   42

Chapter Five

Relationship Marketing and How It Relates to the New Direct Marketing   64

Chapter Twenty-seven

What Do My Customers Look Like? Look at the Stars!   367

Chapter Twenty-eight

Alternative Direct Marketing Response Models: Linear Probability, Logit and Probit Models   371

Chapter Twenty-nine

CHAID for Interpreting a Logistic Regression Model   379

Chapter Thirty

Market Classification Modeling with Logistic Regression   390

Welcome to the third edition of *The New Direct Marketing*. If you are a new practitioner or a student, it's a pretty good bet that you missed the first two editions. But if you are a seasoned database marketer, or a graduate from one of the many universities that now teach direct marketing, you may have already purchased the first or second edition. Therefore, it's my job to tell you what's new in this edition and either convince you that it's time to upgrade, or if you've already purchased this book, reinforce your purchase decision.

What we believe to be unique about *The New Direct Marketing* is that it is the only text that attempts to cover all of the components of what is often referred to as either database marketing or relationship marketing or, most recently, interactive marketing; and some, who have been around longer, still refer to it as just direct marketing. Call it what you like, or do as we do and call it *the new direct marketing,* it encompasses a number of distinct disciplines: **marketing,** both general marketing and direct marketing; **technology,** broadly defined to include an understanding of data as well as an appreciation of all of the hardware and software options available to marketers today; **statistics and modeling,** the tools required for prediction and segmentation, both of which are critical components of the new direct marketing; and **economics,** both the traditional direct marketing economics used to evaluate media purchases and the newer economics, which focuses on increasing the lifetime value of individual customers.

So, if you've not read the earlier editions, here's the one reference you can turn to for an understanding of all the skills that are required to be a well-rounded database marketer.

On the other hand, if you have read one of the earlier editions, here's what's in the new edition for you.

Section One has been significantly expanded to include such topics as contract strategy, relationship marketing, branding, and customer service.

Section Two deals with data and the nontechnical issues associated with developing a marketing database. Three of the five chapters in this section have been revised, and two new chapters, one on data hygiene and householding and another on campaign management, have been added.

Section Three, devoted to technology, has been extensively revised and includes such topics as open systems, data warehouses, proprietary database management systems, client-server systems, and new trends in technology. All of the topics in this section are presented from the perspective of the nontechnical person who wants or needs to be involved in the decision-making processes that will impact the organization's ability to execute a database-driven marketing strategy.

Section Four is devoted to basic direct marketing statistics and predictive and segmentation modeling. This section has always been the signature section of the book, if only because it is the only text we know of that treats some pretty tough material from the unique perspective of the direct marketer. We decided that we would leave this section intact, and add an entirely new section devoted to more advanced modeling and analysis issues, such as genetic algorithms, unique uses for CHAID, a deeper treatment of modeling methodologies such as logistic regression, alternative response modeling techniques, and an introduction to more complex test evaluation procedures.

The last section of the book, Section Six, is devoted to economics and the role of modeling in the new direct marketing and has been revised to include such topics as the use of net present value in the calculation of lifetime value. In addition, we've added a chapter to this section which describes about 20 of the most prevalent modeling and database-driven applications of the new direct marketing. This material was developed from the two-day course we cosponsor with the DMA, the title of which, not surprisingly, is "The New Direct Marketing."

Finally, we would like to remind our readers that this text is a joint product of many authors. The fact of the matter is that no one person knows all the stuff required to implement all aspects of the new direct marketing. George Orme, Russ Rempala, Rajeev Batra, and Robert Kendrick all contributed to the opening section on marketing. Section Two was revised and expanded by Russ and Bob, adding to the work originally done by Andrew Deutch and Dhiraj Sharma. Russ and Dhiraj also collaborated on and expanded Section Three on technology. Section Four was authored by Bruce Ratner, who wrote the original chapters on statistics, predictive modeling, EDA, and neural nets; and by Rajeev, who wrote the chapter on classical segmentation. In Section Five, the six new chapters on modeling were written by Bruce, and Richard Deere wrote the chapter on testing. The material in this section was originally published in the *Journal of Database Marketing*.[1] And, finally, I take responsibility for Section Six, which includes the chapters on economics and the rule of modeling in a database environment.

Again, as in prior editions, a special thanks to our clients—you know who you are—who have lived with us through these last three years as we have jointly tried to expand the boundaries of database marketing applications.

David Shepard

---

1. *Journal of Database Marketing*, Henry Stuart Publications, various issues.

Marketing

Chapters 1 and 2 were written by George Orme; Chapters 3 and 4 by Andrew Deutch and Rus Rempala; Chapter 5 by Rus Rempala; Chapter 6 by Rajeev Batra; and Chapter 7 by Robert Kendrick.

CHAPTER 1

An Overview of the New Direct Marketing

INTRODUCTION

The marketing evolution that began a decade ago is still going strong.

We continue to see marketing change its primary concentration from identifying and exploiting opportunistic product "gaps" and product advantages to focusing on how to position products and customize added-value services to particular market niches.

We continue to see more and more marketers strive to improve performance by using consumer behavior, demographics, and lifestyle information to not only segment the marketplace, but also orchestrate highly targeted marketing communication strategies.

We continue to see more emphasis on customer service and customer loyalty programs as ways to strengthen and sustain customer relationships in today's crowded and highly competitive marketplace.

And we continue to see more and more companies de-massifying their marketing efforts in an attempt to more effectively and efficiently achieve their sales and profit goals.

Don Peppers and Martha Rogers in their book *The One to One Future* summarize what's going on this way[1]:

> The old paradigm, a system of mass production, mass media, and mass marketing, is being replaced by a totally new paradigm, a one-to-one economic system. The 1:1 future will be characterized by customized production, individually addressable media, and 1:1 marketing, totally changing the rules of business competition and growth.

The authors go on to note that in this new paradigm, instead of market share, the goal will be share of customer—one customer at a time. Additionally they suggest that the focus will be less on short-term profits derived from quarterly or annual transaction volumes, and more on the kind of profits that can be realized from long-term customer retention and lifetime values.

Simply put, product-driven marketing has become customer-focused marketing. Consequently, most businesses in the last few years have placed a major emphasis on knowing their customers and using what they know to drive future marketing decisions.

---

1. D. Peppers and M. Rogers, *The One to One Future* (New York: Doubleday, 1993), pp. 4–5.

Significantly, however, most marketers have recognized that to be able to truly address the issues and take advantage of the opportunities of this new age of marketing, it is imperative to understand both the methodology and the economics of database marketing. In some cases this means they will have to learn what data about their customers is important for analysis and decision making and what is not. In other cases it means they will need to expand their knowledge of how a database works, including what is involved in storing, accessing, manipulating, and analyzing data and ultimately turning it into valuable, strategic information.

It also means they will have to apply new thinking, embrace new marketing methods, and focus on the strategic implications of using database marketing in today's fragmented and competitive marketplace.

That is why we have written this book. Our purpose is not to add to what has already been written regarding the changing marketplace of the database marketing evolution, but to provide a practical guide on how to profitably use database technology and new, innovative direct and database marketing methods to become smarter, more efficient, and more effective marketers. As such, it is a handbook for direct marketing companies and users of direct marketing methods.

It is important to note that direct marketing used to be something only direct marketing or direct mail companies did. However, as name and address files were expanded to include huge amounts of marketing information, and as companies began to see the potential marketing benefits that would result from building databases of customers and prospects, the scope and technical complexity of the tasks required to implement marketing programs increased dramatically.

Consequently, the term *database marketing* became a more accurate description of the processes involved, and it has become synonymous with the term *direct marketing* among both traditional and nontraditional practitioners.

Yet for many people, the word *database* has a very strong data processing connotation. In fact, although it is true that advanced computer systems, including database management software and powerful computer hardware, are required to implement the most sophisticated database marketing programs, we intentionally chose not to title this book *Database Marketing* in order to emphasize the broader nature of the new direct marketing. Data processing resources are only one part of the new direct marketing equation, which, when all parts are working together, can dramatically improve the marketing effectiveness of both traditional and nontraditional direct marketing practitioners.

Now we need to define exactly what the new direct marketing is and how companies are using it to enhance their marketing effectiveness.

THE NEW DIRECT MARKETING—WHAT IS IT?

The new direct marketing is an information-driven marketing process, made possible by database technology, that enables marketers to develop, test, implement, measure, and appropriately modify customized marketing programs and strategies.

To implement the new direct marketing you need to know how to:

- Identify and gather relevant data about customers and prospects.
- Use database technology to transform raw data into powerful and accessible marketing information.
- Apply statistical techniques to customer and prospect databases to analyze behavior, isolate relatively homogeneous market segments, and score and rank individuals in terms of their probability of behaving in a variety

of predictable ways (responding, buying, returning, paying, staying or leaving, and so on).

- Evaluate the economics of gathering, manipulating, and analyzing data and capitalize on the economics of developing and implementing data-driven marketing programs.

- Creatively act on the marketing opportunities that emerge from these processes to develop individual customer relationships and to build business.

THE PREMISE OF THE NEW DIRECT MARKETING

Strategically, the new direct marketing is based on the premise that not all customers are alike and that by gathering, maintaining, and analyzing detailed information about customers and prospects, marketers can identify key market segments and optimize the process of planning, pricing, promoting, and consummating an exchange between sellers and buyers that satisfies both individual and organizational objectives.

Given the above premise, the new direct marketing is much broader in scope than what has been regarded traditionally as either direct marketing or database marketing. In the past, direct marketing has been distinguishable from other marketing disciplines because of its emphasis on initiating a direct relationship between a buyer and a seller, a relationship that until recently centered primarily on the exchange of goods and services.

Such a relationship, although often beginning with efforts across various channels of communication and media (e.g., TV, direct mail, print, and so on), was almost always fulfilled through only one *direct* channel of distribution (i.e., mail order). As such it did not involve any intermediary. Significantly, the fact that there was no intermediary resulted in marketers referring to this type of marketing activity as being "closed-loop"; i.e., there was a direct, uninterrupted, measurable communications and distribution channel between the buyer and the seller.

However, in today's marketing environment, with proliferating products, crowded supermarket and retail shelves, overstuffed mailboxes, converging channels of distribution, and the increasing demand for greater marketing efficiencies, smart marketers are not just using the new direct marketing to efficiently consummate a sale; they are also using it in a variety of other ways.

For example, an analysis of past sampling results for a major health and beauty aids company indicated that the best converters (those people who became steady users of the company's brand after they were sampled) were mostly above a certain age, and most often members of slightly more affluent households. Based on these findings, the company stopped mailing certain underperforming segments and significantly improved its marketing efficiencies by targeting according to age and income. These improvements led to this effort becoming the company's primary promotion vehicle in key strategic markets. Moreover, because of the valuable type of store traffic these promotions produce, the company has been able to negotiate better in-store displays and more shelf space during such promotion events.

Another leading package goods marketer has taken targeted promotions even further. In this case, after reviewing the findings from a comprehensive segmentation study, the marketer found a significant number of clusters wherein volume and usage behavior were correlated with certain attitudes about the brand the marketer was promoting and how it fit certain lifestyles. Using a combination of usage and demographic data, the marketer first estimated the size and value of each of these segments and then, using usage and demographic data available from Nielsen, created a customized brand development index (BDI) for each segment of each major market area. Then, depending on the makeup of the market, the marketer developed different types of marketing activities. In those areas where the brand had high levels of loyalty and was the dominant brand, the marketer ran cross-promotions with other brands in the company to optimize the company's chances of capturing a higher share of the customer's overall grocery purchases. In areas where the brand was less dominant, in order to increase usage the marketer offered extra incentives to purchase the brand. And in those areas where the index showed the brand's usage was well below average, the marketer emphasized free trial promotions.

What makes this example noteworthy is that the brand first developed a BDI at the segment level and then used its information to more effectively allocate its promotion dollars and not simply treat all markets and all customers the same.

These examples substantiate why for so many marketers exchanging information is becoming almost as important as exchanging goods and services. In some cases, they are establishing an ongoing dialogue with customers that goes well beyond acknowledging a customer relationship or nurturing customer loyalty. Such dialogues make use of in-package surveys, special questionnaires, opinion polls, and annual tracking studies, as well as point of sale (POS) programs that automatically reward buyers with discounts and special offers while electronically recording what they are purchasing.

Significantly, such dialogues facilitate gathering information of value to both consumers and marketers. For consumers, these dialogues not only provide a mechanism to register preferences regarding merchandise and method of purchase, but also allow them to help mold new products and services based on their interests, lifestyles, and purchase patterns. Additionally, these dialogues enable consumers to continually make known their perceptions and attitudes about a company's products and services. Thus, they offer consumers the chance to play a more active, ongoing role in the buyer-seller relationship and help create a stronger affinity between consumers and companies.

For marketers, these dialogues produce more timely and accurate information about usage and buying habits. For example, they enable companies to track individual usage behavior and identify individual purchase habits so marketers can account for a specific product's or brand's share of a consumer's total category purchases.

In summary, today's marketers are using attitude, lifestyle, and usage information to develop *customized* marketing strategies and programs, both for *individuals* and, where more appropriate, for groups of customers; no longer do marketers have to settle for a single solution or program to best fit their complex marketing situations.[2]

In addition to capturing information, the new direct marketing also enables marketers to use it more easily. Until now, customer data and product data were usually only "linked" after countless hours of analysis and extrapolation. Even the most sophisticated marketers had a tough time matching product sales and

---

2. At times the new direct marketing acts at the individual level; at other times it acts at the group level. For example, in Chapter 5 on relationship marketing we tend to focus on the need to respond to individual customer actions; however, when planning promotions we almost always first place individuals into groups based on a combination of demographic, behavior, and attitudinal information, and then all individuals within the same group are promoted to in essentially the same way, if not with the identical promotion.

individual customer performance. But now, using the new direct marketing, marketers can first marry product sales and data concerning individual customer attributes and characteristics and then, using statistical techniques such as those discussed in Chapters 17 through 22, develop ways to quantify market size and market demand for products or services.

Significantly, companies that are able to marry such individual customer information on an ongoing basis can more accurately and quickly evaluate opportunities and precisely identify who is buying what, how often, and why. And as noted above, they can connect this information to those elements within the market mix that are most likely to motivate consumers to switch or stay with a given brand.

AN OVERVIEW OF SOME OF THE ADVANTAGES AND PRACTICES OF THE NEW DIRECT MARKETING

Lead Grading

One advantage of the new direct marketing is that it allows marketers to know more about various types of customers and prospects and to "grade" prospects by determining, as Lester Wunderman says, if a prospect is willing to buy, able to buy, and ready to buy your goods or services.

A good example of this practice is the way some automotive manufacturers encourage prospects to qualify themselves during the initial stages of the information exchange process. These automotive advertisers often ask prospects to indicate when they are planning to purchase so the sellers can gauge a prospect's readiness to buy. They also ask how much the consumers are willing to spend and what the consumers are currently driving and how long they have been driving it so the sellers can develop a consideration set—the competitive makes and models the consumers are also likely to be considering aside from the company's particular model(s). Then these advertisers use this information to develop a superior competitive position that not only highlights the benefits of their own makes and models, but also is customized to the prospects' needs and wants.

It is important to note that oftentimes the information that companies capture not only is used to grade leads, but also can be used later to reactivate leads and target follow-up promotions. In Chapter 3, we describe how financial services firms have found that the more they learn about customers and prospects, the better able they are to trigger programs that promote appropriate products to selected audiences at the most opportune times.

Customized Targeting at the Right Time

Another way the new direct marketing can help marketers is by enabling them to reach consumers with the right product and the right offer at the right time.

Negative option book and record clubs illustrate this point well. As a *Wall Street Journal* article explains, some clubs no longer send the same set of options to all members. Instead, as Markus Wilhelm of Doubleday Book Club noted, "Segmentation is the wave of the future."[3] Today both Book-of-the-Month Club

---

3. "For the Nation's Troubled Book Clubs, Main Selections of This Year Is Change," *The Wall Street Journal*, July 25, 1992, Section B, p.1.

and Doubleday customize offers based on a member's previous selections and purchases as well as demographic and lifestyle information captured through previous communications.

Two outcomes are resulting from such customization. First, the clubs are seeing a reduction in attrition because members receive selections better suited to their tastes and interests. Second, members are buying more books.

Thus, customizing by treating different types of members differently not only helps minimize the expense of sending offers that are not appropriate for certain customers or prospects, but also helps enhance the company's relationship because it encourages the customer to feel that "this company understands me and knows what I like, what I am interested in."

New Information and Past Results Help Formulate Strategies

The new direct marketing is more than just using a marketing database to selectively target offers to customers and prospects; it allows marketers to continually incorporate new information and results back into the database.

Marketers record each response in the database so they can develop future strategies and executions using the collective results of previous efforts. This means companies can allocate marketing resources based on current, up-to-date results that include a comprehensive performance history for each customer.

Consequently, marketers are able to develop highly targeted customer acquisition and marketing retention programs and, more importantly, profitably customize the sequence and flow of marketing communications.

Using the new direct marketing, leading catalogers have found that they can optimally regulate the number of times they promote to a customer. By selectively targeting, they can also *customize* which version of the catalog a customer receives, the complete catalog or a smaller special-interest catalog. As a result, they have been able to help offset continually rising costs and maximize profits.

Information Can Drive New Programs and Fuel New Revenue Sources

The new direct marketing can also be used by enterprising third-party marketers to bring together companies and customers.

American Express, for example, created a program that used a bill insert promotion to let card members know that buying a new car has "never been easier" because they could use their American Express cards to charge their down payments. The insert then listed over 25 import and domestic manufacturers where the card would be honored.

The card members were asked to indicate which vehicles they would like to know more about so American Express could arrange for *information* and literature to be sent from the manufacturer. Over 100,000 responses were generated.

Aside from demonstrating how the card can produce qualified leads for automotive manufacturers, this effort also enabled American Express to use the information to identify the characteristics of card members who were interested in certain types of cars. Using statistical modeling, American Express was able to create profiles of who responded for each type of car and then segment their entire file accordingly.

As a result, American Express could use its findings to work with key manufacturers to help them target promotions to American Express card members who would most likely respond, and to provide special incentives to charge the down payment for their new purchase on the American Express card.

This is an excellent example of how using the new direct marketing can help everyone win. Consumers win because they can conveniently choose which cars they want to know more about. The automotive manufacturers win because they receive qualified leads. American Express wins because card usage expands when the number of places that honor the card and the number of ways card members can use the card increase.

Information Can Foster New Services and Generate Repeat Orders

Another way companies are using the new direct marketing is to develop special "services" to help make it easy for customers to buy more, more often.

For example, a number of catalog companies now assign customers a unique customer ID number so that each time a customer calls or places an order, customer service representatives can easily and quickly access the customer's record and avoid asking for the same information over and over again.

Not only can these representatives use a person's promotion history and information about products purchased to customize cross-selling opportunities, but they can also use previous purchases as the basis for offering customers a new service, as some gift catalogers have. A leading food cataloger, a well-known fruit cataloger, and a Maine holiday wreath company all send last year's gift list, including the special message associated with each gift, to customers to help them conveniently send the same gifts the following year. For many consumers the receipt of last year's list reminds them to place their order again, and they oftentimes add new names before the revised list is sent back.

Thus, with one well-targeted and service-oriented promotion effort, these companies capture more business and differentiate themselves from other competitors in their category.

Ongoing Communications Efforts Can Increase Customer Loyalty

For many companies another major advantage of the new direct marketing is that it offers the ability to establish a two-way communication with the consumer through a variety of channels. As noted earlier, the purpose of such communication is not only to generate a sale, but also to manage a relationship and develop greater customer allegiance and brand loyalty.

Engendering customer loyalty has become vital to many companies. Good customers are too valuable and too hard to find for companies to risk losing one by being passive, indifferent, or indistinguishable from the competition.

Bob Stone, in his classic book *Successful Direct Marketing,* points out that the heart of building and maintaining customer loyalty is *customized persuasion.*[4] Based on the premise that all customers are not created equal—oftentimes the majority of repeat business for goods and services comes from a relatively small percent of a customer base—proponents of customer loyalty programs target specific marketing efforts to this most fertile percent of their database.

---

4. B. Stone, *Successful Direct Marketing*, 4th ed. (Chicago: NTC Publishing Group, 1988).

It is interesting to note, from a historical perspective, that although book clubs such as Book-of-the-Month Club and the Literary Guild have been offering dividend or bonus points as a means of rewarding purchases for as long as anyone can remember, airlines were among the first nontraditional direct marketers to recognize the opportunity to provide rewards to help retain the loyalty of selected customers. They realized that the more a customer purchases their product and the greater the rewards, the greater the incentive for these customers to keep purchasing their product.

More recently, some marketers have expanded the scope of their reward programs by forming alliances with other programs. One such program offered by American Airlines and Citibank VISA enables members not only to earn points for each mile flown, but also to earn miles for every dollar a member spends with a special *American Advantage VISA card.* In addition, members also can earn bonus miles for flying certain routes, staying in certain hotels, or renting from certain car rental companies. American Airlines offers a similar alliance option with MCI regarding long distance phone calls.

Significantly, these marketers are learning that, aside from constantly keeping in touch with their members, one of the keys to success is targeting promotions and bonus offers based on previous purchases, buying patterns, and the member's stated preferences. Just as with the book clubs' negative option selections that we noted earlier, the customer wants to be recognized as an individual and treated accordingly.

In the future, it will be the companies that can gather, store, and use such information to their competitive advantage by developing new strategies and carefully targeted programs that will benefit the most from the new direct marketing.

Moreover, these companies will develop an ongoing dialogue with their customers and prospects because they know that every contact is an opportunity for an exchange of information and that although a particular effort might not produce a sale itself, the cumulative effect of such communications definitely has an impact on consumer attitudes and loyalty. Thus, managing the communications mix and developing different customer contact strategies for different types of customers has become an important element in the new direct marketing.

SUMMARY

Over the years, regardless of whether marketers operated in a direct marketing environment or the mass marketing arena, one of their major responsibilities has been to develop strategies utilizing products or services that offer the best opportunity of achieving a company's overall business goals.

Today, in an information marketing environment, marketers can execute this responsibility with more precision than ever before. Marketers are analyzing more relevant and timely customer-level information. They are correlating customer-level data with traditional measures of off-the-shelf purchases. They are creating ongoing customer dialogues to funnel relevant information to the marketing database. They are enhancing their databases with survey, demographic, psychographic, and lifestyle data. They are using highly sophisticated mathematical segmentation and predictive models. They are identifying who is buying what, and how often. They are measuring which elements within the marketing mix motivate consumers to make a purchase decision to switch or stay with a given brand. In short, today's information-driven marketers have all the tools necessary to develop new products and new marketing strategies in ways unheard of just a few years ago.

It is important to note, however, that although marketers have access to more powerful tools and more information than ever before, growing consumer sensitivities regarding the misuse of such information seriously threaten future practices.

Consequently, although it seemed just a few years ago that the new direct marketing would only improve sales as more companies came to understand the power of the marketing database in an information-driven economy, today database marketers must find a way to decelerate the growing perception that their activities invade people's "right to privacy" if they are going to be truly successful in the years ahead.

CHAPTER 2
Contact Strategy

INTRODUCTION

In Chapter 1 we defined the new direct marketing, covered its key steps, and highlighted a number of ways marketers are using it to acquire and retain customers. In this chapter we will discuss the role of contact strategy and how companies are using a carefully orchestrated series of contacts with their customers to improve their marketing efforts.

CONTACT STRATEGY—WHAT IS IT?

At its core, contact strategy deals with using information about customer purchases, promotion patterns, interests, and preferences to not only profitably regulate the sequence and frequency of customer contact, but also appropriately customize the offer, creative thrust, and positioning of contacts.

Today's use of contact strategy differs from traditional customer management because all of the key decision criteria are based at the customer or individual level. Whether a customer is included in a promotion or campaign is determined by the incremental profit to be gained from that contact for that customer.

In the past, this was not always the case, as many times marketers grouped customers together based on product ownership and then regulated promotion based on cross-sell opportunities—all customers who did not own Product A would be promoted Product A regardless of their probability of ever buying Product A.

Or in other cases marketers treated all new customers the same regardless of what product or products they bought with the first purchase. As such, customers who bought products outside the mainstream of a company's product line and probably were not very likely to be interested in the majority of the company's offerings were treated the same as any other customer.

But today this is changing. Today marketers are regulating customer contacts by creating model scores to assess the probability of purchase for a forthcoming promotion based on a combination of how long a person has been a customer, what products a person has bought, what a person's previous response rates have been, and what his or her purchase patterns are. Using these probability scores, they then evaluate the return on investment (ROI) for each customer for any particular promotion or series of promotions so they can optimize the yield they get from each customer. Customers who do not have scores above the required ROI goal are not included in the promotion.

To provide a clear understanding of the scope of contact strategy as well as how it applies to different types of marketers later on in this chapter, we will look at three different examples: a traditional cataloger, an automobile manufacturer, and a consumer products company.

First, however, it is important to discuss what types of information marketers use to develop contact strategies. It should be noted that for ease of presentation, this discussion centers on simple, intuitive ways to group customers into actionable segments. It does not cover the use of statistical techniques or quantitative methods as tools to analyze behavior or create segments. In other words, it's possible to read this chapter without first reading the statistical sections that show you how to use models of one type or another to predict behavior or create customer segments.

However, the reader should not get too comfortable with these intuitive "back-of-the-envelope/spreadsheet" techniques, because the modeling tools do produce better results.

RFM: THE WORKHORSE VARIABLES OF BOTH THE NEW AND THE OLD DIRECT MARKETING

Regardless of the tools you'll use to help you think about contact strategy, the key variables you'll need to consider will include purchase data (recency, frequency, monetary value, and product) and promotion history data. You may also find yourself using demographic data and survey data that will help you understand your customers' and prospects' perceptions of you and your competition. Eventually, by the end of this book, we'll get around to explaining the many ways in which all of these bits and pieces of information can be used together. But for now let's focus on one variable at a time and build up from there.

Using Purchase History Information to Develop Contact Strategies

Time or Tenure of Being a Customer
Using the dimension of time might be the easiest way for marketers to use customer information to start to segment customers for the purposes of developing customized contact strategies. For example, *new* first-time buyers can be isolated out from the rest of the file and treated as a special segment; i.e., send them a "welcome new customer" package, for example, as an early contact. Or for these first buyers, perhaps an appropriate strategy is to include a welcome kit with their first product shipment to help stimulate a repeat purchase; including a brief survey with the welcoming package is also not a bad idea and one that we'll propose a number of times, later on in the book.

For customers who have been with the company a longer period of time, some marketers have found that an excellent contact opportunity is a special effort designed to celebrate the anniversary of their original purchase date, or acknowledge a customer's status as a "longtime, valued" customer.

The key point here is that segmenting the customer file by how long each customer has been a customer can, in and of itself, lead to different contact strategies.

Total Sales Dollars and Total Sales Dollars over Time
Total sales dollars is probably the most often used criterion for deciding who are or are not good customers, since it answers the question "How much money have they spent with us since they have been customers?"

Simply stated, evaluating customers according to their total lifetime sales dollars over a certain period of time can easily become the basis for a customer contact strategy. One way marketers do this is to take total dollars spent and divide it by time, say, total months on file. This calculation will result in a revenue "velocity" indicator for each customer.

For example, a customer who has spent $100 with you and been on your file 2 months would have an entirely different score than a customer who has spent that same $100 but been a customer for 20 months.

Intuitively, it would seem to make sense that the customer with the higher revenue velocity score ($100/2 = 50$, $100/20 = 5$) would be a better customer to target for repeat business, and thus a better candidate for more frequent contacts in a contact strategy program.

Product

In addition to looking at dollars, it is important to take product ownership into consideration when developing a contact strategy, if for no other reason than to avoid offending customers by recommending they buy a product they already have.

Obviously if you are a company that offers a portfolio of products, and most of your promotion efforts include multiple-product promotions (i.e., catalogs), selecting which product to promote to which segment is less of a problem. But for financial services companies, insurance companies, automobile manufacturers, and other marketers which promote bigger-ticket items, it is critical that any contact strategy include the ability to carefully regulate both the frequency and the sequencing of single-product promotions.

Contact strategy for insurance direct marketers, for example, focuses on first defining a segment using a combination of product ownership, eligibility, and suppression rules and then using model scores to assess the probability of achieving the highest ROI for each customer for each product.

Every customer who is eligible for a given promotion (i.e., is a resident of a state where the company is licensed to sell its products), who does not have a do-not-contact code, and whose last contact date is outside the too-soon-to-contact window is assigned a probability score for responding to any and all products he or she is eligible for. The marketers then calculate an ROI value for each person for each product by taking each person's estimated response rate times the expected first-year revenue rate for each product.

Product Ownership over Time

Aside from looking at product ownership, another helpful way to use product information is to evaluate customers according to how many products they own and how long they have been customers.

One direct marketer of insurance, for example, was able to identify certain customers who in essence were "too" responsive to cross-sells and upsells. While at first they seemed to be highly profitable, they proved to be just the opposite when many of these recent new customers (less than one year) who had purchased multiple products actually canceled *all* of their policies.

Subsequent research revealed that a primary reason for canceling was the exorbitant combined monthly premium amount. Essentially, when these customers had only one policy, they did not notice the relatively small amount each month on their credit card, but when they began seeing the "sizable" amount for three different policies each month, they realized they had to cut back. Unfortunately for this insurance provider these customers then were unable to decide which one to cancel, so they decided to cancel all of them.

Based on this situation this insurance company developed a much more targeted and customized policy owner marketing cross-selling and upselling contact strategy. Customer promotions were carefully regulated depending on the length of time customers owned a particular policy, their payment history, and their balance-to-credit-limit ratio on their credit card. Customers with balances that were closing in on their credit limit were no longer included in any cross-sell promotions.

Orders

When using a customer's order history as a criterion to segment the file, it is important to look at both the frequency and regularity of orders. The point here is that while some customers don't buy as frequently as others, it might be that they buy in highly regular patterns, even if they buy only during certain times of the year.

One cataloger found that by analyzing the ship to addresses on their database they were able to identify a very valuable segment of customers who primarily bought twice a year once in one location, and once in another. Significantly a review of these *snowbirds*, that is, customers who apparently were migrating each year from the cold dreary winters of the north to the warm climes of the south and southwest regions of the United States, suggested they could be more profitable if they were contacted less, contacted closer to the times when they had ordered in the past, and contacted at the right seasonal address.

Using Promotion History to Define Contact Eligibility and Propensity to Respond

In addition to purchase history, promotion history can help develop meaningful, actionable contact strategy segments.

Many companies have rules, for example, that require each customer have a "rest" period of a certain number of days or months between any two promotions. In addition, companies also have rules regulating how often within a certain time period the same product can be promoted. Consequently, promotion history in its simplest form is often used to define who is eligible for an upcoming contact.

Promotion history can also be very helpful in creating market segments. Some marketers have found that just tracking how many times a person has been promoted can lead to improved contact strategy development. Essentially, people who have been on the file a long time, have not bought, but have been contacted at an above average rate are likely to be sending an important message about their interest in remaining a customer.

One technique some marketers have developed to use promotion history data is to create a propensity indicator for each customer that calculates a person's response rate over time.

Customer A, who has been promoted 6 times and bought twice during the last 12 months ($2/6/12 = .027$), and Customer B, who has been promoted 6 times and bought twice during the last 18 months ($2/6/18 = .018$), are different, with Customer A being the better customer. And Customer C, who has been on the file 6 months, been promoted 4 times, and bought twice, is even better ($2/4/6 = .08$)

The point here is that even without using sophisticated modeling methods, marketers can use simple calculations to help rank a customer's propensity to respond, and in turn use this information to create segments worthy of future contact.

Another type of data—demographic and lifestyle data—can also be used to identify different types of market segments that should be treated differently, oftentimes when marketers do not have access to customer-level transaction data.

Using Demographic Data to Create Actionable Market Segments for the Purpose of Contact Strategy

The goal here is to create relatively homogeneous segments based on a series of lifestyle and/or demographic characteristics, i.e., gender, marital status, age, income, home value, presence of children, educational level, and so on.

For example, one very simple classification scheme that we've seen variations of used a number of times, for a number of different companies in different industries, is created by using a simple 12-way combination of demographic and lifestyle attributes as follows:

- *Young moderate singles*. Males and females between the ages of 21 and 29, unmarried, that earn between $25 and $40K annually
- *Young affluent singles*. Males and females between the ages of 21 and 29, unmarried, that earn over $40K annually
- *Young moderate marrieds*. Couples between the ages of 21 and 29, married, that earn between $25 and $50K annually
- *Young affluent marrieds*. Couples between the ages of 21 and 29, married, that earn over $50K annually
- *Middle-age moderate families*. Families between the ages of 30 and 49, that earn between $25 and $50K annually, with a presence of children
- *Middle-age affluent families*. Families between the ages of 30 and 49, that earn over $50K annually, with a presence of children
- *Older moderate singles*. Males and females between the ages of 50 and 65, unmarried, that are still working and earn between $25 and $40K annually
- *Older affluent singles*. Males and females between the ages of 50 and 65, unmarried, that are still working and earn over $40K annually
- *Older moderate families*. Families between the ages of 50 and 65, that are still working and earn between $25 and $50K annually
- *Older affluent families*. Families between the ages of 50 and 65, that are still working and earn over $50K annually.
- *Retired singles*. Males and females over 65, unmarried and not working full time
- *Retired couples*. Couples over 65 that are not working full time

Companies have found that by using age, marital status, income, and presence of children, they could create segments that were reasonably different from one another, and yet large enough to warrant the targeting of special offers, customized pricing and positioning of products, and different creative thrusts.

Combining Both Purchase History and Demographic Data Can Lead to New Opportunities

Continuing with the above example, companies have also found, not surprisingly, that when they used a combination of purchase data and demographic data, they could develop even more actionable segments.

Based on these behavior/demographic segments, marketers can create new contact strategies for each segment. For example, the best-performing segments can be contacted via mail and phone every month, while those segments that were underperforming could be contacted less frequently, or less expensively, at least until more profitable strategies could be tested and implemented.

Using Attitudinal Data to Create Actionable Market Segments for the Purpose of Contact Strategy

Still another type of data—attitudinal data—can also be used to identify different types of market segments that should be treated differently. Interestingly, this type of data is probably the least used of all data types when it comes to supporting contact strategy, in part because of the long lead times sometimes involved in fielding the research survey required to collect it, and also because many marketers, due to their inexperience or problems with using the data to support contact strategy, have a hard time cost-justifying the financial investment.

Importantly, however, many marketers who have conducted studies of this type have found that just gaining a better understanding of their customers in general, let alone certain segments of their customer base, leads to new ideas about ways to modify creative thrusts, offers, and marketing communications.

Traditionally, whatever the reason one is interested in using attitudinal data—to better understand motivations for purchase, barriers to purchase, ways to enhance a brand's positioning against particular competitor, or ways to leverage brand equity among a highly loyal market segment or within a specific market category—an attitudinal segmentation study begins with a research survey consisting of often hundreds of questions being fielded against a random sample of a customer file.

Using the data captured in the survey, practically any customer file can be segmented into four to eight relatively homogeneous groups. Needless to say, these segments should differ in terms of their members' needs and wants, competitive sets, purchase rates, customer satisfaction, and so on.

Usually in addition to quantifying the attitudinal attributes for each segment, a key step in the study is to profile each segment using demographic and behavioral variables as descriptors. Unfortunately, however, many times these descriptors overlap from one segment to another, and at best can only be viewed as *directional* rather than exclusive.

An insurance company, for example, fielded a segmentation to better understand the needs and wants of extremely loyal and loyal life insurance customers. Significantly, a key finding of the study was that extremely loyal customers averaged much higher face amounts than less loyal customers, preferred to deal with agents, and attitudinally thought insurance was a great value and they could always use more. Less loyal customers did not rank the agents as being so important, and did not think they needed any more insurance.

Interestingly, while the demographic profiles of these segments were different—extremely loyal customers were older, were better educated, and more often held professional and managerial jobs—both groups had their share of what could be termed "average" customers, that is, people between the ages of 35 and 50, married parents earning under $75,000 a year.

As a result, although the segments did differ demographically, the fact that both had a significant number of so-called "average" customers made such differences fuzzy. This fuzziness has two consequences. First, it makes it hard to use behavior and demographic data to predict segment membership, and, second, it oftentimes means that creative strategies targeted to each segment do not do dramatically better than "generic" control creative efforts which are not targeted to any one segment.

One way to deal with this problem is to use each of the above types of data—behavioral, demographic, and attitudinal—sequentially to identify a customer along three separate dimensions.

Here's how such a process works:

- Start with behavior first. Create three to five segments. In the case of one retail company, customers were assigned to categories based on sales within the last year; new customers, those on the file less than six months, were put into their own behavior segment.
- Next, take demographics into consideration. The retail company referred to above used a simple demographic scheme, similar to the one defined earlier, but combined segments into just six major groups.
- Then focus on attitude. The retail company conducted phone research against the most heavily populated segments to probe their attitudes about shopping in the store and specifically why certain segments seemed to satisfy only a minimum of their total requirements through the store, even though the store offered a complete line of clothing and home furnishing items.

No attempt was made to create attitudinal segments within the behavioral/demographic segments, although such segments might exist and might even be predictable. At this stage, the retailer had more than enough information to go on to develop strategies and programs to increase sales from customers within each of the major segments.

The above process is one solution to overcoming the deficiencies of implementing contact strategies and marketing programs built around traditional segmentation practices. Among its benefits is the fact that it is relatively easy to do and also not costly to perform. Much of the expense of fielding the research is kept to a minimum since the surveys are conducted over the phone to a small targeted group rather than a large random sample.

Additionally, sequentially creating the segments, one dimension at a time, by using each data type independently, enables a company to dramatically improve its understanding of its customer file so that it develops more meaningful and compelling creative thrusts and targeted offers for each segment.

Specific Examples of the Role of Contact Strategy
1. The Role of Contact Strategy for Today's Cataloger

For years catalog companies have successfully demonstrated that using a customer's purchase history data, and more specifically, a combination of *recency* of purchases, *frequency* of purchases, and the *monetary* value of purchases (RFM), can be an extremely effective way to choose who should and should not be promoted by the next catalog. Recent buyers generally perform better than customers who have not purchased for a while. Frequent buyers, even those who haven't bought lately, are often better than infrequent, less recent buyers when it comes to subsequent purchases. And big spenders on average perform better than those customers with lower lifetime dollars.

What follows are the traditional steps involved in performing basic RFM segmentation. The intent here is not to suggest that RFM is the recommended strategy or technique for segmenting a life; it's not—at least in our opinion it's not. Rather our purpose in presenting them is to explain what steps are involved in developing RFM cells and how, once they are created, they can support a contact strategy.

- The first step is to create unique segments or cells based on some combination of RFM variables, say, five recency variables, four frequency variables, and four monetary value variables. For example:
  - *Recency.* 0–3 months, 4–6 months, 6–12 months, 12–18 months, more than 18 months
  - *Frequency.* 1 order, 2 orders, 3 orders, 4 or more orders
  - *Monetary value.* <$50, $50–100, $100–250, more than $250
- The next step is to determine the following for each cell:
  - The number of people in the cell, i.e., the *size* of the cell
  - The number of pieces mailed, i.e., *circulation*, for the last promotion effort
  - The number of *orders* generated from the last promotion for this cell
  - The resulting *response rate* from the last promotion for this cell
  - The *revenue* generated from the last promotion for this cell
  - The *average dollars per order* generated from the last promotion for this cell
  - The *marketing cost* for the last promotion effort to this cell
  - The *revenue per thousand catalogs* mailed from this promotion for each cell
  - The revenue divided by the marketing cost, *R:MC*, from the last promotion for each cell
- The next step is to compare the performance of each cell using the above criteria. For example, hypothetically for the cell consisting of recency 4–6 months, frequency 1 order, monetary value <$50, the output might be as follows:
  - Size: 15,000
  - Circulation: 30,000 (each name was mailed twice)
  - Orders: 450
  - Response rate: 1.5 percent
  - Revenue: $52,000
  - Average order: $115
  - Marketing cost: $18,000
  - REV/(000) cat. mld.: $1,733
  - R:MC: (52,000/18,000): 2.88, which means this cell produced $2.88 in revenue for marketing dollar invested
- And for another cell, say, recency 6–12 months, frequency 2 orders, monetary value $50–150, the output might look like this:
  - Size: 21,000
  - Circulation: 42,000 (each name was mailed twice)
  - Orders: 900
  - Response rate: 2.1 percent
  - Revenue: $99,000
  - Average order: $110
  - Marketing cost: $25,200

- REV/(000) cat. mld.: $2,357
- R:MC: (52,000/18,000): 3.92, which means this cell produced $3.92 in revenue for marketing dollar invested

- The next step is to rank all 80 cells according to these key measures. Rather than develop one huge spreadsheet listing all 80 cells (5 × 4 × 4) and each of the above criteria for each cell, most catalogers simplify the analysis by comparing one or two key measures for each cell, say, size and revenue. So, for example, using a cumulative percent of total measure, the cataloger can determine what percent of the total customer file each cell represents and more importantly what percent of the total revenue that cell generated for the last promotion. This simplified spreadsheet allows the cataloger to not only compare each cells' performance, but more importantly determine which cells account for the majority of revenue.

- The last step in the process is to select which cells will be included in the next promotion. At this point most catalogers have a relatively easy time choosing the first 75 percent of the names they will contact. These are the biggest cells, which also produce large volumes of revenue. The harder part is deciding how to fill in the remaining names and from which cells. To help with this situation most catalogers take portions of cells rather than the whole cell and choose cells based on their previous rev per (000) catalogs mailed. Any cell that falls below a certain threshold is not mailed.

The above approach has worked for years. But some catalogers have found that it can be improved in the following ways.

- First, some catalogers have found a way to add product data to the variables that are used to create the segments. This has helped identify certain product affinities that distinguish high-performing repeat buyers from the rest of the file.

- Second, realizing the arbitrary nature of RFM analyses—i.e., who said there should be three breaks of the recency variable, or where those breaks should be, or why recency should come before monetary value or frequency in the tree structure—some catalogers are turning to a method popularized by Arthur Hughes. His method is to divide each of the three RFM variables into five segments (by sorting on each variable and dividing the file into five equal parts) and use a standard 125-cell system. (Cell 234 means second quintile on recency, third quintile on frequency, and fourth quintile on monetary value.)

- Third, catalogers who prefer to use "tree-type" cell analyses are using CHAID or CHAID-like programs to get away from the need to arbitrarily decide where the cells should break, how many breaks there should be of each variable, and what the order of the tree should be.

- Fourth (and most significantly, we think), instead of using ranges of values for each of the three variables, a number of catalogers have developed predictive models that take into account the actual value for each variable for each person on the file. In this way someone who has spent $99 is not put in a different segment from someone who has spent $101 just because the arbitrary break point was set at $100. What's more important is the fact that models can accommodate more variables than the typical RFM&P tree structure, and that variables such as product purchase patterns can be handled in models in ways that cannot be accommodated by trees. For example, in one case, one cataloger found that certain items and combinations of items were either strong positive or negative predictors of catalog response. Using an item-history principal components analysis (PCA),[1] this company found it could produce a much stronger model than just an RFM model. In fact, based on the new model, the company revamped its entire mail planning process as follows:

- It scored all the names on its customer file using a combination of RFM variables and a product PCA.
- Next it ranked the scores in descending order in terms of the probability of response and created 20 even-sized groups (ventiles).
- Then it estimated the response rate for each ventile.
- Finally it created a mail plan for each ventile. If the response rate is above a certain point, mail the ventile three times within the next promotion period. If it is below this point but still above a breakeven, mail it once. If it is below a breakeven, only mail a small portion of the ventile to help validate model performance.

Using this new mail planning process, the company dramatically improved its contact strategy performance. The revenue per (000) catalogs mailed increased by almost 15 percent despite an overall increase in circulation of less than 10 percent, resulting in record-breaking profits.

The key point is that in today's information-rich marketing environment, major benefits have been achieved by finding new ways to use more relevant purchase history including product data. Additionally, using models to put people into ventiles and then developing a mail plan for each ventile can significantly simplify the process—and also lead to substantial improvements in financial results.

2. The Role of Contact Strategy for an Automobile Manufacturer

Catalogers and car companies differ in a number of important ways. For one thing they differ in how they sell. For the most part, catalogers are "closed-loop direct marketers," able to easily track and measure sales results. They enjoy both a direct distribution channel and a direct communications channel to their customers. Car companies do not. They sell through dealers and thus only have a direct communications channel to their customers.

Second, catalogers sell a variety of products all at once. Car companies do not. They sell their products one at a time, and significantly their products are usually referred to as "big-ticket" items, meaning among other things their price tag usually requires some type of financing.

Third, catalogers work hard to have their catalog both sell products and develop an image for their company. With the exception of a handful of catalog companies, most do not use other means of advertising to develop a brand image, differentiate their brand, or support their catalog efforts. Car companies, on the other hand, rely on a variety of media advertising to create awareness for their brand, promote competitive advantages about their models, and reinforce who they are and their brand imagery.

But recently, despite these differences, car companies and catalogers also have something in common. Car companies just like catalogers have turned to

---

1. See our Statistics chapters for a detailed explanation of this statistical technique and how it can be applied to assess a person's product purchase and help rank the probability of subsequent purchase.

contact strategy. What's interesting about the way car companies use contact strategy, however, is their utilization of surveys to capture the critical information they need to regulate carefully timed, customized messages to prospects and customers at key points in their car purchase decision cycle.

These surveys usually consist of eight to ten questions to help the company learn more about a person's hot buttons, purchase window, and monthly payment tolerance regarding their next car purchase. Responses are analyzed so the companies can customize the frequency and contents of their follow-up mailings according to a person's car needs, interests, likes and dislikes, purchase window, and price range.

People who rank safety, for example, as a major factor in their next car purchase receive materials focusing primarily on safety, while those interested in performance receive materials emphasizing the performance features of the brand, and so on.

How often a person is contacted and at what frequency depends on the person's purchase window. Usually those expecting to make a decision within the next month only receive a survey acknowledgment, along with information that appropriately positions how certain models match their needs and price range. Those with longer purchase windows receive a series of communications so the company can further engage the customer in an ongoing dialogue about his or her car needs and interests, and continually demonstrate how its brand is able to satisfy such needs.

Once a person gets closer to his or her purchase window, these companies send one final communication which recommends a particular model as the model that is best suited to the person's price range, driving habits, and hot buttons, i.e., styling, safety, performance, engineering, etc. Additionally, at this point the companies send the lead and a brief summary of the person's needs and wants, as well as monthly payment tolerance, onto a participating dealer.

What's striking about all of this is twofold. First, these marketers have been able to appropriately customize their responses based on the specific needs and wants of the people they are communicating with. Second, these companies have found a way to effectively integrate contact strategy as part of their overall brand and marketing communications efforts.

Moreover, it is noteworthy how some of these car companies are catching up with their direct marketing colleagues when it comes to measuring the results of their programs. At least in one instance that we are aware of, hold-out samples have been created and maintained, to help track the success of the program over time. Names in these statistically valid-sized groups are intentionally "held out" from receiving surveys and other program materials. Each quarter the new-car purchase rates for these sample names are compared with the purchase rates for those names who have gone through the program to measure the incremental gains that can be attributed exclusively to the program.

In summary, what these car companies are doing clearly substantiates the scope and power of customized and carefully regulated contacts They also demonstrate the role of information exchanges to support and even drive the flow and content of communications.

So far in this chapter we have covered the fundamentals of contact strategy—how most marketers use information to develop and implement a variety of different types of contact efforts—and we have taken a closer look at the role of contact strategy in two specific applications, catalogers and automobile manufacturers.

In this next example we will examine how yet another type of marketer, a consumer products marketer, has found a way to take advantage of the benefits of contact strategy.

3. The Role of Contact Strategy for a Consumer Products Company

A leading, well-known and well-respected consumer products company with the number one market share in its category was experiencing higher share erosion than its competition. Initially, it attempted to combat this situation with higher ad spending in hopes that it could stimulate more demand among consumers in its key markets. When this failed, it turned to another proven strategy, targeted trade promotions and special efforts in its recently expanded company-owned stores, but these activities also did not lead to market share improvements.

A comprehensive review of sales and customer traffic patterns indicated a significant fall-off in store visits by previously loyal, higher-spending customers. As a result of this finding, a traditional segmentation study was undertaken which confirmed the need to reverse this waning loyalty among better customers.

A program was developed to target promotions to this group that would not just stimulate store visits, but also engender greater loyalty and reward repeat business. The program would involve a series of customized communications. Significantly the program would not be based on offering price incentives or discounting products. Simply stated, as the market leader the company was not interested in cutting its margins.

Perhaps, however, the most important program element was how the target audience would be defined. Given that the company did not have a customer file, before it could initiate its series of communications it would have to find a way to capture the names and addresses of it customers. Moreover, as noted above, it wasn't interested in just any type of customer. It only wanted the names and addresses of its better customers.

The solution was to give customers a chance to tell the company exactly the type of customer they were via a very simple in-store survey. The surveys would be available on a pad near the register at each of the stores. The motivation to fill it out would be a "buy two, get one free" offer on certain store merchandise. In addition to capturing the customer's name, address, phone number, and birthday (not date) the survey would ask the customer how many of a certain product the customer's household had purchased in the last three months, of the last 10 product purchases how many were in this type of store, and what were the primary reasons or occasions the customer purchased the product.

Essentially, not only did this brief survey enable the company to get the required name and address for its communications; the survey also allowed the company to determine each customer's current and potential category usage and volume of business. Using the survey data, the company selected only those customers who purchased above a certain volume level and specific SOR[2] level to be included in the program.

The contact strategy that was used involved multiple mailings over a 12-month period. Each included a unique "gift" (other company merchandise) plus

---

2. Traditionally the term *share of requirements* (SOR) was used to refer to that portion or share of a person's total category purchase requirements that were satisfied by a specific brand; i.e., if a person buys an average of 10 tubes of toothpaste every 6 months, and 4 of those tubes are Brand x, then Brand x would currently satisfy 40 percent of this person's share of requirements. More recently, marketers have started to use the term *share of customer* to refer to the same thing.

valuable tips on additional product uses every 90 days. A newsletter was also enclosed to provide added recognition and reinforce brand imagery.

The program worked. Market share increased for the product line and also for the overall brand. Diary panel information indicated that customers who were in the program purchased at a higher rate than those who weren't.

This example adds two important points regarding the successful use of contact strategy. First, marketers should not be afraid to ask consumers to share information that if used properly can be mutually beneficial to both parties. Second, if you can determine a customer's total category behavior, including both volume and brands purchased, and your respective share, it is much easier to decide how much money, effort, and time should be expended to sustain or grow your share.

S U M M A R Y

In this chapter we have discussed the role of contact strategy and how different types of marketers are using it to nurture more valuable customer relationships and improve their marketing results. Whether you are a traditional direct marketer, a catalog company, an automobile manufacturer, or a consumer products company, the steps to develop and implement a successful contact strategy are the same:

1. Use one or more of the different data types—behavior data, demographic data, and attitudinal data—to put people into groups or segments based on similar attributes. (It isn't always necessary to use statistical techniques or quantitative methods to develop these segments. Sometimes simple intuitive judgments and common sense can also lead to the development of actionable segments.)

2. Use the past behavior of the group or segment to predict the probability of the future behavior of the segment. (Predictive modeling is the preferred methodology here. However, as indicated by our cataloger RFM segmentation example, such modeling techniques are not mandatory.)

3. Based on the segment characteristics and attributes, plus the probability that the people in the segment will do what you hope they will do (i.e., buy more more often, etc.), determine their ROI and then decide how many times they should be contacted in the next promotion period or campaign.

4. For each contact determine which product(s) will be promoted, with what offer and positioning, using what tone and manner, and in what communications vehicle.

Following the above steps allows the marketer to profitably regulate the type, frequency, and sequence of contacts by sending the right offer to the right person at the right time. It also can enhance the company's relationship because it encourages customers to feel the company or brand understands them, and knows when and how to effectively communicate with them on an ongoing basis.

Marketing Program Strategy Guideline Checklist

Our experience suggests that whether a marketer is initiating a contact strategy program for the first time or trying to find ways to improve an existing program, the thought process can be both overwhelming and paralyzing. There are simply a lot of elements to consider. The checklist below is provided as both a thought starter and a guideline to facilitate the thinking process and provide some relief. By no means is it exhaustive. Nor is it right for every situation. But, we hope, it will be of some assistance particularly with finding ways to appropriately customize the offer, creative thrust, and positioning of contacts.

Section 1   Executive Summary

This section summarizes the key elements of a promotion, including the financials. It lists which product or products are being promoted and in what media. It also provides a place to check off whether the promotion is targeted to prospects or customers, and if to customers, whether it is a cross-sell or upsell effort.

In terms of financials it lists the expected mail quantity (circulation), the expected revenue, the average order amount, the expected number of orders, the response rate, the estimated cost per thousand pieces circulated (mailed), the total cost, and the revenue:marketing costs ratio (revenue divided by marketing costs).

It also lists the drop date and the expected date when the first response will be received, and if any testing is involved, there is a place to check off what elements are being tested: offer, creative, etc.

Section 2   Background

The purpose of this section is to provide a context for why you are doing this promotion. Usually five or six key points will help to highlight recent trends and developments as well as strategic issues, major opportunities, previous research findings, past results, etc., to identify the background and reason this promotion is being developed.

Section 3   Program Objectives

This section outlines the three or four key objectives of the promotion. Needless to say, they must be quantifiable and measurable. Some examples of types of objectives are as follows:

- *Example 1*. Increase the R:MC ratio by 25 percent from xx.x to y..yy using a new approach and offer against the largest segment, Segment 1 of the customer file, at a cost per order of z.
- *Example 2*. Test two new approaches as part of our promotion effort against new customers in the first six months of their customer life, each of which has the potential to lead to increases in revenue of 25 percent and which does not exceed a cost per order of x on a rollout basis.
- *Example 3*. Reduce the fulfillment cost per responder for our contact stream targeted to y customer types by eliminating the special versioning requirements while maintaining current purchase rate levels.
- *Example 4*. Expand the target audience for contact stream x by x percent while holding the current response rate and net paid levels.

Section 4   Target Audience

The purpose of this section is to clearly define the target audience according to two key perspectives: (1) the prime prospect's behavior and demographic and attitudinal dimensions (see the beginning of this chapter for ideas about ways to go about this) and (2) the prime prospect's current perceptions about your brand and your product category or service.

An example of a definition of the prime prospect for an insurance promotion to an oil company credit card file follows:

> It is estimated that approximately 25 percent of the current cardholders drive at least 1,500 miles each month going to and from work and/or traveling either for business or for pleasure. These people are usually heads of households, primary income providers, parents, between the ages of 30 and 50, who aren't always able to provide all they would like to for their family. Their household income is usually slightly above average, ranging between $35 and $55K, and they usually need to revolve rather than pay off their monthly balance. They carry three or four credit cards in their wallet, but prefer to use our card, as evidenced by their frequency of 4.3 purchases monthly. They know the importance of insurance, all have car insurance, and better than 65 percent have a low-face term life insurance policy. Yet given their financial condition and their limited cash flow, they can't seem to justify spending any more on something they personally will never benefit from. Our research shows that most (67 percent) cite lack of time and saving money as their two biggest challenges. And when considering an insurance purchase, they are not sure how to sort out one policy from another or how to find a good value amid all the direct mail and phone solicitations.

An example of the prime prospect's current perceptions (written in the first-person narrative simply to make it more compelling and real) for the same insurance promotion to an oil company credit card file follows:

> Boy, we get called a lot! People always seem to think that we *need* what *they* are selling. More often than not it's some type of "special" insurance offer. Sometimes I go along for 15 seconds or so, and then it all sounds the same—if I die my wife will be rich, but only if I'm hit by a bus. They never give it to you straight. There's always some wrinkle. Nobody understands me, or our needs, ever! I'd love someone to just give the facts in a way I could relate to, and give me something of real value. But it would have to be a reliable company, somebody I'd heard of, and do business with now. Somebody I could relate to, trust—never happen. Especially over the phone. Not in today's hectic world.

Section 5 Competitive Frame

This is the section where you compare the features and benefits of your product or service with your key competition. What are your competitive strengths and weaknesses, major benefits, etc.? Do you offer more channel choices, better service options, longer warranties, higher levels of customer satisfaction, better pricing, wider distribution, etc.? A simple matrix oftentimes can be used to highlight this information. In addition, in this section it is sometimes helpful to include a review of your competitive set's communication materials to add further insight into the competitive frame. Obviously spending levels, market share, etc., are also very helpful, if available, to "frame in" issues and identify opportunities where you can create and sustain a competitive advantage.

Section 6 Selling Strategy

In this section you want to accomplish two things: first define your selling strategy and, second, define the prime prospect's desired perception.

- With regard to defining the selling strategy, given how you define the target audience, their current perception, and your current competitive frame, what is the key need or want that your product or service can really satisfy, and how should the "promise" of satisfying this need be positioned to the prime prospect? In this case, less is more. Since you have already identified specific needs, as well as opportunities, the more concise and disciplined you can be in defining the selling strategy, the better it will precisely convey to your management and eventually to your target audience your unique point of difference.

- With regard to the prime prospect's desired perception, this again is written in the first-person narrative and outlines the prime prospect's reaction after seeing or hearing your promotion and learning about your product and offer. If the materials are on strategy, and well executed, the lasting impression from these materials should mirror your selling strategy.

Section 7   Offer

This section does *not* define what product you are selling. Its intent is to identify exactly what the prime prospect is supposed to do, what action you want your prospect to take immediately after seeing or hearing your promotion. For example, "spend $8 per month starting next month to receive a charter subscription for the next year." Or "send no money now. We will bill your card in six monthly installments starting next month, and we will also send you this free gift as our way of thanking you for becoming a customer." Or "help us help you by returning the enclosed survey as soon as possible; upon receipt of your survey we will send you . . . ."

Section 8   Supportive Evidence for the Promise/Offer

What are the substantiated facts you should use to persuade the prime prospect of your advantage? Are you truly better, or backed by money-back guarantees, or rated number one in customer satisfaction according to a national survey, etc.?

Section 9   Tone and Manner

In this section the goal is to define the "best" way to address your segment, i.e., with authority, as a friend, matter of factly, seriously, humorously, warmly, etc. Said a different way, what personality should your promotion take on, what style, what feeling? How should this tone be conveyed in words and pictures throughout the promotion?

Section 10   Mandatories and Constraints

This is the section where you list what the "legal musts" are regarding product or service claims and compliance issues. Are there corporate mandates regarding trademarks, certain-size type, only certain types of product shots? One company lists in this section that "every photo must have a caption . . . period." Another highlights which type of testimonials can be used, and how they need to be attributed. Insurance companies often list which payment methods, payment modes, and riders must accompany which products for which states. The point is that for the marketer this is the place to highlight all the corporate regulations and product requirements that must be followed by all parties involved with this promotion.

Section 11   Production Highlights

What are the key considerations regarding printing and lettershop requirements? Are there minimum quantities for press run economies? What are the timetable issues and options to ensure that deadlines and financial goals are achieved?

Which pieces need to be personalized? How will this be done? Where will the key code be, and how will you be sure it is captured so the responses can be properly attributed?

Section 12   Media Highlights

The purpose of this section is to highlight the key media factors that will be involved in this promotion. If you intend to use the phone, how are you going to handle wrong numbers? Do you want to speak to one specific person in the customer household? How many attempts can you afford to make to reach this person? If you intend to use the mail, do you plan on mailing bulk rate or first class? Are you willing to co-bundle with other mailers to gain efficiencies? If your promotion involves both mail and phone, how do you plan to ensure optimal synergy? Will you be able to track each medium separately and to accurately attribute orders to each medium?

Section 13   Customer Service/Fulfillment Highlights

In this section any issues regarding new procedures, changes in processing, new script modifications, new materials, etc., that will be required because of this promotion need to be outlined. The point here is that when the responses start coming in, it is important that everyone who will be involved in either speaking with customers or processing responses knows what they are supposed to do, and have been trained to do it.

Section 14   Timing and Key Dates

The items listed below are just some of the key steps to think about regarding a promotion. Again, it is not exhaustive; it's primarily provided to facilitate planning.

- *Concepts.* When will the initial concepts be ready?
- *Comprehensive layouts and headlines.* After approval of concepts, when will you be able to see more detailed layouts and initial copy ideas?
- *Full copy and artwork.* After approval of comps, when can you expect final packages?
- *Release to production.* How long after final approval will it take to get the materials ready for printing and released to printers? How much sooner for envelopes, or brochures, etc.?
- *Presstime.* Once materials have been approved, how long will it take to print?
- *Lettershop.* When will materials begin to arrive at the lettershop, and how long will it take for inserting?
- *Drop date.* When will the packages be delivered to the USPS? Do you plan on using your own transportation sources to deliver packages to regional bulk mail centers (BMCs)? If so, have these steps and dates been accounted for?
- *In-home date.* How long after the packages are "dropped" will it take for them to arrive in home?
- *First-response/order date.* When do you expect to receive the first response at your fulfillment facility?
- *Half-life.* Based on past order patterns, when do you expect that you will have received 50 percent of all the responses the promotion will generate?

- *Last response/Order date.* Is there an expiration date or cutoff date for this promotion? What date are you willing to choose as the date you receive the last response?
- *First analysis.* When will the first results of the promotion be ready for review?
- *Final review.* This is the date when all the learnings from the program and final results will be presented.

Section 15   Approvals

Our experience indicates that having everyone approve and sign off on all of the information contained in a marketing strategy guideline document serves two critical purposes. First it ensures all parties know what to expect when. Second it helps communicate the key facts and rationale behind the program, and just what the company hopes to accomplish.

CHAPTER 3

Buzzwords

A WORD ABOUT BUZZWORDS[1]

Since the first edition of *The New Direct Marketing*, we have attempted to provide nontechnical readers with easy-to-understand translations of technical terms they were likely to encounter in discussions with their own management information systems (MIS) groups and with vendors. As technology has expanded, so has our list of buzzwords.

Some of the definitions of technical terms you will find here are likely to differ from the orthodox definitions of academics and data processing industry leaders. That's because we have attempted to use English language, working definitions that will help marketers understand the technical terms they are likely to encounter in making decisions about hardware and software tools. If nothing else, we hope that reading this chapter will help the nontechnical database marketers get through what otherwise might be a totally incomprehensible series of meetings and presentations. However, our fear is that new buzzwords are introduced faster than we are able to update this book.

BUZZWORD 1: GENERATIONS OF LANGUAGES

In the world of mainframe computing, there are currently four "generations" of languages. First-generation languages speak directly to the computer in machine language.

If you would like to see what machine language looks like, the next time your PC is at the C prompt (C:\>), type TYPE COMMAND.COM. The resulting gibberish of odd lines and happy faces will be meaningless to you. Fortunately, it is meaningful to your computer.

These languages are actually combinations of 1s and 0s that the computer reads directly as positive and negative pulses of electricity. Although machine language is extremely difficult for mortals to understand, it is actually the most efficient way for computers to process instructions.

Second-generation languages such as Assembler are a step closer to languages that humans can understand than are machine languages. They are "machine-like" in the words and syntax they employ but not quite as great a stretch for programmers as writing in machine language. There are actually some relics

---

1. *Buzzwords* are technical terms commonly used by data processing MIS professionals and computer hardware and software vendors.

from the 1960s who can still write programs in Assembler, and, in fact, more programs in use today than you might expect are written in Assembler. It is an extremely efficient language for very large, data-intense programs because it can be compiled into machine language and made to run very efficiently.

Third-generation, procedural languages like COBOL and FORTRAN were invented to make life easier for programmers, and, in fact, they do. One reason is that programming routines are built into these languages so programmers can write in a kind of shorthand, knowing that the COMMAND-level instructions in COBOL will perform fairly complex functions for them.

Third-generation languages are translated or *compiled*[2] into machine language, but because they are even further removed from the simple 1s and 0s that the computer requires than are second-generation languages, a price is paid in processing efficiency. So although third-generation languages help improve the productivity of programmers, they actually lower the productivity of computers. Based on the decreasing cost of computer processing and the increasing cost of programmers, however, this trade-off in efficiencies is one that most companies are prepared to make.

Fourth-generation languages (4GLs) like FOCUS, NATURAL, USER LANGUAGE, IDEAL, or SQL use very simple "verbs" and syntax, and they can be used by both programmers and end users. The apparent simplicity of the 4GLs provides a great deal of power to programmers or nonprogramming end users, but at a great price. Because they are written at such a high level, they can be incredibly inefficient for computers to process.

An apocryphal story holds that several of the fourth-generation languages were developed, and are secretly owned, by manufacturers of hardware because the inefficiencies inherent in fourth-generation languages make it necessary for companies to buy larger, more expensive computers. Fourth-generation languages are available for DBMS products that we refer to in this book. However, many of the DBMS products themselves are written in Assembler to increase processing efficiency.

Procedural Languages

Assembler is more machine-like in its appearance than more familiar languages like COBOL or FORTRAN. In Assembler a program that added two data fields together would look like the following[3]:

```
Load fld 1, R1
Load fld 2, R2
Add R1, R2, R3
Save R3, fld 3
```

Procedural languages like COBOL or FORTRAN provide detailed, line-by-line instructions to programs. A procedural language would include commands within programs like these:

```
GO TO LINE 24
ADD THE QUANTITY SHOWN IN FIELD X TO THE QUANTITY
IN FIELD Y
STORE THE SUM IN FIELD Z
THEN GO TO LINE 30
```

---

2. Compilers are computer programs that translate computer programs written in languages like Assembler, PL-1, COBOL, FORTRAN, or C into machine language, a series of 1s and 0s that computers can read directly. The results of a compiled program can be read only by computers.

3. Where R1, R2, and R3 denote internal machine registers 1, 2, and 3, respectively.

A fourth-generation language would use English-like prose to accomplish the same purpose, and would include commands like this:

FIELD Z = FIELD X + FIELD Y

BUZZWORD 2: SQL

SQL is an abbreviation for Structured Query Language, the American National Standards Institute (ANSI)[4] accepted standard language for relational database technology. Although the name may initially seem as intimidating as all the other unfamiliar acronyms of computer technology, the language itself is fairly simple in concept. SQL (pronounced SE-QUEL by true techies) consists of a very small number of verbs. Because it is a high-level language (fourth generation), each of these verbs packs a lot of power. See the example of SQL code that follows.

Suppose we had a relational database table called CUSTOMER that contained the following data elements: customer number; customer name; address including city, state, and ZIP code; purchase amount; number of purchases; and number of promotions. An extract of this database follows.

If we wanted to create a file of customers who were from Texas and had purchase amounts in excess of $60, we could write the following program in SQL:

CREATE VIEW TEXASBUYERS (CUST#, STATE, PURCHASE$)
AS SELECT CUSTOMER.CUST#,
CUSTOMER.STATE,CUSTOMER.PURCHASE$
FROM CUSTOMER WHERE STATE = 'TX' AND PURCHASE$ > 60;[4]

Although the language may seem a bit foreign, consider how few verbs were required to produce the desired view of the data. CREATE VIEW TEXAS-BUYERS tells the database to create a new table called TEXASBUYERS. The items in parentheses (CUST#, STATE, PURCHASE$) are the elements we wish to include in the new table. The SELECT statement tells us which data elements we wish to extract from the existing table called CUSTOMER. The two WHERE statements, STATE = 'TX' and PURCHASE$ GT 60, specify the conditions that must be met by any records that are to be included in our new table.

Customer Table

Customer Number	State	Purchase Amount	Number of Purchases	Source Code	Number of Promotions
1347	TX	$ 54	6	04	07
0259	NY	126	10	03	15
3268	AR	27	5	01	06
2139	TX	95	4	02	07
0134	NJ	182	12	04	12
0865	AR	315	17	02	06
0932	TX	191	9	04	11
1136	OK	88	8	03	15
2437	MT	113	12	04	09
4521	LA	43	6	08	07

Once the table TEXASBUYERS is created, any number of analyses can be conducted.

BUZZWORD 3: FLAT FILES AND VSAM FILE STRUCTURES

To understand the differences in file structures, think of spreadsheet programs. In the spreadsheet, the rows are records and the columns are fields. The spreadsheet is a file. A flat file doesn't contain any additional intelligence of organization beyond

---

4. SQL and most 4GLs will accept symbols (e.g.,>) or abbreviations (e.g., GT). Both are shown in this text.

the record level. To know the range and average amounts of purchases contained in the file, a marketer would have to perform some data processing operations.

With a spreadsheet a marketer could specify the range and the system could calculate the minimum, maximum, or average levels for any field. Additionally, the file could be sorted in ascending or descending sequence for a primary and secondary sort field. If a marketer using a spreadsheet wanted to know the range and average purchase level of customers who live in Texas, a simple approach would be to sort the file by state as the primary key and then by purchase amount as the secondary key. It would then be relatively simple to calculate the range and average purchase levels for the Texans.

In many ways, spreadsheets function like simple database management systems. If only the mainframe world were as conceptually simple! Unfortunately for marketers, many of whom are extremely facile with spreadsheet products, the data processing complexities of direct marketing require either mainframe systems that, for the most part, are nowhere near as user friendly as end users would like or the use of separate platforms for decision support functions.

In a mainframe environment, a file like the spreadsheet file described above would be considered a flat file because there is no hierarchy of organization that would make it easier for the end users to get the information faster. To answer a question such as we posed earlier (i.e., "How many Texans had purchases greater than $60?"), it would be necessary to search every record in the file sequentially to be certain we had not left out any Texans.

To make life a little simpler, IBM developed a product called VSAM, which is an acronym for Virtual Sequential Access Method. This product enables programmers to establish indexes or keys by which specified fields can be accessed more readily. For example, if STATE were an indexed field in a VSAM file, it would be much easier to answer the Texas query. When the query was entered, the program would use the VSAM file structure to lock in on the STATE field, and within the STATE field it would examine only the Texans.

VSAM enables programmers to establish indexes on a number of different fields at the same time. Thus, if we knew in advance all the fields we would like to be able to reach through indexes and rarely made any changes to this design, we could develop a very efficient application using VSAM file structures rather than the more complex and expensive database management system products.

However, most end users do not know what their requirements will be in the future, and marketers especially must acknowledge that their data requirements are going to change continually over time. Therefore, the functional requirements of marketers rather than a technical limitation of VSAM make DBMS technology essential for the new direct marketing.

BUZZWORD 4: INDEXES[5]

How Indexes Are Used

Indexes in data processing are very much like the indexes readers are familiar with that appear in books. In books, the index indicates the page on which a particular subject, name, or term appears. In database systems, indexes "point" the

5. Two types of indexes are referred to in this text. At times the term is used to describe calculated values for categorical variables. In the present context, the term is used to describe a means of representing locations of data values in records. Readers who wish to know more about the subject of indexes and related technical subjects are referred to C. J. Date, *An Introduction to Database Systems*, vol. I, 4th ed. (Reading, MA: Addison-Wesley, 1986).

programs to the desired data and provide an efficient means of getting there without having to read the intervening records.

One of the most important elements, and one of the major differences between the various commercially available database management system products, is the way in which indexes are structured.

If, for example, we want to easily locate all the people who live in the state of Massachusetts, we would build an index by state. Then, rather than searching sequentially through all our customer records, which might be arranged in customer ID or alphabetical sequence, our search would begin by going to the state index, locating the record numbers of all customers whose entry in the state index is MA, creating a temporary file of those records, and then posing whatever further queries we have about those customers to this Massachusetts-only subset of the file. Reducing the file to include only the relevant set of records makes subsequent processing much more efficient.

Indexes become even more important to ease of access and good performance when we formulate complex queries that require data from a number of different tables or files.[6] If the data fields in question have been indexed, we may be able to answer the query entirely by consulting indexes rather than by reading actual records.

For example, suppose that we want to know the number of people who live in New York, Massachusetts, and Connecticut who purchased products 123, 456, or 789. If address and purchase information were maintained in separate tables, this query could be processed by reading the state index and the product index, selecting the records of only those people who live in the three states indicated, and then selecting the records of only those people who purchased products 123, 456, or 789. The two extracted index files would then be joined on the customer ID field, and the resulting set would provide the desired answer.

If we knew that this type of query would be asked frequently, we would probably design the application so both data elements appear in the same table. This would improve response time because the join would be eliminated.

One of the most challenging issues for database designers is determining which fields in a table should be indexed and how tables in the database should be related. If the database is to successfully support marketing, marketers must provide the system's designers with a great deal of guidance and direction concerning which queries are most important and which data elements are related to each other. The resulting database design optimizes the data capture, storage, and manipulation requirements to achieve the maximum benefit for marketing.

Let's return to our question of how many Texans in the file had total purchase amounts in excess of $60 to see how it could be answered using indexes. To get this information, we would identify Texans within the state index and then do an index search for purchase amount. We would then create a "found set" within the index of records that met the desired conditions. Tables 3-1 through 3-5 show how this works.

Table 3-1 repeats the customer table that illustrated Buzzword 2. In Table 3-2, the original file has been indexed by customer number within state.

If a query were made to find the number of Texans who had total purchases in excess of $60, the database would search the index of the state file until it found the Texans, and then perform all further processing within the found set of Texans. (See Table 3-3.)

---

6. We use the terms *tables* and *files* interchangeably.

Because we are only interested in knowing the range and average purchase levels for Texans (for this specific query) the found set would include only the relevant pieces of data. (See Table 3-4.)

Although we did not specifically request the customer number, it will normally be carried to maintain our link to the actual customer and purchase tables.

The result of the query, based on the found set, would be the count of Texans on the file who have purchases in excess of $60, which equals two. (See Table 3-5.)

T A B L E   3-1

Flat File

Customer Number	State	Purchase Amount	Number of Purchases	Source Code	Number of Promotions
1347	TX	$ 54	6	04	07
0259	NY	126	10	03	15
3268	AR	27	5	01	06
2139	TX	95	4	02	07
0134	NJ	182	12	04	12
0865	AR	315	17	02	06
0932	TX	191	9	04	11
1136	OK	88	8	03	15
2437	MT	113	12	04	09
4521	LA	43	6	08	07

T A B L E   3-2

A File Indexed by Customer Number within State

Customer Number	State	Purchase Amount	Number of Purchases	Source Code	Number of Promotions
0865	AR	$315	17	02	06
3268	AR	27	5	01	06
4521	LA	43	6	08	07
2437	MT	113	12	04	09
0134	NJ	182	12	04	12
0259	NY	126	10	03	15
1136	OK	88	8	03	15
0932	TX	191	9	04	11
1347	TX	54	6	04	07
2139	TX	95	4	02	07

T A B L E   3-3

The Found Set of Texans

Customer Number	State	Purchase Amount	Number of Purchases	Source Code	Number of Promotions
0932	TX	$191	9	04	11
1347	TX	54	6	04	07
2139	TX	95	4	02	07

T A B L E 3-4

The Reduced Found Set of Texans

Customer Number	State	Purchase Amount
0932	TX	$191
1347	TX	54
2139	TX	95

T A B L E 3-5

The Found Set of Texans Who Have Purchases in Excess of $60

Customer Number	State	Purchase Amount
0932	TX	$191
2139	TX	95

Although it may appear, in this example, that the database worked very hard to answer a simple question, consider how well this approach would work with multiple conditions and very large files.

BUZZWORD 5: PRODUCTIVITY TOOLS

Developers of database management systems have long realized that if their products are to be truly successful, they have to put the power of sophisticated data processing in the hands of end users who are not data processing professionals. This goal becomes more difficult if the end users have no knowledge of programming whatsoever.

An initial response was to provide *menus*, that is, tables of processes that could be selected by positioning the cursor over the item or by keying the first letter of the word and hitting the enter key. Users of PC spreadsheet programs will be very familiar with this concept.

More recently, software and hardware developers have offered *mouse* devices as an alternative and often easier means of selecting menu items. Mouse devices are small machines that control a target-like cross-hair image, arrow, or I-Bar on the screen. The end user moves the mouse over a flat surface until the indicator is positioned over the desired menu item and then presses a button on the mouse. This process selects the menu item in exactly the same way that cursor movement or keying the first letter of the desired item would. Some software products include icons, which are visual representations of the functions offered on the menu. The user positions the mouse over the desired icon and clicks a mouse button to make the selection.

BUZZWORD 6: LOGICAL AND PHYSICAL DESIGN

According to C. J. Date,[7] the conceptual or logical database design consists of identifying the entities of interest to the enterprise and the information recorded about those entities. In other words, each firm must decide which of the data elements contained in its various applications will be contained in the database and define the relationships between those data elements. Generally, this is the job of the database administrator (DBA), but it is done in conjunction with the user sponsors.

The *physical design of the database*, again according to Date, is the definition of the storage structure and associated mapping of the system. In other words, the physical design of the database consists of determining which data elements should be contained in which tables, and how the tables are related to each other by primary and secondary key fields.

Key fields are the data elements that appear in more than one table and serve as a link, both logical and physical, between tables.

By *logical design*, we mean the data elements that will be included in the database and the way the elements in the data tables relate to each other. As part of the physical design, the system designer groups the data elements that seem to logically belong together into physical tables so elements that are likely to be involved in the same queries are included in the same tables. This grouping improves response time for queries by reducing the number of table joins,[8] the number of inputs and outputs (I/Os),[9] and the amount of seek time[10] that the system must spend in bringing together the data elements required to answer the query.

Physical design also refers to the size of files. The placement of data on physical devices (generally, direct access storage devices, or DASD) is considered "tuning" and is not technically part of the physical design of the system. However, it is sometimes included under this definition anyway because the database administrator and system designers are responsible for tuning the application to run as efficiently as possible. Proper placement of data helps reduce the time that will be required to get data from DASD into the computer's main memory. So you can see that response time is affected both by the logical and physical design of the system as well as by the placement of data and other tuning issues.

BUZZWORD 7: CPU

The central processing unit (CPU) is the heart of the computer—this is where the work gets done. In a PC, the CPU is defined in terms of the RAM (random access memory) and the processing speed. For example, a 486/33 machine with 2 MB of RAM refers to a PC that has an 80486 chip with a processing speed of 33 megahertz and 2 megabytes of core memory that the computer can use for processing. In a mainframe environment, RAM is referred to as core memory or internal

---

7. C. J. Date, *An Introduction to Database Systems*, vol. 1, 4th ed. (Reading, MA: Addison-Wesley, 1986).

8. *Table joins* are the means that relational databases use to bring together data stored in different tables. The tables are "joined" using a common field in much the same way that third-generation systems merge files using a common data element.

9. Inputs and outputs (I/Os) are the number of times that data must be brought from disk drives into the computer's main memory and the number of times that data that is already in the computer's main memory must be stored on disks. Channel contention is directly proportional to the number of I/Os, and busy channels can delay processing in the same way that traffic jams can occur on highways during rush hour.

10. *Seek time* is the time required for the system to find the right file and data needed to answer the query. See Buzzword 7 for a detailed description of seek time.

memory, and processing speed is generally quoted in a measurement called MIPS (millions of instructions per second).

Channel

Channels are the electronic paths used to get data into and out of the CPU. If data cannot efficiently get into and out of the CPU, processing will slow down. This is like having a car with a very large engine capacity that has a clogged fuel line. Although the engine could make the car go very fast, it is unable to do this processing if it cannot get the fuel it needs.

Channel capacity and channel contention are major concerns to the system designers responsible for the processing efficiency.

Channel Contention

If the physical storage of data on DASD is not efficient, then channel contention will develop in mainframe systems. Channel contention is analogous to a clogged highway or artery in which too many blocks of data are attempting to get through a constrained space. In data processing, the result is that one block of data must wait until the passageway is clear, and end users experience delays in response time.

A PC environment, other than a network environment, generally includes only one disk drive and one channel. Seek time in a PC environment is reduced by storing files in directories or subdirectories to minimize the number of files that must be searched prior to loading data. In a mainframe environment, where there are multiple disk drives and multiple channels, efficiency is increased by physically designing systems so data elements that are likely to be used in the same queries are distributed across multiple DASD units and channels. This distribution reduces channel contention, that is, the number of data requests that are attempting to get through an individual channel at the same time.

Direct Access Storage Device (DASD)

Disk drives (direct access storage devices, or DASD) are the most common form of external memory, or data storage, in on-line computing environments. Companies use disk drives to store data that they know they will need frequently. Programs issue commands or *calls* that tell the system which data files are needed for the process in question. The CPU then sends a message over the channel to find the data that the program needs. A PC environment generally has only one disk drive and one channel over which data enters and leaves the CPU.

Seek Time

When the program requests data, the command goes through the channel to the disk drive(s) to find it. The time required for the request to find the right data and bring it back to the CPU is referred to as *seek time* because the program is seeking the data. System designers attempt to design systems initially to minimize time. However, as a system is used and more and more data is stored, the initial efficiencies of physical data storage tend to erode, and a conscious effort must be made to reposition data to produce greater efficiencies of operation. This function, called *tuning*, is generally the responsibility of the database administrator.

BUZZWORD 8: SUMMARY FILES

Summary files are files that have been created by extracting and summarizing data from one or more tables in the database. Their purpose is to provide quicker response time by grouping data that we know in advance will be important and will be accessed frequently.

A typical case where summary files would benefit system performance would be a situation where a number of different tables must be joined to bring together data for queries or reports. If, for example, we always want to know the counts of products purchased by state and source of purchaser, we would probably want to create a summary file to speed up this process. A fully "normalized" database would maintain data about customers and products purchased in separate tables.

Normalization

Normalization means that each piece of data appears only once, minimizing if not eliminating data redundancy. In a relational database environment, data is normalized as much as possible. One of the functions of the DBMS product itself is to "navigate" through different tables to find the required data.

However, to gain processing efficiency, it may be desirable to *denormalize* the data design to some extent by maintaining selected data elements in more than one table. Although this practice violates the relational model, it is a compromise many companies are willing to make to improve performance.

BUZZWORD 9: TYPES OF DATABASE PRODUCTS

Hierarchical

The oldest and fastest (in certain circumstances) type of DBMS products is hierarchical. These products establish a series of defined paths (not unlike the VSAM description), and data access and processing are very fast. Hierarchical systems are commonly used for banking, airline reservations, and other applications that require very high-speed processing and rarely change the paths of data storage or retrieval.

Inverted File

Inverted files are like hierarchical database structures except that they work from the bottom up rather than from the top down. This enables programmers to design systems that will allow access to virtually any field within the system from any other point. Creating indexes that link key fields enhances high-speed access from point to point. Examples of inverted file systems are Model 204, Adabas, and Computer Associates' Datacom/DB. Inverted file systems are very commonly used for direct marketing applications because their combination of processing speed and flexibility is well suited to this environment.

Relational

Relational systems are essentially collections of relatively simple tables from which the user combines and extracts information in a virtually unlimited number of ways. These are the most flexible of all database management systems, but some performance has been sacrificed to provide their flexibility, and, as a result, they are generally not as fast as inverted file or hierarchical systems. In practice, direct marketers tend to use file applications that are relational in concept and relational applications that are structured like inverted files to achieve the most effective compromise between flexibility and performance.

PROPRIETARY DATABASE SYSTEMS

Proprietary database systems are based on unique, nonstandard architectures that have been optimized for individual business functions, such as marketing. In general, these systems quickly process user-defined ad hoc queries, calculations, and reports; can work efficiently with groups of user-identified records; and can efficiently combine data from different tables according to end-user specifications. These systems offer superior processing performance, i.e., throughput and end-user response time. These systems also offer a variety of marketing-oriented end-user tools, such as customer profiling, campaign planning, list selects, marketing program results evaluation, scoring models, and marketing plan management.

OPEN SYSTEM ARCHITECTURE

Open system architecture is a series of programming conventions that allows software to directly integrate with other software without customized interface programming. The software applications are, therefore, *independent* of the platforms on which they are being operated, hence the term *platform independent*. This creates a very flexible environment where new tools can be added as needed. New PC-desktop applications can be added as end-user needs develop, and new database systems can be implemented as processing volumes grow.

EIS–EXECUTIVE INFORMATION SYSTEM

Executive information systems are PC-based software applications that allow end users to access information in databases operated on the PC or across a network on database server computers. These systems feature extremely user-friendly graphical presentations and are usually custom-tailored for each company. They contain a variety of predefined choices for data items, report formats, and other ways of displaying data such as charts, maps, etc.

OLAP–ON-LINE ANALYTICAL PROCESSING

On-line analytical processing is a method of storing precalculated, summary information. Sometimes referred to as a "multidimensional database," this type of system is essentially a "database of answers" in that the OLAP system stores answers to predefined business reporting needs, i.e., "questions." Data can be stored as individual data elements, as related hierarchies (Corporation → Division → Sales Region → Store Location), or as independent dimensions (time, location, company division, product, etc.).

MDD–MULTIDIMENSIONAL DATABASE

See OLAP.

GIS—GEOGRAPHIC INFORMATION SYSTEMS

Geographic information systems are PC-based end-user applications that present data in geographic formats, i.e., statistical maps. These systems include a variety of reference files for various levels of geography (state, county, city, ZIP code, census tract, etc.), a variety of map types (area shading, dot density maps, feature maps that show roads, etc.), and a variety of mapping-based tools (geocoding, measuring distances, counting customers within a radius of a given point, etc.).

DATA MINING

Data mining is a new class of techniques used to extract useful information from a base of data. In traditional research methods, an individual must take the initiative to identify an issue, state a hypothesis which will be proved or disproved, create an experimental design, and do the needed statistical analysis to reach a conclusion. In the case of the average marketer, he or she must develop a question and then manually create a report to answer the question. These are highly "manual" processes. In data mining, a software system automatically reviews bases of data to identify unusual patterns. These systems are driven by user-specified data evaluation rules, calculations, and limits. They continually review the data, build a set of patterns, dynamically adjust the "model" as changes occur in the data, and report significant trends and occurrences. Currently, data mining is primarily used to focus relatively scarce analysis resources on significant issues. In the future, these systems will no doubt find applications as "intelligent agents" (software assistants) which support individual marketers.

DOMAIN EXPERTS

Domain experts, also known as "subject matter experts," are individuals recognized during the process of designing and implementing information systems as having definitive knowledge on a specific topic. Domain experts can be used to provide background information, standards, and conventions on end-user business processes (campaign planning, list selection, scoring model development, etc.) as well as technical topics (local area networks, data entity relationships, systems interfaces, etc.).

BUZZWORD 10: INTERNET BUZZWORDS

TCP/IP

The Transmission Control Protocol (TCP) and Internet Protocol (IP) form a set of communications conventions that controls how information is exchanged across the networks that compose the Internet. Essentially, TCP/IP is the language of the Internet.

HTML—Hypertext Markup Language

HTML is the computer language used to configure pages on the World Wide Web and tell browser programs how to display a Web page. Hypertext and hyperlinks allow end users to quickly skip to specific parts of a page or connect to other pages.

Browser

Browsers are PC software applications that access and display information stored on local computers or across the Internet via HTML. The two most common browsers are Netscape Navigator and Microsoft Internet Explorer. Besides Internet applications, many companies are implementing internal systems that use browser technology to control data access and support.

Cookies

Cookies are small text files created by Web sites and stored on an end user's PC. They are used to identify new users, track usage of the site, store user preferences, etc.

Internet

Developed between 25 and 30 years ago, the Internet is a global system of computer networks that are made up of millions of local area networks (LANs) and computers (hosts). The Internet is the communications backbone that supports a variety of functions such as:

The World Wide Web (WWW). The interlinked collection of documents, images, animations, sounds, etc., that is accessed interactively via graphical user interfaces

Gophers. The system of databases containing information on specific subjects and accessed via a system of menus

FTP. The system that supports exchanging of files between host computer systems and end users

E-mail system. The system that allows end users to send and receive messages and attached files via the Internet.

Intranet

Intranets are private networks based on Internet technology that are developed by individual companies for proprietary use. Intranets are often developed by interconnecting a company's local area networks and are used to support operational systems, file transfers, report distribution, database access, etc.

CHAPTER 4

Sources and Uses of Marketing Data

The new direct marketing requires vast amounts of data from a variety of internal and external sources: customer and operations-oriented data acquired from many different sources within the enterprise, as well as externally acquired promotion lists and enhancement data (geo-demographic, attitudinal, lifestyle, financial, consumer survey, etc.).

Data makes it possible to identify new business opportunities and develop strategic plans. Data makes it possible to calculate customer value and identify the characteristics associated with our best, worst, and marginal customers. Data provides the basis for segmenting customers into relatively homogeneous groups with similar characteristics, attitudes, or needs. Data is the key to all predictive models. Data is essential to identifying people on prospect files and on rented lists with characteristics similar to those of our best customers. Data makes it possible to evaluate the effectiveness of our marketing programs. Stated simply, without data the new direct marketing does not exist.

CUSTOMER AND PROSPECT DATA

Customer Data

Customer data, which includes all sales, promotion, and customer service activity that has occurred as a result of the customer's relationship with a company, is, of course, the most important information that direct marketers have about their customers.

Direct marketers have consistently found that customer performance data, obtained directly from *transaction* records and customer accounts, is the most relevant when it comes to building reliable predictive models. Key performance measures such as recency, frequency, and monetary value data are no less important in the new direct marketing than they were in classical or traditional direct marketing. Today, these data elements are complemented by additional nontransactional data sources that enable direct marketers to be more efficient and more profitable.[1]

---

1. One of the more promising applications is the use of cross-products, which are new data elements created from the combination of two or more others. One example would be a sales index variable calculated as a given customer's sales divided by the average sales per individual within the customer's ZIP code.

Although performance data is the most important type of data we have about customers, it is not available in equal measure for all customers. The database will have a much richer data history for older customers than for new customers. Accordingly, many direct marketers find it advantageous to calculate new data elements that make it easier to compare all their customers, taking into account length of time that customers have been on file. Typically, these data elements include such measures as total number or value of purchases divided by months on file, allowing us to directly compare "6-month" customers to "18-month" customers.[2]

Cohort or Enrollment Group Reporting

Another strategy is to do statistical analysis broken out by "cohort or enrollment groups"—groups that contain customers that have been on file for similar lengths of time. In fact, enrollment group reporting is one of the most valuable reports that a marketing database is capable of producing, almost regardless of the nature of the business. Among traditional direct marketers, enrollment group reporting is the basis for all of their forecasting systems, and the best early warning measure for changes in customer behavior. It is especially important for alerting management to changes in customer lifespan and customer lifetime value. What's more, it's very easy to accomplish; no sophisticated tools are required. All that is required is that cohort groups be created by summarizing the behavior of all customers acquired during the same enrollment period under the same offer and same communication source. Then selected summary measures are defined, such as total or average sales, returns, or contribution; percent still active, canceled, delinquent, written off; and so on. Monitoring these reports, which are usually produced on a monthly or cyclical basis, can be done on an exception basis or with the aid of simple graphics.

Other Sources of Customer Data

In addition to transaction details, many other types of data generated from internal operations can make significant contributions. Information relating to billing and account status, customer service interactions, back orders, product shipment, product returns, claims history, and internal operating costs all can significantly impact a company's understanding of its customers.

Still another important internal source of data is the marketing department itself. Information about customer classifications, response scoring models, customer value "to date," projected customer value, promotion history, expected sales, expected responses, expected promotion costs, marketing objectives, sources of lists, etc., is essential for supporting the marketing business process.

Response Data

The accurate recording of response information is critical to the success of any direct marketing business. In most cases, this simply involves recording a purchase in response to a coded promotion, but depending on the type of marketing program it may be necessary to track customer inquiries (typically requests for information) and final account activation. A classic example of such a multistep sale process is a lead-generation piece describing the wares of a catalog company,

---

2. More and more modelers are finding that the best way to get around this problem of different amounts of data for different customers is to develop separate models for new, average, and very old customers, measured by their time on the customer file. A CHAID analysis helps in defining the optimal break points.

generating an initial customer response for more information. Instead of the company "prospecting" with expensive catalogs to unqualified leads, a less expensive package is first used to cost-effectively qualify leads. Catalogs are then sent to initial responders, and a portion of them will eventually convert to active customer status.

Problems in Coding Response Data

Today's multichannel marketing environment greatly complicates the capture and use of response information. One major impact is that response transactions must be collected across all channels, such as inbound mail, inbound telephone, Internet Web sites, retail point of sale, sales agents, fax, etc.

Once captured, the response information must be properly attributed to the proper customer/prospect and the proper marketing promotion. In many industries, it is accepted practice to code promotions with "hard match codes" which uniquely identify the individual promoted and the promotion used. In some cases, one code is used to capture both dimensions, and other times separate promotion key code and customer identification codes are used.

However, depending on the response channel, it may be difficult to ensure that these match codes are properly captured and transmitted along with the response transaction. In some cases, the response channel is served by an operational system that cannot be modified to capture and report promotional match codes. This is very typical in the retail environment where many point of sale systems cannot capture customer identification and promotion data.

Difficulties also sometimes arise when marketing does not have direct control over the response channel. In many cases where the company maintains its own inbound cell center, the management of that group places primary emphasis on cost containment via maximizing call volume throughout. In these cases, response matching codes or promotion identification codes are often not captured with full diligence.

Even today, many companies do not utilize "hard match codes" and must rely upon "soft matching techniques," such as name and address matching. Because these techniques are less than 100 percent accurate, a sizable percentage of responses are not matched to a customer/prospect record and fall into the "unattributed" category.

Response Attribution

Major problems can also arise when a customer has been sent multiple promotions. If a soft match indicates that a customer has purchased a software product but the customer has received three different promotions for that item, to which is the sale attributed?

Another factor to be considered is that, depending on the industry, it can be quite common to have a significant portion of responses result from "pass-along" situations. A pass-along situation is one in which the promoted person "passes along" the promotion to another person who makes the purchase. In this case, the purchase will not match any promoted customer name, and it will also fall into the "unattributed" category.

Prospect Data

"Prospects"—those people to whom we have promoted in the past but who have not yet purchased from us—have no performance data at all. The only information typically available for these individuals is a history of the promotions they have been sent, demographic enhancement data, and the fact that they have not responded.

Prospect Databases

Interestingly, creating prospect databases has been a relatively recent development primarily undertaken by large-scale direct marketers operating in industries that extensively use externally acquired promotion lists and have a relatively large variance in potential customer values. The primary applications of these databases are to track prospect promotion history, provide information on the number and type of lists that contain each name, and combine descriptive data for each prospect from the various input sources. Some industries that make extensive use of prospect databases include financial services (especially credit card companies), telecommunications, cable TV, and high-end catalogers.

Obtaining Unlimited Usage Rights

To achieve their information objectives while complying with the ethical guidelines relative to "downstream" use of outside *rented* names, these marketers have negotiated "multiple-usage" rights to these names, or at least the right to retain prospect information for marketing program results analysis. They have negotiated up front the right to maintain a count for each individual of how many input files contain them, how many times prospects receive which promotions, and whatever descriptive information was contained in the original file. Not surprisingly, these firms have found it extremely valuable to use such information to more profitably target their promotions and to reduce the cost of customer acquisition.

Supporting Two-Way Customer Dialogues

Many companies today are shifting to the newest of the new direct marketing methodologies—relationship marketing. Here, the focus is on developing and managing a relationship with each customer across numerous types of marketing communications and many different communication channels. For these activities it is critical to track which customer has received which communications, when the customer received them, and how the customer or prospect responded.

Consider the case of a financial services firm that is generating leads for a variety of investment programs. Some leads or prospects who are actually interested in the programs offered may not be able to invest their funds immediately. In this situation, the financial services marketer may have to make a considerable investment—in both time and money—to nurture the relationship before the prospect can be converted into a customer.

The dialogue between the financial services firm and the prospect may begin as the result of direct mail; direct response media such as print, broadcast, or free standing insert (FSI); or word of mouth passed along by satisfied customers. Once the dialogue has been established, the marketer can use the promotional process to nurture the relationship with the prospect. If used strategically, this dialogue may include gathering data about the prospect through surveys that will contribute to conversion at a later date.

For example, during the relationship-building or "courtship" process, the marketer may learn through surveys that the prospect has a child who will enter college in two years. The marketer can instruct the database to contact the prospect with an appropriate message at that time. Additionally, the marketer may use the promotional dialogue to learn about the prospect's savings and investment goals or "anniversary" dates of time-sensitive deposits at other financial institutions so promotions for the right products can be sent to the right prospects at the right time.

In packaged goods businesses, a customer may initiate a similar dialogue by responding via an in-store display, a rebate coupon, in-pack or on-pack surveys, or direct response media opportunities. Once the customer has responded, the manufacturer can use the information to develop and target programs intended to fulfill specific needs (such as restricted diets), stimulate consumption levels, nurture customer loyalty, and maintain or increase share of wallet.

Thus, in implementing the new direct marketing, all information is potentially important, not just the types of data previously associated only with post-acquisition customer performance. Data gathering is an ongoing process, which often begins prior to the initial purchase, and we must pay careful attention to how we communicate to customers and prospects, when we communicate with them, and what data we attempt to capture at each stage of the relationship-building process.

Nontransactional Data Sources

As suggested above, in addition to data from transactions, two other sources of data are critically important to the new direct marketing and will now be discussed:

1. Data that is provided directly by individuals (customers, prospects, and even nonprospects) about themselves

2. Data about customers and prospects that is purchased from third-party sources

Directly Supplied Data

Directly supplied data consists of data obtained directly from customers, prospects, or suspects.[3] It is generally captured from lead-generation questionnaires, customer surveys, warranty registration cards, customer service interactions, Internet Web site responses, interviews, focus groups, or other direct interactions with individuals. With the advent of relationship marketing, the use of directly supplied data has increased dramatically over the past few years. With the introduction of bar code scanners, interactive voice messaging systems, point of sale systems, home shopping, interactive television, and other electronic media, the number of channels through which data can be collected directly from customers and prospects will increase exponentially.

Directly supplied data consists of three major types:

- *Behavioral* data such as purchase and buying habits, preferred communication channels, language preference, overall product category usage, and company share of wallet
- *Attitudinal* data reflecting attitudes about products, such as satisfaction levels, perceived competitive positioning, desired features, unmet needs, purchase triggers, etc., as well as attitudes concerning lifestyles, brand preferences, social and personal values, opinions, and the like
- *Demographic* data such as age, income, education level, marital status, household composition, gender, home ownership, and so on

In the past, this type of data was often the province of market research, and was collected on small samples of customers and prospects via focus groups,

---

3. Suspects are people who marketers think may be interested in their products or services but who have not yet been promoted.

mall-intercept interviews, mailed surveys, etc. Marketers used this data primarily in a strategic sense to provide direction for programs that addressed large groups of customers and prospects. Market research used demographic and behavioral data to get a better "fix" on the characteristics of a market segment and attitudinal data to provide a sense of which issues were important to various groups of customers and therefore should be emphasized in promotional materials.

Market researchers use directly supplied data to identify new product opportunities or new segments within the marketplace. This is usually done by sending product research surveys to a representative sample of customers or prospects to determine what products and services they are interested in but do not currently purchase from the firm sending the questionnaire.

Although the data gathered by market research surveys has always been valuable for the strategic direction and product development guidance it provides, in the past it has had certain limitations for database marketing. That is, although market researchers for a financial services firm could tell their marketing counterparts that 20 percent of the company's prospects were males between 40 and 45 years old who earn between $50,000 and $75,000 and are interested in investing in mutual funds, they were unable to identify the specific individuals who composed the 20 percent. So although the information about the firm's prospects was important because it described a fairly large segment within the file, it did not provide an opportunity for promotion because the individuals whose characteristics matched the desired profile could not be identified by name.

Relationship Marketing—The Need for Individual Information

More recently, as improved customer communication channels and database technology have enabled companies to capture and manipulate large amounts of individual-level data cost-effectively, the value of surveys has expanded beyond market research and has become an increasingly important component of the mainstream marketing process.

Another important reason for this trend is that purchased enhancement data is now so commonly available that it no longer represents a significant, strategic, competitive advantage to marketers. In fact, it could be argued that external enhancement data now represents a basic requirement that is needed to support the basic elements of targeted marketing programs. In essence, the kind of external data currently available seems to have hit "carrying capacity," meaning that we have already learned how to leverage it to greatest advantage. To advance to a more sophisticated level of marketing requires new data sources with additional potential.

Relationship marketing represents a more sophisticated level of communication requiring much more in-depth information about individual customers and therefore more comprehensive data sources. If a company is going to develop significant, value-added relationships with each customer, then it is necessary to have a great deal of relevant information about that individual. *To accomplish this, many companies are leveraging their investments in service delivery and customer service systems and are directly collecting data from their customers during regular business interactions.*

This approach offers several advantages. Over time, companies will realize better coverage. They have the advantages of focusing on just their customers, asking questions multiple times if necessary, and promising improvements in promotional targeting and customer service if the customer complies with the information request. Also, by controlling the questions that are asked, companies can ensure that the data collected is directly relevant to their marketing objectives. Lastly, if data is collected through service delivery or customer service channels, data acquisition cycles can be as fast as on a daily basis instead of the typical semiannual updates available via outside sources.

Beyond transaction and customer service systems, the Internet represents a growing opportunity to collect information about customers and prospects. Today, almost any company of any significance has implemented a lead-generation Web site. Essentially "automated brochures," theses types of sites provide a wealth of product information and include a number of applications intended to help customers search for specific pieces of information, make product recommendations, assess potential costs and benefits, provide value-added information, and even entertain. A key feature of this type of site is the opportunity to request additional information by providing an e-mail address, postal address, telephone number, etc. Of course, this information is used to provide information kits and also to update the prospect database.

Surveys are another important Web site application. Currently, they are in widespread use as a means to collect additional information from both customers and prospects. Since many Web sites have both a "public" and "private" side, the same survey administration can be used to collect information from all visitors. The more sophisticated applications are context-sensitive, meaning they can ask different questions depending on the answers to previous questions and they can also ask different questions depending on what is already in the customer's or prospect's database record. Also, while it could be a result of the demographic skews of Internet users, there is growing evidence that consumers are less reluctant to respond to surveys administered via personal computer than by any other channel. Despite all we have heard about Internet security issues, consumers seem to feel that this method of responding is less threatening than paper, telemarketing, or interview-based surveys.

Another interesting method of collecting data via the Internet is to record which "areas" of a Web site are visited by consumers and for how long. The utility of this data is still open to question; however, it is easy to see the potential for certain industries, such as on-line booksellers.

Many companies, perhaps fearing a negative reaction by customers and prospects, are reluctant to ask the questions that are most important for improving their business and their customer service. In adhering to ethical and legal standards when requesting information of their customers and prospects and taking care to ask those questions in inoffensive ways, many companies fail to ask the questions that would generate the greatest impact. Companies that do ask the critical questions are often surprised to learn just how willing customers and prospects are to provide information about themselves.

It is essential to establish a solid relationship with customers so that they feel free to share information with the company. While it is commonly known that there is a public movement toward information privacy, both academic studies and practical experience have shown that the vast majority of consumers are reluctant to share information only when there is no clear value proposition. *If the company can demonstrate to the customer that the requested information will be used to deliver tangible benefits and can gain the customer's trust in holding the information confidential, then customers usually are willing to comply.*

EXAMPLES OF THE TYPE OF DATA COLLECTED FROM THREE TYPES OF DIRECT MARKETING BUSINESS

This next section focuses on the kinds of data and the kinds of questions direct marketers in the financial services, clubs, and insurance business collect. If you're not in one of these categories, please use this section to think about the kinds of questions and the kinds of data you should be collecting about your customers.

Financial Services Marketers

Financial services marketers typically want to know the customer's or prospect's:

- Age
- Income
- Occupation
- Employment status
- Credit rating
- Marital status
- Home owner status
- Home value
- Household composition
- Relationships with other financial institutions

Life-stage information is often critical, such as graduation from college, marriage, birth of children, purchase of a home, children entering or leaving college, retirement. Different life stages may require or create different financial services needs.

In addition, financial services marketers may wish to know attitudinal and behavioral information, such as what other financial services products the customer or prospect owns, how satisfied she is with those products, and her intention to buy other products over the next 12 months.

For investment product marketers it is particularly valuable to know:

- If the customer or prospect owns fixed-term investment instruments (such as CDs)
- When the instruments will mature
- The level of funds they will release
- The investment objectives the customer or prospect has for such funds

Each of these pieces of information can help companies define which promotions for which products are most appropriate to the interests and needs of the target audience.

Examples of Questions Asked by Financial Services Marketers

Attitudinal information, such as the amount of risk an investor is willing to take, and information about investment objectives, such as sheltering income from taxes or producing guaranteed monthly income, are critically important if targeted marketing efforts are to be successful for financial services marketers.

Therefore, they tend to ask attitudinal questions like these:

- How do you feel about investing through the mail?
- What is your tolerance for risk?
- How do you decide to make a particular investment?
- How do you keep informed?
- What is your opinion about banks, stockbrokers, insurance agents?

Financial services marketers also use behavioral questions to get at decisions that have actually been made, such as these:

- Are you currently invested in stocks, bonds, mutual funds, real estate?
- Do you use a stockbroker or investment adviser or subscribe to financial newsletters?

And, of course, demographic questions elicit information about age, income, occupation, wealth, and so forth.

Negative Opinion and Continuity Marketers

Many negative option businesses, such as book or music clubs, have traditionally treated all their customers the same once the customers became "members" of the club. That is, these clubs sent announcements with the same frequency and used promotional materials that were identical or nearly identical, differing only in the cover or lead selection offered.

However, today's more progressive clubs are beginning to take advantage of today's desktop publishing and database software technology to vary the promotion frequency, enclosure materials, or catalogs based on customers' stated interests, prior purchase behavior, returns, credit level, and so on.

This type of customization and selective fulfillment, driven by information in the marketing database, can include modifying the basic offer from *negative option* to *positive option*. (In negative option clubs, main selections are automatically sent unless members return an advance announcement card requesting that the selection not be sent. In positive option programs, members must specifically order merchandise and there are no automatic shipments.) These changes can result in significant profit improvements by reducing the clubs' cost of promotion and increasing the average value and total number of customer orders through increased customer satisfaction.

Moreover, customization can be applied not only to the products included in the company's own promotion materials, but also to the *ride-along* or *co-op* promotions that may be included in statements or in the promotion envelopes themselves.

Examples of Questions Asked by Book and Music Clubs

For book clubs the survey questions are, of course, quite different from those asked by a financial services marketer. The key information to support such a data-driven program for book clubs would be reading interests, reading habits and preferences, and current and previous book club memberships. Much of this information can be obtained as part of the initial enrollment form or as part of a brief welcome survey questionnaire sent to new members. A book club survey would include questions such as these:

- How many books do you typically purchase in a year?
- How many of these are general fiction and how many are nonfiction?
- In which special categories do you normally purchase?
- Do you enjoy the convenience of the negative option program?
- Would you prefer to be enrolled in a positive option program?

The relevant behavior questions for a book club would include these:

- How many books did you buy last year in a bookstore?
- Have you previously been a member of a book club?
- If you were previously a member of a book club, what was your primary reason for leaving the club?

The demographic questions for a book club would be similar to those mentioned for financial services marketers, except that they would probably include the highest education level attained.

Insurance Marketers

A direct marketer of insurance products found, not surprisingly, that the single most important data element for its business was the age of the prospect. If the prospect's age were known, the insurance company could target its promotions and generally send the right *first offer*. A prospect's response to the initial offer began a dialogue in which the company was able to learn about other insurance products the customer owned. With this information the company was able to be more successful in its cross-selling efforts.

To develop a reliable source of age data the company had spent a considerable amount of money and several years testing age data from a number of data vendors. But these efforts were disappointing for several reasons:

- Some age data was estimated rather than actual.
- Coverage was limited to only a portion of the file, because the match rate between the prospect file and the external file was often as low as 50 percent.
- The cost of age data was relatively high when applied to a large number of leads.

Because the insurance company mailed promotions to its entire prospect file *four times per year*, managers decided to include a short survey, with an initial communication that asked prospects their date of birth, what other insurance products they owned (from a limited list), and their level of satisfaction with these products.

The result of including a survey as part of its prospect communications enabled the insurance company to accomplish three goals:

- *Better targeting*. Product promotions could be targeted more appropriately because age, product ownership, and product satisfaction information was acquired directly from prospects.
- *Better mailing efficiencies*. Promotion expenses could be better managed because prospects who did not respond to the survey could now be

mailed a different type of offer or could be excluded from further promotion efforts.

- *Reduced dependence on less accurate data sources*. The company avoided relying on purchased data that was both expensive and often inaccurate.

Another way marketers can use survey results is to eliminate or reduce the number of promotions mailed to prospects who do not respond at all based on the assumption that prospects who are unwilling to respond to a brief survey are unlikely to respond to a product promotion.

Additionally, of course, as noted earlier, marketers can use survey information to better target and regulate whom they *should* contact, with what message, and how often.

Using Questionnaires to Gather Data

Using a questionnaire to gather primary data about the target audience is valuable for another reason. Some companies have found that although models may tell us something about a prospect's willingness and ability to purchase based on similarities between the prospect's personal and financial characteristics and those of current customers, models are unlikely to have access to data about the readiness of a prospect to purchase. So although predictive models based on internally available data can reduce the target audience and models that include appended data can further improve the base models, the economics of the promotion still may not work. Information about readiness to purchase is often unavailable unless marketers have already been in direct communication with customers and prospects. This is where the survey data can be very valuable.

One way of capturing the necessary information is to shift from one-step to two-step promotions in which the first step is an inexpensive, simplified attitude and behavior survey. This approach captures data that helps marketers understand the readiness and willingness of customers to purchase and can also improve the economics of the promotion by limiting the number of expensive pieces that will ultimately be mailed.

Another benefit of using a questionnaire as the first step in a two-step process is that some of the people who respond but do not initially convert may provide other valuable information about themselves that will help the marketer in future efforts. The marketer can capture this information in the database and instruct the system to mail a promotion piece when the prospect will be ready to purchase or at a "magic moment."

Magic moment marketing, a well-established technique in the insurance industry, is the concept of mailing a life insurance upgrade or cross-sell promotion to policyholders on their birthdays or at a preset number of days prior to policy renewal. The policyholder's birth date and effective dates of coverage are maintained in the database, and the database is instructed to "wake up" and send a certain promotional piece at a present number of days prior to the event. This is but one example of how an information-oriented communication with customers and prospects can yield valuable results that may extend beyond the promotion at hand.

Using Survey Data to Assign Customers and Prospects to Segments

The assumption underlying all consumer classification techniques is that a single customer or prospect file consists of a small number of relatively homogeneous market segments and that each market segment consists of individuals whose attitudes toward a company's products or services are similar to others within the same segment but different from those in the other segments. Presumably, if you knew to which segment an individual belonged and the average attitude of that segment toward your product or service, you would market to the individuals within that segment differently than you would market to individuals within other segments. The issues, then, are to (1) confirm that the segments exist, (2) determine the attitudes and characteristics of each segment, and (3) figure out a cost-effective way to assign all individuals on your customer or prospect database to the correct segment.

Once the responses to the survey are received, statistical techniques are used to assign all responders to a small number (three to six) of relatively homogeneous segments. If attitude questions are the principal basis for the segmentation, as is frequently the case, then members of each segment have attitudes toward the subject in question that are similar to others within the same segment and dissimilar to those in other segments.

The tradition in segmentation studies is to assign a name to each segment that represents the predominant attitude of the group toward the product or service offered. For example, in financial services analysis, you will likely find such groups as the *new-money risk takers*, the *new-money schizophrenics*, and the *old-money* or *hard-pressed savers*. As you can tell from this naming scheme, each group's attitude toward investing has been combined with the group's ability to invest to provide a more meaningful description of the group.

As stated earlier, general marketers have used this kind of segmentation study for years to gain insights into the composition and needs of individual market segments. However, for this information to be truly useful to direct marketers, we need a cost-effective technique for assigning all customers or all prospects to the appropriate segments. Sending a full-blown segmentation survey to everyone on a multimillion-name database is often not cost-effective.

Direct marketers can assign customers or prospects to the appropriate segment in at least two ways. The first method involves analyzing all the questions asked in the survey to discover a relatively small number of questions that do a very good job of assigning individuals to segments. It is not unusual to discover that the answers to 6 to 10 questions can result in nearly the same assignment (70 to 80 percent correct assignment) as the full-blown questionnaire. If this is the case, then it could be cost-effective to send an abbreviated form of the complete survey to a much larger universe of names.

Of course, even sending an abbreviated survey to a large number of names can be very expensive. Therefore, before executing this approach, attempt to determine if you can accurately predict segment membership by correlating known customer data with survey data in a model that assigns a probability of segment membership to each individual on the database. The exact procedure entails building some form of regression model in which segment membership is the variable to be predicted, and customer data and any available overlay data comprise the independent predictor variables.

In practice, some combination of both methods might work best. For example, suppose a segmentation study discovered four segments within the customer database, with one segment being particularly important. Let's further assume that a mathematical model that predicted membership in this particular segment was strong but certainly not 100 percent accurate. In this case, an abbreviated survey might be mailed to all customers with a higher than average probability of membership in this key segment. The survey would enable the marketer to gather more data about a key market segment without the expense of mailing to everyone on the database. An additional step that some companies take is to develop models that predict survey response based on prior survey mailings. These models can further limit the selection of survey recipients to those names that are predicted to respond to the survey.

Response rates to surveys depend on the strength of the relationship between the company and its customers and may vary from less than 10 percent to better than 50 percent. Some companies, to improve the response rate, include premiums ranging from extra chances in sweepstakes, to price discounts, to cash. The expected response rate is critical to the design of the survey. In general, most segmentation studies require at least 3,000 to 5,000 responses. If the survey response rate is 50 percent, this means sending out 10,000 or so surveys. On the other hand, if the expected response rate is in the vicinity of 10 percent, then a much larger number of questionnaires must be mailed, and the issue of nonresponse bias becomes important. That is, if only 10 percent of the individuals who receive the survey complete it, how representative can these 10 percent be of the entire universe of customers or prospects? The answer is probably not very representative, and care must be taken to ensure the reliability of results. One way marketers sometimes evaluate the reliability of results in situations such as these is to use a telemarketing survey to confirm answers to key questions.

DATA PURCHASED FROM THIRD-PARTY SOURCES

Although directly captured data provides unique information about people's attitudes, expectations, and personal behavior, direct data is not always available to marketers at the initial stages of a targeting process. In many cases, purchasing data from secondary sources can be a cost-effective way of enhancing the strength of models.

Secondary data is defined as data acquired from third-party sources rather than provided by the individuals themselves. This includes data from U.S. census sources as well as commercially developed databases.

Demographic, attitudinal, lifestyle, and financial data are available to varying degrees at both the geographical level and the individual level. Geographical data is based on various levels of small-area geography including census tracts, ZIP codes, ZIP+4, block groups, and postal carrier routes.

A question that is always asked is whether to operate at the ZIP code or census tract block group level when using geo-demographic data. Obviously, ZIP code data is readily available and easy to use. The use of block group data requires "geo-coding" a file to associate each address in it with a block group, census tract, or both. Generally, this process costs a few dollars per thousand and adds some time to the data-appending process.

On the surface, it would appear that the smaller geographic unit would offer superior predictive precision. However, because there is considerable error between either unit's average income, age, or educational level and the true values belonging to individuals within either the ZIP code or the block group, the practical consequence of using the block group over the ZIP code might not be as great as you would expect.

Whether to use the ZIP code or block group also depends on the task at hand. If you were renting a small number of names (50,000 to 100,000) and their incomes had to be greater than, say $100,000, then we would probably recommend using block group data. On the other hand, if you were renting a million or more names or simply overlaying a database for profiling purposes, ZIP code data may be satisfactory. The recommended approach is to pose the specific question to the vendor and perhaps test both methods to see which works best for your application.

Table 4–1 shows the approximate number of each standard geographical unit in the United States for which demographic data are available.

Geography-based demographic data is produced through a series of statistical calculations applied to U.S. census data and proprietary data sources. It is sold under a number of product names by various companies such as First Data Solutions (formerly Donnelley) (ClusterPlus), Claritas (PRIZM), National Decision Systems (MICROVISION), Experian (Mosaic), and others. In fact, the Mosaic product is available for 16 different countries, accounting for a total population of roughly 800 mm. Appendix B contains samples from some of the major clustering products.

The statistical techniques used to produce geography-based demographic data vary according to the type of data being analyzed. Data elements are generally either categorical or continuous. Categorical data elements describe *one-dimensional conditions* such as the customer's state of residence, sex, or occupation. Customers live in only one state at a time, are either male or female, and generally have a single occupation. In each of these cases, the customer or prospect can have only one value for each condition. Because these types of data elements assign customers or prospects to *categories*, they are referred to as *categorical variables*. Categorical variables are analyzed using a special set of statistical techniques, including cross-tabulations, frequency distributions, and CHAID.

Other data elements, such as age and income, are not limited to categorical values. Because these data elements can have *any* values, they are referred to as *continuous*. These data elements are analyzed using different statistical techniques such as averages (means), ranges (minimum, maximum), and so on.

The U.S. Census Bureau captures both categorical and continuous data elements at the census tract and block group levels. Commercial data vendors make this same data available at postal boundary levels, which makes it easier and more convenient for direct mail marketers to use the data. Census Bureau data are broken down by ZIP codes (both five-digit and the nine-digit ZIP+4) and sometimes at the postal carrier route level to develop profiles for small-area geographical units.

Once statistical measures are calculated for each block group, other techniques, notably factor and cluster analysis, are applied to the data to "cluster" block groups with similar characteristics into neighborhood "types." These neighborhood types have similar profiles in terms of average home value, average income, family size, home type, occupation, age, presence of children, and so on.

TABLE   4–1

Unit	Number of Units	Approximate Number of Households per Unit
Residential ZIP codes	36,000	2,400
Carrier routes	210,000	400
Block groups	250,000	340

Geo-demographic data vendors support the notion that "birds of a feather flock together," which assumes that individuals will, for the most part, reflect the characteristics of the neighborhoods in which they live. Neighborhoods with common demographic characteristics may be geographically contiguous or may be located throughout the country. In numerous case studies, marketers have been able to project the purchase behavior of customers to prospects who live in similar geographical clusters in different cities.

Although the "birds of a feather" theory may be true in some respects, such as home value, it may not be true for other characteristics. One reason for disparities is that in a typical suburban neighborhood, other than a new development, immediate neighbors may have bought their homes at different times. Depending on when the home was purchased, the purchase price may vary dramatically. In suburbs of large cities, for example, a four-bedroom house may have cost $30,000 in the 1950s, $60,000 in the 1960s, $120,000 in the 1970s, $360,000 in the 1980s, and $300,000 in the 1990s. So current home value alone may not be as precise an indicator of income, net worth, and lifestyle as we might imagine.

Table 4–2 shows the individual-level demographic characteristics of six neighbors in a typical suburban neighborhood, all of whom have homes of similar value. As you can see, the ages, incomes, and family sizes of each neighbor are dramatically different. Census data would be based on averages, but the ages of only two neighbors are close to the average age and the income of only one neighbor is close to the average income. Similarly, the life stage and lifestyle of each of the neighbors are different, and importantly, the differences are not likely to be picked up by geography-based data.

Another point to consider about geo-demographic data is that neighborhoods change and data gets old quickly. Areas that are undergoing transition—in whatever direction—may be missed, and false assumptions about neighborhoods might be made. In many urban areas, gentrification, or the influx of young, relatively upscale professionals into old, sometimes run-down areas, has changed the characteristics of many neighborhoods.

Young, two-career families have, in many cases, traded proximity to work—and shorter commutes—for the space and comfort traditionally associated with suburban living, i.e., the gentrification trend. Townhouse developments, renovated brownstones, and inner-city apartments have lured many relatively wealthy people into areas that were previously economically disadvantaged.

TABLE 4–2

Neighborhood Comparisons

Neighbor	Age	Marital Status	Home Value (in Thousands)	Household Income (in Thousands)	Number of Persons in Household
Allen	75	Married	300	400	2
Baker	86	Widowed	300	11	1
Corcoran	38	Married	300	149	4
Doyle	59	Married	300	52	6
Everett	38	Married	300	85	5
Freeman	50	Married	300	65	5
Average	58		300	127	3.8

Although the impact of these trends may be well known locally, a national marketer may not be aware of them for a number of key markets and may therefore invest inappropriately in a direct marketing campaign for one of two reasons:

1. A marketer may forgo promoting to people in a certain neighborhood because out-of-date geo-demographic data may not accurately report the neighborhood's ascendancy. In this case, an uninformed marketer may give up a good opportunity.

2. A marketer may be up-to-date on changes that are in progress but may inadvertently market to holdovers from the neighborhood's previous status rather than to the newly arrived group. In this case, by targeting to the wrong people in an area, the marketer may spend promotional dollars on people who are unlikely to respond. This situation can be improved through the use of additional screens, such as change-of-address date, often involving combining data from a variety of sources.

Despite the obvious limitations of geo-demographic data—it is based on average conditions that may in fact not be representative of any of the individuals in a given neighborhood—companies that have not previously applied any external data to their customer and prospect files may find it quite helpful. Using geo-demographic data may be especially cost-effective for companies that market to individuals who live in *contiguous neighborhoods* rather than to individual households that are more geographically dispersed.

In some industries, geo-demographic data may be a very cost-effective means of describing neighborhoods. A cable television multisystem operator (MSO) used Claritas's PRIZM data to find out how similar the neighborhoods in a new franchise were to neighborhoods in which the MSO had previously had successful marketing campaigns for premium services. The MSO tested marketing programs similar to successful ones used in different cities in neighborhoods that were similar in terms of their PRIZM cluster types. The results in the new market were very highly correlated with the results in the original city, and the test significantly outpulled the control. In this situation, the MSO successfully used geo-demographic look-alikes at the neighborhood level.

National Databases as Sources of Data for File Enhancement

Many direct marketers find that they have insufficient data about their customers to make strategic marketing decisions. To develop customer profiles and, it is hoped, to be able to segment their files, additional data concerning age, income, wealth, home value, automobile ownership, presence of children, mail-order responsiveness, and so on may be very helpful.

In this case, compiled lists are very useful, primarily because of their nearly total coverage of U.S. households. Match rates between house files and compiled lists typically are in the range of 45 to 65 percent, and among home owners or mail-responsive individuals they are frequently higher.[4]

---

4. Note that an overall match rate of 45 to 65 percent does not mean that all matching names have values for all data elements. On individual data elements, match rates are typically much lower, often in the range of 5 to 10 percent.

Attitudinal Data

Attitudinal data from third-party data sources usually does not involve a customer's or prospect's attitudes about particular products or services, but rather deals with people's opinions, mores, and perceptions about such diverse subjects as lifestyle, personal values, politics, religion, and other societal issues.

Marketers tend to use attitudinal data when they are planning to launch a campaign or introduce new products into communities where they do not have previous experience. The cable television industry makes extensive use of attitudinal data when deciding whether it should promote pay services that feature R-rated or PG-rated movies. HBO responded to the attitudes of its audience, as well as age and lifestyle characteristics, when it introduced the Cinemax service. Market research showed that a large number of households throughout the country, based on age, education, and moral and religious background, objected to the level of sex, violence, and adult language used in many R-rated films. In response to the attitudes expressed in the market research and the projections of potential viewership among people with similar attitudes, HBO launched Cinemax, which, unlike the more mainstream HBO, offered movies that contained little or no sex, violence, or adult language.

Geography-Based Attitudinal Data

As in the case of demographic data, attitudinal data can be developed internally through surveys or purchased at the geographic level. To use geography-based attitudinal data for its own customer file a marketer would purchase data, such as PRIZM or ClusterPlus, that has been linked to the VALS 2 Segmentation System[5] and overlay it on the customer file or a representative sample if the file is very large. The marketer could then statistically analyze the relationship between people who live in areas where certain types of customer behavior are dominant and the associated VALS categories of those people.[6] The marketer may find that the best customers tend to come from the actualizers and achievers categories. If this is the case, then the marketer would want to promote its products to more people in those categories by looking for clusters that have a disproportionately high percentage of people classified as actualizers and achievers.

Lifestyle Data

The commercial development of lifestyle data grew out of a recognition that geo-demographic data often could not sufficiently describe differences in personal interests and leisure time activities to satisfy the informational requirements of marketers.

A number of geo-demographic data vendors have added value to their databases by combining their geo-demographic clusters with market research data.

---

5. VALS 2 is a revision of VALS, an acronym for *Values and Lifestyles*, produced by SRI International. It offers marketers a classification of customers and markets based on psychographic characteristics. In its revised version VALS 2 uses two fundamental dimensions, *self-orientation* and *consumer resources*, to provide a framework for how and why consumers are motivated to purchase products and services. The VALS 2 topology defines three self-orientations—principle, status, and action—according to a consumer's physical, demographic, and material means to act upon them. As a result, VALS 2 categorizes consumers into such groupings as actualizers, fulfilled, believers, achievers, strivers, experiencers, makers, and strugglers. Consumers are assigned to VALS categories based on their answers to a 30-question survey. Each geo-demographic cluster group is associated with a distribution of the VALS categories.

6. N. J. Olson, K. Ricke, and P. Weisenberger, "Using VALS to Target Market through Package Segmentation," *Journal of Direct Marketing Research* 1, no. 2 (Spring/Summer 1987).

Claritas, for example, combined its geo-demographic cluster data with Simmons market research data. The resulting product enables client companies to link general buyer behavior characteristics that Claritas captured on a neighborhood basis with the actual purchase performance of their customers.

Other data vendors have similarly combined their geo-demographic files with data from Simmons, VALS, MRI, and other sources to add power to their data. First Data Solutions' (formerly Donnelley) Affluence Model provides a means of predicting the affluence of individual households. This product works alone or in combination with First Data Solutions' CONQUEST desktop market analysis tool or with ClusterPlus, which is First Data Solutions' neighborhood segmentation system.

By combining geo-demographic data with purchase behavior and other consumer data, marketers increase the odds that they are placing their advertisements in print or electronic media that have significant reach among people whose characteristics match the profile of their current customers.

In direct mail, the same approach can help identify prospects based on a combination of their neighborhood type and their buyer behavior characteristics.

Vendors of lifestyle data approach the capture and management of behavioral information in a different way. One of the most innovative products in this field is The Lifestyle Selector (TLS), originally developed by National Demographics and Lifestyles (NDL) in the 1970s and subsequently acquired by R. L. Polk.

TLS data is compiled in a unique and fascinating way. The company provides highly automated warranty card processing services to manufacturers, distributors, and retailers. The manufacturer attaches warranty cards to its products and a second card that contains a demographic and lifestyle questionnaire. Once returned, the cards are then sent to Polk for processing. Polk provides the warranty information to the manufacturers in machine-readable form, along with lifestyle data about the purchases of their own products, and NDL adds the lifestyle data it has captured to its own proprietary database. Appendix B describes the data captured by Polk.

Polk then uses the demographic and lifestyle data in a number of ways. It offers a data-appending and list-profiling service for list owners to help them understand the lifestyle characteristics of their own customers beyond what they may have known or inferred based on product purchases and the original list sources. Once a list profile has been developed, list owners can rent from Polk additional names of people whose lifestyle characteristics are similar to those of their current customers.

Marketers also can send rented lists, with the approval of list owners, to Polk for screening, selecting only those names that have the desired sets of lifestyle characteristics or those that have the highest scores according to predictive models.[7] Polk's research staff can develop these models for a marketer, or the marketer can develop the models internally, depending on staff capabilities and cost.

A third approach is for marketers to take the lifestyle profile Polk developed for their house lists and apply it to their prospect files, again on a categorical or a statistical modeling basis. In the categorical approach, the marketer would use cross-tabulation to select prospects who fall into the same categories as currently

---

7. The ethical issues of screening rented lists are well covered in the Direct Marketing Association List Practices Information Task Force's *List Practices Handbook* (New York: Direct Marketing Association), which we urge you to consult.

successful customers. Using statistical modeling, the marketer would apply these characteristics to the prospect file so that promotions would be sent only to those prospects who had the highest scores based on degree of similarity with lifestyle characteristics (and most likely, with other internally available data such as list source and geography).

Marketers could use the Polk lifestyle profile in a fourth way, as a guideline for sources of other rented names. If, for example, a company's best customers all had indicated an interest in tennis, golf, and camping, a marketer might increase its rental of lists oriented to those interests.

Financial Data

Financial data providers are list compilers of a special type. Unlike the Polks, First Data Solutions (formerly Donnelley), and Metromails of the industry, which obtain their data from a variety of sources, financial data providers all get their data through service bureaus that either they own or for whom they perform clearinghouse services.

Among the largest providers of financial data are Experian (formerly TRW Target Marketing Services) and Trans Union. Both companies have access to data about credit card purchases, installment loans, applications for credit, and payment history for a very high percentage of credit-using households in the United States. The type and extent of financial data available from each of these companies change frequently, so marketers interested in using financial data should independently contact representatives of each firm for detailed information.

Taking the geo-demographic data concept of "birds of a feather" a step further, financial data can help further differentiate members of a potential market based on their actual financial performance. Marketers can send their house lists to either of the vendors listed above, as they would to any of the providers of other types of secondary data, and the vendor will produce a financial profile of customers on file. For example, marketers may learn that their best customers tend to have these characteristics:

- More than six revolving credit accounts
- At least four bank cards
- Average revolving credit balances in excess of $500
- Very few payments that are more than 30 days late
- At least two department store credit cards

The service would provide this information as averages or indexes for groups of people, not at the individual consumer level.

Armed with this information, marketers could send their prospect lists to financial data vendors to identify prospects whose financial characteristics are similar to those of their customers—promotions would be sent to those people, but less frequently or not at all to people whose characteristics differed. Additionally, marketers might rent the names of people whose financial characteristics are similar to those of their best customers.

Some marketers have worked with financial data vendors to develop models that predict how well names on the financial data files are expected to perform as customers of their businesses. Then, names from rented lists can be compared with the scored file to screen out names that are unlikely to perform well and either promote them differently or not at all.

This approach enables marketers to avoid mailing to people who are unlikely to be interested in, or unlikely to pay for, their products. By the same token, it can help marketers to find the "needles in the haystack"—those prospects who actually have the financial means and track record to be good prospects for certain products but who live in neighborhoods that models based on geo-demographic data alone might exclude from promotion.

To make data more accessible to marketers while remaining within the ethical and legal standards that govern the use of individual specific data, some vendors of financial data have developed clusters and financial lifestyle overlays that are similar in concept to the neighborhood and lifestyle clusters developed by vendors of other types of secondary data. These overlays can be appended to a company's customer or prospect file, and the company can then either develop its own scoring models or simply use the overlays as categorical selection criteria.

Demographic Data

Several companies, including Polk, First Data Solutions (formerly Donnelley), Metromail, Neodata, Infobase, and others, have compiled household lists of names and addresses and a great deal of individual-specific data for the vast majority of U.S. households. Each of the major vendors of individual-specific data compiles its lists in a slightly different way.

The Polk Company compiles its lists from a number of public record sources, but most notably from state motor vehicle registration information. At present, Polk provides direct marketers with motor vehicle registration data for 33 states. At one time more states participated, but recent concerns about and legislation on privacy have curtailed access to information in some states. This data consists of the make, model, and year of automobiles that individuals currently own and previously owned. It also indicates the value of individual autos and total value of autos by household.

Polk adds a number of other primary data elements, as well as computed data elements such as income, to the base file. In many cases, imputed income is based on a combination of the individual's age, home value, occupation, automobile ownership and ownership pattern, neighborhood type, and other factors. Some computed individual or household-level data is essentially a geo-demographic average of block group data.

Most recently, Polk introduced a new segmentation product called *Niches*. Using all the data available in Polk's national database, the company classified all households as belonging to one of 26 Niches. For marketers requiring further discrimination, each household also belongs to one of 108 *SuperNiches*. Using this scheme, marketers can rent names identified by a predefined segmentation plan and be confident that all the names they rent fall into the segment they're targeting.

Whereas Polk originally compiled its data from state motor vehicle registration departments and from its own city directory business, First Data Solutions (formerly Donnelley Marketing, Inc.) and Metromail originally compiled their data through their telephone directory and city directory businesses. Over the years, each of these companies has expanded its sources to include additional public record agencies, private list compilers, list owners who use their facilities for other computer processing, and new primary name acquisition businesses.

Although many of the variables included in data of this type are similar to geo-demographic data in content, they differ in one critical aspect: all data are specific to named individuals rather than to a set of geography-based summaries.

That is, if the individual-specific age data says that John Smith of 123 Elm street, Anytown, USA, is 37 years old, you can rest assured that the specific John Smith in question is 37 years old. It does not mean that he lives in a block group or ZIP code in which the average age is 37, although this might also be the case.

In the case of some variables, for example, presence of children, implicit data may be used. And in cases where the specific age of an individual is not known, age may be stated in terms of the range that is most probable based on a number of other variables that are known with certainty. For example, if it is known that a household includes children under 5, it will be inferred that the children's mother is not older than 45 and that the father is not older than 50. Although there will certainly be cases in which this inference is inaccurate, for the majority of cases it will be reasonably close when combined with known data elements.

National Databases as Sources of Names

Marketers use national databases in several ways. One way is simply to use a national database as a source of names. The marketer would specify characteristics of people that are desirable for a particular promotion. The national database company's account executive would then work with the programming staff to produce a customized selection of names from the firm's national database file.

Although national databases that include individual-specific data may be a valuable source of names, many marketers find that names from rented lists belonging to mail-order businesses outperform names selected from national databases. In most cases, this is because the source of the rented list indicates two important factors:

1. People whose names are on the list are direct mail–responsive.
2. The content of the magazine or the nature of the catalog or other business that is the source of the list may provide clues about the person's interests.

However, there are notable examples of marketers finding great success using national databases as sources of names. In one case an automobile company (Company A) was planning a campaign with the objective of stealing market share from its principal competitor (Company B). Company A developed an expensive mailing package and sent it to owners of Company B's cars who were at the stage of the car ownership cycle during which people begin to contemplate the purchase of their next car. Using Polk data to determine car ownership and the stage of the ownership cycle, Company A customized the direct mail package to include the name, address, and telephone number of the most conveniently located Company A dealer. This approach enabled Company A to target its offer to the desired segment, support its dealer network, and provide potential customers with the added convenience of local dealer information.

In another case, an automobile company (Company C) planned to launch a customer reacquisition program by targeting owners of selected cars who had previously owned a Company C product. Company C selected names of owners of specific makes and models from the Polk file, matched this list against its own file of former customers, and rolled out a campaign that combined reacquisition with model upgrade strategies.

The Polk file was extremely valuable as a source of names to Company A and Company C in these examples specifically because the file contained automobile data. But numerous examples can be cited by applications that are not primarily related to automobiles and that use national databases quite differently.

Using Acquired Data to Predict Segment Membership

Professional journals have reported a number of innovative marketing programs that rely on gathering, analyzing, and manipulating data. One example involves the use of survey simulators to predict direct marketing response. This approach used surveys to gather data about the characteristics of individuals within the target audience and to link these characteristics to the rate and manner in which people indicated they would respond to a promotion. Green and Moore theorized that people with similar individual characteristics would have similar attitudes and that by "quantifying" a dry run of a promotion, which linked attitudinal data to data about individual characteristics, the results of a promotion rollout could be predicted.[8] By using survey data in this manner prior to mailing, Green and Moore were able to help their clients focus promotion dollars on the campaigns that had the greatest potential for success based on the characteristics of the target audience.

This example is notable because it employed research concepts as part of the mainstream marketing process that would normally be limited to market research. This approach was a cost-effective way to reduce the size of the target audience to those people who were most likely to respond.

---

8. M. E. Green and E. Moore. "Using Survey Simulators to Predict Direct Mail Response," *Journal of Direct Marketing Research* 1, no. 2 (Spring/Summer 1987).

CHAPTER 5

Relationship Marketing and How It Relates to the New Direct Marketing

SOME BACKGROUND AND ATTEMPTS AT DEFINITIONS

As discussed in Chapter 1, what we have chosen to call *the new direct marketing* evolved from traditional direct marketing over the last 20 years or so. During that period a number of attempts have been made to rename what we were tempted to call "this thing of ours," but that name, too, like others we contemplated, we understood to be taken. In the 1980s the name of choice was database marketing, but because the term *database* had, and still has, a technical connotation, other names—names with a more marketing orientation, such as *relationship marketing* or *customer-focused marketing*—have received considerable attention.

It's interesting that the phrase "database marketing persists" and that relationship marketing is treated as a topic within the broader subject of marketing. The two Direct Marketing Association conferences devoted to this subject are still called *The National Center for Database Marketing*. What's also interesting is the DMA/DMEF's[1] decision to change the name of its journal from the *Journal of Direct Marketing* to the *Journal of Interactive Marketing*, a change that might portend the emergence of a new umbrella term which will encompass all of the other components of what we call *the new direct marketing*.

Call it what you like, but when the new direct marketing turns its attention to *marketing*, all versions of this concept involve establishing and maintaining value-added, one-on-one *relationships* with customers. Here then is our understanding of the history, current status, and likely course of development for this important component of the new direct marketing.

Relationship marketing is not so much a bold leap forward as it is a scramble to recapture something from the past. Before the age of mass production, producers and merchants had one-on-one relationships with individual customers. An individual customer's needs were well known and products were routinely custom-produced to meet those needs.

MASS MARKETS

Over time, large-scale mass production and distribution methods revolutionized the way that products were brought to market. These advances created cost-efficiencies

---

1. DMEF stands for the Direct Marketing Educational Foundation, the separate organization within the DMA with the responsibility for attracting students and educators to the field of direct marketing.

that drove lower prices, making a broad range of products affordable to the masses. However, a price was paid for that standardization. Instead of products being configured to the needs of individuals, consumers were placed in the position of evaluating the merits (features and benefits) of mass-produced products and choosing the one that most completely fulfilled their needs.

Along with standardized production and distribution came standardized marketing. In this *product-centric* approach, individuals were grouped into a "mass market" consisting of six or so "macro segments." Effective communication with consumers involved developing half a dozen relevant types of messages and distributing them via "mass media," i.e., very lightly targeted messages blasted out via print, TV, radio, and outdoor advertising. In mass media, marketing communications occurred via impersonal, one-way channels—from companies outbound to consumers.

It is important to recall that people were really no different then than we are today. They all had unique collections of needs. What was different was the fact that production capacity in the post-Depression era was outdistanced by demand, especially in the 1950s and 1960s. *During this time frame, people were happy to get any product at a reasonable cost, let alone one that significantly met their needs.*

TODAY'S MARKETS—THE IMPACT OF TECHNOLOGY

Today, the marketplace is structured quite differently, and consumers have come to hold the advantage in many product categories. Foreign competition and competition from nontraditional suppliers have *increased supply*. Technology-driven advancements in communications and product/service delivery have *increased competitive reach* to the extent that in many industries we have almost achieved a truly global marketplace.

Technology has also vastly increased production capabilities, further lowered manufacturing costs, and *enabled large-scale customized production*. In many industries it is now less expensive to produce custom-configured products than to mass-produce, carry inventory, incur distribution expenses, stock retail sites, and accept closeout losses on unsold merchandise.

As a result, huge multinational companies with heavy investments in retail sites find themselves competing with smaller, more nimble niche providers who remotely service their customers.

TODAY'S MARKETS—THE IMPACT OF DEMOGRAPHIC TRENDS

In most product categories, demographic trends have resulted in a stagnation of growth in the consumer base. Compounding this trend is the fact that the majority of our population is currently in a life stage characterized by relatively low levels of product acquisition. The net impact is a dramatic increase in the cost of customer acquisition for most industries.

Beyond demographics, the vast majority of consumers lead very busy lives with multiple demands on their free time. This factor, combined with the constant introduction of new products and promotions, as well as the constant bombardment of marketing messages, has resulted in a marked decrease in "shopping" as a priority activity. A number of market research studies over the last five years indicate that most consumers today are *convenience-driven* as opposed to being price-driven. Consumers tend to identify suppliers who provide adequate quality at a fair price, simplify their lives, and add value. They tend to stay with suppliers who prove worthy of their loyalty, realizing that it would take time and effort to identify and switch to a new supplier.

RELATIONSHIP MARKETING = CUSTOMER RETENTION + SHARE OF CUSTOMER

Much of the discussion of relationship marketing revolves around the question of how best to relate to the customer. However, we must also consider the inherent profit mechanism, i.e., just what relationship marketing will accomplish in a business sense. Plainly stated, the crux of relationship marketing is retaining customers over the long term and satisfying the largest possible portion of their needs with your products and services. While applications of relationship marketing have been extended over the entire range of the customer life cycle, retention and customer development (share of customer) are really the two key elements.

As a result, customer retention has become a very serious strategic issue in most companies. Contrast this situation with the age of mass marketing, where most companies used a "leaky bucket" approach to drive their businesses. In those times, potential new customers were plentiful, demand outstripped supply, and a number of inexpensive far-reaching media were available and effective.

Today, consumers are rapidly coming to expect that technology should allow companies to adapt to them. They want companies to understand their unique needs and wants and then to adapt products and services to those needs and wants. At a more basic level, customers are saying that they want:

- Reasonable quality at a fair price
- Respect
- Consistency
- Intelligent support
- Convenience and efficient use of their time

Furthermore, most consumers do not have the time to keep abreast of new technologies, applications for existing products, or service options. *Consumers want their "vendors" to become "product usage consultants," helping them to make the correct choice and then gain maximum advantage from the chosen product or service. In this relationship, the company takes partial responsibility for the customer's choice of product relative to the customer's needs, how the product is used, and therefore the customer's level of satisfaction.*

DEVELOPING RELATIONSHIP MARKETING CAPABILITIES

In implementing *traditional direct marketing programs*, marketers first studied customers' needs and the status of competitors in the market. When targets of acceptable opportunity were identified, the marketers next developed marketing programs directed toward specific market segments. Campaign implementation followed with selecting promotional lists, mailing or phoning the customer, collecting responses, and reviewing response tracking reports. Results from that promotional cycle were then used as input to planning the next promotional cycle. The overall objective was to increase long-term customer performance (profitability), with the key measure ideally being customer value, but very often being immediate sales.

In the relationship marketing model, we build upon the traditional direct marketing model. The essential initial steps include building infrastructure capabilities such as:

- Data collection
- Data access and marketing tools
- Product and service customization
- Customer service procedures
- Customer access channels

These capabilities enable the company to use every customer interaction as an opportunity to collect more information and use it to better service and promote customers. The overall objectives are to ease customer access, reduce costs, suggest alternatives, and provide relevant added value. The key measures in relationship marketing are customer satisfaction, share of wallet within product category, and stability of the relationship.

If implemented properly, the company will learn about the customers, provide better service, learn more about the customers, provide still better service . . . The end result is a very stable relationship. The company has long-term customers whose value and satisfaction levels are maximized. The customers have their needs met with minimal effort on their part and would incur a large personal cost if they attempt to switch to and "train" another supplier.

Therefore, the three essential foundation elements of implementing a relationship marketing program are:

- Collecting information about customer demographics, needs, and preferences
- Customizing products, services, and customer support to fit each customer's needs and preferences
- Using customer service via interactive and personalized two-way communications across a variety of channels to determine:
  - Whether needs and preferences have been addressed
  - Levels of satisfaction
  - Any questions that need to be answered
  - Additional customer information and changes in status
  - If presenting new products or options is appropriate

If properly implemented, relationship marketing will deliver a true value-added relationship which the customer will regard as an asset. Additionally, it should provide more stable, longer-term relationships. Since these relationships take time to develop, any customer switching to another vendor with the same skills would have to endure a "learning curve" period while the new vendor:

- Collects behavioral, descriptive, and attitudinal data
- Develops an understanding of the customer's preferences and trends
- Configures appropriate product/service options and marketing programs

CUSTOMER INFORMATION

At its core, relationship marketing is about understanding customers well enough to service them well enough to keep and possibly grow their business over time. Therefore, relationship marketing requires a much more comprehensive set of data sources than traditional direct marketing. While a number of direct and indirect sources of customer information are discussed later on in this book, it is important to point out that the most effective way to get information for relationship marketing programs is to obtain it directly from the customers themselves.

While the optimal types of customer information will vary by industry, company market positioning, and marketing programs, certain broad categories of information are universally useful:

- Demographics
- Life stage
- Lifestyle
- Language preference
- Communication channel preference
- Level of support desired
- Important product attributes
- Attitudes relative to product usage
- Key purchase influencers
- Overall product category usage
- Company's share of wallet in this product category
- Use of related products and services
- Attitude toward company
- Suggestions

Like the relationship itself, building a base of information on a customer will be an iterative, long-term process. In "Stage 1" the customer will have a basic level of interest in the company and will usually provide basic information. As the relationship deepens and the company becomes more important to the customer, the amount of information shared will increase. Also, the base of behavioral (usually transactional) information will grow over time.

A well-known delivery services provider is an excellent example of staged information gathering. Basic information about the customer is collected at the time that a new shipping account is opened. Of course, this is the easiest point at which to acquire information because the customer expects to establish that he or she is a good credit risk. However, because a relationship has not been established and most customers cannot adequately forecast their future usage, the type of information collected is generalized in nature. As the customer conducts transactions, a purchase history database collects the information. Shipping activity levels and patterns, types of shipments, and associated product purchases are analyzed and used to drive follow-up requests for information via outbound telemarketing. High-volume international shippers are prompted for specific types of information, while customers who mostly use domestic letter packages are asked different questions. As explained to the customer, the information is used to customize account statements and recommend new services and cost savings measures as well as sell related products that would provide a benefit relevant to the customer.

Another company, providing cellular telephone services, offers to use customer information provided at the time of sale to suggest optimal initial calling plans and optional services. The company then makes quarterly reviews of calling patterns and uses the customer demographic information to suggest alternative calling plans that would minimize costs.

While it is commonly known that there is a public movement toward information privacy, both academic studies and practical experience have shown that the vast majority of consumers are reluctant to share information only when there is no clear value proposition. If the company can demonstrate that the information will be used to drive tangible benefits in the service level and can gain the customer's trust in holding the information confidential, then customers who have a serious interest in the company as a partner usually are willing to comply.

CUSTOMIZATION AND ADDED VALUE

Customers must derive tangible value from providing information and committing to a relationship with the company. Of course, the scope of specific benefits received will differ by the type of product and/or service being offered.

In the past, companies tended to be product-centric and it was usually up to the customer to decide whether the company provided an appropriate solution and how to use it most effectively. For sure, companies always supplied marketing literature and instructions for using their products, but today it is quite common to have 7-day-a-week, 24-hour-a-day help desks available for products ranging from software to food products to refrigerators.

Perhaps one of the best examples of customized products is the revolution in the way that personal computers are produced and manufactured. While it is still possible to walk into a retail outlet and purchase a preconfigured machine, the majority of the industry now operates through remotely purchased, custom-configured machines. Customers can specify machine characteristics and place orders via telephone customer service, inbound faxes, and Internet systems.

One company, a specialized utilities company, is focusing on servicing customers who have the need to be environmentally conscious. This provider certifies that it will purchase and distribute energy only from "green" sources.

They also provide a variety of environmentally conscious information via newsletters, Internet sites, and interactive voice messaging systems.

The customer service function can leverage information to:

Support the installation and setup process

Provide relevant product specifications

Suggest new products or product features

Remind customers of important dates and events

Custom-configure products and services

Configure pricing bundles, payment options, and account statements

Deliver customers the level of support that they request

Simplify purchase and usage

Suggest options to decrease costs

Tailor promotions and offers to the customer's context

Provide relevant product information

Configure loyalty programs and benefits

Provide consistency and familiarity in customer service

Recommend and schedule product service

Offer proactive advice

This trend is especially evident in service industries like insurance, computer systems, telephone, and financial services. Customer service is rapidly becoming the point of differentiation, not product, price, or promotional offers which can be copied overnight. Sustainable competitive advantage is now driven by corporate culture, customer service training, staff empowerment, and technology infrastructure (data, data usage, and product customization). Being able to develop significant relationships with customers and service them well, on the other hand, has a number of practical barriers to entry:

- Implementing a corporate culture focusing on the customer, i.e., integrating the marketing, advertising, and customer service functions
- Developing a suite of products and services that can be customized to the unique needs of each customer
- Training and empowering the customer service staff
- Developing a technology infrastructure to support collecting customer data, using data effectively, and customizing products and services

TWO-WAY COMMUNICATION AND INCREASED "BANDWIDTH"

Unlike the era of mass media, today we must become focused on our customer's choice of channels. Different lifestyles require different communication vehicles. The same customer will initiate different types of transactions via different channels. One set of options will be used during the workweek, others during weekends. Customers will have different preferences for inbound versus outbound communications and marketing promotions versus product usage or account status information.

Anticipating the entry of new competition, a local telephone service provider has proactively instituted a process of surveying key customers to determine levels of satisfaction, better define the customer, discover any unfulfilled needs, and establish a continuing relationship with a specific customer service representative.

Innovation in communication has introduced the option of two-way communications and has increased the "bandwidth" between customers and companies. Today, we are faced with a dizzying array of communications channels that can be targeted to various degrees:

Telephone customer service

Interactive voice messaging systems

WWW sites

Proprietary PC access systems

E-mail

Fax

Cellular phones

Pagers

Voice mail

Outbound mail

Outbound telemarketing

Account statements and bills

Proprietary newsletters and statements

Retail point of sale sites

Kiosk access sites (ABMs, overnight delivery drop boxes, etc.)

Product servicing and repair services

In traditional media, the marketer can control many communication elements, including timing of delivery, message content, and delivery channel. However, marketing programs using many of the new communication channels will only be able to control the content of messages directed to customers. Access channel preference and delivery timing in many instances will be determined by the customers according to how and when they contact the company.

The key to leveraging existing customer communication channels is being able to integrate information flows across the various customer contact channels and coordinate marketing activity across individual customers, channels, and marketing programs.

Figure 5–1 presents a consolidated framework for the type of systems that several of our clients are implementing. In all cases, these companies had established information systems to support daily operations such as order entry, order status, point of sale purchases, account status, financial transactions, billing, shipping, etc. They also had established a number of electronic channels to give their customers cost-effective and convenient access to the company. Examples include telephone customer service centers, Internet and proprietary PC access systems, interactive voice messaging, retail point of sale promotions, and mailed account statements.

These companies had also implemented marketing operations systems (i.e., next-generation marketing databases) to house information on customers and prospects and provide the tools necessary for strategic planning, marketing program planning, marketing program implementation, and results analysis. While the marketing databases allowed marketers to directly implement marketing programs across traditional channels, such as direct mail and telemarketing, they did not support direct implementation across electronic channels or the ability to drive marketing programs to individuals in a dynamic fashion.

The key to moving forward was to design and implement a new class of

FIGURE 5–1

Marketing Message Delivery System

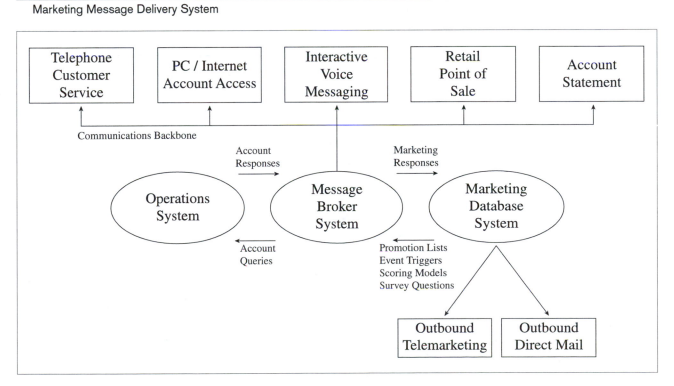

system, referred to here as a "message broker" system. These systems are designed to fit into the information flow supporting existing electronic customer access channels, since all of the various channels must eventually "talk to" the company's operational system that supports its core business functions. In the case of telephone customer service, the service representative inputs the customer's identifier (name and address, account number, telephone number, etc.), and a transaction is sent "downstream" to the operations system. On the way, the message broker intercepts the transaction, creates another marketing-oriented transaction, and then sends the original transaction on to the operations system.

The marketing-oriented transaction is sent to another part of the message broker that makes promotional decisions based on the customer identifier and direction received from the marketing database system. Message delivery decisions are made according to a number of criteria:

- The customer may have one or more marketing messages waiting for him or her in a message database. These messages are created by marketing managers who select lists of names from the marketing database, just as they would for a traditional mail or telemarketing program. Instead of assigning a source code and "cutting a tape" for a lettershop or outbound telemarketing vendor, the marketer assigns a message code and delivery preference information to the selected list and sends it to the message database system. The promotional "creative" or message text (and sometimes graphics) is housed in a separate part of the message database and is referenced via the message code.

- The customer may have met the conditions of an event trigger, such as purchasing a specific item, having a total order value over $150, etc. Event triggers are implemented by marketers setting "selection rules" in the message database, very much like the list selection logic used to pull names for mailing programs, etc. The difference is that these rules are evaluated dynamically each time the customer is active on a channel. This allows the company to immediately react to different promotional situations and to eliminate lag times.

- The customer may also have met the conditions necessary to receive a marketing message as specified by a statistical model. While the selection rules identified above evaluate a customer's current status, scoring models have the ability to predict future status based on present information. For example, a customer may be making a second purchase and the combined values, specific products, and timing of the purchases may result in the customer being classified as a potential high-value customer.

- "Survey questions" represent another type of message that a customer may be eligible to receive. Using a list and event trigger approaches, the company may want to know something specific about the customer. The possibilities are endless, but some examples include demographic information, attitudes toward environmental issues, interest in a particular type of product, satisfaction with the last purchase, etc.

Once the message broker has determined for which messages the customer is qualified, it must decide which ones should be delivered and in which order. These decisions will depend on both the priority of each message and the channel on which the customer is currently active. Different channels will have different effective "bandwidths." For example, a customer standing at a grocery store point of sale will have, at best, the time and patience to receive a very simple offer or request for information. If the same customer is talking to a customer service representative, there is the opportunity to deliver a longer and more complicated message. The service rep also has the advantage of being very conversational and not being limited to a predefined script. One very interesting development is the willingness of customers to provide information via Internet applications. While we do not have sufficient experience to be sure, it appears that people inherently feel that responding via this channel is more confidential or private than providing information when requested by another person.

After deciding on which messages to deliver, the message broker coordinates the marketing communication stream with the customer service communication stream. Depending on channel, type of transaction, etc., the message broker may decide to suspend the customer service exchange until the marketing message is delivered, complete the customer service exchange first, integrate the two communication streams, etc. The message broker will also appropriately format the message transaction according to the needs of the active channel.

Capturing customer response is a critical element of dynamic messaging. The message broker will intercept marketing message response transactions returned from the active channel. If the exchange is intended to be a simple, one-cycle process (one question, one answer), then a transaction will be sent to the marketing database to record the response. However, many exchanges will involve multiple steps, where interest is measured, follow-up information is offered, and lastly the customer is prompted for a delivery channel and location.

Another essential coordination function performed by the message broker is ensuring that messages are not duplicated. Without a central point of coordination, each channel would be free to deliver messages independent of other channels. In one instance, if a customer responded that he was not interested via telephone customer service, the same message would not be delivered when he later contacted the company via the Internet site. Also, the message broker is responsible for balancing a customer's total message load for a given time period. Just as in direct mail or telemarketing where it is possible to saturate a customer and reduce overall value to the company, electronic channels are just as vulnerable, if not more so. An interesting refinement in one of these message broker systems is the use of customer complaint activity in deciding their overall message load.

Of course, this same approach can be applied to contact channels that are not electronic in nature and therefore are not as dynamic. One example is mailed account statements, where customer questions are stored in the message database and the statement preparation system accesses it to determine which questions should be placed on the statement and collected manually when the payment is sent in.

RELATIONSHIP MARKETING AND MARKETING OBJECTIVES

Coordinating marketing communication activity across the available communication channels and marketing programs represents a significant challenge requiring development of business processes and the technical infrastructure to support them. Here are some examples of how the process can be applied across the entire scope of a customer's life span:

> *Consumer awareness and education.* A variety of channels (telephone service center, WWW site, etc.) is made available to the public to deliver information about the company, its products and services, and related "public service" topics. If interested, consumers can directly move into establishing a relationship with the company (provide information and

indicate interest). This interaction also serves to establish the company as a source of value beyond simply providing a product or service.

New Customer Acquisition. Mass media advertising and targeted prospecting programs direct potential customers to contact the customer service center for more information. The relationship marketing process is used to collect information from prospects and appropriately configure the company's response. Beyond being promoted, the consumer comes away from the experience feeling that they have initiated an ongoing relationship and that their needs have been satisfied in an intelligent fashion. The "information value proposition" is clearly established by this interaction.

Customer Acceleration. Once an active relationship has been established, the company can use the customer service process and transactional activity to find out more about the needs of their customer and provide information about new products, new services and uses of current products. Beyond "promoting" the customer, these communications are founded on servicing specific needs. Instead of "Are you interested in this product?" the dialogue is about "Are you interested in us servicing this specific need?" These dialogues offer companies the opportunity to increase product usage levels, increase "share of wallet," as well as cross-sell related products and services.

Customer Retention. At its heart, relationship marketing is about using information to provide value beyond delivering a product or service. Since this is a true learning process, it takes time to collect needed information, understand customer needs/patterns and explore product and service alternatives. Customers have their needs met with minimal effort on their part and would incur a large personal cost if they attempt to switch to and "train" another supplier. Relationship marketing also offers the opportunity to upgrade existing loyalty programs through enhanced customer service and customized benefits packages.

Niche Marketing. In relationship marketing, every customer becomes his or her own niche.

Lapsed Customer Reactivation. Information about customer needs, preferences, patterns and explored options should never be "thrown away," even if the customer deactivates. Since some product usage cycles have a very long period and alternate suppliers can always disappoint the customer, there is a good chance that the customer will come back at some point. Rather than starting from scratch, the company should lead with "Welcome back. We haven't forgotten you."

CHAPTER 6

The Role of Direct Marketing in Building Brands

CONVENTIONAL WISDOM

It has long been asserted that, unlike traditional mass media advertising, the purpose of direct marketing is not to build up a brand's "image," but to get an immediate sale. Bob Stone, for example, in his classic book *Successful Direct Marketing Methods* writes that the objective of "getting the sale" is what leads to the standard principles of direct marketing copywriting: give detailed features; overcome objections; give a reason for acting immediately, such as deadlines and limited offers; etc.[1]

As the reader is no doubt aware, however, building "brand equity" has suddenly become a hot and fashionable topic among marketers and chief executives.[2] Relatedly, there appears to be a widespread belief that in order to build such brand equity a marketer needs to invest heavily in image-building mass advertising. It is time to examine whether direct marketing is in fact only a "one-shot-sale" method of marketing or whether it too has a role in building a brand's longer-term "equity"—and if so, how.

WHAT DOES IT MEAN TO BUILD BRAND EQUITY?

While definitions vary, the term *brand equity* is typically used to describe the financial "asset value" of a brand that derives from the goodwill and loyalty it has built up among customers, as a result of its high awareness, its perceived quality, its imagery and personality associations, and its distribution and other hard-to-copy resources.[3] This overall asset value, in turn, is usually based on the ability of the brand in question to extract higher prices and margins than competing brands of supposedly equal "objective," functional, value. A high-equity brand may also be more valuable as an asset because even though its price and/or market share is no higher than it "should be," the brand has customers who repurchase it more often than they objectively should, so that its marketing costs to retain customers

---

1. Robert Stone, *Successful Direct Marketing Methods* (Chicago: NTC Books, 1995).
2. For example, see David A. Aaker, *Managing Brand Equity* (New York: The Free Press, 1991); David A. Aaker, *Building Strong Brands* (New York: The Free Press, 1996); Jean-Noel Kapferer, *Strategic Brand Management* (New York: The Free Press, 1992); Levin L. Keller, *Strategic Brand Management* (Upper Saddle River, NJ: Prentice Hall, 1998); and Robert Stone, *Successful Direct Marketing Methods* (Chicago: NTC Books, 1995).
3. David A. Aaker, *Managing Brand Equity* (New York: The Free Press, 1991).

are lower than that of competitive brands (and the "lifetime value" of those customers is higher than that of the competition). This would again give the brand "supernormal" profitability.

This greater preference and loyalty exist not because this brand has a functionally superior product or service, objectively speaking, but because of something the consumer perceivedly knows or feels about this brand. This difference is the essence of a "brand," which exists only as a subjective, "imaginary" concept in the mind of the consumer, as an agglomeration of perceived facts and feelings. Beyond the "minimum" necessity of possessing high levels of awareness in the target segment, a strong brand usually evokes many such positive and consistent "thoughts and feelings" in the target consumer, usually referred to as "associations." The relative importance of these "subjective intangibles" in influencing brand choice varies, depending on the product category and the individual (being higher, for example, in socially consumed "badge" categories and among highly influenceable consumer segments such as teens).

The essence of a brand is thus the many associations that the brand's name, symbol, packaging color, etc., evoke in the mind of the consumer. These associations can be about the brand's functional properties and benefits (what it does and how it does it); its overall or attribute-specific level of quality and reliability; the kinds of users and usage contexts the brand is meant for; the company that makes the brand (its reputation for quality, innovativeness, community and environmental orientation, etc.); the country from which that brand originates (e.g., if it comes from Italy, it must be stylish and fashionable); or various other kinds of symbolic and cultural meanings and values (e.g., this is a "fashionable" or "fun" or "high-status" brand). These associations also create a sense of "intimacy" and "relationship" or "distance" toward the brand, leading to higher loyalty toward "high-equity" brands (such as Harley-Davidson or Saturn).

These associations by their very nature can and do vary across consumers and segments. A "brand" can thus be said to consist of those associations that are widely shared and strongly held by its target segment. Clearly, the role of direct marketing and advertising and of other marketer-initiated communications is thus to build awareness to communicate high quality, to create or modify target associations in the minds of its target segment, and to build such loyalty.

BUILDING AWARENESS THROUGH DIRECT MARKETING

It is commonly agreed that strong brands have high levels of awareness among their target consumer segments, with the strongest brands having high "unaided" awareness, coming to mind first when the product or service category is thought of (for instance, FedEx in overnight delivery). The marketer's tools in building such awareness are no secret: spending money in mass media advertising, generating publicity through public relations devices, sponsoring events of various kinds, creating word-of-mouth buzz, etc.

Obviously, direct marketing communications can also be used to create and maintain such brand awareness. It might seem at first glance that most direct marketing vehicles (such as direct mail or telemarketing calls) are not the most efficient marketing communications vehicles for creating such awareness, because the cost per contact (say, $700 per thousand mailing pieces) is much higher than in mass advertising media (say, $20 per thousand exposure opportunities in prime-time network television). This calculus is undoubtedly true in the case of some mass-marketed consumer goods (such as foods or toiletries), but can be deceptive whenever the target segment is narrower and harder to reach through mass media (such as individuals with a certain fashion style). In such cases, because of wastage in mass media, the cost per target consumer actually reached can be much higher there, and the targeting ability of direct marketing can offset these initial cost disadvantages to some extent.

More importantly, building a high level of awareness is usually not the most important part of a brand-building job: building a strong reputation for quality and value is. And this is where direct marketing can shine.

BUILDING A QUALITY REPUTATION THROUGH DIRECT MARKETING

Probably the most crucial element of building a strong brand is creating a reputation for extremely high quality and value. What "quality" means obviously varies across product and service categories, and can very often depend more on post-manufacturing elements (such as speed of delivery, ease of financing, installation assistance, and after-sales service) than on the physical and technical aspects of the product or service. The interpretation of "quality" and "value" can also obviously vary across consumer segments and decision makers in the buying organization (the finance people versus the technical people, for instance). And the claims to "quality" have to be clearly comprehended, and believed, for the quality reputation to get created. Direct marketing can be of great use in these last three aspects.

Communicating Quality

Many direct marketing media—such as direct mail—have the advantage over mass media advertising (such as TV or print ads) of allowing much more space to make, and support, detailed claims about product features and benefits. As a result, they should potentially lead to much stronger communications about why the marketed brand or product is competitively superior, enhancing its quality reputation. And because what "quality" and "value" mean can vary dramatically across consumers and customers, targeted direct marketed communications can do a much better job than less-targeted mass media communications of stressing those features and benefits that are of the highest value to the message recipient, maximizing the perceived degree of value and quality communicated.

Achieving Credibility

Claiming high quality is easy; getting believed is the hard part. Here, again, direct marketing communications typically have an advantage over mass media communications, because they can potentially take the time to understand and refute consumer objections, cite testimonials from satisfied users, and offer guarantees of satisfaction, to a degree not usually possible in space-constrained mass media communications.

Frequency of Post-Sales Contact

To the extent that a reputation for high quality comes from higher frequency of post-sales contact, direct marketing can allow companies to make lower-cost telemarketing calls to monitor and improve customer satisfaction, and to drive home the company's leadership in technology and quality (for instance, through databased-mailing of newsletters).

BUILDING OTHER ASSOCIATIONS THROUGH DIRECT MARKETING

Beyond a reputation for quality, strong brands very often have unique, idiosyncratic, highly valued, and category-relevant associations among target consumers. Think of Harley Davidson and you think of leather jackets and James Dean and Marlon Brando and freedom; think of Coca-Cola and you think of good feelings and Norman Rockwell Americana; think of Budweiser and you think of hard-working men relaxing after a long day's work. Many marketing tools are used in such association building, notably advertising, packaging, and event sponsorships.

If direct marketing communications are to be used more effectively for the association-enhancement part of brand building, they should be designed and written *not only* to convey product features and benefits and value, and to overcome the recipient's inertia to placing the order immediately, but also to strategically use creative elements that build and reinforce the linkage between the brand and symbols that possess the needed "cultural meaning." These can include endorsers and personalities, events and sponsorships, places of origin, etc.

A Starbuck's catalog, for instance, not only provides details about the various kinds of coffee beans it sells, but also goes to considerable lengths to highlight the uniqueness of each source location of coffee bean, and to discuss the expertise with which Starbuck's buyers select them and the special way they are roasted. As a result, the consumer not only places the order for a few pounds of coffee, but begins to believe that coffee beans from Starbuck's will indeed possess superior taste and aroma, and that Starbuck's is *the* unique expert source from which to buy coffee beans.

BUILDING LOYALTY THROUGH DIRECT MARKETING

Suffice it to say that all those reading this book know, or will know by the time they are finished reading, that a smart direct marketer can build and use databases to initiate frequent, timely, and targeted contact with existing customers to upsell and cross-sell products and services, to increase the frequency of purchase and the customer's "share of requirements" satisfied by that vendor, and to reward and incentivize increased loyalty through various kinds of point-style reward schemes.

But a word of warning is necessary. There are two kinds of loyalty. One is created by high "switching costs," such as when I fly an airline simply because I want to accrue my miles in its frequent-flyer program so I can earn my free ticket faster. Such "behavioral loyalty" is important and valuable, but can be fragile if it does not have the underpinning of genuine liking for the airline. It is much more important to create the second kind, a genuine, attitudinal, "deeper-down" sense of loyalty and relationship, where the customer is willing to stick with you even if your offering is a little bit pricier, or a little less convenient. This is also more difficult to create. The mythical advantage of databases and direct marketing is that marketers can potentially offer better, customized, time-saving service to customers so that they feel this deeper attitudinal loyalty to and kinship with the provider. But engendering this kind of loyalty requires an appreciation of the "human element" in customer service, not simply the use of multimillion-name databases and complex software algorithms. It is therefore much more expensive, which obviously limits its use to higher-margin and multiple-purchase situations.

CONCLUSIONS AND SUMMARY

In many ways, the role of direct marketing in building brands is underappreciated. By being identified overly with a "get the sale and who cares about anything else" orientation, you could say that direct marketing itself has a poor "brand image"! Yet, as discussed, direct marketing media and programs are probably superior to other marketing communication vehicles in communicating high quality and value and in building customer loyalty. If used right, they can play a valuable role in building other brand-differentiating associations. And though they will still probably not be as efficient as mass media, they can build the "awareness foundation" that underlies all strong brands.

CHAPTER 7

Customer Service and Direct Marketing

Historically, the customer service department has been a euphemism for the complaint department. In one situation we are aware of, its sole function was to resolve billing disputes. Even with the advent of computers, the staff in many of these departments typically did not have on-line access to up-to-date customer information, requiring them to submit batched transaction slips for overnight generation of account status reports. While this necessitated a delay, in most cases it was sufficiently prompt, as the phone numbers for many early direct marketing firms were unlisted, so that most communications were by mail. When customers did call, in most cases they ended up contacting the company's headquarters, miles away from the fulfillment centers and customer service departments.

Today, less than 10 years later, the use of technology has allowed direct marketers to support inbound-telemarketing-based order processing coupled with overnight (now tending toward same day) shipment. As a result, exemplified by such world-class firms as Lands' End, customer service has become the major contact or touch point between the customer and the company. High levels of quality and significant capabilities are simply expected by customers. Companies that fail to attain even a baseline measurement are finding their business in jeopardy. This is a dramatic shift in the role and importance of customer service. Now, with the shift from product- to customer-focused marketing this role will continue to expand.

In more and more industries that offer goods and/or services to consumers and even to businesses, customer service is becoming the primary channel for contact between the company and the individual, whether a prospect or an existing customer. Consequently, the actions of, and even the responses given by, customer service representatives (CSRs) are critical to establishing and maintaining the relationship between the consumer and the company. Customer service is absolutely vital for customer retention. It will become even more so for customer acquisition, as the first contact with a potential customer imparts a lasting and major impression on the prospective customer as to the character of the company. When the customer, presumably with the intention of buying, initiates this contact, it may present the single defining opportunity for customer acquisition, or in the case of a bad experience, it may be the single defining moment that guarantees customer loss.

Even beyond acquisition and retention, direct customer contact provides a number of other opportunities. Cross-selling, affinity selling, and upselling are most often identified as they imply immediate revenue gains. However, the one subject that is most often overlooked, yet in the long run may be the most important, is the opportunity to collect customer-specific data. While information can be gained in other ways, such as from external demographic databases, it is not comparable to the quality of information provided by a customer when looking to acquire a specific product or service.

REQUIRED CUSTOMER SERVICES CAPABILITIES

To better understand the capabilities that are required of CSRs, in the course of our assignments we have conducted working sessions involving representatives of a number of customer service departments in relatively diverse industries including catalog, insurance, financial services, and consumer products. Attendees at these sessions included the more senior, experienced CSRs who handle the more complex requests and their immediate supervisors, the majority of whom have advanced from CSRs to supervisory positions. These sessions provide the basis for the summarized capabilities listed below.

For customer service to be capable of performing its function, CSRs must be able to quickly respond in an intelligent, courteous manner to all sorts of inquiries. The information provided must be complete, concise, and clear. Cited in the sessions were inquiries pertaining to:

- Products and services
  - Features
  - Technical specifications
  - Availability
  - Warranties
  - Repair/replacement

- Pricing
  - Product
  - Promotional offers
  - Discounts
  - Sales tax

- Catalogs
  - Recent
  - Special focus
  - Promotional

- Offers

- Shipping and handling

- Programs
  - Member get member
  - Gift/donor recipient

- Order status
  - Shipments
  - Missing/delayed
  - Wrong product
    - Defective/damaged products
    - Duplicate shipments
- Billing

- Verification of payment
- Proof of payments/claims paid
- Encoding errors
- Charged wrong price
- Claims not received
- Claims returned
- Misapplied payments
- Credit card payments
- Partial/installment payments
- Shipping and handling
- Sales tax
- Late charges/interest
- Cross in the mail
- Bounced checks
- Due on contract
- Collection agencies/dunning
- Procedures—e.g., How can the customer:
  - Order
  - Return
  - Cancel
- Company's policies with respect to:
  - Returns
  - Negative and positive options
  - Contract fulfillment
  - Redemption of certificates/premiums
  - Shipping limitations/restrictions
  - Credit
  - Cancellation due to:
    - Death
    - Minor
    - Bankruptcy
    - Hardship

As part of responding to the inquiry, the CSR must then be able to initiate processing to resolve any issue that prompted the customer to call including:

- Process changes of address (CHADS)
  - Name
  - Address
  - Phone number
- Make customer and account level changes such as:
  - Negative to positive option
  - Reduce mailings
  - Increase/award bonus points
  - Change commitment
  - Suspend billing
  - Initiate rebilling
  - Change credit limits
  - Reinstate
  - Post service
  - Remove charges
  - Cancel

- - Account
  - Contract
- Process or initiate returns
  - Customer
  - Post office
  - Partial shipment
- Initiate replacement shipments
- Payment-related
  - Applying actual payments
  - Adjustments based upon claim of payment with or without proof
  - Duplicate payments
  - Nonsufficient funds
  - Misapplied
  - Unapplied
  - Collection agency
  - Overpayment
  - Advance
  - Initiating refunds
  - Handling credit balances
- Process orders
  - Rejecting order
  - Rearranging order
  - Installment payments
  - Authorizing credit card payment
  - Alternative ship to/bill to
  - Bonus/free product
  - From canceled accounts
  - Special shipping
    - Express/rush
    - Requiring manual handling

Of course, while the above are listed as independent entries, typically these transactions are interrelated (e.g., in the same call the customer may discuss address changes, payments, and returns). Consequently, the ability to concurrently process transactions is now required to allow the CSRs to perform their tasks in an efficient manner. For example, a customer's address may change and at the same time a rush shipment may be desired. In addition, the occurrence of a combination of transactions may be of interest from a marketing perspective.

INFORMATION NEEDED BY CUSTOMER SERVICE

In order to be able to respond to the inquiries listed above, a significant amount of information must be available to the CSRs. This information must be timely, accurate, and as complete as possible. While these data are too voluminous to list here and vary by company, in general they include:

- Basic information about the customer, such as name, address, and account related data
- Information related to company to customer communications including bills, shipments, and promotions
- Information related to customer to company transactions including payments, returns, and complaints

■ Information about the products, services, policies, and procedures

It must be noted that not all of the information is textual in nature. For example, product and promotional materials usually contain colored images and other graphical information, such that many CSRs cited as a requirement access to either the physical mail piece or a complete image of the page(s) being referenced by the customer.

MARKETING INFORMATION CAN BE COLLECTED BY CUSTOMER SERVICE

Customer service can also prove a valuable resource to marketing, simply as a source of information. This information may come directly from the customer, or indirectly by canvassing the CSRs. Since the CSRs have direct contact, they may be the most knowledgeable people in the company, with valuable insights into the customer base and the customers' wants and needs.

In general, information can be classified as being either static or dynamic in nature. An example of static information is demographic data. While of interest for mass mailings, it is not that strong a determinant of the needs or actions of a particular customer. On the other hand, an example of dynamic information is an event in which a customer participates or an action the customer took. Marketing should take special interest in this event-based information, as it appears in general to be a much more powerful predictor of customer behavior and preferences. Consequently, event-based information should be captured, even if only the most basic information about the event is retained, that is, simply recording the occurrence of the event itself.

As the primary channel of contact, customer service is a logical location for collecting event-oriented data. This is in keeping with the concepts of source data collection, which recommends that the information be collected as close, both physically and in terms of timing, to the occurrence of an event as possible.

For static data, CSRs can also be helpful, even if only by verifying the accuracy of current information such as addresses. They can also obtain missing information, such as phone numbers.

When dynamic data is involved, while the initiator of an event can be either the company or the customer, typically customer service is the contact point when any contention arises. Admittedly, other more frequent company-initiated events, such as promotions and bills, which are intended to effect an expected response from a customer (e.g., order, payment), must be considered when targeting a customer (e.g., outstanding balance, disposition of last contact).

However, it is the unexpected event, which may be broadly classified as a complaint or inquiry, which is of interest—partially because this kind of event reflects the preference of the individual customer. Unfortunately, these events are typically not recorded on the marketing database. Worse yet, in many cases complaints may not be tracked through the customer service support systems to ensure that the incidents are resolved or that they are reoccurring in nature. These inquiries and complaints may also be received in the mail, including annotations on payments, orders, returns, and other forms of white mail. However, a typically overlooked source of this information is included in the standard contacts that CSRs have with customers.

Some customer service support systems are now beginning to include a means of annotating the overall subject of the conversation (e.g., order, complaint); however, typically the information being collected is at too high a level of summarization to be useful, or the CSRs have not been trained to properly record the information, which they may regard as optional at best. Only if the data is useful to them in their role is it likely to be collected. One solution is to ensure that the capabilities exist to track a complaint across multiple contacts and note both when and how it was resolved. As the first contact may have been received by mail, this further requires that the originating source by identified and that all aspects of this complaint and inquiry processing be integrated.

It must be emphasized that information needs to be recorded about the source of the contact. This is especially critical in situations where there are multiple communications channels, including direct calls to customer service as well as messages included with payments and incoming mail (commonly referred to as white mail or masthead letters) if directed to corporate officers. In addition, information about the response and even the customer's reaction must also be recorded. This requires data to be collected for a broad range of events including:

  I. All customer-to-company transaction activity
- *A*. Orders
    - *1*. Accepted orders
    - *2*. Credit rejects
    - *3*. Pending orders
    - *4*. Inventory outage rejects
- *B*. Credits
    - *1*. Credit date
    - *2*. Credit amount
    - *3*. Credit type
    - *4*. Payments
        - *a*. Form of payment
            - *(1)* Check
            - *(2)* Cash
            - *(3)* Credit card
    - *5*. Returns
        - *a*. Opened
        - *b*. Unopened
        - *c*. Source of return
            - *(1)* Customer
            - *(2)* USPS (undeliverables)
    - *6*. Claims
        - *a*. Proof
        - *b*. No proof
        - *c*. Claims paid
        - *d*. Claims returns
    - *7*. Refunds
- *C*. Rejects
- *D*. Enrollments
- *E*. Inquiries
- *F.* Complaints

 II. All company-to-customer activities
- *A*. Promotions
    - *1*. Activity date
    - *2*. Activity type
        - *a*. Cycle mailings
        - *b*. Direct mailings

        c. Telemarketing efforts
      3. Promotion details—for each promotion
          a. Package received
             (1) Each package item
          b. Sale offer
          c. Product offer (rep)
          d. Date selected for promotion
          e. Regression score
          f. Formula used
      4. Rejection reason
   B. Product shipments
   C. Bills
   D. Statements
   E. Correspondence
      1. Form letters
      2. Personalized letters

CAPTURING SURVEY DATA

Historically, when direct marketers survey their customers and prospects, the results are compiled by some market researcher (firm or individual) and presented to management. The detailed survey forms usually end up in some file cabinet for a period of time and are then discarded. The underlying information for which so much effort has been expended, and, it is hoped, which has provided some valuable insight, is then simply "lost."

However, this data, which has proved itself valuable once, could prove itself valuable again. Various potential uses come to mind, not the least of which is customer profiling. This is especially true as most surveys include attitudinal information. From profiling to segmentation is then a relatively short step, as has been discussed elsewhere. In addition, since this information has been collected directly from a specific individual or household, its quality in terms of accuracy and currency must be considered to be better than demographic and lifestyle data obtained from some third-party data provider. This is especially true when the third party's data was obtained from census data and other means (e.g., using a subscription to a pet magazine as the basis for inferring ownership of a pet).

Customer service can play a role in two modes:

1. *When a customer initiates the contact, an effort can be made to obtain survey data.* Since the customer has initiated the contact, it is possible to obtain information of very good quality. Surveys either can be taken on an informal basis of those who call, triggered by specific events (e.g., ordering a specific product), or can be posted in the messages waiting for specific customers to call. The latter capability can be used to verify missing or potentially inaccurate information.

2. *The CSRs may also be used on a time-available basis to initiate contacts.* While CSRs may require some training to effectively conduct surveys, their intimate knowledge of the company, its products, and its services should prove an advantage in collecting quality information. Care should be taken, though, to ensure that the primary objective of these efforts, data collection, is well understood, for this type of initiative verges on becoming outbound telemarketing.

With the advent of database marketing, the obvious solution is to retain the detailed survey data, not just the summarized results. And the place to store this is in the marketing database where it can be analyzed in combination with other information known about the customer.

However, there are some issues to be addressed:

- Only a small number of customers may have been asked to take part in the survey.
- An even smaller number may have responded.
- The information may not be in a format that is traditionally thought of as being machine-readable.

If the marketing database uses a relational data structure that comprises a number of tables organized much like a spreadsheet, with columns as data fields and rows as individual records, then the above issues can be easily resolved. As well, a number of object-oriented database managers allow for other types of data fields in addition to numeric and alphanumeric data. These nontraditional data types include graphics, video, audio, and memos (i.e., lengthy text or documents) that make them ideal for use in association with customer service, especially considering the data requirements of the CSRs. From a marketing perspective these latter data types may not be useful for direct profiling, but could be searched for key words, etc.

If only a few different surveys are to be retained, then each survey could be stored as a separate table. If there are five surveys, then five tables could be established. In each table a key field must be included, such as the customer identifier, to allow data in one table to be associated with data in other tables, including the master customer table.

While the one-table-per-survey approach works when there are only a limited number of surveys, if you expect to produce and retain a large number of different surveys, then another approach should be considered. The second approach is based upon generalizing the data structure to retain data about data, or *meta data*. In this case, it is necessary to retain data about the surveys, the questions on the surveys, and the responses. This results in three basic tables being established:

1. *Survey table.* This table contains a single entry for each survey. Data to be stored in this table could include:

   Survey identifier

   Survey name

   Description or purpose

   Time frame in which the survey was performed

   Number of surveys sent out

   Criteria for receiving survey

2. *Questionnaire table.* This table contains one entry per question for each different survey. If 100 different surveys were issued and each had approximately 25 questions, then this table would contain 2,500 records. Data to be stored in this table includes:

   Survey identifier

   Question identifier

   Question text

   Data type of response

3. *Response table.* This table contains the responses received. A separate record is created for each question. The number of records in the table can be calculated by multiplying the number of survey responses times the number of questions per survey. Data to be stored in this table includes:

Customer identifier

Survey identifier

Question identifier

Question completed (yes/no)

Response data

It should be noted that the format of the response data is dependent upon the data type of question, as identified in the questionnaire table. The capabilities of the database management software will determine how the response data is actually stored in the computer. The important point is to recognize that responses will be in various formats including:

- Boolean yes/no
- Single-valued numeric (i.e., 1 to 5)
- Single alphanumeric value
- Multiple numeric or alphanumeric values

Another important point is to ensure that this is resolved with the designer of the questionnaire prior to its use. This will facilitate data entry and analysis of the results.

In addition to the processing logic needed to load the responses into the marketing database, also remember that logic must be developed to maintain the survey and questionnaire tables.

The major advantage of this generalized approach is that once the data structure and processing logic are developed, then the actual tasks of loading surveys and responses into the marketing database become clerical in nature. However, there is a significant up-front development effort. Consequently, in most situations the recommended approach would be to load the first few surveys as independent tables. Once the volume and frequency of surveying increases, then make the investment.

The use of this approach is applicable to more than traditional market research surveys. It could be used to store data collected:

- From product warranty forms and inquiries
- By customer service representatives handling inquiries and complaints
- As part of an on-line services registration process

In any event, the message is *do not lose the detailed data*! It is valuable and can be used on an ongoing basis to strengthen target marketing.

MARKETING INFORMATION TO BE PROVIDED TO CUSTOMER SERVICE

In addition to providing information about the promotions that have been directed through the more traditional direct marketing communications channels of mail and telemarketing, serious consideration should now be given to providing information to the CSR in order to allow him or her to "steer" or direct the contact. This is typically accomplished by posting "messages" with the other customer data accessed by the CSR. These messages may be generated from the marketing database. It should be understood that in most instances the intent is not to have these messages directly communicated by the CSR to the customer, but rather to have the information available for use by the CSR and interjected or paraphrased during the conversation.

Messages may take many forms including:

- *How to treat special customers.* For example, a " gold or platinum" program could be instituted for very good customers. Conversely, if the customer's profile indicates that he is close to severing his relationship, gentle handling may save or extend the relationship, rather than requiring marketing to attempt to resuscitate the customer through some reactivation or win-back program.

- *Products/services the customer should be made aware of.* There are two reasons that the customer should be made aware of a new product or service. Either the company is offering a new product or service it wants to push, or it has an expectation that this customer would be a buyer based upon the characteristics or prior actions of the customer.

- *Information the CSRs should attempt to collect from the customer.* This may be survey data, or it may be a request to verify the accuracy of customer data or obtain missing data.

It should be noted that since the CSR is in direct communication with the customer, the information could be more extensive than can be presented through other media. Conversely, canned or broadcast-oriented communications may appear stilted and will probably fail. While this places more demands on the CSR, the positive impact in terms of company image is worth it.

CUSTOMER SERVICE AND THE INTERNET

The Internet shows great promise as a channel for servicing many different types of customer needs. On almost a daily basis, new capabilities are being brought on-line to cost-effectively support the customer experience.

The Web sites initially implemented by most companies focused on providing basic information to prospects and customers. Essentially sales brochures displayed on a PC screen, these sites presented basic product information in a relatively static format and then prompted the user to call an 800 number to obtain more details or to place an order.

In a just few short years, the functionality of the Web site has expanded to deliver significant benefits to prospects and customers. Today, commercial Web sites typically offer greatly expanded information along many dimensions:

- Most Web sites open to a page that presents a company overview describing more than what is sold and where the company is located. In these sections companies lay out their unique selling propositions, describe visions for the future, tell the public what they stand for, and detail their involvement with environmental concerns, social programs, charities, etc. Very often, these areas allow end users to drill down into topics of specific interest for more detailed information.

- Either directly or indirectly, end users are often given a choice of different "views" within the Web site. On the home page, they are prompted to indicate how they would like to navigate the site, to indicate areas of interest, or to describe themselves. Choices often include company division, product line, product features, product benefits, product price points, and type of customer (consumer, small business, large business, education, etc.). The general presentation, options offered, and flow of the site will then be configured according to the customer's specified choice.

- Product information areas have been expanded to include product finder tools that recommend products based on specifications provided by customers. When a number of options or features is available, configuration tools that allow customers to decide on options and understand cost ramifications are provided. Of course, most product-oriented sites offer an area for special deals, closeout specials, and remanufactured items. One application that will grow in sophistication and importance is the product recommendation agent that interactively supports cross-selling opportunities. Recommendation systems evaluate a customer's past purchases and then proactively suggest new products that may interest the customer. In the music industry, these systems are being used to recommend other albums in the same music genre or artists in different categories suggested by purchase patterns of other customers.

- Ordering information areas vary greatly according to the type of product being sold and related price points. In many cases, customers are still referred to an inbound 800 number, but increasingly orders are taken directly via secured on-line forms. Many companies have chosen a hybrid approach where basic customer and order information is collected via an on-line form and then the transaction is completed quickly over the phone via voice or fax. While most financial applications still use proprietary networks for security purposes, many are migrating to Internet applications that allow funds transfers and product purchases.

- Customer service applications represent one of the most varied and rapidly growing areas. Depending on the type of business, customers today can check the status of their account, check the status of their order, access installation and troubleshooting instructions, download associated software, etc. One airline even has an application that allows customers to find out the status of every flight and even its current location in the air.

- For companies that do business from physical sites, a retail site locator tool is usually provided that allows customers to find the nearest store according to a number of criteria, such as ZIP code, telephone area code, city name, etc.

- In "what's new" sections, companies present information about new product releases, future product development, new customer service programs, special promotions, partnerships with other companies, etc.

- In a general information section, companies present miscellaneous items that depend on the nature of their business. Common applications include "white papers" that provide background information on industry trends or methodologies, significant news items, "how-to" information that goes beyond product-specific installation instructions, financial calculators, etc. For companies offering accessories and configured products, Internet applications that allow customers to visualize the final product can be very important. For example, one direct marketer of high-performance automobile tires and alloy wheels has an Internet application that shows customers what a given tire (model and size) and wheel (model and size) will look like on their specific year, make, model, and color car.

- Most large companies use the Web site as a channel for acquiring new employees. It is very common to see "jobs" sections that list currently open positions, contain detailed job descriptions, and offer on-line forms that capture employment application data.

- Publicly traded companies often include an investor relations area that presents current and historical stock quotes, annual reports, financial statements, and announcements of upcoming investor meetings.

- Feedback areas provide two-way channels for customers to directly contact the company. Most often, these areas will help the customer format and send an e-mail to the company, but many larger companies now support on-line "chat" sessions where customers can interactively communicate with a customer service or technical support representative.

- Almost all corporate Web sites offer links to other related sites. Depending on the nature of the business, links are commonly offered to providers of related services (financing, accessories, etc.), enthusiast organizations, political action groups, social concerns, etc.

While Internet applications have come a long way, they still require significant development efforts to approach their full potential. Also, companies in many product categories have not been successful in establishing a presence on the Internet. This can be attributed to a number of factors:

- Demographics of the active Internet users limits the products and services that can be successfully sold. At the time this book is being written, the majority of Internet users are males in generation X, who have grown up with technology and are comfortable with its use. For the most significant part of the consumer market, baby boomers, Internet usage varies greatly by lifestyle and socioeconomic position segment.

- For most Internet users, throughput and display functionality remain limited due to the capabilities of current Web browsers and connection channels. Only a very small portion of the consumer base has access to high-performance connections (mostly through corporate gateways) and can take advantage of high-quality graphics or streaming audio and video.

- While substantial advancements have been made in on-line transaction security, this factor still represents a significant issue limiting the growth of purchase activity via the Internet. Besides the technical issues, consumer perception of transaction security remains a major barrier.

- For the most part, the Internet's current culture and etiquette is geared to generation Xers. As a result, many members of older generations are not comfortable with the phrasing, images, terminology, and navigation paths of most Web sites.

Another important factor to be considered in the commercial use of the Internet is that of "push versus pull." Traditional direct marketing efforts have been based upon a "push" strategy where the prospective customer is promoted with an offer. The company chooses the individual to be promoted, the channel, the timing, and the message. However, the Internet has evolved from its origins in the academic community as an information source based on the user first searching for and then "pulling" the desired information. In this environment, the end user chooses the channel, timing, and topics of interest. While there is presently much activity and press relative to incorporating push technology into Internet applications, this functionality will be very limited until new browser software is developed and new communication channels, such as digital TV, are implemented.

For the time being, companies will have to function in an environment where the customer controls the communication process and is able to easily access information from multiple sources. One significant result will be the growth of comparison-shopping applications where consumers evaluate alternative products and points of purchase. As a result, companies will have to provide a great deal of detailed and relevant information to even be included in the customer's list of alternative choices.

In many industries this will require that the same information and capabilities used to support customer service representatives must become available through the Internet. For companies considering developing a Web site, or redeveloping a customer service support system, it seems appropriate to consider developing one system that could support both customers inquiring through the Internet and the CSRs using the company's own network as an "Intranet." Obviously, many issues need to be addressed, including restricting access to customer and competitive product data. However, the development of a common repository of data for use by CSRs and customers is technologically feasible. This approach also overcomes one of the major problems in customer service (regardless of delivery channel): obsolete information—a problem that is demonstrated daily in the often-incorrect answers supplied by the CSRs and by the number of abandoned Web sites.

Data and Marketing Databases

Chapters 8 and 9 were written by Andrew Deutch and Rus Rempala; Chapters 10 and 11 by Robert Kendrick.

CHAPTER 8

What Do You Want Your Database to Do, and Why Do You Think It Will Do It?

INTRODUCTION

In this chapter we discuss a number of issues that marketers should be aware of before embarking on a major database development initiative. It has been our experience that while there are many reasons why specific individual database development projects fail, the most common mistakes have to do with mismanaging responsibilities and expectations. Said another way, there was not a common understanding of:

- What functions the marketing database was expected to perform, both initially and over some longer time period[1]
- What the initial and continuing investment could cost
- How long it would take to install and to complete a set of baseline capabilities
- What would be required, and of whom, to bring the initial system to a point where it begins to recover its costs

KEY ISSUES TO CONSIDER BEFORE STARTING A MARKETING DATABASE PROJECT

Unlike information systems developed to support the more standardized business disciplines, marketing database development projects typically involve many issues caused by misconceptions and unanticipated consequences.

One Size Does Not Fit All

One of the most common misconceptions with marketing database systems is that it is possible to purchase and install a turnkey solution. Considering the broad range of applications software available for computers today, it seems logical that "off-the-shelf" marketing database systems should also be available. In reality, while any number of vendors offer marketing database systems, these systems are at best foundations requiring extensive configuring and development of customized applications for each client company.

---

1. Marketing database systems are never ever complete; there are always new things to do that require enhancements to the system in place.

The primary factor preventing truly standardized marketing systems is that the marketing process itself is not standardized. Unlike accounting, order entry inventory management, etc., marketing is a largely creative process attempting to capitalize on moving targets of opportunity in a very dynamic marketplace. As a result, there are no commonly accepted standards and procedures for marketing business processes. Even within the same industry, different companies build very different marketing database systems due to differences in:

- Corporate culture
- Market position
- Product-centric versus customer-centric emphasis
- Marketing objectives and marketing programs
- Customer expectations
- "Legacy" information systems
- Available data sources
- Budgets
- Marketing staff capabilities
- Marketing staff size and degree of empowerment

Cost-Justifying the Investment in a Marketing Database

Another significant issue impacting the development of marketing database systems is that it is always difficult and often not possible to project a return on investment. In the cost/benefit equation for database systems, costs are the more predictable item. It is possible to estimate initial and ongoing monetary costs, assign values to dedicated staff resources, and factor in the impact of alternative investments that will be forgone. As in any estimation, it is very wise to include an adjustment for unforeseen contingencies.

On the other hand, projecting benefits to be obtained from the system and assigning a monetary value pose quite a problem. Marketing databases are merely tools used to support marketing business processes. As a result, the marketing database will accomplish nothing by itself. The benefits achieved from these systems are directly related to the organization's ability to use them effectively and implement successful marketing programs. Depending on a company's degree of experience with database marketing programs, there may or may not be sufficient background information to support a projection of marketing program results. Further compounding the situation is the fact that database marketing programs are evolutionary in nature and should produce increased results year after year. Estimating escalation factors on top of estimated initial benefits can greatly compound error in the overall estimate.

When a company has no track record with database marketing programs, it is sometimes possible to base estimated benefits on information made public by other companies. However, it is important to consider whether the other companies have accurately measured incremental benefits and whether reported results have been inflated for public relations purposes.

Many companies approach the cost justification issue by applying anticipated costs to "what-if" scenarios that estimate how much of an incremental impact on acquisition, cross-sell, retention, etc., would be necessary to offset incremental system costs. The amount of change that would be needed to offset system costs is then reviewed to determine if it seems reasonable and the degree to which it is likely.

How a Marketing Database Will Affect the Organization

Another group of companies approach the cost justification issue by rationalizing that having a customer database is a forgone conclusion, that this type of resource is becoming a standard cost of doing business in their industry. Companies that take this approach focus on cost issues. They collect estimates of what other comparable companies have paid for their systems and then establish a benchmark amount to gauge their costs against.

One of the most unanticipated consequences arising from implementing marketing database systems is how they tend to impact internal corporate power structures and working relationships. In today's corporate world, data is an extremely valuable resource. Those who control data or have access to its information are in a position of power, or at least significant influence. In many companies, data and access to the data are controlled by one or two departments. Often, the data is owned by information technology, because that department owns the supporting systems. By their very nature, marketing databases greatly expand access to a company's information, and more importantly, provide software tools that empower individual action.

In the traditional structure, access to the data is usually limited to staff in an information technology, research/decision support, or finance department. Other departments must come to these groups to get information that they need, and demand usually exceeds supply. As a result, it is common to see that "bargains" must be struck to allow others to gain access to these scarce resources. It is also common to see that data is readily provided to corporate allies and not so readily provided to those who are not viewed as allies. Of course, these situations are hardly ever overt or obvious. Rather, they are realized as subtle requests for providing collateral support of proposed capital development projects, making adjustments in project priority lists, servicing those in the "chain of command" first, directing that information be delivered to only one individual, etc.

Data: Learning to Live with Imperfect Data

Another very common outcome of marketing databases is an increase in feedback and opinions about data quality and errors in "upstream" systems that feed the marketing database. This is especially true when direct end-user access is introduced for the first time. Prior to this point, access to raw data and its interpretation was handled by experienced analysts who had learned to factor out errors and produce nice, clean, adjusted results. End users, used to adjusted results, are often shocked when they start using a direct access system and gain firsthand experience with raw data. The initial reaction is an opinion that the database is bad. Most novice data users tend to see data quality as an all or nothing issue. The data is either "good" or "bad." In other words, "one bad apple spoils the whole barrel." On the other hand, those experienced with data understand that there is no such thing as perfect data. All data sources contain limitations caused by data entry errors, processing errors, processing rules, limited sources, etc. The result is usually commentary and complaints about the quality of the information systems providing the data and the capabilities of the system managers. In the best of situations, marketing and information technology staffs tend to speak two different languages and have two different sets of priorities. This initial reaction on the part of marketing does not foster improved relations.

The last significant consequence of marketing database projects is very obvious, but often "hides in plain sight." If a company is developing a marketing database for the first time, or is adding significant functionality to an existing system, changes will be required in the marketing department. The new capabilities are being implemented for a reason, usually to implement new marketing programs. New marketing programs usually require revisions to the marketing business process. As a result, job responsibilities are created, altered, or often omitted altogether. These changes require staff training, or sometimes new staff with new skills. It is also important to recall that new marketing programs are developed to service new marketing objectives. If objectives change, success criteria and therefore the criteria for evaluating staff performance and advancement will also change.

Managing Expectations— Everybody's Expectations

The history of marketing database implementation contains many examples of systems that met their design requirements, were delivered on time and on budget, but were deemed to be failures. What most of these situations have in common are expectations that were not in sync with the development plan and functional requirements. Consider basic human nature. Setting and managing expectations must be a conscious effort in marketing database projects. If left in a "vacuum," people tend to establish their own independent expectations. For example:

- *Marketers* tend to assume that the database system will be very fast, able to quickly assimilate new data sources, very flexible, easy to use, intuitive, and tailored to the way that they do their work.
- *Information technology* tends to assume that the database will be consistent with the current system architecture guidelines, will use existing types of hardware and operating systems, will largely be a turnkey installation, will not involve significant staff training, and will be highly automated, not requiring a lot of human intervention.
- *Management* tends to assume that the database will be quickly implemented for a "reasonable" cost and that marketing will be able to use it effectively on "day 1." Management also almost invariably seems to expect that there is still time to favorably impact "this year's bottom line."

At the very beginning of the database planning process there should be agreement on the applications the database is expected to support, anticipated costs, anticipated schedules, and anticipated benefits. As the implementation project moves forward, it will be essential to ensure that expectations remain focused on what will be delivered and that any changes in project scope or delivery schedules are fully communicated to everyone related to the project.

OBJECTIVES, PROCESSES, AND REQUIREMENTS

The next phase of the database development process is concerned with identifying *marketing objectives, the marketing business process,* and *functional requirements for the system needed to support them.*

In theory, marketing objectives, the marketing business process, and functional requirements could be developed independently and sequentially. One team of marketing personnel would define the business needs, and a second team of information technology (IT) professionals would develop the functional requirements necessary to support those needs. In this framework, business needs are essentially marketing's desires, and the functional requirements are IT's translation of those desires into a specific plan for accomplishing marketing's needs. This plan or functional requirements document will include the following:

- Project overview and objectives
- Summary of recommendations
- Business overview and marketing objectives
- Marketing business processes
- Role of the marketing database system
- System processes and functions
  - Information systems environment
  - Data sources
  - Initial system build
  - Ongoing updates and maintenance
- Marketing applications and end-user tools
  - Marketing application software tools
  - End-user query and reporting tools
  - Standardized reporting
  - Research, analysis, and modeling support
- Documentation, support, and training
- Cost estimates and cost/benefit assessment
- Project phases, deliverables schedules

Once the marketing database requirements have been established, the next step is to initiate the detailed design phase by developing a system implementation plan. This plan should include:

- A listing and detailed description of each of the data files to be brought into the database process
- A statement and description of data elements to be retained from individual files
- A plan describing how the records from individual files will be linked together
- A plan for consolidating individual customers into households
- A plan defining how often the database will be updated
- A definition of what new data values will be created during the update process
- A description of how the database will be accessed and manipulated by the marketing department
- A statement of how quickly database queries need to be answered
- Descriptions of how the database will perform the operations included in the business needs analysis such as these, among others:
  - Response analysis
  - Profiling
  - Scoring
  - Selecting names for promotions
  - Selecting data files for external analysis
  - Reporting

As we stated above, in theory, business needs and functional requirements could be developed sequentially, but in practice it makes much more sense for a team of marketing and IT professionals to work together from the very start of the project to develop the business needs document, with the IT team then doing the bulk of the work required to complete the more technical functional requirements portion of the project.

One reason for recommending this team approach to the development of a marketing database is that some of the functions requested by marketing might not be possible to implement in the desired time frame, nor might they be cost-effective or even technically feasible. Very often marketing database requirements involve major and costly changes to one or more of the supporting business systems. IT personnel, who should be familiar with all the supporting business systems, are in a position to point out these situations right away. This joint approach minimizes false starts and disappointments later on in the project and allows a reasonably defined marketing database to be completed quickly.

Many readers may find the notion of marketing and IT people working closely together to agree on anything strange. But cooperation can and must be achieved if the marketing database project is to succeed in a reasonable time frame and at a reasonable cost. One reason for the continuing conflict between IT personnel and marketing staff is that marketing's objectives are frequently "moving targets" requiring tremendous flexibility in supporting systems. Whereas the marketing group typically wants a great deal of flexibility and ad hoc access to data, the IT group is responsible for efficiently managing systems across all user groups. This usually requires standardizing the processing and reporting systems, optimizing systems to support specific, well-defined tasks, controlling data access channels, and adhering to existing production windows.[2]

One of the goals of this chapter is to give both marketing and IT professionals an appreciation of each others' concerns about the implications of the requirements imposed by the database project. Marketing people, to whom this book is principally addressed, should be particularly alert to the problem of imposing requirements that cannot be met without incurring major expenditures. Very often, changing an "upstream" system to meet marketing's requirements will also impact the systems used by many other departments. No marketing professional wants to be in the position of explaining why a seemingly simple request has escalated into a million dollar (or more) project.

MARKETING TOOLS

Another issue to be considered by marketing professionals is that rarely can "a system" provide all of their needs. Because today's marketing environment is so dynamic, marketers should instead focus on having a set of information delivery and usage channels. Some involve software applications; some involve support services. With this strategy, marketers can use different channels on an "as-needed" basis, or add new channels to meet changing requirements. The types of information access channels can be categorized as follows:

- *Research/analytical projects and software* involve the development of strategic segments for customers and prospects, statistical models (for list segmentation, customer value and life span), developing marketing-mix test plans and back-end validation of marketing tests, and scoring models.

---

2. *Production windows* are the time slots during which computer systems perform updates, produce off-line reports, transmit and receive data from other systems, and perform other maintenance activities.

- *Standardized reports*, usually created during the periodic database update process, efficiently service predefined, relatively static information needs, such as database update quality control and "customer inventory" counts, etc. These reports are usually provided on paper.
- *EIS/OLAP systems* provide very graphical, intuitive, flexible delivery of predefined reporting and analysis needs. The executive information system (EIS) is a PC desktop application that collects the end user's information request, formats appropriate queries, retrieves data from the on-line analytical processing (OLAP) database, and then presents the information in the appropriate format (tables, graphs, charts, maps, etc.). The user chooses from a predefined set of options for types of data and display formats. The OLAP database that supports the EIS stores multidimensional summary data and therefore is essentially a "database of answers." It is important to note that while EIS/OLAP systems can be made quite flexible, they do not access raw data and therefore cannot support ad hoc information needs. They can only provide answers to the questions that were designed into them. As a result, they most effectively service predictable information reporting needs such as customer profiles, marketing program results reporting, progress toward the "annual" marketing plan, etc.
- *Ad-hoc query tools* allow marketers to access any and all information in the marketing database, i.e., "raw data." While the EIS/OLAP system gives the marketer a set of predefined choices, the ad hoc system delivers total access to all data and a framework for creating reports. The user has to understand what the overall structure of the database is, what the individual data elements are, how to translate a need for information into "query logic," how to configure the report, etc.
- *Communication and analysis desktop software*—such as spreadsheets, word processing, graphics, presentation packages, geographic information systems (statistical maps), SAS statistical software, chi squared automatic interaction detector (CHAID) segmentation tools, LAN e-mail, Internet e-mail, etc.—is essential to further analyze results from the query and reporting channels and to support effective communication.
- *Promotion implementation support software* consists of the tools that support marketing-specific functions such as:
  - "Annual" marketing plans
  - A reference database tracking details of all marketing programs over time
  - Planning individual marketing campaigns
  - Test cell sizing and experimental design of in-market tests
  - Random sample selection and allocation/splitting
  - Tracking the status of the implementation process
  - Selecting promotional lists
  - Post-selection processing such as file splits, reformats, postal sortation, etc.

BUSINESS NEEDS AND FUNCTIONAL REQUIREMENTS

The marketing database should, at a very minimum, be able to perform several basic marketing functions:

- Answering ad hoc questions (queries) about the characteristics and behavior of customers or prospects

- Selecting names for promotions based on user-specified marketing events or naming scoring models
- Tracking promotion results and profiling responders and nonresponders

We will address each of these subjects individually, starting with ad hoc queries.

Queries

As we stated above, one of the most important issues to address when designing a marketing database is to define the kinds of information needed to plan, implement, and evaluate marketing programs. The more specific the marketing group can be when defining business needs and functional requirements, the better, because the answers to these questions will help IT define the logical and physical design of the system.[3] In our experience, developing sample queries offers the best way (if not the only way) for marketing and technical people to effectively communicate with each other about exactly what data *will* or *will not* be in the database and what data will or will not be immediately accessible.

In effect, the marketing person is saying, "This is what I want to know, and this is how quickly I need an answer." And the technical people are saying, "We can or cannot answer this question given the data that we all agreed to keep," or "We can answer this question but not immediately, given the way we have agreed to design the database."

Only after a good number of truly painstaking sessions will both sides finally understand what is expected of the database application and what is possible. This kind of information is very difficult to absorb from flowchart presentations, and marketing people are well advised to avoid signing off on functional requirements until this question and answer process has been completed.

The ad hoc query function should be capable of providing counts of records that meet the specified criteria as well as subsetting groups of records that meet the criteria. The system should be capable of selecting and manipulating any level of data, i.e., from any table (household, individual, account, orders, promotion history, etc.). The query tool should also be able to calculate fields in the course of a query, such as dividing total sales by months on file to find customers who are averaging at least $100 per month. Once defined, there should be a function to save queries and reports in public or private libraries.

To give you a better idea of the kinds of questions that should be raised in these question and answer sessions, we have posed a set of typical database questions. For the purpose of this discussion queries have been divided into two types:

1. *Type I.* Queries that can be answered directly and fully using the marketing database.
2. *Type II.* More complex queries that require additional analysis beyond what the database has been designed to provide. In this case, the database would be expected to provide *support*, for example, producing files that could readily be downloaded to other computing environments such as statistical analysis system (SAS) or a PC-based spreadsheet.

Type I Queries: Examples
1. Calculate the response rate to Promotion X.

---

3. See Chapter 3, Buzzword 6: Logical and Physical Design.

2. Compare the profiles of customers who responded to Promotion X with those of nonresponders and determine whether there are any differences between these profiles that *appear* to be significant.

3. Count the number of current purchasers of Product A who are also purchasers of Product B.

4. How many purchasers of Product A come from the following states and have household incomes between $25,000 and $35,000?

5. Does there appear to be a regional variation in response to promotions for Product X?

6. Count the number of customers who are purchasers of Product A, who have not purchased Product B, and who have not been promoted for *any* products within the past 12 months, 6 months, 3 months, and so on.

7. What is the age distribution of purchasers of Product A?

8. How many current purchasers of Product A have purchased at least one other product?

9. What is the distribution by age and sex by state of responders to Promotion X?

10. How many former customers of Business A are active customers of Business B?

11. How many current customers make multiple purchases?

12. How many current customers have upgraded their product ownership?

13. Identify customers who have *never* received a cross-sell promotion.

14. What is the average credit balance for customers who have outstanding credit balances?

15. Develop profiles of customers by:
    a. Product category
    b. State
    c. Source media
    d. Demographic cluster type

16. Develop courts of customers who meet criteria for particular product offers.

17. Select, based on predictive models, those customers who are most likely to be responsive to new product offers.

18. How do different customer segments react to different copy?

19. Are customers who once bought through telemarketing more likely to buy again through telemarketing?

20. Flag grandparents and any possible information on the grandchild.

21. What was the customer's original purchase channel (phone, mail, charge, direct, walk-in)?

Type II Queries: Examples

1. Are cross-sell and direct mail promotions optimally coordinated?

2. Can coordination be improved to avoid same-product mailings to *recent* conversions?

3. How many same-product mailings, on average, are required prior to conversion?

4. Based on modeling results, how many promotions for the same product are warranted for given customers?

5. Could the existing calendar-driven sequence of promotions be replaced by a more targeted sequence, and if so, what would be some variations in sequence and packaging?

6. Can calendar-driven promotion sequences be integrated with event-driven promotions?

7. Can targeted promotion frequencies be implemented based on cost per account criteria?

8. What is the optimum level of multibuying to avoid overloading "good" customers?

9. Is there a point in time at which it can be determined that customers will never respond?

10. Does length of residence have any impact on response?

11. How long should historical, inactive records that have not been updated be kept?

12. Can customer profiles from one file be matched to profiles of other files?

Campaign Planning

Marketers should have a software tool that allows them to easily specify the components of a marketing promotion. At a basic level this involves defining all of the "cells" within the promotion and selection logic to identify those customers or prospects who should be assigned to each. The system should provide for both mutually exclusive groups and groups that allow duplicates between them. It should provide the marketer with counts of the records that currently meet the criteria for each group. The more sophisticated tools should automatically feed campaign specifications and counts to update the annual marketing plan management system and automatically assign promotion codes according to the marketing group's conventions. Other significant functions include the ability to select and allocate random samples among cells, to indicate control groups, to set up multistep promotion plans, and to support differential promotional plans based on optimal contact stream.

List Selections

Marketers can use the marketing database to select names and assign to promotions in a variety of ways. Name selections can be the result of an ad hoc query, as discussed above. In this situation the database will tell you how many names meet a particular criterion, and those names can be flagged (split for testing if appropriate), coded, and selected for a particular promotion. Of course, the database will keep track of the entire process so you can analyze responses after the promotion is complete.

Event-Driven Promotions

Another way to use the database for promotions is to have the update process identify particular events that trigger a promotion. For example, the update can check the customer's birth date and, if it is within a specified time limit, say 30 days, select the name to receive a mailing. Or the purchase of a particular product or service may prompt a promotion for another related product, and so on. Event-driven promotions (or *if, then* promotions) can and should be a major source of mailings or telephone contacts in a database environment.

Scoring Models

A third and important type of database-driven promotion results from scoring models. One of the most important tasks of the database is to facilitate the creation of statistical models and the subsequent implementation of model results. The first part of this process is to make the selection of names for statistical analysis easier.

Companies that perform statistical analysis in-house may use any of several platforms, including mainframes, PCs, or workstations, for modeling. If the work is to be done in the same environment where the data resides, the task of the database is to extract a file that contains the desired number of names and the specified data elements and produce an output file in the form that the statistical analysis product requires.

Selecting Names Based on Model Scores

After a model has been built, the database must be able to implement its results by executing scoring equations, storing scores, and providing a facility for selecting customers, based on their scores, for specific direct marketing programs. This process includes these elements:

- Incorporating the model equations into the language used by the database system.[4]
- Executing the scoring equation within the database so all records that meet the conditions specified for the sample group will be scored using the scoring equation. (See Chapters 17 through 23, which discuss statistical analysis and modeling.)
- Storing the scores produced by the scoring equation in the database.
- Sorting the file in descending sequence by score.
- Dividing the file into a number of equal-sized groups (frequently 10 groups or deciles).
- Assigning customer records to their appropriate deciles, based on their scores.
- Storing the decile score for each customer record along with its raw score, the name of the model, and the date on which the model was run.
- Providing a facility for selecting names based on the decile, or raw score, which was assigned by the scoring model.

Post-Selection List Processing

After groups of customers or prospects have been selected for a promotion, a variety of post-selection processing steps is needed to complete preparation of the list. If not handled automatically by the list selection system, promotion history transactions must be generated to update the database with the current selections. At the direction of the marketer and varying cell by cell and promotion by promotion, the database system, information technology group, or external processing vendor will have to handle other final processing steps. Examples include:

Final formatting of records

Merge/purge against outside lists

Matching to suppression files (frauds, do-not-promotes, etc.)

Addition of seed names

Postal sorting

Preparation of postal bag tags and mailing reports

---

4. In some cases, COBOL or FORTRAN may be used for more complex mathematical functions if the database system's fourth-generation language does not support mathematical functions.

Sorting by telephone area code

Creating and shipping computer tapes to vendors

Tracking Promotion Results and Profiling

The third critical database function is tracking promotion results and profiling. In this regard the database should be capable of producing reports that show this information for any promotion or combination of promotions:

- Expected circulation/contact quantities, gross responses, net responses, sales volume, new customer acquisition, promotional costs, etc., broken down by key code or test cell identifier
- Actual circulation/contact quantities, gross responses, net responses, sales volume, new customer acquisition, promotional costs, etc., broken down by key code or test cell identifier
- Profiles of responders and nonresponders
- Comparisons of test and control groups along with statistical confidence intervals
- Predicted versus actual scoring model performance by depth of file and customer segment

Profiles are most easily accomplished by the creation *on demand* of simple tables. For example, the simplest kind of table has only one dimension, such as response rate by state, response by gender, response by PRIZM code, or response by any other variable in the database. A more complicated, but still easy-to-read, table might include two variables, say state and gender, so you could see the response rate for each state and gender combination. More complicated three- or four-way relationships are best depicted using tools such as CHAID, which present such relationships in the form of decision trees.

Another and perhaps more actionable use of profiling is to accomplish these tasks:

- Evaluate scoring model results by customer group.
- Compare performance of scoring model deciles across multiple criteria such as total sales, new customer acquisition, and gross versus net response rates.
- Profile all deciles using demographic data, lifestyle data, or both.
- Compare the profiles of the most responsive segments of the file with the profiles of the least responsive.

If significant differences are found between responsive and unresponsive segments, then there may be reason to believe that different creative approaches might be more effective for the low-performing deciles than the current control, which is probably being mailed to the entire file.

Still another variation on profiling is to use the database to discover product affinities. If, for example, you found that persons who bought Product A also tended to buy Product B, then you might mail a Product B promotion to all Product A owners, of course suppressing those that already own Product B.

USER-FRIENDLY ENVIRONMENTS

The marketing database should provide a user-friendly environment in which marketers can perform all the functions discussed above without requiring programming intervention by data processing professionals.

Since the advent of the personal computer in the early 1980s, marketers who have little or no programming experience have become used to performing analytical tasks independently of their company's data processing professionals. Many PC users are now familiar with software tools such as spreadsheets, databases, and graphics programs. They have become used to working with menus, icons, pop-up screens, point-and-click mouse devices, guided modes of operation, and on-line help screens that assist them in performing complex data analysis tasks.

Because of the power of these tools, many PC users are entirely unaware that to perform the desired tasks the PC-based products are actually writing complex computer programs in the background. Consequently, although all fourth-generation database products include an attractive and *relatively* user-friendly query facility, or front end, users are frequently disappointed in the time it takes to answer what the colorful menus suggest are relatively simple questions. Therefore, to keep user and management expectations in perspective, companies should approve both the screens that will be used to submit queries and the response times associated with queries of differing complexity using prototype versions of applications prior to committing to a final database design.

Some state-of-the-art systems combine the power of mainframe or workstation processing with the ease of use of PCs—end users can simply indicate the functions they wish to perform without being aware of which tasks are being performed on the mainframe or workstation and which on the PC.

TURNAROUND TIME

In the process of defining functional requirements, turnaround times for various types of functions become particularly important. That is, which functions must be performed in seconds, which in minutes, and which ones overnight?

It is a natural tendency for marketers to request that all information, in any combination, be available immediately at all times. The relative importance of various queries should be weighed, however, because system performance does not come free of charge, and quick response time often requires an increased investment in computer hardware.

To better understand the impact that their information requests will have on the cost and performance of their database marketing applications, marketers should work together with their IT groups to determine whether the importance of certain queries and the frequency with which they are made justify the costs. Systems personnel may be able to suggest alternative means of delivering the required information that would have less of an impact on system performance and data storage costs.

Readers who want to know more about this subject should be sure to read Section Three of this book, on technology, especially the parts devoted to improving response times.

In fact, the more that marketers know about how the technology works and the issues that their IT professionals must resolve in designing an application, the more control they can exercise over the quality and functionality of the marketing database system. In recognition of this fact, many vendors of DBMS software, as well as universities and professional associations, offer courses in DBMS technology that are oriented to end users.

The functional requirements issues raised in this chapter have a major impact on how the database will be created and updated and on the hardware and software tools used to build and support the database. These subjects will be addressed in the following chapters.

CHAPTER 9

Building a Marketing Database

A FRAMEWORK FOR IMPLEMENTING A DATABASE PROJECT

In the last chapter we discussed the process of creating a detailed business needs and functional requirements document for a marketing database. This process should be completed prior to detailed design and implementation planning. In this approach, marketing specifies objectives, business processes, and information needs. Next, IT determines how to support those needs and determines likely costs and time frames. The costs are then compared with anticipated benefits, and the project is organized into phases. The initial phase contains the high-priority deliverables, and later phases contain functionality that is not as important, or will take longer to implement. In essence, this approach starts with a "blank sheet" and takes a top-down approach to developing an implementation plan.

However, it is sometimes necessary to begin by identifying the data in the individual business files from which the database will be created and maintained, i.e., a bottom-up approach. This is especially true in marketing databases that must be quickly implemented and therefore make only minimal demands on related systems that are sources of data. In these cases, it is most expedient to start with a listing of data sources that are easily available.

In broad outline form, the process would consist of these steps:

1. Decide whether the database will be created and maintained at an outside service bureau or developed internally. For the purpose of this discussion let's assume that we will be using an outside service bureau and that internal data processing departments will be sending files to the service bureau to update the database.

2. Have the database development team develop a preliminary list of the business needs the database will be expected to support.

3. Identify the individual business and promotional files available for inclusion in the marketing database.

4. Review the data elements contained in each contributing file.

5. Select from each file only the data elements relevant to supporting the marketing needs.

6. On a file-by-file basis define the data elements you might wish to create by comparing end-of-period updates. You can develop cumulative statistics (if only period data exists) or period statistics (if only cumulative data exists).

7. Decide where the data processing work defined above (extracting individual data elements and creating new data elements) is to be done—at one (or more) of the internal data processing departments or at the service bureau.

8. Decide which, if any, *data enhancement files* will be brought into the database.

9. Decide on a methodology for identifying duplicates and consolidating information between duplicate records.

10. Decide on a methodology for consolidating customers into households.

11. Develop a preliminary database design.

12. Decide how frequently the database will be updated.

13. Determine whether the update process will require updating existing records *within the database*, whether database records will periodically be replaced, or whether the optimal approach for your company will be a combination of both update methods.

14. Go back to the preliminary list of business needs and determine if the available data, the consolidation plan, and the database design are capable of meeting the business needs.

15. Revise elements of the plan as necessary.

WILL THE DATABASE BE CREATED AND MAINTAINED IN-HOUSE OR AT AN OUTSIDE SERVICE BUREAU?

Should the entire database marketing process be done in-house, or should a combination of internal and external resources be considered? There are three principal reasons why some companies prefer to do the entire job of developing a marketing database in-house: (1) cost, (2) control, and (3) customization.

Cost

There is always a perception that it is less expensive to develop applications in-house because the programmers on staff are part of a fixed-cost budget. This assumption must be validated, however, based on a number of dimensions:

Existing workload of the in-house staff

Whether additional help will be needed from contract programmers

Other systems development initiatives that will be forgone if resources are directed against the marketing database project

Whether an outside resource familiar with these systems can implement the system more quickly and do it correctly the first time

Oftentimes, a company would end up much farther ahead if it outsourced the marketing database project to a resource with significant experience with these systems and then allocated its internal resources to a project that required inside expertise. As discussed in previous chapters, marketing databases are very different from operations systems in terms of both needs and solutions. Very often, internal IT staffs are surprised at the lack of turnkey solutions and the amount of expertise and personalized service required to support targeted marketing functions. All these factors must be compared with the cost of using external resources.

Control

For many companies control is a more important consideration than cost. The customer list is the lifeblood of most customer-centric companies. Any use of external facilities must, by definition, create additional risk of exposure for the integrity and confidentiality of a company's data. To maintain control of critical data while using external resources, companies must first assess the risk and then manage that risk through procedural and contractual measures in conjunction with the external service provider.

Another essential element of control is familiarity with the company, its initiatives, its processing systems, and its data. While service bureaus have extensive knowledge relative to processing data for marketing databases and targeted campaigns, they often suffer from a lack of "inside" information about the client company itself.

For example, one well-known catalog company used an outside service bureau for its database. One fall, the cataloger decided to institute a purchase discount for its best customers. However, the order entry system would only process discounts for customers identified as employees. The "work-around" solution was to create a special employee code that in fact identified the cataloger's best customers. The change was instituted and everyone was happy. Marketing got its new idea implemented, IT didn't have to reprogram the order entry system, and the best customers got their discounts. Everything went well—until results from the spring catalog started coming in. After a few weeks it was apparent that something was terribly wrong; sales were significantly lower than forecast. List counts had been lower than expected, but only by about 5 percent or so.

After much investigation, the problem was traced to the fact that none of the best customers had received a catalog. You see, the company had a long-standing rule that employees were not to be sent catalogs in the mail. To save postage they could pick them up at work. Unfortunately, no one at the company thought to communicate the change in employee codes to the service bureau. No one at the service bureau noticed that the employee group had grown considerably, nor had anyone reviewed the number of best customers promoted during the list selection quality-control process. Now, nobody was happy. By the time a special mailing was made to the best customers, the cataloger had lost 8 weeks of its spring season.

Customization

Customization is one of the most important reasons to consider doing the project in-house. No matter how committed an external service provider is to the company's project, the service provider must support the needs of many different clients. Unless your company is one of the service provider's major clients, it is unlikely that it will adapt its systems development priorities to meet all of your needs. Consequently, a system developed by an external service provider might not provide the same level of customized screens, menus, and reporting capabilities that an internally developed application would offer.

On the other hand, the marketing function has long suffered from low priorities assigned to its projects by the company's internal IT staff. Another interesting phenomenon when dealing with internal IT departments is transfer pricing. Depending on how a company handles its internal cost accounting, it is very common to see end-user departments "charged" for services provided by the IT function and other cost centers. Very often, the end-user department is charged on a "cost-plus" basis, where the incremental cost of hardware, software, and staff needed to support the system is supplemented by allocations for "overhead" and other such charges.

Sometimes these charges are quite reasonable; other times they are ridiculous. One of our clients wanted to implement a prototype database to build experience for developing marketing database requirements and to drive some initial promotions. IT suggested using "an old machine that it had lying around." The application to which it had originally been assigned has been moved to a newer and more powerful platform. In short, the transfer price quoted by IT for 6 months of use was higher than the cost to do an outright purchase of a more powerful current-generation machine. Besides the usual cost items, it had factored in high maintenance costs because it was an older system, a high salvage value because the company had chosen a long depreciation period and the machine was far from fully depreciated, as well as a substantial charge for "general overhead."

Another significant issue is whether the company's IT staff can work in a "service bureau mode." Service bureaus supporting targeted marketing operations have developed very flexible approaches to working with different clients and each client's changing marketing support requirements. They have also developed a rather unique pool of resources that fully understand address standardization, enhancement data application, merge/purge software, scoring model usage, list reformatting, postal processing software, etc. They are used to receiving large volumes of tapes and sending large volumes of tapes with appropriate documentation to outside resources. Yes, tapes are considered "archaic" by many current standards, but the fact remains that they are still the most common way of transferring data within the targeted marketing industry.

While a client may not have sufficient "pull" to get its service provider to reprogram systems to its liking, it definitely has the complete and full attention of its assigned support staff. Therefore, it can expect its service team to "jump through hoops" to make last-minute changes, fix errors, etc.

On the other hand, most internal IT groups are designed and trained to operate with more standardized business disciplines where needs and business processes are relatively fixed. The types of systems that support those functions tend to be the types that are designed, implemented, and then essentially "just run." Many IT groups are moving toward what is commonly referred to as a "glass house," i.e., an automated system where all data inflows and outflows happen automatically. In these environments, sending and receiving tapes requires several days lead time and a large number of authorizing signatures. Imagine the impact those procedures would have on a dynamic targeted marketing group. In typical IT groups, there is a need to fix systems when they "break," but that is considerably different from the level of support and staff commitment necessary to constantly "do what it takes" to meet marketing's needs.

External Vendors

There are a number of reasons to seriously consider using external resources when developing a marketing database. If the company does not have an RDBMS product in-house or if it uses a different RDBMS product for the marketing database, time (and therefore money) must be invested in getting the IT staff up to speed on the product before any application development work can begin. Also, the licensing costs for RDBMS, desktop access tools, and merge/purge and other needed software can represent a very significant additional cost.

Meanwhile, the application development process will remain stalled until the marketing group and the IT group have developed a functional requirements document, discussed design issues, and, in many cases, reinvented the wheel a few times before the IT group is ready to get down to serious application development work. While all this preparatory work is going on, the marketing group *still* will not have the access it requires to data, and it will continue to make decisions based on the same quality of information that was available before the application development process began.

An external service provider can offer a company very significant value-added support at this point:

Experience with implementing marketing databases

Experience with targeted marketing processes and procedures

Experience with the client's industry

A labor pool from which to draw on an as-needed basis

Sharing of system development costs and licensing fees

A pool of hardware resources that can be allocated as necessary

All of these elements contribute to a generally faster implementation cycle. This enables marketers to load their current data into a marketing database platform, get immediate access to their data so they can make better marketing decisions, and have a chance to develop some hands-on experience with database technology. This hands-on experience will have direct benefits when it comes to defining the final functional requirements of their own applications.

A Combined Approach

A very significant point to consider is that the database support decision doesn't have to be either in-house or an outside service bureau. One approach is to use external services for those functions that are most efficiently done externally, while concentrating the development activities on internal resources. For example, although most companies may be able to define the *rules* for matching and householding, few are as experienced as service bureaus at performing these operations. For database updates that involve flexibility in input files or significant use of enhancement data, it might be more efficient to have a service bureau process updates, but use internal resources to implement an on-line access system.

Another approach is to use external services for the full range of database marketing services at first and then, at a later date, migrate the application in-house. This works well both for licensed versions of a vendor's preexisting database marketing application and for totally customized solutions that have been developed for client companies by vendors. The external vendor's resources and expertise are used to quickly design and implement the system, work out all of the "wrinkles," and establish standardized processes and procedures. After a mutually agreed time period, the vendor will assist client companies in making the transition to maintaining the database in-house (install software, train IT staff, etc.) and will often continue to provide services such as national change of address (NCOA), enhancement data, ad hoc list processing, research services, lettershop, or creative services.

The important point to remember is that using external services and using internal resources are not mutually exclusive approaches. The specific mix of services depends on the company, its available resources, and the development timetable.

WHAT DATA IS NEEDED TO PERFORM THE REQUIRED FUNCTIONS?

The database team should develop a preliminary list of business needs and then define the data elements that will be needed to perform the required functions, a three-step process:

1. Identify the business and promotional files that should be included in the database.
2. Review the data elements contained in each contributing file.
3. Select from each file only the data elements you wish to bring into the database.

Identify the Files to Be Included in the Database

Several constraints affect selecting files for inclusion. Although some marketers would like to include all the data that ever existed about all customers back to the beginning of time, this approach will not be practical, affordable, or even necessarily valuable from an informational perspective. It is possible to build so much data into a marketing database that the data structure, update processes, and access processes become so complex that the system cannot be used effectively.

Some issues to consider:

- Some files may not be available because of company policy decisions, interdivisional politics, or logistical difficulty. Files that are too hard to get can either be replaced with others or simply be excluded from the initial database. If the project team finds that the available files do not offer adequate information to justify the database, then corporate commitment and sponsorship of the project need to be revisited.
- Will the database contain data on customers, prospects, or both?
- How much promotion history is available? If two to three years of history may be available, how much of it is still relevant? Most companies find that one year of detailed data and two to three years of summary data are adequate for building a promotion history. If less data is available, then it will be more difficult to differentiate customers based on their promotion histories. More emphasis would therefore have to be placed on current promotions.
- What level of transaction data is available? Some companies maintain their transaction data as period statistics, such as sales in this month, returns this month, and so on. Other companies maintain their data as current, cumulative snapshots in the customer file, such as sales to date, returns to date, and so on. How the data is captured may determine if preprocessing activities of one type or another are required (more on this subject later in this chapter).
- Is the desired data actionable? Does it provide information that can be used to develop effective strategies and effective marketing programs? Does it provide information needed to effectively implement, manage, or evaluate marketing campaigns?
- Does the data element offer sufficient coverage to be significant? Many pieces of information have great potential value, but offer very sparse coverage of the overall customer universe. Financial companies would benefit greatly by knowing which other providers are servicing their

customers. Insurance companies would like to know when policies held by their prospects are due to expire. Certain catalog companies would like to know who is interested in fly fishing, but this information is not commonly available.

Review the Data Elements Contained in Each Contributing File

The first step in the process is to identify the files to be included in the database based on their availability and their information content. Once the desired subset of available files has been identified, a thorough review of the data elements contained in each file must be conducted. This process will require detailed reviews of each data element with the data processing or end-user personnel who are most familiar with each file to determine the precise meaning of each data element. Adequate time must be allocated for this process, which may take anywhere from one day to a few weeks—there are no shortcuts.

Select the Data Elements That Are Needed from Each File

Two sets of data elements are likely to be identified during the review of data elements:

1. Those data elements that clearly need to be included
2. Additional data elements that are not as clearly necessary but that the team feels uncomfortable about leaving out without further review

Actually, both sets of data elements should be included. Marketers will learn more about the individual data elements as they use the database, and some of the "extra" elements that were initially included will prove to be valuable. In addition, marketers will find that others, as well as some of the "certain" choices, are of little value. Generally, it makes sense to revisit the selection of data elements after about a year of using the database, as the value of each data element becomes clearer, and to modify the database loader programs accordingly.

DEFINE DATA ELEMENTS THAT MUST BE CREATED DURING THE UPDATE PROCESS

Earlier in this chapter, we described two ways in which customer files may be kept, as cumulative statistics or as period statistics. If customer records are kept as *cumulative statistics*, such as sales to date, purchases to date, and so on, then it will be desirable to calculate *period statistics* during each update cycle. Similarly, if customer records are kept as *period statistics*, then it may be necessary to calculate *cumulative statistics* during the update process. Most companies' transaction files contain a small number of cumulative statistic fields and a larger number of period statistic fields. We will discuss *how* these statistics are calculated later in this chapter.

HOW WILL DATA GET INTO THE MARKETING DATABASE?

Once we have identified the data elements that are to be included in the marketing database, the next step in the process is to determine *how* the data elements will get there. This process can be accomplished in three ways, each of which has different cost and processing implications:

1. *Data extraction by data providers.* The desired data elements can be extracted from existing files by a series of programs written and maintained by the data providers. This approach helps minimize the volume of data that must be processed during the initial load and subsequent updates and can reduce the time required and costs associated with these processes. The disadvantage to this approach is that, over time, the data elements to be included in the marketing database are likely to change, and each change in data elements will require corresponding changes not only to the database loader programs, but also to the data extraction programs.

2. *Data extraction including creation of summary calculated data.* In addition to the processes described for the first option, this variation includes calculating summary data fields such as the total sales per customer during the period across all business units, the average purchases to date, and so on. This approach shares all the advantages and disadvantages of the prior process and adds the complexity of performing calculations on data elements during the extraction process.

3. *Providing complete, unextracted copies of existing files to the database loader.* Complete, unextracted copies of all existing files can be provided to the database loader, and the database loader can sort out which records to include and exclude. This is the simplest approach for the data providers, but it involves the greatest amount of work and cost for the database loaders. One advantage that it offers is that over time, as the data elements to be included in the database change, it may be simpler and more cost-effective to modify only the database loader rather than modifying both the database loader and the extract programs.

Each of these approaches has cost, time, and organizational implications, depending on whether the processing work is to be performed in-house or at a service bureau. Although the choices for each company will vary according to such factors as the complexity of the database application, size of the database, number of internal file sources, and availability of internal resources, there is no free lunch for anyone on this issue.

In-House Processing Implications

One of the objectives for most companies in developing a marketing database application is to bring together *all* the information known about customers throughout their relationship with the company. This often requires bringing together files from a number of different business units or profit centers, each of which has its own agenda and priorities.

In companies with a small number of data sources, the internal IT management would have to provide extracts of data on an ongoing basis. Depending on the workload of the IT group and the priorities of other projects, high-level sponsorship for the data needs of the marketing database may be required to get the programming projects and subsequent processing work approved.

In companies where the data sources are from more than one division, it may be necessary to negotiate arrangements with multiple divisions, first to provide data at all and second to gain cooperation for providing data on an ongoing basis. In some cases, divisions will incur personnel or processing costs for performing data extractions that may have to be paid for either by the database project or through some other internal cost transfer mechanism. These issues often need to be resolved at a fairly high level within companies *before* long-term commitments for the support of the database application can be made.

Service Bureau Processing Implications

If a service bureau is to perform the data extraction and other preprocessing activities, companies should consider how the service bureau charges and how these charges will impact the costs of the project. For example, if a large number of records will be preprocessed during each update cycle, the service bureau cost could be significant, particularly if the service bureau charges based on the number of records passed. Companies may wish to consider performing some or all of the preprocessing work internally and then sending the files to the service bureau in these cases:

1. The service bureau's charges for preprocessing files exceed an acceptable level.
2. Adequate and affordable processing services are available in-house.

Although service bureaus offer "painless processing," avoiding any of the political issues associated with internal processing, their services are not free, and the costs may be prohibitive over the duration of the project. Considerations will vary from company to company, but the issues are constant. Each company must evaluate its options and select the approach that is most appropriate based on cost and convenience.

DECIDE WHICH, IF ANY, DATA ENHANCEMENTS FILES WILL BE USED

Several companies are in the business of selling enhancement data either that they have compiled themselves or that they offer on behalf of other data vendor companies. Earlier in this book we described the data elements available for enhancement as secondary data that is purchased from external sources. Secondary data is available on a license basis directly to customer companies or through the major service bureaus. Previously, we described what the data elements are, and in later chapters we describe how you can use these enhancement data elements for modeling or profiling as part of the new direct marketing.

As part of the process of building a database, companies must decide which, if any, of the enhancement data variables they will include in their databases so the database design and the database loader programs can accommodate this data.

CONSOLIDATING RECORDS*

A difficult, time-consuming, and often expensive step in the database loading process is record consolidation. Many firms capture customer records in transaction-oriented systems, and multiple records for individuals and households may

---

* For more information on this topic, please read Chapter 10, "Using Data Hygiene to Identify Individuals and Households."

exist on the file. Before these records are loaded into the database, duplicates must be identified and in some cases "scrubbed" (a process described later in this chapter), so the marketer will have the clearest idea possible of how many customers there are and what their relationships may be to each other.

In a single-product company, if unique customer IDs or match codes are used in the fulfillment system, it is likely that only one record will exist for each customer. However, many companies, particularly in financial services, may have a number of different relationships with a single customer. If the firm's data processing systems are account-based rather than customer-based, it is very likely that the company will be unaware of the total relationship it has with a customer and that each product group will be unaware of the customer's relationships with other parts of the firm.

As part of the initial consolidation process, companies may choose to build a cross-reference file that links all account numbers associated with a given customer using a unique customer ID. The customer ID not only should be unique, but should *not* be based on the customer's name and address because these may change over time, making it more difficult to maintain data integrity within the database.

As shown in Figure 9–1, customer ID is a keyed field, meaning that it is one of the fields used to link a number of different tables together.

Duplicate Identification

To consolidate records at the customer level, a duplicate identification process must be executed prior to loading names into the database to identify which records belong to the same customer. Most often, duplicate identification processes are based on names and addresses. More sophisticated duplicate identification software products use a number of algorithms to predict the probability of two records belonging to the same person. Users can set the criteria to be tighter or looser, as required by the marketing application, and the algorithms within the program will suggest which customers are duplicates and which are unique.

Although the software used to perform duplicate identification is the same as that used to *eliminate* duplicates when preparing mailings from multiple internal sources or from rented lists, the intent of the process is entirely different when building a customer or prospect database. Here the goal is to capture *all the information* related to each customer or prospect and to consolidate data that would otherwise be fragmented across a number of different records into a single and complete picture of that individual's relationship with the company.

The matching algorithms can be set either loosely or tightly, depending on how critical an exact match must be for the company's application. For example,

FIGURE 9–1

	Table I Customer Data	Table II Purchase Data	
Data Elements	Customer ID Name Address Demographic Data	Customer ID Purchase Date Catalog Number Product Code Item Code	Repeating Records

companies that are interested in mailing into *households* rather than to specific individuals within those households may be satisfied if the last name and the address match exactly. In some cases, if they are certain that an address is not a multiple dwelling, they will be satisfied with an address match alone.

Address Standardization

Address standardization software such as LPC's Finalist or Group 1's Code-1 Plus can deal with transposed street addresses and incorrect street names. For example, is *123 Oak Street, 132 Oak Street,* or *132 Oat Street* correct? By comparing these addresses to national databases and by using the Delivery Sequence File (DSF), marketers can automatically determine if:

- The ZIP code matches the city and state portions of the address.
- The ZIP code (or corrected ZIP code) contains an Oak Street, an Oat Street, or both.
- The street numbers along the street in question lie within the bounds of the ZIP code.
- The street number is a valid address.
- The address is a business or residence and whether a residence is a single-family or multifamily dwelling unit.

Matching Issues

It is not unusual to find variations in the spelling of an individual name within a company's files. One company found the names *Robert Smith, Bob Smith, R. Smith,* and *Robt Smythe* all listed at the same address. We may assume that these are the same individual, but it is possible that these are records of a father and son; a grandfather, father, and son; or possibly unrelated individuals. You can set parameters for the matching software to consider these versions of a name as a single name or to retain them as multiple individuals, depending on the requirements of the mailer.

Once all these issues have been addressed, *all iterations of the address* contained in the files can be corrected and the matching process can be completed efficiently.

Often companies that have multiple business files store name and address data in different formats in each file. In this situation, duplicate identification software must be flexible enough to *parse*[1] through the elements of a name and, in some cases, to determine what comprises the first name, last name, middle name or initial, title, suffix, or other elements. Many service bureaus and some large companies have developed dictionaries of first names, last names, titles, and suffixes to use as a reference during this process.

The duplicate identification (or merge/purge process—we use the terms interchangeably) may be equally important for prospect files, since these may contain a history of prior inquiries and related promotions to prospects. For many companies, the number of previous inquiries that a prospect has made is a very strong predictor of eventual conversion. Prior inquiry information about products other than those currently owned by customers may also be available. If so, this data may provide additional guidance for how to market in a cross-selling campaign.

---

1. *Parsing* is a computer process in which data elements are read one position at a time and compared with tables to determine whether the data is valid, and if so, what it means.

Scrubbing

For financial services companies, registration information may be embedded in the customer record as part of the name and address, as shown in Figure 9–2. In this example, we begin an examination of account information for Steven and Christine Smith, who have a number of different relationships with City Federal Bank.

In Figure 9–2, we see that City Federal is the trustee for a trust fund account owned by Steven and Christine Smith as joint tenants. Before we could match this customer record against a customer record like that shown in Figure 9–3, we would first have to strip out registration information unrelated to name and address.

In a specialized application of parsing and dictionary use, scrubbing software would recognize that City Federal, ITF, and JTTNT are all terms that are not names or addresses of individuals. It would strip out this data and prepare a new record that could be matched much more readily using merge/purge software. In addition, scrubbing software interprets and retains the *meaning* of registration data so that its information value is not lost.

Householding

Identifying which customers are actually members of the same household can be a complicated process. Two scenarios follow—one typical householding process based on names and addresses and one that represents more complex and, in the new direct marketing, more common situations.

Householding Based on Names and Addresses

Once the file is scrubbed, we must take some additional steps to accurately and efficiently market to households. Suppose that Steven Smith also had an IRA and that the mortgage for the home where he and his wife reside is in Christine's name alone. To understand the full extent of the Smiths' relationships with City Federal, as well as their household relationship, the bank would have to go through all the steps we described.

First, the software would perform the household match using an algorithm that matched the Smiths by ZIP code, last name, and street address. The first-name comparison would show that Steven and Christine were two different people. Joint account information would further establish the relationship between the two; however, we would have to obtain the fact that they are married to each other either from other account information or from external sources, or we would infer it based on the sex and age of each individual.

Understanding the relationships between customers in a household may be essential to a company's marketing efforts because inappropriate copy or artwork may have a negative impact on response. Accordingly, companies must be careful

FIGURE 9–2

City Federal ITF
Anthony Smith Julia Smith JTTNT IRA
123 Elm Street
Anytown, USA

FIGURE 9–3

Anthony and Julia Smith
123 Elm Street
Anytown, USA

about making assumptions concerning relationships within households and may wish to maintain scores that represent levels of certainty about relationships. These scores in turn could be used to determine how deeply into a file a certain promotion should be mailed.

Let's say that City Federal identified Christine and Steven Smith's relationship as husband and wife based on specific data contained in their trust records. In this case, the value (or confidence level) that Steven and Christine are married could be set at 100 percent. But suppose that this specific data were not available. Based on other information, Steven and Christine's ages were known to be 55 and 53, respectively, and a match of their first names against a dictionary showed that they were male and female, respectively. In this situation, City Federal could not be certain that Steven and Christine were not brother and sister, or even cousins.

If we knew children were in the household, we might have further reason to infer that the Smiths are a conventional family, but even this set of relationships would not provide the same level of certainty as would documentation *within the account*. Therefore, a promotion that featured a conventional family situation and product set might or might not be appropriate. And as many direct marketers have found, promotions with inappropriate or inaccurate personalization can underperform nonpersonalized promotions.

Identifying More Complex Relationships between Customers

Some companies may wish to use householding techniques to identify more complex relationships between customers. Consider a company that has insurance products, retail sales, catalog sales, and house credit cards that may be used for purchases in each of these product lines. To illustrate the complexity of customer relationships, we can describe four situations—Type I, Type II, Type III, and Type IV households. These classifications are not meant to be exhaustive, but rather they are intended to illustrate the kinds of decisions marketers must face when formulating rules to define households.

1. *Type I households.* Type I households are the basic case described above in which customers who have the same last name and who live at the same address constitute a household. In addition to these characteristics, they may have credit card account numbers or insurance policy numbers in common.

2. *Type II households.* Type II households consist of individuals who have different last names, live at the same address, and have credit card account numbers or insurance policy numbers in common. These households may consist of married couples in which the wife has kept her maiden name, parent-child situations in which the parent is responsible for the child's financial obligations or the reverse, or sets of unmarried individuals whose relationships are sufficiently permanent for them to have established shared financial obligations.

3. *Type III households.* Type III households consist of individuals who have common account numbers or policy numbers, live at *different* addresses, and may or may not have a common last name. Type III household structures would be typical of parents who have financial responsibility for dependent children who may be away at school or who at least maintain a separate residence, or of individuals who have financial responsibility for dependent parents who maintain a separate residence.

4. *Type IV households.* Type IV households consist of individuals who live at the same address, have different last names, and do not have account numbers or policy numbers in common. These households would be typical of roommates who share a dwelling, but do not share financial responsibilities.

Each of these household types represents a different marketing opportunity, and marketers could apply the information captured during the data consolidation process to select different groups of customers for different types of promotions.

As part of the data consolidation process the company could obtain counts of the total number of relationships with each customer or related group of customers. Subtotals of the number of relationships could also be calculated by product category. For example, marketers might wish to know the total number of insurance policies for an individual customer or household. This calculation could be based on the number of policies owned by individuals who make up each of the household types described above.

Similarly, credit card account numbers used for retail or catalog purchases could be linked, either within a single residence or across multiple residences. The number of relationships at the customer or household level may be used in combination with information about individual customer purchases and promotion history to develop statistical models that predict response to promotion efforts.

DEVELOP A PRELIMINARY DATABASE DESIGN

Once a company's data had been consolidated at the individual and household level, the next step in the process would be to populate a marketing database with this data. This requires that a preliminary database design has been developed by data processing professionals, either within the company or at the service bureau if the marketing database application is being developed externally. Figure 9–4 contains a series of tables that together compose a preliminary database design for a catalog company. Although the specific data elements would vary for different types of companies, this example will help you understand the types of tables that a marketing database likely includes and the organization of data elements within each table.

Figure 9–5 illustrates data that would be stored in summary form in a typical marketing database after the summary fields had been created either during the data extraction or the data loading process.

FREQUENCY OF UPDATE OR REPLACEMENT

The frequency of update or table replacement is generally driven as much by operational processing windows as by marketing's information needs. Both replacement and updating are time-consuming processes. The frequency of updating or replacement determines how well the database represents the actual customer master file. If promotional decisions (for example, who should be mailed what) are based largely on buyer behavior, most marketers will want information to be as current as possible to avoid excluding active customers from promotion.

Updates need not be more frequent than the decision-making interval requires. If, for example, a company makes two mailings a year, it may only be necessary to update the file sufficiently in advance of the two mailings to provide the data required for name selection. As long as the intervening months' files are stored so they will be accessible for update processing, the company can put off processing the information until it is actually required for decision making.

Although less frequent updating may make financial sense, particularly in situations where a company's marketing database is maintained at a service bureau, many companies opt to update more frequently to support ongoing analysis and reporting between mailing cycles.

A nightly update schedule that includes the following information is typical for many companies:

- Purchase and return data for current customers, including total sales, by:
  - Department
  - Item/SKU
  - Product type
- Customer data, including new customers and customer change-of-address data
- Performance by list source during a campaign

Other companies update the following information less frequently, often quarterly:

- Address correction from external sources
- Assignment of customers to product groups
- External demographic data about customers
- Performance index by demographic or ZIP cluster

Creating Separate Databases for Marketing to Avoid Conflict

As will be discussed in detail later on in Section Three of this book, which deals with technology, many companies have a priority conflict between analytical users of data, such as marketers, and operational or production users of data, such as customer service or data processing operations. In general, if a company has only one system to support both analysis and operations and if the two functions are being operated simultaneously, conflicts in processing priority are inevitable. This is one of several reasons that a number of direct marketing companies create separate databases for each function. Then, each application can be separately tuned to operate at optimal efficiency. Performance may be further enhanced by decoupling the operations support and decision support functions and operating them on separate hardware and software platforms, each of which has been optimized to support the requirements of its application.

From a data standpoint, the separation of functions requires maintaining separate files of data for operations and for decision support, which requires spending more money for data storage, in either the mainframe, workstation, or PC environment, depending on the configuration selected. However, data storage is relatively inexpensive.

For example, the space required to store 2 million records, each containing 1,000 bytes (characters) of data in a mainframe environment, ranges from about $500 to $800 per month.[2] Even with the additional space required to store indexes for the files, the cost would be less than $1,000 per month.

---

2. In a workstation or PC environment, data storage can be purchased for as little as $200 to $500 per gigabyte.

FIGURE 9–4

Data Tables

	Customer Table	Repeat Purchase Table	Item Table	Catalog Promo Table	Print/FSI Promo Table	Broadcast Promo Table	Catalog Source Table
Key Fields							
	Customer ID	Customer ID	Item Code	Catalog Number Item Code	Key Code	Key Code	Catalog Number Key Code Offer Code
Nonrecurring Fields							

	Name
	Address
	Match Code
	Prior Name
	Prior Address
	Individual Demographic Data
	Original Source Code
	Date of First Purchase
		Purchase IDs
		Actual Catalog Number
		Attributed Catalog Number
		Purchase Date
		Purchase Amount
		Payment Mode
		Ordering Mode
			Item Cost
			Subject Code
			Product Code
			Description
				Date Mailed
				Quantity Mailed
				Item Price
				Percent of Page
				Page Number and Position
				Key Code
				Offer Code
				Test Code
				Production Costs
				  Fixed
				  Variable
				Total Cost
				Description
					Ad Code
					Release Date
					Media Cost
					Circulation
					Offer Code
					Production Costs
					  Fixed
					  Variable
					Total Cost
						Ad Code
						On Air Date
						Air Time
						800 Phone Number
						Production Costs
						  Fixed
						  Variable
						Total Cost
						Description
							Duplication Rate versus House File
							Quantity Ordered
							Quantity Mailed
							Costs
							Broker ID
							Creative Code
							Test Code

Data Tables (Continued)

Print/FSI Source Table	Medium Table	Offer Code Table	Deciles Table	Model Table	Purchase Item Table
		Key Fields			
Key Code	Medium Code	Offer Code	Customer ID	Model Code	Item Code
Offer Code	Key Code	Catalog Number	Model Code		Purchase ID
		Nonrecurring Fields			
Circulation	Major Media Code(s)	Description	Model Score	Model Name	
Creative Code	Description		Date of Scoring	Model Description	
Test Code			Decile Code		
Description					
Costs					

Customer Table	Data Element	Description
		Key Fields
	Customer ID	A unique customer identification code that, once assigned, will always remain associated with that customer. This is used to link the customer table with a number of other tables in the database and to help identify repeat customers who may have been archived from the system because of inactivity.
		Nonrecurring Fields
	Name	Customer's current name.
	Address	Customer's current address.
	Match Code	A match code based on the customer's current name and address. This code makes customers who are already on the database easily identifiable when new orders or inquiries are received. Match codes are associated with the unique customer ID.
	Prior Name	Some marketers like to carry at least one prior name on the database.
	Prior Address	Similarly, some marketers like to carry one or two prior addresses on the file for ease of identifying customers who have moved.
	Individual Level Demographic Data	Through modeling, many marketers have found that demographic data, for example, individual age, income, lifestyle, home value, and so on is useful in predicting response to a particular promotion and lifetime value of customers. A number of fields are usually made available for storing this data in the customer table, even though the specific data elements that will fill these fields may not be known at the time the database is created.
	Original Source Code	This field links individual customers with their original source. Although it would also be possible to link customers by source via the purchase table, there are many instances in which it is desirable to determine the number or the characteristics of customers who come from a particular source without having to sort through their purchase behavior. Also, since the original source code will not change, it makes sense to maintain this as one of the static fields in the customer table.
	Date of First Purchase	Although the purchase table will capture dates of all future purchases, the date of first purchase defines a class of purchasers, and is therefore often maintained separately.

Repeat Purchase Table	Data Element	Description
		Key Fields
	Customer ID	The unique customer ID is the link between purchases made and the customers who made them.
		Purchase Data Elements That Recur with Each Purchase or Return Transaction
	Purchase ID	The purchase ID identifies individual purchase or return transactions so detailed information about purchases could be obtained if desired.
	Actual Catalog Number	The catalog number (catalog) that the customer bought from.
	Attributed Catalog Number	In situations where the actual catalog number is unknown, an attributed catalog number is calculated, usually based on the most recent catalog that contained the purchased item that was mailed to the customer prior to ordering.
	Purchase Date	For all subsequent purchases, the date of the purchase is maintained in the purchase table.
	Purchase Amount	For each purchase, the purchase amount is maintained.
	Payment Mode	An indicator is often maintained to show whether a purchase was made using cash or a credit card. This data may be important in the future when selecting customers for certain promotions.
	Ordering Mode	An indicator is maintained to show whether an order was placed by mail or by telephone.

Item Table	Data Element	Description
		Key Fields
	Item Code	This field links the item table with other tables, including purchase, product, and catalog, and through them with customers.
		Nonrecurring Fields
	Item Cost	The cost of an item to the cataloger.
	Subject Code	The subject with which each item in the table is associated.
	Product Code	The product type with which each item is associated.
	Description	A free-form description of the item.

	Data Element	Description
Catalog Promotion Table		
		Key Fields
	Catalog Number	Each catalog has a unique identification number.
	Item Code(s)	Item code field links specific items purchased to the catalog from which they were purchased. Because prices and costs of items may vary depending on quantities ordered or special promotions, each combination of catalog code with item code is able to support unique prices and costs. This data is carried in detail in the item table.
		Nonrecurring Fields
	Date Mailed	Each catalog has a unique value for date mailed, which will be maintained in the database.
	Quantity Mailed	The mailing quantity of each catalog is maintained for subsequent analysis.
	Item Price	The standard (or default) price for an item. This may change for special offers or for certain catalogs. The combination of item code and catalog code is linked with a unique price.
	Percent of Page	Indicates the percent of page in a catalog given to a specific item.
	Page Number and Position	Indicates the page of the catalog on which the item appeared and the position of the item on the page.
	Key Code	Links catalog number to specific mailing source(s).
	Offer Code(s)	Provision for unique codes to describe the offers being conducted in a specific catalog.
	Test Code(s)	Provision for unique codes to describe the offers being conducted in a specific catalog.
	Costs	Costs associated with mailing.
	Production Costs	For each catalog mailing, costs, including list rental, postage, and detailed production, are maintained so that return on promotion can subsequently be calculated.

	Fixed Costs
	  Color Separations
	  Type
	  Mechanicals
	  Creative
	Variable Costs
	  Printing
	  Lettershop
	  Lists
	  Postage
	  Return Postage	

	Total Costs	Total of all fixed and variable costs associated with production and distribution of catalog.
	Descriptive Data Number of Pages	The number of pages in the catalog is maintained.
	Free-Form Description	Free-form text describes the seasonality, theme, coloration, or other relevant data about the department.

Print/FSI Promotion Table

Data Element	Description
Key Fields	
Key Code	Links to other tables.
Nonrecurring Fields	
Ad Code	Unique ID for each ad.
Release Date	The date on which the periodical issue will be released.
Media Cost	Cost per page for print, cost of production, and distribution for FSIs.
Circulation	Circulation of periodical or guaranteed distribution volume for FSIs.
Offer Code	As in direct mail, specific offers can be tested in other media.

Production Costs
  Fixed
    Color Separations
    Type
    Mechanicals
    Photography
    Creative
  Variable Costs
    Printing
    Media
	Cost associated with print or FSI promotions. For each promotion, costs include production, creative, and other fixed costs, as well as variable costs such as printing and distribution.

Response Cost
    Lettershop
    Postage
    Return Postage
	Inbound coupon or telephone response cost.

Total Costs	Total of production, response, and media expenses.

Broadcast Promotion Table

Data Element	Description
Key Fields	
Key Code	Links to other tables.
Nonrecurring Fields	
Ad Code	Unique ID for each ad.
On-Air Date	Date on which promotion airs.
Air Time	Media cost for airtime used.
800 Phone Number	In-bound response costs.
Production Costs Fixed	Costs of developing broadcast promotion including creative, talent, studio expenses, and so on.
Variable	Airtime, response expenses, and so on.
Total Costs	Total of production, airtime, and response expenses.
Description	Free-form description of ad content.

Catalog Source Table

Data Element	Description
	Key Fields
Catalog Number	Unique catalog ID that source is being used for.
Key Code	Specific use of a particular medium, for example, the *New York Times,* November 9, issue.
Offer Code	
	Nonrecurring Fields
Duplication Rate versus House File	Many direct marketers have found that the density of the duplication rate between the house file and an external source is predictive of response the next time that the source is used for promotion.
Quantity Ordered	Number of names considered for promotion from a source.
Quantity Mailed	Net number of names mailed after merge, purge, suppression, and so on.
Costs	List rental.
Broker ID	Unique identifier for each list or media broker.
Creative Code(s)	Different creative packages are constantly being tested. This code links sources with the specific creative packages they are being mailed.
Test Code(s)	Within an offer or creative package, a variety of tests may be used in each mailing. The source table captures a code that identifies the specific test people are being subjected to.

Print/FSI Source Tables

Data Element	Description
	Key Fields
Key Code(s)	This unique identifier links the source table with the print/FSI promotion table so the cataloger will know which sources received which promotions.
Offer Code(s)	A unique identifier that links specific offers with the sources to which the offers were mailed.
	Nonrecurring Fields
Circulation	For print sources, this is the number of guaranteed names that have direct visual access to an ad. Response is calculated against the circulation number in much the same way that response rate is calculated against quantity mailed for direct mail promotions.
Creative Code(s)	Different creative packages are constantly being tested. This code links sources with the specific creative packages they are being mailed.
Test Code(s)	Within an offer or creative package, a variety of tests may be used in each mailing. The source table captures a code that will identify the specific test people are being subjected to.
Free-Form Description	Free-form text that identifies the list source in detail.
Costs	Costs in relevant units, for example, per page, black and white versus color versus four-color bleed.

Medium Table

Data Element	Description
	Key Fields
Medium Code(s)	Specific periodical or newspaper, for example, the *New York Times*, *Time*.
Key Code(s)	Specific use of a medium for a particular promotion or subset of a promotion.
	Nonrecurring Fields
Major Media Code(s)	Indicates whether medium is a rented list, broadcast, space, and so on, and for space, the type of medium, for example, magazine, newspaper.
Description	Free-form description of medium.

Offer Table

Data Element	Description
	Key Fields
Offer Code(s)	Identifies a specific offer that may include discounts, special premiums, and so on.
Catalog Number	Ties specific offers to specific department numbers.
	Nonrecurring Fields
Description	Free-form description of offer.

Deciles Table

Data Element	Description
	Key Fields
Customer ID	Provides link to customer table and customer data.
Model Code	Unique code for each scoring model.
	Nonrecurring Fields
Model Score	Score produced by model.
Date of Scoring	Date model was used to score names in customer table.
Decile Code	Indicates the decile that customers or prospects are assigned to by the various models.

Model Table

Data Element	Description
	Key Fields
Model Code	Unique code for each scoring model. Link to decile table.
	Nonrecurring Fields
Model Name	Name of each scoring model.
Model Description	Free-form description of each scoring model.

Purchase Item Table

Data Element	Description
	Key Fields
Item Code	Links purchases to the items purchased. There may be several items purchased in one transaction.
Purchase ID	Links to repeat purchase table so that data about purchase transactions can be related to items purchased.

F I G U R E   9–5

Examples of Summary Information

By Customer
    Total purchases
    Total orders
    Total mailings
    Product frequency (how many times a product code ordered)
    Subject frequency (how many times a subject code ordered)
By Source
    Key code (specific mailings)
    Total sales
    Total costs
    Profit calculations:
    1. CPM
    2. CPO
    3. Average sales
    4. Sales per thousand pieces mailed
    5. Profit per thousand pieces mailed
    6. Average lifetime value for customers
By Department
    Total sales
    Total costs
    Profitability measures:
    1. CPM
    2. CPO
    3. Average sales
    4. Sales per thousand pieces mailed
    5. Profit per thousand pieces mailed
    6. Average lifetime value for customers
By Item
    Item number
    Total sales
    Total usages (departments)

Marketers should evaluate the additional cost of data storage required to support their database marketing applications in the same way that they evaluate all other business investments. That is, the incremental value of the data, in terms of increased profitability to the company, must outweigh the incremental cost of data storage. Marketers should be able to calculate the increased revenues or savings that would occur based on the decisions they would be able to make if the additional data were available.

The potential disadvantage of maintaining separate data for operations and decision support is that marketers will not have up-to-the-minute, or real-time, data in their file. Marketing's data will be accurate only through the time that the marketing database was last updated. Many companies update key files daily, twice a day, or in some cases on a real-time basis. However, some data pertaining to customers, list sources, items, or departments does not change on a daily basis except when new records are added.

Purchase or return transaction data, on the other hand, may change several times during the course of a day. A large-sized catalog company, for example, could have anywhere from 50,000 to 100,000 customer transactions per day. Although these transactions are extremely important to the company's business, marketers rarely require real-time transactions. For calculation of trends, distribution by list source, or the comparative performance of items or product type, real-time data is not necessary.

Levels of Detail of Data

Data may be brought into the database at the detailed transaction level or at some level of summarization. If the data does not enter the database at the detailed transaction level, then marketers will not be able to analyze relationships in the database at this level of detail.

Although it is only logical that data can't be viewed at a lower level than it exists in the system, many IT professionals have experienced the frustration of trying to explain this fact to their marketing colleagues six months after the database project is completed. This is one more reason why dialogue between the marketing and IT members of the database team referred to earlier in this chapter is so essential.

Although it may be desirable to have data available at the lowest possible level of detail, cost and operational considerations must be weighed. Detailed transaction-level data, in virtually all cases, requires more data storage, higher processing costs, and a longer update processing window than would be required for summary data.

WILL THE DATABASE BE UPDATED OR REPLACED?

Will data actually be updated, that is, modified, in the database, or will the system replace the current database tables with more current snapshots of customer data? If the update is performed within the database, then more complex programming is required so the application can actually find previous records and then perform adds, changes, and deletes to existing tables.

Alternatively, if the update is done in the transaction system and the database tables are to be replaced by fresh information, it may be necessary to modify existing transaction systems so data at the detailed level will be available to the database. The extent of the modifications will depend on the level of detail the transaction system currently maintains. For example, if a customer had $100 in sales from six purchases at the time of the last update and $160 in sales resulting from nine purchases in the current update, what was the value of each purchase during this period? Were there three equal purchases of $20? Were there two purchases at $10 and one at $40? The answers to these questions may determine the type of promotion the marketer wishes to send. If detailed transaction-level data is not made available to the database, then the opportunity to differentiate customers at this level may be lost.

If the *replacement* approach is used, the database may be required to maintain a history of prior snapshots of the files. In this case, pseudo-transactions may be calculated based on the difference in values between current snapshots and prior snapshots of selected variables. Then, in addition to replacing prior values, counter-oriented fields showing the activity during the current month may be populated using the values produced by the pseudo-transactions. Many companies combine the replenishment and update approaches, updating frequently changing fields, such as sales, each month using detailed transaction records and updating less frequently changing fields, such as customer demographics, periodically.

In companies that wish to maintain historical data in their marketing databases, marketers must decide these issues:

- How much historical data should be maintained?
- What level of detail should be maintained?
- For how long a period should the data be retained?

Many companies work with a rolling 24- or 36-month view of their data.

RETURN TO THE BUSINESS NEEDS AND DETERMINE THE ADEQUACY OF THE PLAN FOR MEETING THOSE NEEDS

Prior to proceeding with the database project, the project team should reconvene to evaluate how well the data elements that have been incorporated into the preliminary database design and the functional capabilities designed for the database meet the original business needs. Typically, as projects progress, decisions are made based on such issues as data availability, cost and complexity of processing, cost of data storage, and anticipated costs of development and implementation that cause changes in original specifications. In more than a few cases, final applications were significantly different from the original business requirements, and in too many cases, they failed to meet the original business requirements entirely.

For these reasons, a thorough review should be performed *prior* to beginning the implementation phase of the project to ensure that the database marketing application, as planned, meets the business requirements as stated.

If, during this review process, the database team determines that, in light of information discovered during the project, the company's business needs have actually *changed* and the database application will have to perform somewhat different functions from those originally anticipated, three actions are available to companies:

1. If the changes are relatively minor, then the design should be revisited to incorporate those changes and then proceed.
2. If the changes are major and consist primarily of additions to the original set of functions, then the original project can proceed as planned and the enhancements can be added as part of the next version of the application.
3. If the changes are major and are a significant departure from the original business requirements, then the project should be stopped and the entire process, beginning with business needs assessment, should begin again.

By maintaining continuity of team members from the marketing and data processing groups throughout the project, the original business needs and the resulting database design should be a close fit. However, some companies have found that projects can take on a life of their own, with the result that the differences between the system design and the original requirements come as a complete surprise even to those who have participated throughout the process. The step-by-step approach in this chapter should minimize the likelihood of that occurring.

CHAPTER 10

Using Data Hygiene to Identify Individuals and Households

Elsewhere in this book, the importance of *defining* the targeted audience, be it an individual, household, or some other grouping, has been addressed along with techniques for defining these groupings and testing their appropriateness. The majority of these decisions are strategic or at least tactical in nature. In this chapter we will address the operational challenges that the real world poses, the majority of which revolve around the ability to *identify an individual* from among the records that are included on the house files and any rented lists. This identification process may seem operational in nature, but the degree of success (or failure) plays a key role in determining the viability of the promotion both economically and in meeting its marketing objectives.

Targeting the audience for a direct marketing promotion is critical to success. However, sometimes even if the individual to whom the promotion is directed is clearly defined, the vagaries of contacting the individual come into play. For a direct mail effort, it may be whoever opens the mail, while for a telemarketing contact it may be whoever answers the phone. In any event, the requirement is still to direct the contact to the individual or group of individuals who are most likely to accept the offer.

In most cases, the target of the promotion is typically an individual who either is an existing customer or is identified by a name and address obtained from a rented list. Some direct marketing efforts may target an aggregation of individuals, such as the traditional household. In any event, all of these efforts require some means of identifying the unique individuals or groups, though to varying levels of precision, who are the target of the promotion.

REAL-WORLD ISSUES

Beyond who opens the mail or answers the phone, there are a number of real-world issues that intrude on or complicate the process of identifying individuals or groups. These include:

- *People using multiple versions of their names including nicknames and initials, for example:*
  John Robert Smith
  Jack Smith
  J. Smith
  John Smythe

J. R. Smith

J. Robert Smith

Bob Smith, and so on

- *People with similar names.* In the United States, there is a society of individuals with the name Jim Smith comprising some 500,000 members. In other cultures, using such things as clan names (e.g., in Scotland) or a last name such as "son of" (e.g., in Norwegian countries) imposes even more difficulties.

- *People having multiple relationships, and consequently multiple records on file.* On customer lists of companies that maintain their data in transaction-oriented files, including at the policy and account level, individuals that have multiple relationships (e.g., one person has both life and property insurance policies) could possibly be treated as multiple customers. If so, this may result in multiple mail pieces (e.g., one for each statement) each month and multiple promotional pieces, assuming that the individuals meet the selection criteria based on more than one of their relationships. In addition to being costly, this practice is also bad from a customer relations and image perspective as it may appear that the company does not know what it is doing.

- *Customers who become dormant.* Such customers who you think are new are really old customers.

- *People who move.* While down from prior years, over 15 percent of the population of the United States moves annually.

- *People who provide incomplete addresses.* Incomplete addresses adversely affect deliverability. For example, depending upon the situation an individual may omit an apartment number in multifamily dwellings, a box number on rural routes, etc.

- *Various data transcription errors.* This category of discrepancies covers a number of sins including misspelling, transposing numbers, etc.

- *Individuals who change their names.* For example, as a result of marriage women may assume their spouse's last name or include it using hyphenation.

- *People who do not want to be promoted.* Thus, the existence of the DMA's TPS and MPS files.

When rented lists are used, a further complication is added by the high propensity to have duplication, especially across lists within a special-interest category (e.g., outdoors, fashion, etc.). Also, information ages (remember, over 15 percent of the population of the United States moves annually), making the retention of some types of data, such as promotion history, of decreasing value as time passes.

DATA HYGIENE

A number of techniques are available that, while not offering a complete solution to the above, when taken as a group improve the effectiveness of identifying and contacting the targeted audience. They can broadly be defined as being based upon performing some hygiene on the name and address data.

The effort required to perform data hygiene can be justified because it:

- *Increases mail efficiency.* For example, being able to perform postal sortations at the carrier route level, which simplifies mail handling, or being able to add bar coding to the package, which can be read by automated postal equipment

- *Reduces nondeliverables*. For example, by being able to recognize in advance that a piece of mail cannot be delivered or that a phone number is invalid

Of course, this all comes down to a decrease in expense. In the first example, the post office gives a price break, while for the second example there is the savings in wasted postage and promotional material.

As a case in point consider the numbers presented in the following diagram for the fictional Electronic Netwaves Corporation (ENC). ENC illustrates the point in showing that the 2 million mailing pieces actually represent only 1.6 million unique customers (a duplicate rate of 20 percent). This is expensive for mailers, since most customers would only respond to one offer, regardless of how many copies they received. Each extra piece that is mailed to an individual (and sometimes to a household) is likely to be wasted.

Let's assume that each person mailed will only respond once to an offer regardless of the number of pieces mailed. At a typical in-the-mail cost of $500 per thousand names, it would cost ENC $200,000 to mail the 400,000 duplicates. Eliminating these is either a direct improvement to a company's bottom line or a potential reinvestment in customers or prospects who are more likely to respond, either as initial mailings to segments in additional lists or as repeat mailings to the highest potential segments on current lists.

Equal in importance to duplicate identification is the identification and suppression of names that are not deliverable. There are absolute conditions of nondeliverability, such as addresses that do not exist or addresses that are incomplete. The existence of an address can be verified using the USPS delivery sequence file, to be described further below. Again the ENC example illustrates that 15 percent of the names mailed were later identified as undeliverable.

The cost of undeliverability to house lists can be calculated as the production cost per thousand plus the postage cost per thousand times the number of undeliverable pieces. In the ENC example 15 percent undeliverables at the in-the-mail cost of $500 per thousand results in a $120,000 cost of undeliverability (15 percent* 80 percent *2,000,000*$.50).

Electronic Netwaves Corporation
  Marketing Fact Sheet
  Using Data Hygiene to Make an Unprofitable Mailing Profitable

Names mailed last year	2,000,000
Duplication rate within file (%)	20.00
Unique names mailed	1,600,000
Responders	29,000
Gross response rate (%)	1.45
"Net" response rate (%)	1.81
Names undeliverable (%)	15.00
Net mailable names	1,360,000
CPM	$500
Actual cost of mailings	$1,000,000
Potential cost of mailings	$680,000
Potential "savings"	$320,000
Actual cost per order (CPO)	$34.48
Potential cost per order	$23.45

Average selling price	$60.00
Unit margin (%)	50.00
Unit margin ($)	$30.00
Break-even CPO	$30.00
Sales	$1,740,000
Contribution	$870,000
Profit/(loss)	($130,000)
Required response rate for break-even under current mail quantity and cost conditions (%)	1.67

Other Benefits of Data Hygiene

In addition to all of the above, the application of data hygiene techniques may provide other benefits or information that can be exploited. For example, many companies fail to understand and exploit the additional information value of duplicate identification. Namely, that as a by-product of the duplicate identification process they can create *counts* of the number of lists on which each name appears, and discover any *specific pattern* of lists on which names appeared. The former may be an indication of a prospect's responsiveness. The latter may define potentially actionable market segments.

APPLYING HYGIENE

Data hygiene should be applied in the proper sequence in order to be most effective. This sequence can be thought of as being performed in two stages:

1. *Upon individual records.* Individually, the various techniques are applied to the individual records within each of the files in order to provide the best-quality data.
2. *Comparisons among files.* During this stage the files and records are compared in order to find duplicates, enhance the files with external data, and consolidate data at the individual and household levels.

Once the final list of candidates is compiled, prior to the actual mailing, the individual is targeted, tests are defined, and segmentation is applied. When the results of the promotion become available, the overall promotion and the various tests are reviewed to determine whether segments and/or models performed as expected.

The individual forms of data hygiene are described briefly below. Unfortunately, each could easily be the subject of its own chapter in a book, but as space limitations preclude this, the information presented in the following sections should be considered a primer on the subject.

NAME STANDARDIZATION

A full name can be *parsed* into its individual components:

- Title
- First name
- Middle name or initial
- Last name
- Suffix

In addition, first names can be standardized. For example, nicknames can be replaced, such as *Bob* with the formal *Robert*. Further, the individual's gender can be determined with a fairly high degree of precision.

Depending upon the strictness of the matching to be performed later, a decision to include/exclude components must be made. Options to be considered include using a component if it is available, but not precluding a match if it is missing in one or more records. For example, a suffix (e.g., Jr., Sr.) is not present on one of the input files. Similarly, it may be appropriate to include the derived gender in the comparison.

ADDRESS STANDARDIZATION

Like a name, an address can be divided into its elements:

- First address line
- Second address line
- City
- State
- ZIP code

In addition, various types of edits and validations can be performed including:

- Order the data on the address lines
- Standardized abbreviations for words such as *road*, *apartment*, *street*, and even *state names*
- Verify that the ZIP code is valid and matches both the state and city names
- Replace vanity names with postal names

As an example of a vanity name, I live in an area sometimes called Harbor Heights, yet the branch post office is Halesite, New York. And for those who want even more generalization, my local post office is a substation of the main post office for Huntington, New York. I receive mail addressed in all three ways.

Some key facts that explain why address hygiene is important:

- As much as 7 percent of all unendorsed third-class mail goes directly into the trash bin due to bad or incorrect addresses
- At one time there were 130,878 duplicate street names in the United States, and there are probably more now. The top seven are:

Street Name	Number of Cities
1. Main	7,102
2. Maple	5,444
3. Oak	5,394
4. Park	5,346
5. Second	4,861
6. Third	4,861
7. First	4,656

Postal Address Standards

To facilitate address standardization, the U.S. Postal Service (USPS) has developed a series of standards. They fall into 11 categories:

1. General
2. Last line of address
3. Delivery address line
4. Rural route addresses
5. Military addresses
6. Highway contract route addresses
7. General delivery addresses
8. Postmaster addresses
9. Post office box addresses
10. Puerto Rican addresses
11. International addresses

Per USPS a standardized address is one that contains all delivery address elements matched against the ZIP+4 file and contains the correct city name, state, and ZIP+4 code. These standards are documented in USPS Publication 28. Since the first four apply to most direct marketing situations, they will be discussed below.

The general standards require all lines to be formatted with a uniform left margin and be printed in an acceptable font. Uppercase letters are preferred on all lines of the address block, though lowercase styles are acceptable provided they meet postal guidelines for OCR readability. In addition, the delivery address line and the last line of the address that are output to a mail piece must be standardized and validated with a ZIP+4 file and city-state file, respectively. These files are available from the USPS. Only approved city place names are included, and all suffixes, directionals (e.g., east, west), and abbreviations must appear as they are in the ZIP+4 file.

The last line of address standard strongly recommends that only approved last-line (city or place) names as described in the Postal Service city-state file be used. This includes only using abbreviations as contained in the file when 13-character abbreviations are needed, due to labeling constraints. In addition, other than the hyphen in the ZIP+4 code, punctuation should be omitted. Standards are also defined for overseas military addresses (e.g., they must include the APO or FPO designation along with a two-character "state" abbreviation of AE, AP, or AA and the ZIP code or ZIP+4 code). Finally, the preprinted POSTNET bar code must be correct for the delivery address, city, state, and ZIP+4 code that appear on the mail piece.

The delivery address line standard requires that the line be broken down into its components with one space between address elements. There are standards for each of these components addressing abbreviation, punctuation, numeric street names, corner addresses, and even highways. The components are:

- Primary address number
- Predirectional
- Street name
- Suffix
- Post-directional
- Secondary address identifier
- Secondary address range

Rural route address standards are based upon the format RR N BOX NN. This replaces the use of "rural," "route," "number," "RD," and "RFD." Inclusion of additional designations, such as town or street names, is specifically prohibited. A similar structure is used for highway contract route addresses, with "HC" replacing "RR."

When taken as a whole, this presents a large number of standards with which to comply. If developed in-house, this would require significant development and maintenance effort on the part of data processing staff. However, software packages available from vendors can be used to accomplish this. The key issue is to understand that these standards exist and that to obtain maximum postal discounts they must be adhered to. This will allow you to incorporate the most appropriate way of satisfying them in your plans.

FILE SCRUBBING

Some marketers, particularly those in financial services, may have extraneous data included in the address portion of their records. Examples include:

> City Federal FBO
> Anthony Smith Julia Smith JT
> 1123 Elm Street
> Anytown, USA

> City Federal ITF
> Julian Smith UGMA
> 123 Elm Street
> Anytown, USA

JT refers to joint tenant status, FBO indicates "for benefit of," UGMA refers to the uniform gift to minors act, ITF refers to "in trust for," and so on. Also, note that two individuals were listed as joint tenants.

For purposes of matching names within and across files effectively, the extraneous information should be removed from the address fields. However, the information has value, and therefore the terms should be captured and stored elsewhere. A few companies maintain dictionaries of terms, such as those listed above. The name and address fields are parsed searching for these terms. This *scrubbing* process is used to improve the ability to match names and addresses and still retain the desired information.

DETERMINING DELIVERABILITY

The USPS has made available the following information with which to determine deliverability:

1. *ZIP+4 file*. This file contains all valid ZIP codes in the United States. The records in the house file or rented lists can be compared by ZIP code with this file. If the ZIP codes do not match, then the record should be considered nondeliverable.
2. *Delivery sequence file (DSF)*. This file, which is available at licensed service bureaus, lists all deliverable addresses in the United States. It is compiled from letter carrier data. In addition, the number of postal delivery sites per address is indicated, depicting whether an address is single family, multiple unit, business, etc.

The file can be used as part of the file comparison process following address standardization to determine if the address exists and, thus, is deliverable by USPS.

3. *National change of address (NCOA) processing.* Approximately 15 percent of the U.S. households change their addresses each year. A very common means of improving the potential deliverability is by using the information compiled by the licensed service bureaus that maintain the NCOA file. When used in conjunction with the DSF, this provides the additional ability to identify the one in six households that moves each year.

The file is compiled from cards that people fill out and mail to their postmasters when they are moving. The information, presently consisting of approximately 70 million change of address records, is maintained for three years and is updated biweekly. NCOA processing can often identify 60 to 70 percent of the households moving each year, as the remainder provides no forwarding address.

In order to use NCOA data, your file must be sent to a licensed service bureau where it will be matched. From the time you send your file to the time it is returned is typically less than five elapsed days. To encourage its use, the USPS has ensured that its use is very competitively priced.

COMPARISON AMONG FILES

Up until this point the techniques described above should have been individually applied to the source files. Once individual records have been through data hygiene, comparisons among the records will be more effective. Since the objective is to identify (and if desired, eliminate) duplicate records within a single file or across multiple files, this has been known as the *merge/purge* process. Historically, this activity was used to combine multiple rented lists; thus, the focus has been on the purge activity. However, the ability to combine multiple records for use in marketing database consolidation processes allows more information to be known about a customer than would be known from a single file, so the term *consolidation* is becoming associated with the process.

The major processes of this stage are to:

1. Identify duplicates
2. Enhance files with external data
3. Consolidate data at the individual and household level

Duplicate Identification

Duplicates are any group of records that, when promoted, will result in more than one offer going to a single target. By identifying (and eliminating) duplicates you can:

- Eliminate duplicate pieces of mail going to one target
- Analyze and evaluate list sources
- Identify likely prospects
- Save on postage, printing, and preparation costs
- Identify abusers of limited-edition offers

- Reduce your computer shop's secondary storage requirements by eliminating redundant records
- Reduce required processing time

Identification of duplicates is not always simple; it depends on what you are looking for. All three addresses in a table may or may not be duplicates, depending on what you want to accomplish with your promotion. For example, there are different levels of aggregation:

- At the individual level a unique person at each address is targeted.
  - ✓ This is applicable to political canvassing and marketing surveys.
- At the household level each family at an address is targeted.
  - ✓ This may be used for catalog mailings and magazine subscriptions.
- At the residence level each address is targeted.
  - ✓ This is useful for promotion of product samples and U.S. census forms.

In addition the tightness of the comparison can be varied by controlling the individual criteria and parameters used in the algorithms. For example, apartment numbers can optionally be included as extensions of the street address if a tighter address fit is desired.

Householding

Householding is a term for the process intended to identify an aggregation of individuals. Traditionally, members in a household have had a common last name and address. However, complicating this are:

- Hyphenated last names
- Women not taking the last names of their spouses
- Extended households or superfamilies
- Individuals with multiple residences including retirees and college-age children

Many companies want to identify the households that customers belong to so they can communicate to the customers at the household level as well. For some businesses, such as catalogers, music clubs, or book clubs, it may be desirable to market differently to each customer in a household. For them householding may not be appropriate and is an unnecessary expense.

For other marketers, such as financial services, it may be more appropriate to market to households rather than individuals. For example, homeowners insurance or mortgage insurance will typically be sold only once within a given household. Therefore, multiple mailings to the same household would have much the same effect as duplicate mailings to individuals. The cost of inappropriate multiple mailings to a household would be calculated in the same way as duplicate mailings were calculated for individuals.

Other Uses for Duplicate Information

The information obtained as a result of identifying duplicates can be used to:

1. *Measure list fatigue.* It is possible to create a history of the percentage of matches for the individual lists and/ categories of lists. These can be compared over time with your house file. The information can be used to

negotiate the CPM rate on net and net-net name arrangements with list brokers/managers.

2. *Estimate how a new list should perform.* Evaluate the percentage of matches for new names as compared with lists that are proven winners. Assuming the unmatched names of a given list are similar to those which matched, intuitively it would seem that a higher than average incidence of matching would indicate a better chance of success for a new list.

   An important issue to consider is which method to use regarding where a name "survives." Your choices and the implications are:

   - *If you use random selection,* then the new list will retain more matches and thus does better. However, the previous winning lists will lose previous "survivors" and thus are likely to perform lower than earlier results.

   - *If you use some priority scheme,* such as retaining matches on past best performers, then you are likely to be favoring these lists, making it harder for new lists to succeed. As a consequence, it is best to test the impact of each of your situations to determine the best method for your promotions.

3. *Identify new market segments.* Review the number of matches by lists and list categories. Develop strategies and programs to increase penetration by promoting more and/or deeper into those categories that perform above average.

   It may be appropriate to enhance the names with demographic data. This will allow you to evaluate the probability of different prospects responding to your promotions based upon demographic profiles. Consider the profiles of current customers and promote only those prospects that have comparable attributes.

4. *Identify the best-performing areas (i.e., states, SCFs, ZIPs).* Identify areas, such as states, where you have the most customers. Then evaluate the lists according to how the names match and are apportioned. That is,

   - Do certain lists have a higher than average number of poor-performing areas?

   - Have certain lists omitted certain areas all together, and thus their results will possibly be afffected?

Finally, remember that all names and lists are not created equal. Which method you choose for selecting "survivors" depends upon your marketing objectives. If you choose to use a priority method, the priority you assign will affect individual lists' performance. For example, you could prioritize based upon:

- *Past results.* The best lists retain the matches.
- *CPM.* The least expensive lists retain the matches.
- *Universe size.* The biggest lists retain the matches.
- *Expected universe growth.* The fastest-growing lists retain the matches.

MERGE/PURGE TECHNIQUES AND SOFTWARE

Various techniques are available to identify duplicates. Most of these originated with the need to combine multiple external lists, where the objective was to purge or eliminate the unwanted duplicates.

Since these external lists were provided as sequential tape files, one of the first approaches was to develop a "match code." A match code is a concatenation of encoded name and address elements, which results in a code that represents a relatively unique name and address. The files to be matched could then be sorted into match code sequence and then compared. The issue is that the encoding became quite complex as the need for more precise matching increased.

Today, several companies offer more sophisticated software that is based upon algorithms, and, in one case, is based on rules or artificial intelligence. These packages can be "tuned,' in that the tightness or looseness of the match can be specified by the user. In addition, they provide the ability to perform individual, household, residential, as well as custom-defined aggregation.

USING ADDRESS HYGIENE FOR MARKETING DATABASES

Marketing databases are consolidated views of all information companies know about their customers as it pertains to:

- Product ownership
- Prior purchase history
- Lapse or renewal data
- Demographic data
- Survey data
- And any other data available from internal or external sources

Marketing databases usually contain "snapshots" of information showing what customers looked like at a point in time. They are typically updated weekly or monthly, depending upon the marketing requirements. In addition, they may contain information from transaction files that manage individual business or product relationships.

Marketing databases allow data to be consolidated at the individual level. This is especially important for businesses that have historically been more transaction- or product-focused. For example:

- Banks maintain data at the account level.
- Insurance companies maintain data at the policy level.
- Telecommunications companies maintain data at the phone number level.
- Customers who have multiple accounts or policies are often treated as multiple customers.
- Companies with multiple businesses may have multiple relationships with customers that cross product lines.

In these situations customers may perceive that companies do not know them. In addition, scarce promotion dollars are wasted.

In order to effectively consolidate data at the individual level, address hygiene and merge/purge techniques need to be applied. As with external lists, the quality of the name and address data varies by source.

The Consolidation Process

Unlike the traditional merge/purge process, which results in the elimination of duplicate records, the marketing database wishes to retain the data contained in each list or file and establish the relationships between them. In a relational database environment, each file would be viewed as a separate table. An identifier, termed a *key*, such as an individual number, would be created that would allow records in these individual tables to be associated.

For processing efficiency the following process flow has evolved:

1. *Load records into the marketing database*. This allows other edits and validations to precede the consolidation process.

2. *Identify new or changed records*. This includes both new records and records where it appears some name and address changes have occurred.

3. *Perform data hygiene on the individual records*. Apply the techniques as described previously.

4. *Extract existing records that the new records appear to be candidates for matching*. This is a fairly loose match, possibly only by ZIP code, or more tightly by first character(s) of street name, once the address has been standardized and parsed. The objective is not to eliminate potential matches, but rather to keep the processing volumes manageable.

5. *Perform a merge/purge process at the household level*. Rather than deleting duplicate records, segregate the records into two groups: duplicates and uniques. Unique records will have no corresponding match on the database, so they can be considered new individuals. Records that exist in duplicate groups can be considered as being associated with the same traditional household. If among these records is a record extracted from the database, then all records are presumed to be associated with this existing household. Otherwise, they are assumed to be associated with a new household.

6. *Perform a merge/purge process at the individual level*. This need only be performed using records in duplicate groups at the household level. Again, segregate them into groups. Unique records can be deemed as new members of the database. Records that exist in duplicate groups can be considered as being associated with the same individual. If among these records is a record extracted from the database, then all records are presumed to be associated with this existing individual. Otherwise, they are assumed to be associated with a new individual.

7. *Maintain a table of individual names*. In addition to identifying the individuals and households, it is appropriate to retain a table containing one record for each individual. This table should also contain the individual address components, derived gender, bar code, and any other information, such as deliverability.

8. *Match back processing to associate records in the source tables*. During this process the unique identifiers of the individual and household are appended to the source tables. This will allow the data in the various tables to be associated or "joined" together.

The above discussion has been simplified for presentation purposes. For example, the inclusion of change of address records into the process flow requires that they be treated appropriately. A change of address record for one individual already on the marketing database may be found to have a corresponding record extracted from the database at the new address (e.g., they are in the same individual duplicate group). It will then be necessary to consolidate all references to the one individual.

Establishing More Complex Relationships

Once data is consolidated at the individual level, further levels of aggregation can be applied, for example, at the traditional household level. In addition, further aggregations can be established, such as people with a financial relationship—for example, payment of extended warranties by individuals located in a different address from that of the appliance. Similarly, a policyholder may be considered to be in the same aggregate household as the person whose credit card was used to purchase the policy, regardless of the name and/or address of either individual. Identifying and then delving further into these extended households may provide insights into the relationship that a customer has with the company.

Consolidating data as effectively as possible will support smarter marketing and promotion decisions based upon an understanding of the total relationship a company has with the individual and all members of the household.

CHAPTER 11

Campaign Management

In previous chapters we have discussed the requirements of a marketing database. One of those requirements is the ability of the database to support name selections, promotion file creation, and response analysis. In this chapter we will focus on a subsystem within the larger marketing database system, called the *campaign management system*.

A campaign management system (CMS) must be able to support marketing throughout the entire life cycle of a promotion, from conception through completion, not for just one campaign but for all campaigns.

This chapter will present the capabilities required of a campaign management system based upon the major life stages or phases of a campaign and the business functions that need to be supported and monitored at each stage. Using this approach, we will explore in detail the major activities (or business processes) that marketing performs throughout the life span of a campaign and identify the capabilities that are required of a campaign management system. (See Figure 11–1.)

CAMPAIGN PHASES

For purposes of this discussion, a campaign should be viewed as a group of related promotional efforts undertaken to achieve a set of marketing objectives. For most companies, campaigns may span a season, but are rarely longer than a calendar year. An example is a series of promotions aimed at new customer acquisition, or a series of promotions to selected customers intended to stem attrition. In this context a promotion is a specific initiative with a fixed time frame. A campaign is composed of one or more promotions.

Conceptually, there are four distinct phases in the life of a marketing campaign:

1. *Planning*. During this phase strategic decisions are made about the campaign, beginning with definitions of its purpose and objectives.
2. *Development*. Here the tactical issues dealing with the creation of the offer, the design of the marketing collateral, and the selection of the names are addressed.
3. *Execution*. These are operational tasks that may vary based upon the media and product being offered. For example, an outbound telemarketing effort includes all of the activities performed by the call and distribution center during the calling period.

Major Marketing Processes

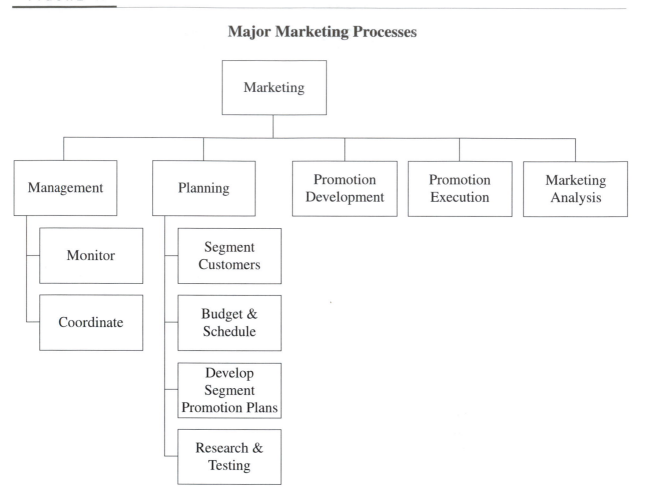

4. *Analysis.* Finally, these are the tasks associated with evaluating the results of the campaign.

In practice, the boundaries between these phases are fuzzy. Planning may not be completed until execution begins, and analysis begins as soon as management can begin to see results. In addition, from one campaign to the next these tasks are highly iterative. Unless a new product or service is being offered for the first time, the typical marketing campaign is a refinement of the prior one, modified by the results of any successful testing and augmented with additional tests.

MANAGEMENT PROCESSES

In addition to the four phases of the campaign life cycle, there is an overall management process. The two major management activities are:

1. *Monitoring.* Due to the large numbers of activities in progress at any one time, management must have a facility to keep track of the status and schedule of each campaign.

2. *Coordination.* Similarly, as schedules invariably slip, management must be aware of the interdependencies among the tasks, whether there are precedence relationships or there is simply a need to utilize some limited resource. This includes activities performed by internal staff and vendors.

From this perspective, the requirements that management places on a campaign management system can be viewed in terms of project scheduling and resource allocation.

THE CAMPAIGN PLANNING PHASE

Campaigns are defined in two phases. During the campaign planning phase, marketing executives make the strategic decisions that define the overall scope, approach, and target audience. Once these strategic boundaries are established, then the development of the specific promotions begins. This development, which is described in the next phase, is much more tactical in nature.

In a customer-focused direct marketing company, in order to define a campaign and begin to outline individual promotions, the following major activities occur (see Figure 11–2):

1. *Identifying customer segments.* Individuals within a customer segment are expected to have similar needs, wants, and perceptions with respect to a company and its products or services. Consequently, marketing campaigns are targeted toward each segment.

   The tools and techniques (e.g., statistical modeling, CHAID) needed to identify customer segments are beyond the scope of a campaign management system. Nevertheless, the characteristics or attributes (e.g., variables) which distinguish a segment are the same as those that are needed in response analysis. Consequently, the CMS's purpose at this juncture is simply to serve as a repository of descriptive

FIGURE 11–2

Promotion

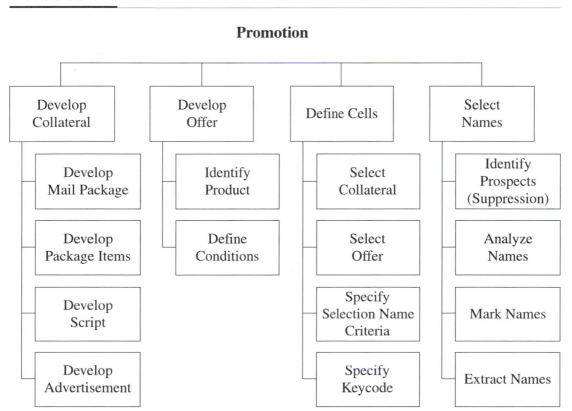

information about customer segments. Later, the information will be used to ensure that details about the customers (e.g., these variables) are captured for both profile and response analysis.

2. *Developing segment-level promotion plans.* As high-level plans are formulated, basic information about the time frame, objectives, gross volume estimates, and even major media decisions are recorded in the CMS. This information serves as the guidelines within which the more detailed promotion-level design activities are conducted.

3. *Budgeting and scheduling.* Typically, all of the campaigns that are proposed for an entire year are evaluated and a campaign calendar is created, which forms the basis for the firm's marketing budget. Revisions are made to the individual segment-level plans, and they are integrated into an overall marketing plan for the year. At this point resources begin to be assigned and major milestones are identified. These milestones are needed to coordinate and manage the promotion process. Again, the CMS should be updated to reflect these plans. It should also contain the planned financial expenditures and returns.

4. *Research and testing.* Even though specific tests may not be defined until the next phase, strategic decisions on the methodologies to be used and types of testing to be performed, either as part of a promotion or as part of market research, are already being formulated. These decisions will have an impact on the profitability of the entire campaign, because the addition of test and control groups will always increase absolute costs, but in direct marketing these costs are considered to be a necessary cost of doing business. Campaigns that don't include testing are rarely done, at least be experienced direct marketers that appreciate the value of testing.

THE CAMPAIGN DEVELOPMENT PHASE

Over the course of a year, a campaign may have more than one promotion. Promotions have a definite beginning and end. Promotions are conducted using a specific medium and are usually intended to promote one or more related product lines, businesses, or clubs.

In addition, the results of one promotion may affect a subsequent effort. For example, when a car manufacturer launched a new line of sports utility vehicles, an early promotion identified a concern among the prospective buyers that the vehicle's cargo capacity was limited. To address that, both text and images were altered in subsequent promotions to depict the car's ability to carry a number of large containers within the cargo area.

The following major activities occur as each promotion is developed:

1. *Developing collateral material.* The components of collateral material will vary by media. For telemarketing, it is the development of a script. For direct mail it involves the design of each of the mail pieces including selection of images and associated text. Again, this may not be fully developed from scratch for each promotion, but rather shared among several.

    By recording this information in the CMS, it is possible to identify other promotions in which the same collateral is used. This is useful in such activities as ordering and inventory control by using the planned volumes already recorded in the CMS to determine the approximate quantities needed by each mail piece over the course of the year.

2. *Developing the offer*. Depending upon the company and product, some type of promotional offer will be made. Offers may range from simple requests for more information, to straightforward discounts, to more complex arrangements. For example, record and book clubs may offer "Buy one at full price and get two, three, or even four other books free" with or without a commitment to buy more products within some specified time frame. Whatever the offer, estimates of profitability, based on both up-front response and back-end performance, are recorded in the CMS. These estimates will be compared against actual results during analysis and may form the basis for further refinement, as more offer testing is conducted.

3. *Defining cells*. A cell, sometimes called a panel, is a unique combination of collateral and offer made to a specific subset of the names to be promoted. For a telemarketing promotion, where the collateral is the script, it may be desired to further separate the cell based upon the telemarketing agency selected to make the contact. A cell is uniquely identified by a key code, which is used to identify the promotion, and is typically the lowest level of summarization in all later analysis.

   One complication arises when combinations of offers are presented during one promotion. This typically occurs during telemarketing promotions. In this situation the key code identifies the audience, script, and offers presented, but does not reflect the offer accepted. This requires that analysis be performed at a level of detail that is lower than the cell. Some systems have resolved this by having an outbound key code that depicts what is offered and a series of inbound key codes that depict the actual offer that is sold. The CMS must be able to portray the relationships among these key codes in order to avoid double counting.[1]

4. *Selecting names*. The process of selecting names from a marketing database can be viewed as occurring in three phases:
   - *Preparation*. A marketing database operations or support group will be responsible for maintaining the database. The group will perform all of the necessary processing to ensure that the database contains the latest data, that any consolidation at the individual and/or household levels is performed, and that any suppression files (i.e., DMA's MPS or TPS) are reflected in the database. If external files are used, in addition to the "house list," they ensure that these are loaded and prepared also.
   - *Analysis*. The marketing team responsible for the promotion is then provided access to the marketing database. Using interactive features, the team makes all decisions needed to identify the names to be selected including key code splits.
   - *Extraction*. The operations group is then given control of the processing to perform the extract and send it to the telemarketing vendor, lettershop, etc. At this time the actual number of names extracted can be recorded, by key code, in the CMS and summarized for the promotion as a whole. In addition, a profile of the selected names can be taken. In order to do ongoing profiling, the values of the

1. The same situation occurs in club offers where the new member may choose to take an additional book or CD at a large discount from the regular club price. These kinds of choice offers are very common in direct marketing, and very often the decision the customer makes is a good indication of the customer's lifetime value, so this information must be closely tracked and related back to the average cost per customer in order to measure the profitability of the offer.

variables to be used in profiling must be retained for each name. This "snapshot" data should be retained within the marketing database in order to allow solicitation responses and sales to be matched to them for purposes of analysis (to be discussed further).

THE CAMPAIGN EXECUTION PHASE

Execution of the promotion is frequently outside of marketing's direct control, as it is typically outsourced to one or more vendors (e.g., telemarketing agencies and lettershops). In some situations the vendors perform additional processing. For example, direct mail may involve some mailstream processing that could result in a decrease in the number of pieces mailed. These changes at both the individual customer level and the key-code level should be reflected in the CMS so that accurate comparisons and response analysis can be performed at a later date.

Telemarketing promotions offer an additional opportunity, as it is possible to obtain information about the disposition of each solicitation. These dispositions can be broadly categorized as:

- Sale
- Contact, including sale
- Contact, excluding sale
- Noncontact
- Contact not attempted (when calling terminated)

This information is useful for both profiling and analyzing responses. It may also lead to the development of a contact strategy. For example, if an individual has said no to an offer multiple times, there is usually not much chance that further calls will succeed. Thus, a simple contact strategy may place a limit on the number of calls or on the frequency with which an individual or household is contacted. Again, the point is that only by recording the information can the analysis be performed on a quantitative basis.[2]

THE CAMPAIGN ANALYSIS PHASE

Many types of analyses, financial and otherwise, can be performed, depending upon the needs of company management. However, for purposes of campaign management these will be broadly classified into two categories: profile analysis and response analysis:

- *Profile analysis* is used to identify and compare the composition of responders with the composition of customers or prospects (individuals, households, or businesses) to whom the promotion was addressed. The characteristics of both groups are defined in terms of database variables or fields on the marketing database.
- *Response analysis* in a campaign management context refers to the need to calculate results to date, to project final results (responses, inquiries, or leads), and to analyze such results by segments. Some of the more

2. The recording of accurate telemarketing disposition information is absolutely critical to companies that rely on outbound telemarketing. Almost all outbound telemarketing vendors have systems that can capture this information, but it is up to the client company to make sure that the information provided to them is both accurate and timely.

sophisticated applications also perform financial calculations, such as return on promotion as discussed elsewhere in this book.[3]

Profile Analysis

Profile analysis can be performed at many different points in time:

- As part of defining customer segments
- As part of designing tests
- When developing selection criteria
- As responses are received
- Periodically, after a promotion is completed to see attrition

Profile analysis can be performed using any field in the marketing database that is attributable to the name, whether individual or household. These fields are typically those identified through the process of defining customer segments or through development of statistical models. They may be fundamental attributes (e.g., birth date) or derived (e.g., age, score). What is important is that they provide some reasonable expectation of being able to predict the actions of the names and as a result should be useful in refining the marketing strategy.

An important issue for profile analysis is the ability to provide information about a combination of fields (i.e., gender and age). Traditionally, this has been accomplished by predefining the breaks and creating a derived field. Unfortunately, this method has a tendency to mask the results. For example, consider what would happen if the ages were split into age ranges and then the age ranges were combined with gender. If the profile resulted in a cluster near the age range break, chances are that the insight would be hidden. A potential solution is to use a CHAID-type presentation. In order to accomplish this, the detailed data by individual must be available. By saving it earlier as part of the "snapshot" of the profile variables and storing in the marketing database, this can be accomplished.

Response Analysis

Response analysis includes the ability to present and project trends. In order to do this, responses have to be summarized by date, or some reasonably granular time period, such as a week. This is especially true when management is interested in viewing the results as the promotion progresses. Afterward longer time frames, measured in months, are typically used to analyze attrition.

For analysis to be as useful as possible the campaign management system should provide the flexibility to perform response analysis at various levels of summarization including:

- Customer segment
- Market
- Product line
- Product
- Campaign
- Promotion

---

3. Some definitions of response analysis also include the process of creating regression models so that customers can be scored in terms of their probability of responding to a future similar promotion. That aspect of response analysis takes up much of the content of the modeling section of this book, and will therefore not be addressed in this chapter.

- Promotion offer
- Collateral (script or package)
- Mail piece
- Media
- Telemarketing agency

One problem that is often encountered is matching a sale back to the promotion. This is further complicated when the desire is to match the sale back to the individual who was promoted. In reality, there are many situations where this is simply not possible, such as when a catalog is given by one person to another, or in business-to-business situations where the decision maker is not the person to whom the promotion was directed, nor the person from whom the order was received. One solution is to apply some kind of allocation or attribution scheme that results in the cell or key code being inferred from some knowledge about the sale — for example, some combination of date and time of the sale, shipping address, etc.

CAMPAIGN CONTENT AND STRUCTURE DATA

The accompanying diagram presents a simplified pictorial of the data contained in the CMS that pertains to campaigns. The boxes represent data entities, which are people, places, things, or events in which we are interested in retaining information. A review of the diagram will show that these are the very topics that have been discussed throughout this chapter.

Planning Data Model

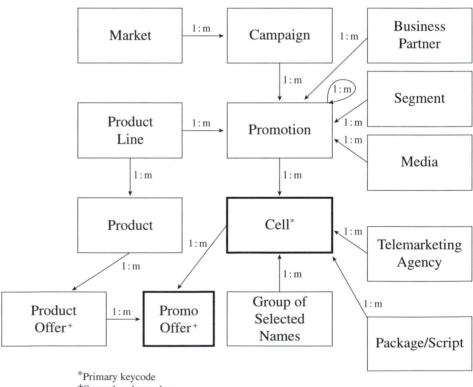

*Primary keycode
+Secondary keycodes

The arrows in the diagram depict the relationships between two entities. The annotation "1:m" indicates that one occurrence of an entity can be related to many of another. For example, a market will typically have many campaigns associated with it.

The specific detail that is retained about each entity is dependent on the company. However, the basic relationships are consistent within the direct marketing industry, though again terminology varies.

ACTUALS DATA

The accompanying diagram depicts the information that could be retained on a summary basis. This particular one is created for the insurance industry.

It should be noted that, while it is possible to retain the detailed information in the marketing database, after a period of time, its usefulness diminishes. In addition, there are the practical problems associated with storing significant numbers of records. Consequently, one solution is to summarize.

Another solution, at least for profile analysis, is to retain the detail on the database until you are reasonably comfortable that the resulting profiles are static. At this time, a complete set of profiles is created. The information, especially the breaks identified by the CHAID, can be retained either on the database or in some reporting package that summarizes the results of the campaigns for the year.

Actuals Data

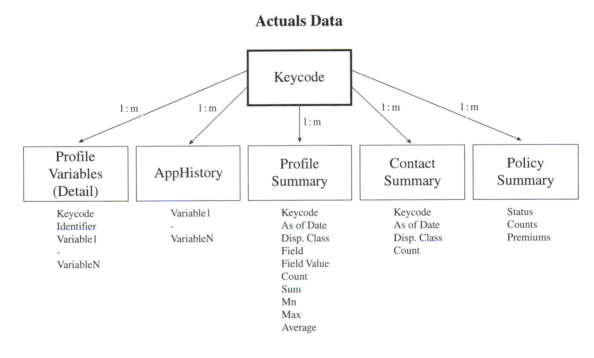

CONCLUSION

Campaign management is about the management of a process. The process can be likened to a positive feedback loop as seen in engineering. The process begins with planning and then goes on to development and execution. Analysis then takes the results and allows them to be factored into the next plan.

A campaign management system by itself contains the information needed to monitor and coordinate all phases of the process. When coupled with a marketing database, all of the information necessary to both manage and perform the process is available. As the use of marketing databases matures, expect to see the integration of these into the database management software, data access and reporting tools, and the CMS.

What Direct Marketers Need to Know about Technology

Chapters 12, 13, 14, and 16 were written by Dhiraj Sharma; Chapter 15 by Rus Rempala.

CHAPTER 12

Operations and Decision Support Systems

A VERY BRIEF HISTORY OF COMPUTER APPLICATIONS IN BUSINESS

Since the advent of the personal computer in the early 1980s, the nature of computer applications in business has changed, and today's technology has further accelerated the rate of change. Prior to the personal computer, most business applications were *transaction*-oriented, including such functions as payroll, accounts payable, accounts receivable, general ledger, inventory management, order entry, and shipping. Because computers in those days were primarily thought of as *counting* machines, counting functions predominated in their use. Periodic, scheduled reports were produced, generally as printouts; and business analysts, including marketers, used the available *hard-copy* reports for decision making. Reports were rarely modified because the modification process was time-consuming and expensive.

When the personal computer arrived on the scene, many analysts and executives began to use spreadsheets and basic database products on their PCs to perform analytical tasks. However, these tasks exceeded the capability or flexibility of existing mainframe applications, particularly for reporting and for asking all the what-if questions that are the lifeblood of marketing users and the bane of data processing managers.

In the early years, many companies' data processing professionals viewed PCs as novelties and did not develop or support applications for them. As a result, many analytical users would *rekey* data that had appeared in mainframe-produced reports so the data could be viewed or analyzed in different ways. Leading-edge companies, at this time, were those that downloaded mainframe-produced data to PC environments to avoid at least the rekeying aspect of the operation. In a technological sense, downloading eliminated the need for marketers to carry around heavy printouts and hunch over keyboard to rekey data, enabling them to walk upright and emerge from the role of secondary data entry clerks to that of decision makers.

Although most companies have evolved beyond this prehistoric stage of information management, even functions such as downloading to more user-friendly platforms have not yet become universal. This chapter shows how some companies are using today's technology to accomplish the decision-making processes of database marketing cost-effectively *without* disrupting or degrading day-to-day operations.

OPERATING SUPPORT SYSTEMS FOR DAY-TO-DAY PROCESSING

Most companies can divide their information processing functions into two categories: day-to-day operations and decision making. Day-to-day operations include all the transaction-oriented processes that were the initial thrust of business computing, including customer transactions such as orders, invoices, and statements; accounting transactions such as payroll, accounts payable, and accounts receivable; and batch jobs including posting transactions and producing preprogrammed reports.

Because these functions support day-to-day operations, we refer to them as operational support system (OSS) technology. The repetitive, predictable, machine-resource-intensive nature of OSS applications makes them well suited to mainframe computing environments. Although a great deal of work is required to make them operate smoothly, they are often referred to as *production* jobs and are perceived as background activities that somehow happen automatically.

Operations managers frequently lament that OSS jobs are only noticed when something goes wrong and are rarely appreciated when everything works as expected. They are the utility applications of most companies that we expect to function with certainty—lights going on when we flip a switch or a dial tone sounding when we raise a telephone handset. Most data centers use software products that schedule which jobs will run at which time and in which sequence and that identify which jobs have prerequisite jobs that must be successfully completed before others can be initiated.

The on-line aspects of these applications, such as data entry, customer service, and production management, generally use software products such as CICS[1] to manage transaction sessions and tune computer systems to provide maximum operating efficiency for these transaction-oriented on-line functions during business hours. After business hours, many data centers change their computers' internal software configurations to provide maximum operating efficiency for batch jobs, including transaction posting, updates, backups, and so on.

As more and more information is captured through business transactions and more and more reporting is required within companies and by regulatory agencies, transaction windows become tighter and tighter and most companies find themselves chronically in need of additional processing cycles. In mainframe processing environments, additional processing cycles are expensive, and because of the way machines are configured, companies must often purchase additional capacity in steps larger than immediately required for each increment.

In addition to processing windows, data center managers are always cognizant of their requirements for direct access storage device (DASD) space. As more and more transactions shift from tape storage to disk storage, the number of disk drives in most data centers increases dramatically. Some large data centers have so many acres of floor space dedicated to disk drives that they refer to this section of their machine room floor as the *DASD farm*. Like processing power, DASD is expensive in the mainframe environment. Although manufacturers somewhat alleviated the problem by increasing the capacity of each DASD unit so that today three times the amount of data can be stored in the same footprint[2] required for single-density DASD units a few years ago, the cost of DASD units for mainframe computers is still relatively high.

---

1. CICS is IBM's on-line teleprocessing monitor.
2. *Footprint* is defined as the amount of floor space occupied by a computer hardware device, such as a CPU, tape drive, or DASD unit.

DECISION SUPPORT APPLICATIONS CAN BE A DRAIN ON MAINFRAME RESOURCES

Because the additional data processing and data storage costs that must be incurred to support ad hoc processing are hefty and because the traditional OSS world is so predictable in it schedules, inputs, outputs, and resource consumption, data center managers are loathe to support decision support system (DSS) activities in the same computing environment. During business hours ad hoc DSS requirements, which are often intensive users of computer resources, can disrupt on-line customer service and data entry functions because they divert some of the computer's power away from these tasks.

DSS applications can further contend for limited computer space if they require data that is also being sought by on-line OSS applications. Contention between these disparate types of applications can result in processing delays that keep customers on the telephone longer, and in turn productivity decreases for both OSS and DSS users within the company. Many direct marketing companies are able to measure the costs of these delays in terms of increased toll call charges and abandoned calls that could not be serviced because customer service personnel were not available to handle the calls in a timely manner.

DECISION SUPPORT SYSTEMS

Unlike operating support systems, decision support systems are used to analyze customer data. Marketers can use them to gain insights into customer performance, identify promotable or nonpromotable segments within the customer and prospect files, detect trends in product purchasing or particularly successful types of promotions, and so on. Marketing analysts use this data to make informed resource allocation decisions for advertising and promotion expenses, product development, and name selection for future promotional efforts.

In addition, marketers (and most upper management) find it more effective to communicate their findings and recommendations using graphical and tabular representations of data rather than the raw data that traditionally results from preprogrammed reports.

Need for Flexibility and Quick Response

The what-if types of analyses that marketers use require flexibility in the way questions are posed and in the way data can be accessed and also quick response so interaction with the company's data will be as close to conversational as possible. Studies have shown that with delays of more than 20 seconds from the time the enter key has been pressed until the response appears on the computer monitor, analysts initiate other activities, such as returning telephone calls. By the time the analyst returns to the analysis task, his train of thought has been broken and his productivity reduced.

DSS Technology

DSS technology, like OSS technology, may be mainframe-based. However, unlike OSS technology, DSS technology requires custom programs for analysis and reports. In addition, in the mainframe environment DSS activities may degrade response time for critical activities such as customer service. Mainframe systems, with few exceptions, are not as flexible as other platforms, particularly when it comes to presentation tools such as graphics and analysis tools such as spreadsheets. In fact, the more of these tools available in the mainframe environment, the worse will be the performance for other mainframe applications. As we discussed, marketers will not tolerate slow response time. In Chapter 16 we'll discuss in detail client-server systems, for the most part, combinations of workstations and PCs that make up most of the decision support systems in use today by direct marketers.

INTEGRATING OPERATIONS SUPPORT SYSTEMS AND DECISION SUPPORT SYSTEMS

When we were researching and writing the first edition of *The New Direct Marketing*, we limited our descriptions of database technology to mainframe-based products. In the years since, a virtual technological revolution has occurred; new hardware and software platforms have been introduced, and the price performance of the tools available to direct marketers has dramatically improved.

The selection of a database management system (DBMS) solution no longer requires a compromise between high-speed transaction processing and the flexibility needed by marketers for analysis and decision support. As is often the case, those compromise solutions were ultimately satisfying to neither group. Operations groups found that transactions could not be processed as quickly as they could in traditional third-generation systems using flat files with VSAM keys; marketers found that the turnaround time for routine queries was unacceptably slow.

The technological improvements and price-performance advances of the last five to ten years have made this compromise unnecessary and have made it possible to decouple the systems that support operations and the systems that support decisions, thereby reflecting the fundamental functional differences of each corporate group. That is, in the same way that operations and marketing analysis functions tend to be performed by different personnel or departments within companies, the computer systems that support each group can also be separated. To the extent that these systems share data, the integration of data can be accomplished by *communication* between systems rather than through structural integration as in the past.

In one sense, the separation of systems across multiple platforms is revolutionary. In another sense, it merely reflects the way in which people work together within companies. When marketing people need to obtain information from operational staff, they hold meetings, send memoranda, or make telephone calls. In much the same way, marketing professionals can *extract* selected data from operational support systems and load it into decision support systems where they can access and analyze it. In many cases, the results of their analyses are passed back to the operational support systems as files for implementation by fulfillment or other systems, thereby closing the loop.

CHAPTER 13

The Unique Requirements Direct Marketers Place on Their Decision Support Systems

Database technology has been used for many years in many different ways to support a variety of marketing analysis and reporting needs. The most common such usage has been to support product and geography-centric marketing. These applications involve, for example, analysis of sales and item counts for cells that are defined by combinations of:

- Product groups and subgroups
- Geographical entities such as state, marketing regions, and subregions
- Time periods such as year, quarter, month, and week, in cases where time-related details are important

Such analysis may involve, for example, examining the movement of leather goods in a given market region by season, the revenue from perfume by week after an advertisement campaign, and so on. Based upon the reports obtained from the database, marketing programs are designed to influence the sales and item counts for different cells in a way that is desirable for the company. Such marketing is generally supported by creating summaries of sales, item counts, etc., for the predefined calls. It seldom requires direct access to detailed-level data about customers' behavior and never requires modifications to the database.

Direct marketing, in contrast, is quite different from the product and geography-centric marketing described above. Its focus is the individual customer, and its goal is to influence the buying behavior of that customer through properly designed marketing programs. Actually the targets of marketing promotions are individual purchasers, who may be customers, households, or companies, but we refer to them simply as customers in this discussion. Direct marketing is thus customer-centric, and this has strong ramifications for the performance of databases that are used to support it.

DIRECT MARKETING'S FUNCTIONAL REQUIREMENTS

Let us further explore the nature of direct marketing from a technological viewpoint. The targeted customers are generally selected using behavioral, attitudinal, and demographic data about them. Some of this data may be owned by the company in the form of prior transactions, which include past purchases, returns, inquiries, prior promotions, telemarketing contacts, etc. In addition, some of the data may have been purchased as add-on data from external sources. Such customer-level data is used to group customers with similar characteristics into segments by using a combination of ad hoc criteria and deciles based on statistical model scores. These segments may be further divided into control and multiple test groups for tracking purposes. The ultimate goal is to place each promotable customer in a segment in which each member will be assigned the same promotion code and receive the same promotion. By its very nature, this type of marketing requires direct and repeated access to detailed-level data on customers' behavior.

Thus, from the data processing viewpoint, we need the following capabilities to support direct marketing:

1. Consolidate and store in one database large amounts of data (including transactional, promotional, geographical, and attitudinal data) on a large number of customers (and prospects).

2. Incorporate additional purchased data on a when-needed basis.

3. Process the above data to identify customer segments by using techniques such as RFM, ad hoc criteria, and statistical model scores.

4. Modify the files and fields entering the database as well as database reports with a minimum of data processing effort. Keep in mind that in order to keep in step with changing business requirements, the analysis steps, models, data layouts, etc., must also keep changing in a marketing database that is being actively used. Therefore, the database system must be capable of evolving in lockstep with business needs.

5. Create output files to communicate marketing decisions to other systems. This step must include all the business rules adopted by the company, such as not promoting a product to the same customer twice in any 60-day period or not offering a particular product in selected markets.

6. Because segment creation may also involve a fair amount of ad hoc querying and report generation, we need interactive response times for such operations.

7. Because the marketing staff may consist of several analysts, all those analysts should be able to carry out their work at the same time. Technically, this involves read as well as modify access to the shared data by multiple users at the same time.

To summarize, on the one hand we have product- and geography-centric marketing in which we work with aggregates over multidimensional cells (defined by product, geographical, and time dimensions), and on the other hand we have customer-centric marketing in which we form segments and select specific names by examining a variety of detailed data (transactional, promotional, etc.) on customers.

Several tools and technologies have been deployed to support both types of marketing efforts. Of late, relational DBMSs have been extensively used for this purpose. As it turns out, the relational systems support product- and geography-centric marketing moderately well, but are not very effective in supporting customer-centric marketing for all but the smallest databases. In the following chapters, we will (1) explain the technical factors behind the above observation and (2) describe ways in which performance of marketing databases can be improved.

CHAPTER 14

Hardware and Software Fundamentals

In this chapter we'll review the different hardware and software products that database marketers will most likely be working with as they build their marketing database systems. In Chapter 15 we'll go into more depth with regard to the benefits and limitations of relational database management systems, and in Chapter 16 we'll expand on the combinations of products that make up client-server systems.

HARDWARE

Mainframes

The mainframe computer hardware environment at most companies is either IBM or non-IBM. IBM has about a 60 percent share of mainframe installations, with the balance going to Unisys, the larger Wang systems, IBM plug-compatibles (e.g., Amdahl, Hitachi, etc.), and clusters of midframe computers (e.g., Digital Equipment). For the purposes of this discussion, we will focus on the IBM mainframe environment and separately discuss the midframe computers, whether configured in clusters or as stand-alone machines.

Although the IBM (and plug-compatible) machines are among the largest computers available for most commercial applications, their capacity is not limitless. Memory and processing power can be added on, but incremental growth for mainframe computers is relatively expensive. MIS management, like any other corporate management, attempts to scale the available capacity of computer resources to the known and anticipated resource level required. Unless major growth is expected in the immediate future, few MIS directors would want to incur the expense of significant excess computer capacity.

Typical data centers achieve optimal system performance when 65 to 75 percent of available CPU capacity is being consumed. At this level of use, applications get the processing power they need to provide generally acceptable response time for on-line transactions while sufficient capacity remains available to support the requirements of background transactions and the operating system.

A key hardware issue facing most companies today is downsizing. Improvements in price performance and flexibility of midframes, workstations, and microcomputers have led many companies to consider taking at least some of their applications off the mainframe. There are many reasons for this trend, including lower cost for incremental hardware growth; lower cost for application development, maintenance, and operation; lower cost for data storage; and greater flexibility in application use.

Therefore, from the perspective of building a decision support system, among the key hardware issues to consider are these:

1. Is the firm's current hardware environment mainframe only, or does it include other platforms?

2. Is the firm's technology plan restricted to mainframe processing, or are other platforms either designated or under consideration?

3. Can the firm's existing hardware communicate with additional platforms such as midframes, workstations, or PC networks?

The answers to these questions may limit the list of DBMS software products that can be considered.

Midframes

As suggested above, increasing numbers of companies are finding midframe computers to be a cost-effective alternative to mainframe computer systems. This is especially true for companies that configure several midframe computers into clusters that can easily rival or exceed the capacity of mainframe computers at a lower total cost. In addition, midframe computers can be configured to redirect work to other parts of the cluster if one CPU in the cluster goes down. In this situation, companies may attempt to continue operating all their applications at a degraded performance level or, alternatively, shutting down less critical applications so the most critical applications can operate at their normal levels. This is one reason that midframe clusters have been adopted by a number of companies for whom continuous uptime is a critical issue. Companies in fields as diverse as financial services and publishing have based their technology strategies on midframe clusters.

Another reason that this approach has increased in popularity is that the cost of incremental growth is often considerably less than comparable growth in a mainframe computing environment. If additional processing requirements develop, the firm can simply add an additional CPU to the cluster, thereby increasing CPU processing power and memory.

A third reason for recent growth in this segment is that midframe computers are often thought of as departmental machines. Because each unit is relatively inexpensive and can support a number of users ranging from fewer than 8 to more than 100, depending on the size of the cluster, the purchase price of midframe computers is often within the annual computing budget of a single large department, rather than requiring a capital investment that would necessitate corporate approval and would normally go through the MIS department. In decentralized companies, this factor alone may drive the hardware acquisition decision.

For some companies, developing a marketing database in a stand-alone, midframe computer environment may make far greater economic sense than expanding the mainframe computer environment solely to support the new application. The final hardware decision for the database marketing application will be a function of what the existing hardware environment is, how much capacity within the existing environment is available and whether alternative platforms are part of the company's strategic direction. These factors are different for each company.

Companies that are considering midframe computers as part of their database marketing application should be familiar with such vendors as Digital

Equipment Corporation (DEC), which is by far the leader in this segment; Data General; Hewlett-Packard (HP); Stratus; Perkin-Elmer; Prime; and Wang. IBM's AS/400 computers serve a dual role:

1. They provide an unbounded migration and growth path for IBM's Series 3 computers (Systems 34, 36, and 38).

2. They can be a cost-effective solution for companies that are either bringing computer processing in-house for the first time or downsizing from mainframe computers. AS/400 systems include an integrated DBMS platform as part of their operating systems.

Key issues for midframe environments include these:

1. Is there an existing DBMS product in place, and if so, can it support the functional requirements of the database marketing application?

2. If not, does the existing midframe environment support other DBMS products that *do* support the functional requirements?

3. Can the existing midframe environment be expanded cost-effectively if necessary to support the database marketing application?

4. If the existing environment *cannot* be expanded cost-effectively, *or* if DBMS products that will support the company's functional requirements will not operate in the existing hardware environment, other hardware must be brought in to support the DBMS product selected.

5. If another hardware platform were brought in, can data be extracted from existing applications and loaded into the new hardware environment as electronic file transfers, or must a tape transfer approach be used?

Workstations

The word *workstation* is used to denote a wide variety of computer systems, ranging from a single-user, single-display workstation to multiuser network servers. All these workstations are built using the recent vintage central processing units (CPUs) called reduced instruction set computer (RISC) chips, which provide very high performance for modest prices. Such workstations run Unix or Unix-like or Windows operating systems. In addition, they can all be networked with each other and with mainframes and minis. Such computers are offered by SUN Microsystems, IBM, HP, DEC, SGI, NCR, and others.

One of the most important changes of the past few years has been the dramatic improvement in workstation price performance. Workstations, compared with mainframes, offer not only superior price performance, but also increased flexibility and ease of connectivity. As costs continue to drop, the financial advantages of workstation technology will become even more compelling.

In addition to providing good price-performance ratios, these computers offer flexibility, ease of software programming, comprehensive facilities for system administration, and elaborate tools for implementing user-friendly interfaces. They can be networked among themselves and with mainframes or minis for rapid data transfer. Thus, a company's operations data could continue to reside on existing mainframe(s), mini(s), or both. From time to time, selected parts of this data could be sent down to one or more workstations configured and programmed to perform decision support functions (analysis, name selection, etc.). The addition of a workstation computer would not disrupt the existing computer system(s) and would enable the marketing department to carry out analysis without affecting daily operations.

Although the *functional* requirements of the marketing group will primarily drive the selection of a database management system product to be used as the core software for the marketing database, a number of very important technical issues concerning hardware, configuration, data communications, and software must be addressed as part of the selection process, and the company's MIS management should be actively involved in addressing them.

Another caveat in this context is that in addition to acquiring the workstation computer, a company needs access to qualified systems administration personnel to perform routine software maintenance and backups on the Unix operating system. Such personnel could be hired or subcontracted on a part-time basis, or in-house personnel could be trained in Unix through courses offered by the vendors and several third parties.

Microcomputers

Microcomputer processing power and storage capacity continue to increase at a dramatic rate. The advent of microcomputer networks has increased potential processing power and storage capacity by such an extent that large networks easily rival the power of midframe computers and begin to approach the power of small mainframe configurations as well. Equally important is the flexibility that microcomputer networks provide end users in terms of file sharing and the use of common, professionally managed applications.

Compared with stand-alone microcomputer environments, which were the only option a few years ago and remain the predominant configuration for microcomputers, networks now provide many companies with full-function computer applications at a fraction of the cost for comparable applications operating in mainframe or even midframe configurations.

Although microcomputers and microcomputer networks today offer companies a much wider range of hardware choices for their marketing databases, the issues of cost, technical support, data integrity, updating, and system management have become increasingly complicated.

The major players in the microcomputer marketplace—IBM, Apple, Compaq, Toshiba, Zenith, Dell, and so on—have become household words. All the major microcomputer products being used for database applications are IBM-compatible, including the newer products from Apple. Companies also are becoming more familiar with networking products and the companies that make them, such as Novell, Pyramid, Banyan, Ethernet, and the like.

A key issue concerning microcomputers is that many users still think of them as stand-alone PCs rather than computer environments that can support complex, often critical applications. As a result, many companies fail to provide adequate support for PC applications because they don't realize that microcomputers and networks must be supported by the same level of data processing professionals that support companies' other computer applications. Companies that anticipate developing database marketing applications using microcomputer environments must be aware of these points:

- The role of the database administrator (DBA) is just as critical in this environment as in any other.
- Data integrity must be maintained. Therefore the ability to alter codes, data, or both must be strictly limited and enforced.

- Data security is increasingly important. Many companies programmatically limit the data that can be downloaded or use diskless PCs to reduce the risk of data theft or loss.

All Database Management Systems Require a Great Deal of Computer Capacity

Regardless of which hardware decision companies make, they should keep one thought in mind when evaluating database management systems to support their database marketing applications: *all database management systems require a great deal of computer capacity*. This should not be surprising, especially when you consider all the work they do. Remember that the ease of use, menu-driven screens, pop-up windows, and all the other tools that enable marketing end users to directly access information about their customers, without having to rely on the intervention of data processing professionals, require greater processing power and data storage. As in all resource allocation considerations, there is no such thing as a free lunch. All the productivity and user-friendly features that we want in a database management system can only be made available by including large numbers of very complicated computer programs as part of the packages.

The trade-off for increased access to data and increased productivity on the part of end users is the increased cost of CPU hardware and, often, of data storage as well. Companies must evaluate the additional benefits to the firm as a result of increased end-user productivity in the context of increased computer hardware expenses and in terms of the firm's strategic technology plan.

For marketing-driven firms, this evaluation usually comes out on the side of the database management system. In any event, marketing and MIS management must be prepared to discuss the issues of the company's strategic technology plan, function, flexibility, and cost in the context of overall benefit to the firm.

SOFTWARE

File Structures

Flat Files versus Relational Files

The terms *flat files* and *relational files* describe two broad classes of data storage in computer systems. Within each class of system exist a number of options, or "subarchitectures." For example, in a flat file system, each customer is represented by an individual record where all of the information is stored in the same location. These records can be of *fixed length* with a specified number of data fields, or *variable length* where certain fields are allowed to repeat as necessary (purchases, promotions sent, etc.). On the other hand, relational database systems can be based on *open systems architecture standards*, which allow easy integration of new applications software, or can be based on *proprietary architectures*, which are optimized for the marketing function and offer a signficiant speed advantage.

Flat Files   In fixed-length file systems, the same data items (such as first name) are carried in exactly the same position (i.e., first name in position 1-15) across all records. This approach is most appropriate for mailing lists and simple marketing databases that contain only basic information such as name, address, source of name, etc. While fixed-length records can be used to capture customer transaction activity, recall that the number of transactions will vary from customer to customer and every record must carry a predefined number of occurrences. In some cases the customer record will contain "blank occurrences," while in other information will be lost because the customer has more transactions than provided for.

In systems that contain transaction-type information, the variable-length format is generally more efficient. If a customer has one transaction, that customer's record will use considerably less space than a customer who has 50 transactions. The same holds true for promotion history, coupon redemptions, insurance claims, etc. On the other hand, it is much more complicated (time and expense) to develop programs that update and generate reports from these types of systems. Regardless of whether flat files are fixed or variable length, any reports stemming from these files must be written in a third-generation language such as COBOL where the programmer is required to know the layout of the files that will be worked on. In short, marketing end users do not have direct access to their information.

Relational Databases

In systems that employ relational file structures, each customer is represented by one or more rows in one or more files or tables that are linked together through the use of common keys. Unlike flat file systems, this approach delivers fast access to individual pieces of information (customers, order status, payments, etc.), and using tools to be described shortly, end users can access their own data, write their own reports, and generate their own files. What's more, in these types of systems, there is no need to limit the number of transactions carried, nor is there any wasted space from reserving an area for 10 purchases when a given customer has only one purchase on record.

Because the information for a given customer is split up and stored in many different places, relational database systems rely on "key fields" to associate rows in different tables with each other. For example, the field "customer number" may link the customer table row for a particular customer to that customer's orders, represented by rows in the order table. In a similar fashion, a unique order number may link an order to all of its items in the item table.

The "master plan," or "map," for all of this linking is called a *database schema*. Schemas are typically presented as diagrams that show the various tables in the database, summarize the types of data they contain, and indicate how they are associated with each other. It is very important to fully understand how the proposed database design, or schema, will impact desired marketing functions. A well-designed schema will optimize throughput and functionality, while a poorly designed schema will result in poor performance or even unsupported needs.

Deciding between Flat Files and Relational Databases

In deciding between flat files and relational database management systems, there are a number of trade-offs that must be considered. Flat files are easier and less expensive to set up. In their simplest form, fixed-length records, limits have to be set on transactions tracked for all customers. Set the limit too high and the system is inefficient (lots of blank transaction fields). Set it too low and many customers will have an incomplete history of transactions (i.e., lost information). It's important to note that the amount of data lost will increase with the customer's activity—i.e., the most data will be lost for your best customers.

In variable-length file systems even fields that are allowed to repeat must have a specified maximum number of occurrences. This fixed-field aspect of flat files makes it difficult to add new data items after the system has been implemented. To add new characteristics such as age and income means that all records must be converted to the new format via a customer-developed, one-time-use conversion program. Additionally, all programs designed to read the file (both update and reporting) must be modified to reflect the new format.

Flat files can only be accessed by "passing" the entire file. In a practical sense, this means that using them involves computer programmers setting up and running "batch mode" programs. Under this approach, counting how many customers have purchased in the past 30 days in certain product categories will require that a computer program be written and tested and a computer production run be scheduled. Depending on available resources, this process often takes between several days and several weeks.

This same process holds true for customer profiles, cross-sell analyses, custom reports, and selection of promotional lists. In flat file–based marketing databases, marketers rely heavily on standard reports produced during the database update process. Very often the type of information needed by marketers has not been built into the various standard reports, and the marketers must either wait for custom reporting programs to be developed or try to do without the needed information.

Relational databases are more complicated to implement, but provide more efficiency and flexibility. There are no practical limits on the number of transactions tracked for individual customers, so there is no loss of information. Relational databases provide different options for using the data. As with flat files, computer programmers can still write programs to pass the file in "batch mode."

Sophisticated on-line relational database access tools allow marketers to use the database "hands-on" in real time. This means that instead of waiting several days or weeks for a report, marketers can sit down at their PCs and design their own reports, ask their own questions, etc. A very important, but nonquantifiable, benefit of on-line marketing systems is that they allow marketers to work in a "stream of consciousness." In other words, it is possible to run a query or report, see something interesting or unusual, run another query or report to investigate, and so on.[1] In the world of batch reporting, marketers have to contact someone in "programming" and explain what they want, review the programmer's summary of requirements, wait for programming to be completed, wait for the report to be run, review the report, see something interesting or unusual, again contact someone in programming, and so on.

It's also important to understand that many of these systems are designed specifically for marketers. By "pointing and clicking" they can directly get customer groups defined, counts and custom reports generated, campaign plans defined, promotional lists selected, and the results of marketing campaigns evaluated.

With many of the systems currently available, the PC desktop part of the system directly interfaces with other PC software. This allows marketers to feed the counts, reports, etc., from the marketing system into other applications such

---

1. As will be discussed in more detail later on in this chapter, on-line decision support systems strive for a response time under 20 seconds. But depending upon the size of the database and the complexity of the query, such response times may not be possible. When databases become large, relational systems become slow and summaries are required for real-time decision support, but then flexibility is compromised. To some extent, proprietary systems can overcome this trade-off, but have their own set of issues to contend with. So, if the system you're using is returning response in minutes or in some cases hours, you make take some solace in knowing that you are not alone. Much of the following material will address this issue and offer alternative strategies for increasing response times, at least to some of your queries.

as graphics packages, spreadsheets, statistical mapping systems, word processing, presentation packages, and even e-mail.

Depending upon the size of the database, and/or the amount of presummarization work performed in a matter of minutes, it is possible to profile customers based on income and age, look at cross-selling patterns between different products, compare the value of customers acquired via "Media A" compared with "Media B," look at regional variations in response patterns, "cut and paste" results into a spreadsheet package, create tables and graphs, "cut and paste" the tables and graphs into a word processing package, put text around them to create a short report and then distribute the report via company local area network or across the Internet—just to point out a few possibilities.

The flexible nature of relational databases makes it much easier to add new data items downstream. New characteristics such as age and income either will be added to an existing "table" or will have a new "table" created. Since the software that uses the database refers to a "data dictionary" to determine the location and format of data items, there is no need to modify programs already in use. However, flexibility in relational databases does have a price. Creating additional key fields and indexes creates additional system overhead (data storage and update time) and significantly increases the complexity of the system, which impacts all phases of its maintenance and use.

As usual, there is a trade-off between functionality, flexibility, speed, and power on the one hand and cost on the other. Depending on a number of factors, the cost differential between flat file–based and relational database–based marketing databases can range from 150 percent to well over 10 times.

One of the most important factors to consider is the anticipated volume of changes to reports and data elements. To set up a new flat file report involves both time and cost to configure a reporting utility or write a new reporting program to tabulate and present the needed information. Like the development of any software, there is a design process followed by programming, testing, and prescheduled production runs. If a business is very dynamic and/or the targeted marketing program is rapidly evolving, the batch report approach will most likely be too slow and costly.

Another consideration is the degree to which the database will track summary information (total number of purchases, etc.) versus tracking individual transactions or events (list of every purchase made). The greater the emphasis on individual transactions, the more appropriate the relational database approach.

From the marketer's standpoint, the most important factors are speed and ease of getting needed information and implementing marketing programs. An interactive, on-line marketing system offers much greater utility than static reports presented on paper. With an on-line system, the marketer works interactively, posing a question and getting the answer, posing another question based on the first result, and getting the answer. . . . In a batch reporting system there is an unnatural break in the thought process because it takes days or weeks to develop answers to questions. On-line systems allow the marketer to link with other desktop PC functions. Also, since reporting is not a variable-expense item in on-line systems, the cost per query or report actually decreases with the volume of queries and reports run.

Database Management System Software
In the prior section we focused on the distinction between systems based on flat file structures and systems based on relational file structures. However, in the

world of database management systems products, not all of the file structures employed can be correctly defined as being strictly relational. In fact, three different file structures are used. The next section describes two file structures not previously mentioned—hierarchical and inverted files—and goes into more detail with regard to relational file structures.

Hierarchical Systems   The first DBMS products, for example, IBM's IMS, used a hierarchical structure. Hierarchical databases are designed for efficiency in high-volume transaction environments. Although they are much more flexible than non-DBMS systems, their structure can often limit the flexibility required for the types of ad hoc queries that marketing end users typically require.

Hierarchical systems were designed primarily to support limited analytical flexibility while providing support for high-volume transaction applications. As a result, many companies use hierarchical DBMS products to support customer service, airline or hotel reservation, or financial applications. Although these DBMS products offer greater analytical and reporting flexibility than traditional third-generation systems, they are not designed to support the multiplicity of views or the ad hoc query requirements of today's database marketing applications.

IBM's DB2 and SQL/DS products, along with Computer Associates' IDMS/R, were developed partly to bridge the gap between today's requirements and the hierarchical DBMS products that are ideal for large-volume transaction environments. A number of utility programs have been developed that make it relatively easy to load data from hierarchical systems to relational database environments.

So, although existing hierarchical DBMS products themselves may not be ideal for database marketing applications, companies that are already using them for order entry, customer service, or other transaction-oriented applications may find that their hierarchical systems, when used in combination with other DBMS products, provide a great deal of the information required for marketing.

Inverted File Systems   If the company's existing database has an inverted file structure, for example, Computer Associates' Datacom/DB, Computer Corporation of America's Model 204, or Software A. G.'s Adabas, the marketing group would find these software products especially well suited for database marketing applications. In fact, a number of major direct marketing companies, including Scudder Stevens & Clark, RL Polk, Metromail, and Kraft General Foods (for its original marketing database), had (or still have) database marketing applications that were (are) based on these software products.

One major difference between these products is that CCA's Model 204 and Computer Associates' Datacom/DB are designed to run exclusively in IBM or IBM-compatible environments, whereas Adabas is designed to run on IBM, DEC, and a variety of other vendors' hardware. Companies that do not currently have IBM environments should be cognizant of this fact when they evaluate products.

Inverted file systems are popular for direct marketing applications because they are very good at providing quick counts of records that meet specified conditions. To produce quick counts, inverted file systems can create indexed versions of the data stored in their files. If queries can be answered by index-only processing, that is, not actually reading raw data records, they can produce counts for databases of several million records in a matter of a few minutes at most. In many cases, the database can return query responses in seconds.

To take full advantage of the power of index-only processing, marketers must be very conscious of which variables are important enough to be indexed and which data relationships should be predefined. Although marketers have a natural tendency to create indexes for every variable field, this approach will result in significantly slower updates and data loads. Whereas the indexing approach is satisfactory for simple counts, it tends to be slow if additional conditions are added in the analysis process—for example, reports comparing year-to-date performance this year with corresponding numbers for previous years for a specified set of product codes.

Developing a true understanding of the trade-offs involved in designing the database to be efficient for both processing and updating requires years of experience. That is one reason many firms hire consulting systems analysts and designers who have several years of hands-on experience with the database product they selected. Consulting expertise during the early stages of the database design process can save literally years of development time and processing headaches.

Relational Systems   Relational technology is based on the premise that data redundancy should be minimized and that the most logical arrangement of data within a database is in a series of tables that can be logically joined by key fields.

From a logical standpoint, this arrangement of data makes a great deal of sense. From a practical standpoint, however, logical joins, if done on a dynamic basis (that is, while the application is operating on-line and while end users are waiting for results) have proved to be an inefficient way to link data for the types of queries that are typical for direct marketers.

As a result, relational databases used for the kinds of quick counts described above tend to be designed to look like inverted files. If quick counts are a requirement, relational databases are generally structured as one large file in which virtually all fields are indexed.

In some cases, summary files that already contain counts known to be important may be produced as part of the regular production process so key pieces of information for the firm are prepared in advance. The query process can then function more like a "look-up table" and avoid actually counting records.

Although the ability to perform quick counts is not an essential function for all marketing users, it is particularly important to direct marketers. For this reason, you would expect the number of direct marketing users whose systems are based on relational database systems to be small. However, this is not actually the case.

Relational database technology has been used for database marketing for several reasons. One is that the way in which relational databases are structured, using a process called *normalizing*, is very similar to the way in which marketers visualize their data. Relational technology organizes data elements into logical tables and links them by common data elements.

The utility and dictionary functions available within relational database product families make it relatively easy to extract the desired data elements from the numerous, often fragmented, files in which they are currently captured, and to load the data elements into logical groupings that are more appropriate for the kinds of questions marketers tend to ask. Once the data has been loaded into the relational table format, all the queries and reports that marketers require can be readily defined and, if their database is not too large, readily produced.

Another reason for using a relational database is that IBM, which controls about 60 percent of the mainframe computing marketplace in the United States, has made the strategic decision to support relational technology. To stimulate usage of its relational products, IBM has placed its DB2 and SQL/DS products in thousands of data centers that are committed to the IBM product line.

Because the cost of database management system software is relatively high and technical support staff are expensive, it is only natural that companies with a database management system in-house would want to develop new applications using whatever system is in place.

One of the criticisms of DB2 has been that it is difficult for end users who are not data processing professionals to use. For that reason, a number of products have been developed to bridge the gap between the kinds of menu-driven, PC-based screens that end users are comfortable with and the database management system itself.

Some user-interface products, for example, Natural/SQL, are add-ons to the product lines of other mainframe DBMS products—in this case, Software A.G.'s Adabas. Oracle also has a number of user-friendly tools that can readily be used in conjunction with DB2 or with its own line of DBMS products. Because the Oracle database product itself supports SQL,[2] any programs written using its products will, by definition, be compatible with an SQL product environment like DB2's.

Metaphor, an independently developed product that has been acquired by IBM, can be operated on IBM PS2 platforms and can be used as a user-friendly bridge to IBM's DB2, SQL/DS, or OS/2 databases.

Metaphor's screens consist of a series of menus and icons that resemble Apple's Macintosh, Microsoft's Windows, or other products that are the staples of the point-and-click approach to end-user computing. All these products tend to lower the resistance that computerphobes have toward using technology.

Metaphor enables end users to have access to data that may be stored in a number of different tables and to perform very complex data analysis tasks without requiring any knowledge of programming or systems. All end users need to do is point the Metaphor mouse at the appropriate icons on the screen and click. Once a listing of the available database files is displayed, end users can select the desired files by pointing and clicking the mouse. A display of the fields contained within the table is readily available, and end users can select fields from within tables, combine these with fields selected from other tables, and dynamically create the database needed to solve the marketing questions they have in mind.

Another relational product that has had considerable success in the last few years is Oracle, a relational database developed and marketed by the Oracle Corporation. Oracle's success has come about for two primary reasons:

1. It is an exceptionally good relational database product.
2. The Oracle Corporation is committed to platform independence (see the definition that follows).

From its inception as a company, Oracle has been committed to the concept of platform independence. That is, Oracle's products are developed so they can be used on virtually any computer hardware and with virtually any operating system. It is one of the very few products that can be used on the full range of IBM mainframe machines, the full line of DEC midframes, and virtually any IBM-compatible workstation or microcomputer.

This flexibility is ideal for companies that use DEC or other midframe equipment as departmental machines because programs can be written in any of

---

2. SQL is the abbreviation for Structured Query Language, which is the American National Standards Institute (ANSI) standard language that underlies all relational database management systems.

the environments and then be run in any of the other environments without changing a single line of program code.

If properly designed, relational database systems, if not too large (not over 1 million records) and/or if integrated with other performance-enhancing software, can be well suited to the requirements of database marketing; and in some cases, if the marketing database is to be linked with other applications that the company is running, it may be cost-effective for firms to go with a single-vendor, single-DBMS strategy. Again, a company's strategic technology plan is a very important component of the DBMS selection process.

Products for the Unix Environment   As stated earlier in this text, Unix-based workstation products are becoming increasingly important platforms for database marketing. A number of high-performance database management system products have been developed for this environment, including Sybase, Informix, Ingres, and the Unix-based version of Oracle.

Direct marketers can think of these platforms as consisting of two distinct parts: the core DBMS and application development tools.

The core DBMS in all these products functions as a data repository that allows data manipulations using the SQL language. These cores support on-line transactions and provide a variety of locking features for implementing concurrent updates from simultaneous users. In addition, they can also perform functions related to rollback and recovery. In short, they provide all the facilities needed to build *mission-critical* applications that must be reliable and crash-resistant.

In addition to the core DBMS, the above-mentioned products also provide programming tools to build applications that can be used by the end users and data administrators. These tools can support full-screen applications on a variety of access terminals ranging from plain ASCII terminals to dial-up PCs. They can also support batch and command-line operations intended for data administrators. In almost all cases, the core data can be accessed outside the *relational paradigm* using a conventional (third-generation) language, for example, COBOL, Pascal, or C, in combination with SQL. Such a combination is called *embedded SQL*. Report generators are another kind of access tool which are provided by the vendors and various third parties. Some report generators are based upon fourth-generation report-writing languages, whereas others are screen-based and provide an interactive interface.

To summarize, the set of facilities available for data storage and manipulation and for building applications provides a rich environment suitable for building software applications even for the most demanding needs.

Customized Applications for Direct Marketing

Over the last five to ten years literally dozens of products have come on the market to support the special needs of database marketers to manage direct marketing campaigns and analyze the results of their efforts. Some of these products are built on top of relational, or relational-like, database management systems; other are built on top of proprietary file structures and access methods.

Proprietary Systems   What sets proprietary systems apart from systems built on top of standard relational systems is that proprietary systems are based on unique, nonstandard architectures that have been optimized for the marketing function—namely, to handle ad hoc queries quickly and work efficiently with groups of user-identified records, to quickly combine data in different ways from different tables and efficiently implement user-defined calculations.

The primary benefit of these systems is that they offer superior processing performance, i.e., throughput. The systems currently on the market offer query speeds in the range of 2–10 million rows per second. What this means is that a marketer working for a company that has 30 million customers can find out how many are over age 65 in 3 to 15 seconds. This is roughly the same amount of time needed to pull a predefined answer from an OLAP system. On the other hand, today's open relational database systems would require approximately 2 minutes (if the field was indexed) and up to 30 minutes (if the field was not indexed and a "full table scan" was required).

The difference in performance may seem trivial. Both systems can resolve a simple one-data element, one-table query in a reasonable amount of time. However, extremely few marketing queries are that simple. Effective marketing requires consideration of many pieces of information. Very quickly marketing queries grow into the "complex range." What makes queries complex is that they require many data elements from several or more database tables. For example, a query could easily involve customer-level information, demographic enhancement data, purchase data, and even item-level data. In this example the query requires a four-way table join. If each customer had 1 demographic enhancement row, 2 order rows, and 3 item rows, the query now involves 300 million records! The slower proprietary systems would resolve this new query in 2.5 minutes, while the faster systems would take 30 seconds. In most open relational database systems, this same query would involve overnight processing.

While the number of records or rows involved in a query is an important factor in determining throughput, the number and type of table join operations also have a major impact. One nice feature of most proprietary systems is that adding new tables to a query has a linear impact on throughput. There is no additional penalty for adding a different table. Rather the only impact is the increased number of records. If you have 30 million customers and 60 million purchases, a query involving both tables would take just as long as if you had one table of 90 million customers. On the other hand, open RDBMSs suffer large penalties when additional tables are included in a query. In fact, there is often a geometric increase in query processing time where adding another table to a query could take 5 to 20 times as long.

The relational engines built into proprietary systems achieve their speed by not being general purpose in nature. Rather than being optimized for individual lookups, they are optimized to work in an ad hoc manner with user-defined groups of records. This focused mission allows proprietary systems to handle ad hoc queries, ad hoc reports, inclusion of new data, and list selections.

Since they are focused on the targeted marketing function, these systems also offer a variety of specialized end-user tools. These applications use marketing terminology and conventions and allow ad hoc query, campaign planning, list selects, scoring models, and marketing plan management.

As with any system, this concentrated group of benefits comes at a price. When proprietary databases were optimized for the marketing function, they were developed outside the conventions that allow a system to meet open system architecture standards. This means that you cannot easily add new software from other vendors. As long as you use the system, you are tied into one vendor. You are tied to that vendor's development plans, ability to add tools, and ability to customize the system for your needs. Proprietary systems often require that the system be maintained at a service bureau because many system developers do not have the resources to support the information technology departments of many customer companies with installation guidance, operational training, help desk, etc.

As a result, information technology departments tend to regard these systems as oddball technology. Because these systems are usually not consistent with the company's current system architecture, they result in significant and constant exceptions. As a result they do not contribute to IT's overall mission to make systems more simplified and consistent, as well as reduce system maintenance and operations costs. These systems often involve:

- Special operational schedules and procedures
- Unique software conventions
- Special training or new staff
- New hardware and communications interfaces
- Custom interface programming
- Different vendors

The impact from the IT perspective is more work, more complexity, and, therefore, extra resources (hardware, software, staff).

Systems to Support Database Marketing

As mentioned previously, literally dozens of systems are now available to support database marketers. Many of these products take advantage of the improved price performance of PC and client-server platforms to provide increased end-user access, flexibility, and processing speed, and as said before, some are built around standard relational products and some are built around proprietary systems.

A sampling of some of these products is shown in the Table 14–1. For a complete list of database marketing systems, readers may wish to contact David Raab, who publishes *The David Raab Guide to Database Marketing Systems* (610-565-8188).

TABLE 14–1

A Sampling of Products That Support Database Marketing

Company	Product
Computer Corporation of America	MarketPulse
Customer Development Corporation	CDC/mdm
Customer Insight Company/Metromail	AnalyiX
Db INTELLECT	Marketing Database Architecture and Tool Kit
Decision Software	TopDog
Epsilon Data Management	Epsilon Campaign Manager
Exchange Applications	ValEX
Harland	Pinnacle
Hart-Hanks Data Technology	P/CIS
MarketVision	Relationship Management System
MBS/Multimode	Klondike
MegaPlex Software/David Shepard Associates	Fast-Count DBMS
Paradigm	Ovation
Prime Response	Prime Vantage
Retail Target Marketing System	Archer
RMS	MarketEXPERT
STS Systems	STS Open MarketWorks

CHAPTER 15

Trends in Technology

In this chapter we will discuss trends in price performance, the use of multiple CPUs, open systems, and standard interfaces. We will also touch on the evolution of relational technology, noting its strengths for operations support systems and its limitations for decision support, and how these limitations are being overcome, at least to some extent, through hardware and software solutions. Finally, we will discuss the issues surrounding the creation of enterprise-wide data warehouses and their offshoot, data marts.

IMPROVEMENTS IN PRICE PERFORMANCE

For the past decade, there have been yearly improvements in price performance in every aspect of data processing and of 25 to 35 percent in the price performance of mainframe computers. In other words, the same level of data processing costs 25 to 35 percent less each year, or in each year companies can gain 25 to 35 percent improved performance for the same price. During the same period, comparable rates of improvement in price performance have not occurred in any other industry. If comparable improvements in price performance had occurred in the automobile industry during the same period, an automobile that cost $20,000 in 1982 would cost less than $1,000 today.[1]

Many economists and historians compare this rate of improvement in price performance with the economic changes associated with the Industrial Revolution. Whereas the Industrial Revolution dramatically reduced costs by shifting production from manual to mechanical means, the Information Revolution is extending the computational and analytical abilities of today's workers to levels previously unimaginable.

And that's just the beginning of the story. Price performance for microcomputers is improving at eight times the rate of mainframes, and that for RISC[2] technology is improving at four times the rate of microcomputers.

The net effect of these improvements is evident from advertising in trade and general-interest publications where workstation computers with 300 MIPS[3]

---

1. Assuming annual price improvements of 25 percent.
2. RISC is an acronym for reduced instruction set chips, the technology used in workstation platforms.
3. MIPS is an acronym for millions of instructions per second, a commonly used measure of computer processing power.

of processing power are being offered for approximately \$4,000.[4] Data storage, which can be prohibitively expensive for mainframe computing environments, now can be *purchased* for \$200 to \$500 per gigabyte.[5] Functionality has also been improved.

These costs demonstrate the dramatic improvements in the price performance of individual computing devices. But earlier we discussed using multiple platforms to support the new direct marketing. What opportunities do the trends in technology offer for multiple-platform environments?

MUTIPLE CPUs

Multiple platforms, with separate computing platforms for each functional group within a company, require multiple CPUs. To work together effectively, these multiple CPUs must be able to communicate efficiently and effectively using standard, inexpensive communications and data processing links. This is conceptually no different from people who work in different departments being able to exchange information by telephone. As in the case of telephones, particularly those attached to PBXs,[6] computers can communicate with each other through *networks*.

Computer networks, like telephone networks, are hard-wired physical circuits that support communications between and among the computer devices attached to them. The next chapter describes in more detail the different types of computer networks currently in use, the speeds at which they can transfer data, the protocols they use, the functions they can perform, and their cost. For purposes of this discussion, be aware that computer networks exist and that they are a critical component of getting computers to communicate with each other.

OPEN SYSTEMS ARCHITECTURE

A very important trend in computer technology during the past few years has been the evolution and adoption of open systems architectural standards. In the not too distant past, computer operating systems were different for each manufacturer's set of products. For example, IBM had its DOS, MVS, and CMS operating environments that IBM computers and some compatibles, notably Amdahl and Hitachi, could use. Digital Equipment Corporation (DEC) had different operating systems, which did not communicate directly with IBM's. Data General had still another set.

In the Unix world, there were three different Unix operating systems, Berkeley Unix, AT&T Unix (now Hewlett Packard), and SCO Unix. IBM's entry into Unix-based products produced the AIX environment, still another version of Unix. In addition, Sun has Solarris and SGI has IRIX. The mainframe-based operating systems tended to be proprietary, whereas the Unix-based products tended to be more similar. Manufacturers liked proprietary environments because they helped justify higher profit margins for their products. In addition, closed or proprietary environments encouraged many companies to use software products

---

4. As of mid-1998. This figure will change by the time you read this book; either the cost will drop, the number of MIPS will increase, or both.

5. A gigabyte is equal to 1 billion bytes, roughly 600,000 pages of text, or 500 copies of *War and Peace*.

6. A private branch exchange (PBX) is an internal telephone switch that enables people using telephones attached to the same network to call from extension to extension without using external telephone lines.

from a single vendor or a very limited set of vendors because vendors would naturally make every effort to ensure that their own suite of products would work together in a customer's data center. Customers in multiple-vendor environments, by contrast, tended to experience problems with each manufacturer's technical support team if their software products did not work together smoothly.

However, because of a recognition of computing requirements in the marketplace and a desire to be part of any future configurations, computer hardware manufacturers have more or less agreed upon open systems architecture, which allows many manufacturers' products to work cooperatively in their customers' data centers. This development was critical for businesses to consider using workstations in their computing environments because these devices all use Unix-based operating systems.

Standard Interfaces

Open systems require a standard set of interfaces between operating systems, DBMS products, communications protocols, and graphical user interfaces (GUIs).[7]

It is not enough, however, just to *have* open systems. Companies must have well-defined and published interfaces so software developers know exactly how their software will work in each environment and how data communications will flow from one platform to another within the same configuration or between configurations.

Standard interfaces make it possible for software developers to produce applications that can be operated in a number of different operating system environments. Standard interfaces make it possible for companies to use applications on a number of different computer platforms, generally without having to modify their applications. The applications are, therefore, *independent* of the platforms on which they are being operated, hence the term *platform-independent*.

The advantages of using platform-independent applications are numerous. They enable companies to use their computer applications on one computer platform and, when they have outgrown the capacity of that platform, to seamlessly move the application to another, larger platform, whether or not the new platform is manufactured by the same manufacturer as the former device.

In addition, companies may wish to simultaneously operate the same application on numerous platforms if, for example, a number of different business units all use the same set of applications. A single applications maintenance team can then support all versions of the application, regardless of differences in the platforms on which the application is being operated, because the application itself is platform-independent.

Many DBMS products, for example Oracle, Informix, Sybase, and Ingres, are also platform-independent. All these DBMS products can be operated in any Unix-based environment, on any manufacturer's computers, and several can be operated in *non-Unix* environments as well, for example, in PC-DOS or even in mainframe environments.

Platform independence becomes critically important when applications that use GUI tools on PCs are linked to DBMS products on individual PCs or on PC

---

7. Graphical user interfaces are software products that provide users with user-friendly screens. These products include tools like mouses and screen images in the form of icons. Apple's MacIntosh, Microsoft's Windows, and IBM's OS2 are examples of GUI environments.

networks and subsequently to DBMS products on workstations or mainframe computers that are connected using local area networks. In this type of environment, it is essential that all components within the configuration work smoothly together and that they work in precisely the way they are expected to work together each and every time.

Evolution of Relational DBMSs

Early development of relational DBMSs took place to support operations systems, which are collections of software systems used to support day-to-day operations of businesses and are characterized by transactions processing for applications such as customer service and accounting. The primary objectives behind this development were:

1. All data stored in the database should be accessible without COBOL programming.

2. Application code need not have any knowledge of where data is stored in the database, and the data structure should be amenable to change without extensive programming effort.

3. As far as possible, any given piece of data should be stored in only one place. For example, address of a household should be stored only once, and not with each customer who belongs to that household. This is intended to simplify update processing and reduce possibilities of creating inconsistencies within the database.

4. The database should provide for the storage of linked information at all levels; for example, a household could have multiple customers, a customer could have multiple transactions and accounts, etc. The database should not impose any limit to the number of linked items.

5. Data records should be quickly accessible using certain key information such as customer number and account number.

6. MIS reports should be easy to run on the database, that is, without much COBOL-level custom programming.

Salient Characteristics of Relational DBMSs

The above-listed objectives are met by relational DBMSs by providing the following facilities:

1. All data is stored in *tables,* which consist of rows and columns (or fields and records), in such a way that the rows in each table contain data on similar business entities. For example, data about households is stored in the households table, while data about customers is stored in a separate customers table. Each customer record contains a household number, and the customers table can have any number of customer records for a household—there is no limit on the multiplicity.

2. A high-level language, SQL, is used to work with data. Any changes to the table structure do not need COBOL-level programming, and therefore can be implemented more quickly. This powerful language has numerous capabilities for performing arithmetic calculations, identifying records using Boolean conditions, and doing many other tasks.

3. Certain fields in tables can be designated as primary keys, which allow very quick access to records containing specified values of these fields.

For example, the customer number field is often a primary key for the customers and transactions tables; given a customer number, records in both tables can be quickly accessed from the database.

4. Fields in data tables can be indexed for quick report generation. For example, if the state field in the households table is indexed, a report on the number of households for each state can be generated more quickly than when the state field is not indexed. The same holds for queries, too; for example, the query, "How many households in a specified set of states have more than $25,000 annual income?" will run faster if the state field is indexed.

5. Normalized storage, in which each piece of data is stored in only one place, leads to efficient disk storage and update processing, and also leads to numerous joins to support the queries. The join operation provides a great deal of flexibility and power, but it is slow and consumes a lot of temporary disk space.

For example, to determine the number of customers for each state, the households and customers tables will have to be joined on the household number field. The result of the join operations is a temporary, hypothetical table in which records would contain (1) fields from the customers table and (2) fields from the households table, which would be repeated for each customer. For instance, if a household has three customers, the state information (which resides in the households table) will be repeated in each of the three customer records. The records in the temporary table are then used to finish the query by counting the number of customers in each state.

Capabilities and Performance of SQL

Performance of relational DBMSs varies depending upon the task being performed. The following points illustrate the salient aspects of their performance:

1. As illustrated by the design criteria listed in the above section, relational DBMSs perform very effectively all tasks related to on-line transactions processing (OLTP). Such tasks call for identification and extraction of records using one or more key fields and do not involve a large amount of data.

2. Relational DBMSs provide good performance for several tasks that use indexed fields—for example, condition evaluation using indexed fields, distribution of counts for distinct values of such fields, and distribution of aggregates (such as average income and minimum account balance) for distinct values of such fields.

   In the context of marketing analysis, a few problems tend to arise with indexed fields. For one thing, as more and more fields are indexed, the update times for the database become long, and the indexes consume more and more disk space. For example, if additional records are added to the customer table at the refresh time, all the indexes are generally dropped, new records are added to the table, and the indexes are recreated.

   A second problem is that marketing databases tend to have a large number of attributes for customers (400 is not uncommon). Some relational DBMSs do not allow storing and indexing this many fields in one table. If the table is split, what otherwise would be a simple query becomes a query with a join operation; that would take considerably longer to run and would need much more disk space. Note that operations systems do not tend to have such wide tables, as they do not need to maintain a large number of attributes for customers. Direct marketers need those attributes because they use this information to create customer segments. The segment definitions in the end may not involve many attributes, but the process of arriving at the desirable (that is, predictive) attributes calls for examining all the available attributes.

Finally, short of indexing all fields in a table, there is no practical way to assure nontechnical marketing users that the database will provide uniform performance for all or most of their queries.

3. Relational DBMSs provide poor performance for condition evaluation and distribution of counts and aggregates using unindexed fields. The main problem here is that a lot of data has to be transported from the disk drives to the CPU, which takes time. However, once the data is in the CPU, the actual calculation does not take very long at all. By the way, the main reason why indexes expedite certain operations described above is that they reduce the amount of data that needs to be brought from disks to the CPU.

4. Multitable operations involving joins are very slow in relational DBMSs. This aspect of performance is not a big problem for operations systems because they are mostly concerned with OLTP as described above and do not need to perform joins of big tables all that often. They need the joins for batch updates and MIS reports, which are carefully programmed to be as efficient as possible and are run during off hours in batch, not interactive, mode — still, such operations tend to take a long time to run.

The situation in direct marketing is quite different. Many queries and reports for direct marketing require the join operations and must be performed often and in interactive mode. One such report displays counts by state for customers who purchased Item A and not B between any two specified dates. This report would require joining the customers, transactions, and items tables, and on most relational DBMSs might take anywhere from 10 to 40 minutes for a million customers (the timings given here are very approximate and are intended as ballpark figures). In the world of direct marketing, this is not an unusual query, neither is it a rare one, nor is a million-customer database a large one.

On the other hand, in product- and geography-centric marketing, monthly summaries of counts and amounts generally suffice and do not require the join operations. Major time investment in this case is in creating the summary tables (often called the star-schema tables), but that is done once during a refresh period and not while the user is waiting for the answer.

5. Relational DBMSs are very effective in providing read-only access to several simultaneous users for analysis and reporting purposes, and that is quite adequate for product- and geography-centric marketing applications. Direct marketing, in contrast, requires supporting several simultaneous users who would need to modify the database based upon how they would be developing their campaigns on the system. For example, they might identify different sets and subsets of users, they

might score using different models, they might assign different promotion codes, etc. Such multiuser read-modify access is clumsy at best in relational DBMSs.

Post-SQL Processing for Direct Marketing

Direct marketers often require several functions that are not supported in relational DBMSs through SQL. For example:

1. Calculate score using several dummy variables.
2. Determine deciles based upon the score.
3. Split cells into *N*-way random subcells and assign test and control codes to them.

Such functions are performed by extracting data from the relational DBMS by using embedded C or COBOL and then storing the results back in the database. This would require additional software development, which comes with all the cost and time problems associated with either buying or developing specialized software in C and COBOL. Since such processing cannot be done in SQL, we call it post-SQL processing—and direct marketing requires a lot of it.

The Performance Dilemma

To summarize the ideas presented in the above sections, we note that:

- Relational DBMSs were created to address the high cost and long development times associated with building operations systems using pre-relational systems (such as flat files, ISAM, VSAM, and hierarchical DBMSs).

- Relational DBMSs:
  1. Are easy to program
  2. Meet operations systems requirements very well
  3. Satisfy marketing requirements for product- and geography-centric marketing, even though the creation of summary tables tends to be slow and such tables tend to take up huge amounts of disk space
  4. Do not meet many direct marketing requirements in terms of both speed and capabilities

The primary impediment to relational DBMSs delivering good performance for direct marketing applications is that these applications make full passes on the tables, as opposed to finding a few records using a few key fields (as operations systems do). Such processing necessitates transferring large amounts of data from disk drives to the CPU, which is a slow process. Once the data is available to the CPU, the remainder of the processing steps are done very quickly.

Solutions to the Database Performance Problem

Several techniques have been used to eliminate or at least mitigate the speed problem described above. Some of them are entirely in software, while others use hardware improvements. These techniques are briefly described below.

Software Solutions

Middleware Systems These software systems sit between the relational database and the end-user query tool. Their main purposes are to monitor the kinds of queries and operations requested by the user, to store data in their temporary store that they deem might be useful in future end-user requests, and to perform the requested function at a faster speed using the temporary data store. These systems do expedite some direct marketing queries such as those that call for reports on unindexed fields, but are not able to help in the queries that need access to the detailed data. These systems seem to be much more effective in expediting product- and geography-centric marketing functions.

Post-Relational DBMSs   These are special-purpose DBMSs that are designed to provide high-speed support for direct marketing. They use a variety of software techniques to move the data queries along at a fast pace, such as bit vectors, data compression, inverted lists, etc. Such techniques strive to reduce the disk input/output that is the main source of slowdown.

Hardware Solutions   Several hardware solutions have been widely used to expedite database functions. Some of the salient ones are listed below:

1. *Parallel computers*. These computers deploy several CPUs simultaneously to try to expedite database queries. For direct marketing type of queries which tend to be data-intensive, this technique alone does not yield much improvement in the speed because it does not address the basic problem of a slow data transfer rate between the disk and the CPUs.
2. *Parallel data transfer paths*. Disk data transfer rates can be improved if data is split across several disks and is transferred in parallel on those paths.
3. *Faster disk drives*. Making the disk drives themselves faster has the obvious advantage of improving the transfer rate and is a good way to expedite the database functions.
4. *RAID drives*. RAID stands for redundant array of independent drives. As the name indicates, several disk drives are used to store the data in a way such that one out of nine drives is redundant. This arrangement provides the high speed of transfer due to several drives working in parallel and also has the added benefit of improved reliability.

DATA WAREHOUSES AND DATA MARTS
Enterprise Data Warehouses

Almost every company today is supported by a very complicated combination of information systems that have been developed independently throughout the company's history. Some of these systems are based on the newest technology (relational databases, local area networks, rapid application development methods, etc.), while others are based on older, third-generation software (flat files, VSAM structures, COBOL programs, access via CICS, etc.).

These systems, often referred to as *legacy systems*, represent significant challenges to information technology groups because they are often difficult to maintain and modify as new needs arise. Also, because legacy systems were usually developed as "silos" supporting individual business functions, it is very difficult to bring information together from various parts of the company for comprehensive reporting, business management functions, and new "downstream" systems.

In response to these needs, the information technology world has developed a concept called the *enterprise data warehouse*. Based on relational database platforms, the data warehouse provides a central point into which all company "legacy" systems feed their data. The data warehouse provides a single comprehensive source for enterprise-wide data. In the data warehouse, differences between legacy systems in how individual data items are defined, formatted, and coded are resolved. For example, differences in how name and address data is carried are resolved into one set of standardized fields. (See Figure 15-1.)

The data warehouse also provides a central "data dictionary" that describes, in detail, all data in the system. While data dictionaries differ between systems, they usually contain for each data element its original source system, what information it represents, known limitations or errors, translations of codes it contains, how the field is formatted, where it is stored in the data warehouse, etc. The data dictionary has several important uses:

As an administration tool, it ensures that differences in data sources are resolved and duplication of fields only occurs when intended.

As a reference source, it is available to systems analysts, programmers, and even end users so that they can understand what the data represents and how it should be used.

As a guide for software that uses data from the data warehouse, it eliminates "hard-coding" data formats into the software, which allows the database to

FIGURE 15-1

Enterprise Data Warehouse

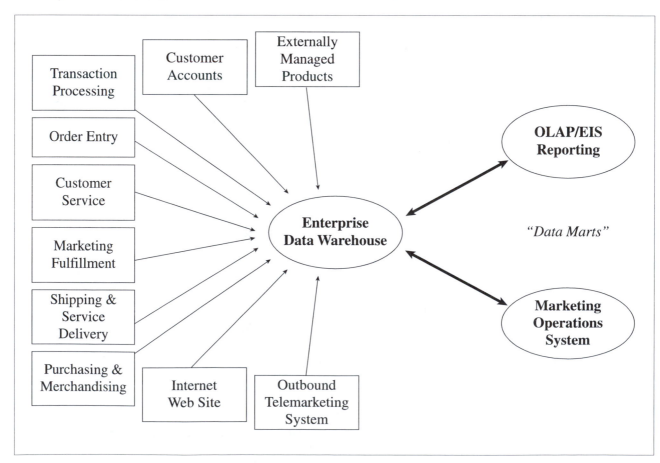

be modified without having to reprogram all of the software that accesses the database. In traditional legacy systems, every time there is a change to record formats, all software that uses those records must be updated. That means maintenance programming—more time and cost, and fewer resources to support new applications.

Data Marts

In the introduction to relational databases, we mentioned that it was possible to use one database system to concurrently support many applications, but that it was not always practical to do so. While task-specific "views" can simplify database schemas for specific uses, and offer alternative ways of associating tables, they cannot always overcome the general-purpose nature of data warehouse designs. In many cases, the capabilities and performance of downstream applications are restricted.

Alternatively, every application that accesses a data warehouse contributes to the data warehouse's overall processing load. This impacts throughput, which is a major concern in data warehouse operations. In fact, the processing necessary to support data requests from downstream applications must compete with the processing that keeps the data warehouse updated—and updating consumes significant amounts of resources. In the case of one well-known retailer, it was discovered that the retailer's daily update processing load required 32 hours of machine time! Besides slipping further behind every day on updates, there simply was no capacity to handle applications intended to use the database.

In response to these issues, the conceptual architecture of data warehouses was extended to include "data marts." Typically, these are separate relational database systems combined with task-specific end-user applications that are intended to support a particular business function, such as targeted marketing, financial reporting, sales management, etc. Data marts receive subsets of data from the data warehouse that are relevant to the specific tasks they support. The database tables, data elements, primary keys, secondary keys, indexes, etc., are structured to optimize throughput and the unique capabilities needed to support the specific task.

Many companies that have developed data warehouses have found the data mart approach to be an excellent way of handling the needs of targeted marketing. Unlike many other business functions, targeted marketing requires the ability to work in a user-defined, ad hoc fashion with groups of records from different levels of the database (households, customers, accounts, promotion history, etc.). Supporting this set of needs requires:

Heavy use of processing resources

A very flexible data model

Unique data structures

Unique record-linking (relational) capabilities

Unique end-user and list processing tools

All of these factors point to having a separate database system for marketing.

OLAP/EIS

One of the primary reasons for developing a data warehouse is to provide a comprehensive, consistent source of data for enterprise-wide reporting. Like most downstream applications, reporting often runs into throughput issues caused by the data warehouse's processing of data updates and real-time feeds to operational systems. Therefore, many companies with data warehouses have implemented a special type of data mart intended to handle reporting. The current architecture of choice for this function is the OLAP/EIS system—actually, two concepts combined into one information delivery channel.

On-Line Analytical Processing

On-line analytical processing (OLAP) is a method of storing summary information. It was originally developed to support sales reporting and financial reporting applications. Essentially a "database of answers," the OLAP system stores answers to predefined business reporting needs, i.e., "questions."

Sometimes referred to as *multidimensional databases*, OLAP databases store important values such as sales, profit, and customer counts for predefined dimensions of the business (time, sales region, product, salesperson, etc.). Another characteristic of OLAP databases is that the structure of the dimensions (Worldwide Sales → U.S. Sales → Western Region Sales → Metro Denver Territory Sales) is also predefined. Therefore, a user can only "drill down" into increasingly more detailed levels of data according to the structure built into the system. End users access the database via any number of "front-end" applications (usually EIS applications) that help them format their information requests and then display the answers in tables, graphs, statistical maps, etc.

While OLAP systems deliver answers very quickly, that speed comes at a price. It is important to understand that OLAP systems can deliver only information that has been anticipated well in advance and has been built into the system—hence, the repeated use of the term *predefined* in the last paragraph. In that way, OLAP systems are similar to the batch reporting systems used with flat file databases. Adding new information to the system involves working through the information technology group to define new requirements; design, implement, and test software changes; and then wait for the next production run before the data is available.

It is this characteristic that often directly conflicts with the needs of the marketing group. Part of what the marketing group needs is predictable, generally 30 to 60 percent of the overall reporting need. However, that means that 40 to 70 percent of a typical marketing group's needs cannot be supported by an OLAP-based system. In addition, keep in mind that even for the product and geography summary reporting, the creation of summary tables may be very slow for large databases; as more dimensions are added to provide more flexibility, space requirements tend to rapidly increase; and fast analysis is limited to high-level summaries.

Executive Information System

The usual delivery channel used to access OLAP databases is the executive information system (EIS). Some industry insiders claim that EISs were named to reflect the fact that they delivered "reporting and analysis so easily that even executives can use them." EISs are characterized by extremely user-friendly graphical interfaces that are typically custom-tailored to the needs of each company—using the company's terminology, its accounting categories, its products, its geography, etc.

The EIS prompts the user to choose from a set of predefined options (usually by clicking on an icon, a row in a report, a state on a map, etc.) and then displays the results. Sometimes the end user is given options on how the results should be displayed (tables, graphs, maps, etc.).

Besides reporting options, another key to the success of an EIS is building in appropriate "drill-down paths." These are data structures inherent in the reporting applications that allow users to further investigate what they have seen by requesting increasingly more detailed reports.

In an EIS, choices on data elements, calculated values, drill-down paths, and report formats must be predefined. However, that does not necessarily mean that these systems are inflexible. It is possible to build in many, many end-user options. But there are some disadvantages:

The size of the associated OLAP database grows quickly.

The end-user system becomes expensive to build and maintain.

The system becomes very complex for end users.

With this type of system, end users can use a spreadsheet-like application on their PC to link to the OLAP database and pull up a report presenting sales by marketing program compared with what was expected in the annual marketing plan. If they see that the expected sales for "the September catalog" are much lower than expected, they can "click" on that catalog's row in the report table to get more detail. The predefined "next level" of detail is to present each of the rollout and test cells within that promotion. If they see that results are uniformly low across all cells, they can then click on the "product detail button" at the bottom of the screen. The next screen to occur shows actual and expected sales by product for the September catalog. There, the problem appears—sales of the new silk blazers are much lower than what the buyer had projected. See Figures 15-2 to 15-4 for examples of the kinds of reports that an EIS can produce.

FIGURE 15-2

Customer Performance by Source Report

Customer Performance by Source of Name						
Customers Acquired in 1Q93–Status As of 4Q94						
Source of Name	Number of Names	Times Promoted	Number of Responses	Annualized Customer Value	Composite Response Rate	Average Annualized Sales per Customer
Scored Names from Commercial Lists	124,332	875,324	19,507	$1,404,490	2.23%	$72
Site Radiation Selection	101,870	717,090	12,648	$569,160	1.76%	$45
Joint Venture Partner List	79,492	557,444	9,349	$448,742	1.68%	$48
Affinity List	75,117	529,819	9,597	$547,018	1.81%	$57
Survey Responders	51,873	361,111	8,522	$570,987	2.36%	$67
Inbound 800 Number	42,995	295,965	3,913	$242,606	1.32%	$62

FIGURE 15–3

Customer Acceleration Matrix						
1Q97 Status versus 4Q97 Status						
–4Q97–						
1Q97	**Inquiry**	**Light User**	**Medium User**	**Heavy User**	**Total**	
Inquiry	**175,392**	153,737	98,070	54,332	481,531	28%
Light User	1,651	**453,728**	98,727	35,002	589,108	35%
Medium User	322	33,465	**332,465**	19,044	385,296	23%
Heavy User	29	9,807	11,221	**227,521**	248,578	15%
Total	177,394	650,737	540,483	335,899	1,704,513	100%
	10%	38%	32%	20%	100%	

Members Increasing	458,912	27%
Members Static	1,189,106	70%
Members Decreasing	56,495	3%
	1,704,513	100%

The Marketing Operations System

The phrase *marketing database* is most commonly used to describe information systems that support targeted marketing efforts. However, the industry is coming to realize that it falls short of adequately describing the application. While many new phrases have been offered up, we are hearing the phrase *marketing operations system* used more and more. This wording seems to convey the idea that the marketing function involves more than collecting data and producing standardized reports (See Figure 15-5).

The marketing process is part creativity and art, part science, part planning, part inspiration, and part luck. The system needed to support this business function must capture and assimilate data that is not only relevant to the marketing function, but in a format that optimizes it. This system must also be able to manipulate data according to marketing's needs. It must provide standard reports as well as ad hoc query and reporting. And, very importantly, it must provide a number of specific marketing software tools, such as customer group identification and selection, customer classification and tagging, customer profiles, promotion scoring model development, customer value calculation, annual plan management, campaign planning, list processing, campaign management, marketing program results analysis—just to name a few.

While it is still common for companies to operate without data warehouses and link the marketing operations system directly to feeds from legacy operations

FIGURE 15–4

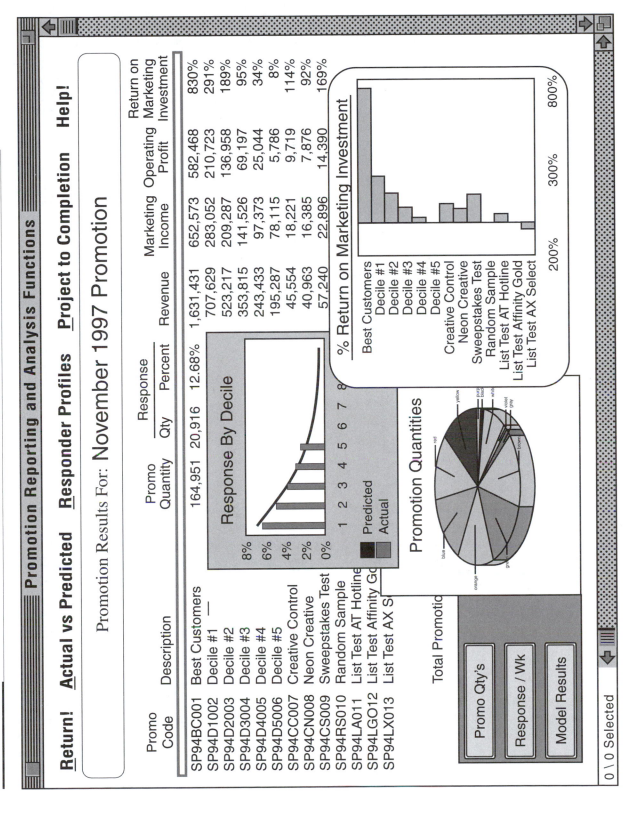

FIGURE 15-5

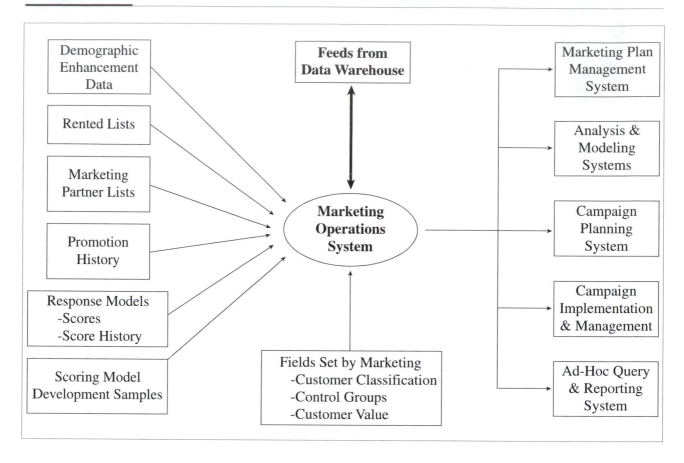

systems, the growing trend is for companies to have data warehouses at the core of their information technology architectures.

In the theory of enterprise data warehouses, one of the fundamental, underlying assumptions is that they should contain all the data in the organization. In this way, all the data necessary for operations, reporting, and analysis is contained in one consistent source. However, data warehouses tend to be focused on customers and "line operations." In the world of marketing, there exist some types of data that are relevant only to the marketing group, are very significant in size, and have high associated processing loads.

While this issue is not black or white, there are a number of data types that many information technology professionals are coming to believe should only be housed in the marketing data mart. One example is prospect data. Due to the increasing costs of list rental and promotion, many companies find it necessary to build prospect databases. These systems help trim promotional costs in two ways. First, by identifying duplicates across multiple prospect list sources, they are able to reduce multiple promotions to the same individual and thus avoid "renting the same name several times." Second, by maintaining promotion history for prospects, it is possible to effectively "score" prospect names and eventually allow the cost of acquisition to be calculated when the prospects purchase.

Depending on the size of the company and industry in which they operate, it is common to see prospect databases that range in size from 10 million to 90 million individuals. Imagine the reaction from the data warehouse staff when they manage a system designed to house between 1 million and 2 million customers and marketing wants to add 20 million prospect names that are constantly being input, deleted, matched/merged against each other, profiled, selected for promotions, etc.!

Response scoring models are another type of data that represents a significant challenge to data warehouses. While the amount of data storage required is not excessive, scoring models require large amounts of processing resources and flexibility in their calculation and use. Scoring models are constantly being implemented in an ad hoc fashion. Calculating response scores requires bringing together large amounts of customer data from the many different tables that hold a customer's information. The data required is unpredictable in that each model uses different data. End users want to be able to implement scoring models directly, and response scores are of very little use to other parts of the company.

A related type of data is scoring model development samples. While many types of data have been used to develop response scoring models, the most effective approach continues to be selecting a random sample of a file, mailing it, and then modeling the characteristics of responders versus nonresponders. This requires keeping a copy of each person's record "frozen" at the time he or she was selected for the random sample. When a list of responders is available, it is "matched back" to the original promotion file. The scoring model then uses what was known about the person at the time of selection to determine what characteristics are indicative of eventual response. This data is another example of data that is not relevant to other business functions. Depending on the use of scoring models at the company, there can be a significant amount of data and it requires match-back capabilities that are not used for other purposes. Also, records tend to sit unused for a long period of time (the promotional period) and then are used only once.

Promotion history is another type of data that typically is not used by other departments. Depending on the promotional activity of a company, this can represent a very significant amount of data. Also, where there exists promotion history data, there exists the need to associate it with response data from multiple inside and outside sources and use many different methods of matching.

Inclusion of demographic enhancement data is a very "gray" area in data warehouse designs. Many companies have use for demographic data in areas other than marketing; others do not. Update cycles are infrequent, usually once or twice a year. However, the system must be able to match data on name and address from multiple outside sources and often prioritize which data to retain when duplicate hits occur. Another important issue is the data usage license and whether it applies to only the marketing group and marketing purposes, to only the division that marketing is part of, or to other divisions, etc.

Similar to demographic enhancement data is the issue of whether to include customer survey data in the data warehouse. In some companies, measuring customer satisfaction, attitudes, and opinions is integral to supporting all business functions that touch the customer. In others, it is not as important and probably should be kept out of the data warehouse. Depending on how the data is captured, it can represent a very significant processing load to keep it updated.

One topic seems to consistently generate a lot of discussion when integrating marketing functions into a data warehouse environment. In marketing it is very important for end users to be able to create data. They must be able to classify customers, calculate customer values, apply scoring models, create new fields to be used in reports, etc. These functions require the ability to select groups of customer and change fields, to calculate new values in real time, and even to create new data fields. While necessary, these functions conflict with the information technology world's view of how to efficiently manage databases. Typically the database is "owned" by a database administrator. This person carefully manages the database schema to ensure that a change for one system does not affect another, that data is not duplicated, and that the system remains in optimal configuration and security. On this issue, every company develops a different solution that meets its unique needs. Some restrict end users to working through the DBA, others allow full access to restricted tables, and others allow any changes as long as they are restricted to the marketing data mart.

CHAPTER 16

Client-Server Systems

Based on information in the preceding chapter, if we could develop a wish list of the information management functions required for the new direct marketing, what would we include?

Certainly we would want to include modular growth, so we could add inexpensive modules for additional processing capacity and upgrade the functions of existing modules. We would want to have an adequate number of data processing cycles and adequate data storage for both the OSS and the DSS environments, but we would want to acquire these at lower costs than currently available in the mainframe environment. To avoid the data contention and resource contention issues we discussed, we would ideally want to have separate computers for the OSS and the DSS functions tuned to optimally support the needs of each environment. Separate platforms must, however, be able to communicate with each other, readily exchanging data through data extraction and electronic file transfer for downloads and uploads. In addition, we would want the DSS computing environment to have flexible tools for analysis and presentation.

The major trends in computer technology that were discussed in the previous chapter, namely, improvements in the price-performance ratio, the availability of local and wide area networking, and the evolution of open systems architecture, support both types of business needs efficiently by *utilizing client-server configurations*. In this chapter, we present a brief, nontechnical overview of client-server technology, explain its salient benefits, and discuss several configurations that businesses can use to meet the needs in the wish list we developed at the start of this chapter.

CLIENT-SERVER TECHNOLOGY

As its name indicates, client-server technology consists of clients and servers whose roles are very similar to those encountered in everyday business: clients make certain requests, and the servers carry out those requests. The main difference, of course, is that the clients and servers are both computers, albeit of different sizes and capacities. In addition, because the clients and servers cannot communicate using the communication media used by human beings, they exchange requests and responses over a computer network that forms the backbone of any client-server configuration (see Figure 16-1). Thus, not only are the clients and servers computers, but also they must be equipped with appropriate communication hardware and software.

FIGURE 16-1

Client-Server Technology: What Is It?

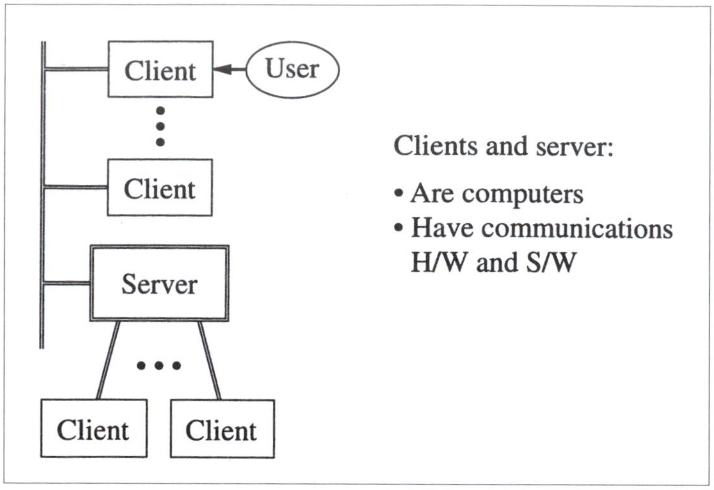

Typically, end users interact with their respective client computers (or client stations) to *compose* work requests. A work request, for example, may be to examine a customer record, to perform an analysis or a name selection step, or to make a report. The client computer transforms that request into a message that the server computer can understand and sends it to the server over the network.

The server analyzes the message to identify the requesting client and the work requested. It then carries out the request and communicates the results back to the requesting client by sending a message the client can understand. The server sends the response message over the same network on which it received the request. The client computer, upon receiving the response message, extracts the results from it and displays them on the screen for the end user.

As shown in Figure 16-1, the simplest client-server configuration must have at least one server; it may, however, have several client computers. The networking hardware and software is set up to allow all clients to communicate with the server and vice versa. The clients may not be able to communicate with each other—that type of communication is not necessary for client-server interactions.

As the above example indicates, the client computer's primary responsibility is to support end-user interactions and to provide a user-friendly human interface. This may involve screen painting, echoing keyboard input, displaying results, supporting point-and-click actions using the mouse, and so on. While these operations are going on, the server on the network is not disturbed at all. The server is contacted (and therefore interrupted) only when a request has been fully formed and requires server action.

The primary responsibility of the server is to receive requests from all the clients on the network and carry out those requests as fast as possible, without worrying about how the work request was composed and how the results will be displayed on the screen.

Due to the nature of the workload, clients are generally small, single-user computers, whereas servers are much more powerful computers that can support multiple clients. In addition, depending upon the type of user interaction, clients, servers, or both could be specialized for different users' needs (more on specialization later in this chapter).

BENEFITS OF CLIENT-SERVER CONFIGURATIONS

The primary benefit of using client-server configurations is a good price-performance ratio. Because the clients and servers use an open systems approach, you can mix and match different vendors' products to design the most suitable configuration for a given set of needs. The competition between the products that can fulfill any role in the system tends to drive the quality up and prices down. In contrast, as Figure 16-2 shows, the proprietary mainframes and minis have vendor-specific hardware and software, which tend to be more expensive and less flexible than the equivalent products in the open systems marketplace.

Another factor that improves the price-performance ratio of client-server configurations is the division of labor between the clients and the server (see Figure 16-3). The clients are small, inexpensive computers largely responsible for the human interface and are deployed one per user. On the other hand, the servers are more expensive shared computers assigned the responsibility of carrying out

FIGURE 16-2

Client-Server Technology: Different from Mainframes and Minis

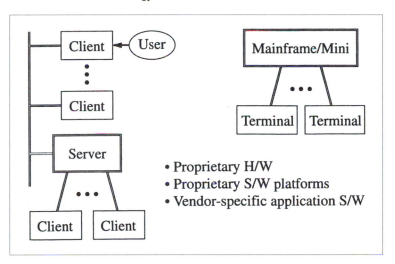

FIGURE 16-3

Client-Server Technology: Division of Labor

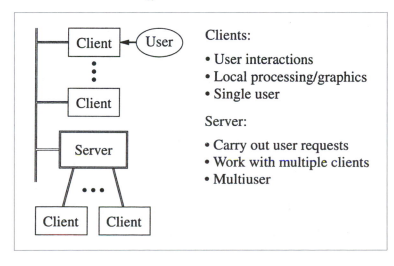

client requests. Servers are not interrupted for human interface, and thus they can perform their own tasks more efficiently. Such a division of labor is not easily achieved by mainframes and minis because the main computers also provide human interface, which slows down their performance of back-end tasks.

In addition to providing attractive price-performance ratios, the client-server configurations provide flexibility and incremental growth. We can match client computers to the human-interface needs of their end users. We can also connect multiple servers on the networks that are specialized for different classes of requests. If we need more computing power, we can add more servers of the same type. If we need more storage capacity, we can add more disk drives to any server. In contrast to conventional mainframe configurations, these changes would all be incremental and would not necessitate major upgrades of the overall system. If managed properly, these changes would not create major disruptions in service either.

DIFFERENT KINDS OF CLIENTS

Based upon the type of work to be performed by the end users, the client computers could be of several types. These different types of client computers offer different local disk storage, type of display (text, graphics, high-resolution graphics), and type of operating system (single-user or multitasking).

A relatively inexpensive client computer may be a DOS PC with small, low-capacity disks and human-interface tools for text applications. Such a configuration would be adequate for data entry applications.

If the end users require a graphical interface for their work, the client PC would need to be equipped with a faster processor, additional disk storage, and a Windows-based front end for human interface.

For more elaborate applications, the client computer could be a multitasking Unix station with local disk storage, high-resolution display, and X-Windows human interface.

If the network has enough capacity, the clients may not have any local disk at all—all their storage requirements could be served by shared disks on the network.

These different types of client computers could coexist in the same client-server configuration, as long as the networking aspects of the system are well managed and the requests from the client computers are routed to the appropriate servers.

DIFFERENT KINDS OF SERVERS

Just as client computers can be of different types, so can the servers. Different types of servers satisfy specialized requests that they are specially equipped to carry out. Figure 16-4 shows three different types of servers.

The database server should have fast disk drives and a large amount of disk capacity. In addition, it should have enough main memory (RAM) to satisfy several simultaneous requests and a database management system to store and manage data. All the data-related requests, for example, retrieving customer records, would be routed to this server.

The file server's needs are similar to those of the data server, except the file server may not need as much disk capacity and those disks may not have to be as fast. It would be used to store files shared by different end users. Thus, all requests related to retrieving shared files, such as word processing files, would be routed to this server.

FIGURE 16-4

Client-Server Technology: Different Kinds of Servers

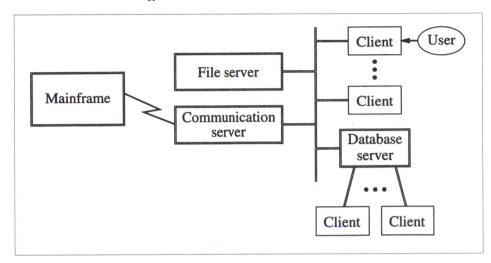

The communication server, on the other hand, should be equipped with specialized communication equipment to connect to computers outside the client-server cluster. The communication server shown in Figure 16-4 can connect to a mainframe over a dial-up or T-1 line. Specialized communication servers are available to connect from one local area network to another, from a local area network to a wide area network, or from one wide area network to another.

DIFFERENT TYPES OF NETWORKS

In the discussion above, we talked about the client computers and servers exchanging messages over a network. In open systems architecture, the network, just like the clients and servers we just described, can also be of several different types. All that matters is that it is able to transmit all the required messages at a satisfactory rate of speed so the clients do not have to wait too long for a response.

If all the computers in a client-server configuration resided in a single building, for example, within a campus environment in which buildings are less than a mile apart, they could be connected using a local area network such as Ethernet or Token Ring. The information-carrying capacity of such networks can range from 10 to 100 megabits per second, and the networks can easily connect hundreds of computers in one cluster.

If, on the other hand, the computers to be connected are spread apart over distances of more than one mile, they would have to use a wide area network. Such networks usually carry less information than local area networks—they can carry as much as 10 kilobits to 1 megabit of information per second. They may be configured using leased telephone lines, T-1 lines, or even fiber-optic links.

EXAMPLES

So far, we have discussed a variety of affordable computer and communication hardware available from a variety of vendors. We thus have the building blocks we can use to configure client-server systems to meet most requirements. These building blocks can be used in endless ways to create practical solutions to business needs. In the following section, we present three examples of increasing complexity to illustrate the flexibility of the building blocks.

Happy Combination of Old and New Technologies

The first example, shown in Figure 16-5, assumes that the day-to-day operations are already being supported by a mainframe (or a mini). That system, although perennially in need of more computing cycles and disk space, does help run the business satisfactorily.

The mainframe, however, is not adequate for decision support work, which would put an additional burden on its already stretched resources and demand a level of flexibility that the mainframe is not designed to handle. In addition, the decision support work would interfere with the production windows of the *next* batch run.

To provide decision support capabilities, we add a bit of new technology on the left in the form of a simple client-server cluster with one server. This new technology will happily coexist with the old technology and will communicate with the latter using either a dedicated line or a wide area link depicted by the jagged line in the figure.

From time to time, selected data will be extracted from the mainframe database(s) and sent down to the decision support server over the communication link. That data will be stored on the server in a form that allows the end users (for example, marketing analysts) to perform analysis, name selection, and similar tasks. After a marketing campaign has been fully *defined* in the decision support environment, predefined data sets will be created and uploaded to the mainframe where they will be acted upon by the operations software. Responses to the marketing campaign thus created will flow to the decision support server as part of future data downloads from the mainframe.

The primary benefit of this configuration is that it does not call for major changes to the mainframe side, but it still manages to provide much-needed flexibility at an affordable price.

All New Technology

The second example, shown in Figure 16-6, portrays a configuration in which the daily operations are also performed by a server on the network. This server can

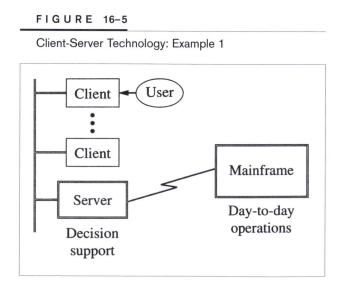

FIGURE 16–5

Client-Server Technology: Example 1

FIGURE 16-6

Client-Server Technology: Example 2

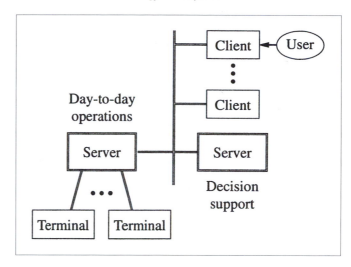

communicate with decision support servers right over the network—the link to the mainframe is not needed anymore. The operations server is connected to several data entry terminals using point-to-point lines or a wide area network.

The primary benefits of this configuration are modular growth and a high-speed connection between the operations and decision support servers. As the need for computing power expands on either side, additional servers can be added on the network incrementally. Because these additional servers will be able to exchange data over the network, they will be seamlessly integrated with the existing set of servers.

Multilocation Installation Using All New Technology

Our last example builds on the previous one to support a remote office location. The remote office has a client-server cluster of its own, shown on the left in Figure 16-7. The server there supports the daily operations of the remote office and is connected with the central server by a wide area link. Thus, the remote server could exchange information with the central operations server to provide users on either side of the wide area link an up-to-date view of the operations data.

The decision support server is not at all affected by adding the remote server. It continues to exchange information with the central operations server that is located on the same local area network.

REVISITING THE WISH LIST AND OUTLINING FUTURE STEPS

As illustrated by the three examples we just discussed, the use of new technology has made it possible for us to achieve most of the items on our wish list for decision support work. We can provide different computing systems to support the daily operations and decision support work. We can supply ample computing power for decision support work to provide adequate response time, without interfering with daily operations. Lastly, we can achieve affordable incremental growth in computing power and disk space.

FIGURE   16–7

Client-Server Technology: Example 3

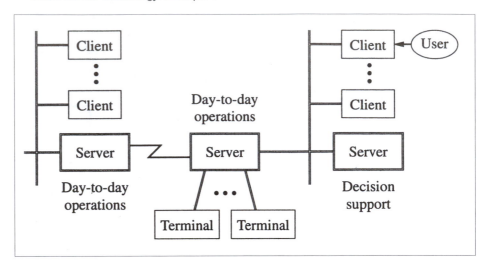

The use of new technology, however, is only one component of a complete solution to business needs. The deployment of new kinds of systems creates challenges for personnel because the new systems have very different programming and administration requirements from traditional systems.

The old systems were mostly batch-oriented, whereas the new ones are more interactive. They involve the use of new operating systems (e.g., the Unix operating system) and are heavily dependent on communication software for exchanging information with other computers.

All this implies that computer support personnel have to be retrained in the care and feeding of the new kinds of systems on several fronts, including new operating systems, networks, application software, database management systems, and programming languages. Such training is readily available from the vendors themselves or even from independent training organizations.

In addition to the training issue, the use of new technology involves thinking about computer systems in a different way, most notably, recognizing modularity and incremental growth. We need to think about small, powerful computers that can be interconnected to accomplish bigger tasks. We also need to think of specialized computer systems for selected tasks. As planners and decision makers embrace this new thinking, businesses would be better able to harness the newly evolved computer technology to provide cost-effective solutions for their ever-expanding needs.

Basic Statistics and Modeling

Chapter 17 was written by David Shepard and Bruce Ratner; Chapters 18, 19, 20, 22, and 23 by Bruce Ratner; and Chapter 21 by Rajeev Batra.

The Basics of Statistical Analysis

THE PROCESS OF DATA ANALYSIS

Data analysis is a process. It starts with observations of an event, a behavior, or an outcome that are first encoded into data (called variables), then analyzed, and eventually turned into information. (See Figure 17-1.)

EXAMPLE 1

An example will illustrate the process.

Let's consider a catalog marketer who sells woodworking tools and supplies. Catalogs are mailed four times a year to all customers. The company has 1 million names on its customer file (database). For each customer on the database, there is a fairly complete history that includes dates of all purchases, items purchased, purchase dollar amounts, and a code indicating the source from which the name was originally acquired.

The cataloger would like to know if "new" customers buy more than "old" customers. Classifying new customers as anyone whose first purchase was made within the last 12 months and old customers as anyone whose first purchase was made over a year ago, the mailer's analyst draws a sample of 100,000 names and calculates the following:

5,000 orders were received in the last month.

3,000 orders (60 percent) were from new customers.

2,000 orders (40 percent) were from old customers.

Even in this simple example, the analyst was involved in a fairly complicated and very structured process. First, observations of customer purchasing were encoded based on dates of first purchase, thereby creating the variable CUSTOMER TYPE with two values, new and old. Similarly, purchase data was encoded into the variable PURCHASE with two values, yes and no.

Finally, the resultant variables were analyzed by calculating the percentages of new and old customers among the total number of buyers in the period analyzed. The resulting information is that new customers accounted for 60 percent of sales volume and old customers represented 40 percent of sales volume.

Let's examine the process in more detail and discuss what else could have been done. The analyst transformed the observations into *categorical* data; that is,

F I G U R E   17–1

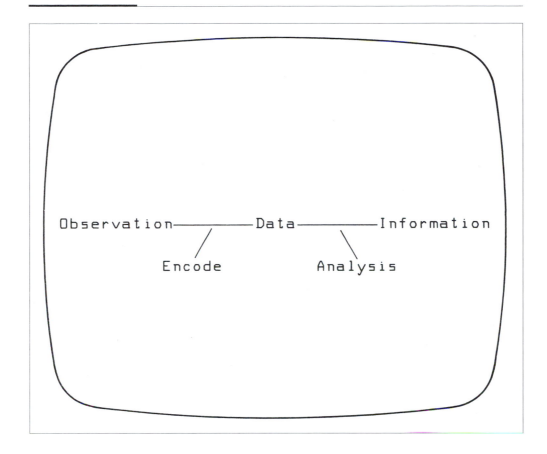

observations were classified into two distinct and nonoverlapping categories or groups. For CUSTOMER TYPE, a customer is either new or old; for PUR-CHASE, a customer either did purchase or did not purchase.

Data at this gross level of detail provides no discrimination among the customers within either group. For example, a customer whose first purchase is 11 months old is "equal" to a customer whose first purchase is 11 days old.

Similarly, customers who purchased any item, regardless of how many or their cost, are considered equal. Clearly, information is *lost* when using categorical data.

The analyst could just as easily have created *scalar* data or *continuous* data, which provide more information. The PURCHASE variable could use actual purchase amounts as its values. This new PURCHASE variable is scalar, by definition, because it satisfies the required condition: the four operations of arithmetic $(+, -, \times, \text{ and } /)$ can be meaningfully performed on the variable's values.

For example, the sum of two purchases may be added together—$5 and $2 equals $7—to produce a meaningful number. In contrast, if CUSTOMER TYPE, a categorical variable, is coded 1 for new customers and 0 for old customers, adding the two category numbers together results in a number that is obviously not meaningful.

If this scalar PURCHASE variable had been used, the analyst might have found that the average purchase amount among new customers was two or three times larger than the average among the old customers. This information adds to the understanding of the new-customer group. Not only do new customers purchase more, but also their purchases are worth more.

Hopefully, this short walk through the data process conveys the intended impression that the process of analyzing data requires a feeling for the data. However, because we never really know whether or not we have the right feeling, we need more tools to help us get that feeling, to help us better understand what we are about to analyze.

PICTURES OF DATA: STEM AND LEAF

Actually, we can see what the data looks like — in a picture statisticians call *stem and leaf*.

The stem-and-leaf picture is easy to draw, either by hand or by computer, and easy to understand. Because it's easier to illustrate the method of construction than it is to describe it, let's go to an illustration.

EXAMPLE 2

Consider a small sample of a mailing consisting of 20 observations of purchase dollar amounts. Ranking the dollar amounts from low to high, we have:

5 6 7 8 10 12 14 15 17 18 20 30 40 45 47 50 50 50 66 90

Each number can be broken up into two parts: a stem and a leaf.

The stem is the first part of the number. In this case, because we are dealing with two-digit numbers, the stem is the digit representing the 10s position. The leaves are the unit digits.

Thus, the data can be first expressed as follows:

		Stem	+	Leaf
5	=	0	+	5
6	=	0	+	6
7	=	0	+	7
8	=	0	+	8
10	=	1	+	0
12	=	1	+	2
14	=	1	+	4
15	=	1	+	5
17	=	1	+	7
18	=	1	+	8
20	=	2	+	0
30	=	3	+	0
40	=	4	+	0
45	=	4	+	5
47	=	4	+	7
50	=	5	+	0
50	=	5	+	0
50	=	5	+	0
66	=	6	+	6
90	=	9	+	0

Accordingly, the stem-and-leaf picture of purchase amounts in dollar units looks like this:

Stem	Leaf
0	5678
1	024578
2	0
3	0
4	057
5	000
6	6
7	
8	
9	0

The stems are written vertically. The leaves are put on the stems horizontally in rank order, and if necessary they are repeated according to the actual number of occurrences (e.g., 50 occurs three times, resulting in stem 5 with three 0 leaves).[1]

At a glance, we can see the overall *shape* of the variable PURCHASE. The shape of the variable is dependent on *wild observations* (e.g., 90), *gaps* (70 through 89), and *clumps* (10 through 18) in the data.

Why this emphasis on the shape of the data? The answer is that traditional statistical techniques such as regression, which will be the focus of this section, work better if the shape of the data (or variables) conforms to a specific profile. If the data does not match this profile, then either certain techniques (like regression) should be used with caution, or the data must be "massaged" or reshaped to fit the desired profile.

The desired profile is the well-known bell-shaped curve, formally referred to as the *normal curve* or *distribution*. Figure 17-2 shows a stem-and-leaf display of normal data and Figure 17-3 shows a traditional graph of the normal curve.

The normal distribution is important to many traditional statistical methods. However, in order to understand its importance, we should understand two other basic concepts first. So let's present these basics and then discuss the role the normal distribution plays in data analysis and statistical model building.

NUMERICAL SUMMARIES

The two basic concepts are the *center* of a set of numbers of data, more commonly known as the *average*, with which everyone is familiar, and the *spread* or variation in the data set, a concept few of us who aren't statisticians think much about, if at all. There are three ways to find the center and several alternatives to measure spread.

---

1. When we are working with numbers having more than two digits, we must decide on the appropriate break for the stem and leaf. This depends on the data at hand and the objective of the analysis; therefore, rule of thumb for splitting the data cannot be made. However, let's consider the two possible breaks for data in the hundreds. One break is between the 100s and 10s positions, in which case we ignore the units digit. For example, 345 = 3 plus 4. This stem-and-leaf display implies the stem is multiplied by 100 and the leaf is multiplied by 10.

   The second possible break is between the 10s and units positions. For example, 345 = 34 plus 5. This implies the stem position is multiplied by 10 and the leaf is multiplied by 1.

FIGURE   17–2

0	13
1	009
2	3333
3	1111112
4	11112223346
5	112223334566
6	0003345699
7	444445
8	3333
9	5

FIGURE   17–3

Probability Distributions

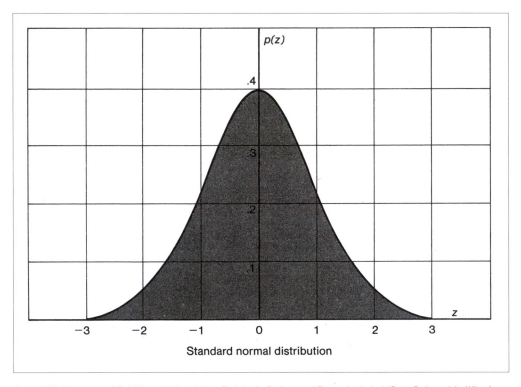

Standard normal distribution

Source: T. H. Wonnacott and R. J. Wonnacott. *Introductory Statistics for Business and Economics*, 2nd ed. (Santa Barbara: John Wiley & Sons: 1977), p. 92.

Center of Data

EXAMPLE 3

Let's consider the following set of nine numbers, or observations:

$$1\ 2\ 3\ 5\ 5\ 5\ 7\ 8\ 9$$

The sum of these nine numbers is 45. The sum of the observations (45) divided by the number of observations (9) is called the *mean*, which is the everyday average. In this case, the mean is 5.

It is also true, in this case, that the mean is equal to the number in the center or middle of the set of numbers. The number in the center of a set of numbers ranked from high to low (or low to high) is called the *median*. Thus, in our example, the median equals the mean.

If we look closely at our set of nine numbers, we will see that one number, the number 5, appears more frequently than any other number. The number that appears most frequently in a set of numbers is called the *mode*. Thus, in our example, all three measures of center are equal.

Variation within the Data

The notion of *variation* is more complicated but equally important. For example, three persons with incomes of \$49,000, \$50,000, and \$51,000 could all be meaningfully described as coming from a fairly homogeneous group with a mean income of \$50,000. But three persons with incomes of \$25,000, \$50,000, and \$75,000 are clearly not alike even though their mean income is also \$50,000.

To assess variation, we can use several summary measures.

Range

Going back to our simple example, we see that the numbers go from a high of 9 to a low of 1. We can measure the variation by the distance or difference between the high and low numbers. In this case, the difference or range is equal to 8.

Differences about the Mean

We can measure variation by observing the differences of the numbers about their center, say, the mean. The set of differences about the mean of 5 are:

$$-4 \ -3 \ -2 \ 0 \ 0 \ 0 \ 2 \ 3 \ 4$$

Thus, we can summarize the differences by using the sum of the differences, or the mean of the differences. In either case, the value is zero:

$$\text{Sum:} \quad -4 + -3 + -2 + 0 + 0 + 0 + 2 + 3 + 4 = 0$$

$$\text{Mean:} \quad \frac{-4 + -3 + -2 + 0 + 0 + 0 + 2 + 3 + 4}{9} = \frac{0}{9} = 0$$

Intuitively, a numeric summary intended to represent variation should equal zero only when there is no variation, which is clearly not the case here. The pluses and minuses, in this case, cancel each other out and cause the zero. Although canceling out might not be a problem for a different set of numbers, we'd rather use a measure that is not sensitive to this problem. To avoid canceling out, we must eliminate the minuses. There are at least two ways to do this.

Absolute Difference

The first way to eliminate minuses is to use only the absolute value of the difference; that is, to ignore the sign and use only the value. Accordingly, the set of absolute numbers is:

$$4 \ 3 \ 2 \ 0 \ 0 \ 0 \ 2 \ 3 \ 4$$

Using this approach, the sum and the mean of the differences are 18 and 2, respectively.

Squared Difference

The second way to avoid minuses is to use the square of the difference, which produces a positive number. (Remember, a negative number times a negative number results in a positive number.) Accordingly, the squares of the differences are:

$$16\ 9\ 4\ 0\ 0\ 0\ 4\ 9\ 16$$

The sum and mean of the squared differences are 58 and 6.4, respectively.

Thus, for summary measures of variation for the set of the nine numbers 1, 2, 3, 5, 5, 5, 7, 8, and 9, we have:

    8.0 = Range
    0.0 = Either sum or mean of the difference about the center.
  18.0 = Sum of the absolute difference.
    2.0 = Mean of the absolute difference.
  58.0 = Sum of the squared difference.
    6.4 = Mean of the squared difference.

Aside from the effects of the canceling-out issue, all the measures work the same way: the larger the value, the greater the variation.

To assess which of two or more sets of numbers has the greatest variation, we select *one* summary measure and calculate its value for all sets. The set with the largest numerical value has the greatest variation. Why have we taken you through all this? First, we want to demonstrate that the subjectivity or preference of the analyst can affect the objectivity of data analysis. Second, and more importantly, we want to give you a basic understanding of three very important measures that are used in a variety of statistical applications:

- *Total sum of squares*. The sum of the squared differences, used in all regression theory
- *The variance*. The sum of the squared differences divided by the number of observations
- *Standard deviation*. The square root of the variance

The concept of variation, expressed in terms of the standard deviation, is integral to the understanding of *confidence intervals* and *tests of significance*—formal statistical procedures for determining the level of confidence with which we can assert that the findings of a study are real or due to chance (i.e., what the statisticians call *sample variation*). This is our next topic.

CONFIDENCE INTERVALS

EXAMPLE 4

Returning to our catalog example, let's assume our analyst is now interested in knowing the average purchase dollar amount of the customers on the house file. The analyst draws a sample of 75 customers and calculates the mean purchase amount, which turns out to be $68. This mean value seems small, so another sample of 75 is drawn and the mean turns out to be $122. Although the analyst knows that the means will vary from sample to sample due to the nature of randomly selecting different groups of customers, the analyst feels the two means are too far apart to provide an indication of the true mean purchase amount. Accordingly, the analyst draws another 38 samples of 75 customers and calculates the mean of each sample.

FIGURE   17–4

Stem	Leaf
12	22
11	24
10	00222268888
9	0222444446688
8	00224466
7	048
6	8

Mean = 94.85
Median = 94.00
Variance = 166.75
Standard error = 12.91

The analyst creates a stem-and-leaf display of the *sample means*. The shape of the distribution of sample means looks normal. (See Figure 17-4.) The variation and standard deviation of the 40 sample means can be calculated using the following formulas[2]:

$$\text{Variance of sample means} = \frac{\text{Sum (each sample mean} - \text{average of all sample means)}^2}{\text{Number of samples} - 1}$$

$$\text{Standard deviation of sample means} = \text{Square root of the variance of sample means}$$

Note that it is customary to refer to the standard deviation of sample means as the standard error of the sample mean, and we will follow that custom from this point on.

In this case, the variance among the 40 sample means turns out to be 166.75 and the standard error is 12.91. The mean of the sample means is 94.85.

At this point, the analyst is prepared to consider $94.85 as the true mean purchase amount, that is, the average that would have been discovered if all customers on the database were included in the calculation. How confident should the analyst be in this mean of means? The analyst knows that the mean is affected by the variation of the data on which it is calculated. That is, if the variation is small, the mean is more representative of the true mean than if the variation is large. Thus, if the variation of the mean of the means is small, the analyst would have more confidence in the mean of means representing the true purchase amount. On the other hand, if the variation is large, then we would have less confidence.

Now, the analyst has three important pieces of information:

1. The shape of the data appears to be normal.
2. The mean of means is $94.85.
3. The standard error is $12.91.

To put the pieces together and establish a sense of confidence about the assertion of the true mean purchase, the analyst needs one of the fundamental rules (statisticians call them theorems) of statistics.

---

2. A statistical note: when working with a sample instead of the entire population, which is almost always the case, the variance is calculated by dividing by the number of observations minus 1.

Theorem 1

95 percent of the time (95 out of every 100 sample means) the true mean purchase amount lies between plus or minus 1.96 standard errors from the mean of the sample means.

Thus, we can create a *95 percent confidence interval* around the mean of $94.85, which includes all values between the mean plus 1.96 standard errors and the mean minus 1.96 standard errors.

In our example, we get these figures:

$$1.96 \text{ times the SE} = 1.96 \times \$12.91 = \$25.30$$
$$\text{The mean plus 1.96 times the SE} = \$94.85 + \$25.30 = \$120.15$$
$$\text{The mean minus 1.96 times the SE} = \$94.85 - \$25.30 = \$69.55$$

Thus, the 95 percent confidence interval includes all values between $69.55 and $120.15.

The theorem also allows for varying the levels of confidence, though 95 percent is a widely used standard. By increasing the confidence, the interval becomes wider; conversely, by decreasing the confidence, the interval becomes narrower. For example, the factor for a confidence interval that would include 99.7 percent of all observations is calculated by multiplying the standard error by 3.0 rather than 1.96. The factor for a 90 percent confidence interval is 1.64.

Where do these factors—1.64, 1.96, and 3.0—come from? The normal distribution! When a variable is normally distributed or nearly normal, we have the following facts (see Figure 17-5):

90 percent of the observations or values fall between plus and minus 1.64 standard deviations.

95 percent of the observations fall between plus and minus 1.96 standard deviations.

99.73 percent of the observations fall between plus and minus 3.0 standard deviations.

The center or middle value is the mean of the variable.

In practice, we do not have to draw many samples to construct a *confidence interval for a mean*. We work with only one sample. However, to describe this one-sample approach, we need to have another way to calculate the standard error of the mean:

Standard error of the mean = Standard deviation from a single sample, divided by the square root of *n*, the number of observations

We use the following example to illustrate the one-sample approach.

EXAMPLE 5

Let's say we want to know the mean age of all customers on a house file; that is, the true mean age. The file is too large to calculate the mean directly, so we pull a sample of 30 names from the house file and draw an inference from the data contained in the sample. (See Figure 17-6.)

We have the following pieces of information:

- The sample size, $n = 30$.
- The same mean age, $\bar{x} = 44.03$.

Areas under the Normal Curve for Various Standard Deviations from the Mean

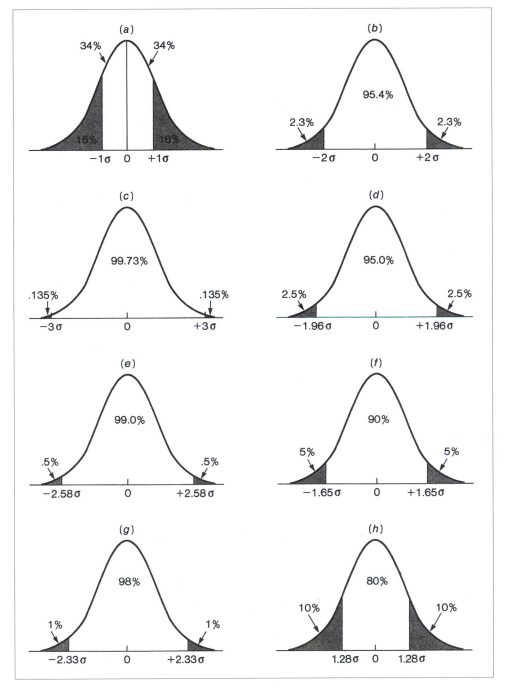

Source: S. K. Kachigan. *Statistical Analysis* (New York: Radius Press, 1986), p. 61.

- The sum of squared differences = 3,682.966.
- The variance equals the sum of squared difference divided by $n - 1$, which equals 126.9988.
- The standard deviation is the square root of the variance, and the square root of 126,9988 = 11.26937.

FIGURE 17-6

Sample from House File

Observations	Age	$(x - \bar{x})$	$(x - \bar{x})^2$
1	45	0.967	0.934
2	45	0.967	0.934
3	45	0.967	0.934
4	65	20.967	439.601
5	45	0.967	0.934
6	36	−8.033	64.534
7	45	0.967	0.934
8	56	11.967	143.201
9	62	17.967	322.801
10	43	−1.033	1.068
11	34	−10.033	100.668
12	54	9.967	99.334
13	57	12.967	168.134
14	59	14.967	224.001
15	47	2.967	8.801
16	38	−6.033	36.401
17	38	−6.033	36.401
18	32	−12.033	144.801
19	23	−21.033	442.401
20	28	−16.033	257.068
21	47	2.967	8.801
22	49	4.967	24.668
23	58	13.967	195.068
24	61	16.967	287.868
25	26	−18.033	325.201
26	32	−12.033	144.801
27	34	−10.033	100.668
28	36	−8.033	64.534
29	38	−6.033	36.401
30	43	−1.033	1.068
Average	44.03		3,682.966
n	30		
$n-1$	29		
Variance			126.9988
Standard deviation			11.26937
Standard error			2.057497
95% confidence			1.96
Range = + or −			4.032694
Range =			40.00063
			48.06602

- The standard error of the mean equals the standard deviation divided by the square root of n. The square root of 30 is 5.477. Therefore, the standard error is equal to $11.26937/5.477 = 2.0574$.

We want to use the sample mean to estimate the true mean age, with 95 percent confidence. For this, we need another theorem, which is very similar to Theorem 1.

Theorem 2

95 percent of the time (95 out of every 100 samples) the true mean lies between plus or minus 1.96 standard errors from the sample mean.

Accordingly, we can say that the sample mean age will differ from the true mean age by less than 4.03 (1.96 $\times$ 2.0574) years with 95 percent confidence. That is, we can assert with a confidence of 95 percent that the true mean age lies between

$$44.03 \pm 4.03$$

or

$$40.00 \text{ and } 48.07$$

Confidence intervals apply not only to means but also to percentages or, in case of direct marketing, to response rates.

CONFIDENCE INTERVALS AND TESTS OF SIGNIFICANCE FOR RESPONSE RATES

The theorem needed to calculate the 95 percent confidence interval for response rates is very similar to the theorem for means.

Theorem 3

95 percent of the time (95 out of every 100 samples) the true response rate lies between plus or minus 1.96 standard errors from the sample response rate,

where

$$p = \text{Sample response rate}$$
$$n = \text{Sample size}$$
$$\text{Standard error} = \text{Square root of } p \times (1 - p) \text{ divided by } n$$

Let's consider an example.

EXAMPLE 6

Our cataloger wants to test 1,000 names selected at random from a new list. However, to break even the list must be expected to have a response rate of 4.5 percent on a rollout mailing. The cataloger wants to be 95 percent certain that the list test will hold up on the rollout.

Prior to mailing the list, the cataloger could calculate a confidence interval based on the number of pieces mailed (1,000) and the desired level of confidence (95 percent). Using the formula,

$$\text{Confidence interval} = \text{Expected response} \pm 1.96 \times \text{SE}$$

or

$$\text{CI} = p \pm 1.96 \times \text{SE}$$
$$\text{CI} = .045 \pm 1.96 \times \sqrt{[(.045) \times (1 - .045)/1{,}000]}$$
$$\text{CI} = .045 \pm 1.96 \times \sqrt{(.04298/1{,}000)}$$
$$\text{CI} = .045 \pm 1.96 \times 0.00656$$
$$\text{CI} = .045 \pm 0.0128$$
$$\text{CI} = .0578 \text{ to } .0322 \text{ or } 3.22\% \text{ to } 5.78\%$$

Based on this confidence interval, a statistician would say that any response rate between 3.33 and 5.78 percent supports the hypothesis that the true response rate *is* 4.5 percent. However, this does not mean that the true response rate is definitely 4.5 percent. Therefore, the cataloger would say that any response rate within the confidence interval would support the conclusion that the true response rate *may be* 4.5 percent. If a response rate is achieved that is outside the interval, the cataloger is prepared to accept the conclusion that the true response rate is not 4.5 percent. The list is mailed and pulls a 3.5 percent response. Based on the confidence interval we just calculated, we can conclude that the true response rate is 4.5 percent.

On the other hand, we now have more information. We have an actual 3.5 percent response rate on a test mailing of 1,000 pieces. Therefore, we could calculate a confidence interval based on this information:

$$p = .035$$
$$(1 - p) = 0.965$$
$$n = 1,000$$

Standard error = Square root of $(.035 \times .965)/1,000 = .006$

$$.035 - (1.96 \times .006) = .035 - .012 = .023$$
$$.035 + (1.96 \times .006) = .035 + .012 = .047$$

Thus, we can be 95 percent certain that the true response rate lies in the interval between 2.3 to 4.7 percent. Of course, the confidence interval around 3.5 percent had to include the desired 4.5 percent response rate because the confidence interval around the 4.5 percent response rate included 3.5 percent.

How do we interpret this new information? Again, if 4.5 percent were *not* included in the interval, we could say with 95 percent confidence that the true response rate was not 4.5 percent. But, as we said before, and it bears repeating, the converse is not true. Even though 4.5 percent is included in the confidence interval, we cannot say with 95 percent confidence that the true response rate is 4.5 percent, but we can say that the true response rate may be 4.5 percent, and that the list should be tested again.

This phenomenon of a test result being different from the true result is often associated with the concept of *regression to the mean.* More often than not, regression to the mean is referred to in the context of a list that tests well but does not do as well when rolled out in larger quantities. What's happening here is that part of the high response is due to chance or sample variation. For example, a list with a true response rate of 4 percent on a test of 5,000 names might pull as high as 4.5 percent just due to chance. However, when rolled out in large quantity, in all likelihood the list will respond closer to its true mean of 4.0 percent. In statistical parlance, the performance of the list will regress back to its mean. Because direct marketers usually don't retest lists that fall below a cutoff rate, the reverse side of this phenomenon is seen less frequently. We don't often see lists that initially tested poorly do well on larger rollouts because we don't do larger rollouts on lists that initially don't test well. Our hope is that this discussion will cause marketers to give more thought to lists whose cutoff rate is within the confidence interval of the test result—and to be cautious when a test result is above the break-even point.

A clear implication of this analysis is that the size of the confidence interval is related to the number of pieces mailed. Remember, the confidence interval is equal to the response rate plus or minus 1.96 standard errors. And the standard error is calculated using this equation:

$$SE = \sqrt{[p \times (1 - p)]/n}$$

In the case where the response rate is 3.5 percent, $[p \times (1 - p)]$ will always be equal to $(.035 \times .965)$ or 0.034, no matter what the size of the sample. Therefore, the larger the sample, the smaller the standard error. If $n = 1,000$, then the standard error is $\sqrt{.034/1,000}$ or .005811. If n were 10,000, then the standard error would be $\sqrt{.034/10,000}$ or .001837, and so on.

Following this example, it is clear that if we have some idea of how large an error we are prepared to tolerate, and if we have some idea of the expected response rate, we can use the above information to solve for the number of pieces to mail.

For example, if we think the true response rate is 3.5 percent, but we want to be 95 percent certain that our test mailing will tell us if the true response rate is between 3.3 and 3.7 percent, we are in effect saying that we want 1.96 times the standard error to be equal to .002 or 0.2 percent—because 3.5 percent plus or minus 0.2 percent is equal to 3.3 to 3.7 percent. Statisticians use the term *precision* to describe the amount of error we are willing to tolerate on either side of the expected response rate.

Therefore, in this example:

$$\text{Precision} = .002 = 1.96 \times \text{SE (standard error)}$$

Then, solving for SE we get this result:

$$\text{SE} = .002/1.96 = .001020$$

and

$$\text{SE} = \sqrt{[p \times (1 - p)/n]}$$

Thus,

$$.001020 = \sqrt{[p \times (1 - p)/n]}$$

and, substituting .035 for p and .965 for $(1 - p)$, we get:

$$.001020 = \sqrt{(.033775/n)}$$

and, squaring both sides of the equation, we get:

$$0.00000104 = .033775/n$$
$$n = .033775/.00000104 = 32,437$$

In general, then, the rule for determining the number of pieces to mail (at the 95 percent level of confidence) is equal to:

$$n = \frac{(p) \times (1 - p) \times 1.96^2}{\text{Precision}^2}$$

where

$$p = \text{Expected response rate}$$
$$\text{Precision} = \text{One half the length of the 95 percent confidence interval}$$

EXAMPLE 7

Suppose the cataloger mailed not only one new list but two new lists, and suppose the second list consisted of 1,200 names and pulled 4.5 percent. Are the true response rates for the two lists unequal? Can we declare with 95 percent confidence that the true response rates are different?

What are we really asking? If we believe the two lists have the same true response rate, then we are in effect saying that we think the difference between the two true response rates is equal to zero, and the difference we observed is due to chance.[3]

In this case, the difference in response rates is equal to 1 percent (4.5 − 3.5 percent). So then we are really asking how likely it is to find a difference in sample response rates of 1 percent, when there is no difference in true response rates.

If this test of the two lists were repeated many times, there would always be differences between the lists, but statistical theory tells us that the differences would be approximately normally distributed—and if the two lists had the same true response rate, the average or mean difference would be zero.

Our discussion of the normal distribution told us that in any normally distributed population, 95 percent of all observations would fall within a range equal to 1.96 standard errors, and that 90 percent of all observations would fall within a range of 1.64 standard errors. In the latter situation, 5 percent of the observations would be below 1.64 standard errors from the mean and 5 percent above 1.64 standard errors from the mean. In situations where we want to be 95 percent sure one number is greater than another, not just different but greater, we use 1.64 standard errors as our factor to determine statistical significance.

Now the question of whether 4.5 percent is different from 3.5 percent starts to come into sharper focus. The question can now be restated to read, "Can we be 95 percent certain that an observed difference of 1 percent is more than 1.64 standard errors away from a mean value of zero?" Well, if 1.64 is the benchmark, all we have to do is divide 1 percent by the correct measure of the standard error and see if the result is more or less than 1.64. If it is more than 1.64, we will say that this difference couldn't be due to chance and we'll declare the difference to be statistically significant. If the result is less than 1.64, we'll say the difference may be due to chance and we will not declare the lists to be different.

It is algebraically cumbersome to calculate the standard error of a difference between two response rates. Because the concept is important we'll try the algebra anyway, but don't worry if you get lost.

First, we must estimate the true response rate, given the two results and the number of pieces mailed on both sides of the test. In effect, we calculate a weighted average response rate.

Remember, the first list test was mailed to 1,000 persons and the response rate was 3.5 percent:

$$p1 = .035$$
$$n1 = 1,000$$

The second list test was mailed to 1,200 persons and the response rate was 4.5 percent:

$$p2 = .045$$
$$n2 = 1,200$$

3. In statistics, the argument that there is no difference between two percentages (two response rates in direct marketing language) is referred to as the *null hypothesis*. When a statistical test indicates that there is no difference between response rates, a statistician would say that we accept the null hypothesis; conversely, when we find a statistically significant difference, a statistician would say that we reject the null hypothesis.

The average value, called p, is equal to:

$$p = \frac{p1 \times n1 + p2 \times n2}{n1 + n2}$$

$$p = \frac{.035 \times 1,000 + .045 \times 1,200}{1,000 + 1,200} = \frac{89}{2,200} = .04045$$

The standard error of p equals:

$$SE = \sqrt{p \times (1 - p) \times \left(\frac{n1 + n2}{n1 \times n2}\right)}$$

$$SE = \sqrt{(.040450) \times (1 - .040450) \times \frac{1,000 + 1,200}{1,000 \times 1,200}}$$

$$SE = \sqrt{.03881379 \times \frac{2,200}{1,200,000}}$$

$$SE = \sqrt{.03881379 \times .001833}$$

$$SE = \sqrt{.00007159}$$

$$SE = .0084355$$

Now we divide the observed difference by the standard error of the difference:

$$.01/.0084355 = 1.185 < 1.64$$

Because the observed difference divided by the standard error of the difference is less than 1.64, we can say that the difference is not statistically significant at the 95 percent level of confidence.

What if the same response rates were achieved but the quantity mailed on each side of the test were 5,000? Without going through all the arithmetic, the answer is that the observed difference of 1 percent would be divided by a standard error that would now equal .003919 and the result of 2.55 would be greater than 1.64, so we would say that there is a statistically significant difference in response rates. Again, the point is that the larger the sample size, the more confident we can be in the results. The result is no real surprise, but it is a factor that will come up again and again as we move into statistical modeling.

The questions of statistical significance and sample size can be answered through the formulas presented in this chapter; however, to make life a little easier for you, we've included in Appendix A three Lotus 1-2-3 programs that automatically calculate confidence intervals and sample size and test for statistical significance. We have included sample screens and the cell formulas supporting each screen.

TESTS OF SIGNIFICANCE—TWO TYPES OF ERRORS AND POWER

We hope the relationship between confidence interval and significance testing is apparent by now. In a test versus control situation, if the test result lies within the confidence interval of the control, then the finding is that the test is not different from the control. If the test result lies outside the confidence interval of the control, then we say the test result is significantly different from the control.

Implicitly related to both confidence intervals and significance tests are two kinds of errors. Recall that we state our findings with a confidence level of less than 100 percent but typically greater than 95 percent. Thus, if we are confident 95 percent of the time, what about the other 5 percent of the time? The other 5 percent of the time we make errors. Statisticians call them Type I and Type II errors.

To understand Type I and Type II errors, let's think about them in our test versus control situation and assume that the observed test result is greater than the observed control result.

A *Type I* error occurs when we:

Reject the null hypothesis H when it is true.

The null hypothesis states that there is *no* difference between response rates. Therefore, when we reject the null hypothesis, we are in effect accepting the conclusion that the difference in observed rates is significant. So, if we make a Type I error—rejecting the null hypothesis when it is true—we therefore are also making the error of believing that (in our test/control situation) the test result is greater than the control result. We would therefore act to replace the control, when in fact the control should be maintained.

The probability of making this kind of error is defined by the alpha level you establish. The alpha level is equal to 1 minus the confidence level. A decision to work at the 95 percent confidence level means that you have established a 5 percent alpha level. Having established a 5 percent alpha level, you are in effect saying that 5 percent of the time you may be making this kind of error. If you want to be even more sure of not making this kind of error, reduce alpha to, say, 1 percent. This will have the effect of increasing the confidence interval of the control, thereby requiring an even higher test response before the observed response rate can be declared to be statistically different—in this case, greater.

A *Type II* error occurs when we:

Accept the null hypothesis when it is false.

Again using the test versus control situation where the observed test result is greater than the control result, acceptance of the null hypothesis when it is false means not recognizing a test that really beat the control.

Now we would also like to make the chances of making a Type II error as small as possible. But here's the catch: the probability of making a Type II error, called beta, is mathematically related, in a complicated way, to alpha. As alpha decreases, beta increases. So if you want to make the probability of making a Type II error small, you have to make alpha, the probability of making a Type I error, large.

What do you want to do as a businessperson? Suppose you have a good solid business, with a control offer that makes money. You run a test of a new offer and it appears to beat the control. But what if this is one of the situations in which acting on the test results will result in implementing a Type I error? You never know when this is happening! Clearly, as a prudent businessperson, you don't want to roll out a test that is really no better than your control. One approach is to set a low alpha, between 1 percent and 5 percent, if the economics of the situation warrant such care, and not worry about making a Type II error.

To summarize, in most situations you want to be conservative—if you are going to make an error, you don't want to accept a difference as significant when it is not. In statistical terms, therefore, you want to minimize the probability of making a Type I error. Beyond lowering alpha, this can be accomplished by increasing sample size, not surprising because we know that confidence intervals decrease when sample size increases. It is even possible to state statistically how certain you are of not making a Type II error. This is called the *power* of the test. The mathematics are complicated, but the point to remember is that the power of the test increases as sample size increases.

CHAPTER 18

Relationships between Variables

With some of the fundamentals of statistical analysis behind us, we can now begin to study the *relationship between variables*, which is the subject matter of statistical modeling. Simply stated, two variables are related if they move together in some way.

Variables can be related in varying degree from strong to weak, from a perfect relationship to no relationship at all. With a strong relationship, knowing the value of one variable will tell us a lot about the value of the other variable; knowing everything, we have a perfect relationship. With a weak relationship, knowing one variable will tell us little about the other variable; knowing nothing, we have no relationship at all.

EXAMPLE 8

Let's return to our cataloger, who just tested a mailing of two different catalogs (A and B) to both new and old customers. The mailer wants to know which customers, new or old, buy more from which catalog, A or B.

To address this query, our cataloger's analyst pulls a small sample of 100 names to see if there is a relationship between customer type and catalog received.

The sample results are in Table 18–1.

From Table 18–1, we see that all new customers buy only from Catalog A, and all old customers buy only from Catalog B. In terms of percentages, we have:

1. 100 percent of new customers buy from A and 0 percent from B.
2. 100 percent of old customers buy from B and 0 percent from A.

TABLE 18–1

Catalog	Customer Type				Total	Percent
	New	Percent	Old	Percent		
A	50	100%	0	0%	50	50%
B	0	0%	50	100%	50	50%
	50	100%	50	100%	100	100%

FIGURE 18-1

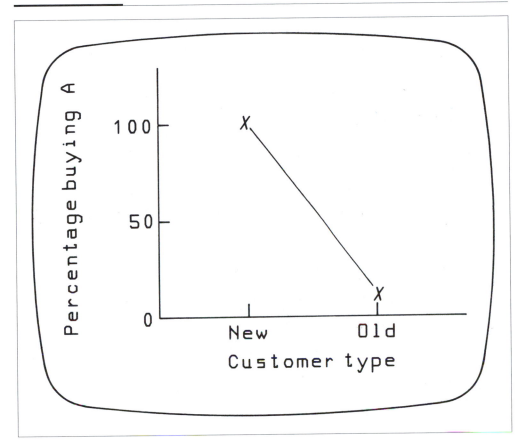

Apparently, there is a perfect relationship between the variables CUS-TOMER TYPE and CATALOG.

It is interesting to plot the percentages of Table 18−1. Figure 18−1 plots the percentages with a vertical axis of percentage of customers buying from Catalog A and a horizontal axis of CUSTOMER TYPE. We see a line with a steep slope, which tells us in some obscure way that the relationship is perfect.

Although the analysis seems convincing, the analyst wants to validate the finding with another somewhat larger sample. Table 18−2 shows the results of a second sample of names.

The findings of Table 18−2 look drastically different from the findings of Table 18−1:

TABLE 18-2

Catalog	Customer Type					
	New	Percent	Old	Percent	Total	Percent
A	500	50%	500	50%	1,000	50%
B	500	50%	500	50%	1,000	50%
	1,000	100%	1,000	100%	2,000	100%

FIGURE 18–2

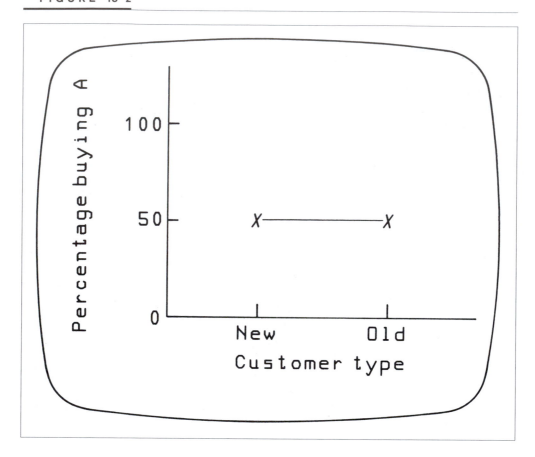

1. 50 percent of new customers buy from A and 50 percent from B.

2. 50 percent of old customers buy from B and 50 percent from A.

Clearly, there is no relationship between the CUSTOMER TYPE and CAT-ALOG; for every new customer buying from B there is an old customer buying from A.

In Figure 18–2, the plot for the percentages of Table 18–2 shows us a horizontal line, or a line with no slope, which, following the logic of the plot in Figure 18–1, tells us there is no relationship.

The analyst, somewhat disturbed by the two conflicting sample results, pulls a third and much larger sample to obtain a truer picture of the house file. The sample results are shown in Table 18–3.

TABLE 18–3

| Catalog | Customer Type | | | | | |
	New	Percent	Old	Percent	Total	Percent
A	110,300	84%	11,500	13%	121,800	56%
B	20,700	16%	76,600	87%	97,300	44%
	131,000	100%	88,100	100%	219,100	100%

FIGURE 18-3

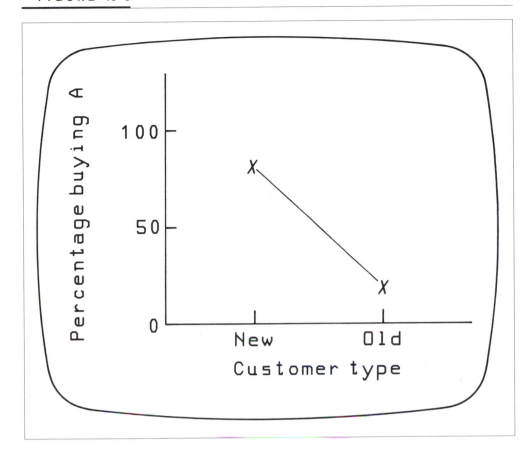

From Table 18–3, we have:

1. 84 percent of new customers come from A and 16 percent from B.
2. 13 percent of old customers come from A and 87 percent from B.

The corresponding plot is in Figure 18–3. The slope of this line is between the slopes of the perfect line (in Figure 18–1) and the no-relationship, horizontal line (Figure 18–2). It would seem that the closer this line's slope is to the perfect line's slope, the stronger the relationship; conversely, the more this line's slope conforms to the no-relationship line's slope, the weaker the relationship. How do we measure this relationship between CUSTOMER TYPE and CATALOG? Between any two variables?

CORRELATION COEFFICIENT

As you may suspect, there are statistical measures to indicate the degree of relationship between two variables. The most popular measure is the *correlation coefficient* (*r*), which is the workhorse of many statistical theories, applications, and analyses. The correlation coefficient is used either directly or indirectly in statistical work ranging in complexity from 2 × 2 tables (like Tables 18–2 to 18–3), to simple regression models, to multiple regression models, factor and cluster analyses, and more.

For categorical variables, the correlation coefficient *r* takes on values ranging from 0 to 1, where

0 indicates no relationship.

1 indicates a perfect relationship.

Values between 0 and 1 indicate a weak to moderate to strong relationship.

These values are depicted in Figure 18–4.

Returning to Table 18–3, our analyst calculates the correlation coefficient using a formula that applies to categorical variables and determines that $r = .702$. Accordingly, the relationship between CUSTOMER TYPE and CATALOG is strong.

Descriptively, we declare the relationship as strong; but is the relationship significant? Again, the analyst may choose to call the finding significant or not important based on experience. Or the analyst can defer to the objectivity of tests of significance, which address the issue of whether or not the finding of $r = .702$ is due to chance (sample variation) or is beyond chance. The former implies that the finding is not statistically significant, and the latter implies statistical significance. Fortunately, all computer programs you are likely to encounter calculate the correlation coefficient and a measure of the statistical significance of the correlation for you automatically, so we won't burden you with formulas for these calculations. The measure of statistical significance is, as you might imagine from Chapter 17, related to the concept of the normal distribution and confidence intervals. However, instead of declaring the coefficient of correlation to be statistically significant at the 95 percent confidence level, the programs produce a measure called the p value. The p value indicates the likelihood or probability of the

FIGURE 18–4

Strength of Relationships as r Goes from 0 to 1

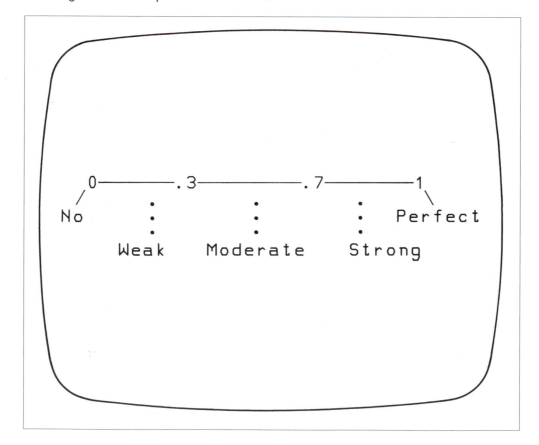

sample correlation coefficient occurring given that there is no true relationship between the variables. If the p value is less than .05 or 5 percent, then we conclude that the true coefficient is not zero and that there is a significant relationship. If the p value is greater than 5 percent, then we conclude the true correlation coefficient is zero and that there is no significant relationship between the variables.

Correlation Coefficient for Scalar Variables

To the extent that scalar variables provide more information than categorical variables, the correlation coefficient for scalar variables gives more information about the relationship. Specifically, the correlation coefficient for scalar variables indicates both the *direction* and *degree* or strength of a straight-line relationship.

These concepts are best explained with an illustration.

EXAMPLE 9

Consider two scalar variables x and y, whose pairs of points are depicted in Figure 18–5. We see that large values of x correspond to large values of y, and that the reverse is also true—small values of x correspond to small values of y. The dots or points on the graph each represent a single observation of an x-y relationship. The entire set of points is called a *scatter plot* or *scatter diagram*. Finally, you can easily imagine drawing a straight line through the points, as in Figure 18–6.

FIGURE 18–5

Scatter Plot

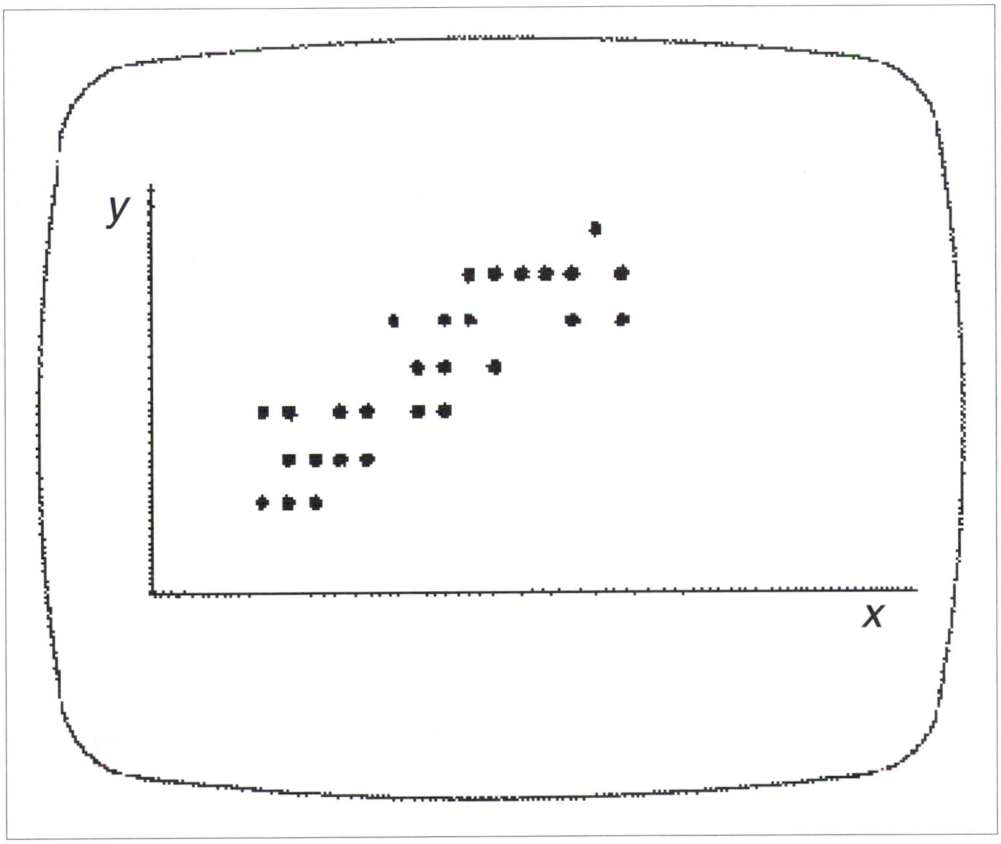

FIGURE 18-6

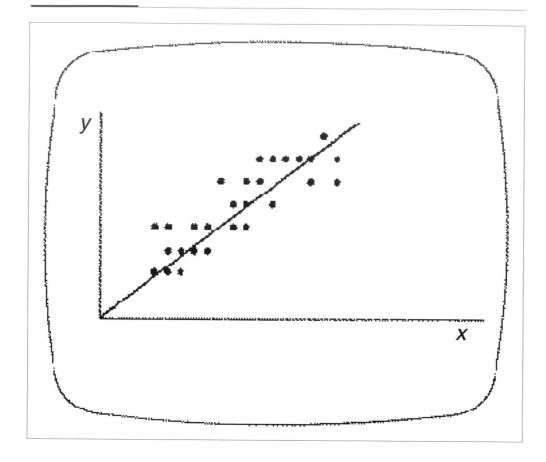

The straight line has a positive slope; that is, as *x* increases in value, *y* also increases in value. So we say there is a positive straight-line relationship between *x* and *y*.

In Figure 18-7, we have an opposite pattern of scatter points: large values of *x* corresponding to small values of *y*. A straight line could still be drawn through the scatter points, but in this case the slope of the line would be negative. As *x* increases, *y* decreases. Therefore, we would say that a negative straight-line relationship exists between *x* and *y*.

Accordingly, when working with scalar or continuous data, as opposed to categorical data, the correlation coefficient can range in values between −1 and +1 where

0 indicates no relationship.

+1 indicates a perfect positive relationship.

−1 indicates a perfect negative relationship.

Values between 0 and 1 or 0 to −1 indicate a weak to moderate to strong relationship.

Figure 18-8 depicts these relationships.

Correlation Coefficient in Practice

There are two basic issues when working with correlation coefficients in practice. First, are the data straight or linear? Pictorially, can the relationship between the

FIGURE 18-7

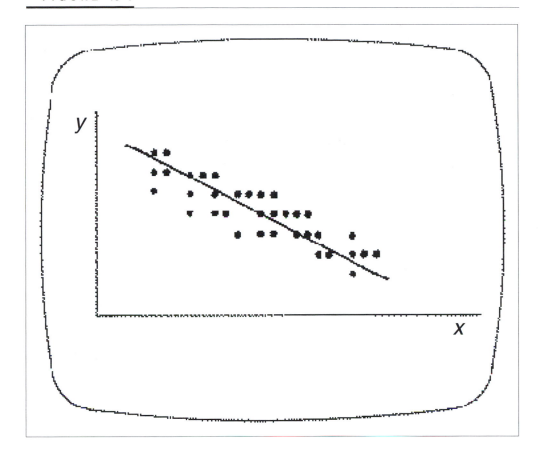

FIGURE 18-8

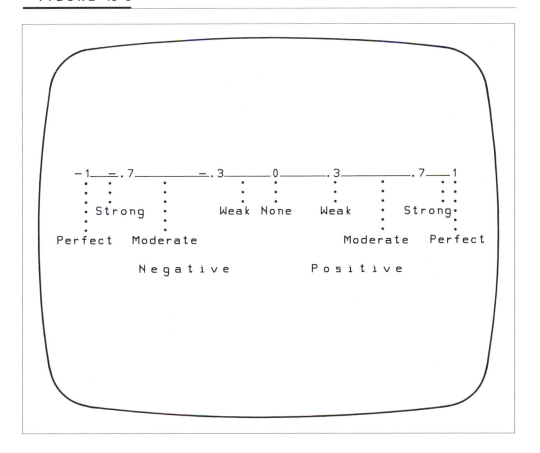

x variable and the *y* variable be adequately expressed by a straight line? Second, as previously discussed, is the relationship between the two variables significant?

Are the Data Straight?

The correlation coefficient for scalar variables should be used to measure the strength of a straight-line relationship. That is, the use of *r* is only valid when the data suggest a straight-line relationship. To the extent that the data do not support a straight-line or linear relationship, *r* can be misleading. In other words, an *r* of 1 does not guarantee that the data are straight, nor does an *r* of 0 indicate that the variables are not related. Accordingly, we use scatter plots to see what the data suggest. An illustration will make this point.

EXAMPLE 10

Consider the four sets of data for *x* and *y* in Table 18–4. Although the sets have equal means, variances, and correlation coefficients, the scatter plots clearly show different relationships. (See Figures 18–9 through 18–12.)

In Figure 18–9, the relationship is straight; therefore, we can confidently use *r* to assess the straight-line relationship between *x*1 and *y*1.

In Figure 18–10, the relationship is curved down and the use of *r* is not necessarily recommended; however, certain measures can be taken to salvage the relationship (more about this later).

In Figure 18–11, the relationship appears straight except for the wild point at (13, 12.74), which must be examined. If the point is a "typo-mistake," then *r* should be calculated after removing the point and the resultant *r* value can be used with confidence.

If the point is a valid but unusual observation, then either more data should be collected to firm up the shape of the relationship or the special situation in which it occurred should be investigated because the information surrounding the situation may be more helpful than *r* itself.

TABLE   18–4

Four Data Sets with Equal Descriptive Measures

	*x*1	*y*1	*x*2	*y*2	*x*3	*y*3	*x*4	*y*4
	10	8.04	10	9.14	10	7.46	8	6.58
	8	6.95	8	8.14	8	6.77	8	5.76
	13	7.58	13	8.74	13	12.74	8	7.71
	9	8.81	9	8.77	9	7.11	8	8.84
	11	8.33	11	9.26	11	7.81	8	8.47
	14	9.96	14	8.10	14	8.84	8	7.04
	6	7.24	6	6.13	6	6.08	8	5.25
	4	4.26	4	3.10	4	5.39	19	12.50
	12	10.84	12	9.13	12	8.15	8	5.56
	7	4.82	7	7.26	7	6.42	8	7.91
	5	5.65	5	4.74	5	5.73	8	6.89
Mean	9	7.50	9	7.50	9	7.50	9	7.50
Variance	10.96	4.12	10.96	4.12	10.96	4.12	10.96	4.12
r		.81		.81		.81		.81

Source: S. Chatterjee and B. Price. *Regression Analysis by Example* (New York: John Wiley & Sons, 1977), p. 8.

FIGURE 18–9

Plot of *Y*1, *X*1

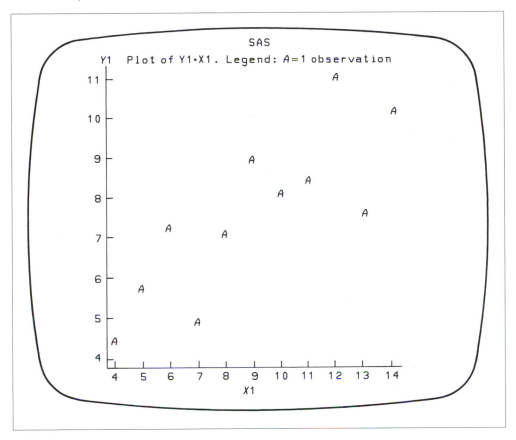

FIGURE 18–10

Plot of *Y*2, *X*2

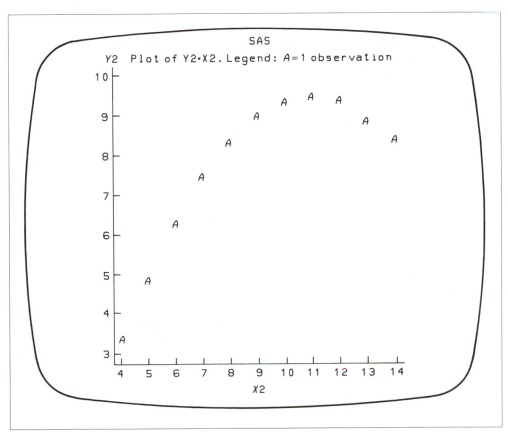

FIGURE 18-11

Plot of *Y3*, *X3*

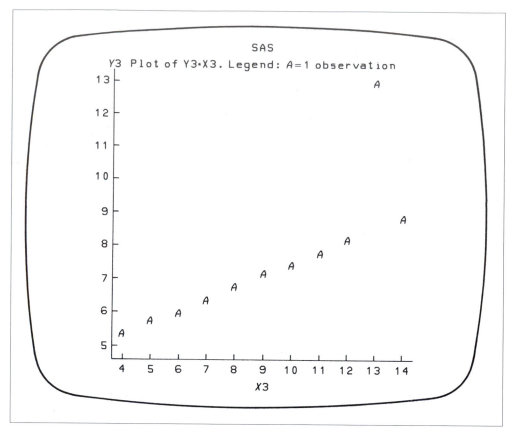

FIGURE 18-12

Plot of *Y4*, *X4*

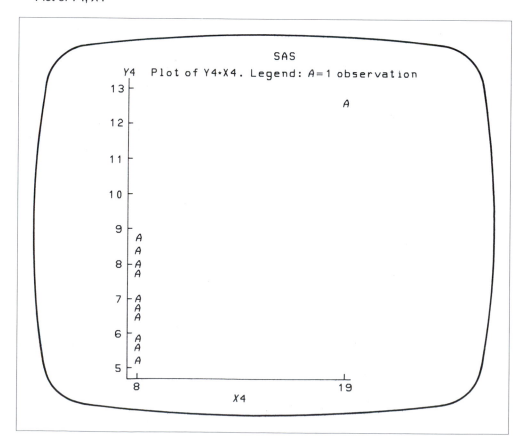

The relationship shown in Figure 18–12, which is really no relationship at all, is an example of how misleading statistics can be and why it is always important whenever possible to look at pictures of data, not just summary statistics.

SIMPLE REGRESSION

Now that we have a way of measuring the extent to which knowing one variable tells us something about the other variable, let's see how to extend this process to *predict* the value of one variable based on the value of the other variable, or from the value of many other variables. The technique is called *regression*: *simple* regression when there is only one other variable and *multiple* regression when there are many other variables.

In statistics, the variable we want to be able to predict or forecast is called the *dependent* or *criterion variable*. The variable (or variables) used to make the prediction or forecast is called the *independent* or *predictor* variable(s).

The input for a simple regression is a table, where the first column consists of data for the independent variable (*X*) we always know, and the second column consists of data for the dependent variable (*Y*), the variable we are trying to predict. The output of the regression is an equation that permits us to:

1. Explain why the values of *Y* vary as they do.

2. Predict *Y* based on the known values of *X*.

The equation is based on the relationship between *X* values and *Y* values for simple regression and on the relationship between each *X* and *Y*, and among the *X*s themselves, for multiple regression.

The Regression Line

What makes regression tick?

EXAMPLE 11

Let's return to our catalog example, where we learned that there was a relationship between the length of time our customers have been on the file and sales. Remember, new customers purchased more orders and produced greater sales than old customers.

If we define length of time on file more specifically as the independent variable *X*, the number of months since the date of first purchase, and the dependent variable, the variable we would like to be able to predict (*Y*), as the dollar value of sales within the last month, we can build a model that will relate date of first purchase to sales.

Suppose our analyst draws a sample of 15 customer records from the house file and puts the data into a table format. (See Table 18–5). Let's begin our analysis with a scatter plot of the observations, where *Y* (sales) is plotted on the vertical axis and *X* (months since date of first purchase is the horizontal axis. (See Figure 18–13).

We would like to draw a straight line using a ruler and our eye that passes through the middle of the cloud of points. Our objective should be to draw the line so a more or less equal number of points lie above and below the line. The

TABLE 18–5

X Months since First Purchase	Y Dollar Sales in Past Month
3	10
3	9
3	12
5	15
5	13
5	11
7	14
9	18
9	17
9	15
13	23
13	21
13	16
15	26
15	23
15	20
19	30
19	27
19	23

FIGURE 18–13

Plot of Y, X

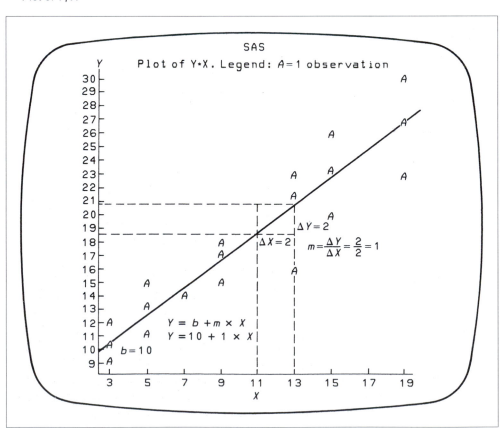

reader will recall (we hope) from simple algebra that the equation of a straight line is:

$$Y = mX + b$$

where

b = the point at which the line would cross the Y axis
m = the slope of the line, or the rate at which Y increases as X increases

We'll review this in more detail below.

In Figure 18–13, we draw such a line through the points and estimate that the line has a slope of 1.0 and intercept of 10.0. The "eye-fitted" regression line is therefore:

$$Y = 10.0 + 1.0 \times X$$

The goal of drawing a line with as many points above it as below it relates to the statistical objective of minimizing the difference between the actual observations and the estimated observations, referred to as the *fit*. The difference between an actual observation and a fitted point is called a *residual*. This leads to a very important identity:

An actual observation = A fitted observation + a residual

or more simply:

Residual = Actual − fit

Recalling the canceling-out problem when measuring variation, a reasonable way to measure the *goodness-of-fit* of a line, fitted by eye or by formal statistical methods, would be to use the total sum of squares of residuals. Accordingly, the line or equation with the smallest total or mean *residual sum of squares* is said to have the best fit of the data.

It turns out that the most common fitting rule, referred to as *least-squares*, uses residual sum of squares as just described and produces the smallest residual sum of squares. Accordingly, the resultant equation, called the *ordinary least-squares regression equation*, produces the best fit of the data and is considered the best equation. The equation for the simple regression is:

$$Y = b0 + b1 \times X1$$

where

$b0$ = a constant called the Y intercept because it is the point on the Y axis
through which the regression line passes when the value of X equals 0.
$b1$ = the slope of the regression line, referred to as the *regression coefficient*.

Most algebra texts use the letter m to represent the slope, but statistics texts use b to represent this concept.

Simple Regression in Practice

Simple regression in practice is easy and fun because it takes only five steps to complete the regression analysis:

1. Turn observations into data (variables).
2. Assess whether the relationship between the X and Y variables is linear or straight.

3. Straighten out the relationship, if needed.
4. Perform the regression analysis using any one of a number of computer programs.
5. Interpret the findings.

We will illustrate the steps with a new example.

EXAMPLE 12

Let's build a regression model to support the argument that customers who purchase more frequently also buy bigger-ticket items. Accordingly, we would like a model to predict largest-dollar-item (LDI) amounts based on frequency of prior purchases.

Again, the first step is to transform observations into data:

1. Define a period of time in which to measure frequency of purchase. Let's choose the past 12 months.
2. Find the LDI amount among customers who made only one purchase in the past year, among customers who made two purchases, and so on.

Based on a large random sample, the resulting data array consists of an independent variable X, the number of purchases in the past 12 months, and a dependent variable Y, the LDI amount. (The largest number of purchases in 12 months was 9; thus the X ranges from 1 to 9.) (See Table 18–6).

To assess the relationship between X and Y, we review the scatter plot in Figure 18–14, which reveals that the relationship is more or less straight except for what looks like a curved relationship in the lower left corner. The curve is not too terrible, and we choose for now, at least, not to attempt to straighten it out. Thus, we feel the assumption of straight-line relationship has been met, which enables us to confidently use the correlation coefficient.

A regression analysis on the data (using one of the standard statistical software packages, in this case SAS) resulted in the following output:

Variation of Y: Variance = 792.94

Total sum of squares: 6,343.55

Correlation coefficient: $r = +0.97254$

TABLE 18–6

X Number of Purchases	Y LDI
1	2
2	3
3	10
4	15
5	26
6	35
7	50
8	63
9	82

F I G U R E   18–14

Plot of Y, X

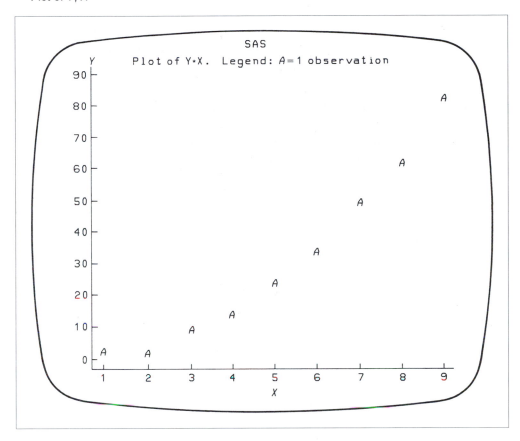

Intercept, $b0$:   −18.22

Regression coefficient, $b1$:   10.00, with p value of .001

The regression equation is

$$Y = -18.22 + 10.00 \times X$$

The large positive value of r indicates there is a positive and strong straight-line relationship between X and Y, which is consistent with the hypothesis that large sales are associated with frequent purchase.

We can obtain a second and perhaps more useful interpretation of r by squaring its value and relating it to the amount of variation of Y that is accounted for by X.

The r-squared statistic is probably the most popular statistic associated with the output of a regression model. The name *coefficient of determination* has been given to r squared, and it ranges in value from 0 to 1.

In this case, r squared is .946, or 94.6 percent. Therefore, we can say that 94.6 percent of the variation of Y can be accounted for by X. (Technically, of the variation [total sum of squares] of Y, 6,343, X accounts for 94.6 percent, or 6,000).

The intercept has limited meaning and in most cases can be viewed as a "placeholder" in the equation. When the equation is built with X values that include zero, the intercept has meaning and the predicted value of Y when X equals zero can be used reliably. In the present example, the intercept must be treated as a placeholder because the predicted LDI amount is a nonsensical negative \$18.22.

The regression coefficient $b1$ represents the change in Y for every change in X. That is, every additional purchase made (in the past 12 months) is associated with an increase in average LDI dollars (Y) of \$10.

Is this \$10 increase significant? Maybe it is due to the sample drawn, sample variation. The p value, the probability that a value of $b1$ will equal \$10 by chance only, is .001. Because this is less than the usual .05 level, we conclude that the regression coefficient is statistically significant and the \$10 increase for every additional purchase is meaningful.

The use of the regression equation as a predictive model is easy: To predict the expected largest-dollar-item amount from a customer who has made, say, three purchases in the past 12 months, simply plug in a value of 3 for X in the equation and calculate Y:

$$Y = -18.22 + 10.00 \times 3$$
$$= 11.78$$

Thus, the expected dollar amount of the largest dollar item made by a customer with three purchases in the past 12 months is \$11.78.

STRAIGHTENING OUT THE DATA

This just about wraps up the simple regression analysis of the data. However, what about the curve in the data? Since the analysis rests on the data being straight, *perhaps* the regression results will be better—in terms of explanatory and predictive powers—if we can straighten out the data to remove the curve. We say *perhaps*, because straightening out the data may not necessarily make things better. Straightening out the data involves transforming or reexpressing the data (variables) by means of arithmetic operations, which include taking logs, squaring, and raising to powers. The choice of which operation or combination of operations to use may involve more art than science.

Accordingly, we use the reexpression that raises Y to the $1/2$ power, more commonly termed as *taking the square root of Y* ($\sqrt{Y}$). The effect on Y values from the square root reexpression is in Table 18–7. The range of the new values is much smaller than the original values ($9.05 - 1.41 = 7.64$ compared with

TABLE 18–7

X	Y	$\sqrt{Y}$
1	2	1.41
2	3	1.73
3	10	3.16
4	15	3.87
5	26	5.09
6	35	5.91
7	50	7.07
8	63	7.93
9	82	9.05

$82 - 2 = 80$), and the new values are also much closer to one another than are the original values.[1]

The scatter plot of X and $\sqrt{Y}$ is in Figure 18–15. The curve is gone. The data look very straight. The new r is .99750, which is an improvement of 2.56 percent over the original r of .97254. Is this 2.56 percent improvement enough to make a difference, enough to bother with reexpressing?

Explanatory Power

An r of .99750 implies that virtually all, 99.5 percent, of the variation of the new reexpressed variable $\sqrt{Y}$ is explained by X. The 2.56 percent represents "topping the gas tank" and appears not to be a substantial improvement. Thus, reexpression here does not help in terms of explanatory power.

Predictive Power

The new (predictive) regression equation is:

$$\sqrt{Y} = .108845 + .984016 \times X$$

FIGURE 18–15

Plot of $\sqrt{Y}$, X

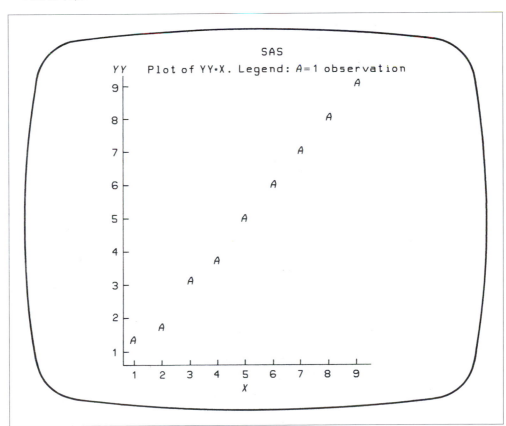

---

1. The "magic" of reexpression, which is beyond the scope of this chapter, lies in the property that the reexpression preserves the order of the values. That is, the smallest original value is also the smallest new value, and the largest original value is the largest new value. The same holds true for all the values in between.

To assess the predictive gain of the new regression model over the original regression model, we look to see which model predicts better, that is, produces the smallest residual. (See Table 18-8).

An examination of Table 18-8 shows that the errors or residuals resulting from the transformed data are clearly smaller than the residuals produced from the model built on the original data. In particular, the errors around the extreme values of X are smaller. When X equals 1 or 9, the errors are very large, which is characteristic of linear regression models applied to curved data.

In Table 18-9, we calculate the sum of the residuals squared to demonstrate that the straightened model produces a much smaller sum of squares. The sum of the errors or residuals squared using the original data is equal to 339.01. The sum of the residuals squared using the transformed data, the straightened model, is 10.79.

T A B L E   18-8

Data			Estimated Y Original Model	Error	Estimated Value $\sqrt{Y}$	Estimated Value Y-sqrt Model	Error
X	Y	$\sqrt{Y}$					
1	2	1.41	-8.22	10.22	1.09	1.19	0.81
2	3	1.73	1.78	1.22	2.08	4.31	-1.31
3	10	3.16	11.78	-1.78	3.06	9.37	0.63
4	15	3.87	21.78	-6.78	4.05	16.36	-1.36
5	26	5.09	31.78	-5.78	5.03	25.29	0.71
6	35	5.92	41.78	-6.78	6.01	36.16	-1.16
7	50	7.07	51.78	-1.78	7.00	48.96	1.04
8	63	7.93	61.78	1.22	7.98	63.70	-0.70
9	82	9.05	71.78	10.22	8.97	80.38	1.63

T A B L E   18-9

Data		Estimated Y Original Model	Error	Error Squared	Estimated Value Y-sqrt Model	Error	Error Squared
X	Y						
1	2	-8.22	10.22	104.04	1.19	0.81	0.64
2	3	1.78	1.22	1.44	4.31	-1.31	1.71
3	10	11.78	-1.78	2.89	9.37	0.63	0.39
4	15	21.78	-6.78	44.89	16.36	-1.36	1.84
5	26	31.78	-5.78	32.49	25.29	0.71	0.49
6	35	41.78	-6.78	44.89	36.16	-1.16	1.32
7	50	51.78	-1.78	2.89	48.96	1.04	1.08
8	63	61.78	1.22	1.44	63.70	-0.70	0.47
9	82	71.78	10.22	104.04	80.38	1.63	2.85
Total				339.01			10.79
Mean				37.06			1.19

CHAPTER 19

Multiple Regression

Multiple regression is used in situations where it is believed that more than one independent variable affects the dependent variable. Because in practice there is almost always more than one independent variable affecting the dependent variable, we almost always use multiple rather than simple regression.

The form of the multiple regression model is given by the following equation:

$$Y = b0 + b1 \times X1 + b2 \times X2 + b3 \times X3 + \ldots + bn \times Xn$$

where

$$
\begin{aligned}
X1, X2, X3, \ldots, Xn &= \text{Independent variables} \\
Y &= \text{Dependent variable} \\
b0 &= \text{A constant again, but this time it's impossible to visualize because the intercept is going through a multidimensional plane} \\
b1, b2, b3, \ldots, bn &= \text{Regression coefficients associated with the } n \text{ variables } X1, \ldots, Xn
\end{aligned}
$$

Multiple regression is obviously much more complicated than simple regression. In simple (one-variable) linear regression, we always know what the two variables in the model are, and we simply decide which variable is the dependent variable and which is the independent variable. In a simple two-variable regression model, it is also fairly easy to look at a scatter plot of the relationship and determine if the relationship is linear or if the relationship needs to be straightened by the use of some transformation.

With multiple regression the tasks are more complicated in practice. Assuming for the moment that we know the dependent variable we want to predict (which is not always the case), we have to make the following decisions:

1. Which variables in our database should be included in the model and which should not? A direct marketing company may have literally hundreds of variables to choose from, making variable selection a difficult and time-consuming task.

2. Is the relationship between the dependent variable and each of the variables to be included in the model linear, or must transformation be performed?

3. Is the dependent variable normally distributed for all values of the

independent variables? This is one of the basic assumptions of regression, needed for tests of significance. If nonnormality exists, transformations can be used to induce normality.

4. Without regard to their relationship with the dependent variable, are the independent variables each normally distributed? This condition is often overlooked in practice when building regression models. We'll talk about the consequence of this later in the chapter.

5. Are there variables that affect the dependent variables that we might have overlooked because they are not "natural" variables themselves but really contrived variables made from combinations of two or more independent variables? These are called *interaction variables* and we'll talk more about them later as well.

6. When we add many variables to our models, are the independent variables themselves highly correlated, causing a condition known as *multicollinearity?* If so, what effect will this have on the reliability of the models we produce?

Despite all these complexities, the procedures for performing multiple regression are a straightforward extension of simple regression. We'll illustrate these procedures and present solutions to all the issues raised above through a number of examples.

EXAMPLE 13

Let's return to our cataloger, who now believes that by knowing the age (AGE) and income (INCOME) of customers, a model can be built using these two variables to predict dollars spent in the last six months (DOLLSPENT). The analyst draws a sample from the house file, captures the three variables, and performs a multiple regression of DOLLSPENT on INCOME and AGE, which results in the output shown in Table 19–1.

The multiple regression equation is:

$$\text{DOLLSPENT} = 351.29 - .65 \times \text{INCOME} \ .86 \times \text{AGE}$$

MULTIPLE REGRESSION STATISTICS – HOW TO READ THEM

The first thing we notice about multiple regression statistics is that they look very much like the statistics associated with simple regression. We have variance and total sum of squares of the dependent variable (DOLLSPENT). We also have an *R*-square with the adjective *multiple* to indicate that multiple or many variables are being used.

The *R*-square for a multiple regression indicates the proportion of variation in DOLLSPENT "explained" by all the independent variables in the equation. In this example, *R*-square is .5480, indicating that INCOME and AGE together account for 54.8 percent of the variance in DOLLSPENT.

It is important to note that although it is desirable to have a regression model with high *R*-square values, a large *R*-square does not necessarily guarantee a better model. By a mathematical necessity of the regression calculations *R*-square can never get smaller, and it typically increases on adding variables to the model, so we can arbitrarily increase *R*-square by just loading up the model with variables until we reach a comfortably large value of *R*-square.

T A B L E   19-1

Income (thousands)	Age (years)	DOLLSPENT
$35.6	52.5	$54.1
40.9	57.2	52.4
38.6	58.0	56.1
48.7	52.9	41.4
43.9	53.0	58.0
51.2	52.5	47.1
48.1	57.4	52.5
42.0	54.5	50.8
45.9	66.3	64.9
49.8	60.2	54.0
48.9	51.1	46.4
42.5	51.7	54.7
36.4	51.8	57.1
33.3	51.3	55.4
30.6	57.8	57.7
33.5	54.7	62.8
44.4	62.6	58.7
36.5	56.3	69.9
43.0	60.3	63.2
37.4	50.8	59.1

Variation of DOLLSPENT: Variance = 4,427.65

Total sum of squares: 84,126.55

Correlation coefficient: multiple R-square = .5480

Intercept, b_0:   351.29

Regression coefficients:

b_1 for INCOME: -0.65 with a p value of .0020

b_2 for AGE: .86 with a p value of .0038

Clearly, such a model built on a helter-skelter selection of variables will not assure good predictions and reasonable explanatory power despite its large R-square. Thus, the analyst must be guided by past experience when building a regression model instead of striving for a model with a large R-square. Statistical search strategies can help the analyst systematically and logically add variables into a model. We'll discuss these in detail later.

The interpretation of the intercept, as in the simple regression model, must be treated as a placeholder in the regression equation because DOLLSPENT equals the intercept only when a customer has zero INCOME and is not born yet (AGE = 0), clearly a ridiculous condition.

The interpretation of the regression coefficients, however, requires careful explanation. Let's take the coefficient of AGE, .86:

.86 = the average change in DOLLSPENT associated with a unit change (i.e., every one-year increase in AGE)

when INCOME *is held constant*.

By this means of control, we are able to separate the effects of AGE itself, free of any influence from INCOME.

Thus, for every one-year increase in a customer's age, the predicted DOLL-SPENT increases by $0.86, regardless of the customer's income. Or, in other words, if there are two customers one year apart in their ages, the older customer has an associated DOLLSPENT of $0.86 more than the younger one, regardless of their incomes.

Similarly, for the coefficient of INCOME, $-.65$, we can say that for every additional $100 in INCOME, there is an associated decrease in DOLLSPENT of $0.65, regardless of (controlling for) the influence of AGE.

Are these associated increases in the DOLLSPENT significant? Statistically speaking, the coefficients are statistically significant because the p values are less than the usual .05. However, if any one of the variables had a p value greater than 0.5, then it would be declared nonsignificant and would be deleted from the equation by redoing the regression analysis without that variable. If both variables were declared nonsignificant, there are two options:

1. Find new independent variables.
2. Use the mean value of DOLLSPENT based on the full sample of customers to predict DOLLSPENT. In other words, when good predictors cannot be found, the mean is the best predictor.

EXAMPLE 14

Let's go a little further with our catalog example. Our cataloger would now like to build a model to identify those customers who are most likely to buy from the catalog scheduled to be mailed next month. The cataloger wants to be sure to include the best customer in the mailing. By the same token, if those customers most unlikely to buy from the next catalog could be identified, the cataloger might exclude them from the next mailing.

In other words, the cataloger wants a model that predicts response so each customer can be assigned a score indicating the propensity to respond. After all customers on the file are scored, they can be ranked from most to least likely to respond. Assuming the cataloger does not wish to mail to all customers on the file, the cataloger can use the ranked file to mail to as many names as desired or as many as the budget allows.

Unfortunately, our cataloger has never tracked responses to individual catalog mailings and so isn't able to build a model based on the results of a similar prior mailing.

However, for the last year, while learning statistics, our cataloger started keeping extra data on a 10 percent sample of customers. Two of the statistics kept included the total number of pieces mailed (TOT_MAILED) and a record of the total number of orders received (TOT_ORDERS).

Our cataloger now hypothesizes that the ratio of total orders to total pieces mailed for an individual is a good measure of a person's likelihood of responding to the next planned mailing.

This seems to make sense. It may not be true, but it seems to make sense. Remember, we said the choice of a dependent variable is not always simple. Very often, the variable you want to use is not available and you have to improvise. This is an example of improvising.

In any event, the decision is made to make the ratio of TOT_ORDERS to TOT_MAILED the dependent variable. To make life simpler, we'll call this new variable RESP.

Our choice of independent variables must be sure to include only variables that appear on both the sample file and the total customer file so the model can be applied to all customers. For both files, we have the following variables that we will use as the independent variables:

TOT_DOLL—Total purchase dollars to date

AVG_ORDR—Average dollar order

LAST_BUY—Number of months (from today) since last purchase

We draw two samples of 100 customer records from the 10 percent sample file that includes these three variables. One sample will be used to build the model and the other will be used to test or validate the model.

We always need to validate a model on a fresh sample because evaluating a model using the same data that produced the model would overestimate the model's predictive power. The data for building and validating the model is in Tables 19–2 and 19–3, respectively.

Quick and Dirty Regression

The cataloger is anxious for a model, so we perform a quick and dirty (Q&D) model regressing: RESP on TOT_DOLL, AVG_ORDR, and LAST_BUY. In other words, we expect to see a regression equation that has this form:

$$\text{RESP} = b0 + b1 \times \text{TOT\_DOLL} + b2 \times \text{AVG\_ORDR} + b3 \times \text{LAST\_BUY}$$

The SAS regression output is in Table 19–4.

We see a lot of output in Table 19–4, more than we previously discussed. We'll still focus on what we know: R-square, coefficient estimates, and p values, but we will explain the rest of the printout as we go along. In SAS, p values are shown in the column labeled Prob > |T|.

TOT_DOLL and AVG_ORDR are very significant, with p values much less than .05. LAST_BUY is not significant, with a p value of .8204. Before deciding what to do about this nonsignificant variable, let's review the other new statistics and measures shown in Table 19–4.

Analysis of Variance Table

Table 19–4 reports how the total sum of squares is broken up into parts corresponding to the:

Model—the sum of squares that can be accounted for or explained by the variables in the model

Error—the sum of squares that is unexplained by the model

Sum of squares (SS) has associated with it numbers called *degrees of freedom* (DF). DF for the model is the number of independent variables in the model; DF for the total SS is the number of observations minus 1; DF for the error is the difference between the total and model DFs.

We can obtain R-square from the ratio of sum of squares explained by the model to the total sum of squares:

$$
\begin{aligned}
R\text{-square} &= \text{Model SS/total SS} \\
&= .50495/.90722 \\
&= .5427
\end{aligned}
$$

Data for Building Regression Model

OBS	TOT_DOLL	AVG_ORDR	LAST_BUY	RESP
1	265.02	26.502	0.33333	0.05952
2	242.98	15.186	0.58333	0.09195
3	109.72	13.715	0.25000	0.06400
4	1990.12	73.708	0.16667	0.14286
5	307.82	11.839	0.25000	0.14525
6	416.04	32.003	0.16667	0.07647
7	534.89	7.429	0.16667	0.40449
8	773.58	17.990	0.16667	0.23118
9	285.65	20.404	0.08333	0.07865
10	579.76	23.190	0.08333	0.13812
11	370.43	24.695	0.41667	0.06818
12	143.26	6.822	0.91667	0.13816
13	479.35	8.410	0.08333	0.32571
14	555.40	29.232	2.58333	0.09314
15	427.35	11.550	0.91667	0.20670
16	256.63	12.220	0.83333	0.13208
17	1093.74	109.374	0.16667	0.05587
18	299.78	7.687	2.16667	0.19024
19	376.52	8.011	0.75000	0.26257
20	290.97	6.191	0.33333	0.21860
21	883.51	25.986	1.66667	0.19101
22	368.94	6.961	0.83333	0.28962
23	195.42	4.248	1.08333	0.28221
24	528.11	12.282	1.33333	0.24294
25	518.19	11.515	0.75000	0.24725
26	199.56	7.127	0.08333	0.18301
27	297.07	14.146	0.75000	0.12883
28	516.24	14.340	0.50000	0.18947
29	309.82	8.606	1.66667	0.20690
30	427.30	11.245	0.25000	0.21111
31	2722.85	42.545	0.00000	0.17827
32	1556.99	16.742	0.50000	0.52542
33	463.94	14.966	0.08333	0.16848
34	260.22	12.391	1.58333	0.12651
35	191.56	9.578	1.33333	0.12121
36	518.53	16.204	1.16667	0.18286
37	229.51	17.655	1.33333	0.07738
38	1033.03	19.130	0.50000	0.24000
39	382.97	8.510	0.41667	0.25568
40	430.83	21.541	0.41667	0.10929
41	843.90	21.097	0.50000	0.21277
42	965.85	16.370	0.91667	0.21533
43	276.14	4.315	1.91667	0.32323
44	1042.32	14.477	0.25000	0.37895
45	697.28	24.044	0.00000	0.14573
46	884.73	12.120	0.16667	0.38421
47	485.09	8.222	1.16667	0.34104
48	353.24	10.093	0.25000	0.20468
49	3092.58	44.820	0.00000	0.23549
50	1519.39	41.065	1.33333	0.16667

Continued

OBS	TOT_DOLL	AVG_ORDR	LAST_BUY	RESP
51	640.34	14.553	0.83333	0.20091
52	1965.66	23.1254	0.08333	0.46703
53	514.83	9.7138	2.66667	0.31737
54	861.86	57.4573	0.25000	0.07979
55	260.32	18.5943	1.41667	0.10072
56	267.11	7.0292	0.41667	0.23457
57	207.75	20.7750	0.83333	0.06211
58	432.63	21.6315	0.75000	0.11173
59	583.20	25.3565	0.75000	0.12169
60	311.60	8.2000	0.50000	0.21229
61	1359.44	26.1431	1.16667	0.27513
62	456.68	11.7097	1.91667	0.20745
63	236.22	11.2486	0.00000	0.13816
64	476.55	12.8797	0.25000	0.20330
65	505.85	8.8746	0.58333	0.30978
66	845.57	31.3174	0.25000	0.14439
67	358.84	22.4275	0.75000	0.09581
68	103.93	3.8493	0.50000	0.18750
69	686.72	18.0716	0.50000	0.20430
70	586.02	10.6549	0.58333	0.25463
71	673.51	13.4702	1.25000	0.24272
72	364.15	17.3405	0.08333	0.12000
73	397.88	18.9467	0.33333	0.11351
74	2038.75	30.4291	0.16667	0.34359
75	322.07	12.8828	1.83333	0.14535
76	921.64	28.8013	1.08333	0.14545
77	686.71	16.7490	0.00000	0.20098
78	549.22	22.8842	0.33333	0.12698
79	724.27	38.1195	0.75000	0.10270
80	437.21	54.6512	0.58333	0.04848
81	256.18	8.5393	0.83333	0.18293
82	595.82	17.5241	1.25000	0.18085
83	792.00	34.4348	0.91667	0.12849
84	779.18	31.1672	0.50000	0.15625
85	859.21	13.4252	0.08333	0.28319
86	1716.75	30.1184	0.50000	0.31319
87	319.88	11.8474	0.50000	0.15882
88	627.58	14.2632	0.08333	0.24309
89	774.58	21.5161	0.16667	0.21429
90	559.81	27.9905	0.50000	0.10526
91	597.83	11.7222	0.25000	0.28492
92	691.70	20.3441	0.00000	0.20482
93	1964.13	22.5762	0.33333	0.46774
94	158.01	7.1823	0.08333	0.14103
95	420.93	15.5900	0.75000	0.14362
96	1061.77	16.0874	1.66667	0.31884
97	335.43	23.9593	0.75000	0.08383
98	768.71	23.2942	0.00000	0.18539
99	673.18	15.6553	0.58333	0.23118
100	453.98	15.1327	0.25000	0.15075

Data for Validating Regression Model

OBS	TOT_DOLL	AVG_ORDR	LAST_BUY	RESP
1	1679.13	40.954	0.83333	0.18062
2	574.61	22.100	0.33333	0.13265
3	586.64	19.555	0.75000	0.17143
4	513.03	10.470	0.91667	0.28324
5	1561.91	58.859	0.25000	0.15591
6	274.26	13.713	0.75000	0.11765
7	477.19	22.723	0.08333	0.12209
8	232.09	8.596	0.41667	0.15976
9	879.43	39.974	0.08333	0.09692
10	432.25	36.021	0.08333	0.07643
11	350.53	21.908	0.16667	0.09249
12	311.95	12.998	0.83333	0.13953
13	236.54	14.784	1.08333	0.09357
14	440.33	17.613	0.75000	0.13298
15	1097.03	47.697	0.66667	0.12105
16	344.67	13.257	2.16667	0.15758
17	737.44	67.0404	2.00000	0.06748
18	319.66	9.133	1.00000	0.19774
19	1930.83	22.986	0.16667	0.44920
20	303.59	12.650	0.08333	0.12565
21	1009.29	59.370	0.08333	0.09140
22	1088.09	24.180	0.08333	0.24064
23	378.98	10.243	1.25000	0.22289
24	536.41	16.255	0.08333	0.19298
25	304.03	13.219	1.00000	0.12366
26	417.28	34.773	0.66667	0.06977
27	1080.00	30.000	0.25000	0.18947
28	501.70	3.890	0.66667	0.12000
29	376.15	34.195	1.00000	0.05612
30	817.06	28.174	0.08333	0.15676
31	1883.37	117.711	0.25000	0.07729
32	230.95	5.922	1.33333	0.24375
33	457.21	9.525	0.33333	0.24615
34	446.43	24.802	0.08333	0.10405
35	749.20	32.574	1.91667	0.10952
36	110.26	4.794	0.75000	0.14744
37	1664.19	46.228	0.00000	0.19149
38	183.75	12.250	0.25000	0.09934
39	249.64	7.801	0.50000	0.20126
40	196.55	16.379	1.41667	0.08955
41	852.11	23.030	0.08333	0.20330
42	914.48	35.172	0.16667	0.12322
43	892.33	21.764	0.41667	0.11549
44	2281.84	17.827	0.33333	0.47059
45	122.38	6.441	1.25000	0.11728
46	1800.32	47.377	0.41667	0.15323
47	752.08	19.792	1.16667	0.20879
48	448.52	12.122	1.25000	0.20670
49	756.85	42.047	0.00000	0.09677
50	536.83	16.776	0.00000	0.14884

Continued

OBS	TOT_DOLL	AVG_ORDR	LAST_BUY	RESP
51	145.07	6.307	0.16667	0.15033
52	769.18	18.7605	1.00000	0.22043
53	1092.98	52.0467	0.50000	0.11538
54	547.62	19.5579	0.50000	0.11290
55	333.49	12.8265	0.00000	0.15205
56	859.70	26.8656	0.25000	0.17778
57	426.97	11.8603	0.08333	0.20225
58	288.86	11.1100	1.91667	0.15569
59	376.68	9.4170	0.08333	0.21978
60	511.88	15.9962	0.00000	0.18182
61	1766.24	47.7362	0.00000	0.19892
62	930.93	23.2732	0.66667	0.18957
63	690.51	36.3426	2.91667	0.11446
64	554.32	34.6450	1.41667	0.08889
65	1189.95	56.6643	0.00000	0.11351
66	805.75	73.2500	0.25000	0.05238
67	227.14	16.2243	0.33333	0.07143
68	556.49	20.6107	0.50000	0.13846
69	602.23	25.0929	0.58333	0.11111
70	1156.40	22.2385	0.50000	0.27660
71	349.65	13.4481	1.41667	0.15385
72	324.02	8.5268	0.08333	0.22353
73	515.43	13.5639	2.08333	0.21839
74	347.12	26.7015	0.66667	0.07429
75	227.91	9.1164	0.41667	0.15152
76	349.74	19.4300	0.41667	0.11043
77	320.61	14.5732	1.25000	0.12571
78	447.28	16.5659	0.00000	0.14211
79	2777.47	27.7747	0.16667	0.18975
80	501.86	33.4573	0.25000	0.08621
81	1130.55	32.3014	0.25000	0.17766
82	733.18	13.5774	0.58333	0.27411
83	295.82	10.2007	1.58333	0.12719
84	1115.04	38.4497	0.25000	0.15676
85	484.19	17.2925	0.16667	0.16000
86	255.10	28.3444	1.41667	0.05844
87	234.52	18.0400	0.66667	0.07602
88	991.80	70.8429	0.50000	0.06512
89	453.94	17.4592	0.33333	0.14943
90	426.52	25.0894	0.50000	0.09189
91	513.76	24.4648	0.25000	0.11538
92	345.89	15.7223	1.75000	0.09322
93	95.99	9.5990	1.25000	0.07937
94	854.35	32.8596	0.50000	0.13978
95	846.52	16.2792	2.08333	0.29050
96	1233.51	44.0539	0.33333	0.14973
97	1363.34	34.0835	0.08333	0.19048
98	1742.23	31.1113	0.16667	0.21374
99	389.75	16.9457	0.58333	0.12500
100	309.53	8.1455	0.08333	0.23313

The ratio of model SS divided by its DF to error SS divided by its DF is the F statistic, which is used to test the significance of all the independent variables in the model. If the p value of the F value is less than 5 percent, then the model is considered statistically significant with 95 percent confidence.

Another way to interpret the F statistic is to check to make sure the value of F is greater than 4; a value greater than 4 will correspond to a p of less than 5 percent. The reason for looking at the F statistic two ways is that when comparing two or more models with each other, each may have p values of less than .05, but an examination of the difference in the F statistic can provide a sense of which model is most significant, when all models are significant.

Also of note is the relationship between R-square and F:

$$F = \frac{R\text{-square}/(k-1)}{(1-R\text{-square})/(n-k)}$$

where k equals the number of variables, including both the dependent and the independent variables included in the model. In a simple regression model k would be equal to 2. In a model with two independent variables k would be equal to 3, and so on.

From this definition of F, we see that when the number of variables increases without significantly increasing R-square, the F value becomes smaller, thus decreasing the statistical significance of the model. It is also clear for the formula that F increases as the number of observations increases.

Another way of considering the effects of adding variables to the model is as follows: As we mentioned, R-square typically increases when variables are added to the model even if they are not important; thus, to offset their unimportant contribution to R-square, we often consider adjusted R-square:

$$\text{adj } R = 1 - (1 - R\text{ sq}) \times \frac{(n-1)}{(n - \text{number of variables})}$$

Parameter Estimates Table

Table 19–4 reports the regression coefficients (called *parameter estimates*), their corresponding standard errors, t values (T for H0:), and p values (Prob > |T|).

The t value is the ratio of parameter estimate to standard error. If the t value is less than -1.96 or greater than $+1.96$, then we conclude that the true parameter or regression coefficient is greater than zero and the variable in question is significantly related to the dependent variable, with 95 percent confidence. For a t value inside this interval, the true regression coefficient is zero and there is no relationship between the variable and the dependent variable.

Often it is useful to know which variables in the model are most important. The parameter estimates or regression coefficients cannot be used because the units are not comparable. In our example, we have dollars (for TOT_DOLL), number of orders (for AVG_ORDR), and number of months (for LAST_BUY) with a coefficient of .000141 for TOT_DOLL versus .002589 for LAST_BUY. We cannot say LAST_BUY contributes more than TOT_DOLL in predicting RESP on the basis of the apples-to-oranges comparison of the size of the coefficients.

One way around this problem is to use standard coefficients (standardized estimates), which are the regression coefficients converted into a common unit by multiplying the coefficient by the standard deviation of the independent variable divided by the standard deviation of the dependent variable. Thus, TOT_DOLL

T A B L E   19–4

SAS					

Model: MODEL1
Dependent Variable: RESP

Analysis of Variance

Source	DF	Sum of Squares	Mean Square	F Value	Prob>F
Model	3	0.50495	0.16832	40.168	0.0001
Error	96	0.40227	0.00419		
C Total	99	0.90722			

Root MSE	0.06473	R-square	0.5566	
Dep Mean	0.19586	Adj R-sq	0.5427	
C.V.	33.05019			

Parameter Estimates

Variable	DF	Parameter Estimate	Standard Error	T for H0: Parameter = 0	Prob>|T|
INTERCEP	1	0.194386	0.01508134	12.889	0.0001
TOT_DOLL	1	0.000141	0.00001443	9.780	0.0001
AVG_ORDR	1	−0.004708	0.00051457	−9.150	0.0001
LAST_BUY	1	0.002589	0.01137582	0.228	0.8204

Variable	DF	Standardized Estimate
INTERCEP	1	0.00000000
TOT_DOLL	1	0.78196276
AVG_ORDR	1	−0.72689782
LAST_BUY	1	0.01589971

and LAST_BUY have standardized coefficients of .7819 and .0158, respectively, which indicate that the former is roughly 49 times more important than the latter.

More Quick and Dirty Regression

Now that our review of the regression output from an SAS program is complete, let's review the regression equation and decide what to do about that nonsignificant variable LAST_BUY.

The regression equation derived from Table 19–4 is:

$$RESP = .19 + .00014 \times TOT\_DOLL - .0047 \times AVG\_ORDR + .0025 \times LAST\_BUY$$

As we said before, the model includes TOT_DOLL and AVG_ORDR, and both variables are significant with p values of .01 percent. But the LAST_BUY variable has a t value of less than 2 and a p value of .82. Clearly, the variable should not be used according to either of our rules: that t should be greater than 2, or that the p value should be less than .05. However, before redoing the model with this variable removed, let's note that the model has an R-square of 55.66 percent and an F value of 40.1. We'll want to compare these values with the values produced from a new model with only two independent variables,

TABLE 19-5

SAS

Model: MODEL1
Dependent Variable: RESP

Analysis of Variance

Source	DF	Sum of Squares	Mean Square	F Value	Prob>F
Model	2	0.50473	0.25237	60.820	0.0001
Error	97	0.40249	0.00415		
C Total	99	0.90722			

Root MSE	0.06442	R-square	0.5563	
Dep Mean	0.19586	Adj R-sq	0.5472	
C.V.	33.88825			

Parameter Estimates

Variable	DF	Parameter Estimate	Standard Error	T for H0: Parameter = 0	Prob>|T|
INTERCEP	1	0.196591	0.01150215	17.092	0.0001
TOT_DOLL	1	0.000141	0.00001421	9.897	0.0001
AVG_ORDR	1	−0.004718	0.00051005	−9.251	0.0001

Variable	DF	Standardized Estimate
INTERCEP	1	0.00000000
TOT_DOLL	1	0.77937273
AVG_ORDR	1	−0.72849090

TOT_DOLL and AVG_ORDR. Table 19–5 shows the results of running the model with the variable LAST_BUY removed.

The new model has this form:

$$RESP = .19 + .00014 \times TOT\_DOLL - .0047 \times AVG\_ORDR$$

In this case, the regression coefficients did not change with the removal of the nonsignificant variable LAST_BUY. We see that the two variables are still significant. Their t values are well above 2, and their p values are below the .01 percent level. The F value has improved from 40.2 to 60.8, indicating that this model in total is stronger, in a statistical sense, than the prior model. The reason for this improvement is that the R-square value has not changed appreciably; its value is still 55.6 percent, but this R-square has been achieved by a model with one less variable, and you'll recall from our previous discussion that the F value tends to increase as the number of variables decreases.

So we have a good model, but should we stop here? Remember, this was a quick and dirty model; it was built with almost no examination of the data. We did not check to see if the independent variables were normally distributed. We did not check to see if the relationship between the independent variables and the dependent variables was linear or straight. We did not probe for interaction variables. We did not check for multicollinearity. We did a quick and dirty job — but we still got a pretty good model. Let's see what a better, more thorough, job would produce.

REGRESSION BUILT WITH CARE

A thorough regression analysis often begins with an examination of a correlation matrix. A correlation matrix simply consists of correlation coefficients and p values for each combination of all independent and dependent variables.

Step 1 — Examination of the Correlation Matrix

Table 19–6 shows a correlation matrix of the four variables in our example.

In practice, the analyst will scan the correlation matrix to get an idea of which independent variables appear to be related to the dependent variable. The reason for doing this is that in most real situations, there may be hundreds of potential independent variables, and it's literally impossible to deal with all of them thoroughly. So the analyst looks to include, for further analysis, only those variables that seem to have a good chance of being related to the dependent variable, that is, a good chance of entering a final regression model.

An examination of Table 19–6 indicates that the variables TOT_DOLL and AVG_ORDR both have relatively high correlation coefficients (.39032 and −.32488) with the dependent variable. The p values of both are less than .05, indicating statistical significance.

On the other hand, LAST_BUY has a relatively low correlation coefficient (.09807) and its p value is greater than .05.

At this point, the analyst looking at the correlation matrix may guess that LAST_BUY will fall out of the picture, but we'll try to salvage this variable. Maybe the variable is correlated with response, but the relationship is not linear, and this could account for the low correlation. We'll see.

Step 2 — Normalization of All Variables

After deciding which variables are worthy of further consideration, the next step is to check to see if the variables in their raw form are more or less normally distributed. Does their shape correspond to the shape of the bell-shaped curve or normal distribution? If not, what can we do to make their shape appear normal?

T A B L E   19–6

SAS CORRELATION ANALYSIS 4 'VAR' Variables: RESP TOT_DOLL AVG_ORDR LAST_BUY Pearson Correlation Coefficients/Prob > |R| under Ho: Rho = 0/N = 100				
	RESP	**TOT_DOLL**	**AVG_ORDR**	**LAST_BUY**
RESP	1.00000	0.39032	−0.32488	−0.09807
	0.0	0.0001	0.0010	0.3317
TOT_DOLL	0.39032	1.00000	0.57381	−0.29063
	0.0001	0.0	0.0001	0.0034
AVG_ORDR	−0.32488	0.57381	1.00000	−0.15539
	0.0010	0.0001	0.0	0.1226
LAST_BUY	−0.09807	−0.29063	−0.15539	1.00000
	0.3317	0.0034	0.1226	0.0

In Figures 19–1 through 19–4, we see stem-and-leaf pictures of all four variables.

In each case, we see that the distributions are skewed toward the lower numbers in the stem. On the right-hand side of each figure we see something called a *boxplot*. The boxplot is simply an aid to answer the question, "Is the distribution normal or skewed?" When the bar with the stars on each end (*------*) is in the middle of the box, the distribution is normal. As you can see, these distributions are not normal.

So we'll normalize them. Distributions are normalized by transforming the original variable into some other variable. Often, this is done by replacing the original variable with its logarithm or by taking the square or the square root of the original variable. There are lots of ways to do this and these techniques are part of the statistician's bag of tricks. It really doesn't matter which method of transformation is used; what matters is that the final shape of the variable be as normal as possible before entering the regression mode. Having said that, we should keep in mind the fact that a final regression model may have to be applied to a customer file of millions of names, and the more complicated the model, the more difficult it may be for programmers, who are not statisticians, and who may not have the programming tools required to deal with logs, to score the database. We'll come back to this point in later chapters.

In Figures 19–5 to 19–8 we see the effect of transforming each variable into its logarithm. (We used logs to the base 10, but natural logs would have accomplished the same objective.) The result is that the distribution of each variable comes closer to the shape of the normal distribution. The importance of this to the final regression model will become clearer in a few minutes.

Step 3—Checking for Linearity

To check for linearity or straight-line relationships, we ask the computer program (again we are using SAS) to produce scatter diagrams of the relationships between each independent variable and the dependent variable.

In Figure 19–9, we see the relationship between RESP and TOT_DOLL. The relationship isn't great, but it seems to be linear and positive. In other words, an argument could be made that a straight line drawn through the points fits the points just as well as any curved line. To illustrate this observation, we've drawn a straight line through the scatter points.

Figure 19–10 plots the relationship between AVG_ORDR and RESP. The relationship is clearly negative. The negative correlation sign told us this, and the scatter plot simply describes the relationship pictorially. If we assume for the moment that the three data points that stand apart from the rest of the data points are real, not errors, then we could argue that a curved line fits the points better than a straight line and some straightening is required.

Figure 19–11 simply reinforces the argument that there is no relationship between LAST_BUY and RESP.

At this point, you might be curious about what scatter plots of the transformed variables might look like and about what effect transforming the variables has on the question of linearity.

To assist in this analysis, we should also produce a new correlation matrix using the transformed variables. The new correlation matrix is shown in Table 19–7.

If we compare the results of Table 19–6 with those of Table 19–7, we note some interesting things:

SAS Univariate Procedure

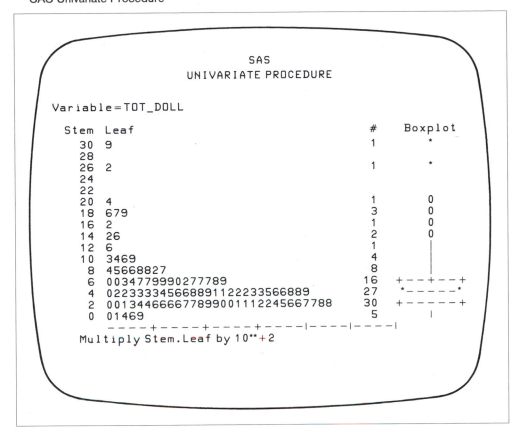

```
                        SAS
                UNIVARIATE PROCEDURE


Variable=TOT_DOLL

   Stem  Leaf                                      #   Boxplot
     30  9                                         1      *
     28
     26  2                                         1      *
     24
     22
     20  4                                         1      0
     18  679                                       3      0
     16  2                                         1      0
     14  26                                        2      0
     12  6                                         1      |
     10  3469                                      4      |
      8  45668827                                  8      |
      6  0034779990277789                         16   +--+--+
      4  022333345668891122233566889             27   *-----*
      2  00134466667789900111122456677 88        30   +-----+
      0  01469                                     5      |
         ----+----+----+----|----|----|
         Multiply Stem.Leaf by 10**+2
```

SAS Univariate Procedure

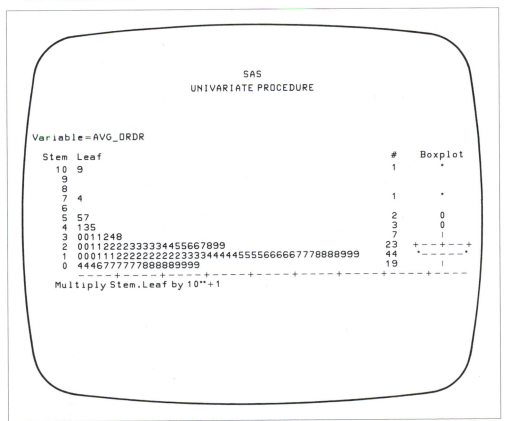

```
                        SAS
                UNIVARIATE PROCEDURE


Variable=AVG_ORDR

   Stem  Leaf                                      #   Boxplot
     10  9                                         1      *
      9
      8
      7  4                                         1      *
      6
      5  57                                        2      0
      4  135                                       3      0
      3  0011248                                   7      |
      2  00112222333334455667899                  23   +--+--+
      1  00011122222222223333444445555666667778888999  44   *-----*
      0  4446777777888889999                      19      |
         ----+----+----+----+----+----+----+----
         Multiply Stem.Leaf by 10**+1
```

FIGURE 19–3

SAS Univariate Procedure

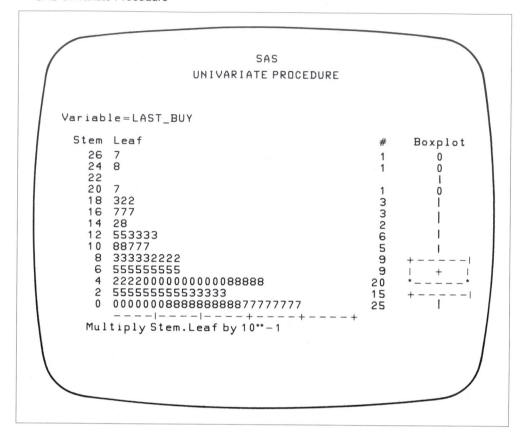

```
                              SAS
                    UNIVARIATE PROCEDURE


     Variable=LAST_BUY

        Stem  Leaf                                      #     Boxplot
         26   7                                         1        0
         24   8                                         1        0
         22                                                      |
         20   7                                         1        0
         18   322                                       3        |
         16   777                                       3        |
         14   28                                        2        |
         12   553333                                    6        |
         10   88777                                     5        |
          8   333332222                                 9     +-----|
          6   555555555                                 9     |  +  |
          4   22220000000000088888                     20     *-----*
          2   555555555533333                          15     +-----|
          0   00000008888888888877777777               25     |
             ----|----|----+----+----+
             Multiply Stem.Leaf by 10**-1
```

FIGURE 19–4

SAS Univariate Procedure

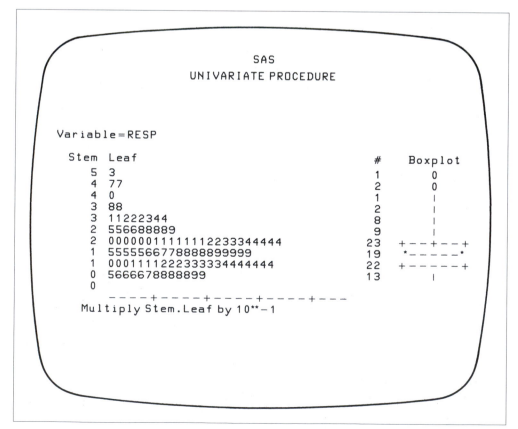

```
                              SAS
                    UNIVARIATE PROCEDURE


     Variable=RESP

        Stem  Leaf                                      #     Boxplot
          5   3                                         1        0
          4   77                                        2        0
          4   0                                         1        |
          3   88                                        2        |
          3   11222344                                  8        |
          2   556688889                                 9        |
          2   00000011111112233344444                  23     +--+--+
          1   5555566778888899999                      19     *-----*
          1   0001111222333334444444                   22     +-----+
          0   5666678888899                            13        |
          0
             ----+----+----+----+---
             Multiply Stem.Leaf by 10**-1
```

SAS Univariate Procedure

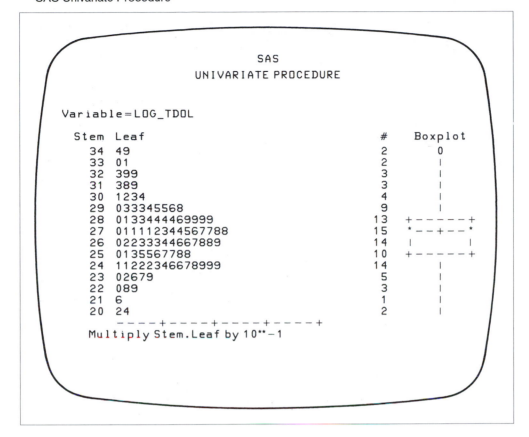

```
                              SAS
                      UNIVARIATE PROCEDURE


      Variable=LOG_TDOL

        Stem  Leaf                                #   Boxplot
         34   49                                  2      0
         33   01                                  2      |
         32   399                                 3      |
         31   389                                 3      |
         30   1234                                4      |
         29   033345568                           9      |
         28   0133444469999                      13   + - - - - +
         27   011112344567788                    15   * - - + - - *
         26   02233344667889                     14   |         |
         25   0135567788                         10   + - - - - +
         24   11222346678999                     14      |
         23   02679                               5      |
         22   089                                 3      |
         21   6                                   1      |
         20   24                                  2      |
              - - - + - - - - + - - - - + - - - - +
              Multiply Stem.Leaf by 10**-1
```

SAS Univariate Procedure

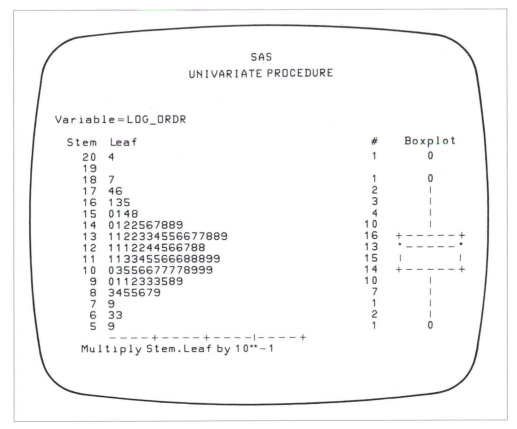

```
                              SAS
                      UNIVARIATE PROCEDURE


      Variable=LOG_ORDR

        Stem  Leaf                                #   Boxplot
         20   4                                   1      0
         19
         18   7                                   1      0
         17   46                                  2      |
         16   135                                 3      |
         15   0148                                4      |
         14   0122567889                         10      |
         13   1122334556677889                   16   + - - - - +
         12   1112244566788                      13   * - - - - - *
         11   113345566688899                    15   |         |
         10   03556677778999                     14   + - - - - +
          9   0112333589                         10      |
          8   3455679                             7      |
          7   9                                   1      |
          6   33                                  2      |
          5   9                                   1      0
              - - - + - - - - + - - - - | - - - - +
              Multiply Stem.Leaf by 10**-1
```

FIGURE 19–7

SAS Univariate Procedure

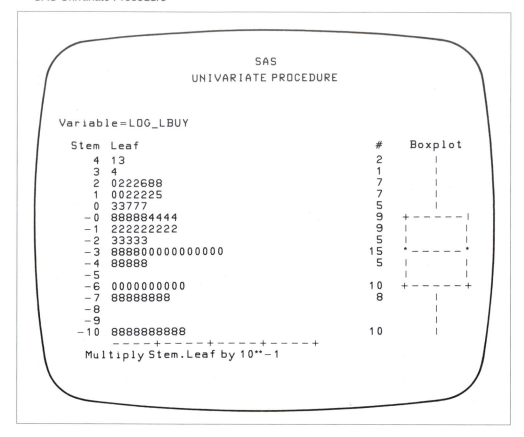

```
                              SAS
                      UNIVARIATE PROCEDURE


      Variable=LOG_LBUY

        Stem Leaf                                    #   Boxplot
           4 13                                      2     |
           3 4                                       1     |
           2 0222688                                 7     |
           1 0022225                                 7     |
           0 33777                                   5     |
          -0 888884444                               9   +-----|
          -1 222222222                               9   |     |
          -2 33333                                   5   |     |
          -3 888800000000000                        15   *-----*
          -4 88888                                   5   |     |
          -5                                             |
          -6 0000000000                              10  +-----+
          -7 88888888                                8     |
          -8                                               |
          -9                                               |
         -10 8888888888                              10    |
             ----+----+----+----+
             Multiply Stem.Leaf by 10**-1
```

FIGURE 19–8

SAS Univariate Procedure

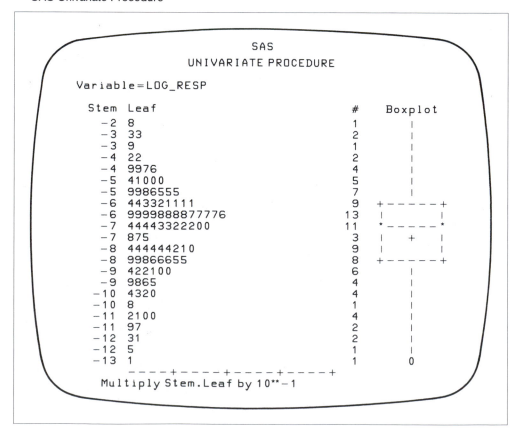

```
                              SAS
                      UNIVARIATE PROCEDURE
      Variable=LOG_RESP

        Stem Leaf                                    #   Boxplot
          -2 8                                       1     |
          -3 33                                      2     |
          -3 9                                       1     |
          -4 22                                      2     |
          -4 9976                                    4     |
          -5 41000                                   5     |
          -5 9986555                                 7     |
          -6 443321111                               9   +-----+
          -6 9999888877776                          13   |     |
          -7 44443322200                            11   *-----*
          -7 875                                     3   |  +  |
          -8 444444210                               9   |     |
          -8 99866655                                8   +-----+
          -9 422100                                  6     |
          -9 9865                                    4     |
         -10 4320                                    4     |
         -10 8                                        1    |
         -11 2100                                     4    |
         -11 97                                       2    |
         -12 31                                       2    |
         -12 5                                        1    |
         -13 1                                        1    0
             ----+----+----+----+
             Multiply Stem.Leaf by 10**-1
```

FIGURE 19–9

Plant of RESP, TOT_DOLL

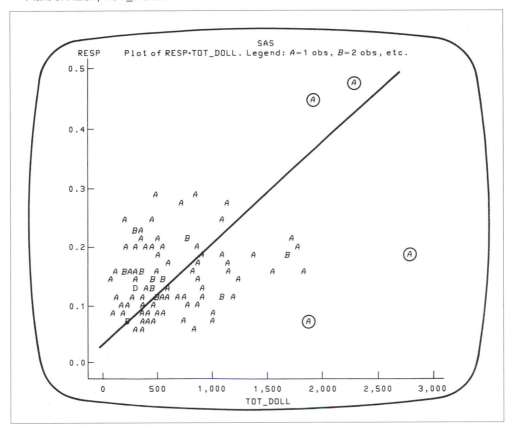

FIGURE 19–10

Plot of RESP, AVG_ORDER

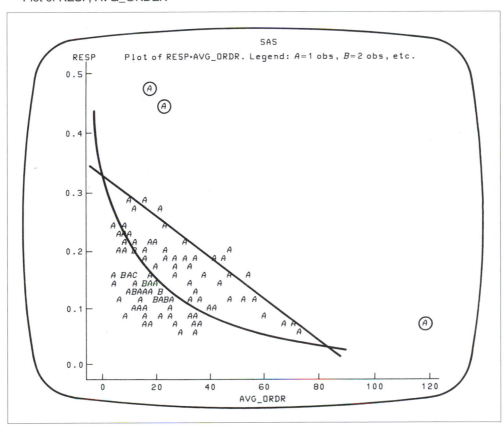

F I G U R E   19–11

Plot of RESP, LAST_BUY

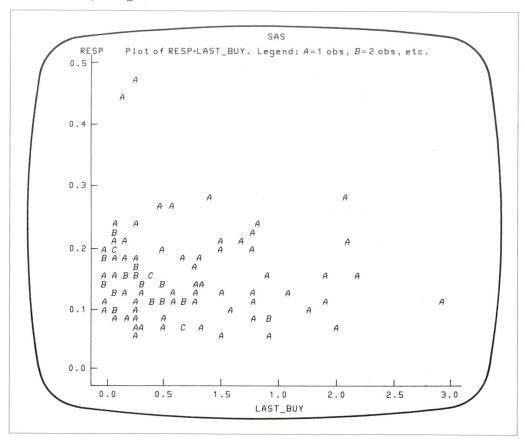

T A B L E   19–7

	LOG_RESP	LOG_TDOL	LOG_ORDR	LOG_LBUY
SAS				
CORRELATION ANALYSIS				
4 'VAR' Variables: LOG_RESP LOG_TDOL LOG_ORDR LOG_LBUY				
Pearson Correlation Coefficients / Prob > |R| under Ho: Rho = 0				
/ Number of Observations				
LOG_RESP	1.00000	0.30066	−0.38477	−0.16945
	0.0	0.0024	0.0001	0.1064
LOG_TDOL	0.30066	1.00000	0.73874	−0.28732
	0.0024	0.0	0.0001	0.0055
	100	100	100	92
LOG_ORDR	−0.38477	0.73874	1.00000	−0.14667
	0.0001	0.0001	0.0	0.1630
	100	100	100	92
LOG_LBUY	0.16945	−0.28732	−0.14667	1.00000
	0.1064	0.0055	0.1630	0.0
	92	92	92	92

- The correlation coefficient between RESP and TOT_DOLL decreased from .39032 to .30066.
- The correlation coefficient between RESP and AVG_ORDR increased from −.32488 to −.38477 (the direction sign can be ignored).
- The correlation coefficient between RESP and LAST_BUY also increased from −.09807 to −.16945.

The decrease in correlation between RESP and TOT_DOLL suggests that we might have been better off by not transforming the data. However, even though we lost some "correlation" points from TOT_DOLL, we prefer to use relationships that are symmetrical or approximate the normal distribution because the underlying mathematics of regression analysis assumes linearity of all variables with the dependent variable, which is enhanced when the variables are as close to a normal distribution as possible. Also, models built on variables that do not violate these assumptions have a better chance of holding up in practice.

Another reason for sticking with variables that conform more closely to the normal distribution assumption is that, to the extent that the normality assumption is violated, the interpretation of the t and F statistics becomes difficult. In other words, the ts might not be as reliable estimates of significance as we assume them to be, and since variables are evaluated on the basis of their t scores, it's important that their interpretation be correct.

Now let's look at the scatter plots of the transformed variables.

In Figure 19–12, we see the relationship between LOG_TDOL and

FIGURE 19–12

Plot of LOG_RESP, LOG_TDOL

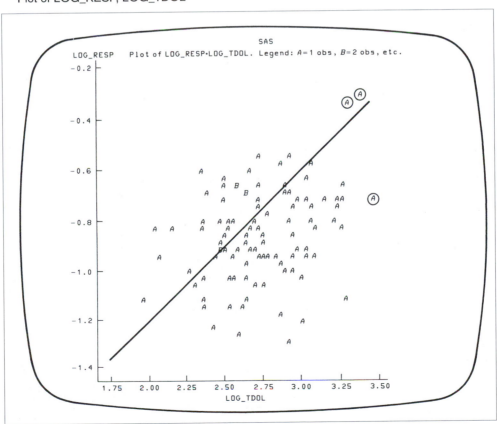

LOG_RESP. Compared with the raw data relationship shown in Figure 19–9, we see that the extreme values of response are somewhat closer to the rest of the data points, which is a function of the log transformation. To the naked eye it appears that the relationship is a bit more straight, but the difference does not appear to be significant.

We see a bigger difference when we compare Figure 19–13 with Figure 19–10. Here the transformations have clearly resulted in a straighter relationship between LOG_ORDR and LOG_RESP. This example points to a very interesting and valuable conclusion: *reexpressing most of the time normalizes and straightens the data simultaneously*. This means that by taking care of one problem, normality, most of the time you will take care of the second problem, the linear relationship assumption of regression.

Finally, the transformation of the LAST_BUY variable, Figure 19–14, doesn't make very much difference. It's getting close to the time when we should disregard this variable from further consideration.

RERUNNING THE MODEL

Now we're ready to build the model using the transformed variables. The first model we'll try will take the form:

$$LOG\_RESP = b0 + b1 \times LOG\_TDOL + b2 \times LOG\_ORDR + b3 \times LOG\_LBUY$$

FIGURE 19–13

Plot of LOG_RESP, LOG_ORDR

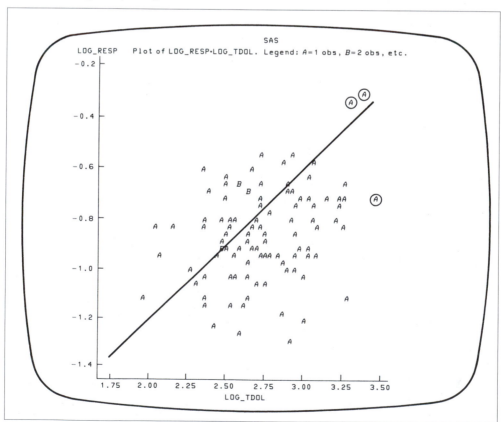

F I G U R E   19–14

Plot of LOG_RESP, LOG_LBUY

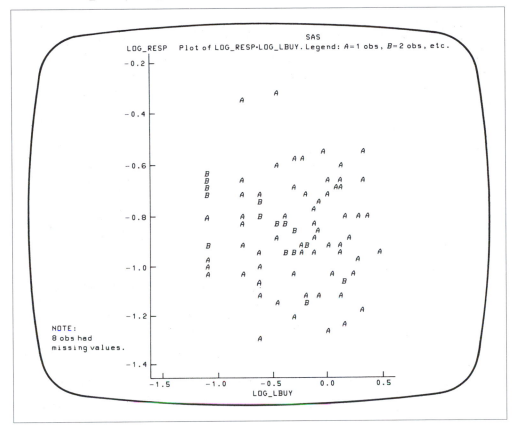

The regression printout (see Table 19–8) for this three-variable model shows a *t* value close to (but still less than) 2 for the variable LOG_LBUY, and a correspondingly large *p* value. The *p* value of the transformed variable is much smaller than before but is still greater than the .05 or 5 percent rule we established for entry into a model, so we'll drop this variable and run the model again with only two transformed variables.

Rerunning the model without LOG_LBUY results in the following model (see Table 19–9):

$$\text{LOG\_RESP} = -1.89 + .084 \times \text{LOG\_TDOL} - 0.959 \times \text{LOG\_ORDR}$$

Both transformed variables are very significant, with high *t*s and low *p* values. The *R*-square for this model is 96 percent, which represents a large improvement over the Q&D model's *R*-square of 55 percent.

Based on *R*-square values, we may be tempted to say that the carefully built model is clearly better than the Q&D model because its *R*-square is larger. However, we cannot say this for two reasons.

First, a model with a larger *R*-square would be better than a competing model with a smaller *R*-square *provided* that the dependent variables were the same for both models. To compare models using different variables is, in effect, making the proverbial comparison of apples and oranges. And a transformed variable is equivalent to a different variable.

T A B L E   19–8

SAS

Model: MODEL1
Dependent Variable: LOG_RESP

Analysis of Variance

Source	DF	Sum of Squares	Mean Square	F Value	Prob>F
Model	3	4.60627	1.53542	1052.486	0.0001
Error	89	0.12984	0.00146		
C Total	92	4.73610			

Root MSE		0.03819	R-square	0.9726	
Dep Mean		−0.76149	Adj R-sq	0.9717	
C.V.		−5.01583			

Parameter Estimates

Variable	DF	Parameter Estimate	Standard Error	T for H0: Parameter = 0	Prob>ITI
INTERCEP	1	−1.973401	0.0393574	−50.092	0.0001
LOG_TDOL	1	0.875307	0.01787217	48.976	0.0001
LOG_ORDR	1	−0.961115	0.01887344	−50.924	0.0001
LOG_LBUY	1	0.015471	0.00991300	−1.561	0.1222

Variable	DF	Standardized Estimate
INTERCEP	1	0.00000000
LOG_TDOL	1	1.06809616
LOG_ORDR	1	−1.10992738
LOG_LBUY	1	−0.02768440

The second and more important reason for not using *R*-square as the ultimate measure in evaluating a model, as previously pointed out and to be repeated, is simply because it has been shown that models with large *R*-squares put to use under real situations or simulated conditions do not always perform better than their small *R*-square model counterparts.

To sum up, we have two models with the following equations:
The Q&D model:

$$\text{RESP} = .19 + .00014 \times \text{TOT\_DOLL} - .0047 \times \text{AVG\_ORDR}$$

The carefully built model:

$$\text{LOG\_RESP} = -1.89 + .84 \times \text{LOG\_TDOL} - .95 \times \text{LOG\_ORDR}$$

The model using log transformations has an *R*-square of 96 percent; the quick and dirty model has an *R*-square of 55 percent. It appears that the carefully built model is almost twice as good as the quick and dirty model. Is it?

VALIDATION – CHOOSING THE BEST MODEL

If we cannot rely solely on *R*-square, then how can we choose the best model? The answer lies in the validation of the candidate models under simulated conditions. That is, we apply the model to a file of names for which the dependent variable is

TABLE 19-9

SAS

Model: MODEL1
Dependent Variable: LOG_RESP

Analysis of Variance

Source	DF	Sum of Squares	Mean Square	F Value	Prob>F
Model	2	4.58193	2.29096	1124.797	0.0001
Error	97	0.19757	0.00204		
C Total	99	4.77949			

Root MSE	0.04513	R-square	0.9587	
Dep Mean	−0.76009	Adj R-sq	0.9578	
C.V.	−5.93756			

Parameter Estimates

Variable	DF	Parameter Estimate	Standard Error	T for H0: Parameter = 0	Prob>|T|
INTERCEP	1	−1.890376	0.04300760	−43.954	0.0001
LOG_TDOL	1	0.844590	0.01995868	42.317	0.0001
LOG_ORDR	1	−0.959345	0.02220746	−43.199	0.0001

Variable	DF	Standardized Estimate
INTERCEP	1	0.00000000
LOG_TDOL	1	1.12039211
LOG_ORDR	1	−1.14375208

known, and then evaluate the predicted values of the dependent variable with the actual values. The model that *performs best* in the validation test *is the best*.

For validating the cataloger's two models, we use the second sample of 100 fresh names for which the response rates are known. We score each name for each model and compare predicted and actual response rates by a decile analysis. A decile analysis starts by ranking the scored file from high to low score and dividing the ranked names into 10 equal groups or deciles. The mean value of the actual dependent variable for each decile is calculated. In this case, the model with the largest mean response rate for the top two or three deciles is declared the best model.

The decile analyses for the two models are in Table 19–10. We see that the carefully built model beats the Q&D model in the top decile with a mean response rate of 29 versus 27 percent, but performs the same in decile 2 with a mean response rate of 20 percent. Thirty percent into the file, both models perform the same. Depending on how deeply the cataloger plans to mail, the 2 percent difference could represent a significant gain in dollars per response, in which case the preferred model is the one built with care. However, if the cataloger plans to use the model to mail to 50 percent of the file, not just the top 10 percent, then either model will produce the same result.

This example was intentionally designed to produce a result in which two models produce very different R-squares, but have little difference in practical results, to convince you to pay less attention to the R-square statistic and more attention to the validation results.

T A B L E   19–10

Decile Analysis — Mean Response Rate

	Careful Model		Q&D Model	
Decile	Decile	Cum	Decile	Cum
1	29.0%	29.0%	27.0%	27.0%
2	20.0	24.5	20.0	23.5
3	19.0	22.6	21.0	22.6
4	16.0	21.0	16.0	21.0
5	14.0	19.6	14.0	19.6
6	14.0	18.6	13.0	18.5
7	11.0	17.6	13.0	17.7
8	11.0	16.7	10.0	16.8
9	08.0	15.8	08.0	15.8
10	06.0	14.8	06.0	14.8
House file average response rate	14.8		14.8	

In practice, users will discover that the R-squares associated with most models, particularly response models, where only a very small percent of the population responds, are generally under 10 percent, very often under 5 percent. Nevertheless, these models can be used with confidence, provided (1) the individual variables are significant (ts greater than 2 and the corresponding p values less than .05); (2) the F value for the entire relationship is greater than 4 or 5; and (3) most importantly, the model validates, that is, produces a meaningful difference in decile performance when applied to a fresh validation sample.

MULTIPLE REGRESSION – SOME ODDS AND ENDS

Through our illustrations, we hope that you've obtained some feel for how multiple regression works in practice. At this point, hands-on experience with regression models is the only way you will become proficient in the application of regression and your company will become efficient in its direct mail programs.

In Chapter 20, we will outline a how-to for building regression models. But before doing so, we would like to take care of three loose ends.

Interaction

We note that in the regression model, each independent variable is multiplied by a weight (its coefficient) and then all the weighted variables are added to obtain a score or predicted value of the dependent variable. In effect, we are saying that the regression model is an *additive* model—the independent variables in the models are said to have additive effect on the dependent variable.

Let's recall the model in Example 13, where we predict DOLLSPENT based on income and age:

$$\text{DOLLSPENT} = 351.29 - .65 \times \text{INCOME} + .86 \times \text{AGE}$$

As the model stands, AGE and INCOME are in the model and contribute to the prediction of DOLLSPENT additively. That is, regardless of the age of a customer, the DOLLSPENT will decrease $.65 for every thousand dollars of income. The equation tells us that if you hold age constant, there is a negative relationship between sales and income. In other words, the product line appeals more to lower-income persons than to upper-income persons. This may be true, but what if it's "really" true for younger people and only "a little" true for older persons?

What if the effect of income on sales is much greater than −$.65 for younger people, but much less than −$.65 for older people? If this is true, then the $.65 regression coefficient is really an average that reflects the behavior of both older and younger people. Clearly, we would like to have a technique that would do better than simply average out the behavior of both older and younger people.

In regression analysis, there are a couple of ways to handle this problem. You could run two models, one for older people and one for younger people. You could create a categorical "dummy" variable to represent age and include this variable in the model. Or you could create what is called an *interaction variable*.

An interaction variable is needed when the additive effects of the independent variables do not adequately explain the relationship between the dependent variable and independent variables. An example we often use has to do with the sale of opera tickets. A statistical profile of opera ticket buyers would reveal that they are both highly educated and upper income. This observation could be used in building a model of opera ticket buyers. We would want both variables, education and income, to be included in the model as independent variables. However, as we all know, not all highly educated persons have high incomes, nor are all upper-income persons highly educated. What we would like in the model, therefore, is a third variable that reflects the fact that a person is *both* highly educated and upper income. As noted earlier, this third variable, which is the combination of the two original variables, is called an *interaction variable*.

If an analyst were building a regression model of opera ticket buyers and had correctly identified income and education as important independent variables but had failed to create the interaction variable, the regression model *would not* include the interaction variable. An analyst has to create interaction variables and include them in the set of variables to be considered by the regression program. Fortunately, interaction variables can easily be added into regression models.

Going back to our example where we believe there might be an interactive effect between AGE and INCOME, we create an interaction variable to take the suspected effect into account by simply defining a new interaction variable AGE_INCOME as the product of the AGE and INCOME: AGE_INCOME = AGE × INCOME.

Putting interaction variables into a model is easy because all we have to do mechanically is instruct the regression program to create a new variable by multiplying two old variables together. However, in practice, finding which two variables (or even three or four variables for higher-order interaction effects) is not easy. Although a working knowledge of the variables is the best guide for creating interaction variables, a statistical method called automatic interaction detection (AID/CHAID) has been expressly developed for finding interaction. (We'll discuss AID/CHAID in Chapter 20.)

Multicollinearity

For multiple regression to produce good and reliable coefficients for its independent variables, there must be the absence of perfect mutlicollinearity. That is, none of the independent variables has a correlation coefficient of 1 with any of the other independent variables or with any weighted sum of the other independent variables. When perfect multicollinearity exists, the regression coefficients cannot be calculated. In such cases, the problem is always identified—the program literally won't run.

The real problem arises when there is high multicollinearity; however, there are some practical rules for identifying multicollinearity:

1. Multiple R-square is high and all or most of the p values are greater than 5 percent.
2. The magnitude of the regression coefficients changes greatly when independent variables are added or dropped from the equation.
3. There are unexpectedly large regression coefficients for variables thought to be relatively unimportant and/or small regression coefficients for variables thought to be relatively important.
4. There are unexpected signs of the coefficients.

Remedies for Multicollinearity

OK, now that you know what multicollinearity is, what it does, and how to detect it, here's how to alleviate the problem:

1. Try to get more observations, more data. That's right, more data. Often, multicollinearity can be a data problem rather than a modeling problem and increasing the sample size will make the problem go away. Actually, although texts on statistics discuss multicollinearity extensively, in most direct marketing applications where we are dealing with thousands of observations, multicollinearity is generally not a problem.
2. If you cannot get more data, try to examine all correlation coefficients to spot those with Rs greater than .90. Then, eliminate one of the two "culprit" variables.
3. Review all the independent variables to try to combine those that seem to measure the same content. For example, three variables capturing the number of hours spent listening to MTV, playing the stereo, and watching movies on the VCR can be summed or averaged to obtain a measure of passive media interest. Factor analysis, a technique we'll describe in Chapter 21, can be used for this purpose.

Selection of Variables

Perhaps the most important step in the building process is finding the right variables to include in the model. Without a relevant set of predictors, no amount of data manipulation can produce a good model.

There are three basic approaches to variable selection. The first one we recommend is by far the most important. It's not statistically elegant, but it satisfies the validity test of logic and reasonableness and, accordingly, will be accepted by all. It's the selection based on knowledge of the data. Nothing replaces the analyst's experience with the data in terms of what it measures, what it suggests, and how it behaves.

The second approach helps the analyst when her experience with the data is limited or she cannot distinguish among a subset of very good variables. The approach of (forward) stepwise selection starts off by finding the variable that produces the largest R-square with the dependent variable. Then, given that the "best" variable is in the model, it finds the next best variable in terms of adding to the R-square. This process of finding variables that add to R-square stops when variables can no longer add to R-square according to certain statistical criteria.

This approach is helpful in paring down a large number of variables; however, it is notorious for finding subsets of variables that do not "hang" together. That is, the selected variables are difficult to justify because they appear not to be related in any logical or reasonable way to the dependent variable.

Even if a subset of variables produced by the stepwise approach hangs together well, the fact that it is declared best because it has the largest R-square is no guarantee, as we pointed out, of it being the best. In sum, the stepwise selection is only a good first step in finding the right variables.

The third approach uses a relatively new measure of total prediction error, denoted by Mallow's C(p). Using the approach, which is produced automatically by one of the procedures in SAS, we obtain many subsets or combinations of independent variables to choose from. Each combination of variables is associated with a C(p) statistic. The rule of thumb for using C(p) is to work with sets of variables whose C(p) value is equal to or less than 1 plus the number of variables in the subset. However, even though we favor this approach, selection based on C(p) is just like the first two approaches in that there's no guarantee of getting the best set of predictor variables.

If we've made variable selection into "mission impossible," that's because it sometimes seems that way. When the final model is not as strong as desired, we assume it's because we cannot find the right set of variables. This problem gets us back to the need to collect better data, which was the theme of Chapter 4 on primary research data.

CHAPTER 20

Response Analysis

In Example 14 in Chapter 19, we discussed building a regression model to predict response. The dependent variable was undoubtedly a response variable but not of the usual kind found in most DM response modeling projects. In most response analyses, the dependent variable is a categorical "dummy" variable. Each person mailed is given a score of 1 or 0 on the variable RESPONSE. A 1 means the person responded, and a 0 means the person did not respond. As we all know, the vast majority of recipients unfortunately do not respond; this is the problem.

INTRODUCTION

The technique of regression analysis was originally developed for scalar or continuous dependent and independent variables. When independent variables are categorical, there are ways (for example, using dummy variables, which will be discussed shortly) to include such variables in the analysis without violating the assumptions of the technique. Use and interpretation of a regression model with categorical variables is similar to that of a model with scalar independent variables.

When the dependent variable is a categorical response variable with two levels, response yes/response no, or 1/0, the regression model is formally called the *linear probability model* (LPM). This label is appropriate because the predicted value of the response variable is interpreted as the probability of response. However, this label gives a false sense of form (linear) and correctness (probability) of the model. It turns out that the presence of a yes/no response-dependent variable violates a number of the assumptions of the regression technique, which renders questionable the model and its utility. One assumption that is violated is that the dependent variable conforms to the shape of the normal distribution. A variable that can have only two values, 1 or 0, cannot be normally distributed. If the response rates to direct marketing offers were greater than 20 percent, this violation would have little practical consequence. However, because this is rarely the case, and many of our response rates hover around the 1 to 3 percent area, this violation of the normality assumption cannot simply be dismissed.

Without going too deeply into theoretical issues, the LPM suffers from *potentially* excluding important predictors from the final model. This can happen because the *t* and *F* statistics can give false signals, potentially causing the analyst to either include insignificant variables or exclude significant variables. In addition, the LPM often results in estimates with probabilities less than 0 or greater than 1.

Not all model builders consider these potential problems terribly serious. Knowing the subject matter, they feel it is easy to identify the important variables and put them into the model. As for the "outside" probabilities, if the number of occurrences is small (which is usually the case), they view the model as more than acceptable.

In practice, if a marketer is only interested in ranking a file of customers from most to least likely to respond, then the LPM and alternative techniques (such as logistic regression and discriminant analysis, which will be described shortly) all produce essentially the same ordering of a customer file.

The following are more important issues: Does each technique have access to the correct set of variables? For example, are interaction variables available to all techniques? Is each technique being used properly? Are variables being transformed to approximate normality? Are linear relationships sought out, and so on?

However, for those analysts who just do not want to use a model that is flawed or who really need to go beyond ranking the names on a file to have reliable probabilities of response, there are alternative techniques.

Before getting into the mechanics of these techniques, it might be helpful to clarify some terms that are used almost interchangeably but in fact have slightly different meanings: (1) *log-linear models*, (2) *logit models*, (3) *logit regression*, (4) *logistic models*, and (5) *logistic regression*.

The terms *regression* and *models* in this context mean the same thing, so we have only to define the differences among log-linear models, logit models, and logistic models.

Logit models and *logistic models* are essentially the same thing. In both cases, the dependent variable is the categorical yes/no, or 1/0, or respond/did not respond variable we work with in direct marketing. However, some of the computer programs that perform these analyses distinguish between logistic models and logit models. In statistical packages such as SAS where there is a difference, logistic models or programs are run when the independent variables include one or more continuous variables; logit programs are run when all the independent variables are categorical. However, there are other statistical packages in which logit programs accept both continuous and categorical independent variables.

Log-linear models are used when all variables are categorical. Technically, log-linear models do not distinguish between independent and dependent variables. We can, however, take the results of a log-linear model and declare one variable as the dependent variable and run what is essentially a logit model.

Log-linear and logit models, as well as ordinary regression models, can accept interaction variables but cannot systematically identify them—the models can only test the variables for significance. However, the CHAID technique (which we will discuss in detail shortly) does identify significant interaction variables that can then be used as variables in any of the three techniques just mentioned.

With that as background, let's examine logistic regression in more detail. It should be pointed out that the following material is mathematically difficult and some readers may want to skip ahead to the sections on discriminant analysis and CHAID.

Just remember, for most direct marketers, the bottom line with regard to logistic and logit modeling is that they are perfectly appropriate techniques and should be used provided your statistician is familiar with them. Not all statisticians are. On the other hand, if, as we said, you are using modeling to rank a large file in terms of each individual's probability of responding, the rankings developed with ordinary regression are likely to be equivalent to the rankings found using these more appropriate statistical techniques.

As a practical matter, most of the work involved in modeling projects has to do with understanding and massaging the available data. After all this preliminary work is done, it's a relatively simple matter to run the data through all three techniques: the LPM or ordinary least-squares regression, discriminant analysis, or logit or logistic regression. Figure 20–1 shows the results of such a process. As you can see, from a ranking perspective the differences are not terribly different. More often than not we find this to be the case.

LOGISTIC REGRESSION

Concepts and Definition

The concepts that hold the logistic regression model together are these:

1. Probability
2. Odds
3. Logit
4. Odds ratio
5. Log odds

It takes a fair amount of algebra to transform raw yes/no data into a form that can be used in a logistic model. The algebra that follows is no more than a transformation, but the logic of the steps is not intuitively obvious. The reader who wishes to follow along is welcome, but again, understanding how the transformation is accomplished is not necessary to understanding how to use the results.

To begin, let Y stand for the response to a mailing, where Y equals 1 for a yes response and 0 for a no response.

FIGURE 20–1

Comparison of Statistical Methods: OLS Regression, Logistic, and Discriminant

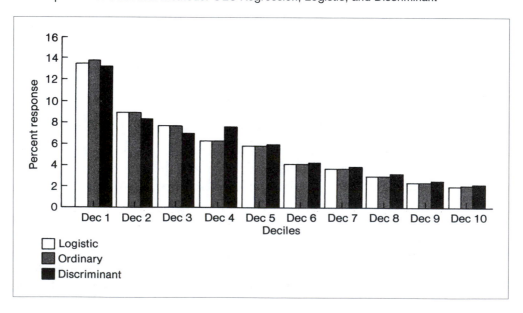

Let's define the probability of a response as p, and therefore the probability of a nonresponse is $(1 - p)$. (If the probability of a response is 5 percent, then the probability of a nonresponse is 95 percent.)

The next concept is the concept of *odds*. By definition, the odds of a yes response is the ratio of the probability of a response divided by the probability of a nonresponse:

$$\text{odds} = \frac{p}{(1 - p)}$$

With a little algebra, the probability p can be expressed in terms of odds:

$$(1 - p) \times \text{odds} = p$$
$$\text{odds} - p \times \text{odds} = p$$
$$\text{odds} = p + p \times \text{odds}$$
$$\text{odds} = p \times (1 + \text{odds})$$
$$p = \frac{\text{odds}}{(1 + \text{odds})}$$

We'll use this relationship later.

If the odds of a yes response are given by $p/(1 - p)$, then the natural log of the odds of a yes response (log to the base e), denoted by ln, is:

$$ln(\text{yes}) = ln(p/1 - p) = ln(p) - ln(1-p)$$

This difference, the natural log of a yes response, is called the *logit* of yes.

Now, let's consider another variable X that takes on two values, a and b. Also, assume that Y depends on X, where

The probability of a yes response when $X = a$ is $p(a)$.
The probability of a no response when $X = a$ is $1 - p(a)$.
The probability of a yes response when $X = b$ is $p(b)$.
The probability of a no response when $X = b$ is $1 - p(b)$.

The odds of a yes response given $X = a$ is $p(a)/1 - p(a)$. The log of a yes response given $X = a$ is:

$$ln(\text{yes given } X = a) = ln\, p(a) - ln(1 - p(a))$$

This difference is called the *logit of yes given $X = a$.*

The odds of a yes response given $X = b$ is $p(b)/1 - p(b)$. The log of a yes given $X = b$ is:

$$ln(\text{yes given } X = b) = ln\, p(b) - ln(1 - p(b))$$

This difference is called the *logit of yes given $X = b$.*

The ratio of the odds of yes for $X = a$ to the odds of yes for $X = b$, called the *odds ratio*, is:

$$\frac{p(a)/1 - p(a)}{p(b)/1 - p(b)}$$

The log of odds ratio, called the *log odds*, is:

$$ln(\text{odds ratio}) = (\text{logit of yes given } X = a) - (\text{logit of yes given } X = b)$$

Logistic Regression Model

All of the above algebra allows us to introduce the concept of a logistic regression model. The logistic regression model is a linear model in this form:

$$G = b0 + b1 \times X1 + b2 \times X2 + \ldots + bn \times Xn$$

where

G = the logit of a yes response given specific values of $X1$, $X2$, ..., Xn. (Implicit in the phrase *yes response* is a categorical dependent variable with two values of yes and no)

$b0$ = the intercept, which, as in ordinary regression, can be viewed as a placeholder necessary to make the equation work well

$b1, \ldots, bn$ = logistic coefficients (to be discussed shortly)

EXAMPLE 15

Logistic Equation

Let's consider a sample of 20 customers from our cataloger's latest catalog mailing. The cataloger would like to build a model to predict response to this mailing for use in developing a list for future mailings of similar catalogs. The goal is to identify new customers on the file who have a high likelihood of responding to a similar program.

The 20 records consist of three variables: RESPONSE to the mailing (1 = yes/0 = no), AGE (in years), and GENDER (0 = male/1 = female). (See Table 20–1.)

The variables of the model are the categorical dependent variable RESPONSE, the scalar independent variable AGE, and GENDER, a categorical independent variable.

Up to this point, all our independent variables were scalar. Can linear models, whether ordinary, logistic, or otherwise, handle categorical independent variables? Yes.

Dummy Variables

The trick for putting categorical independent variables into any regression model is to create dummy variables. Suppose, for example, that the categorical variable is SOURCE OF ORDER, which has been coded as direct mail, print, and other. This case requires two dummy variables. The first dummy variable, $D1$, is coded 1 if the individual's source is direct mail, and 0 if the individual's source is print or other. The second dummy variable, $D2$, is coded 1 if the individual was acquired from a print source, and 0 if acquired from direct mail or other.

Accordingly, if an individual was acquired from a direct mail source, then for that person, $D1$ equals 1 and $D2$ equals 0; if an individual was acquired from a print source, then $D1$ equals 0 and $D2$ equals 1; and if the source was neither direct mail nor print, that is, an other, then $D1$ and $D2$ are both equal to 0. Table 20–2 shows the dummy variables for SOURCE OF ORDER.

Thus, whenever a categorical independent variable is to be put into a model, we simply create a set of dummy variables (the number of variables in the set is equal to the number of category values minus 1).

T A B L E   20-1

Response	Age	Gender
0	21	1
0	23	1
0	25	1
0	29	1
0	32	1
0	33	0
0	34	0
0	34	0
0	45	1
0	45	1
1	46	1
1	46	1
1	57	1
1	57	1
1	58	1
1	58	0
1	59	1
1	63	1
1	64	1
1	64	1

T A B L E   20-2

Source of Order	D1	D2
Direct mail	1	0
Print	0	1
Other	0	0

Because the GENDER variable has only two values, which implies that only one dummy variable coded 1 if female and 0 otherwise (for male) is needed, GENDER is already a dummy variable. GENDER, as is, can go directly into the model.

Running the data through a logistic regression program produces the logistic equation shown below[1]:

$$G = -10.83 + .28 \times \text{AGE} + 2.30 \times \text{GENDER}$$

G is the logit of a yes response to the mailing given specific values of AGE and GENDER.

Let's see what G is all about. Consider a male customer age 40 (GENDER = 0 and AGE = 40). His G or logit score is:

$$G(0,40) = -10.83 + .28 \times 40 + 2.30 \times 0$$

---

1. This solution was obtained by using SAS 6.08. Due to the artificial nature of the data set, a unique solution does not exist. Thus, different statistical packages produce either no equation or a quasi-equation. For example, SAS 6.12 produces $G = 223.8 - 6.2070*\text{AGE} + 58.6739*\text{GENDER}$.

$$= -10.83 + 11.2 + 0$$
$$= .37 \text{ logit}$$

A female customer of the same age would have a score of 2.67:

$$G(1,40) = -10.83 + .28 \times 40 + 2.30 \times 1$$
$$= -10.83 + 11.2 + 2.30$$
$$= 2.67 \text{ logits}$$

Logits, with the aid of tables, can be converted into odds, which can be converted into probabilities.

Accordingly, we have:

Odds of yes response for a 40-year-old male $=$ .37 logit $=$ 1.44
Odds of yes response for a 40-year-old female $=$ 2.67 logits $=$ 14.44

recalling from above that:

$$p = \frac{\text{odds}}{(1 + \text{odds})}$$

For the 40-year-old male:

$$p = 1.44/(1 + 1.44)$$
$$p = .59$$

For the 40-year-old female:

$$p = 14.44/(1 + 14.44)$$
$$p = .93$$

Thus, the 40-year-old male customer has a 59 percent probability of response. The female customer has a probability of 93 percent.

Logistic Coefficients

Because G is in logits, the coefficients are also in logits. Because we can unlog G logits to obtain odds, we can unlog the coefficients, too. Doing this will give us the meaning of the coefficients and add to our understanding of a logit.

Let's consider the coefficient of AGE, .28, that is, .28 logit. Unlogging the coefficient of .28, we have 1.32, that is, the odds of a yes response is 1.32. Thus, for every one-year increase in age, the odds of a yes response increase 1.32 times. Let's see.

The G logit score for a male 41-year-old is:

$$G(0,41) = -10.83 + .28 \times 41 + 2.30 \times 0$$
$$= -10.83 + 11.48 + 0$$
$$= .65 \text{ logit}$$

The odds corresponding to .65 logit is 1.92 and the odds for a 40-year-old male corresponding to .37 logit is 1.44 (as calculated above); thus, the increase in the odds for a male when his age increases one year is 1.32 times (1.92/1.44 = 1.32).

Now that we have some idea of where logits come from, let's remind ourselves of how they are used. If everyone on a file is scored and the scores are in terms of logits, the scores, that is, the logits, can still be ranked from high to low and the traditional decile analysis can be performed. You recall that we, and others, argue that most of the time the ranking based on a logit analysis will be equivalent, from a practical decision-making perspective, to the rankings resulting from an ordinary regression analysis. On the other hand, each individual logit score can be transformed back into a specific probability of response, a probability that will always be between 0 and 1, which is not always the case in regression.

One last point. Although it is one thing to find a statistician who can build a logit model, it is another thing to find computer programmers who have the skills and tools available to translate logits back into probabilities. Scoring in logits and ranking in logits are simple, because to the computer a logit is just another number. This is a similar problem to the one of presenting a programmer with an ordinary regression equation that requires the use of logs or exponential functions. The point to be remembered is to always check with data processing to make sure any solution you come up with can be implemented.

DISCRIMINANT ANALYSIS

In the preceding discussion, we mentioned discriminant analysis as an alternative to regression when the dependent variable is a categorical yes/no or 1/0 response variable. The independent variables can be either scalar or categorical with the use of dummy variables, and interaction variables can also be included, just as in multiple regression.

Discriminant analysis is a statistical technique that was developed to identify variables that explain the differences between two or more groups (e.g., responders and nonresponders of a mailing) and that classify unknown observations (for example, customers) into the groups. The discriminant model looks like a multiple regression model where the categorical dependent variable is again expressed as a sum of weighted independent or discriminant variables:

$$Z = b0 + b1 \times X1 + b2 \times X2 + b3 \times X3 + \ . \ . \ . + bn \times Xn$$

The weights (the bs), called *discriminant coefficients*, are derived such that the resultant discriminant model maximizes the statistical difference among the groups. It is interesting to note that in regression, the coefficients are derived to maximize R-square. Thus, both techniques are very similar in their maximizing derivation. In addition, both methods depend on certain assumptions about the normality of the variables that go into the model.

In a simple two-group discriminant analysis, if an individual's Z score is greater than some critical value determined by experience, the individual is placed in Group 1; if the Z score is less than that value, the individual is placed in Group 2. The evaluation of the model is based on whether or not the model places persons into groups more accurately than would occur by chance.

However, in practice discriminant analysis is more sensitive to violations of normality than regression. This is particularly true when the size of the two groups is very different, as is the case in response analysis when the yes group is generally below 10 percent. Although we try to reshape the data as best we can for those situations where the best we can do in reexpression is not enough, discriminant models will not perform as well as regression models. Therefore, a conservative approach is to stick with ordinary regression or logistic regression over discriminant analysis.

AUTOMATIC INTERACTION DETECTION—AID/CHAID

Thus far, we've described and illustrated two regression methods. If the dependent variable is scalar and the independent variables are scalar, categorical, or both, then ordinary regression is the appropriate method to use. If the dependent variable is a categorical 0/1 response variable and the independent variables are scalar, categorical, or both, we can, in most circumstances, still use ordinary regression if the application is only to rank a file from most to least likely to respond. If good reliable estimates of probability of response are needed, then we must use the logistic regression method.

Now, we discuss two complementary methods to ordinary and logistic regression: automatic interaction detection (AID) and CHAID. In an AID analysis, the dependent variable is scalar. In CHAID, the dependent variable is categorical, and the independent variables in either are categorical. If an independent variable is scalar, it must be transformed into a categorical variable. This is not hard to do—the analyst simply breaks the scalar variable into ranges. For example, sales, which is a scalar variable, can be expressed in ranges of $0 to $9.99, $10 to $19.99, $20 to $49.99, and so on.

Notice the word *interaction*. This is the same interaction as previously discussed in the context of interaction variables. AID/CHAID was originally developed for the express purpose of finding interaction variables for inclusion into a regression, logit, or log-linear model.

As it turns out, today AID/CHAID is often used as an "end" analysis rather than as a "means" to provide insight for further model building. We'll discuss the use of AID/CHAID both as a complement to regression and as a stand-alone technique.

First, let's explain the differences between AID and CHAID. AID was developed in the 1960s at the University of Michigan as a method to identify segments of a market. It defines the segments in terms of *two-level* categorical independent variables. For example, an AID "model" with two independent variables (MARITAL STATUS and COLLEGE EDUCATED), each with two possibilities (MARRIED/NOT MARRIED, COLLEGE/NO COLLEGE), can divide a market into four segments:

1. Married, with college
2. Married, without college
3. Unmarried, with college
4. Unmarried, without college

Later, two significant improvements to the method were introduced. First, multiway splits of the independent variable were allowed—no longer was it necessary for the independent variables to be limited to two-way splits. Second, the differences between end-point cells in an AID analysis were not subject to a test of statistical significance. This deficiency was eliminated with the introduction of the chi-square test for statistical significance—thus, the addition of CH in CHAID, which stands for the chi-square test of statistical significance. Dr. Gordon V. Kass is credited with the development of the CHAID methodology.[2] Jay Magidson enhanced the basic CHAID program with a series of features that make CHAID more useful to direct marketers and produced a product called SI-CHAID™, which is now marketed by SPSS. (SI stands for Statistical Innovation, the name of Magidson's company.)

2. G. V. Kass, "Significant Testing in, and Some Extensions of, Automatic Interaction Detection" (doctoral dissertation, University of Witwatersrand, Johannesburg, South Africa, 1976).

EXAMPLE 16

Let's illustrate the use of CHAID by making one last return to our cataloger, who now believes that it is possible to build a predictive response model based on knowledge of these basic factors:

1. How long a customer has been on the database (HOW_LONG).
2. What part of the country the customer lives in (REGION).
3. Whether or not the customer is married (MARITAL).

A random sample of approximately 40,000 customers who received a recent mailing was drawn. The data was coded as follows:

1. HOW_LONG
   a. Less than 1 year (coded 1)
   b. 1–2 years (coded 2)
   c. 2 years, plus (coded 3)
   d. Years unknown (coded 4)

2. REGION
   a. Northeast (coded 1)
   b. East (coded 2)
   c. Southeast (coded 3)
   d. Midwest (coded 4)
   e. Midsouth (coded 5)
   f. Northwest (coded 6)
   g. Southwest (coded 7)

3. MARITAL
   a. Divorced/separated (coded 1)
   b. Married (coded 2)
   c. Single (coded 3)
   d. Widowed (coded 4)
   e. Unknown (coded 5)

4. RESPONSE (to the last mailing)
   a. Yes (coded 1)
   b. No (coded 2)

TABLE 20-3

Results by Segments of Individual Variables (in Percents)

HOW_LONG 1 = 13.98%	MARITAL 1 = 13.66
HOW_LONG 2 = 13.40	MARITAL 2 = 12.95
HOW_LONG 3 = 11.12	MARITAL 3 = 12.21
HOW_LONG 4 = 14.24	MARITAL 4 = 5.76
	MARITAL 5 = 12.25
REGION 1 = 9.44	
REGION 2 = 13.00	
REGION 3 = 15.53	
REGION 4 = 12.85	
REGION 5 = 14.93	
REGION 6 = 11.29	
REGION 7 = 13.20	

TABLE 20-4

Model: RESP_HAT
Dependent Variable: RESPONSE

Analysis of Variance

Source	DF	Sum of Squares	Mean Square	F Value	Prob>F
Model	5	33.00807	6.60161	58.295	0.0001
Error	40581	4595.56640	0.11324		
C Total	40586	4628.57447			

Root MSE	0.33652	R-square	0.0071	
Dep Mean	0.13127	Adj R-sq	0.0070	
C. V.	256.34856			

Parameter Estimates

Variable	DF	Parameter Estimate	Standard Error	T for H0: Parameter = 0	Prob>|T|
INTERCEP	1	0.149570	0.00270699	55.253	0.0000
MARITAL4	1	−0.070960	0.00784734	−9.042	0.0001
HOW_LNG3	1	−0.027374	0.00335740	−8.153	0.0001
REGION1	1	−0.034529	0.00434860	−7.940	0.0001
REGION3	1	0.028100	0.00564363	4.979	0.0001
REGION5	1	0.024340	0.00566267	4.298	0.0001

Variable	DF	Standardized Estimate
INTERCEP	1	0.00000000
MARITAL4	1	−0.04497071
HOW_LNG3	1	−0.04052533
REGION1	1	−0.04058342
REGION3	1	0.02524823
REGION5	1	0.02181160

The average response rate was 12.59 percent. Table 20−3 shows response rates by each level of the variables HOW_LONG, REGION, and MARITAL. In a regression model, each break will be treated as an independent variable. Not yet having heared of CHAID, the analyst runs an ordinary dummy variable regression analysis. Table 20−4 shows the results of that analysis.

Table 20−4 depicts a result that direct marketers are becoming accustomed to seeing: a significant model ($F = 58.295$), with significant independent variables (ts range from 4.2 to 9.0, and all p values are less than .0001), and an almost nonexistent R-square of .0071 or .71 percent.

As we said, the real proof of the usefulness of a predictive model is in the analysis of a validation sample. In Table 20−5, we apply the model to a second sample of 40,000 names and look to see how well the model "spreads" the average response rate.

The model spreads the average response rate fairly well. The best 14.4 percent of the names mailed pulled 17.1 percent, the bottom 13.9 percent pulled 8 percent, and another 9.8 percent pulled 11 percent. The question is, "Can we do better?" and specifically, "Can CHAID identify important interactions between the independent variables that regression did not explicitly take into account?" Remember, regression has no provision to automatically look for interactions; it has to be told that interactions exist.

T A B L E 20–5

Ordinary Dummy Variable Regression Model

Regression Segments	Quantity	Number of Responses	Percent Mailing	Cumulative Percent Mailing	Percent Response	Cumulative Percent Response
1	2,097	361	5.2%	5.2%	17.2%	6.8%
2	3,756	642	9.3	14.4	17.1	18.8
3	12,194	1,829	30.0	44.4	15.0	53.1
4	1,948	269	4.8	49.3	13.8	58.2
5	10,975	1,339	27.0	76.3	12.2	83.3
6	3,986	438	9.8	86.1	11.0	91.5
7	5,691	450	13.9	100.0	8.0	100.0
Total	40,647	5,328	100.0%		13.1%	

THE SI-CHAID ANALYSIS OF THE SAME DATA

The SI-CHAID program begins by presenting the response rates for each segment of each variable, and then uses the chi-square test to combine segments that are not statistically different from each other. (See Table 20–6.)

Table 20–6 tells us that the SI-CHAID program has found no statistical difference among the HOW_LONG variables 1, 2, and 4, so it has combined them into HOW_LONG 124. Similarly, it has combined REGIONS 2, 4, and 7 and REGIONS 3 and 5 into two new variables: REGION 247 and REGION 35. The five original marital variables have been reduced to two variables.

The solution of the CHAID analysis is in the form of a tree diagram, found in Figure 20–2. There are seven end segments defined by the three independent variables HOW_LONG, REGION, and MARITAL, even though there were 105 possible segments (3 times 7 times 5) before the segments within variables were combined and 16 possible segments after the segments within variables were combined (2 times 4 times 2).

T A B L E 20–6

Before Merging	After Initial Merging
HOW_LONG 1 = 13.98%	HOW_LONG 124 = 14.06
HOW_LONG 2 = 13.40	HOW_LONG 3 = 11.12
HOW_LONG 3 = 11.12	
HOW_LONG 4 = 14.24	
REGION 1 = 9.44	REGION 1 = 9.44
REGION 2 = 13.00	REGION 247 = 12.96
REGION 3 = 15.53	REGION 35 = 15.23
REGION 4 = 12.85	REGION 6 = 11.29
REGION 5 = 14.93	
REGION 6 = 11.29	
REGION 7 = 13.20	
MARITAL 1 = 13.66	MARITAL 1235 = 12.94
MARITAL 2 = 12.95	MARITAL 4 = 5.76
MARITAL 3 = 12.21	
MARITAL 4 = 5.76	
MARITAL 5 = 12.25	

Notice that of the three "main effects" variables (MARITAL, HOW_LONG, and REGION), the CHAID program determined that MARITAL with the two new levels of 1, 2, 3, and 5 versus 4 was the single best predictor of response.

Next, CHAID treats the two segments of MARITAL as the starting point for two new analyses. CHAID now attempts to split the MARITAL cell (MARITAL 1235) by either REGION or HOW_LONG. CHAID determines that MARITAL 1235 is "best" (largest statistically significant difference) divided by REGION, resulting in three new levels (REGION 1 versus REGION 2467 and REGION 35). On the other hand, the cell identified as MARITAL 4, at this point, is "best" further divided by the variable HOW_LONG with two new levels HOW_LONG 14 and HOW_LONG 23.

Notice how REGION 6 has been combined with REGIONS 2, 4, and 7. Originally REGION 6 could not be combined with any of the other REGIONs, but after MARITAL 4 is removed from consideration, those persons in REGION 6 look statistically similar to those in REGIONS 2, 4, AND 7. This is what we mean when we say that the process is repeated from the beginning at each new level in the tree.

The two HOW_LONG segments (Segments 6 and 7 on the CHAID tree) are considered end or final segments because the remaining variable (REGION) does not provide any further predictive splitting power. The same holds true for Segment 1, which cannot be split by HOW_LONG.

FIGURE 20-2

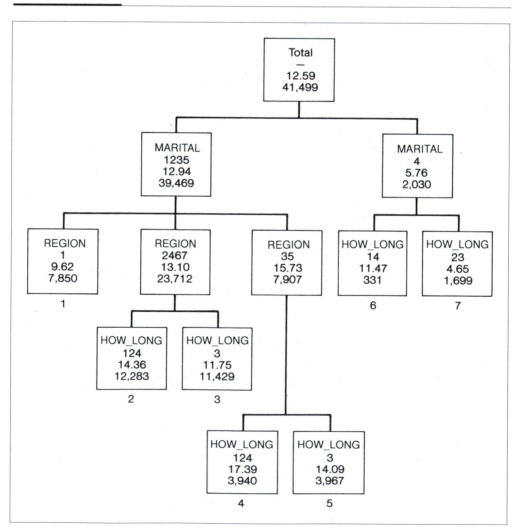

Thus, at this "depth" of the tree, there are three final segments defined as follows:

Segment 1. Customers who are either divorced/separated, married, single, or marital status unknown *and* live in the northeast region of the country. These customers have an average response rate of 9.62 percent, somewhat below the house file average of 12.59 percent, which is indicated in the top box of the tree.

Segment 6. Widowed customers who have been on the database less than one year or for an unknown number of years; these customers have an average response rate of 11.47 percent and consist of approximately 1 percent of the file (331/41,499).

Segment 7. Widowed customers who have been on the file two years or more. These customers have an average response rate of 4.65 percent.

The remaining two cells (defined by REGION 2467 and REGION 35) are both split by the HOW_LONG variables with the same combined levels (HOW_LONG 124 and HOW_LONG 3), resulting in four final segments. Segment 4 has the largest average response rate of 17.39 percent, significantly above the overall average 12.59 percent, and consists of a reasonable market size of 9.5 percent of the house file.

At this point, we could stop and use the results of the SI-CHAID analysis as the sole basis for segmenting the database, or we could use the results of the CHAID analysis as input to a regression model. If we were to stop here, we would have the model shown in Table 20–7.

As mentioned previously, many mailers will stop at this point and use the CHAID output to segment their file and mail accordingly. Others may use the CHAID output as input into a regression or a logit model, attempting to build a model with more predictive power than the CHAID model.

How does the CHAID solution compare with the dummy variable regression solution? Essentially, the results are the same. The CHAID solution appears to have identified a small, poor-performing segment of the file (4.1 percent of the names mailed that pulled only 4.65 percent) that the regression model missed, but we really can't be sure of that without looking much more closely at a ranking of the bottom 4.1 percent of the file scored with the regression model. And that's not

T A B L E 20–7

Model Based on CHAID Analysis

CHAID Segments	Quantity	Number of Responses	Percent Mailing	Cumulative Percent Mailing	Percent Response	Cumulative Percent Response
4	3,940	685	9.5%	9.5%	17.39%	13.1%
2	12,283	1,764	29.6	39.1	14.36	46.9
5	3,967	559	9.6	48.7	14.09	57.6
3	11,429	1,343	27.5	76.2	11.75	83.3
6	331	38	0.8	77.0	11.47	84.0
1	7,850	755	18.9	95.9	9.62	98.5
7	1,699	79	4.1	100.0	4.65	100.0
Total	41,499	5,223	100.0%			

easy to do. Another, easier way to see what CHAID has added to our understanding is to use the results of the CHAID analysis in a regression model.

USING CHAID IN REGRESSION ANALYSIS

There are lots of ways to use the information gained by CHAID in a regression model. One way is to take advantage of what the CHAID model tells us about the breaks within the main variables HOW_LONG, MARITAL, and REGION, as well as what CHAID tells us about the important interactions among the main variables.

For simplicity let's examine just the second-level breaks shown in Figure 20–2. If we use a * to indicate the interaction between two main variables, we see the following:

Second-Level Breaks

MARITAL_1235 * REGION_1 = 9.62
MARITAL_1235 * REGION_2467 = 13.10
MARITAL_1235 * REGION_35 = 15.73
MARITAL_4 * HOW LONG_14 = 11.47
MARITAL_4 * HOW LONG_23 = 4.65

Given these five mutually exclusive categories we can create four dummy variables and use these dummy variables in a regression equation. Because the response rate to MARITAL 1235 * Region 2467 is closest to the average response rate of 12.59, we will use this category as the neutral or base case in setting up the dummy variables.

Conditions	Dummy Variables			
	M1R1	M1R3	M4H1	M4H2
MARITAL_1235 * REGION_1	1	0	0	0
MARITAL_1235 * REGION_35	0	1	0	0
MARITAL_4 * HOW LONG_14	0	0	1	0
MARITAL_4 * HOW LONG_23	0	0	0	1

The results of a regression model using all the dummy variables defined above is presented in Table 20–8. The significant variables turned out to be REGION 1, REGION 35, HOW_LONG 3, and the interaction variables M4H2, M4H1, and M1R3.

Did the regression model provide the user with a better model? The answer to this question is in Table 20–9, which presents the validation results for the model built with the CHAID variables, and in Table 20–10, which compares the two regression models, the one built without the knowledge of interactions (Table 20–5) and the one just built with knowledge of interactions (Table 20–9).

As you can see from a comparison of the two models, the CHAID-enhanced model does the better job at the extremes. It identifies a small group (about 5 percent) that pulls 19.7 percent, compared with a similar-sized group that pulled only 17.2 percent, and on the bottom it identified a relatively large group that pulls only about 6 percent, as compared with a similar-sized group that pulled about 8 percent.

T A B L E   20–8

Model: RESP_HAT
Dependent Variable: RESPONSE

Analysis of Variance

Source	DF	Sum of Squares	Mean Square	F Value	Prob>F
Model	6	34.53475	5.75579	50.842	0.0001
Error	40580	4594.03972	0.11321		
C Total	40586	4628.57447			

Root MSE		0.33647	R-square	0.0075	
Dep Mean		0.13127	Adj R-sq	0.0073	
C. V.		256.30914			

Parameter Estimates

Variable	DF	Parameter Estimate	Standard Error	T for H0: Parameter = 0	Prob>|T|
INTERCEP	1	0.149459	0.00271559	55.037	0.0000
REGION1	1	−0.034585	0.00434798	−7.954	0.0001
REGION35	1	0.048844	0.00906417	5.389	0.0001
HOW_LONG3	1	−0.026411	0.0033888	−7.794	0.0001
M4H2	1	−0.084690	0.00883210	−9.589	0.0001
M4H1	1	0.044651	0.01928074	−2.316	0.0206
M1R3	1	0.028018	0.00980542	2.857	0.0043

Variable	DF	Standardized Estimate
INTERCEP	1	0.00000000
REGION1	1	−0.04064964
REGION35	1	0.05834542
HOW_LONG3	1	−0.03910062
M4H2	1	−0.04918049
M4H1	1	−0.01165782
M1R3	1	−0.03087002

T A B L E   20–9

Regression Model Using Information from CHAID

Regression Segments	Quantity	Number of Responses	Percent Mailing	Cumulative Percent Mailing	Percent Response	Cumulative Percent Response
1	1,976	379	4.6%	4.6%	19.7%	7.3%
2	3,554	608	8.6	13.2	17.1	18.9
3	12,202	1,830	29.4	42.7	15.0	53.9
4	3,302	466	8.0	50.6	14.1	62.8
5	10,975	1,218	26.5	77.1	11.1	86.1
6	4,034	403	9.7	86.8	50.0	93.8
7	5,456	322	13.2	100.0	5.9	100.0
Total	41,499	5,227	100.0%			

　　　Are these results typical? That's a very hard question to answer. The results can be more (or less) dramatic than those shown in the example used. Certainly, when the effect of interaction does not work in the same direction for all combinations of variables, the results can be much more important. For example, take two variables—SEX and ADVERTISING COPY—each of which was split two ways—MALE/FEMALE and COPY A/COPY B. If COPY A had a positive effect on men and a negative effect on women, and COPY B worked in the reverse way, that is, a positive effect on females and negative on males, a model that took these two variables (SEX and COPY) into consideration but failed to look at the interaction of SEX and COPY would be incomplete and potentially misleading.

　　　An examination of Table 20–11 indicates that a test of MALE versus FEMALE would conclude that females respond better than males. Without looking at the different effect COPY has on each SEX, one would also conclude that COPY had no effect on response when in fact COPY A increases response among women and decreases response among men. COPY B has the reverse effect; it increases response among men and decreases response among women. A regression model that had only two dummy variables, one for SEX and one for COPY, would not discover this interaction effect, and could in fact produce misleading results—an incorrect ranking of the four combinations of the variables. However, a regression analysis that included an interaction variable that was the

TABLE 20–10

A Comparison of Regression Results

Regression Segments	Regression without Interaction Effects			Regression with Interaction Effects		
	Quantity	Percent Mailing	Percent Response	Quantity	Percent Mailing	Percent Response
1	2,097	5.2%	17.2%	1,976	4.6%	19.7%
2	3,756	9.3	17.1	3,554	8.6	17.1
3	12,194	30.0	15.0	12,202	29.4	15.0
4	1,948	4.8	13.8	3,302	8.0	14.1
5	10,975	27.0	12.2	10,975	26.5	11.1
6	3,986	9.8	11.0	4,034	9.7	50.0
7	5,691	13.9	8.0	5,456	13.2	5.9
Total	40,587	100.0%		41,499	100.0%	

TABLE 20–11

The Effect of Interaction When the Effect of Variable A Depends on the Value of Variable B

Average response rate = 4%
Response among men = 3%
Response among women = 5%
Response to COPY A among both groups = 4%
Response to COPY B among both groups = 4%
Response to COPY A among men　　　 = 1%
Response to COPY B among men　　　 = 5%
Response to COPY A among women　　 = 7%
Response to COPY B among women　　 = 3%

product of the two dummy variables would take the interaction into account and produce a correct ranking of the four combinations of SEX and COPY.

The lesson to be learned is that interactions can be very important and a search for interactions should be one of the first steps in the modeling process. A summary of that process follows.

MULTIPLE REGRESSION: GUIDELINES FOR BUILDING A MODEL

The following are basic guidelines for building a multiple regression model:

1. Know your data, or work with someone who does. A data analyst without a working knowledge of your data is a data analyst who's going to get you in trouble.

2. Start with an examination of a correlation matrix to develop ideas about candidate variables and to check for two-variable multicollinearity.

3. Look at your data using stem-and-leaf displays. If the data is not normal, attempt to normalize it using the transformations we suggested.

4. Plot your original and transformed data two variables at a time, for all pairs of variables. Examine all the relationships to make sure they are straight.

5. Try some interaction variables, using your knowledge of the business or CHAID.

6. Select variables for inclusion into the model using all the approaches discussed: your choice of variables, stepwise selections, and models based on the C(p) statistic.

7. Validate the model on fresh data.

CHAPTER 21

Segmentation Analysis

In Chapters 18 through 20 of this section, we concentrated on predictive models. Predictive models are designed, as their name implies, to predict some outcome, for example, response to mailing, returns, bad debts, sales volume, and so on.

In this chapter, we turn our attention to segmentation models. Segmentation models are designed to assign people or geographic areas to groups or clusters on the basis of the similarities in characteristics or attributes that describe them rather than on the basis of some specific action such as response to a mailing.[1]

In Chapter 4 we discussed the many segmentation products available to direct marketers: PRIZM, ClusterPlus, ACORN, MicroVision, and so on. All these products combine small geographic units, usually census block groups, into larger units or clusters based on similarities among the block groups. The characteristics or attributes examined in making this decision include each area's values on the many census (and other) variables collected by the Census Bureau and other government and private agencies.

In this chapter, we will discuss the two primary statistical techniques used in building segmentation models: factor analysis and cluster analysis. These techniques can be used to build customized segmentation models of customers and prospects based on survey and customer or prospect performance information, as well as segmentation models based on census data.

One of direct marketing's unique strengths as a promotional medium is its potential ability to make customized promotional offers to individual customers through the use of available or inferred information about each customer. Unfortunately, all too often, this potential capability is still not adequately utilized. Most direct mail packages are still not customized for the recipient: the same package is usually sent to every name on the mailing. True, laser technology is often used to print the recipient's name in a dozen places in the package, and the recipient's address may be mentioned in the letter, but the guts of the offer are for the most part not customized. The product, the price, the terms, and the strategy are most often identical. And yet one would expect, intuitively, that just as different recipients have different buying preferences, a mailing would work better if its offer were tailored to each individual's specific needs.

---

1. In Chapter 20, we treated CHAID as a tool to be used in predictive modeling. CHAID also may be used as a segmentation tool when the final step in the analysis is the CHAID model itself.

Such targeting and customization of the offer is different in concept from the kind of list segmentation and decile analysis covered earlier in the discussions of predictive modeling. Predictive modeling is used to indicate *which* segment of a list should be mailed, or how often. It does not tell you *how* the segment of the list, or that individual name, should be mailed, in terms of the kind of offer that is most likely to be successful with that segment.

DATA NEEDED FOR SEGMENTATION MODELING

In customizing offers for each segment, the direct marketer uses the data on hand about the customer. At minimum, the direct marketer knows each customer by name, address, and ZIP code, and the list the customer's name came from. If this list is a response list of some kind, the mailer knows what kind of product or service the name responded to. It is sometimes possible to negotiate even more detailed information from the list owner, such as the amount of money spent, previous buying history, and so on. Even better, if promotion and sales history is maintained on a customer database, the direct marketer will know what this customer purchased in the past, how often he or she purchased, how purchases were paid for, and so forth. To this data could be added individual information from customer surveys on, for example, demographic characteristics, attitudes, and interests. Finally, actual or inferred demographic or lifestyle characteristics or both could be overlaid on the existing data; these could come from census, or survey sources (see Chapter 4 on sources of primary and secondary data).

The marketer's task now is to "beat the data till it confesses" on what kind of offer to mail each customer. Because it is usually impractical, infeasible, and financially ruinous to customize the offer to every individual mailing recipient, the best we can usually do is to assign names to a relatively small number of homogeneous groups, so we can send the people in each group the same mailing and different groups, clusters, or consumer segments (the three terms are used interchangeably) different mailings.

In discussing factor and cluster analysis, the techniques that make up segmentation analysis, our objective is to provide enough information to make you an *informed user* of these techniques—but definitely not an expert. To become an expert in these techniques usually requires several years of instruction and experience, and such expertise is more effectively "bought" than "made." After reading the following pages, you should know when to call for these kinds of analyses, how to conduct or manage a segmentation study yourself, how to understand the most important elements of the computer output that accompanies these procedures, and what questions to ask of an expert, if you decide to work with one.

FACTOR ANALYSIS: WHAT IT IS AND WHEN YOU SHOULD USE IT

Factor analysis is a technique used to reduce data to a workable form so it can then be used for some other analysis (like cluster analysis, discussed below, or response modeling using multiple regression, discussed earlier). Technically, the output of a factor analysis can be quite revealing in and of itself, and some researchers find it unnecessary to go further. However, we will treat the output of a factor analysis as input to another procedure.

Factor analysis is usually called for when there is too much data to deal with intuitively or statistically. It may seem paradoxical to marketers who are continually searching for more and better information about their customers to talk about situations where you have too much data, yet these situations can easily occur. Leaf through an information vendor's catalog and you will often find hundreds of pieces of information available. Look through what the Census Bureau has to offer, and you will find each ZIP code or census block described on more than 200 different variables. Conduct a customer survey on attitudes, lifestyles, opinions, interests, and values, and you will probably ask 200 different questions.

Two things happen when you get a huge amount of information. First, it just becomes too much to absorb and comprehend. (There is a well-known psychological principle that says humans cannot, at one time, hold more than seven pieces of information in working consciousness.) Second, it can become difficult to work with this mass of data, both statistically and operationally. Not only can it eat up huge amounts of computer memory, but it can actually seriously distort the results of many statistical analyses, as we discussed earlier in Chapter 19 under multicollinearity. If you get, say, 150 pieces of information about a person or a ZIP code, it is very likely that some of those pieces of information will be highly related. For example, if you try to explain response rates to a mailing across different ZIP codes in terms of the average education and income levels of each ZIP code, your statistical coefficients for these two variables can get distorted because income and education are often highly related. This could threaten the validity of some statistical analyses.

In such situations, you need factor analysis. What factor analysis does is to take your 150 different pieces of information and reduce them to far fewer, say, 20 (or 10 or 30). The reduced pieces of information are now called *factors* or *components*. The bulk (say, 75 percent) of the information contained in the 150 original pieces of information is now contained in the 20 factors. Factor analysis enables you to sacrifice some of the information you began with (in this example, 100 percent minus 75 percent, or 25 percent), for the benefit of greatly improved economy of processing and parsimony of description.

As an example: Suppose you buy Census Bureau data describing every ZIP code on 150 different variables such as percent male population, percent white, percent earning above $35,000, percent with two or more cars, median monthly mortgage, percent homeowner, percent with four or more years of college education, percent in white-collar occupations, and so on. These variables represent 100 percent of the raw information. You wish to use these census data to help you analyze statistically the results of a mailing. Having read this book, you know that (1) 150 raw variables are too many to work with and (2) factor analysis is the way to cope with this surfeit of data. After you or your statistical analyst factor-analyze the data, you will be able to describe each ZIP code in terms of its scores on (perhaps) 20 factors, instead of the 150 original variables. In doing so, you will lose—willingly—some of the richness of the original data. Sacrificing perhaps 20 to 30 percent of the raw information you started out with is the price you pay for the benefit of a dramatic reduction in the number of ZIP code descriptors (from 150 variables to 20 factors) that you now have to work with.

HOW FACTOR ANALYSIS WORKS

There are actually many variations of factor analysis techniques. The one we are describing here is more accurately labeled *principal components analysis*, and what we are referring to as factors are what finicky statisticians would call *components*. But we will continue, for our purposes, to call them factors, for that is what nonstatisticians call them.

You need to understand essentially three key things about how factor analysis works. First, each factor is really a composite, or combination, of original raw variables. The score of each person or ZIP code on each factor is thus a weighted combination of the scores of each person or ZIP code on each of the original, raw variables. Factor analysis combines those raw variables that are highly related among themselves into composite factors, thereby allowing you to let this combination replace those original raw variables. Thus, if average income levels, average monthly mortgage payments, and the percent of households with two or more cars were highly correlated in the actual data, factor analysis would combine these three into a factor (which you might label "affluence"), and you could then create factor scores for each ZIP code for this factor. (In actual practice, the factor score would use information on all the raw variables, but these three would be the ones carrying the highest weights.)

If a ZIP code had average income of $40,000, average monthly mortgage payments of $1,500, and 30 percent of households owning two or more cars, the factor analysis computer output would tell you what weights to apply to these raw numbers to create the factor score (for example, .0035, .25, and 300.17). Thus, the factor score on this factor for this ZIP code would be $(.0035 \times 40,000) + (.25 \times 1,500) + (300.17 \times .30)$, which equals 605.0510. So in subsequent analyses you would not use those three original numbers ($40,000, $1,500, and 30 percent) but one composite factor score (605.0510). This is the data-reduction service of factor analysis.

Importantly, when factor analysis gives you these factor coefficients (similar to regression coefficients), called *loadings*, it does so in a manner that the factor scores you create (for the first, second, and third factor, and so on) have a zero correlation with each other. Thus, you can use them as independent (predictor) variables in a multiple regression without any danger of the problems of multicollinearity, which occurs when the independent variables are highly related to each other. These factor scores, as we just said, are not related to each other at all because of the way we do factor analysis. (A technical note: to get such uncorrelated factors, your analyst will have to ask the computer for *orthogonal* factors.)

The second key idea is that factor analysis "shifts" the information you feed to it for analysis. Suppose we give it 150 census variables to analyze. Let us say that each of these raw variables has a value, going in, of one *information unit*. (Statisticians call this an *eigenvalue*.) So we are feeding the computer a total of 150 units of information, with each raw variable having exactly one unit. Factor analysis is a little like performing a centrifugal operation on milk to let the cream float to the top. If you think of the cream as being rich in information, factor analysis shifts the information when it creates the factors so that the first factor it creates is richest in information content, the next one a little less so, and so on, till the last one barely contains any—its information value (or eigenvalue) is close to zero.

In fact, the mathematics of factor analysis is such that if you feed it 150 raw variables (each with a raw information value of 1), the computer solution will initially give you 150 factors—as many as the number of variables you put in—but with this key difference: the first factors now contain most of the raw information that went in (the cream), whereas the rest are, from an information standpoint, trivial and unimportant. Therefore, the analyst tells the factor analysis program to retain only the first few (high-information value, or high eigenvalue) factors, and to drop the rest from consideration.

Although there are many rules concerning which factors should be kept and which ones dropped, one frequently used rule is to drop those factors that have an eigenvalue of less than 1. The reasoning here is that if a raw variable starts out with an eigenvalue of 1, a final factor must, after the analysis, have at least that same amount of information if it is to be worth keeping.

There are many other ways to decide how many factors to keep, however, and you and your analyst should try several, ending with one that leaves you with a factor analysis output you can most easily and intuitively interpret and implement.

For example, you might decide to keep as many factors as are necessary to retain some fixed amount of information. This might be 70 percent, 80 percent, and so on. Alternatively, you might simply decide that 5 (or 6 or 10) factors are the number of factors you wish to keep. If you really want to be scientific, you could apply what is called a *scree test*. In this approach, you ask the computer to give you a graph of the eigenvalue of the first through last factors, and try to find the factor at which the curve bends sharply—what statisticians with anatomical bents call an *elbow*. This is very often the point where subsequent factors really add very little by way of extra information (i.e., where they begin to have small eigenvalues), and so it is reasonable to stop at the factor where the elbow occurs.

Before we get to interpretation, however, there is one last idea you need to grasp. Doing a factor analysis is a lot like taking a photograph with a camera. Just as you would focus the lens—by rotating it—to get a sharp (not blurred) picture on film of whatever it is that you are photographing, so also are you expected to "rotate" the factor analysis table of loadings (the output) to get a more focused interpretation of what is in the data. By focused, we mean a situation where you can look at the output table and read off unambiguously which raw variables are key to forming each factor. There are many ways to rotate the output, but one called *varimax rotation* is frequently used. Once again, you should try a few rotation alternatives to find one that yields an output table you find easiest to interpret.

RUNNING AND INTERPRETING FACTOR ANALYSIS

Let's walk through the steps you need to use factor analysis on your own and talk about how you would interpret what you get.

Let's suppose you are managing a negative option book club. You decide that instead of mailing the same negative option selection to all of your million-member file, you would like to customize the negative option to the reading preference of the member. You are thinking of dividing your file into perhaps five segments, or clusters, and featuring a different negative option selection in your monthly mailing to each segment. What you need is information to let you create these segments. So you mail a sample of 5,000 customers a 100-question survey on reading habits, lifestyle, demographics, attitude, and interests, and get 2,500 responses. Eventually, you will use cluster analysis to create these groupings of people, but first you want to use factor analysis to reduce these 100 questions into fewer factors so that you can later use these factor scores in your subsequent cluster analysis.

You first create a data file where the rows are the 2,500 people and the columns (or fields) are the answers to the 100 questions. A few things need to be quoted here. You can only use factor analysis on data that is continuous or scalar, such as age and income. Attitude questions answered on a 5- or 7-point agree/disagree scale also meet this requirement. You cannot legitimately use factor analysis on data where people are put into arbitrarily coded categories (such as male/female, coded 0/1). Note, also that you should usually have many (e.g., 10 or more) times the number of rows (people or areas) than you have columns (questions or attributes). Since we have 25 times more people than we have questions to analyze, we have no cause for worry here.

Next, you pick factor analysis from your statistical software package's menu. In submenus, you pick principal components analysis. You tell the software package where your data file is and what the 100 raw variables are called, and you ask it to create *orthogonal* factors (those that have a zero correlation to each other) from those 100 variables.

In its first output solution, it will give you a table of the eigenvalues (remember, this was analogous to the amount of information) for each factor. There will be 100 factors because you used 100 raw variables. You notice from the table that, after the 20th factor, the eigenvalue drops below 1. You also note that the first 20 factors (of the 100) explain 80 percent of the variance, or raw information, that went in. You decide to ask the factor analysis program to rerun the output, but this time to keep only the first 20 factors (and retain 80 percent of the raw information). Though you are sacrificing 20 percent of the information, you are gaining the ability to work with just 20 factors instead of five times as many raw variables. (In later computer interactions, you can experiment with other cutoff rules.)

You also ask the software program to rotate the output table using varimax rotation (or another one from the menu). This time around, the output contains the key table of interest, called *rotated factor loadings*. The rows here, 100 in all, are the original question variables. The 20 columns correspond to your 20 retained important factors, with the first one being the most important (it has the highest eigenvalue). The numbers in the table, called *factor loadings*, represent the correlation relationship between each factor (column) and each variable (row), measured from -1.00 (strong negative relationship) through 0.00 (no relationship) to $+1.00$ (strong positive relationship). Mathematically, to create the first factor's score for each of the 2,500 people, you would multiply each person's score on each of the 100 raw variables by the loading for each variable on the first factor, and add up the results. Usually the computer program will do this automatically, if you ask it to, for each of the 20 factors. You can then create a new data file of 2,500 rows (people) and 20 columns (factors) and now use this second data file, instead of your first raw data file, in susbsequent modeling (such as regression and cluster analysis).

To interpret the rotated loadings table, however, all you have to do is look down each column (factor) and see which variables have a high loading (e.g., 0.50 or above—use your judgment) on that factor. A positive and high loading means that a high factor score is created by a high score on that particular raw variable. A negative and high loading means that a high score on that raw variable *decreases* the factor score. Because the factor score is essentially based on those raw variables that have a high loading, you can now give the factor a name to summarize what those high-loading variables appear to have in common. For example, if the raw variables with a high loading on a factor all deal with aspects of religion and morality (such as attitudes toward sex on TV, prayer in public schools, and abortion), you might want to label that factor the "religious" factor. Giving names to factors is often the most enjoyable part of factor analysis, so savor this opportunity!

CLUSTER ANALYSIS: WHAT IT IS AND WHEN YOU SHOULD USE IT

Cluster analysis, as we said previously, is appropriate whenever you want to assign people or areas to groups so those people within a group are similar to each other and those in different groups are different from each other. After forming such groups (clusters) through cluster analysis, you can then tailor offers and packages to each group, thus (you hope) increasing response and profitability. This is the promise and technique of market segmentation.

You can assign not only people or areas to clusters, but also other things as well, for example, brands within a category. Any "thing" that is given a number for each of a reasonably large number of variables (such as ZIP codes rated on average age, average income, percent white population, and so on) is fair game for a cluster analysis. When we are dealing with consumers, we typically score each individual or household on demographic variables, previous purchases (what was purchased, when purchased, how much, how often, how paid), source of name, lifestyle and attitudinal data (perhaps from overlays), benefit preference data from surveys, and so on. This data is more easily handled in cluster analysis if it is of the continuous scalar type, but methods do exist for working with binary (yes/no) information as well. Thus, if your house file contains data on how each name responded in the past to different offers, that yes/no response history can also be used in certain kinds of cluster analysis to put your file into response segments.

The most common use of cluster analysis is with geo-demographic data—the kind discussed in Chapter 4 and marketed as ClusterPlus, PRIZM, Acorn, and so on. In essence, what these companies have done is to take census data on various variables by block group, update the data, add other data (such as auto registration statistics), and then use cluster analysis to create clusters of these block groups. Those block groups within a cluster are very similar to each other in terms of their scores on these variables (no mater where they happen to be geographically), and the clusters themselves are different from each other.

Thus, for example, Cluster S01 in the *ClusterPlus* scheme is described by the cluster concept of "established wealthy," which includes (among other things) the highest socioeconomic status indicators, highest median income ($75,000), homeowners living in prime real estate areas (73 percent in single-family homes), high education levels (64 percent college graduates, 26 percent with graduate degrees), professionally employed people (58 percent so employed), and parents whose children go to private schools. Towns across the country having a large proportion of people in this cluster include Los Altos, California; Westport, Connecticut; Bethesda, Maryland; Scarsdale, New York; and Highland Park, Illinois. While forming only 1.4 percent of the nation's population, people in this cluster buy disproportionately large amounts of expensive clothes, financial products, imported wines, vacations, and expensive cars, and they fly more often. Not surprisingly, people in such a cluster respond more readily to high-priced offers, and packages sent to them most profitably appeal to upscale values. In contrast, people in the bottom clusters are not good targets for such offers and appeals.

These syndicated geo-demographic cluster assignments to ZIP codes or census block groups are used most often, and most easily, for name selection purposes in a mailing—to decide which names in a list you wish to mail to and which ones you wish to suppress. Yet the technology of cluster analysis is also used to classify customers or prospects, at an individual level, into benefit segments (people who value similar benefits in a product category, such as reading preference segments in a book club), or lifestyle and psychographic segments (people with similar attitudes, values, and interests).

HOW CLUSTER ANALYSIS WORKS

There are many different varieties of cluster analysis, so many that statisticians don't really know which ones are best or standard. In fact, these different varieties work in different ways and very often yield different cluster results. The practical consequence of this variety, and a very important one, is that you should often use more than one technique, and you should be satisfied only when two or more techniques yield outputs that look reasonably similar. Otherwise, you may be seeing clusters that exist only as figments of the computer's imagination. Always ask your analysts to try more than one technique and to demonstrate some convergence.

When you work with continuous, scalar data (such as income, years of education, age, and agree/disagree attitude scales), cluster analysis works much like the coordinate geometry that we all learned way back in high school. As we said earlier, the objective of cluster analysis is to put similar things together in a group. How do we know when things are similar? The computer calculates a statistical measure of similarity called *distance*—obviously, things that are similar are not distant, and things that have high distance (that are far apart) are not similar.

The distance between any two things is calculated much as we would calculate the distance between the two points A and B on a graph with two axes or dimensions (X and Y). If point A is located at ($X1$, $Y1$) on this map, and point B is located at ($X2$, $Y2$) on this map, coordinate geometry tells us that the distance between A and B is given by the square root of the squared total of ($X2 - X1$) and ($Y2 - Y1$). (If you don't remember, or don't care, that's OK; we are simply giving you an intuitive feel for what's inside the black box of cluster analysis.) Now, suppose we're dealing with ZIP codes instead of points. The same logic applies; the axes become the variables (such as average age, average income, or average education), and each ZIP code has a location (its score) on each axis. The computer first calculates a total distance between every pair of points (ZIP codes or people), and then uses some rule to put points that are closest to each other in the same cluster.

If you are working with binary (yes/no, bought/didn't buy) kinds of data, the methods of calculating similarity use a different approach. Suppose you market collectibles, and in the last year you mailed 10 offers to each of a million people. For each offer, some people bought, and most didn't buy. You had the good sense to record in your files how they responded (bought/didn't buy) to each of the 10 mailings. For such data, the computer will define similarity for every pair of names as the proportion of times they acted the same way (both bought, or both didn't buy) to the total number of offers mailed; if one name in the pair bought one offer while the other didn't, then that should count as dissimilar behavior.

The user has to tell the computer program which method it should use to calculate distance, which method it should use to bring close points together, and how many clusters it should create. Obviously, statisticians spend lifetimes studying which rules are best for making these methodological decisions. Although we will skip the details here, we will now give you some guidelines.

RUNNING AND INTERPRETING CLUSTER ANALYSIS

First, you have to create a data file in which each of the things you want to cluster (the rows) is scored on each of the variables you want it to be clustered on (the columns). These might be ZIP codes scored on various census variables. The columns might be factor scores, which (as we saw in the earlier section) are combinations of variables. (Some statisticians recommend that you *standardize* these column scores before using cluster analysis. Standardizing means mathematically converting each number to another equivalent one, with the new set of numbers having an average of 0 and a standard deviation of 1. Most computer programs do this painlessly, on request).

When you pull up the cluster analysis portion of your statistical software, the menu will ask you (1) which kind of program you want to use, (2) how you want distance computed, (3) which method you want it to use to put points into clusters, based on their distances, and (4) how many clusters you want it to create. It may also ask you in what shape and form you want to see the output, that is, tables or trees (called *dendograms*).

The first decision—what kind of program—really depends on how large your data set is. Calculating and storing the distance between *every* pair of 35,000 residential ZIP codes, for example, is beyond the capacity of most computers and software. For really large data sets, therefore, you should pick a cluster analysis program that doesn't require these pairwise calculations and that works somewhat differently. Though the name may vary with the software package, such programs are often called *K-means* clustering programs (the software will usually tell you clearly that it is meant for large data sets). Smaller data sets are handled by most cluster analysis programs.

The second decision—what kind of distance measure to use—typically depends on your data as well. Binary (yes/no) data have their own types of distance measures (which not all software programs have, so check before you pick your software if you want to work with such data). If you are working with continuous, scalar data, you would normally pick Euclidean or squared Euclidean distance measures. (Your software might recommend which kinds of distance measures work best with different kinds of grouping methods, discussed next. The programs for larger data sets typically have a default measure and grouping method.)

The third decision—what kind of grouping rule you want to apply to the calculated distance—offers a big array of possibilities. Statisticians again have their preferences, but one called *Ward's method* works well in many situations.

The fourth decision—how many clusters you want the program to form— is, unfortunately, the most judgmental. Although some statistical packages offer ways to help you here, most often how many clusters you want is simply a subjective question. It depends on your economics, the number of logical segmentation possibilities, and your production capabilities—how many customized offers or mailings you can profitably and feasibly handle.

After you indicate your choices to the computer, it will eventually give you (among a host of other output) a table in which each thing (person/ZIP code, and so on) you have clustered is given a cluster number. You can, optionally, get a tree diagram telling you the exact sequence of the clustering process; this will give you a visual idea of how the clusters and cluster members related to each other in terms of overall similarity, and the sequence in which the method split up the total mass of things into a greater and greater number of clusters. Finally, the program may give you an average score for each cluster on each raw variable used for the clustering (if not, you can do this separately by computing the average scores on these variables for each of the things in that cluster); you use average scores to profile each cluster and to understand these clusters intuitively.

One final point on validation. We have already mentioned the need to repeat your analyses using different methods to see if you get similar solutions. Another method of checking the validity of your cluster solution is to first get a cluster output on a randomly selected half of your data, and then on the other half. Check to see that the clusters look similar—trust them only if they do.

USING SMALL-SAMPLE SURVEY DATA TO SEGMENT A MUCH BIGGER FILE

One of the practical issues that database marketers face is this: If I want to create cluster-based segments in my many-million-name house file, using data on customers obtained through a questionnaire mailing, must I mail that survey questionnaire to every individual on my file? Since that is obviously an expensive and impractical undertaking, how can I feasibly use cluster analysis on my entire file, while still benefiting from customer survey techniques?

Fortunately, there is indeed an answer to this problem. The steps you need to go through are as follows:

First, randomly select a small Nth-name sample from the huge file you want to create segments in. You could, for example, select 10,000 names to mail to. Mail each of these 10,000 people or households your questionnaire, which is probably quite long, with lots of questions on benefits sought in the product category, their attitudes and values, demographic data, product/brand usership, and so on. Consider (or test) giving them some incentive for responding to boost the response rate. You should develop this questionnaire through conventional marketing research techniques. It is very important to remember here that as many scales as possible in the questionnaire should be "continuous" (e.g., 5- or 7-point "agree-disagree"-type scales).

The second step is to create segments among the responders (let's say 4,000 responded) through cluster analysis, using the data on this questionnaire (perhaps after you've reduced the data through factor analysis first). As suggested earlier, try to make sure you've got valid clusters by doing split-half replication, multimethod replication, and the like.

Let's say you end up with four clusters among these 4,000 people, and that these clusters make intuitive sense and also relate to differences in the customer performance data your earlier had on these customers from your file. Note that it is very important that you only accept clusters that differ meaningfully on some performance or response dimension relevant to your business.

The trick now is to take this information on these four clusters from these 4,000 people and use it to put each of your many-million house file people into the "most likely" cluster—even though only the 4,000 got the questionnaires.

This brings us to step three, which is to develop a predictive model for cluster membership, USING ONLY YOUR HOUSE FILE DATA AND NOT YOUR SURVEY DATA. You begin by taking your 4,000 responders, each of whom has been placed into one of these four new clusters. To the file that has the cluster membership scores for these 4,000 people, append all the house file information you already had without the survey (which is information you would also have for everybody else on your file).

Now, in step four, see if you can build a logistic regression or discriminant analysis to create a predictive model, for just these 4,000 people, using that "old and plentiful" house file data to predict which of the four "new" clusters each of them belongs to. Note that you already "know" this cluster membership from the cluster analysis you did earlier from the survey data. You are trying to see if you can come up with a model that would predict the cluster each of these 4,000 people belonged to IF ALL YOU KNEW was the standard house file data that you have on them—and on everyone else.

You should—it is hoped—come up with a model that works reasonably well, though it will obviously misclassify some of these 4,000 people. In the final step, use the computer-estimated coefficients (weights) from this predictive model to score everyone else on your house file, using the house file data you have on everyone (which should be the same variables that you used in your predictive model in step four earlier). Use this score to place everyone in your file into a "predicted" cluster.

Then—and here's the payoff—use this predicted cluster membership to mail different offers or packages to the people you're mailing to. If you do the process right (and if you're lucky), response rates and performance should improve over a one-mailing-for-all-strategy.

CONCLUDING EXAMPLE AND REVIEW

The example that follows came about as a result of what began as a simple use of one of the commercially available clustering products. An analysis of our client's mailing of an upscale product indicated that, contrary to expectations, response was not coming from the very top socioeconomic clusters but from middle and lower socioeconomic clusters. The client questioned the reliability of the clustering product. To verify the analysis, we created our own clustering scheme for just New York state, based on available census data at the ZIP code level.

We selected 40 census variables (of the more than 150 available) as the raw data for summarization through factor (principal components) analysis. Each of 2,000 New York ZIP codes was rated on these 40 census variables; this formed the raw data file. Initial analysis showed that only the first 10 of the 40 factors extracted had an eigenvalue (amount of information) that exceeded 1, so only these 10 factors were retained in the next round. The table showed that these 10 factors retained 70 percent of the information (variance) that originally came in with the 40 raw variables, and we considered this an acceptable trade-off.

Table 21–1 shows abbreviated varimax-rotated factor loadings for the factor analysis of New York state ZIP code data. Figure 21–1 shows the scree diagram that suggested a 10-factor solution.

Table 21–1 describes the original census variables (the rows) and gives the loadings (the numbers relating each row to each of the factor columns). For brevity, we have reproduced only the first 26 rows and first 3 columns here. (The full table had 40 rows and 10 columns.) The computer would automatically create 10 factor scores for each ZIP code for use later. For interpretation, note that the first factor related highly negatively to the percentage of homeowners, percentage of households with two or more cars, percent white population, and percent born in the state where they now live. It related highly positively to the percentage of renter homes, percent homes with elevators, percent foreign born, percent Hispanic, and percent single-person households. This factor should paint an easily interpreted picture in your mind's eye. What the analysis suggests is that ZIP codes that will score high on this one factor will represent urban areas with large Hispanic populations.

As a contrast, the second factor is very different—almost the reverse image of the first but still urban. These ZIPs appear to represent educated, upper-income professionals with children in preschools. Yuppies! Factor 3 scores high

TABLE 21-1

Varimax-Rotated Factor Loadings for Census Variables (First Three Factors)*

	Factors		
Raw Census Data at ZIP Code Level	**1**	**2**	**3**
1. Percent homeowners	−.91	−.05	.00
2. Percent renters	.91	.05	.00
3. Percent two-car households	−.87	.14	.14
4. Percent households with elevators	.82	.06	.12
5. Percent born in foreign countries	.71	.29	.07
6. Percent Hispanic	.68	.02	−.14
7. Percent white	−.66	−.04	.18
8. Percent single-person households	.66	−.20	.12
9. Percent born in the same U.S. state	−.62	−.17	−.04
10. Percent income of $25,000+	−.21	.80	.34
11. Median household income	−.30	.78	.30
12. Percent with central air conditioning	−.10	.70	.16
13. Median monthly mortgage	.03	.69	.18
14. Median monthly rent	.09	.67	.13
15. Percent in professional occupations	.10	.62	.18
16. Percent with four+ years college education	.17	.61	.42
17. Percent who work in a place different from where they live	.01	.60	−.03
18. Percent urban population	.54	.59	.08
19. Percent educated high school+	.03	.53	.47
20. Percent of children in nursery schools	−.02	.48	−.07
21. Percent in administrative occupations	.28	.47	.15
22. Percent of English origin	−.38	−.65	.10
23. Percent of population in total labor force	.06	.28	.90
24. Percent of females in labor force	−.11	.24	.78
25. Percent of males in labor force	.18	.24	.74
26. Percent of households with two or more workers	−.35	.13	.63

* Loadings have been sorted so that factor 1 has high (positive or negative) loadings on variables 1 through 9; factor 2, variables 20 through 22; and factor 3, variables 23 through 26. Factor 1 appears to be urban Hispanics; factor 2, affluent, white-collar, suburban commuters; and factor 3, level of employment in that ZIP code.

on two-income families, suggesting ZIP codes populated by hard-working, low-to middle-income families.

Factor scores were then derived for each of the 2,000 ZIP codes, for each of the 10 factors; this formed the new data file for later input into cluster analysis. We used a program suitable for large data sets and requested 50 clusters (to be consistent with the commercial product that was being questioned). The program output told us which of the 50 clusters each of the 2,000 ZIP codes belonged to, as well as how close each ZIP code was to the center of that cluster. For each cluster, we then selected the one ZIP code that was closest to that cluster's center and used that ZIP code's profile on the 10 factor scores as a proxy for the factor score profile of the entire ZIP code. Finally, we compared the resulting cluster profiles with that provided by the commercial product for these 16 center ZIP codes.

Table 21–2 shows the factor loadings for the three factors discussed above for three entirely different ZIP codes or neighborhoods.

As you can see, there is a strong relationship between the factor scores and the vendor's abbreviated description of the ZIP code. ZIP code 10504, described

SPSS Factor Analysis

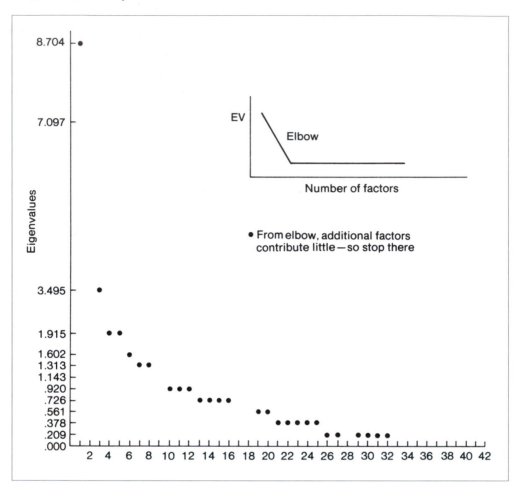

as wealthy, scores highly negative on factor 1 and highly positive on factor 2. Center city ZIP code 10026 scores highly positive on factor 1 and highly negative on factor 2. ZIP code 14146, commercially described as small town, scores high on factor 3, which you will recall represented areas with large percentages of two-income families.

T A B L E   21–2

ZIP Code	Abbreviated Commercial Description	Factor 1	Factor 2	Factor 3
10504	Wealthy	−1.04107	2.67803	.75684
10026	Center city	2.98245	−.92635	−1.88863
14146	Small town	.42019	−1.14470	3.36004

Thus, our analysis supported the integrity of the commercial product. But what about the conclusion that upscale ZIP codes were not responding as well to an upscale product as middle- and low-income ZIP codes were? Well, it turns out that we haven't been telling you the whole story. The key fact we omitted to tell you is that the upscale product was being promoted with the aid of a downscale premium, which did not appeal to an upscale market but did appeal to middle- and lower-level markets. The final result was that the premium offer was changed to an offer more attractive to the client's desired market.

CHAPTER 22

A Closer Look Back

[A note to our readers: Chapters 17 through 21 on statistical analysis, modeling, and segmentation were primarily intended to provide the users of models with enough information so that they could ask intelligent questions of those actually charged with responsibility for developing working models. This chapter and the ones that immediately follow are intended to provide modelers with some additional insights and tools they may wish to incorporate into their modeling procedures. Nonstatisticians, users, are encouraged to follow along, but if the material gets a little too theoretical, just go on to Chapter 34 where we discuss the role of modeling in the new direct marketing and where the emphasis is on the issues associated with the use and implementation of models.]

This chapter will further develop your understanding of some of the more important ideas introduced in the preceding chapters. From a practical perspective the material it covers will help you both develop new measures of the effectiveness of your models and improve the power of your models.

A CLOSER LOOK AT *r*, THE CORRELATION COEFFICIENT

In this section we'll discuss the key measure of most statistical analyses, *r*, the correlation coefficient first introduced in Chapter 18. After a brief review of the basics we'll introduce the concept of rematching, a technique that provides the analyst with a basis for evaluating the power of the models.

Review of *r*

The correlation coefficient *r* (Pearson's product-moment) measures the strength of the *linear* relationship between two variables.

In theory, *r* can range in value between +1 and −1 where

0 indicates no relationship
+1 indicates a perfect positive relationship
−1 indicates a perfect negative relationship

Values between 0 and 1 or 0 to −1 indicate a weak to moderate to strong relationship, as depicted in Figure 22–1.

Remember that *r* was originally built for two continuous variables, and it is

FIGURE 22-1

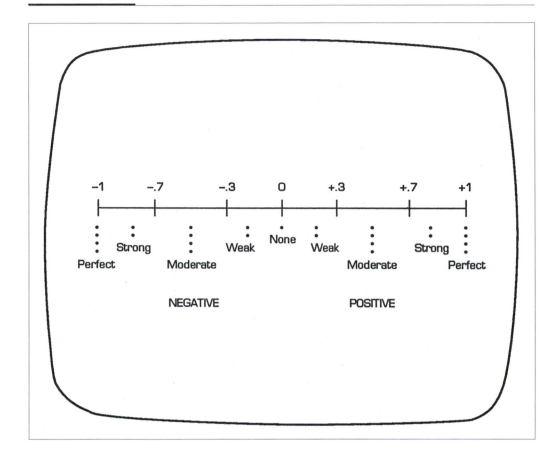

expressed in the form of *standard scores* (each variable is reexpressed to have a mean of zero and a standard deviation of 1).

Let $Z(X)$ and $Z(Y)$ be standardized variables for X and Y, respectively:

$$Z(X) = \frac{X - \text{mean}(X)}{\text{std}(X)} \quad \text{and} \quad Z(Y) = \frac{Y - \text{mean}(Y)}{\text{std}(X)}$$

Then r is defined as the average product of paired standardized scores:

$$r = \frac{\text{sum of } [Z(X) \times Z(Y)]}{n}$$

where n = the number of (x, y) pairs, and std = standard deviation. See Table 22-1 for a simple illustration.

In the illustration in Table 22-1 r is equal to $+.59625$, so we would declare the relationship between X and Y as moderate using the schematic defined in Figure 22-1.

REMATCHING

The strength of a relationship as depicted in Figure 22-1 and as measured by the correlation coefficient is based on theoretical extreme values of plus and minus one. That is, if the data (X and Y) itself has the potential of a perfect correlation

T A B L E   22-1

Calculating the Correlation Coefficient Data Set $A - (X, Y)$

	X	Y	Z(X)	Z(X)	Z(X) × Z(Y)
	124	779	−1.42313	−1.70114	2.42095
	153	988	−1.10020	1.04221	−1.14664
	170	759	−0.91090	−1.96366	1.78869
	192	933	−0.66591	0.32028	−0.21328
	235	922	−0.18708	0.17589	−0.03291
	267	891	0.16926	−0.23102	−0.03910
	292	942	0.44765	0.43841	0.19626
	316	924	0.71491	0.20214	0.14451
	347	946	1.06011	0.49092	0.52043
	422	1002	1.89529	1.22598	2.32357
mean	251.8	909.6		sum	5.96248
std	89.80	76.18		r	0.59625
n	10	10			

($r = +1$ or $r = -1$), then the nominal weak/moderate/strong categories are valid. To the extent that X and Y cannot achieve the most positive value of $r = +1$ and the most negative value of $r = -1$, then the schematic in Figure 22–1 is not quite valid, and an adjusted r is needed.

We can realize the full potential of the data by using a technique called *rematching*. We know intuitively that for any set of X, Y values, the most positive relationship possible would come about when the highest X value was paired with the highest Y value, the second highest X value was paired with the second highest Y value, and so on until the lowest X is paired with the lowest Y. Equally intuitive, the most negative relationship would come about when the highest X value was paired with the lowest Y value, the second highest X was paired with the second lowest Y, and so on until the lowest X is paired with the highest Y.

Suppose that we took the data set we are working with and created positive and negative rematched data sets and then calculated the correlation coefficient for each rematched set. The result would be the largest positive r and the largest negative r possible.

Rematch Example

So, let's rematch X and Y to obtain the largest positive value and the largest negative value r for the data set A.

The data set named P (for positive) has X ordered from low to high and matched with Y, which is also ordered from low to high. Data set N (for negative) has X ordered from low to high and matched with Y ordered the other way, from high to low. Table 22–2 shows the correlation coefficients for the rematched data sets and the original data set.

We see that, given this data set, the most positive value that r can have is $+.875$ and not $+1$; and the most negative r is $-.926$ and not -1. Accordingly,

T A B L E   22–2

Rematched Data Sets

A Original Pairing			P Remached for Most Positive			N Rematched for Most Negative	
X	Y		X	Y		X	Y
124	779		124	759		124	1002
153	988		153	779		153	988
170	759		170	891		170	946
192	933		192	922		192	942
235	922		235	924		235	933
267	891		267	933		267	924
292	942		292	942		292	922
316	924		316	946		316	891
347	946		347	988		347	779
422	1002		422	1002		422	759
$r = +.596$			$r = +.875$			$r = -.926$	

we adjust r by simply dividing the original r of $+.596$ by its potential or actual (not theoretical) most positive value of $+.875$. Thus:

$$r_{adj} = +.596/+.875 = +.681$$

Now, referring to the schematic, we still must consider the relationship between X and Y as nominally moderate, but its numerical r has increased by 14.3 percent. We now have a more accurate numerical assessment of the relationship between X and Y. (Note: If r was negative, then we would have divided by the most negative r value.)

Rematching Phi

As we've seen, when two variables are continuous, the calculations for r are messy. When the variables take on only two values (referred to as *dichotomous* or *binary* variables), the formula changes. Technically, the correlation coefficient r is now referred to as the *phi coefficient*.

Let X and Y take on values 0 and 1. This implies that there are only four possible combinations or pairs of X and Y:

$$a = 1, 1$$
$$b = 1, 0$$
$$c = 0, 0$$
$$d = 0, 1$$

Let a represent the number of times the pair $(1, 1)$ occurs; b, c, and d are the number of times the pairs $(1, 0)$, $(0, 0)$, and $(0, 1)$ occur, respectively. Accordingly, we can present the data in the following table, and *phi* is defined as follows:

$$Y$$

$$0 \quad 1$$

		0	1	
X	1	a	b	a + b
	0	c	d	c + d

$$a + c \qquad b + d$$

$$\text{phi} = \frac{ad - cb}{\text{square root of } [(a + b) \times (c + d) \times (a + c) \times (b + d)]}$$

Simple Illustration

Let X = Sex   [(male, female) = (1, 0)]

Y = Response   [(yes, no)   = (1, 0)]

Suppose a sample of 100 names from a mailing with a 10 percent response from a list composed of 70 males and 30 females produces the table below:

Response (Y)

$$0 \quad 1$$

			0	1	
X	Males	1	a	b	70
	Females	0	c	d	30

$$90 \quad 10$$

The phi coefficient is calculated as follows:

$$\text{phi} = \frac{65 \times 5 - 25 \times 5}{\text{square root of } [(70) \times (30) \times (90) \times (10)]}$$

$$= +.145$$

The relationship between response and sex is declared weak if the most positive value phi could be is +1.

To determine the most positive value that phi can be, assume we must find the a, b, c, and d that make phi large with the restriction that the row and column totals (the marginals) remain fixed. In other words, we must fill in the empty cells in the table below to make the corresponding phi the most positive it can be:

Response (Y)

$$0 \quad 1$$

			0	1	
X	Males	1			70
	Females	0			30

$$90 \quad 10$$

The most positive phi occurs when the a-c diagonal is largest. This occurs when $a = 70$ and $c = 10$, which in turn forces $b = 0$ and $d = 20$. Thus, we have:

Response (Y)

		0	1	
Males	1	70	0	70
Females	0	20	10	30
		90	10	

X and phi $= +.509$.

Similar to adjusting r by its extreme value, the adjusted phi is .285 ($= .145/.509$), still indicating a weak relationship but representing a numerical increase of 97 percent [$(.285 - .145)/.145 \times 100$] over the original and unadjusted r of $+.145$.

The "unadjusted" assessment of the effect of sex on response indicates that sex explains 2.1 percent (r squared $= .145 \times .145$) of the response variation. In contrast, an "adjusted" assessment indicates that sex explains 8.1 percent of response variation and that it has promise as a candidate predictor in developing a response model. With the addition of a few more powerful predictors an excellent response model can be anticipated.

Although not needed here, the most negative value of phi is $-.218$ and occurs with the table below:

Response (Y)

		0	1	
Males	1	60	10	70
Females	0	30	0	30
		90	10	

X

IMPLICATION OF REMATCHING

Rematching provides an accurate assessment of the relationships between variables by taking into account their "shapes." For a categorical variable, the shape refers to the marginals—the frequency distribution among the variables' categories or cells. The shape can be flat, indicating equal distribution among the cells, or skewed, indicating unequal distribution among the cells.

The shape of a continuous variable is the frequency curve as depicted by a stem-and-leaf picture, box-and-whisker plot, or a regular histogram. The shape can be symmetric or skewed. *To the extent that the shapes of variables are not the same, the rematching adjustment will improve the assessment of relationships between variables.*

Thus rematching is telling us that our variables should be in the same shape, the "best" shape being symmetry. However, as previously mentioned, symmetry and straightening go hand in hand. Accordingly, if we strive for the trio of symmetry, straightening, and rematching, our whole modeling results should be as close to optimal as possible.

Clearly, in direct marketing where a zero-one response is always very skewed (typical response rates are between 2 percent and 15 percent), rematching offers an effective way of performing more sensitive analyses and developing more precise predictive equations.

Consider a house file mailing with a known response rate and the usual key selection criteria. The analyst can properly assess the effects of the selection factors on response by taking into account both the level of the house file's response rate and the shape of the factors.

At a multivariate level of analysis, for example, response modeling, the analyst can adjust all the pair correlation coefficients of the correlation matrix and directly input the adjusted correlation matrix instead of the raw data into any regression routine. Model development will proceed as usual, but the results will reflect more accurate interrelationships among the predictor and response variables.

A CLOSER LOOK AT A MODEL'S POWER

In direct marketing a model's predictive power is typically assessed in terms of how well the model can identify the best customers, either the most responsive or the most profitable. The model's dependent variable, Y, is either a binary response variable (Y = yes or no) or a continuous performance variable (e.g., Y = sales dollars).

Models are used to predict Y, thus providing an estimate of Y, $\hat{Y}$ (pronounced Y-hat). The model scores a customer file to produce a score value, $\hat{Y}$. The scored file is ranked from highest to lowest value on $\hat{Y}$.

The ranked file is then divided into 10 groups or deciles, and the average (actual) Y (average response rate or average sales) is calculated for each decile. The results are typically displayed in a decile analysis, which provides the information needed to assess the model in terms of how well it finds the best groups of customers.

To make sense of all this, let's go to an example.

An Example

A regression model was built to predict increased total net sales within a specified period. The dependent variable Y was defined as *increased total net sales*, and because returns or credits were possible, this variable could have had, and did have, negative values.

The final model consisted of five variables and produced the decile analysis shown in the first three columns in Table 22–3, under the heading *Model*.

The Impact of the Model

The actual average increase in the dependent, variable increased total net sales, was $75. The top decile consists of those customers predicted to be our best-performing customers, and these customers had an actual average increase of $150.

The top decile shows a lift of 200, which indicates that the decile produced two times the file average of $75 in increased total net sales. That is, without a model any 10 percent of the file would have had an average increased total net sales of $75; but with this model the top 10 percent of the file produces an average of $150, or two times better than average.

The next best decile, decile 9, had a mean or average increased total net sales of $112. The top two deciles combined have a cumulative increased total net

TABLE 22-3

Assessing a Model's Power Using Rematching

	Model			Rematch			AID		
Decile	Decile Average Increased Total Net Sale	Cum Average Increased Total Net Sale	Cum Lift	Decile Average Increased Total Net Sale	Cum Average Increased Total Net Sale	Cum Lift	Decile Average Increased Total Net Sale	Cum Average Increased Total Net Sale	Cum Lift
1	$150	$150	200	$337	$337	449	$170	$170	226
2	$112	$131	175	$172	$255	339	$134	$152	201
3	$94	$119	158	$117	$209	278	$119	$141	187
4	$80	$109	145	$82	$177	236	$85	$127	168
5	$89	$105	140	$57	$153	204	$67	$115	152
6	$73	$100	133	$33	$133	177	$63	$106	141
7	$62	$94	126	$12	$116	154	$62	$100	132
8	$65	$91	121	$0	$101	135	$52	$94	124
9	$25	$83	111	($17)	$88	117	$18	$86	113
10	$0	$75	100	($42)	$75	100	($15)	$75	100
Average	$75			$75			$75		

sales averaging 131 or a lift of 175. That is, without a model any 20 percent of the file would have an average increased total net sales of $75, but with the regression model the top 20 percent of the file produces an average of $131, or 1.75 times better than average.

The combined top four deciles had an average increase of $109 and a lift of 145.

The BIG Question

How *good* is the regression model's predictive power?

The answer lies in how well the *model* decile analysis—reflecting the model's ranking of Y—compares with the best or *maximum* decile analysis— reflecting the full potential of the best ranking of Y, which is obtained by *rematching*.

To rematch to obtain the *maximum* decile analysis, take these steps:

1. Rank the file of Y (not $\hat{Y}$) from high to low values.
2. Divide the ranked file into 10 equal parts and produce a decile report.

The maximum decile analysis is shown in the next three columns of Table 22–3, under the heading *Rematch*.

Maximum Decile Analysis

The ranked file still, of course, shows an average increase of $75. Now rematched, the top "maximum" decile shows an average increase in increased total net sales of $337 and lift of 449.

The next best maximum decile, decile 9, has an average increased total net sales of $172. Combining the top two maximum deciles, there is a "maximum" average cumulative increased total net sales of $255, and a "maximum" lift of 339.

The combined top four maximum deciles show a maximum mean increase of $177 and maximum lift of 236.

Comparing the Regression Model and the True Model

A maximum decile analysis reflects the results of the one and only true model—the model that has the correct variables in their optimal functional form. Accordingly, a comparison between a regression model's decile analysis and the true model's decile analysis is an indication of how good the regression model actually is.

Because model performance varies at different depths of file, comparisons are made at different "local" levels. At the level of 40 percent of the file, the comparison between the regression model's and the true model's performance indicates that the regression model has a local efficiency of 62 percent (145 divided by 236). This means that the model captures 62 percent of the maximum cumulative increased total net sales. NOT BAD!?

Rematching with AID

The regression model with 62 percent of the maximum fares quite well, but is the comparison fair? The example compared the regression model based on available variables and the true model reflecting the correct variables, which are probably neither known nor available to the model builder. So, a more reasonable comparison is between the regression model with its set of selected variables and the best model possible using only the variables actually available to the modeler.

To calculate the best or maximum decile analysis *given* the known potential independent variables, we must rematch with the aid of an AID program.

To rematch an AID analysis to obtain a maximum decile spread based on model variables, take these steps:

1. Perform an AID analysis on the dependent variable Y with the set of available variables.
2. Rank each of the resulting AID end-point cells from high to low with respect to the dependent variable.
3. Within each AID end-point cell, rank the individuals (or geographic areas) within the segment from high to low with respect to the dependent variable.
4. Divide the resulting file into 10 equal parts.
5. Calculate the various columns of the decile report.

The result of the AID rematching is shown in the last three columns of Table 22–3. Under the heading AID we find the following:

> The file, now rematched with the help of an AID program, shows the top decile with a mean of $170 and a lift of 230.
>
> The next best maximum-AID decile, decile 9, has a mean increased total sales of $134.
>
> Combining the top two AID-maximum deciles, we arrive at an AID-maximum cumulative mean increased total net sales of $152, and an "AID-maximum" lift of 201.

The combined top four AID-maximum deciles account for 40 percent of the file with a mean increase of $127 and a lift of 168. As before, because model performance varies at different depths of file, comparisons are made at different "local" levels. At the usual level of 40 percent of the file, the comparison between the regression model's and the AID-maximum model's deciles indicates that the regression model has a local (at the fourth decile) efficiency of 87 percent (a lift of 145 for the model divided by a lift of 168 for the AID-maximum model). This means that the model captures 87 percent of the AID-maximum cumulative in-creased total sales. Not bad? Very good!

You may now reasonably ask, "Why bother with a regression model if the AID analysis produces better results?" We are using the output of the AID analy-sis as a *maximum* benchmark of the potential predictive power of the variables available to the modeler. Our justification is as follows: AID is an optimal proce-dure (i.e., it finds the best splits of a variable such that the spread in the depen-dent variables is as large as possible), which unfortunately implies it capitalizes on the idiosyncrasies of the sample data at hand (even though there are explicit adjustments to minimize this capitalization). As such, AID finds predictive power that may or may not be real (also known as a positive bias). We assume the "ex-tra" predictive power *is real* and use it to set a maximum benchmark for the de-pendent and set of independent variables under study.

A CLOSER LOOK AT STRAIGHTENING DATA

When we observe in an *x-y* plot that the relationship between two variables ap-pears to bend or bulge, for example, as in Figure 22–3, every effort should be made to straighten the bulge. The importance of "straight" data bears repeating. Straight data is important, primarily for the sake of simplicity. Straight data, such as in Figure 22–5, clearly depicts the relationship between the two variables in question; the relationship is easy to see, understand, and interpret—as one vari-able increases so does the other variable.

The second reason straight data is important is that most models, including the ones most often used in direct marketing, belong to the general class of linear models that assume the relationship between the dependent variable and each in-dependent variable is linear or straight-line.

Bulges in the data can be generalized into four simple shapes, as depicted in Figure 22–2. When a curved relationship has a shape close to any one of the four, we can use the mnemonic plots, called the *bulging rule*,[1] along with the *lad-*

FIGURE 22–2

The Bulging Rule

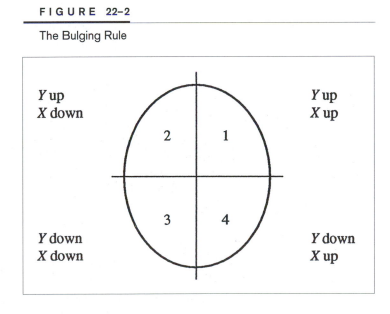

---

1. John Tukey, *Exploratory Data Analysis* (Reading, MA: Addison Wesley, 1977).

der of powers to guide us in choosing the appropriate reexpression of the variables to straighten the data.

LADDER OF POWERS

When we go up the ladder of powers we try reexpressions that raise the variable, either X or Y, to powers of p where p is greater than 1. The most common p values used are 2 and 3, but sometimes we may have to go farther up the ladder and use 4 and 5, or find in-between values and use mixed numbers like 1.333. Accordingly, the common "up-the-ladder" reexpressions are:

$$X \text{ is reexpressed to } X^2 = X \text{ squared}$$
$$X \text{ is reexpressed to } X^3 = X \text{ cubed}$$
$$Y \text{ is reexpressed to } Y^2 = Y \text{ squared}$$
$$Y \text{ is reexpressed to } Y^3 = Y \text{ cubed}$$

When we go down the ladder we try reexpressions that raise the variable, X or Y, to powers of p where p is less than 1. The most common p values used are 1/2, 0, $-1/2$, and -1, but sometimes we may have to go farther down the ladder or use in-between values. Some common down-the-ladder reexpressions are given below.

Note that the reexpression for $p = 0$ is not mathematically defined, but conveniently defined as log to base 10. And for negative power we again conveniently add a negative sign. The reasons for all this convenience are theoretical and beyond the scope of this chapter.

$$X \text{ is reexpressed to } X^{1/2} = \text{square root } X$$
$$X \text{ is reexpressed to } X^0 = \log_{10} X$$
$$X \text{ is reexpressed to } X^{-1/2} = -1/\text{square root } X$$
$$X \text{ is reexpressed to } X^{-1} = -1/X$$
$$Y \text{ is reexpressed to } Y^{1/2} = \text{square root } Y$$
$$Y \text{ is reexpressed to } Y^0 = \log_{10} Y$$
$$Y \text{ is reexpressed to } Y^{-1/2} = -1/\text{square root } Y$$
$$Y \text{ is reexpressed to } Y^{-1} = -1/Y$$

BULGING RULE

The bulging rule states that:

If the data has a shape similar to that shown in the first quadrant, then we try to reexpress by going up the ladder for X, Y, or both.

If the data has a shape similar to that in the second quadrant, then we try to reexpress by going down the ladder for X and/or up the ladder for Y.

If the data has a shape similar to that in the third quadrant, then we try to reexpress by going down the ladder for Y, X, or both.

If the data has a shape similar to that in the fourth quadrant, then we try to reexpress by going up the ladder for X and/or down the ladder for Y.

Before we go to an example we must emphasize that the rule only offers hope that the data can be straightened—no guarantees and no one solution. The only way we fail in reexpressing is if we fail to reexpress.

An Example of the Bulging Rule

Let's consider the data set shown in Table 22–3:

The plot of X and Y in Figure 22–4 indicates that the relationship has a shape similar to the one in quadrant 4 of the bulging rule. Accordingly, to straighten out this bulge we must try reexpressing X, Y, or both by going up the ladder for X and/or down the ladder for Y.

Starting with X we reexpress it by creating X^2 and X^3. We can plot these new variables with Y, but instead we can just look at the correlation coefficients. Because the reexpressions straighten data, we assume the new relationships with the new variable are as straight as possible; thus to find which reexpression works better, we just need to look at the correlation coefficient. The larger the value, the better the reexpression.

The rs for Y and X, X squared, and X cubed are .736, .707, and .651, respectively. Clearly, the best reexpression for X is no reexpression, or X itself. Reexpressing X actually weakens the strength of the relationship as r decreases from .736 to .707 and .651. (See Table 22–5.)

So we leave X alone, for the time being, and reexpress Y by going down the ladder, creating eight new variables corresponding to the powers of 1/2, 1/3, 1/4, 1/5, 1/6, 0, $-1/2$, and -1. The corresponding r value for each of these transformations is .825, .844, .850, .853, .854, .855, .794, and .678. (See Table 22–6.)

The best reexpression is log Y.

Plotting log Y and X, we see in Figure 22–5 that the bulge has changed direction; now, the shape is like that in quadrant 2 of the bulging rule. Thus, we must try to reexpress X by going down the ladder. We have already reexpressed the Y variable in the plot, namely log Y.

Going down the ladder for X we create six new variables corresponding to the powers of 1/2, 1/3, 1/4, 1/5, 1/6, and 0. The r values for Log Y with each of the six transformations of the X value are .886, .891, .892, .892, and .889. (See Table 22–7). The best reexpression for X is the fifth root of X.

Hence the best pair of reexpressions is $F5\_RT\_X$ and log Y. The plot for

TABLE 22–3

Sample Nonstraight Data

X	Y	X	Y
1	0.6	6	3.4
1	1.6	6	9.7
1	0.5	6	8.6
1	1.2	7	4.0
2	2.0	7	5.5
2	1.3	7	10.5
2	2.5	8	17.5
3	2.2	8	13.4
3	2.4	8	4.5
3	1.2	9	30.4
4	3.5	11	12.4
4	4.1	12	13.4
4	5.1	12	26.2
5	5.7	12	7.4

F I G U R E   22–4

Model $Y = X$ — Plot of $Y \times X$

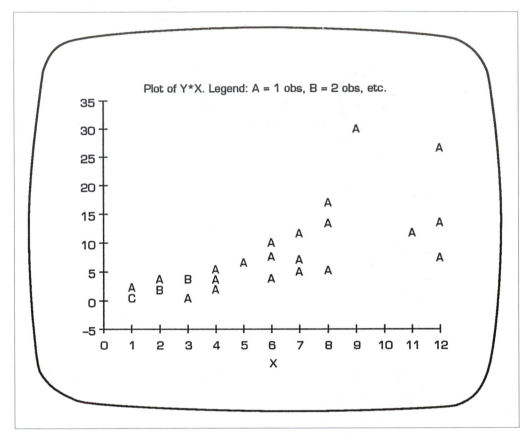

Plot of Y*X. Legend: A = 1 obs, B = 2 obs, etc.

T A B L E   22–5

Correlation Analysis : X up with Y

	1 'WITH' Variables: Y		
	4 'VAR' Variables: X	SQUARD_X CUBED_X SQRT_X	
	Pearson Correlation Coefficients / Prob > |R| under Ho: Rho = 0 / N = 28		
	X	**SQUARD_X**	**CUBED_X**
Y	0.73636	0.70770	0.65111
	8.E−06	3.E−05	.00018
power	1	2	3

these two new reexpressed variables, given in Figure 22–5, reveals a very nice straight-line relationship. We obtained the equation for this relationship by running a simple linear regression program. Its output in Table 22–8 indicates:

$$\text{Log } Y = -2.07 + \text{F5\_RT\_}X \times 2.00$$

For those who are familiar with residuals, the residual plot, showing residual versus Y-hat, further indicates that this is the right reexpression. If the residual plot shows a random scatter of points above and below the zero line in the residual plot, then the model is a good fit and the correct representation of the data. Clearly, we have that situation, as depicted in Figure 22–6.

TABLE 22-6

Correlation Analysis : *Y* down with *X*

1 'WITH' Variables: *Y*   SQRT_*Y*   CBRT_*Y*   F4_RT_*Y*   F5_RT_*Y*   S6_RT_*Y*
              LOG_*Y*
1 'VAR' Variables: *X*

Pearson Correlation Coefficients / Prob > |R| under Ho: Rho = 0 / N = 28

Power		X
1	*Y*	0.73636
		8.E−06
1/2	SQRT_*Y*	0.82501
		7.E−08
1/3	CBRT_*Y*	0.84428
		2.E−08
1/4	F4_RT_*Y*	0.85078
		1.E−08
1/5	F5_RT_*Y*	0.85353
		8.E−09
1/6	S6_RT-*Y*	0.85487
		7.E−09
0	LOG_*Y*	0.85521
		7.E−09
−1/2	RCPRT_*Y*	0.79410
		5.E−07
−1	RECIP_*Y*	0.67875
		7.E−05

FIGURE 22-5

Model log_*Y* = *X*—Plot of LOG_*Y* × *X*

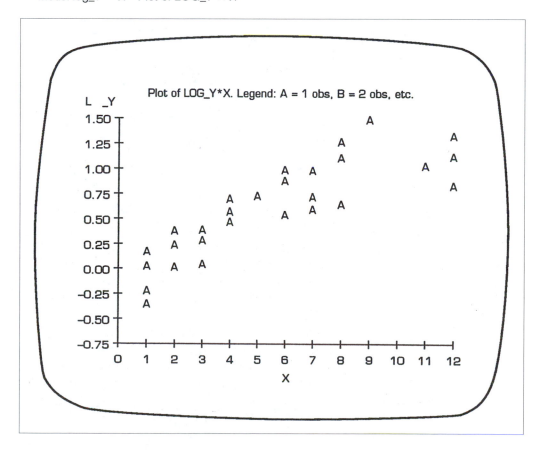

315

T A B L E   22–7

Correlation Analysis: *X* down with log_*Y*

'WITH' Variables: LOG_Y							
7 'VAR' Variables: *X*		**SQRT_*X***	**CBRT_*X***	**F4_RT_*X***	**F5_RT_*X***	**S6_RT_*X***	
LOG_*X*							
Pearson Correlation Coefficients / Prob > IRI under Ho: Rho = 0 / N = 28							
	X	**SQRT_*X***	**CBRT_*X***	**F4_RT_*X***	**F5_RT_*X***	**S6_RT_*X***	**LOG_*X***
LOG_Y	0.85521	0.88663	0.89130	0.89233	0.89252	0.89246	0.88996
	7.E−09	3.E−10	2.E−10	2.E−10	2.E−10	2.E−10	2.E−10
power	1	1/2	1/3	1/4	1/5	1/6	0

This example illustrates the value and the process of reexpressing variables. The approach is sometimes subjective (we could have started with *Y* instead of *X*) and based on trial and error (how far up or down should we go), and, of course, there is no guarantee of success. But as we mentioned when we began the example, we really only fail if we fail to try.

F I G U R E   22–5

Model log_*Y* = *f5_rt_X* — Plot of LOG_*Y* × *F5_RT_X*

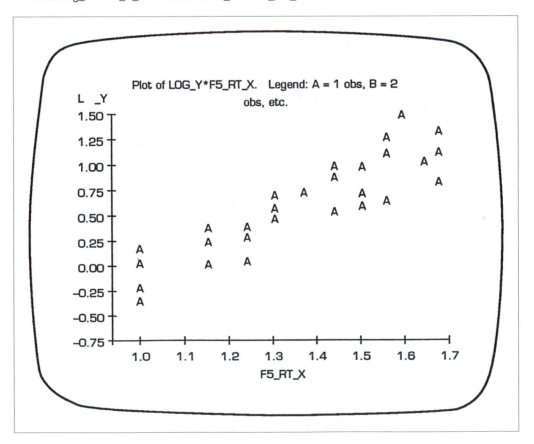

TABLE 22–8

Model log_Y = f5_rt_X

Model: MODEL1
Dependent Variable: LOG_Y

Analysis of Variance

Source	DF	Sum of Squares	Mean Square	F Value	Prob>F
Model	1	4.67556	4.67556	101.816	0.0001
Error	26	1.19396	0.04592		
C Total	27	5.86951			

Root MSE	0.21429	R-square	0.7966	
Dep Mean	0.63665	Adj R-sq	0.7888	
C. V.	33.65964			

Parameter Estimates

Variable	DF	Parameter Estimate	Standard Error	T for HO: Parameter = 0	Prob>|T|
INTERCEP	1	−2.071624	0.27143839	−7.632	0.0001
F5_RT_X	1	2.001498	0.19835637	10.090	0.0001

FIGURE 22–6

Model log_Y = f5_rt_X — Plot of RES_LOG5 × LOG5_HAT

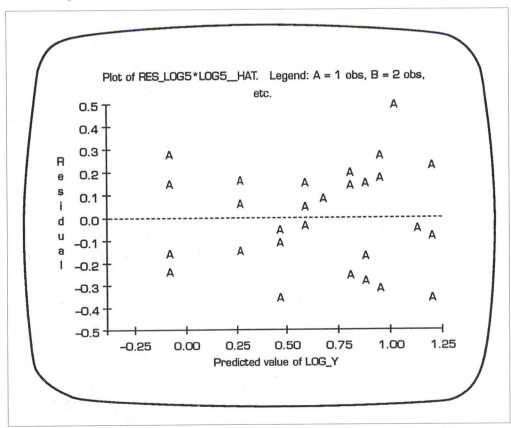

Plot of RES_LOG5*LOG5__HAT.   Legend: A = 1 obs, B = 2 obs, etc.

A CLOSER LOOK AT REEXPRESSIONS FOR MANY VARIABLES

In the prior chapter on segmentation we introduced the topic of factor analysis, specifically principal component analysis (PCA). In this section we'll go into much more detail about the subject, emphasizing reexpression.

PCA is an exploratory technique that uncovers the interrelationships among *many* possibly correlated variables by reexpressing them into a smaller number of *new* variables such that *most* of the information or variation contained within the original set of variables is accounted for or retained by the smaller number of new and uncorrelated variables.

Formally, PCA reexpresses or transforms an original set of p variables $X1 \ldots Xp$ into a new set of p variables, called principal components (PCs), such that the newly created PCs are a weighted sum of the original variables. The weights are the coefficients of the principal components and are determined in somewhat the same way that we determine regression coefficients.

For convenience, let's assume we are working with the standardized versions of the original variables, or Xs. That is, the Xs have been replaced by their standardized counterparts, the Zs:

$$Zi = \frac{Xi - \text{mean of } Xi}{\text{standard deviation of } Xi} \quad \text{for all } i$$

So, the principal components, PC1, PC2 . . . , PCp, look like this:

$$PC1 = a11 \times Z1 + a12 \times Z2 + \ldots + a1p \times Zp$$
$$PC2 = a21 \times Z1 + a22 \times Z2 + \ldots + a2p \times Zp$$
$$PCp = ap1 \times Z1 + ap2 \times Z2 + \ldots + app \times Zp$$

As we said before, the PCs are weighted sums of (standardized) variables. The number of PCs produced by the process is equal to the number of original variables, namely p. (In English, if we start with 36 variables we'll wind up with 36 PCs.) But, to reiterate the objective of PCA, we want to eventually come out at the end of the process with just a few PCs (much less than the number of original variables) that contain a large amount of the information (statisticians prefer the term *variation*) that was contained in the original set of variables.

These principal components have three important properties:

1. The variance of principal components, sometimes called *eigenvalues* or *latent roots*, will be presented in a sequence in which the first-named principal component contains the most information (the largest variance) and each successive principal component contains an amount of information, or a variance, equal to or less than the previous one.
2. The mean of a principal component is zero.
3. The correlation between any two principal components is zero.

Let's go to a simple example.

A Simple PCA Example

Consider four variables $X1$, $X2$, $X3$, and $X4$, representing education in a geographical unit, say, a ZIP code:

$X1 = $ Percentage of persons in a ZIP code with less than a high school education.

$X2$ = Percentage of persons in a ZIP code that graduated high school.

$X3$ = Percentage of persons in a ZIP code with some college education.

$X4$ = Percentage of persons in a ZIP code with college or more education.

Because PCA is performed on a correlation matrix (which is why we defined the principal components in terms of standardized variables), let's consider Table 22–9, the correlation matrix for $X1$ through $X4$.

Table 22–9 indicates that there is a positive correlation between *some college* and *college or more*, and a negative correlation between *less than high school* and *college or more*. This correlation table, then, reflects the observation that in a ZIP code that contains more than the average percentage of college graduates you will find more than the average percentage of persons with more than a college education and less than the average percentage of persons with just a high school degree—just as you would expect.

The standard output of a PCA also consists of variances and coefficients, or latent roots and latent vectors, respectively, as found in Table 22–10.

The variance of the principal component (LRi) corresponds to each latent root. The variance of the first principal component is 2.66, the largest. The variance of the second principal component is .8238; the third is .5141; and the fourth is zero! (A variance of zero indicates a special case, which we'll address later in this chapter.)

We can draw several conclusions from Table 22–10:

1. Because there are four variables, it is possible to extract four PCs from the correlation matrix.
2. The basic statistics of PCA are the four variances or *latent roots* (LR1, LR2, LR3, LR4), which are ordered by size, and the associated weight (i.e., coefficient) vectors, or *latent vectors* ($a1$, $a2$, $a3$, $a4$).
3. The total variance in the system or data set is four—the sum of the variances of the four (standardized) variables.
4. Each latent vector contains four elements, one corresponding to each variable. For latent vector $a1$ we have:

$$-.5514, -.4041, .4844, .5457$$

which are the four coefficients associated with the first and largest PC whose variance is 2.6620.

5. The first PC is the linear combination:

$$PC1 = -.5514 \times Z1 - .4042 \times Z2 + .4844 \times Z3 + .5457 \times Z4$$

TABLE 22–9

Correlation Matrix for X1 to X4

	X1	X2	X3	X4
% Less than H.S.—X1	1.000	.2689	−.7532	−.8116
% Graduated H.S.—X2		1.000	−.3823	−.6200
% Some college—X3			1.000	.4311
% College or more—X4				1.000

TABLE 22–10

PCA OUTPUT: Latent Roots (Variances) and Latent Vectors (Coefficients) of
Correlation Matrix

Standardized Variables	Latent Vectors			
	a1	a2	a3	a4
Z1	−.5514	−.4222	.2912	.6655
Z2	−.4042	.7779	−.3595	.3196
Z3	.4844	.4120	.6766	.3710
Z4	.5457	−.2162	−.5727	.5721
LRi	2.6620	.8238	.5141	.0000
Prop. Var %	66.55	20.59	12.85	.0000
Cum. Var %	66.55	87.14	100	100

6. PC1 explains that $(100 \times 2.6620/4) = 66.55$ percent of the total variance of the four variables.

7. The second PC is the linear combination:

$$PC2 = -.4222 \times Z1 + .7779 \times Z2 + .4120 \times Z3 - .2162 \times Z4$$

8. PC2 with next-to-largest variance .8238 explains that $(100 \times 8.238/4) = 20.59$ percent of the total variance of the four variables.

9. Together the first two PCs account for 66.55 percent plus 20.55 percent, or 87.14 percent of the variance in the four variables.

10. For the first PC, the first two coefficients are negative and the last two are positive; accordingly, PC1 is interpreted as a *contrast* between persons who at most graduated high school and persons who at least attended college.

 High positive scores on PC1 are associated with ZIP codes where the percentage of persons who at least attended college is *greater* than the percentage of persons who at most graduated high school.

 Low scores (high negative scores) on PC1 are associated with ZIP codes where the percentage of persons who at least attended college is *less* than the percentage of persons who at most graduated high school.

ALGEBRAIC PROPERTIES OF PCA

PCA has a lot of very appealing algebraic properties, some of which we list below. The previous example should provide you with "empirical" proof of these properties, and, it is hoped, an appreciation of the value of the PCA method.

1. Almost always PCA is performed on a correlation matrix; that is, the analysis is done with standardized variables (means = zero and variance = 1).

2. Each principal component:

$$PCi = ai1 \times Z1 + ai2 \times Z2 + \ldots + aip \times Zp$$

 has a variance also called a latent root or eigenvalue such that:
 a. Var(PC1) is maximum.
 b. Var(PC1) > Var(PC2) > ... > Var (PCp).

    c. Equality can occur but it is rare.

    d. Mean (PC*i*) = 0.

3. All PCs are uncorrelated.

4. Associated with each latent root *i* is a latent vector:

$$(ai1, ai2, \ldots , aip)$$

that is the weight for the linear combination of the original variables forming PC*i*:

$$PСi = ai1 \times Z1 + ai2 \times Z2 + \ldots aip \times Zp$$

5. The sum of the variances of the PCs (i.e., sum of the latent roots) is equal to the sum of the variances of the original variables. Since the variables are standardized, the sum of latent roots equals *p*.

6. The proportion of variance in the original *p* variables that *k* PCs account for is equal to the:

$$\frac{\text{sum of latent roots for first } k \text{ PCs}}{p}$$

7. Correlation between an original variable (*Xi*) and its principal component (PC*j*) equals:

$$aij \times \sqrt{[\text{Var}(PСj)]}$$

This correlation is called a PC *loading*.

8. The sum of the squares of loadings across all the PCs for an original variable indicates how much variance for that variable is accounted for by the PCs (communality of the variable).

9. Var(PC) = 0 implies that a perfect collinear relationship exists.

10. Var(PC) = small (less than .001) implies high multicollinearity.

Properties 9 and 10 provide us with a way to identify whether the variables are highly correlated. Recalling our simple example in which the fourth PC has zero variance, the question we must address is how the four variables are perfectly correlated.

Actually, the answer is somewhat intuitive. The perfect relationship among the four variables is such that:

$$X1 + X2 + X3 + X4 = 100\%$$

That is, the percentages of the four education variables or levels must sum to 100 percent. Thus, knowing any three of the education variables automatically provides us with the remaining variable's value. Such data, which add to 100 percent, are known as compositional data. Such data, which add to 100 percent, are known as compositional data. Suffice it to say that census data frequently take this form and that modelers should be aware that compositional data can present difficulties not always associated with principal components analysis. However, the techniques needed to use this data correctly are well beyond the scope of this book.[2]

2. Interested readers are referred to J. Aitchison, "The Statistical Analysis of Compositional Data," *J. R. Statistical Society B,* 44, 1982, pp. 137–177.

MODEL BUILDING WITH PCA – TWO CASE STUDIES

1. A Continuity Example

A continuity company wanted to develop a geography-based model that could be used against outside rented lists. The plan was to perform the usual merge/purge and then apply the scoring model to the resulting mail file. The decision was made to score the file at the block group level.

A principal components analysis was done on all the census categories. (There are about 300 census variables that can be collapsed into about 40 categories. Education, for example, as we discussed before, represents four variables, but on census category.) In this case study, a number of categories proved to be significant (i.e., correlated with response), but three categories were found to be exceptionally significant, and these three categories were the only categories to enter the model. One of the categories was household income, consisting of nine individual variables, and the other two categories will remain nameless for reasons of confidentiality.

Tables 22–11 and 22–12 describe PCA output having to do with the household income factor. In Table 22–11 we see that the analysis produced nine principal components, equal to the number of original variables shown in Table 22–12.

In Table 22–11 the first principal component contains 47 percent of the information or variance contained in all of the original nine variables. The second principal component contains 20 percent of the total variance. Thus, the first two PCs account for 67 percent of the total information in the entire data set.

In Table 22–12 we see the eigenvector or weights for the first principal component against which each ZIP code will be scored. Notice the contrast. The lower-income variables have negative weights, and the higher-income variables have positive weights.

In Table 22–13 we see the scores produced by a relatively low income block group that we'll label Case 1 and the scores produced by a relatively high income block group, labeled Case 2. Because a greater percentage of Case 1's population have lower incomes and because lower incomes are associated with

TABLE 22–11

Household Income Principal Components Output — The Proportion of Total Variance Explained by Each Principal Component

Principal Component	Eigenvalue	Proportion	Cumulative
Principal component 1	4.213	47%	47%
Principal component 2	1.826	20	67
Principal component 3	0.837	9	76
Principal component 4	0.579	7	83
Principal component 5	0.497	5	88
Principal component 6	0.357	4	92
Principal component 7	0.300	4	96
Principal component 8	0.279	3	99
Principal component 9	0.109	1	100
Total	9.000	100%	

TABLE 22–12

Household Income First Principal Component Output — Eigenvector

Census	Variable Description	Eigenvector/Weight
1	%HH < $15	−0.342
2	%HH $15–$25	−0.370
3	%HH $25–$35	−0.261
4	%HH $35–$50	−0.003
5	%HH $50–$75	0.304
6	%HH $75–$100	0.404
7	%HH $100–$125	0.412
8	%HH $125–$50	0.376
9	%HH $150+	0.339

negative weights in this data set, it's not surprising that this particular block group has a negative score with regard to income. The converse is true for Case 2, a block group with a relative upscale income distribution. Now let's use this principal component in a logistic regression model to see if it helps us predict response.

The top of Table 22–14 presents the logistic regression model. As we mentioned before, the actual model contained two other principal components that are not shown in this example. The coefficient of the income variable is a negative number (−0.7324). Because, as we have seen, block groups with relatively low income distributions have negative scores, or low positive scores, the model tells us that low-income block groups will have higher scores than upper-income block groups. (Remember a negative value times a negative coefficient yields a positive number, which will increase a block group's final score or probability of response.)

TABLE 22–13

Using Principal Components in Logistic Regression Models

Description	Eigenvector	Case 1 Lower-Income Block Group		Case 2 Upper-Income Block Group	
		Distribution	Eigenvector Contribution	Distribution	Eigenvector Contribution
%HH < $15	−0.342	25%	−0.0855	2%	−0.0068
%HH $15–$25	−0.370	10	−0.0370	3	−0.0111
%HH $25–$35	−0.261	10	−0.0261	6	−0.0157
%HH $35–$50	−0.003	30	−0.0009	4	−0.0001
%HH $50–$75	0.302	10	0.0302	10	0.0302
%HH $75–$100	0.402	4	0.0161	30	0.1206
%HH $100–$12	0.410	6	0.0246	10	0.0410
%HH $125–$15	0.374	3	0.0112	25	0.0374
%HH $150+	0.332	2	0.0066	25	0.0830
	Total Score	100%	−0.0608	100%	0.2785

TABLE 22–14

Scoring a Principal Components Logistic Regression Model

The Model	
The constant is equal to	−3.4964
The coefficient of HH INC 1 is equal to	−0.7324
Scoring Case 1	
Case 1's score for the HH INC 1 variable from Table 22–13	−0.0608
The product of Case 1's score × the coefficient of HH INC 1: −0.7324	0.0445
Adding the constant back to get Case 1's total score	−3.4519
Converting the score, which is a logit, to odds by exponentiating the logit	0.0317
Converting odds to probabilities using the formula Probability = Odds/(1 + Odds)	3.07%
Scoring Case 2	
Case 2's score for the HH INC 1 variable from Table 22–13	0.2785
The product of Case 1's score × the coefficient of HH INC 1: −0.7324	−0.0204
Adding the constant back to get Case 2's total score	−3.7004
Converting the score, which is a logit, to odds by exponentiating the logit	0.0247
Converting odds to probabilities using the formula Probability = Odds/(1 + Odds)	2.41%

Note how the difference in the distribution of incomes between block groups changed the expected probability of response from 2.41 percent for the block group with the higher-income distribution to 3.07 percent for the block group with the lower-income distribution.

Finally, we believe that census data-based models that use principal components turn out to be more stable over the long term than models that use individual census variables (percent of households with incomes between $100,000 and $125,000, for example), and we encourage their use. Too many companies have had the experience of developing models that validate but do not hold up over the long haul. We think this approach will help.

2. A Packaged Goods Example

A packaged goods manufacturer with a large database wanted to mail a promotion to customers on the database likely to buy Category A products. A significant percentage of customers on the database were known users of Category A products, but the promotion was budgeted to go to more than just these known category users.

A modeling file was created in which known users of Category A were coded 1 and customers on the database who were not known users were coded 0. We could now develop a logistic regression model on this data set, similar to a 0/1 response model. We are assuming that if we could identify users of Category A products through modeling (modeling data other than Category A usage), the model could be used to rank customers not known to be users on the database in terms of their probability of being a Category A user.

In this case the potential independent variables included the answers to 60 categorical (yes/no) lifestyle questions that a large majority of persons on the database (both users and nonusers of Category A products) had answered.

TABLE 22–15

Comparison of Regression Models Using Dummy Variables versus Principal Components as Independent Variables

	Dummy Variables			Principal Components		
Decile	Decile Usage Rate %	Cumulative Usage Rate %	Cum Lift	Decile Usage Rate %	Cumulative Usage Rate %	Cum Lift
1	45%	45%	294	50%	50%	330
2	21	33	215	20	35	232
3	16	27	178	15	28	187
4	17	24	161	15	25	166
5	21	24	157	19	24	158
6	14	22	146	13	22	147
7	9	20	133	8	20	134
8	10	19	125	10	19	125
9	0	17	111	0	17	111
10	0	15	100	0	15	100

We analyzed the data two ways. First, we created 59 dummy variables and produced a model in the traditional way by coding each person in the data set a 0 or a 1 on each of the lifestyle questions. Next we completed a principal components analysis and ran the regression model on the resulting principal components. Five raw lifestyle variables entered the dummy variable regression model and two principal components (now used as independent variables) entered the principal components model. Table 22–15 compares the two models. Not only did the principal components model do somewhat better, but also the principal components model is expected to be more stable than the dummy variable model because it looks at all 60 lifestyle variables, not just the 5 that entered the model.

This concludes our discussion of principal components analysis, a tool we find to be increasingly useful in building stable regression models stemming from data sets that contain large numbers of potential independent variables such as retail SKUs or items within a mail-order catalog.

CHAPTER 23

Artificial Neural Networks

INTRODUCTION

Unless you have been under a rock building statistical models, you must have heard something about neural networks. Most probably you heard something like the following: *"Neural networks outperform traditional regression models by 20, 30, or even 1,000 percent."* Or *"Neural network technology is so advanced it virtually builds models by itself, and very quickly, too!"* Or *"Neural networks find interaction variables automatically and also work especially well when the data are nonlinear. That's right, neural networks thrive on nonlinear data."* What more can we direct marketers ask for? Perhaps a clear-cut expository on neural networks, specifically artificial neural networks (ANN).

The key word in ANN is *artificial*. Here, *artificial* does not mean fake, false, or sham. It means it's not the real thing. The real neural network (RNN) is the human brain. However, ANNs are a serious effort at imitating or simulating the real thing. Otherwise, there is nothing artificial about ANNs. ANNs are based on rock-solid computational processing logic that is carried out by well-accepted mathematical algorithms.

The claims quoted above are made by salespeople who either are good at selling by hyperbole or believe so much in the underlying concept of ANNs that they forget the A in ANN. They think they are selling a brain in a box. On the other hand, the die-hard ANN analysts, so absorbed in the theoretical beauty and mathematical elegance of ANNs, also get carried away and treat ANNs like RNNs. But that's only because they love their nets.

In this chapter we provide you with everything you need to know about ANNs, without a black belt in statistics. In discussing ANNs, we draw parallels to statistical modeling to set the stage for the final comparison of which technique is better; this is the real issue today in the direct marketing industry.

WHEN ARE ANNs USED

The two most popular applications of ANNs correspond to the two most popular applications of statistical modeling in the direct marketing industry: classification and prediction.

Classification

This type of application is the mainstay of direct marketing modeling: to find individuals in a population defined by distinct and separate classes. Specifically, the population is either a house file or an outside list, and the classes are customers/prospects that can be labeled as responders or nonresponders. The classification problem is usually performed by developing a logistic regression response model.

Prediction

Prediction in the direct marketing industry, and in every industry, focuses on finding customers or prospects most likely to generate significant dollar and/or volume sales. This task is typically performed by developing an ordinary least-squares regression model.

If ANNs and regression-based techniques do the same things, why bother with the newer and perhaps not-as-well-tested ANN? The answer lies not only from the emotional aspect of "something new is something better," but from a theoretical vantage point. ANNs are more complex than regression models by virtue of the fact that regression models are a special case of ANN. Accordingly, the potential gain of the more complex and encompassing ANN is real.

However, just because ANNs have more theoretical muscle does not imply that they can outperform regression techniques. In other words, the proof of the pudding is not how the pudding is made, but how the pudding tastes. Before we do a taste test comparison between ANNs and statistical modeling, let's formally discuss what ANNs are and how ANNs are built.

WHAT ARE ANNs?

Definition

ANNs are multi-input nonlinear models with weighted interconnections between input and output layers, as depicted in Figure 23–1. The multi-input layer holds the information to be modeled, namely the independent/predictor variables. The independent variables are connected by weights to the middle layer, which is referred to as the hidden layer. A nonlinear function, called a *transfer* or *squashing function*, resides in the hidden layer. The hidden layer is also known as the black box of the ANN, because even the experts cannot figure out at all times how the

FIGURE 23–1

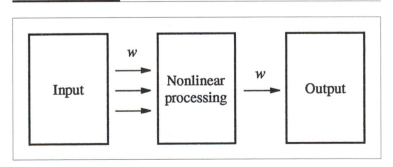

nonlinear function treats the independent variables. Regardless, the independent variables are processed in such a way that when they reach the output layer the desired outcome is—it is hoped—achieved.

This broad definition of ANN is proved to set the stage for a closer look at ANN—its basic structure.

Basic Structure

The basic structure of an ANN is:

1. the weighted sum u of $n + 1$ inputs (variables) $X_0, X_1, X_2, \ldots, X_n$, where $X_0 \equiv 1$, $w_0 \equiv 0$,
2. which passes through a nonlinear function ψ,
3. thus producing output y.

$$y = \psi \left(\Sigma w_i X_i + \theta \right)$$

where

ψ is called the transfer or squashing function.

w_i are the interconnection strengths, or weights.

θ is called the bias, similar to the intercept term in a logistic regression equation in that it adjusts the weighted sum into a usable range.

Y is the output, whose values are called the activation levels produced by the (feedforward) relationship between input and output layers.

The basic structure of an ANN is depicted in Figure 23–2. We see that input elements $x_1, x_2, \ldots, x_n$ and the bias element are fully connected to the single hidden element, denoted by the encircled Σ. The weighted sum of these elements, u_j, passes through the transfer function, typically the S-curve.

Basic ANN

This basic structure is actually an ANN itself; however, the basic ANN consists of many basic structures, resulting in an input layer of many input elements, a hidden layer of many hidden elements, and, lastly, an output layer of many output elements. The connections among the input elements to hidden elements, and

FIGURE 23–2

Basic Structure

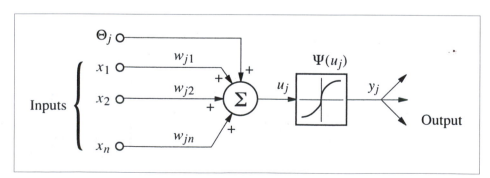

FIGURE 23-3

Basic ANN

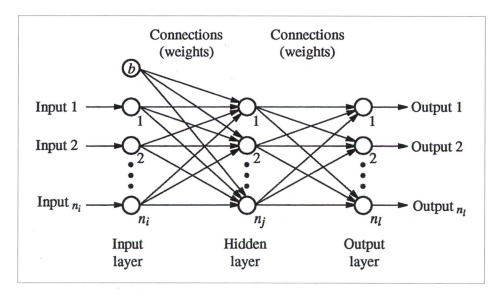

hidden elements to output elements, may be either fully or partially connected. See Figure 23-3 for the basic ANN structure or architecture.

Basic Architecture

With the basic structure of an ANN presented, we can characterize ANN in terms of how it is organized—its architecture. There are five components of the architecture; each one is briefly discussed below:

1. *Number of layers*. With the necessity of input and output layers, the question of how many hidden layers are needed is very important, from both a theoretical and practical standpoint.

2. *Number of elements per layer*. This component relates to the issue of too many variables in a regression model. Too many variables is a good indication the model builder either had a problem developing an adequate model or did not know there was a problem. In other words, too many variables in regression and too many elements in a layer are signs of trouble, also known as *overfit*.

3. *Type of connections*. Information within the ANN can flow in several directions. Although we have only described forward information flows, there are feedbackward and laterally connected ANNs.

4. *Degree of connectivity*. The elements within a layer can be connected to other layers either fully or partially connected. Partially connected layers minimize an overfitted ANN, but the trade-off is less predictive power.

5. *Type of transfer function*. The choice criterion for transfer function is simply the one that provides good performance with minimum training time. See Figure 23-4 for the types of transfer functions available.

As mentioned previously, the transfer function is also known as a squashing function because it takes u_j values, which can range from plus to negative infinity and

FIGURE   23–4

Types of Transfer Function

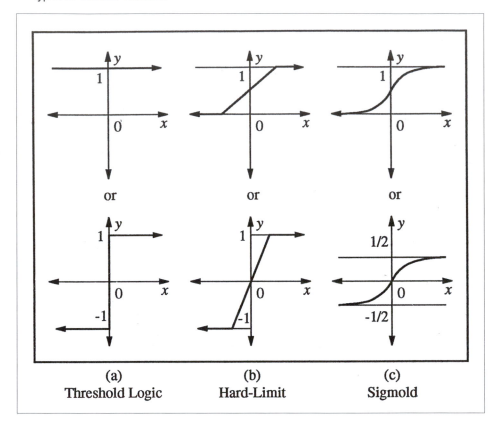

(a)   (b)   (c)
Threshold Logic   Hard-Limit   Sigmold

"squashes" them into small output y_j ranges. This nonlinear structural component is what makes the ANN robust, or reliable. The squashing minimizes the effects' "far out" input values by replacing them with values restricted to a small range (e.g., values between plus and negative 1, or plus and negative 1/2, or 0 and 1). See Figure 23–4.

HOW ANNs ARE TRAINED

When humans want to master a task, they practice or train themselves until the task is learned. ANNs do the same: train, train, and train until the task is learned. Humans sometimes need a teacher, and sometimes are self-taught. The same is true for ANNs. (A note on ANN terminology: where the statisticians say the regression model is estimated, the ANN analysts say the ANN undergoes learning or training.)

ANN learning/training can be either supervised by a teacher or unsupervised. Supervised learning is based on pairs of information: for every input there is a matched and known output. Specifically, for every input value, which is essentially a set of values for the independent variables $X_1, X_2, \ldots, X_n$, and for the corresponding output value, which is a set of values for the dependent variables $Y_1, Y_2, \ldots, Y_n$, the ANN learns the patterns within the X values that are associated with known Y values. The training is successful when the learned (i.e., observed or estimated) output agrees with known paired (i.e., desired or correct answer) output. The goal of supervised learning is to get correct answers.

In contrast, unsupervised learning does *not* use pairs of information; it uses only input values. There are no direct comparisons between learned and known output; there are no correct answers. The goal is to discover patterns in the data using only the input itself and no external information. We will not discuss unsupervised ANNs, for they are second in application to their supervised counterpart, and offer no real potential in the direct marketing industry.

Supervised Training Method

Mathematically, learning means adjusting the weights so the desired outputs are produced by using an adaptive or optimization algorithm. Specifically, supervised learning involves adjusting the weights so the total error, *E*, defined below, is minimized:

- For a given training pair or single presentation, *p*, and for an output layer with *n* elements, the error is the mean-squared of *desired minus observed* outputs:

$$E_p = \frac{1}{n} \Sigma (d_{pj} - o_{pj})^2$$

- For *m* presentations (training sample/epoch size *m*), total error is the mean of all presentation errors:

$$E = \frac{1}{m} \Sigma E_p$$

The method of gradient steepest descent is the adaptive algorithm used in most ANN training. This method, which iteratively changes the weights to (it is hoped) achieve an *absolute minimum* total error proceeds as follows:

1. Initial weights are randomly set to small values.
2. All training pairs, *p*, one at a time, are presented to the *ANN*.
3. The error *E* is calculated.
4. The weights are adjusted to minimize *E*.
5. Repeat Steps 2 to 4 (called an epoch) until *E* converges.

It turns out that the algorithm is a "cruncher" requiring long training time, with no guarantee of convergence or convergence to an absolute minimum.

DESIGNING AN OPTIMAL MULTILAYER FEEDFORWARD ANN

Building an ANN is like cooking pudding; you need a well-tested recipe with quality ingredients and, of course, a good cook. Here we outline the best ingredients for the most popular and well-tested multilayer feedforward ANN:

1. *Degree of connectivity*. Fully connected between all layers.

2. *Type of transfer function*. The logistic function provides good performance with minimum training time.

3. *Number of hidden layers.*
   a. Theoretically, it is sufficient to use no more than two.
   b. Practically, it is necessary to use only one.

4. *Number of elements per layer.*
   a. Output layer—problem dependent.
   b. Hidden layer—$\sqrt{(\#inputs) \times (\#outputs)}$
      (1) Too few; network won't train/calibrate.
      (2) Too many; network won't validate/generalize.
      (3) Strategy—start with "too few" and end before "too many."
   c. Input layer—become an artist.
      (1) Less is "more":
         (a) Use PCA to reduce the number of input variables.
         (b) Use CHAID to combine input variables.
      (2) Linear scaling of input so values fall in [0, 1] interval.

         (a) Use $X = \dfrac{(x - x_{min})}{(x_{max} - x_{min})}$

      (3) Nonlinear transformations—use ladder of powers to symmetrize input.

5. *Training set*: Should include:
   a. Every input (covariate) pattern for a complete network.
   b. Some noise in every pattern for a robust network.
   c. Large number of pairs to minimize overfit tendency.
      (1) 16 inputs with 4 hidden and 1 output elements result in 72 weights/*free* parameters that will *cost* the network!
   d. Number of training pairs $\geq 10 \times \#weights$.
   e. Present many subsets of the training sets in random batches of increasing size.

THE BLACK BOX ANN

Theoretically, we now know how an ANN works. Practically, we will most probably never know how an ANN works, because, as previously mentioned, the hidden layer is considered the black box of the ANN. The hidden layer with all its weights coming in and going out is virtually impossible to interpret. But perhaps its worth a try. Here are some approaches to better understand what's going on in the hidden layer:

1. To determine which variables are important, train in a forward, stepwise approach and check performance. Be careful. As in stepwise regression, the order of variable selection is dependent upon which variables are in and which variables are not.

2. Examine weights directly. Be careful. Also, as in regression, the coefficients are dependent upon which variables are in and which variables are not.

3. Perform cluster analysis on the training set based on the activation levels of all hidden elements. Be hopeful. Cluster-analyze the activation levels; then compute means on the original input variables for each cluster. The hope is that the centroids make some sense. (Note: For each training input, there is a set of activation levels whose number equals the number of hidden elements.)

PROOF OF THE PUDDING

We conclude that at this stage in its development, ANN appears to not significantly outperform logistic regression. Interestingly, exploratory data analysis (EDA) appears to be *even* more important for the building of an ANN than for a logistic regression model (LRM).

The following two examples typify our experience with the two techniques:

Problem. To identify financial investors most likely to purchase additional investment vehicles based on a current mailing to stimulate such activity.

Solution. Response rate of the mailing was 4.5 percent. The mail file was appended with over 50 internal and external variables.

EDA boiled down the variables to four candidate predictors:

1. RECENCY—number of months since last inquiries.
2. FREQUENCY—number of previous inquiries.
3. LIFE—number of months investor is active.
4. PRODUCTS—number of services an investor subscribes to.

ANN Model

The ANN optimally selected all four independent variables and decided on three hidden elements. The decile analysis shows a top decile with a 7.9 percent response rate and a lift of 174. However, the second decile has a higher response rate, 8.8 percent. Also, decile 3 has a higher response rate than decile 4, and decile 5 higher than decile 6. See Table 23–1.

Such "unsmooth" performance of any model (i.e., response rates not decreasing smoothly down through the deciles) is an indication the model was not given the "right" variables to train or estimate with. Whether we are modeling with ANN or LRM, we *never* know the right variables; and even if we do, they may not be available to us. Apparently, the ANN was not given the right set of input variables.

This ANN has three hidden elements, which may be one too many. Perhaps, in learning the training pairs and not having all the right variables, the ANN used

TABLE 23–1

ANN Decile Analysis (4 variables/3 hidden elements)

Decile	Number of Customers	Number of Responses	Decile Response Rate	Cum Response Rate	Cum Lift
Top	2,410	190	7.9%	7.9%	174
2	2,410	212	8.8%	8.3%	184
3	2,410	106	4.4%	7.0%	155
4	2,410	114	4.7%	6.5%	143
5	2,410	88	3.7%	5.9%	130
6	2,410	91	3.8%	5.5%	122
7	2,410	88	3.7%	5.3%	117
8	2,410	74	3.1%	5.0%	110
9	2,410	69	2.9%	4.8%	105
Bottom	2,410	58	2.4%	4.5%	100
Total	24,100	1,090	4.5%		

an "extra" hidden element to find some pattern in the data to help the training and inadvertently modeled noise. This may result in a *negative-bias* overfit, which results in deterioration of performance, such as unsmooth response behavior. This kind of overfit is not as common as *positive-bias* overfit, in which the model's performance is spuriously enhanced by the inclusion of a redundant (highly correlated) variable.

LOGISTIC REGRESSION MODEL

We ran an LRM with all four candidate predictors and found that PRODUCTS should be dropped from the model because it is declared nonsignificant with a *p* value of .36980.

(Note: Although our peddlers of ANN say that you can put all the variables you have in an ANN—the more the better—we have no way of knowing if a variable is really needed in an ANN, let alone that it may be hurting the ANN performance. The working assumption is that the weights from input to hidden layers will affect the importance of a variable. Is PRODUCTS hurting our ANN?)

Variable	DF	Parameter Estimate	Standard Error	Wald Chi-Square	Pr > Chi-Square
INTERCEPT	1	−2.9531	0.0838	1242.3272	0.E+00
RECENCY	1	−0.00889	0.00177	25.1787	5.E−07
FREQUENCY	1	−0.1889	0.0337	31.3892	2.E−08
PRODUCTS	1	0.0285	0.0317	0.8043	.36980
LIFE	1	0.2839	0.0337	71.0918	3.E−17

We reran the LRM without PRODUCTS, and the model looks fine with *p* values indicating all variables are statistically significant. We see that the coefficients do not significantly change from those in the first LRM, which indicates that PRODUCTS was providing noise.

The three-variable LRM decile analysis looks quite good with a top decile having a response rate of 8.1 percent, and the second decile having 6.7 percent. There is, however, as with the ANN, some unsmooth response behavior within the deciles 8 and 9. Again, this reflects that we do not know and/or have all the right variables; that is, we have a data problem, not a modeling issue. See Table 23–2.

Variable	DF	Parameter Estimate	Standard Error	Wald Chi-Square	Pr > Chi-Square
INTERCEPT	1	−2.9537	0.0838	1242.5492	0.E+00
RECENCY	1	−0.00882	0.00177	24.8038	6.E−07
FREQUENCY	1	−0.1870	0.0337	30.8287	3.E−08
LIFE	1	0.2942	0.0315	87.1062	0.E+00

Reruns

Perhaps we should rerun the ANN without PRODUCTS. We do so and get an ANN with three hidden elements and a decile analysis, which looks much im-

TABLE 23-2

LRM Decile Analysis (3 variables)

Decile	Number of Customers	Number of Responses	Decile Response Rate	Cum Response Rate	Cum Lift
Top	2,410	196	8.1%	8.1%	180
2	2,410	162	6.7%	7.4%	164
3	2,410	135	5.6%	6.8%	151
4	2,410	122	5.1%	6.4%	141
5	2,410	102	4.2%	6.0%	132
6	2,410	89	3.7%	5.6%	123
7	2,410	65	2.7%	5.2%	114
8	2,410	78	3.2%	4.9%	109
9	2,410	85	3.5%	4.8%	105
Bottom	2,410	56	2.3%	4.5%	100
Total	24,100	1,090	4.5%		

proved. Notwithstanding a possible positive-bias overfit as indicated by three hidden elements as opposed to the preferred two hidden elements, the top decile response rate is 8.4 percent (the first ANN top decile is 7.9 percent). The top five deciles have smooth response rates; however, there is still some unsmooth response behavior at deciles 6 and 8. See Table 23-3.

Apparently, PRODUCTS is hurting the performance of the first ANN. Since there is no *internal* ANN device to detect when a variable can deteriorate an ANN, EDA is very important to the building of a reliable ANN. Possibly, a more rigorous EDA assessment of PRODUCTS would have removed it from the initial training input set.

LRM has such devices. For a variable's overall contribution, we have the simple correlation coefficient; for a variable's unique contribution, taking into

TABLE 23-3

ANN Decile Analysis (3 variables without PRODUCTS/3 hidden elements)

Decile	Number of Customers	Number of Responses	Decile Response Rate	Cum Response Rate	Cum Lift
Top	2,410	203	8.4%	8.4%	186
2	2,410	179	7.4%	7.9%	175
3	2,410	123	5.1%	7.0%	154
4	2,410	121	5.0%	6.5%	144
5	2,410	83	3.4%	5.9%	130
6	2,410	94	3.9%	5.6%	123
7	2,410	72	3.0%	5.2%	115
8	2,410	86	3.6%	5.0%	110
9	2,410	80	3.3%	4.8%	106
Bottom	2,410	49	2.0%	4.5%	100
Total	24,100	1,090	4.5%		

TABLE 23-4

LRM Decile Analysis (4 variables with PRODUCTS)

Decile	Number of Customers	Number of Responses	Decile Response Rate	Cum Response Rate	Cum Lift
Top	2,410	192	8.0%	8.0%	176
2	2,410	153	6.3%	7.2%	158
3	2,410	148	6.1%	6.8%	151
4	2,410	116	4.8%	6.3%	140
5	2,410	106	4.4%	5.9%	131
6	2,410	83	3.4%	5.5%	122
7	2,410	68	2.8%	5.1%	113
8	2,410	75	3.1%	4.9%	108
9	2,410	93	3.9%	4.8%	105
Bottom	2,410	56	2.3%	4.5%	100
Total	24,100	1,090	4.5%		

account the presence of other variables in the model, we have partial correlation coefficients.

Just for the sake of completeness, let's look at the performance of LRM with the "noisy" PRODUCTS (Table 23–4). The top decile has a response rate of 8.0 percent (the first LRM top decile is 8.1 percent). The second and third deciles have response rates of 6.3 percent and 6.1 percent, respectively (the first LRM second and third deciles are 6.7 percent and 5.3 percent, respectively). The response rates are still unsmooth in the same deciles as the first LRM, deciles 8 and 9.

The top three deciles have the same cum lift of 151, for the three- and four-variable LRM, respectively. The differences below 30 percent of the file are clearly nonsignificant but reflect the slight but nonetheless negative-bias overfit from the noise of PRODUCTS.

Discussion

We feel this example typifies two important implications. First, every attempt at the identification of unnecessary variables, carrying either redundant information or noise like that from PRODUCTS in the first ANN, must be made. Since ANNs do not have any internal devices for such analysis, EDA is important to ANN and should be part of the ANN building process. Interestingly, EDA may be more important to ANN than it is to LRM.

The second relates to modeling strategy. This example clearly suggests the modeling processing should be a partnership between the analyst and his/her tools. We should use both LRM with its EDA devices and ANN with its optimal components, not to pit one technique against the other but to gain predictive power in the synergy of using them together.

One question remains: Does ANN without PRODUCTS outperform LRM without PRODUCTS? We tested for significant differences in response rates between models for the top decile, and the top 20 percent and top 30 percent of the file:

	Response Rate			
Percent of File	ANN	LRM	Difference	*p* value
Top decile	8.4%	8.1%	0.3%	35%
Top 20%	7.9%	7.4%	0.5%	18%
Top 30%	7.0%	6.8%	0.2%	32%

In all cases the differences were not statistically significant at any reasonable level. Thus, we must conclude that the ANN does not outperform the LRM.

The larger question for direct marketers is whether ANN models will hold up better than regression models over time. Given all that we have learned up to this point about ANNs, our conclusion is that if they are *used correctly*, as demonstrated by the work done in this case study, ANN models should not do any worse or any better than regression with regard to deterioration.

Of course, the reality is that if marketers think that they can blindly use ANN without the aid of an experienced statistician or an AI expert, they are making, in our opinion, a very serious mistake and may well find that ANN models, given their tendency to "overfit" the data, will deteriorate even faster than regression models. And it won't be the fault of ANN; it will be the fault of marketers looking for a quick, simple, and inexpensive alternative to solid analysis. With ANN, as is the case everywhere else, there's no free lunch.

Advanced Modeling Applications

Chapters 24 through 30 were written by Bruce Ratner; Chapter 31 by Richard Deere.

CHAPTER 24

Assessment of Direct Marketing Response Models

Direct marketers assess the accuracy of a response model by evaluating a decile analysis. The purpose of this article is to present two additional concepts of model assessment—precision and separability—and to illustrate these concepts by further use of the decile analysis.

We begin our discussion with the traditional concept of accuracy, and illustrate its basic measure, proportion of total correct classifications. Then we introduce the accuracy measure used in direct marketing, cum lift. Our discussion of cum lift is set in the context of a decile analysis, which is the usual approach direct marketers use to evaluate the performance of response models. We provide a step-by-step procedure for conducting a decile analysis with a real case study.

We continue with the study to present and illustrate the new concepts, precision and separability. Lastly, we provide guidelines for using all three measures in assessing direct marketing models.

ACCURACY

How well does a response model correctly classify individuals as responders and nonresponders? A popular measure of accuracy is the proportion of total correct classifications (PTCC), which can be calculated from a simple cross-tabulation.

Let's consider the classification results of a response model. The validation sample consists of 100 individuals with a 15 percent response rate. The cross-tabulation of the *actual* classification and the *predicted* classification (produced by the response model) is shown in Table 24–1. The "Total" column indicates there

TABLE 24–1

Classification Results of Response Model

		Predicted		
		Nonresponder	Responder	Total
	Nonresponder	74	11	85
Actual	Responder	2	13	15
Total		76	24	100

are 85 actual nonresponders and 15 actual responders in the sample. The "Total" row indicates the model predicts 76 nonresponders and 24 responders. The model correctly classifies 74 nonresponders and 13 responders. Accordingly, the PTCC is (74 + 13)/100 = 87 percent.

Although PTCC is frequently used, it may not be appropriate for the given situation. For example, if the assessment criterion imposes a penalty for misclassification,[1] then PTCC must be either modified or discarded for a more relevant measure.

Direct marketers have defined their own measure of accuracy for response models: cum lift. They use response models to identify individuals most likely to respond to a solicitation. They create a solicitation list of the "most likely" individuals to obtain an advantage over a random selection of individuals. The cum lift is an index of how many more responses are expected with a selection based on a model over the responses expected with a random selection without a model. The calculation of the cum lift is best illustrated with a decile analysis.

DECILE ANALYSIS

The decile analysis is a tabular display of model performance. Construction of the decile analysis consists of the following steps (see Table 24–2):

1. Score the validation sample or file using the model under consideration. Every individual receives a model score, Prob_est, the model's estimated probability of response.

2. Rank the scored file in descending order by Prob_est.

3. Divide the ranked and scored file into 10 equal groups. The *decile* variable is created, which takes on 10 ordered "values": top (1), 2, 3, 4, 5, 6, 7, 8, 9, and bottom (10). The top decile consists of the best 10 percent of individuals most likely to respond; decile 2 consists of the next 10 percent of individuals most likely to respond; and so on, for the remaining deciles. Accordingly, decile separates and orders the individuals on an ordinal scale ranging from most to least likely to respond.

4. *Number of individuals* is the number of individuals in each decile—10 percent of the total size of the file.

5. *Number of responses (actual)* is the actual—not predicted—number of responses in each decile. The model identifies 911 actual responders in the top decile. In decile 2, the model identifies 544 actual responders. And so on, for the remaining deciles.

6. *Decile response rate* is the actual response rate for each decile group. It is *number of responses* divided by *number of individuals* for each decile group. For the top decile, we have 12.3 percent (= 911/7,410). For the second decile, we have 7.3 percent (= 544/7,410). Similarly for the remaining deciles.

7. *Cumulative response rate* for a given depth of file (the aggregated or cumulative deciles) is the response rate among the individuals in the

---

1. For example, there is a $2 loss if a responder is classified as a nonresponder; and a $4 loss if a nonresponder is classified as a responder.

TABLE 24–2

Decile Analysis

Decile	Number of Individuals	Number of Responses (Actual)	Decile Response Rate	Cumulative Response Rate	Cum Lift
Top	7,410	911	12.3%	12.3%	294
2	7,410	544	7.3%	9.8%	235
3	7,410	437	5.9%	8.5%	203
4	7,410	322	4.3%	7.5%	178
5	7,410	258	3.5%	6.7%	159
6	7,410	188	2.5%	6.0%	143
7	7,410	130	1.8%	5.4%	129
8	7,410	163	2.2%	5.0%	119
9	7,410	124	1.7%	4.6%	110
Bottom	7,410	24	0.3%	4.2%	100
Total	74,100	3,101	4.2%		

cumulative deciles. For example, the cumulative response rate for the top decile (10 percent depth of file) is 12.3 percent (= 911/7,410). For the top 2 deciles (20 percent depth of file), the cumulative response rate is 9.8 percent [= (911 + 544)/(7410 + 7410)]. Similarly for the remaining deciles.

8. *Cum lift*—for a given depth of file—is the *cumulative response rate* divided by the overall response rate of the file, multiplied by 100. It measures how much better you can expect to do with the model than without model. For example, a cum lift of 294 for the top decile means that when soliciting to the top 10 percent of the file based on the model, you can expect 2.94 times the total number of responders found by soliciting 10 percent of the file without any model. The cum lift of 235 for the top two deciles means that when soliciting to 20 percent of the file based on the model, you can expect 2.35 times the total number of responders found by soliciting 20 percent of the file without any model. Similarly for the remaining deciles.

Rule: The larger the cum lift value, the better the accuracy, for a given depth of file.

PRECISION

How close are the predicted probabilities of response to the true probabilities of response? We cannot determine "closeness" directly, because we do not know an individual's true probability. (If we did, then we would not need a model!) We propose the method of smoothing to provide estimates of the true probabilities.

Smoothing is the averaging of values within "neighborhoods." In this application of smoothing, we average *actual* responses within "decile" neighborhoods formed by the model. The average actual response rate for a decile is the estimate of true probability of response for the group of individuals in that decile. See Column 3 in Table 24–3.

Next, we calculate the average *predicted* probabilities of response (based on the model Prob_est scores) among the individuals in each decile. We insert these

T A B L E   24–3

Decile Analysis with HL and CV Indexes

	Column 1	Column 2	Column 3	Column 4	Column 5	Column 6	Column 7
Decile	Number of Customers	Number of Responses (Actual)	Decile Response Rate (Actual)	Prob_est (Predicted)	Square of (Column 3 Minus Column 4) Times Column 1	Column 4 Times (1 − Column 4)	Column 5 Divided by Column 6
Top	7,410	911	12.30%	9.60%	5.40	0.086	62.25
2	7,410	544	7.30%	4.70%	5.01	0.044	111.83
3	7,410	437	5.90%	4.00%	2.68	0.038	69.66
4	7,410	322	4.30%	3.70%	0.27	0.035	7.49
5	7,410	258	3.50%	3.50%	0.00	0.033	0.00
6	7,410	188	2.50%	3.40%	0.60	0.032	18.27
7	7,410	130	1.80%	3.30%	1.67	0.031	52.25
8	7,410	163	2.20%	3.20%	0.74	0.031	23.92
9	7,410	124	1.70%	3.10%	1.45	0.030	48.35
Bot	7,410	24	0.30%	3.10%	5.81	0.030	193.40
Total	74,100	3,101	4.20%				
	Separability CV		80.33		Precision HL		587.40

averages in the column "Prob_est" in the decile analysis. We can now assess model precision.[2] See Column 4 in Table 24–3.

Comparing Columns 3 and 4 is informative. We see that for the top decile the model underestimates the probability of response: 12.3 percent actual versus 9.6 percent predicted. Similarly, for deciles 2 through 4 the model underestimates. Decile 5 is perfect. As we go down Deciles 6 through the bottom, we experience the model overestimating. This type of evaluation for precision is perhaps too subjective. We need an objective summary measure of precision.

We present the HL index[3] as the measure of precision. The calculations for the index are detailed below. See Table 24–3.

1. Columns 1, 2, and 3 are available from the conventional decile analysis.

2. Calculate the average predicted probability of response for each decile from the model scores, Prob_est (Column 4).

3. Calculate Column 5: Take the difference between Column 3 and Column 4. Square the results. Then multiply by Column 1.

4. Column 6: Column 4 times 1 minus Column 4.

5. Column 7: Column 5 divided by Column 6.

6. HL index: sum of the 10 elements of Column 7.

Rule: The smaller the HL index value, the better the precision.

---

2. This assessment is considered at a 10 percent level of smooth. If we constructed a ventile analysis with the scored and ranked file divided into 20 groups, we would have an assessment of model precision at a 5 percent level of smooth. There is no agreement among statisticians on a reliable level of smooth.

3. This is the Hosmer-Lemeshow goodness-of-fit measure.

SEPARABILITY

How different are the individuals (in terms of likelihood to respond) across the deciles? Is there a real variation or separation of individuals as identified by the model? We can measure the variability across the decile groups by calculating the coefficient of variation (CV) among the decile estimates of true probability of response.

CV is the standard deviation of the 10 smooth values of Column 3, divided by the overall response rate, 4.2 percent, multiplied by 100. CV = 80.33. See Table 24–3.

Rule: The larger the CV value, the better the separability.

ALL TOGETHER NOW (DISCUSSION)

In general, a good model has high precision and large separability; but such a model is not necessarily the best model for a given situation. If the purpose of the model is to maximize response rates, then a model with the largest cum lift value is preferred. To ensure a large cum lift, it is necessary but not sufficient to have high precision and large separability.

If individual probability of response estimates are needed,[4] then we seek a model with high precision, i.e., a small HL value. To ensure precision throughout the deciles we should search among models that have small HL values *and* large CV values. Accuracy is irrelevant for this purpose, and particular cum lift values are not necessary to ensure high precision.

The measure of separability has no real practical value by itself. A model that is selected solely on a large CV value will not necessarily have good accuracy or good precision. Separability should be used in conjunction with the other two measures of model assessment as discussed above.

---

4. For example, in calculating expected revenue: revenue per response times probability of response.

CHAPTER 25

Direct Marketing Models Using Genetic Algorithms

Data analysts in direct marketing seek to build models that maximize the expected response and profit from solicitations. Their tool kit consists of statistical techniques, including classical discriminant analysis, logistic regression and ordinary least-squares regression, and the recent addition of the artificial intelligence (AI) method of neural networks. The purpose of this chapter is to present the newest entry in the tool kit, the hybrid AI-statistics DMAX model.

We first provide a background on the concept of optimization, because optimization techniques provide the estimation of all models. We then discuss genetic algorithms, a new AI optimization approach, which is used in the DMAX model. Lastly, we present the DMAX model and discuss real case studies to demonstrate its potential.

WHAT IS OPTIMIZATION?

Optimization theory and methodology involve the selection of the best or most favorable condition within a given environment. Optimization is central to any problem dealing with decision making, whether in business or building models. Decision making requires choosing the best alternative among possible choices. A decision rule or objective function is necessary to distinguish between choices. The choice corresponding to the extreme[1] value of the objective function is to declare the best alternative and thus the solution to the problem. Accordingly, optimization techniques are used to solve decision-making problems.

Modeling techniques are developed as solutions to decision problems. For example, the ordinary least-squares regression technique was developed as a solution for predicting an outcome variable, e.g., sales. The "regression" problem is formulated in terms of finding the regression equation such that the prediction errors (the difference between actual and predicted sales) are small.[2] The objective function is prediction error. The best equation is the one which minimizes the prediction error. Calculus-based methods are used to find (estimate) the best regression equation.

---

1. If the optimization problem seeks to minimize the objective function, then the extreme value is the smallest; if it seeks to maximize, then the extreme value is the largest.
2. The definition of "small" (technically called mean squared error) is the average of the squared differences between actual and predicted values.

As we will later discuss, each modeling method addresses its own decision problem. The DMAX model addresses a problem specific to direct marketing, and uses a genetic algorithm as the optimization technique for its solution.

WHAT IS A GENETIC ALGORITHM?

A genetic algorithm (commonly called GA) is a series of mathematical procedures for search and optimization that transforms a set (population) of mathematical objects or individuals, each with an associated objective (fitness) function value, into a new population, using operations patterned after both Darwin's principle of survival of the fittest and natural occurring genetic operations.

Genetic algorithms consist of three basic operations:

1. Reproduction,[3] based on the principle of survival of the fittest, assures that individuals who are better able to perform tasks in their environment (i.e., fitter individuals) survive and reproduce at a higher rate. Less fit individuals survive and reproduce, if at all, at a lower rate.

2. Crossover (sexual recombination) allows new individuals to be created. Two "parent" individuals with high fitness will likely produce, through sexual recombination, new individuals, or "children," with higher fitness.

3. Mutation is an asexual operation in that it operates on only one individual. It is a random alteration of an individual, which expectantly increases the individual's fitness.

ILLUSTRATION OF A SIMPLE GA[4]

Let's say we want to maximize the objective function $f(X) = X^2$, where X is between and including 0 and 31. Clearly, the maximum value of the function is 31^2, or 961. Let's see how the GA finds the solution.

We code X as a binary integer, a *string* of length 5. With a five-bit (*binary digit*) integer, we can obtain numbers between 0 (00000) and 31 (11111).

We select an initial population (Generation 0) at random. By tossing an unbiased coin[5] 20 times, we obtain four strings or individuals.[6] See Table 25-1. The first randomly generated individual is represented by string (01101), which equals 13. The corresponding objective or fitness function value is 13^2, or 169. The remaining three individuals and their fitness values are shown in Table 25-1. The most fit individual in the population is Individual 2 (fitness value 576); the least fit individual is Individual 3 (fitness value 64). The sum of the fitness values—1,170—represents the total fitness in the population. The average fitness in the population is 293.

The last column of Table 25-1, "Fitness/Sum," is the ratio of fitness value divided by the total fitness of the population. The ratio represents fitness *proportional to total fitness* (PTF). These indexed fitness values sum to 100 percent, and are used as probabilities of selection for reproduction.

---

3. Also known as selection.

4. This illustration is used by D. E. Goldberg, *Genetic Algorithms in Search, Optimization and Machine Learning* (Reading, MA, Addison-Wesley, 1989).

5. The coin appears to be unbiased because we obtain 9 out of 20 heads (cf., 10 out of 20 heads).

6. The population size for this example is set at four, for ease of illustration. The population size can affect the results of the GA solution. The setting of population size is a current issue of GA research.

Initial Population

i	String	X_i	Fitness $f(X_i)$	Fitness /Sum
1	01101	13	169	.14
2	11000	24	576	.49
3	01000	8	64	.06
4	10011	19	361	.31
	Sum		1,170	
	Worst		64	
	Average		293	
	Best		576	

Reproduction

After the initial population is randomly drawn, the operation of reproduction takes place. Reproduction is the process by which individuals are duplicated or copied according to their fitness PTF. Such copying means individuals with a higher fitness PTF value have a higher probability of contributing one or more offspring in the next generation. The reproduction operator is implemented with a biased roulette wheel, where the slices are sized according to fitness PTF. See Figure 25–1.

To reproduce, we simply spin the biased roulette wheel four times.[7] Say, we obtain one copy of String 1, two copies of String 2, none of String 3, and one

F I G U R E 25–1

Biased Roulette Wheel. Slices Sized According to Fitness

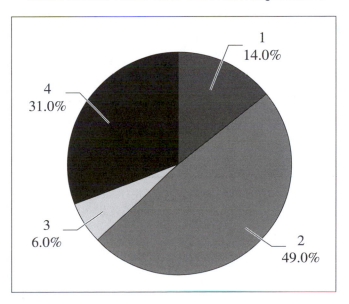

---

7. We reproduce four times so the new population is the same size as the initial population.

copy of String 4. We put them into a *mating pool*, a tentative population for further operations. See Table 25–2. The total fitness of the new population has increased to 1,682 from the initial population fitness of 1,170. This increase occurs, in part, because of the fitness contribution of the two copies of Individual 2, a highly fit individual. The best of the population is still Individual 2, with a fitness value of 576. Because reproduction does not do anything to make Individual 2 or any other individual more fit, the best of the population cannot increase.

Crossover

To increase the fitness of an individual we sexually recombine genetic material of two individuals to produce offspring for the next generation. Sexual recombination or crossover is a three-step process of creating new and more fit individuals.

In the first step, crossover starts with individuals or parents, who are randomly selected from the mating pool to mate. The parents are called mating pairs. In the second step, the pairs are considered for crossover on the basis of a crossover probability test. A probability of crossover is preselected, usually a value between 0.60 and 0.90. A random number between 0 and 1 is assigned to each pair. If the random number is less than the crossover probability (i.e., passes the crossover probability test), then the pair is selected for crossover mating in the third step.

We illustrate how the genetic material is swapped in crossover mating. Say, we have randomly selected parents 1 and 2 (from Table 25–2) to mate, and they pass the crossover probability test. See Table 25–3. We then randomly select a cross site, a number between 1 and L, where L is the length of the string. In our example $L = 5$. Each parent is split at the cross site into a crossover fragment and remainder. Say, our cross site is between bits 4 and 5. In Tables 25–4 and 25–5, we show the Crossover Fragments 1 and 2, and Remainders 1 and 2, corresponding to Parents 1 and 2.

In Table 25–6, we show the results of crossing fragment 1 with remainder 2, and fragment 2 with remainder 1: two "children" represented by strings (01100) and (11001).

We return to the mating pool, Table 25–7, left-side panel. Individuals 1 and 2 mate at the cross site between bits 4 and 5, and their two children (new strings)

T A B L E   25–2

Mating Pool
(Created after Reproduction)

i	String	X_i	Fitness $f(X_i)$	Fitness /Sum
1	01101	13	169	0.10
2	11000	24	576	0.34
2	11000	24	576	0.34
4	10011	19	361	0.22
	Sum		1,682	
	Worst		169	
	Average		421	
	Best		576	

TABLE 25–3

Parents for Crossover

(Randomly Selected to Mate, and Pass Crossover Probability Test)

Parent 1	Parent 2
01101	11000

TABLE 25–4

Crossover Fragments

(Cross Site Is Randomly Selected between Bits 4 and 5)

Crossover Fragment 1	Crossover Fragment 2
0110_	1100_

TABLE 25–5

Crossover Reminders

(Cross Site Is Randomly Selected between Bits 4 and 5)

Crossover Remainder 1	Crossover Remainder 2
_ _ _ _1	_ _ _ _ 0

TABLE 25–6

Results of Crossover

Child 1	Child 2
01100	11001

are in Table 25–7, in the right-side panel, "Generation 1 after Crossover." Individuals 3 and 4 mate at the cross site between bits 2 and 3; their children are also in Table 25–7.

The new population, *Generation 1 after crossover*, has total fitness 1,754. The best of the generation is the child from the crossover between parents 3 and 4, who have fitness values 576 and 361, respectively. The child has an *X* value of 27 and a fitness value of 729. Thus, crossover has created a new and more fit individual.

We summarize the GA process thus far, in Table 25–8. From an initial population randomly generated, we have a total fitness of 1,170, with a best of generation fitness 576. After reproduction, just copying according to fitness PTF, we increase the total fitness of the population to 1,682 without increasing the best of generation. We find a better-fit individual in the generation after crossover. Crossover, which swaps genetic material to produce a better individual, yields a most fit individual, with fitness value 729.

T A B L E   25–7

	Mating Pool (after Reproduction)		Generation 1 after Crossover		
i	String (Cross Site Shown)	Mate (Randomly Selected)	New String	X_i	Fitness $f(X_i)$
1	0110|1	2	01100	12	144
2	1100|0	1	11001	25	625
3	11|000	4	11011	27	729
4	10|011	3	10000	16	256
		Sum			1,754
		Worst			144
		Average			439
		Best			729

T A B L E   25–8

GA Process

	Initial Population (before Reproduction)	Mating Pool (after Reproduction)	Generation 1 (after Crossover)
Sum	1,170	1,682	1,754
Worst	64	169	144
Average	293	421	439
Best	576	576	729

There is one more single operation we can perform to increase the fitness of an individual, namely, mutation.

Mutation

Mutation is introduced to increase genetic diversity into the population. As in natural genetic systems, mutation in GAs occurs occasionally. Mutation randomly selects with low probability a string bit, and replaces it with another character on the basis of a mutation probability test. When a string bit passes the test, mutation negates the bit value. If a 0 bit passes the test, mutation alters it to a 1; otherwise the bit remains unchanged. Similarly, if a 1 bit passes, mutation turns it to 0.

We illustrate how mutation works in Table 25–9. The left-side panel shows the population after crossover. Random numbers in the center panel are assigned to each bit of the four strings. A bit passes the probability test if the associated random number is less than some preselected "cutoff" low probability. In our example, the probability test with cutoff value .005 only passes once, for the third bit of the third string. The results change string 11011 to 1111. The X value of this mutated string is 31, and its fitness value is 961. This is the best of the generation, of all generations previously produced, and it is the solution to the original problem: $X = 31$ produces the maximum value of X^2 on the interval between 0 and 31.

TABLE 25-9

Generation 1 (after Crossover)						Generation 1 after Mutation		
String	Random Numbers (Test: Random Number Less Than .005)					String	X_i	Fitness $f(X_i)$
01100	.801	.102	.266	.373	.201	01100	12	144
11001	.181	.222	.636	.743	.241	11001	25	625
11011	.641	.502	**.001**	.344	.401	11111	31	961
10000	.231	.322	.928	.713	.136	10000	16	256
			Sum					1,986
			Worst					144
			Average					497
			Best					961

GAs TODAY

This illustration is simple and trivial but does not oversimplify the GA procedure for search and optimization. Since its inception by John Holland in the early 1970s, GAs have experienced tremendous growth in their theory. GAs today are way beyond the binary-integer representation of a problem. Research indicates that real number representation along with new sophisticated operators (e.g., arithmetic, exchange, and heuristic crossover operators, and uniform and nonuniform mutation operators) yields more powerful, efficient, and reliable GA solutions. Despite the improvements made to GAs, the basic technique has not changed: GAs still consist of randomly seeding a population, and finding new generations which are better than the previous ones through reproduction, crossover, and mutation.

Applications of GAs have also experienced tremendous growth since the early days. GAs offer feasible approaches to problems where traditional methods either do not exist or are inappropriately used because of weighty assumptions, which cannot be met. Complex problems, correctly formulated in terms of a fitness function, can now be implemented with a GA and the crunching power of the desktop PC.

GAs: STRENGTHS AND LIMITATIONS

GAs have strengths and limitations, like any methodology. Perhaps the most important strength of a GA model is that it is a workable alternative to traditional methods, which are highly parametric with sample size restrictions. Traditional methods have algorithms depending on smooth, unconstrained functions with the existence of derivatives (well-defined slope values). In practice, the functions (response surfaces) are noisy and multimodal with discontinuities. In contrast, GAs are robust, assumption-free, nonparametric models, which perform well on large and small samples. The only requirement is a fitness function, which can be designed to ensure that the GA does not perform worse than any other method.

GAs have been shown to be effective for solving large optimization problems and searching very large data sets. In addition, GAs can learn complex relationships, making GA a viable data mining tool for digging among the data to find "golden nuggets" of information.

A potential limitation of a GA is in the setting of the GA parameters: population size and crossover and mutation probabilities. The parameter settings are, in part, data- and problem-dependent; thus proper settings require experimentation. Fortunately, new theories and empirical studies are continually providing rules of thumb for these settings as application areas broaden. These guidelines make GA methodology an accessible approach to analysts not formally trained in GAs.

Even with the "correct" parameter settings, GAs do not guarantee the optimal (best) solution. Further, GAs are only as good as the definition of the fitness function. Precisely defining the fitness function sometimes requires expert experimentation.

THE GENETIC ALGORITHM DMAX MODEL

The DMAX model is a technique developed for the direct marketing industry, where maximizing response and profit from solicitations are the primary objectives. The model is estimated by a genetic algorithm with a fitness function that seeks to "maximize the deciles." Consequently, the DMAX model allows data analysts to build response and profit models in ways that are not possible with traditional methods.

DMAX Fitness Function

Although the formulation of the DMAX fitness function is beyond the scope of this chapter, the GA estimation procedure for the DMAX model is easy to understand. We perform the three GA operations of reproduction, crossover, and mutation until the operational definition of maximizing the deciles, namely, the *cum lift*, is optimized. In the discussions below, we review and illustrate the concept of cum lift, which is the core of the GA application of the DMAX model.

DMAX Response Model

DMAX response models identify individuals most likely to respond by uniquely taking into account how the model will be implemented. It is common knowledge that direct marketers always have a resource limitation, which results in mailing to only a fraction of their entire database or mail files. DMAX incorporates the "resource limitation" in the modeling process.

Let's say resources allow mailing to only 20 percent of the names in a database. A DMAX response model can be built with the usually chosen predictor variables *and* knowledge that only 20 percent of the database will be mailed. The model ensures that the number of responders, among the 20 percent of the individuals identified by the model as most likely to respond, is maximized. (Note: Any prescribed percent of file can be used, the usual deciles or any specific percentage point.)

We review the standard measure of model performance, the cum response lift, before presenting an illustration. The cum response lift—at a given depth of file—is the ratio of the total number of responders identified by the model (at the given depth of file) over the total number of responders obtained with no model, just by chance (at the given depth of file), multiplied by 100. For example, a cum response lift of 220 for the top 10 percent of a file, the top decile, means that when mailing to 10 percent of the customer file based on the model, you can expect 2.20 times the total number of responders found by mailing 10 percent of the file without any model.

Illustration—Real Case Study 1

The response cum lifts in Table 25–10 show the results of four DMAX response models and one logistic regression model, built on a universe with a 2 percent response rate. All models have the same predictor variables.[8] We see that the DMAX model outperforms logistic regression: 220 versus 194, for 10 percent of file; 195 versus 165, for 20 percent of file; 179 versus 148, for 30 percent of file; and 161 versus 154, for 40 percent of file.

This illustration points to the fact that the DMAX response model is unparalleled because alternative response modeling techniques do not integrate percent-of-file information into the model-building process.

Powerful Response Modeling

DMAX response models can also be used when there is *no prior knowledge* of how many pieces will be mailed. In this case, the DMAX response model is theoretically superior to a response model built with alternative response techniques because of the explicit search heuristic of the genetic algorithm used to estimate the model. The model is defined to *explicitly* maximize the desired criterion: the total probability of correctly classifying both groups of responders and nonresponders, *and* the accuracy of estimating an individual's probability of response.

Discriminant analysis, logistic regression, and artificial neural networks only *implicitly* maximize the desired criterion:

- Discriminant analysis, with the assumption of bell-shaped data, is defined to explicitly maximize the ratio of between-group sum of squares to within-group sum of squares.
- Logistic regression, with the two assumptions of independence of responses and an *S*-shape relationship between predictors and response, is defined to maximize the likelihood function.
- Artificial neural networks, nonparametric assumption-free methods, are defined to explicitly minimize the residual sum of squares without regard for the accuracy of estimating an individual's probability of response.

These three techniques use their optimization criteria as a surrogate for the desired criterion. The DMAX response model has a theoretical advantage because all other alternative response modeling techniques do not explicitly address the desired modeling criterion.

DMAX Discrete Profit Model

The DMAX approach also provides a unique and powerful method of modeling profit.[9] The DMAX discrete profit model identifies individuals who are most likely to both respond and contribute maximum profit. Just as with the response

---

8. We use the same variables for the comparison of DMAX and alternative models. To do otherwise would confound the results by the variable selection process used in each method.
9. We use the term *profit* to stand for any continuous measure related to the bottom line, such as sales dollars, units sold, margin, and lifetime value.

version of DMAX, the DMAX discrete profit model incorporates the resource limitation in the modeling process.

Consider the situation where an individual is classified as either a responder or a nonresponder, each having an associated profit value. Nonresponders have an associated "negative" profit related to the cost of mailing; unpaid responders also have a negative profit, but typically larger because they "take the offer" without fulfilling the commitment; and paid responders have a true and large profit because they are good customers who participate in the program and generate revenue.

We provide the definition of a cum *profit* lift before presenting a profit illustration. The cum profit lift—at a given depth of file—is the ratio of the total profit identified by the model (at the given depth of file) over the total profit obtained with no model, just by chance (at the given depth of file), multiplied by 100.

TABLE 25–10

Response Cum Lifts

Decile	DMAX (10%)	DMAX (20%)	DMAX (30%)	DMAX (40%)	Logistic Regression
Top	220	186	191	192	194
2	174	195	166	166	165
3	157	173	179	150	148
4	148	158	158	161	154
5	139	145	146	146	146
6	131	135	136	138	138
7	122	124	126	127	127
8	114	116	116	117	117
9	108	108	108	109	109
Bottom	100	100	100	100	100

TABLE 25–11

Profit Cum Lifts

Decile	DMAX (20%)	Logistic Regression
Top	444	385
2	371	294
3	277	235
4	223	190
5	191	184
6	169	163
7	151	146
8	130	123
9	114	111
Bottom	100	100

Illustration—Real Case Study 2

The profit cum lifts in Table 25–11 show the results of one DMAX discrete profit model and one logistic regression (modeling paid responders), built on a universe with a .45 percent "paid" response rate and $.32 average profit. Both models have the same predictor variables. We see that the DMAX model at 20 percent of file outperforms logistic regression: 371 versus 294. Clearly, this DMAX (20 percent) model can be used for 10 percent-, 30 percent- and 40 percent-of-file mailings, as it outperforms the logistic regression model, for these depths of file.

The DMAX discrete profit model is unparalleled because it is the only explicit method for modeling profit related to groups of individuals. The model is flexible, as it can handle any number of predefined groups. Furthermore, it can be extended to the situation where each and every individual, not just groups of individuals, can have its own associated profit value. Effectively, we have the DMAX regression model, which serves as an alternative to ordinary regression.

DMAX Regression

Ordinary regression is the oldest and most popular statistical technique for predicting an outcome or continuous dependent variable, such as sales, lifetime value, or any other profit[10] measure. The adjective *ordinary*, perhaps, suggests "good old favorite" to the layperson. However, to the statistician, the word means something very specific. It refers to the method used to estimate the regression model, namely, ordinary least squares.

Ordinary least squares (OLS) should remind us that there is a key assumption of the regression technique; namely, the dependent variable data must be a "normal" curve, or bell-shaped. If the assumption is violated, the resultant model may not be accurate and reliable.

Unfortunately, profit data is not bell-shaped. For example, a 2 percent response rate yields 98 percent nonresponders with profit values of zero dollars or some nominal cost associated with nonresponse. Data with a concentration of 98 percent of a single value cannot be spread out to form a bell-shaped distribution. As another example, consider lifetime value (LTV) data, which is typically positively skewed. The log is the appropriate transformation to reshape the data into a normal curve. However, using the log of LTV as the dependent variable in an OLS regression does not guarantee that other OLS assumptions are not violated.[11] Accordingly, attempts at modeling profit with ordinary regression is questionable and/or difficult.

In contrast, the DMAX regression model has no restriction on the dependent variable: it does not require the dependent variable to be bell-shaped. This is because DMAX regression is actually a nonparametric[12] model because its estimation method is due to its genetic algorithm estimation, which is inherently without any assumptions, parametric or otherwise.

In addition, nonparametric DMAX models have no restriction on sample size. The DMAX regression model can be built on small samples as well as large samples. Ordinary regression, however, requires at least a "moderate"-size

---

10. Again, we refer to profit as any continuous variable which reflects the bottom line.
11. The error structure of the OLS equation may not necessarily be normally distributed with zero mean and constant variance, in which case the modeling results are questionable and additional transformations may be needed.
12. We will not split hairs here; we do not distinguish between assumption-free and nonparamteric methods.

sample. (Statisticians do not agree on how moderate a moderate sample size is. Therefore, I drew a sample of statisticians to determine the size of a moderate sample; the average was 5,000.)

Similar to the other DMAX models, a DMAX regression model can be built with the usually chosen predictor variables *and* knowledge that only a given percent of the database will be mailed. The model ensures that the total profits, among the given percent of the individuals identified by the model as most likely to contribute maximum profit, are maximized.

Illustration—Real Case Study 3

An ordinary regression model with three predictor variables was built on a universe with an average profit of $.37. The decile analysis in Table 25–12 shows the performance of the model over chance (i.e., no model). The top decile has a cum profit lift of 189, which indicates the model has a good predictive range.[13] The "Cum Profit Lift" column appears to show a model with good performance.

However, a closer look at the decile analysis reveals that the model may not be as good as initially believed. The "Total Dollar Profit" column shows unstable performance through the decile; i.e., profit values do not decrease steadily through the deciles. This unstable performance, which is characterized by major "jumps" in deciles 4, 7, and 10 (bottom), indicates the model is inadequately representing the universe. The probable cause for this "lack of fit" is the violation of the dependent variable assumption of bell-shaped data. The implication is that the model is not reliable. It should be pointed out that only perfect models have perfect performance through the deciles. Most models have some jumps, albeit minor.

A DMAX regression profit model was built for a 10 percent-of-file mailing with the same three predictors on the same universe and data. The decile analysis

TABLE 25–12

Decile Analysis
Ordinary Regression Profit Model

Decile	Number of Customers	Total Dollar Profit	Average Profit	Cum Average Profit	Cum Profit Lift
Top	8,083	$5,582	$.69	$.69	189
2	8,083	$4,655	$.58	$.63	173
3	8,083	$3,342	$.41	$.56	153
4	8,083	$5,258	$.65	$.58	160
5	8,083	$2,219	$.27	$.52	143
6	8,083	$992	$.12	$.45	124
7	8,083	$2,196	$.27	$.43	117
8	8,083	$3,034	$.38	$.42	115
9	8,083	$896	$.11	$.39	106
Bottom	8,083	$1,351	$.17	$.37	100
Total	80,830	$29,525	$.37		

---

13. A predictive range is technically measured by the ratio of top-to-bottom decile average profit. Here, we have $.69/$.17 = 4.058. However, because the model is not smooth, this measure is not reliable.

TABLE 25-13

Decile Analysis
DMAX Regression 10% Profit Model

Decile	Number of Customers	Total Dollar Profit	Average Profit	Cum Average Profit	Cum Profit Lift
Top	8,083	$6,444	$.80	$.80	218
2	8,083	$4,548	$.56	$.68	186
3	8,083	$4,547	$.56	$.64	175
4	8,083	$3,098	$.38	$.58	158
5	8,083	$2,521	$.31	$.52	143
6	8,083	$2,990	$.37	$.50	136
7	8,083	$1,850	$.23	$.46	126
8	8,083	$1,968	$.24	$.43	118
9	8,083	$1,000	$.12	$.40	109
Bottom	8,083	$559	$.07	$.37	100
Total	80,830	$29,525	$.37		

in Table 25–13 indicates the model has good performance as evidenced from the "Cum Profit Lift" column (top decile, 218), as well as a very good representation of the universe as evidenced by the "Total Dollar Profit" column (only two minor jumps in Deciles 6 and 8).

DMAX Improvement over Ordinary Regression

Additional DMAX models were built with the same three predictors on the same universe and data for 20 percent-, 30 percent-, 40 percent-, 50 percent-, and 60 percent-of-file mailings. See Table 25–14. We see that DMAX outperforms ordinary regression in terms of greater cum profit lifts: 218 versus 189, for 10 percent

TABLE 25-14

Cum Profit Lifts
DMAX and Ordinary Regression Models

Decile	DMAX (10%)	DMAX (20%)	DMAX (30%)	DMAX (40%)	DMAX (50%)	DMAX (60%)	Ordinary Regression	DMAX Improvement
1	218						189	15.3%
2		187					173	8.1%
3			179				153	17.0%
4				164			160	2.5%
5					151		143	5.6%
6						139	124	12.1%
7							117	
8							115	
9							106	
Bottom							100	

of file; 187 versus 173, for 20 percent of file; 179 versus 153, for 30 percent of file; 164 versus 160, for 40 percent of file; 151 versus 143, for 50 percent of file; and 139 versus 124, for 60 percent of file. The performance gain by using DMAX over ordinary regression is showed in Table 25–14. The percent improvement ranges from 2.5 percent for a 40 percent-of-file mailing to 17.0 percent for a 30 percent-of-file mailing.

DMAX Guarantee

The three case studies discussed are typical DMAX results when DMAX outperforms other techniques. DMAX does not guarantee to find improvement; and finding improvement does not guarantee how much. DMAX only guarantees to look for improvement with respect to the depth-of-file constraint. The other techniques cannot make that claim. When DMAX cannot find improvement, the DMAX model's performance is equivalent to the other models by definition of the fitness function.

CHAPTER 26

Bootstrapping in Direct Marketing: A New Approach for Validating Response Models

Traditional validation of a response model is based on a "holdout" sample, which consists of individuals who are not part of the sample used in building the model itself. The validation results are probably biased and definitely incomplete—unless a resampling method is used. This chapter points to the weaknesses of the traditional validation, and then presents a new approach for validating response models using the bootstrap.

TRADITIONAL RESPONSE MODEL VALIDATION

The analyst's first step in building a model is to split randomly the original data file into two parts: a calibration sample for developing the model and a validation or holdout sample for assessing the reliability of the model. If the analyst is lucky to draw a sample which has favorable characteristics, then a "better-than-true" biased validation is obtained. If unlucky, and the sample has unfavorable characteristics, then a "worse-than-true" biased validation is obtained.

Lucky or not, or even if the validation sample is a "true reflection" of the population under study, a single sample cannot provide a measure of variability, which would otherwise allow the analyst to make inferences about the validation.

To sum, the traditional single-sample validation provides neither assurance that the results are not biased nor any measure of confidence in the results. An illustration will make these points clear.

ILLUSTRATION

Let's consider the validation of a response model[1] in terms of the decile analysis, as reported in Table 26–1. The validation is based on 181,100 customers with a .49 percent response rate. The measure of the predictive power of the model is the cumulative lift (commonly called *cum lift*), which indicates the expected gain of mailing *with* a model over mailing *without* a model.

---

1. Any response model built from any modeling technique (e.g., classical discriminant analysis, logistic regression, artificial neural network, genetic algorithms, or CHAID).

TABLE 26-1

Single-Sample Validation

Decile	Number of Customers	Number of Responses	Response Rate	Cum Response Rate	Cum Lift
Top	18,110	88	0.49%	.49%	182
2	18,110	58	0.32%	.40%	151
3	18,110	50	0.28%	.36%	135
4	18,110	63	0.35%	.36%	134
5	18,110	44	0.24%	.34%	126
6	18,110	48	0.27%	.32%	121
7	18,110	39	0.22%	.31%	115
8	18,110	34	0.19%	.29%	110
9	18,110	23	0.13%	.28%	105
Bottom	18,110	27	0.15%	.27%	100

For example, the cum lift for the top decile is 182. This means that when mailing to the top decile, the top 10 percent of the customer file identified on the model, you can expect 1.82 times the number of responders found by mailing 10 percent of the file without any model. Similarly for the second decile, the cum lift 151 indicates that when mailing to the top two deciles, the top 20 percent of the customer file based on the model, you can expect 1.51 times the number of responders found by mailing randomly any 20 percent of the file.

As luck would have it, our analyst has two additional samples on which two additional validations are performed. See Table 26-2. Not surprising, the cum lifts for a given decile are somewhat different. The reason for this is due to an expected sample-to-sample variation attributed to chance. We notice a large variation in the top decile (range is $15 = 197 - 182$), and a small variation in decile 2 (range is $5 = 153 - 148$). These results raise obvious questions.

THREE QUESTIONS

With many validations of a given response model, we expect variation within each decile. If we observe a large variation within a decile, we have less confidence in the cum lifts for that decile; if we observe a small variation, we have more confidence in the cum lifts. Thus, the following questions:

1. With many validations, how do we define an "average" cum lift (for a decile) to serve as an honest estimate of the cum lift? Additionally, how many validations are needed?

2. With many validations, how do we assess the variability of an honest estimate of cum lift? That is, how do we calculate the standard error of an honest estimate of the cum lift?

3. With only a single validation data set, how can we calculate an honest cum lift estimate and its standard error?

The answers to these questions, and more, lie in the bootstrap methodology.

T A B L E   26–2

Cum Lifts for Three Validations

Decile	First Sample	Second Sample	Third Sample
Top	182	197	186
2	151	153	148
3	135	136	129
4	134	129	129
5	126	122	122
6	121	118	119
7	115	114	115
8	110	109	110
9	105	104	105
Bottom	100	100	100

THE BOOTSTRAP

The bootstrap is a computer-intensive approach to statistical inference.[2] It is the most popular resampling method,[3,4] which uses the computer to extensively re-sample the sample at hand. By random selection with replacement from the sample, some individuals occur more than once in a bootstrap sample, and some individuals occur not at all. Each same-size bootstrap sample will be slightly different from the others. This variation makes it possible to induce an empirical sampling distribution[5] of the desired statistic, from which estimates of bias and variability are determined.

The bootstrap is a flexible technique for assessing the accuracy[6] of any statistic. For well-known statistics, such as the mean, the standard deviation, regression coefficients, and R-square, the bootstrap provides an alternative to traditional parametric methods, which require large sample size. For statistics with unknown properties, such as the median and cum lift, traditional parametric methods do not exist; thus, the bootstrap provides a viable alternative over the inappropriate use of traditional methods, which yield questionable results.

The bootstrap falls also into the class of nonparametric procedures. It does not rely on unrealistic parametric assumptions. Consider testing the significance of a variable[7] in a regression model built using ordinary least-squares estimation. Say, the error terms are not normally distributed, a clear violation of the least-squares assumptions.[8] The significance testing may yield inaccurate results due to the model assumption not being met. In this situation, the bootstrap is a feasible approach in determining the significance of the coefficient without concern

2. E. W. Noreen, *Computer Intensive Methods for Testing Hypotheses* (New York: John Wiley & Sons, 1989).
3. Other resampling methods include the jackknife, infinitesimal jackknife, delta method, influence function method, and random subsampling.
4. B. Efron, "The Jackknife, the Bootstrap and Other Resampling Plans," *SIAM*, 1982.
5. A sampling distribution can be considered as the frequency curve of a sample statistic from an infinite number of samples.
6. Accuracy includes bias, variance, and error.
7. That is, is the coefficient equal to zero?
8. N. R. Draper and H. Smith, *Applied Regression Analysis*, (New York: John Wiley & Sons, 1966).

of any assumptions. As a nonparametric method the bootstrap does not rely on theoretical derivations required in traditional parametric methods. Consider the well-known parametric construction of a confidence interval for the population mean. Say, we draw a random sample of five numbers from a population. The sample consists of 23, 4, 46, 1, and 29. The sample mean is 20.60, the sample median is 23, and the sample standard deviation is 18.58.

The parametric method is based on the central limit theorem, which states that the sample mean is normally distributed and its standard error is analytically defined.[9] The 95 percent confidence interval (CI) for the mean is sample mean value $+/- |Z_{0.025}|*$standard error, where

- Sample mean value is simply the mean of the five numbers in the sample.
- $|Z_{0.25}|$ is the value from the standard normal distribution for a 95 percent CI; the value is 1.96.
- Standard error (SE) of the sample mean has an analytic formula: SE = the sample standard deviation divided by the square root of the sample size. SE = 8.31.

The 95 percent CI for the population mean is between 4.31 and 36.89. That is, we are 95 percent confident that the population mean lies between 4.31 and 36.89.

If we want a confidence interval for the median or the cum lift, we must rely on a resampling method like the bootstrap, because the theoretical sampling distributions of the median and cum lift are not known.

HOW TO BOOTSTRAP[10]

The key assumption of the bootstrap is that the sample is the best estimate[11] of the unknown population. Treating the sample as the population, we repeatedly draw same-size random samples with replacement from the original sample. We estimate the desired statistic's sampling distribution from the many bootstrap samples. We are then able to calculate a bias-reduced[12] bootstrap estimate of the statistic and a bootstrap estimate of the SE of the statistic.

The bootstrap procedure consists of 10 simple steps:

1. State desired statistic, say, Y.
2. Treat sample as population.
3. Calculate Y on the sample/population; call it SAM_EST.
4. Draw a bootstrap sample from the population, i.e., a random selection with replacement of size n, the size of the original sample.
5. Calculate Y on the bootstrap sample to produce a pseudo-value; call it BS_1.
6. Repeat Steps 4 and 5 m times.[13]
7. We have: BS_1, BS_2, . . . , BS_m.

---

9. J. Neter and W. Wasserman, *Applied Linear Statistical Models* (Irwin, 1974).
10. This bootstrap method is the normal approximation. Others are percentile, B-C percentile, and percentile-t.
11. Actually, the sample distribution function is the nonparametric maximum likelihood estimate of the population distribution function.
12. The bias-reduced estimate adds precision to the decile analysis validation when conducting small mailings, and has no effect on large mailings. Some authors argue against use of the bias correction in various situations; however, there is no danger in the proposed application.
13. Studies show the precision of the bootstrap does not significantly increase for $m > 250$.

8. Calculate the bootstrap estimate of the statistic:

$$BS_{est}(Y) = 2*SAM\_EST - mean(BS_i).$$

9. Calculate the bootstrap estimate of the standard error of the statistic:

$$SE_{BS}(Y) = \text{standard deviation of } (BS_i).$$

10. Calculate the 95 percent bootstrap confidence interval:

$$BS_{est}(Y) +/- |Z_{0.025}|*SE_{BS}(Y)$$

SIMPLE ILLUSTRATION

Let's consider a simple illustration. We have a sample from a population (no reason to assume it's normal), which produced the following 11 values:

Sample A: .1 .1 .1 .4 .5 1.0 1.1 1.3 1.9 1.9 4.7

We want to develop a 95 percent confidence interval for the population standard deviation. (Of course, if we knew the population was normal, we would use the parametric chi-square test and obtain the confidence interval: .93 < population standard deviation < 2.35.)

1. The desired statistic is the standard deviation, StD.
2. Treat Sample A as the population.
3. We calculate StD on the original ample/population. SAM_EST = 1.3435.
4. We randomly select 11 observations with replacement from the population. This is our first bootstrap sample.
5. We calculate StD on this bootstrap sample to obtain a pseudo-value, $BS_1 = 1.3478$.
6. We repeat Steps 4 and 5 an additional 99 times.
7. We have $BS_1, BS_2, \ldots, BS_{100}$ in Table 26–3.
8. We calculate the bootstrap estimate of StD:

$$BS_{est}(StD) = 2*SAM\_EST - mean(BS_i) = 2*1.3435 - 1.2034 = 1.483$$

9. We calculate the bootstrap estimate of the standard error of StD:

$$SE_{BS}(StD) = \text{standard deviation } (BS_i) = 0.5008.$$

TABLE 26–3

100 Bootstrapped StDs

1.3476	0.6345	1.7188	. . .	. . .	. . .	. . .	1.4212	1.6712	1.0758
. . .	. . .	. . .	. . .	. . .	. . .	. . .	. . .	. . .	. . .
. . .	. . .	. . .	. . .	. . .	. . .	. . .	. . .	. . .	. . .
. . .	. . .	. . .	. . .	. . .	. . .	. . .	. . .	. . .	. . .
1.3666	1.5388	1.4211	. . .	. . .	. . .	. . .	1.4467	1.9938	0.5793

10. We calculate the 95 percent bootstrap confidence interval for the population standard deviation:

$$0.50 < \text{population standard deviation} < 2.47$$

BOOTSTRAP PERFORMANCE

As you may have suspected, the sample was drawn from a normal population (NP). Thus, it is instructive to compare the performance of the bootstrap with the theoretically correct parametric chi-square test. The bootstrap (BS) confidence interval is somewhat wider than the chi-square–based interval. From Figure 26–1, we see that the BS confidence interval covers values between .50 and 2.47, which also include the values within the NP confidence interval (.93, 2.35).

These comparative performance results are typical. Performance studies indicate that the bootstrap methodology provides results that are consistent with the outcomes of the parametric techniques. Thus, the bootstrap is a reliable approach to inferential statistics in most situations.

Note that the bootstrap estimate offers a more honest[14] and bias-reduced[15] point estimate of the standard deviation. The original sample estimate is 1.3435, and the bootstrap estimate is 1.483. There is a 10.4 percent (1.483/1.3435) bias reduction in the estimate.

BOOTSTRAP DECILE ANALYSIS VALIDATION

Continuing with the decile analysis validation illustration, we perform a bootstrap validation with 50 bootstrap samples.[16] The size of each bootstrap sample is equal to the original sample size of 181,100. The bootstrap cum lift for the top decile is 183, with a bootstrap standard error of 10. Accordingly, the 95 percent bootstrap confidence interval for the top decile is 163 to 203. The second decile has a bootstrap cum lift of 151 and a 95 percent bootstrap confidence interval between 137 and 165. Similar readings can be made for the other deciles. See Table 26–4.

This bootstrap validation tells us the following. Using the given response model to select the top 30 percent of the most responsive individuals from a customer file of size 181,100, we can expect a cum lift of 135. The cum lift is expected to lie between 127 and 143 with 95 percent confidence. Similar statements can be made for other depths of file from the bootstrap validation in Table 26–4.

FIGURE 26–1

Bootstrap Performance

NP: .93xxxxxxxxxxxxx2.35
BS: .50xxxxxxxxxxxxxxxxxx2.47

---

14. Due to the many samples used in the calculation.
15. Attributable, in part, to sample size.
16. We experience high precision in bootstrap decile validation with just 50 bootstrap samples.

T A B L E   26–4

Bootstrap Decile Validation

Decile	Bootstrap Cum Lift	Bootstrap Standard Error	95% Bootstrap Confidence Interval
Top	183	10	(163, 203)
2	151	7	(137, 165)
3	135	4	(127, 143)
4	133	3	(127, 139)
5	125	2	(121, 129)
6	121	1	(119, 123
7	115	1	(113, 117)
8	110	1	(108, 112)
9	105	1	(103, 107)
Bottom	100	0	100

Bootstrap sample size $n = 181,100$

Number of bootstrap samples $m = 50$

If the standard error is too large for your business objectives, what can be done? We look toward the bootstrap for the answer.

ONE MORE QUESTION

It is a well-known relationship in statistics that as the sample size increases, so does the level of confidence we can have in our estimates.[17] We can use this fact to decrease the bootstrap standard error, and to answer the question, "How can we increase our confidence in the bootstrap cum lift estimates?"

If there are additional customer names available to append to the original validation data set, then we increase the data set until the corresponding bootstrap validation produces the desired standard error. If additional names are not available, then we simulate an increase in the data set by increasing the bootstrap sample size. For a desired standard error, the increase in the bootstrap sample size can be determined. Using the increased bootstrap sample, the validation for the desired standard error and confidence intervals is obtained.

Returning to our illustration, we gain a slight decrease in the standard error (from 4 to 3) for the top 30 percent by increasing the bootstrap sample size to 225,000. See Table 26–5. This validation indicates that using the given response model to select the top 30 percent of the most responsive individuals from a customer file of size 225,000, we can expect a cum lift of 142 and a 95 percent confidence interval between 130 and 142. Note that the bootstrap cum lift estimates also change, because their calculations are based on new larger samples. If the gain is not acceptable, a further increase in the bootstrap sample size can be made.

---

17. W. L. Hayes, *Statistics for the Social Sciences* (New York: Holt, Rinehart and Winston, 1973).

TABLE 26-5

Bootstrap Decile Validation

Decile	Bootstrap Cum Lift	Bootstrap Standard Error	95% Bootstrap Confidence Interval
Top	185	5	(175, 195)
2	149	3	(143, 155)
3	136	3	(130, 142)
4	133	2	(129, 137)
5	122	1	(120, 124)
6	120	1	(118, 122)
7	116	1	(114, 118)
8	110	0.5	(109, 111)
9	105	0.5	(104, 106)
Bottom	100	0	100

Bootstrap sample size $n = 225,000$

Number of bootstrap samples $m = 50$

BOOTSTRAP COMPUTATION

The time and effort required to generate a bootstrap validation is minimal. With the appropriate bootstrap program secured, the time needed to input the data, generate the many bootstrap samples, and calculate the BS statistics is only a matter of minutes.

Following the step-by-step outline as discussed in this chapter, a proficient programmer can write a bootstrap routine in most computer languages, such as Fortran, C, and Pascal. An all-purpose bootstrap package is available from Resampling Stats, 612 N. Jackson Street, Arlington, Virginia, 22201. The specific bootstrap program used for this chapter, BS CumLifts, is available from the author.

SUMMARY

We discussed the weaknesses and limitations of the traditional holdout validation of a response model. After introducing the bootstrap philosophy and methodology, we illustrated how the bootstrap can provide honest, less-biased estimates of cum lifts. Additionally, the bootstrap provides measures of stability for the bootstrap estimates, which affords us a level of confidence when implementing the model.

CHAPTER 27

"What Do My Customers Look Like?" Look at the Stars!

Direct marketers use response models to find their potential customers, after which they ask, "What do my customers look like?" The purpose of this chapter is to present a visual display—a star graph—of the individuals identified by a response model.

STAR GRAPH BASICS

A tabular display of numbers shows neatly "important facts contained in a jungle of figures."[1] However, more often than not, a table leaves room for further untangling of the numbers. Graphs can help us out of the "numerical" jungle with a visual display of where we've been and what we've seen. A good graph can leave you starry-eyed.

A star graph is a visual display of multivariate data, i.e., many rows of many variables. The basics of star graph construction are as follows:

1. Consider an *observation* defined by a row or an array of *k variables*, $X_1, X_2, \ldots, X_k$.

2. There are *k* equidistant rays emitting from the center of the star.

3. The lengths of the rays correspond to the array of *X* values. The variables are assumed to be measured on relative similar scales. If not, the data must be transformed to induce comparable scales.[2]

4. The ends of the rays are connected to form a polygon or star.

5. A circle is circumscribed around the star. The circumference provides a reference "line," which aids in interpreting the star. The centers of the star and circle are the same point; the radius of the circle is equal to the length of the largest ray.

---

1. Tukey, EDA.

2. There are two methods to accomplish comparable scales. Normalizing transforms the variables such that the rescaled variable values lie within a common interval, typically [0, 1]. Normalizing destroys the information about location and scale of a variable. Standardizing transforms the variables to have the same mean and standard deviation, typically 0 and 1, respectively. When negative values exist, adding a constant to all values of the variable(s) is required.

6. A star graph typically does not contain labels indicating the X values.[3] The evaluation of the shapes of the stars untangles the numbers to reveal the patterns and trends in the numbers.

ILLUSTRATION

Direct marketers use response models to identify potential customers. The model provides an analysis that orders the individuals into 10 equal-sized groups or deciles, ranging from the top 10 percent most likely to respond to the bottom 10 percent least likely to respond. The traditional approach of describing or profiling the individuals is to calculate the means of variables believed to discriminate among individuals and assess their values across the deciles.

Let's consider the means of four demographic variables across the deciles. See Table 27–1. The tabular display of the decile analysis shows:

1. *Age.* Older individuals are more responsive than younger individuals.
2. *Income.* High-income earners are more responsive than low-income earners.
3. *Education.* Individuals with greater education are more responsive than individuals with less education.
4. *Gender.* Females are more responsive than males.

STAR GRAPHS FOR SINGLE VARIABLES

The first step in interpreting a star graph is to identify the "units" that serve as the *observation* and the *k variables.* A single variable star graph uses the variable itself as the observation and the 10 deciles (top, 2, 3, . . . , bottom) as the *k* variables. The star graphs for each of the four variables are shown in Figure 27–1.

TABLE 27–1

Means by Deciles

Decile	Age (Yrs)	Income ($000)	Education (Years of Schooling)	Gender (1 = male/ 0 = female)
Top	63	155	25	0.05
2	51	120	21	0.10
3	49	110	14	0.20
4	46	111	13	0.25
5	42	105	13	0.40
6	41	95	12	0.55
7	39	88	12	0.70
8	37	91	12	0.80
9	25	70	12	1.00
Bottom	25	55	12	1.00

---

3. If transformations are required, then the transformed values are virtually meaningless.

Star Graphs for Age, Income, Education, and Gender

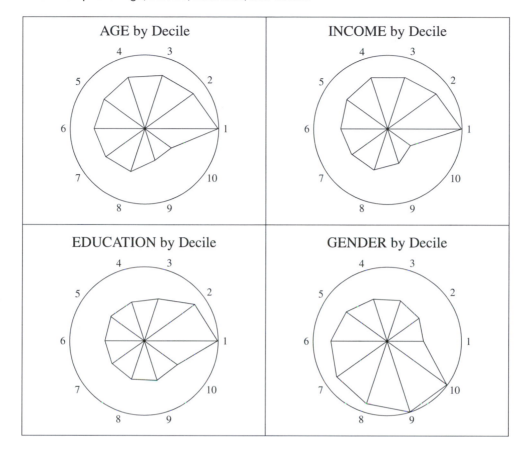

We interpret the star graph as follows. Starting with the top decile, and going about the perimeter of the star in a counterclockwise direction:

1. For age, income, and education, we observe a decreasing trend in the values of the variables as we go down the deciles.

2. Stars for age and income are virtually identical, except for the ninth decile. Implication: Age and income have very similar effects on response. That is, standardized unit increases in age and income produce very similar changes in response.

3. For gender, we observe an increasing trend in the incidence of males as we go through the deciles. (Keep in mind that gender is coded zero for females.)

STAR GRAPHS FOR MANY VARIABLES CONSIDERED JOINTLY

Now, let's consider a star graph for the array of the four demographic variables *considered jointly*. The *observation* is a decile, and the *k variables* are the four demographics. Accordingly, there are 10 star graphs, one for each decile; each star has four rays, corresponding to the four variables. See Figure 27–2.

We interpret star graphs for an array of variables as a comparative evaluation. Because star graphs have no numerical labels, we assess the shapes of the

F I G U R E   27–2

Star Graphs for the Array of Four Demographic Variables Considered Jointly

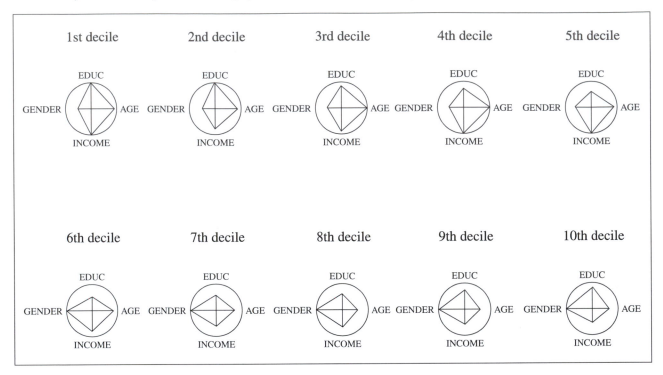

stars by observing their "movement" within the reference circle as we go from the top to bottom deciles:

   A. *Top decile star.* The rays of AGE, INCOME, and EDUCATION touch or nearly touch the circle circumference. These long rays indicate older, more educated individuals with higher income. The short ray of GENDER indicates these individuals are mostly females. These individuals in the top decile constitute the reference group for a comparative analysis of the other decile stars.

   B. *Second decile star.* Individuals in this decile are slightly younger, with less income than individuals in the top decile.

   C. *Third to fifth decile stars.* Individuals in these deciles are substantially less educated than the individuals in the top two deciles.

   D. *Sixth decile star.* The shape of this star is a significant departure from the top five decile stars. This star indicates individuals who are mostly males (because the GENDER ray touches the circle), younger, less educated, with less income than the individuals in the upper deciles.

   E. *Seventh—bottom decile stars.* These stars hardly move within the circle as we go through the lower deciles (sixth—bottom). This indicates that the individuals across the least responsive deciles are essentially the same.

CONCLUSION

We presented the star graph as a visual display of multivariate data. We illustrated the technique by addressing a question often posed in direct marketing: "What do my customers look like?" Our answer: Look at the stars!

CHAPTER 28

Alternative Direct Marketing Response Models: Linear Probability, Logit and Probit Models

Direct marketers use response models to create lists of individuals most likely to respond to solicitations, thereby maximizing response rates. Despite their substantial reliance on models, direct marketers have some misunderstanding over the distinctions among the alternative response methods: linear probability, logit and probit models. The purpose of this chapter is to insure the proper use of these models by reviewing their theoretical and practical differences.

LINEAR PROBABILITY MODEL

The objective of a direct marketing response model is to predict or estimate the probability of an individual responding to a solicitation. Let Y be the response (dependent) variable that assumes two outcomes: yes (coded as 1) and no (coded as 0). Also, let $X1$, $X2$, . . . , X_n be the predictor (independent) variables believed to be related to response.

The linear probability model (LPM) states that the probability of an individual responding yes, denoted by $\Pr(Y = 1)$, can be expressed as:

$$\Pr(Y = 1) = b0 + b1X1 + b2X2 + \ . \ . \ . \ + bnXn$$

In other words, LPM provides a probability estimate in the form of a weighted sum of the predictor variables. The b's are the "weights" or coefficients, which are estimated by the method of least-squares. Actually, LPM is the Ordinary Least-Squares (OLS) regression model with the dependent variable defined as the binary (yes-no) response variable.

OLS regression assumes that the dependent variable is continuous. Thus, when the dependent variable is binary, the utility of the model is questionable. Specifically, LPM has theoretical problems: it violates some of the OLS *assumptions*[1] that can lead to incorrect inferences; and it can produce nonsensical predictions. Some variables may be excluded from the model because significance tests may be invalid. Probability estimates are highly dependent on the sample values, making extrapolation suspect.

Perhaps, the most fundamental problem with LPM concerns the formation of the model itself. The left-hand side of the model equation is a probability, which must lie inside the restricted [0, 1] interval. The right-hand side is an "unrestricted" weighted sum, because the coefficients and the values of the predictor variables

---

1. Heteroscedasticity, nonnormal error term, and nonlinearity.

can take on any value, negative or positive, large or small. Thus, probability estimates can result in nonsensical scores, which lie outside the [0, 1] interval.

Hence, LPM is not theoretically perfect. Why is it popular? Is there any merit in building a LPM? The LPM is popular because it is simple to understand, and computer programs are readily available to encourage its (mis)use. Regarding its merit, first, let's take a look at the two alternative response models.

LOGIT AND PROBIT MODELS

Essentially, the problem with LPM is that it explicitly uses the unrestricted weighted-sum scores as probability estimates. The "unrestricted scores" problem can be eliminated if we *transform* the scores such that:

1. As the weighted-sum scores becomes large, the transformed scores that represent $Pr(Y = 1)$ approach 1.

2. As the weighted-sum scores becomes small, the transformed scores that represent $Pr(Y = 1)$ approach 0.

We are suggesting a continuous S-shaped transformation of the weighted-sum scores.

There are many S-curve *transformations*.[2] Two transformations have been studied extensively, namely, the normal cumulative distribution function (cdf) and the standard logistic cdf. Their shapes are very similar, with the logistic having heavier tails and a flatter midsection than the normal. Accordingly, analysis and modeling based on these two cdfs produce very similar results except when the weighted-sum scores are extreme. When the weighted-sum scores are very small (large), the logistic tends to give larger (smaller) probabilities to $Y = 1$ than the normal. See Figure 28–1.

The mathematical expressions for the two transformations are below:

$$Pr(Y = 1) = \frac{\exp(b0 + b1X1 + b2X2 + \ldots + bnXn)}{1 + \exp(b0 + b1X1 + b2X2 + \ldots + bnXn)}$$

$$Pr(Y = 1) = \int^{\Sigma biXi} \frac{1}{\sqrt{2\pi}} \exp\left(-\frac{t^2}{2}\right) dt$$

The integral is evaluated between negative infinite and weighted-sum scores less than/equal to $b0 + b1X + b2X2 + \ldots + bnXn$.

The logit and probit models are defined as above, respectively. The weighted-sum scores from the models are called logits and *probits*,[3] respectively.

The assumptions of the Logit and Probit models are as follows:

1. The data are generated from a random sample.

2. Y assumes only two values, 0 and 1.

3. The Y observations are statistically independent of each other.

4. The probability of $Y = 1$ is defined by the standard logistic cdf for the logit model, and by the normal cdf for the probit model.

5. There is no exact linear relationship between two or more of the Xs.

The method of maximum likelihood is used to estimate the coefficients of logit and probit models.

---

2. Angular, Gompetz, Burr, and Urban.
3. Readers may recognize that Probit scores are actually z-scores.

F I G U R E   28–1

Logistic cdf(L) and Normal cdf(P).

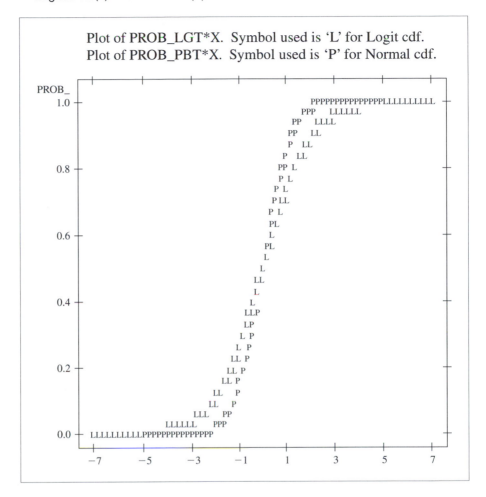

Plot of **PROB_LGT*X**. Symbol used is 'L' for Logit cdf.
Plot of **PROB_PBT*X**. Symbol used is 'P' for Normal cdf.

Illustration

Let's build response models using the data in Table 28–1. We have response variable *Y*, two predictor variables *X*1 and *X*2, and the ID number for 18 individuals. The LPM and the logit and probit models are in Tables 28–2 to 28–4, respectively.

DISCUSSION OF TABLE 28–5

1. The LPM model produces explicit probability estimates, LPM_prob, defined by:
   a. LPM_prob = 1.315076 − 0.003490 X1 − 0.032546 X2.

2. The logit model produces logit scores, defined by the equation below. To obtain the corresponding probability estimates, LGT_prob, we apply the logit transformation.
   a. Logit = 12.059738 − 0.001287 X1 − 0.503354 X2.

T A B L E   28-1

18 Observations

ID#	X1	X2	Y
1	23	9.5	1
2	23	27.9	0
3	27	7.8	1
4	27	17.8	1
5	39	31.4	0
6	41	25.9	0
7	45	27.4	1
8	49	25.2	0
9	50	31.1	0
10	53	34.7	0
11	53	42.0	0
12	54	29.1	0
13	56	32.5	0
14	57	30.3	0
15	58	33.0	0
16	58	33.8	0
17	60	41.1	0
18	61	34.5	0

3. The probit model produces probit scores, defined by the equation below. To obtain the corresponding probability estimates, PBT_prob, we apply the probit transformation.

  a. Probit $= 6.9182165 + 0.0021827\,X1 - 0.2929096\,X2$.

4. Not unexpectedly, there are LPM estimates with values less than zero.

  a. Individuals 11, 17, and 18 have negative probability estimates (LPM_prob):

  i) -0.23679, -0.23193 and -0.02062, respectively.

  b. The "correct" probability estimates for these individuals from the Logit and Probit models are [ID#:(LGT_prob, PBT_prob)]:

  i)   ID 11 $= (0.00011, 0.0000)$,

  ii) ID 17 $= (0.00017, 0.0000)$, and

  iii) ID 18 $= (0.000457, 0.00113)$.

  c. The implication is that individual LPM probability estimates cannot be used in subsequent *analysis*.[4]

5. For unknown individuals with $(X1, X2)$ values outside the range of the observed/tabled values of $X1$ and $X2$, say, $(20, 5)$ and $(62, 43)$, we have LPM probability estimates 1.08, and -0.30, respectively. Clearly, extrapolation is problematic.

  a. The extrapolation predictions based on the logit and probits models are meaningful:

  i) $LGT(20, 5) = 0.9999264321$, and $PBT(20, 5) = 0.9999999807$.

  ii) $LGT(62, 43) = 0.0000635082$, and $PBT(62, 43) = 0.000000014989$.

---

4. For example, in calculating expected revenue: revenue per response times probability of response.

TABLE 28-2

Linear Probability Model (OLS Regression)

Variable	DF	Parameter Estimate	Standard Error	T for H0: Parameter = 0	Prob > |T|
INTERCEPT	1	1.315076	0.25261062	5.206	0.00011
X1	1	−0.003490	0.00850083	−0.410	0.68725
X2	1	−0.032546	0.01228740	−2.649	0.01824

TABLE 28-3

Logit Model

Variable	DF	Estimate	Std Err	ChiSquare	Pr > Chi
INTERCEPT	1	12.059738	9.604729	1.576542	0.20926
X1	1	−0.001287	0.116314	0.000122	0.99117
X2	1	−0.503354	0.380351	1.751373	0.18570

TABLE 28-4

Probit Model

Variable	DF	Estimate	Std Err	ChiSquare	Pr > Chi
INTERCEPT	1	6.9182165	5.227334	1.751571	0.18568
X1	1	0.0021827	0.066933	0.001063	0.97398
X2	1	−0.2929096	0.213761	1.877632	0.17060

6. The theoretical relationship between the logit and probit scores is:

  a. $\dfrac{\text{logit}}{\text{probit}} = \dfrac{\pi}{\sqrt{3}} \sim 1.8$

  b. We can empirically test this relationship by creating the ratio variable (logit/probit). We observe that relationship holds satisfactorily for all individuals, except two.

   i) Ratio values for individuals 2 and 8 are 1.67264 and 1.93136, respectively.

  c. The implication for these two individuals is that they may not "fit" the logit and probit models.

7. We evaluate the *precision* of a model by *Mean Absolute Difference*[5] (MAD). Smaller MAD values imply greater precision.

  a. The logit and probit models have greater precision than LPM.

   i) MAD(probit) = 0.0993

---

5. MAD is the mean of the absolute differences between actual *Y* values and the predicted *Y* values.

TABLE 28–5

Model Scores and Probabilities

ID#	X1	X2	Y	LPM_prob	LGT_prob	PBT_prob	Logit	Probit	Ratio
1	23	9.5	1	0.92563	0.99929	0.99999	7.24827	4.18578	1.73164
2	23	27.9	0	0.32679	0.11780	0.11434	−2.01345	−1.20376	1.67264
3	27	7.8	1	0.96700	0.99970	1.00000	8.09883	4.69246	1.72592
4	27	17.8	1	0.64154	0.95544	0.96108	3.06528	1.76336	1.73832
5	39	31.4	0	0.15705	0.02197	0.01412	−3.79578	−2.19402	1.73006
6	41	25.9	0	0.32907	0.26310	0.28141	−1.02990	−0.57865	1.77984
7	45	27.4	1	0.26629	0.14306	0.15642	−1.79008	−1.00928	1.77362
8	49	25.2	0	0.32393	0.33451	0.36086	−0.68785	−0.35615	1.93136
9	50	31.1	0	0.12842	0.02511	0.01867	−3.65893	−2.08213	1.75730
10	53	34.7	0	0.00079	0.00417	0.00087	−5.47487	−3.13006	1.74913
11	53	42.0	0	−0.23679	0.00011	0.00000	−9.14935	−5.26830	1.73668
12	54	29.1	0	0.17956	0.06554	0.06843	−2.65737	−1.48758	1.78637
13	56	32.5	0	0.06192	0.01248	0.00659	−4.37135	−2.47911	1.76327
14	57	30.3	0	0.13003	0.03678	0.03344	−3.26525	−1.83253	1.78183
15	58	33.0	0	0.03867	0.00970	0.00438	−4.62560	−2.62120	1.76469
16	58	33.8	0	0.01263	0.00651	0.00215	−5.02828	−2.85553	1.76089
17	60	41.1	0	−0.23193	0.00017	0.00000	−8.70534	−4.98940	1.74477
18	61	34.5	0	−0.02062	0.00457	0.00113	−5.38449	−3.05402	1.76309

ii) MAD(logit) = 0.1003, and

iii) MAD(PM) = 0.1877.

8. We assess the predictive *accuracy* of a model by the *Total Correctly Classified*[6] (TCC).

    a. All three models have TCC = 15. See Table 28–6.

        i) None of the models correctly identify ID 6 and ID 8.

        ii) Logit and probit models correctly classify ID 2; but not LPM.

        iii) LPM correctly classifies ID 7; but neither the logit nor the probit models.

9. We gauge the predictive *power* of a model by analyzing the ranking of responders. A preferred model is one that ranks the largest number of responders at the "top" of the file.

    a. From Table 28–7, we see that the logit and probit models produce identical rankings.

    b. The logit and the probit models have a better ranking than LPM, as they place one more responder, namely ID 7, at the top of the file.

CONCLUSION

We reviewed the LPM and showed that it is theoretically flawed. As for its practical value, there is only one use: LPM serves well as a starting point for a discussion on response models. The theoretically preferred logit and probit

---

6. See Table 7 for the calculation of TCC.

TABLE 28-6

Model Classifications

ID#	X1	X2	Y	LPM_pred	LGT_pred	PBT_pred
1	23	9.5	1	1	1	1
2	23	27.9	0	*1	0	0
3	27	7.8	1	1	1	1
4	27	17.8	1	1	1	1
5	39	31.4	0	0	0	0
6	41	25.9	0	*1	*1	*1
7	45	27.4	1	1	*0	*0
8	49	25.2	0	*1	*1	*1
9	50	31.1	0	0	0	0
10	53	34.7	0	0	0	0
11	53	42.0	0	0	0	0
12	54	29.1	0	0	0	0
13	56	32.5	0	0	0	0
14	57	30.3	0	0	0	0
15	58	33.0	0	0	0	0
16	58	33.8	0	0	0	0
17	60	41.1	0	0	0	0
18	61	34.5	0	0	0	0
	Total Correctly Classified (TCC)			15	15	15

* = incorrect classification. If an individual's probability estimate is less/equal .22 then the individual is incorrectly classified. (E.g., if LPM_prob < / = .22, then LPM_pred = 0; otherwsie LPM_pred = 1). See Table 28-5 for probability estimates: LPM_prob, LGT_prob, and PBT_prob.

TABLE 28-7

Model Rankings

Ranking by LPM		No Match (x)	Ranking by Logit and Probit	
Y	ID#		Y	ID#
1	3		1	3
1	1		1	1
1	4		1	4
0	6		0	8
0	2		0	6
0	8		1	7
1	7	x	0	2
0	12	x	0	12
0	5	x	0	14
0	14	x	0	9
0	9		0	5
0	13	x	0	13
0	15	x	0	15
0	16	x	0	16
0	10		0	18
0	18		0	10
0	17		0	17
0	11		0	11

models were presented and illustrated to provide reliable and almost identical estimates.

The logit is the response model of choice, at least in direct marketing, because it is easy to interpret. The coefficients of the logit model can be explained *directly,* unlike with the probit model. Exponentiating a coefficient produces the factor by which the odds (of responding) change for every unit change in the corresponding independent variable.

CHAPTER 29

CHAID for Interpreting a Logistic Regression Model

The logistic regression model is the current standard technique for modeling response in direct marketing. The theory is well established, and the estimation algorithm is available in all major statistical packages. The literature on the theoretical aspects of logistic regression is large and rapidly growing. However, little attention is paid to the interpretation of logistic regression results. The purpose of this article is to present CHAID as a graphical method for understanding how the variables in a model work individually and together.

LOGISTIC REGRESSION MODEL

We begin by reviewing the logistic regression model. Let Y be a binary (yes/no) dependent response variable, and $X1, X2, \ldots , Xn$ be the independent predictor variables. The logistic regression model defines the logit, from which the probability of an individual responding yes is obtained:

$$\text{Logit} = b0 + b1{*}X1 + b2{*}X2 + \ldots + bn{*}Xn$$

$$\text{Prob}(L = \text{yes}) = \frac{\exp(\text{logit})}{1 + \exp(\text{logit})}$$

The logit stands for the log of the odds of an individual responding yes. The bs are the logistic regression coefficients, which are estimated by the method of maximum likelihood. Once the coefficients are determined, an individual's probability of response is calculated by plugging in the values of the predictor variables for that individual in equations.

DIRECT MARKETING RESPONSE MODEL (REAL STUDY)

A woodworker's supply cataloger wants to increase response rates. The cataloger commissions the building of a response model, which is based on the most recent mailing of the general catalog. The model is developed using standard procedures for variable selection and model assessment and validation. The variables in the model are CUST_AGE = customer age, LOG_LIFE = log of lifetime dollars, and PRIOR_BY = purchase made in prior three months (yes = 1, no = 0). The logistic regression output is in Table 29–1. The "Parameter Estimate" column contains the coefficients, the bs in the logistic or logit regression equation.

The "Odds Ratio" column (in Table 29–1) is the traditional measure of assessing the effect of a variable on response, actually on the odds of responding yes. It is obtained by exponentiating the coefficient of the variable in question. For PRIOR_BY, we have exp(.8237) = 2.279. This means that for a unit increase in PRIOR_BY, i.e., going from 0 to 1, the odds (of responding yes) for an individual who has made a purchase within the prior three months is 2.279 times the odds for an individual who has *not* made a purchase within the prior three months, given that the other variables in the equation are "held constant."[1]

CUST_AGE has an odds ratio of 1.023. This indicates that for every one-year increase in a customer's age, the odds increase by 2.3 percent. LOG_LIFE has an odds ratio of 2.102, which indicates that for every one "log lifetime dollar" unit increase, the odds increase by 1.02 percent.

As informative as the odds ratio is (notwithstanding the need for most analysts to convert odds into probability,[2] and an ability to work with log lifetime dollars units), it does not provide a complete assessment of a variable's effect with respect to the *variation* of the other variables in the model.

CHAID

CHAID is a technique that recursively partitions a population into separate and distinct subpopulations or segments such that the variation of the dependent variable is minimized within the segments and maximized among the segments. CHAID was originally developed as a method of finding "combination" or interaction variables. Today in direct marketing, CHAID primarily serves as a market segmentation technique.

Here, we propose CHAID as a method of enhancing interpretation of a logistic regression model through the examination of the estimated probability of response. In this application of CHAID, we benefit from the visual displays of the trees to show us how the variables in a model work individually and together.

It is worth emphasizing that CHAID in this application is not being used as an alternative method for analyzing or modeling the data at hand. It is assumed

TABLE 29–1

Analysis of Maximum Likelihood Estimates

Variable	DF	Parameter Estimate	Standard Error	Wald Chi Square	Pr > Chi Square	Odds Ratio
INTERCPT	1	−8.4349	0.0854	9760.7175	0.E + 00	
CUST_AGE	1	0.0223	0.000409	2967.8450	0.E + 00	1.023
LOG_LIFE	1	0.7431	0.0191	1512.4483	0.E + 00	2.102
PRIOR_BY	1	0.8237	0.0186	1962.4750	0.E + 00	2.279

1. For given values of CUST_AGE and LOG_LIFE, say, a and b, respectively,

$$\frac{\text{the odds ratio}}{\text{for PRIOR\_BY}} = \frac{\text{odds(PRIOR\_BY} = 1, \text{given CUST\_AGE} = a, \text{LOG\_LIFE} = b)}{\text{odds(PRIOR\_BY} = 0, \text{given CUST\_AGE} = a, \text{LOG\_LIFE} = b)}$$

2. The conversion formulas: Probability = odds/(1 + odds); Odds = probability/(1 − probability).

that a model is built. Based on the final model, CHAID is being used to understand how the variables in the model affect response rates, one variable at a time and all variables simultaneously.

In general, to perform a CHAID analysis we must define the dependent variable and select a set of independent variables. For this application of CHAID, the model's estimated probability of response is the dependent variable. The estimated probability, call it Prob_EST, from the model in Table 29–1 is defined as:

$$\text{Prob}\_\text{EST} = \frac{\exp(-8.43 + .02*\text{CUST}\_\text{AGE} + .74*\text{LOG}\_\text{LIFE} + .82*\text{PRIOR}\_\text{BY})}{1 + \exp(-8.43 + .02*\text{CUST}\_\text{AGE} + .74*\text{LOG}\_\text{LIFE} + .82*\text{PRIOR}\_\text{BY})}$$

The set of independent variables consists of the variables, in their raw form, used in the model: CUST_AGE, PRIOR_BY, and the raw variable *lifetime dollars*. We do not consider the explicit model variable LOG_LIFE, because, as we will later see, it hinders the interpretation of the CHAID analyses.

Also, for ease of interpretation, we require categorizing the continuous variables into *meaningful* ranges. Our woodworker cataloger views his or her customers as follows:

1. Two age groups: less than 35 years, and 35 years and up
2. Lifetime dollars in three groups: less than $15,000; $15,001 to $29,999; and equal to/greater than $30,000

Accordingly, CHAID denotes these ranges[3] for the sample under study as follows:

1. Customer age — [18, 35) and [35, 93].
2. Lifetime dollars — [12, 1500), [1500, 30000), and [30000, 675014].

The CHAID trees for the three independent variables are shown in Figure 29–1. The CHAID tree is read as follows: For PRIOR_BY in Figure 29–1a, the top box indicates that for the sample of 858,963 customers the average estimated probability[4] (AEP) of response is .0235. The left-side box represents the segment (size 333,408) of the total sample which has PRIOR_BY = no. These customers have *not* made a purchase in the prior three months; their AEP of response is .0112. The right-side segment of 525,555 customers have made a purchase in the prior three months; their AEP of response is .0312.

For CUST_AGE in Figure 29–1b, customers who are less than 35 years old have an AEP of response 0.0146; customers who are 35 years and up have an AEP of response .0320. For lifetime dollars in Figure 29–1c, the AEP of response is .0065, .0204, and .0332 for the lifetime dollar ranges [12, 1500], [1500, 30000], and [30000, 675014], respectively.

At this point, we have easy-to-interpret trees, which show the effect of a variable. However, these trees, like the odds ratio, do not enhance the understanding of the effect of a variable with respect to the *variation* of the other variables in the model. For a graphical display of a variable's effect on response accounting for the presence of other variables, we must go to a full CHAID tree.

---

3. CHAID denotes the ranges as a closed interval, or a left-closed/right-open interval. The former is denoted by [a,b] indicating all values between and including a and b. The latter is denoted by [a,b) indicating all values greater than/equal to a and less than b.

4. The average estimated probability or response rate is always equal to the true response rate.

F I G U R E　29-1

CHAID Trees for (a) PRIOR_BY, (b) CUST_AGE, and (c) Lifetime Dollars

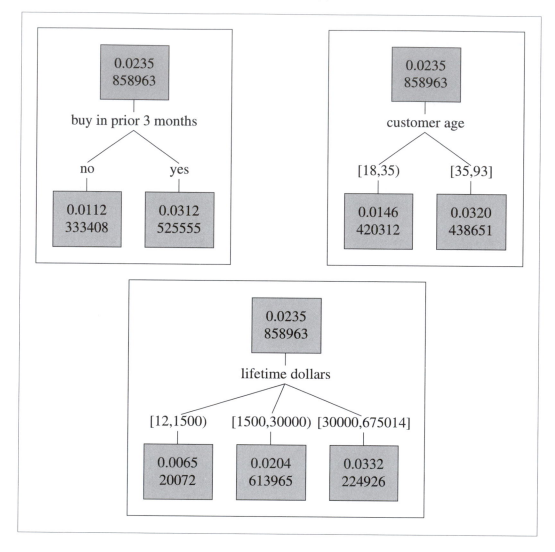

CHAID TREES

In Figure 29–2 below, we have a full CHAID tree showing the effect of lifetime dollars on response with respect to the variation of CUST_AGE and PRIOR_BY. The AEP of response ranges from .0032 to .0076 to .0131 for customers who are less than 35 years old *and* have not purchased in the prior three months. The AEP of response ranges from .0048 to .0141 to .0192 for customers who are 35 years old and up *and* have not purchased in the prior three months.

Similarly, in Figure 29–3, the AEP of response ranges from .0077 to .0186 to .0297 for customers who are less than 35 years old *and* have purchased in the prior three months. The AEP of response ranges from .0144 to .0356 to .0460 for customers who are 35 years old and up *and* have purchased in the prior three months.

Note: A closer look at the two full trees shows there is a pair of segments with equal performance.

FIGURE 29-2

Full CHAID Tree: Effect of Lifetime Dollars, Accounting for CUST_AGE and PRIOR_BY = no

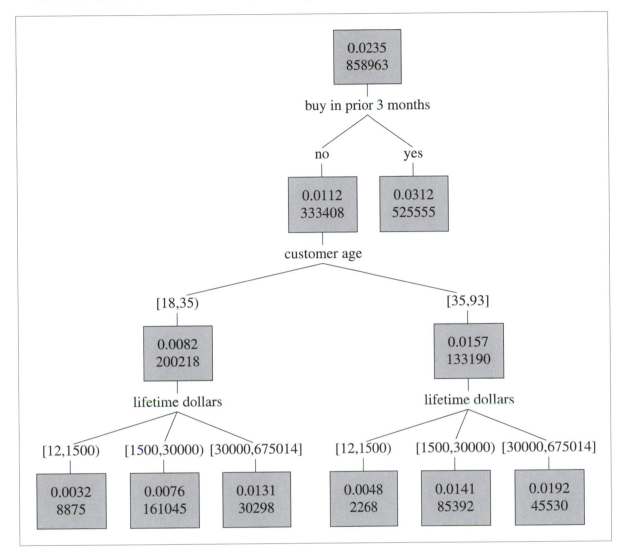

1. Customers who are less than 35 years old and have *not* purchased in the prior three months and have lifetime dollars in the range [1500, 30000). The AEP of response is .0076. See Figure 29–2.

2. Customers who are less than 35 years old and have purchased in the prior three months and have lifetime dollars in the range [12, 15000). The AEP of response is .0077. See Figure 29–3.

In fact, there are two more pairs of segments with equal performances.

This type of segment identification illustrates the value of CHAID as a market segmentation technique. At this point, CHAID provides the cataloger with insight into high and low-performing segments. Marketing strategy can be developed to stimulate the high performers with, say, cross-selling, and low performers with, say, incentives and discounts.

FIGURE 29-3

Full CHAID Tree: Effect of Lifetime Dollars, Accounting for CUST_AGE and PRIOR_BY = yes

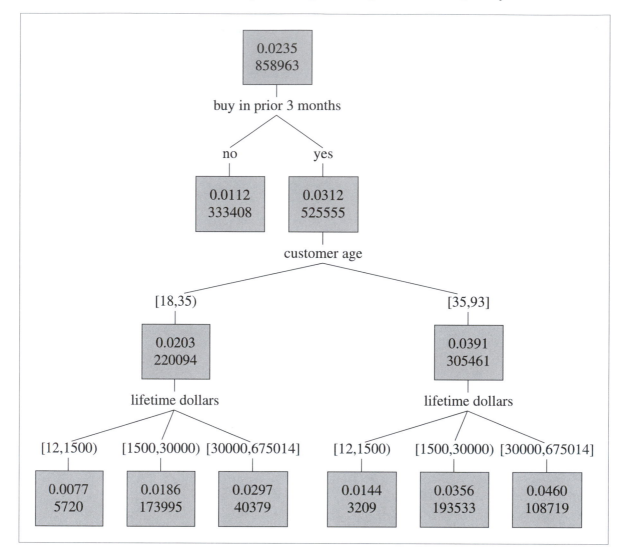

CHAID TREE GRAPHS

Displaying CHAID trees in a *single* graph facilitates the evaluation of a variable's effect. We plot the AEP of response by the minimum values[5] of the ranges for the end nodes (i.e., for the boxes in the last row of the trees). Each resultant line segment represents a market segment defined by the other variables in the model. The shape of the line indicates the effect of the variable on response for that segment. A comparison of the lines provides a total view of how the variable affects response.

For lifetime dollars, we plot the AEP of response by the minimum values of the ranges for the end nodes in Figures 29–2 and 29–3. There is only one line segment with a significant "bend," which corresponds to older customers (age 35 years and up) who have made purchases in the prior three months. This indicates

---

5. The minimum value is one of several values that can be used; alternatives are the mean or median of each predefined range.

that lifetime dollars has a nonlinear effect on response (for this customer segment). The other line segments are straight lines,[6] which indicate that lifetime dollars has a constant effect on response (for each of the remaining customer segments). See Figure 29–4.

For PRIOR_BY, we focus on the slopes of the lines.[7] The evaluation rule is the steeper the slope, the greater the constant effect on response. The line segment of older customers (age 35 years and up) with lifetime dollars equal to/greater than $30,000 has the steepest line among all segments. This segment experiences the greatest difference in response between customers who have and have not made prior purchases in the past three months. See Figure 29–5.

The other segments experience differences in response between customers who have and have not made prior purchases, but not as large as that by the former segment. This is indicated by the magnitude of the their slopes. See Figure 29–5. The CHAID trees for PRIOR_BY are shown in Figure 29–7.

For customer age, the two parallel lines, corresponding to customer segments defined by (1) PRIOR_BY = no/Lifetime = $1,500 and (2) PRIOR_BY = yes/Lifetime = $1,500, indicate these customers experience the same difference in response between those who are less than 18 years old and those who are older than 18 years. See Figure 29–6.

FIGURE   29–4

Effects of Lifetime Dollars on Response by CUST_AGE and PRIOR_BY

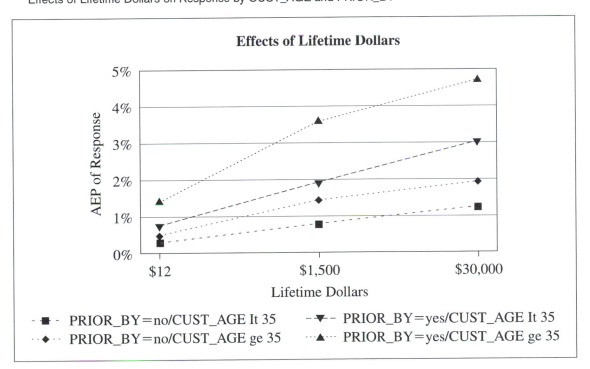

6. Segment PRIOR_BY = no/CUST_AGE 35 appears to have a very slight bend. However, we treat the line as straight because the bend is very slight.

7. The lines are necessarily straight because two points (PRIOR_BY points "no" and "yes") always determine a straight line.

F I G U R E   29–5

Effects of PRIOR_BY on Response by CUST_AGE and Lifetime Dollars

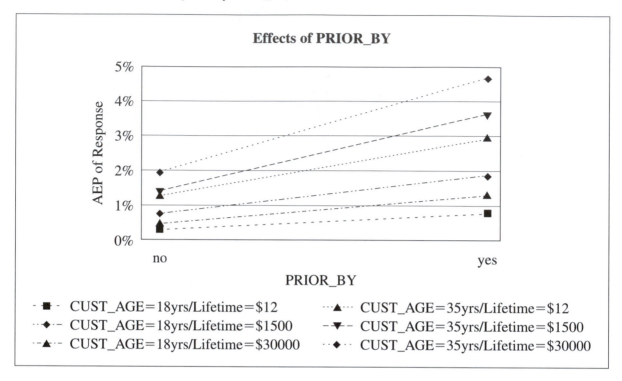

F I G U R E   29–6

Effects of Customer Age on Response by PRIOR_BY and Lifetime Dollars

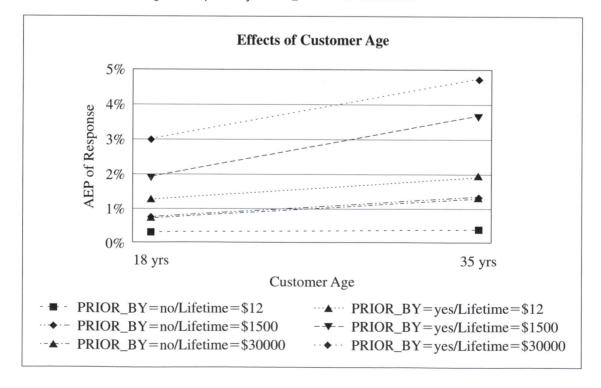

FIGURE   29-7

CHAID Trees: Effect of PRIOR_BY, accounting for CUST_AGE and Lifetime Dollars

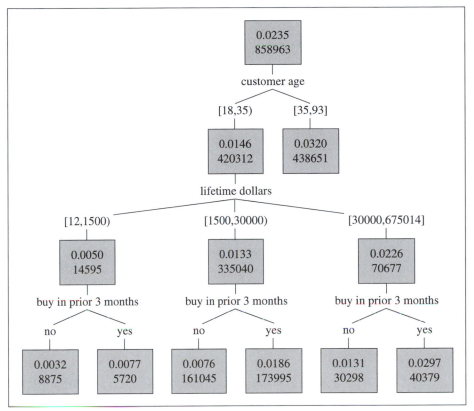

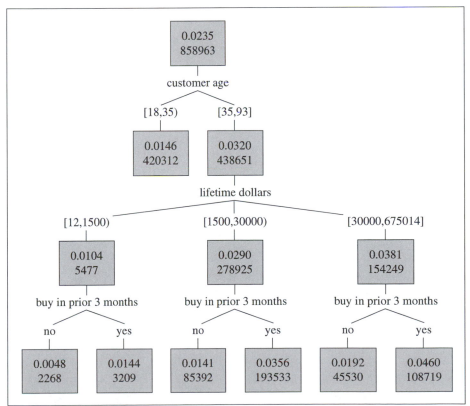

The three parallel lines, corresponding to customer segments defined by (1) PRIOR_BY = no/Lifetime = $3,000, (2) PRIOR_BY = no/Lifetime = $1,500, and (3) PRIOR_BY = yes/Lifetime = $12 (the latter two lines virtually overlap each other), indicate these customers experience the same difference in response between those who are less than 18 years old and those who are older than 18 years. In contrast with the former two parallel lines, these three lines have lesser slope. This indicates that customer age has a lesser effect on response for the corresponding three segments than for the former two segments. See Figure 29–6.

Lastly, the line segment defined by PRIOR_BY = no/Lifetime $12 is nearly flat. This indicates that customer age has no effect on response for this customer segment. See Figure 29–A-1. The CHAID trees for customer age are shown in Figure 29–A-2.

SUMMARY

We discussed the traditional odds ratio as a measure of assessing the effect of a variable in a logistic regression model. Noting that the odds ratio does not provide a complete assessment, we proposed CHAID as a graphical method to display a variable's effect on response accounting for the presence of the other variables in the model. The three-variable response model was used to illustrate the new CHAID application.

FIGURE 29–A–1

CHAID Trees: Effect of PRIOR_BY, accounting for CUST_AGE and Lifetime Dollars

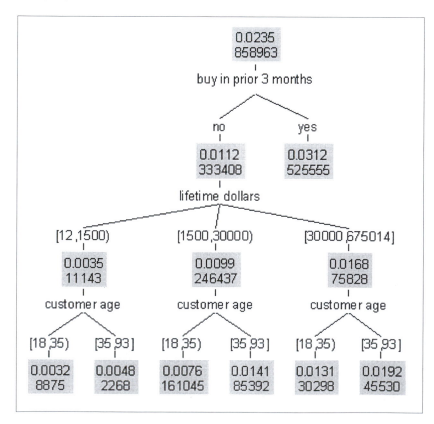

CHAID Trees: Effect of CUST_AGE, accounting for PRIOR_BY and
Lifetime Dollars

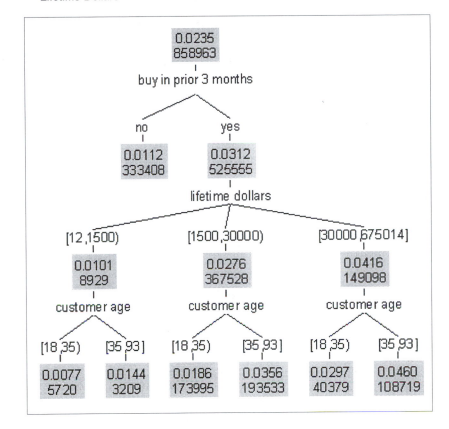

CHAPTER 30

Market Segment Classification Modeling with Logistic Regression

Logistic regression is a well-known technique for classifying individuals into two groups. Perhaps less known but equally important, polychotomous logistic regression is used to classify individuals into more than two groups. The purpose of this article is to present this multigroup classification technique as an extension of the two-group binary logistic regression, and to illustrate the building of a classification model based on a cellular phone market segmentation study.

BINARY LOGISTIC REGRESSION

Let Y be a class variable that assumes two outcomes or categories, coded as 0 and 1. We want to classify individuals into one of the two categories based on the values the individuals have for variables $X1, X2, \ldots, Xn$. The binary logistic regression (BLR) model allows such classifications to be made. BLR defines the logit, from which the probability of an individual belonging to class 1, Prob($Y = 1$), is obtained:

$$\text{Logic}(Y = 1) = b0 + b1*X1 + b2*X2 + \ldots + bn*Xn$$

$$\text{Prob}(Y = 1) = \frac{\exp(\text{logit})}{1 + \exp(\text{logit})}$$

The logit stands for the log of the odds of an individual belonging to class 1. The b's are the logistic regression coefficients, which are estimated by the method of maximum likelihood. Once the coefficients are determined, an individual's probability of belonging to Class 1 is calculated by plugging in the values of the predictor variables for that individual in equations.

Needless to say, the probability of an individual belonging to Class 0 is 1 − Prob($Y = 1$).[1]

In direct marketing, binary logistic regression models are built to classify customers as either most likely or least likely to respond to a solicitation. Response to a solicitation is the class variable, which is typically coded as 1 and 0 for responder and nonresponder, respectively. As such, the BLR model serves as a response model for creating a list of customers most likely to respond to future solicitations.

---

1. Because Prob($Y = 0$) + Prob($Y = 1$) = 1.

SOME NOTATION

Let's introduce some notation, which is needed for the next section. There are several formal expressions of the logit of Y that can be used, although they are superfluous when Y takes on only two values, 0 and 1.

1. $\text{Logit}(Y)$ $\quad\quad\quad\quad = b0 + b1 \ast X1 + b2 \ast X2 + \ldots + bn \ast Xn$
2. $\text{Logit}(Y = 1)$ $\quad\quad\quad = b0 + b1 \ast X1 + b2 \ast X2 + \ldots + bn \ast Xn$
3. $\text{Logit}(Y = 1 \text{ vs. } Y = 0) = b0 + b1 \ast X1 + b2 \ast X2 + \ldots + bn \ast Xn$
4. $\text{Logit}(Y = 0 \text{ vs. } Y = 1) = -[b0 + b1 \ast X1 + b2 \ast X2 + \ldots + bn \ast Xn]$

Expression 1 is the standard notation for the BLR mode; it is assumed that Y takes on two values, 1 and 0, and Class 1 is the outcome being modeled. Expression 2 indicates that Class 1 is being modeled, and assumes Class 0 is the other category. Expression 3 formally states that Y has two classes, and Class 1 is being modeled. Expression 4 indicates that Class 0 is the outcome being modeled, which is actually the negative of the first expression.

POLYCHOTOMOUS LOGISTIC REGRESSION

When the class variable takes on more than two outcomes or classes, the polychotomous logistic regression (PLR) model, an extension of the BLR model, can be used to predict class membership.

For ease of presentation, let's discuss the class variable Y with three categories, coded 0, 1, and 2. We can construct three binary logits.

1. $\text{logit\_10} = \text{Logit}(Y = 1 \text{ vs. } Y = 0)$
2. $\text{logit\_20} = \text{Logit}(Y = 2 \text{ vs. } Y = 0)$
3. $\text{logit\_21} = \text{Logit}(Y = 2 \text{ vs. } Y = 1)$

It can be shown that from any pair of logits the remaining logit can be obtained.[2] Accordingly, we use the first two logits because of the familiarity with the standard expression of the BLR.

Accordingly, the PLR model is defined as

$$\text{Prob}(Y = 0) = \frac{1}{1 + \exp(\text{logit\_10}) + \exp(\text{logit\_20})}$$

$$\text{Prob}(Y = 1) = \frac{\exp(\text{logit\_10})}{1 + \exp(\text{logit\_10}) + \exp(\text{logit\_20})}$$

$$\text{Prob}(Y = 2) = \frac{\exp(\text{logit\_20})}{1 + \exp(\text{logit\_10}) + \exp(\text{logit\_20})}$$

Recall, each logit is a weighted sum of the same independent variables $X1, \ldots, Xn$.

The PLR model is easily extended when there are more than three classes. When $Y = 0, 1, \ldots, k$ (i.e., $k + 1$ outcomes), the model is defined as

$$\text{Prob}(Y = 0) = \frac{1}{1 + \exp(\text{logit\_10}) + \exp(\text{logit\_20}) + \ldots + \exp(\text{logit\_}k0)}$$

---

2. From logit_20 we have $\ln[(\text{Prob } Y = 2)/(\text{Prob } Y = 0)] = \ln[(\text{Prob } Y = 2)] - [\ln(\text{Prob } Y = 0)]$. From logit_10 we have $\ln[(\text{Prob } Y = 1)/(\text{Prob } Y = 0)] = \ln[(\text{Prob } Y = 1)] - [\ln(\text{Prob } Y = 0)]$. Subtracting the latter from the former, we have on the right-hand side: $\ln[(\text{Prob } Y = 2)] - [\ln(\text{Prob } Y = 1)] = \ln(\text{Prob } Y = 2)/(\text{Prob } Y = 1)] = \text{logit\_21}$.

$$\text{Prob}(Y = 1) = \frac{\exp(\text{logit}\_10)}{1 + \exp(\text{logit}\_10) + \exp(\text{logit}\_20) + \ldots + \exp(\text{logit}\_k0)}$$

$$\vdots$$

$$\text{Prob}(Y = k) = \frac{\exp(\text{logit}\_k0)}{1 + \exp(\text{logit}\_10) + \exp(\text{logit}\_20) + \ldots + \exp(\text{logit}\_k0)}$$

where

$$\text{logit\_10} = \text{Logit}(Y = 1 \text{ vs. } Y = 0)$$
$$\text{logit\_20} = \text{Logit}(Y = 2 \text{ vs. } Y = 0)$$
$$\text{logit\_30} = \text{Logit}(Y = 3 \text{ vs. } Y = 0)$$
$$\ldots$$
$$\text{logit\_k0} = \text{Logit}(Y = k \text{ vs. } Y = 0)$$

Note: There are k logits for a PLR with $k + 1$ outcomes.

MODEL BUILDING WITH PLR

PLR is estimated by the same method used to estimate BLR, namely, maximum likelihood estimation. The theory for stepwise variable selection, model assessment, and validation has been worked out for PLR, but these features are not available in the major statistical software packages. Some theoretical problems still remain. For example, a variable can be declared significant for all but, say, one logit. Because there is no theory for estimating a PLR model with the constraint of setting a coefficient equal to zero for a given logit, the PLR model may have some noise.

Choosing the best set of predictor variables is the toughest part of modeling, and is perhaps more difficult with PLR because there are k logit equations to consider. However, we do not view the lack of a stepwise procedure for the PLR as a major drawback. Without arguing the pros and cons of the stepwise procedure, its use as the determinant of the final model is questionable.[3] The stepwise approach is best as a rough-cut method for boiling down many variables (about 50 or more) to a manageable set (about 10). Once there are several candidate predictor variables, we recommend performing a CHAID analysis and constructing tree graphs to identify the final set of important variables and interaction terms, and their structure (e.g., log or square root). In the next section, we illustrate the use of CHAID in building a market classification model with PLR.

MARKET SEGMENTATION CLASSIFICATION MODEL

Survey of Cellular Phone Users

A survey of 2,005 past and current users of cellular phones from a wireless carrier was conducted to gain an understanding of customer needs and the variables that affect churn[4] and long-term value. The survey data was used to segment this market of consumers into homogeneous groups, so group-specific marketing programs could then be developed to maximize the individual customer relationship.

---

3. Briefly, the stepwise procedure is misleading because all possible subsets are not considered; the final selection is too data-dependent and sensitive to influential observations. Also, it does not automatically check for model assumptions and does not automatically test for interaction terms. Moreover, the stepwise procedure does not guarantee to find the globally best subset of the variables.

4. Cancellation of cellular service.

Segment Name	Segment Size
Hassle-free	13.2% (265)
Service	24.7% (495)
Price	38.3% (768)
Features	23.8% (477)

A cluster analysis was performed, which produced four segments. See Table 30–1 for segment names and sizes. The *hassle-free* segment is concerned with the ability of the customer to design the contract and rate plan. The *service* segment is focused on the quality of the call (e.g., no dropped calls and clarity of calls). The *price* segment values discounts (e.g., 10 percent off the base monthly charges and 30 free minutes of use). Lastly, the *features* segment enjoys the latest technology (e.g., long-lasting batteries and free phone upgrades). A model is needed to divide the carrier's entire database into these four actionable segments, after which marketing programs can be used in addressing the specific needs of these predefined groups.

Data

The survey was appended with information from the carrier's billing records. For all respondents, which are now classified into one of four segments, we have 10 usage variables, such as number of mobile phones, minutes of use, peak and off-peak calls, airtime revenue, base charges, roaming charges, and free minutes of use (yes/no). We use CHAID to identify the important variables and their structure.

CHAID Analysis

Briefly, CHAID is a technique that recursively partitions a population into separate and distinct subpopulations or nodes such that the variation of the dependent variable is minimized within the nodes and maximized among the nodes. The dependent variable can be binary, polychotomous, or continuous (e.g., sale dollars or units sold). The nodes are defined by independent variables, which pass through an algorithm for partitioning. The independent variables can be categorical or continuous.

To perform a CHAID analysis we must define the dependent variable and select a set of independent variables. For this application of CHAID, the set of independent variables is the set of usage variables appended to the survey data. The class variable Y identifying the four segments from the cluster analysis is the dependent variable. Specifically, we define the dependent variable as follows:

$$Y = 1 \text{ if segment is hassle-free}$$
$$= 2 \text{ if segment is service}$$
$$= 3 \text{ if segment is price}$$
$$= 4 \text{ if segment is features}$$

The CHAID analysis identifies four significant[5] variables[6]:

1. *Number of mobile phones.* The number of mobile phones a customer has
2. *Monthly off-peak calls.* The number of off-peak calls averaged over a three-month period
3. *Free minutes, yes/no.* Free first 30 minutes of use per month
4. *Monthly airtime revenue.* Total revenue excluding monthly charges averaged over a three-month period

The CHAID trees for these variables are shown in Figures 30–1 to 30–4. The CHAID tree is read as follows. For the number of mobile phones in Figure 30–1:

1. The top box indicates that for the sample of 2,005 customers the sizes (and incidences) of the segments are 265 (13.2 percent), 495 (24.75 percent), 768 (38.3 percent), and 477 (23.9 percent), for hassle-free, service, price, and features segments, respectively.
2. The left node represents 834 customers of the total sample, who have one mobile phone. Within this subsegment the incidence rates of the four segments are 8.5 percent, 21.8 percent, 44.7 percent, and 24.9 percent, for hassle-free, service, price, and features segments, respectively.
3. The middle node represents 630 customers, who have two mobile phones, with incidence rates of 14.8 percent, 35.7 percent, 31.3 percent, and 18.3 percent, for hassle-free, service, price, and features segments, respectively.
4. The right node represents 541 customers, who have three mobile phones, with incidence rates of 18.5 percent, 16.3 percent, 36.4 percent, and 28.8 percent, for hassle-free, service, price, and features segments, respectively.

For monthly off-peak calls in Figure 30–2:

1. The top box is the sample breakdown of the four segments; it is identical to the top box showing the number of mobile phones.
2. There are three nodes: the left node is defined by the number of calls in the half-open interval (0,1), which means zero calls; the middle node is defined by the number of calls in the half-open interval (1,2), which means one call; and the right node is defined by the number of calls in the closed interval [2, 270], which means calls greater than or equal to 2 and less than or equal to 270.
3. The left node represents 841 customers, who have zero off-peak calls. Within this subsegment the incidence rates of the four segments are 18.1 percent, 26.4 percent, 32.6 percent, and 22.9 percent for hassle-free, service, price, and features, respectively.
4. The middle node represents 380 customers who have two off-peak calls, with incidence rates of 15.3 percent, 27.1 percent, 43.9 percent, and 13.7 percent for hassle-free, service, price, and features, respectively.
5. The right node represents 784 customers who have off-peak calls inclusively between 2 and 270, with incidence rates of 6.9 percent, 21.7 percent, 41.6 percent, and 29.8 percent for hassle-free, service, price, and features, respectively.

5. Based on the *p* values of the CHAID chi-squared statistic.
6. We did not consider interaction variables identified by CHAID because the sample was too small.

F I G U R E S   30–1 A N D 30–2

CHAID Trees: Number of Mobile Phones and Monthly
Off-Peak Calls

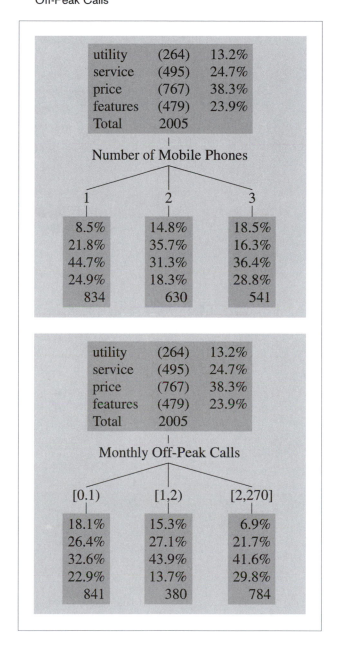

Similar readings can be made for the remaining two variables identified by CHAID.

Analytically, CHAID declaring a variable significant means the segment incidence rates (as a column array of rates) differ significantly across each of the nodes. For example, monthly off-peak calls has three column arrays of segment incidence rates, corresponding to the three nodes, {18.1 percent, 26.4 percent, 32.6 percent, 22.9 percent}, {15.3 percent, 27.1 percent, 43.9 percent, 13.7 percent}, and {6.9 percent, 21.7 percent, 41.6 percent, 29.8 percent}. These column arrays are significantly different from each other. This is a complex concept, which really has no interpretive value, at least in the context of identifying variables with classification power. However, the corresponding CHAID tree can

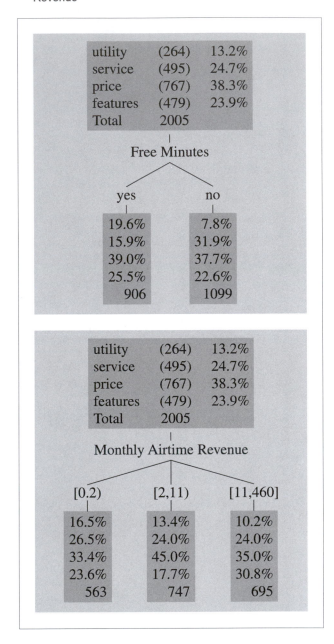

FIGURES 30-3 AND 30-4

CHAID Trees: Free Minutes and Monthly Airtime
Revenue

help us descriptively evaluate the potential predictive power of variables when it
is transformed into a tree graph.

CHAID Tree Graphs

Displaying a CHAID tree in a graph facilitates the evaluation of the potential predictive power of a variable. We plot the incidence rates by the minimum values[7]
of the ranges for the nodes, and connect the "smooth" points to form a trace line,
one for each segment. The shape of the line indicates the effect of the variable on

---

7. The minimum value is one of several values which can be used; alternatives are the mean or median of each
   predefined range.

identifying individuals in a segment. The baseline plot, which indicates a variable with no classification power, consists of all the segment trace lines being horizontal or "flat." The extent to which the segment trace lines are not flat indicates the potential predictive power of the variable for identifying an individual belonging to the segments. A comparison of all lines (one for each segment) provides a total view of how the variable affects classification across the segments.

The PLR is a linear model,[8] which requires a linear or straight-line relationship between predictor and segment. The tree graph suggests the appropriate re-expression when the empirical relationship is not linear.[9] The tree graph for number of mobile phones in Figure 30–5 indicates the following:

1. There is a positive[10] and nearly linear relationship between number of mobile phones and the identification of customers in the utility segment. This implies we only need the variable number of mobile phones in its raw form; no reexpression is needed.

2. The relationship for the features segment also has a positive relationship but with bend from below.[11] This implies we may need the variable number of mobile phones in both its raw form and its square.

3. Price has a negative effect with a bend from below. This implies we may need the variable number of mobile phones in both its raw form and its square root.

4. Service has a negative relationship with a bend from above. This implies we may need the variable number of mobile phones in both its raw form and its square.

F I G U R E   30–5

CHAID Tree Graph: Number of Mobile Phones

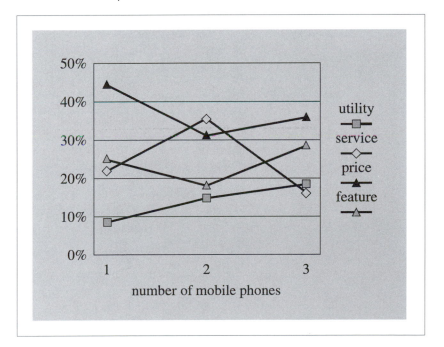

---

8. That is, each logit is a weighted sum of the predictors.

9. The suggestions are determined from the ladder of powers and the bulging rule, found in John Tukey, *EDA* (Addison-Wesley, 1997).

10. A relationship is assessed by determining the slope between the left and right node smooth points.

11. The position of a bend is determined by the middle node smooth point.

The tree graphs for the other variables are in Figures 30–6 to 30–8. Interpreting the graphs, we diagnostically determine the following:

1. **Monthly off-peak calls.** We may need this variable in its raw form, its square, and its square root.
2. **Monthly airtime.** We may need this variable in its raw form, its square, and its square root.
3. **Free minutes.** We may need this variable as is, in its raw form.

F I G U R E   30–6 A N D 30–7

CHAID Tree Graphs: Monthly Off-Peak Calls and Monthly Airtime

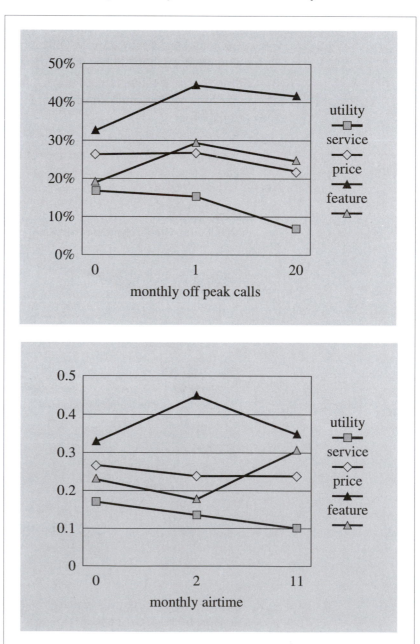

FIGURES 30-8

CHAID Tree Graphs: Free Minutes

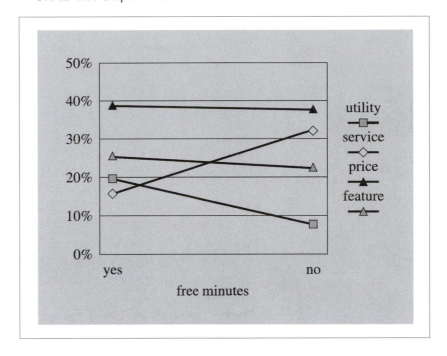

Market Segment Classification Model

The final polychotomous logistic regression model[12] for classifying customers into one of the four cellular phone behavioral market segments has the following variables:

1. Number of mobile phones (NMP)
2. Square of NMP
3. Square root of NMP
4. Monthly off-peak calls
5. Monthly airtime (MAT)
6. Square of MAT
7. Square root of MAT
8. Free minutes

Without arguing the pros and cons of validation procedures,[13] we draw a bootstrap sample of size 5,000 to assess the total classification accuracy of the model. The results of the model are shown in Table 30–2, and are explained here:

1. The row totals are the *actual* counts in the sample. The sample consists of 650 hassle-free customers, 1,224 service customers, 1,916 price customers, and 1,210 features customers. The percent figures are the percent compositions of the segments with respect to the total sample.

---

12. The criterion used was: a variable must be significant at the .05 level on all but one logit.
13. Here is a great opportunity to debate and test various ways of calibrating and validating a "difficult" model under the best of conditions.

T A B L E   30-2

		PREDICTED				
		Hassle-Free	Service	Price	Features	Total
Actual	Hassle-free	326	68	158	98	650
		50.0%				13.0%
	Service	79	460	410	275	1,224
			36.3%			24.5%
	Price	147	431	922	416	1,916
				49.0%		38.3%
	Features	103	309	380	418	1,210
					34.6%	24.2%
	Total	655	1,268	1,870	1,207	5,000
		13.1%	25.4%	37.4%	24.1%	100.0%

For example, 13.0 percent of the sample consists of actual hassle-free customers.

2. The column totals are *predicted* counts. The model predicts 655 hassle-free customers, 1,268 service customers, 1,870 price customers, and 1,207 features customers. The percent figures are the percent compositions with respect to the predicted counts. For example, the model predicts 13.1 percent of the sample as hassle-free customers.

3. Given that the sample consists of 13.0 percent hassle-free customers and the model predicts 13.1 percent hassle-free customers, the model has no *bias* with respect to classifying hassle-free. Similarly, the model shows no bias in classifying the other groups: for service the actual incidence is 24.5 percent versus the predicted 25.4 percent; for price the actual incidence is 38.3 percent versus the predicted 37.4 percent; and for features the actual incidence is 24.2 percent versus the predicted 24.1 percent.

4. Although the model shows no bias, the big question is, "How accurate are the predictions?" Among those predicted to be hassle-free, how many are actually hassle-free? Among those predicted to be service how many are actually service? Similarly, for price and features. The percents in the table cells provide the answer. For hassle-free the model correctly classifies 50.0 percent of the time (326/655). Without a model we would expect 13.0 percent correct classifications of hassle-free. Thus, the model has a lift of 385 (50.0 percent/13.0 percent); i.e., the model provides 3.85 times the number of correct classifications of hassle-free customers obtained by chance.[14]

5. The model has a lift of 148 (36.3 percent/24.5 percent) for service, a lift of 128 (49.0 percent/38.3 percent) for price, and a lift of 143 (34.6 percent/24.2 percent) for features.

6. As a summary measure of how well the model makes correct classifications, we look at the total correct classification rate (TCCR).

---

14. Or a monkey.

Simply, TCCR is total number of correct classifications across all groups divided by total sample size. Accordingly, we have 326 + 460 + 922 + 418 = 2,126 divided by 5,000, which yields TCCR = 42.52 percent.

7. To assess the improvement of total correct classification provided by the model we must compare it with chance. TCCR by chance is 28.22 percent.[15] Thus, the lift is 151. That is, the model provides 51 percent more total correct classifications across all groups than obtained by chance.

SUMMARY

We presented the polychotomous logistic regression, an extension of the well-known binary logistic regression, as a method for classifying individuals into more than two groups. We illustrated the building of a classification model using a cellular phone market segmentation study. CHAID was used for variable selection and structure.

---

15. TCCR(chance) = the sum of the sqaured actual group incidence.

CHAPTER 31

Modern Methods of Testing in Direct Marketing

INTRODUCTION

This chapter presents a brief introduction to the use of statistical experimental design in testing components of direct marketing programs like lists, offers, creative, copy, etc. These techniques are contrasted to some commonly accepted procedures to conduct direct marketing tests, and the comparative advantages of experimental designs are pointed out. Specifically, the use of blocking and factorial designs to make tests more sensitive and economical is presented by way of example.

COMMON DIRECT MARKETING TESTING RULES

Although there are a number of rules or procedures for conducting direct marketing tests, almost all share the desirable characteristic of being simple to set up and easy to administer. Simple tests can be set up and results evaluated by marketers without specialized training in testing methods, while ease of administration decreases the chances of making mistakes in conducting the tests (like sending the wrong package to a list) or measuring results (such as attributing responses to a wrong subkey).

However, as is demonstrated later, in many instances conceptual simplicity and ease of administration are false economies. Somewhat more complex ways of setting up tests using statistical experimental designs, which require some specialized training, can more than pay for themselves by reducing testing costs and providing additional insights, leading to improvement in direct marketing campaigns.

The two rules used most often in testing components of direct marketing programs are:

- Test one thing at a time.
- Test all things.

Each rule is described below in terms of its advantages and disadvantages, and then each is contrasted against rules for setting up tests using statistical experimental designs.

Test One Thing at a Time

A widely followed axiom in direct marketing is to "test one thing at a time" while keeping all other components constant. The resultant variation in the outcome being measured can then be attributed solely to the one component being tested.

However, direct marketers usually test several components in a mailing, using two or more alternative approaches for each. Since this rule requires a different group of customers to be exposed to each alternative, the total number of pieces of mail—or telephone calls—can quickly add to large numbers with a concomitant increase in cost. Therefore, fewer marketing components—and fewer alternative approaches to each—can be tested for a fixed testing budget.

This procedure also ignores the positive effect of selected combinations of factors, as is discussed later. For example, in a test of alternative copy strategies and various acquisition lists, a particular copy may work exceedingly well on certain lists while doing poorly overall (as on a random sample selected from all the lists being tested).

Finally, as direct marketers usually practice it, testing one thing at a time sometimes leads to misleading results. When more than two approaches to a direct marketing component are tested, and the results ranked in decreasing order of performance, the probability of making an error in the rank order is higher than that associated with the significance level being used.

A ranking of alternative approaches implies conducting multiple tests between each pair of approaches, so that while the significance level of any one test may be at the stated level, the actual significance level of *all* pairwise tests taken together decreases geometrically as a function of the number of pairs. In comparing the performance of a dozen lists at the 95 percent significance level, for example, this method results in an actual confidence level of 54 percent. That is, there is a 46 percent probability of finding a significant difference in one or more pairs of lists when there is none in reality—a level most direct marketers would not accept. Tests which use the true experiment-wise significance level are available for such situations, but they are rarely used in database marketing: Duncan's multiple range test is the one used most, while Dunnett's multiple range test should be used when comparing all factor levels with a control.

Test All Things

Another commonly accepted rule for direct marketing tests is to "test all things the way they should be at rollout" by selecting appropriate combinations of the components of packages, and then rolling out the combination which produces the best results. The advantage of this approach is that many fewer pieces of mail are required to read results with acceptable accuracy since only a few combinations are usually selected.

However, most direct mail pieces have many components, each of which can be chosen from a wide array of possibilities. In order to conduct tests in this manner, the best combinations of components have to be decided in advance based on previous results or by judgment. Since dozens, sometimes hundreds, of combinations may be possible, selecting the few that are likely to perform better than others is a difficult task even for experienced marketers. There is frequently the nagging thought—impossible to disprove—that a better combination may have been possible, but was not selected for testing.

Moreover, the reason for the top performance of a package is not evident from the results of this rule of testing. If different types of copy, promotion incentives, or envelopes were used in each package, it is not possible to say, with any confidence which component, i.e., copy, incentive, or envelope, was responsible for the superior performance of the winning package.

Nor is it feasible to identify the relative importance of each component to the success of the package as a whole. Measurement of the relative importance is valuable to direct marketers because the cost of package components varies widely, and small improvements in results can justify the use of the components with little or no incremental cost—like copy or color of envelope—whereas larger gains are needed to build a business case for using more costly alternatives like premiums.

The shortcomings of both these direct marketing testing rules can be overcome by using statistical experimental designs. Hundreds of designs, ranging from simple ones for testing a single component to quite complex ones for many components, are available to direct marketers for achieving various testing objectives. The following sections describe two simple designs and some important principles, and illustrate them with examples.

STATISTICAL EXPERIMENTAL DESIGN

Designed Experiments

Direct marketing lends itself much more readily to designed experiments— where subgroups within a population can be treated in different ways—as compared with mass marketing using other means of advertising. Since different offers can be made by mail or phone to people living next door without one affecting the other, the outcome of each offer is independent of the other. Therefore, there is a wide variety of testing situations in direct marketing where experimental design can be profitably applied.

Like any other scientific discipline, experimental design uses terminology unique to it. Therefore, a few concepts need to be defined at the outset. The components of a direct marketing campaign—list, copy, incentive, price—are called *factors*. Factors used in designed experiments may be qualitative (lists, copy, reply devices, etc.) or quantitative (e.g., product price, coupon value, etc.). Variations of a component are called *levels* of the factor: long copy, short copy, and humorous copy are three levels of the factor "type of copy."

The combination of levels of each factor in an experiment is called a *treatment*. For example, a long copy with a high price is a treatment produced by levels of the factors copy and price. A treatment formed by levels of three factors (shipping offer, type of envelope, and coupon value) might be a free shipping by Federal Express offer when combined with an outgoing express mail envelope and a $5 coupon for early reply. Direct marketing allows for relatively easy application of many different treatments to random segments of the population.

Experimental Designs

Statistical experimental designs are ways of assigning treatments to experimental units, which are usually groups of names—people or companies—selected in some way to be homogeneous in important characteristics. The objective is to assign treatments in such a way that the amount of reliable information obtained is maximized while minimizing the cost of obtaining it. Good statistical experimental design aims to keep sample sizes relatively small while increasing reliability.

As direct marketers are keenly aware, the reliability of conclusions from a test increases with larger sample sizes. However, so does the cost of conducting the test. But reliability only increases asymptotically with sample size while costs increase linearly with it. Therefore, after a certain sample size is reached, diminishing returns set in, and larger samples cannot be justified.

Fortunately, reliability also increases with decreases in the variability or heterogeneity — statisticians use the term *variance* — of the population being tested. So if ways could be found to reduce the variance in the population without a corresponding increase in the sample size, reliability could be increased at little or no additional cost. Good experimental design allows that to be done, though, it should be added, with the additional cost of a qualified statistician's time. In fact, most experimental designs are clever ways of applying treatments to subgroups of a population created such that the variance is less than that of the entire population. Sometimes they allow the extraction of more reliable information while using a smaller number of mail pieces than traditional direct marketing testing procedures.

Analyses of Experimental Designs

The results of tests based on statistical experimental designs are analyzed using analysis of variance (ANOVA) or analysis of covariance (ANCOVA) techniques. The tests are set up to test the null hypothesis that all treatment means are equal, and that none of the treatments makes a difference to the outcome like response rate, average order, etc. If the hypothesis is rejected, then it is concluded that at least one treatment mean is not equal to the others — i.e., the outcome of one or more treatments varies significantly from the others.

In addition, the relative contribution of factors to differences in the outcome is calculated using deviations from a common mean as a measure. ANOVA is based on the sum of squared deviations of the outcome variable for each experimental unit from the grand mean — called the *total sum of squares*. This is composed of two parts. The sum of squares between treatments is a measure of variation in the outcome attributable to different treatments, usually abbreviated SSB. The sum of squares within treatments (SSW) measures variation in the outcome of units treated identically, and hence is a measure of the "natural" variation inherent in the response of consumers. It is also referred to as the *experimental error*.

Tests of the difference in means are based on the ratio SSB/SSW. Larger values of this ratio are desirable since they imply higher sensitivity of the statistical test, or being able to read the results with more confidence. Therefore, the larger is SSB, the variation attributable to marketing components or treatments, the higher is this ratio. But for a given set of treatments this effect is fixed and not amenable to manipulation.

On the other hand, SSW can be manipulated to become smaller with the use of clever experimental designs, thus producing a larger SSB/SSW ratio and more sensitive tests. Indeed, the aim of most experimental designs is to reduce SSW. Appreciable reduction in SSW leads to being able to use smaller sample sizes and results in tighter confidence intervals or more reliability.

Blocking

The experimental error, or SSW, can be reduced by identifying subgroups within the population which are homogeneous and so have smaller variances. The act of identifying homogeneous subpopulations before assigning them to treatments is called *blocking*. Most experimental designs are clever uses of blocking.

Essentially, a variable used to block an experiment is one whose variation is not of interest in the experiment, possibly because there is no control over it. Therefore, variables with high variance are better candidates for blocking. By identifying the variance due to a blocking variable and taking it out of experimental error, SSW can be reduced.

Many such situations arise in direct marketing. For example, a not-for-profit mailer may raise funds by setting up different membership categories with varied fees—a one-year membership may cost \$25 while the charge for a five-year membership may be \$100. In trying to predict the average contribution to a related fund-raising solicitation, it is usually not of interest that the five-year people give more than the one-year members—attractive names from both categories will be solicited anyway. Rather, the effect of different types of copy of various "thank you" gifts may be the outcome of interest. Blocking by membership level can identify the variation due to it, and then it can be removed from the experimental error, allowing a clearer estimation of the copy or gift effects.

Other variables that are often desirable to use as blocks are individual lists or list groups, telemarketing firms, day of week that calls are made, month of year, or seasonality. When conducting experiments on house files, it may be especially useful to block by recency, frequency, or monetary value since the outcome being measured can vary significantly along with their values.

Example 1

The use of blocking in testing the components of a direct marketing campaign can be illustrated by the following example. A test was conducted to test the effect of shipping offers on response rates. Three types of shipping offers were tested: free two-day FedEx for orders \$50 or more; free UPS ground for orders \$50 or more; and no special offer was used as the control.

Five lists were chosen at random from among the many which were regularly used to prospect for customers, and all three offers were tested on each list. Therefore, there were 15 treatments (3×5).

Three samples of 5,000 names each were chosen at random from each list, or 75,000 names in all. Each set of three samples was sent one of the packages with different shipping offers. The results are shown in Figure 31–1.

The overall response rate was 1 percent, while the response rate to the offers were FedEx 1.12 percent, UPS .96 percent, and control .93 percent. The F-test for significance of the shipping offer effect had a p value of .059, which is not significant at a 95 percent significance level. Therefore, it can be concluded that the shipping offer did not produce a large enough difference in response rates to be rolled out.

However, the response rates by list showed larger variations, as shown in Figure 31–2, which affected the significance test since this variation was included in experimental error. Since the variation by list is of little consequence to the decision regarding the shipping offer—these are only five lists out of many, and they represent the variation to be expected when using the rest of them—list can be treated as a blocking variable and its variation taken out of the experimental error.

With list being used as a block, the F-test for significance of the shipping offer yielded a p value of .0003, which is significant at the 95 percent level (or indeed at the 99 percent level as well), while the p value for the model was less

FIGURE 31-1

Variation by Offer

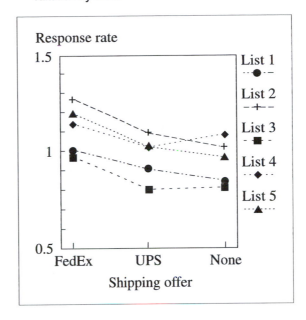

FIGURE 31-2

Variation by List

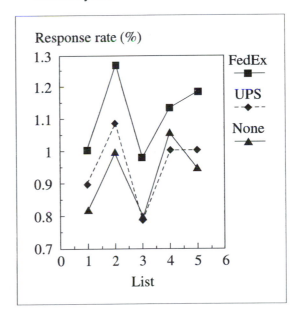

than .0001. Therefore, it can be concluded that the shipping offer *did* produce a significant difference, and if the increase in response rate due to the FedEx offer is enough to justify its incremental cost, it should be rolled out.

EFFICIENCY OF EXPERIMENTAL DESIGNS

It is useful to measure the efficiency of experimental designs in order to evaluate whether the results justify their complexity of administration and analysis. Usually the efficiency of a particular experimental design is evaluated by comparison with a completely randomized design (CRD), since the latter is the simplest kind and usually requires the largest number of experimental units (or pieces mailed or telephone calls made). Fortuitously, a CRD is also the design underlying the test-one-thing-at-a-time rule commonly used by direct marketers, when:

- Random samples (or Nth selects) of names are chosen to get homogeneous groups.
- The "thing" being tested is randomly assigned to groups, one to each sample.
- The outcome is measured by subkeying each group separately.
- Each outcome is compared with the others or with a control.

Of course, in statistical experimental design terminology this completely randomized design is a single-factor experiment where the "thing" being tested is a factor and each type of "thing" is a factor level. So the usual measure of efficiency of a statistical experimental design also serves as a measure of improvement over the traditional method of conducting direct marketing tests. The relative efficiency of an experimental design is the ratio of the error variance that would result by using a completely randomized design to the error mean square obtained from the ANOVA of that experimental design.

The design in Example 1, with lists used as a block, is called a randomized block design because the five lists were chosen at random from all lists in order to infer about the universe of lists. In this example its efficiency as compared with the completely randomized design is almost 6.6. That is, in order to get the same power the CRD would have to use 6.6 replications, or 99 (15×6.6) experimental units. Since each experimental unit contained 5,000 pieces of mail, 495,000 pieces would be required in a CRD or the usual direct marketing test-one-thing-at-a-time design compared with the 75,000 actually used in the randomized block design.

Obviously, it is not possible to find a blocking variable which is so effective in all cases, but in many instances direct marketing tests can be undertaken with considerably fewer pieces when an experimental design with blocking is used. This is especially true when two or three variables are not of interest to the test but are associated with large variations in the outcome variable.

MULTIFACTOR EXPERIMENTS

Standard experimental designs are also available to test two or more components of a campaign—they are called *multifactor experiments*—and provide more efficient ways of testing than the usual direct marketing rules. For example, it may be of interest to test a high-value coupon against a low-value one, bargain positioning against quality, and a cheap envelope against an expensive version. Each of the three factors could be tested on different groups of people by changing only the one factor and keeping all others constant. However, much more information can usually be obtained by testing combinations of factor levels on the same names—a common practice in survey research conducted by mass marketers or in manufacturing quality control.

Factorial Experiments

A simple type of multifactor experiment is a factorial experiment in which responses are observed for every combination of factor levels. Its main advantage is that it allows the estimation of main and interaction effects. Main effects are differences in mean response across levels of each factor, e.g., coupon, copy, and envelope. Interaction effects are inconsistencies of main effect responses for one factor across levels of another factor. An interaction may arise when, for example, a cheap envelope lifts response with a bargain copy but not with a quality copy.

The estimation of interaction effects can be important because they modify inferences on main effects and sometimes even nullify them. They can be very useful in direct marketing because positive interaction effects can be used to increase response without incremental expenditure, while negative interactions point to combinations of factors to avoid.

Moreover, interaction effects cannot be estimated in single-factor experiments like the completely randomized designs following the test-one-thing-at-a-time rule. Nor, for that matter, can they be isolated by using the test-all-things rule.

Interaction effects are estimated and tested in factorial experiments by replicating treatments. Replication in experimental designs is the process of applying the same treatment to two or more similar experimental units—that is, sending the identical piece of mail to groups which are selected independently of each other and subkeyed separately.

Replication allows the calculation of sampling error or the variation in response among different samples of observations which are treated the same. It is an indication of the natural variability of the outcome variable relative to the treatment, and is used to gauge the magnitude and significance of the treatment effect.

In many cases replication can also enhance the power of a test without calling for a higher number of pieces to be mailed: instead of assigning the same subkey to, say, 10,000 pieces, more information can be obtained by keying the same names in two subkeys of 5,000 each. The beneficial effects of dividing the same number of pieces into replicates diminishes as the number of groups increases, with the most benefit resulting from subkeying the same number of pieces into two subkeys rather than one. As might be expected, obtaining a better estimate of the natural variation in the outcome variable by replication is most important when sampling error is large.

Example 2

As an example of the importance of interaction effects, consider the case of a cataloger seeking to increase average order by offering a $5 coupon with each order over $25. Two new copy strategies for the mail piece are also to be tested against the existing control: one exemplifies a quality positioning, while the other positions the catalog as a bargain.

The coupon factor is set at two levels—$5 coupon and no coupon—and the copy factor is at three levels: control, quality, and bargain. A two-factor factorial design is chosen so that there are 6 (3 × 2) cells, with each combination of coupon and copy being sent to the same number of people. Each cell is mailed 5,000 catalogs, but they are randomly keyed into groups of 1,000 each—that is, each treatment is replicated five times.

Table 31–1 shows the resulting average order amounts for each subkey.

A traditional analysis looking at the effect of coupon alone would conclude that since the average order with a coupon was $24.49 compared with $22.25 without, the increase of $2.24 being statistically significant, offering a $5 coupon was desirable.

The average order from all groups exposed to the quality positioning was $1.22 more than those receiving the control, while the bargain positioning lifted it

T A B L E   31–1

	Coupon	Replication	Copy Positioning			Mean
			Control	Quality	Bargain	
1	No	1	23.60	23.50	21.40	
2	No	2	21.70	22.80	20.70	
3	No	3	20.30	24.60	20.50	22.25
4	No	4	21.00	24.60	23.20	
5	No	5	22.00	22.50	21.30	
6	Yes	1	22.60	23.70	26.00	
7	Yes	2	24.50	24.60	25.00	
8	Yes	3	23.10	25.00	26.90	24.49
9	Yes	4	25.30	24.00	26.00	
10	Yes	5	22.10	23.10	25.40	
Mean			22.62	23.84	23.64	

F I G U R E   31–3

Catalog Average Order

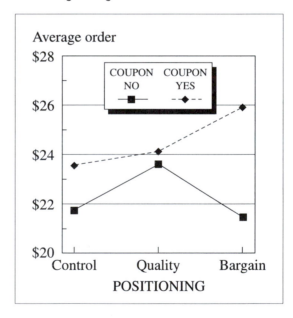

by $1.12 over the control. Therefore, since the type of copy does not result in appreciably higher costs, it seems that the quality positioning should be used.

So, a test-one-thing-at-a-time approach would conclude that the best results would be had by offering a $5 coupon with quality positioning. But as Figure 31–3 shows, the coupon main effect is inconsistent at different levels of positioning, showing a strong interaction effect between copy positioning and coupon.

Offering the coupon in conjunction with quality positioning hardly increased average order, though in the presence of bargain positioning it showed the largest increase. In fact, the highest average order comes from groups given the coupon in conjunction with a bargain positioning—higher than those given a coupon along with a quality positioning.

TABLE 31-2

	ANOVA Sum of Squares	% Sum of Squares	P value
Model			.0001
Coupon	37.6	57	.0001
Positioning	8.6	13	.0329
Coupon*positioning	20.3	31	.0010

An analysis of variance on these data, in Table 31–2, clearly shows that the coupon should be offered along with the bargain copy:

- Coupon main effect is most important.
- Interaction of coupon and positioning is next in importance.
- Main effect due to positioning is the least important, but is significant at 95 percent.

Had the effects of coupon and copy positioning been tested on separate groups of names—as is traditional in direct marketing—their interaction would not have been identified and quality positioning would have been used with a $5 coupon.

STATISTICAL EXPERIMENTAL DESIGN RULES

Rules applicable to direct marketing tests can be summarized by the following generalizations:

- *Test a few important factors at a time*. Rather than testing each component of a direct marketing program on separate groups of individuals, the use of statistical experimental designs can yield more insight, often with fewer pieces mailed, when a few important components (factors) are tested on the same group of people. The relative importance of each factor can be calculated in terms of the amount of variance in the outcome variable (response rate for example) each explains.

- *Set each factor at a handful of different levels*. Each marketing component (e.g., length of copy, peel-off sticker, or levels of money-back coupons) should be set at two or more levels, but not more than a handful, that are far enough apart to make a measurable difference in the outcome (coupon levels of $0, $1, $5, and $10, for example). Results for values between those tested can be interpolated for numeric variables like money, number of remails, etc.

- *Look for important interactions*. It is especially important to test interactions when offering a new product or new version of a catalog or making significant changes in the components of a direct marketing program for which there is little or no prior experience.

- *Replicate each treatment*. Replication is always desirable for the light it sheds on the natural variation in response among people treated the same, but it is necessary when interaction effects are to be estimated in a factorial experiment.

- *Use the same number of pieces for each treatment.* It is not necessary to do so, but doing so results in more power for the same number of pieces mailed.

- *Block for important sources of variation.* Most direct marketing tests can be conducted with fewer number of mail pieces or telephone calls if important extraneous sources of variation are used as blocks. Often two sources are sufficient to reduce sample sizes dramatically when used with Latin square or other multifactorial experimental designs. Previous mailing experience is a good guide to the factors which should be used for blocking.

Economics, Lifetime Value, and the Role of Modeling in the New Direct Marketing

Chapters 32 through 36 were written by David Shepard.

CHAPTER 32

An Introduction to the Economics of the New Direct Marketing

What if this chapter were titled "The Economics of Direct Marketing?" Would the contents be any different? The answer is yes. The difference between the economics of the *new direct marketing*, or, to use the more conventional term, *database marketing*, and the economics of *direct marketing* is fundamentally the same as the difference between database marketing and what is generally thought of as *classical direct marketing*.

So before jumping into equations, formulas, and P&Ls, let's spend a few minutes on the differences we see between classical direct marketing and modern database marketing, the new direct marketing. Let's also take this time to define the important differences between a *traditional* direct marketing company, which may employ both classical direct marketing methods and database marketing methods, and companies that are not traditional direct marketing companies (*nontraditional* direct marketers) but that use classical direct marketing methods, database marketing methods, or both, as just one part of their marketing mix. (See Figure 32–1.)

The differences are important and have much to do with the popularity of database marketing and the changes that are taking place within traditional direct marketing companies and within what is generally referred to as the direct marketing industry, as represented by the members of the Direct Marketing Association.

Traditional direct marketing companies or divisions of companies are operating units that depend entirely on acquiring and servicing customers through direct marketing methods. This definition would encompass all the business-to-business and consumer catalogers, fund-raisers, and continuity, club, and subscription businesses, as well as all financial service organizations that use only direct media to acquire and retain customers. If we include direct sales as part of direct media, this definition could also accommodate firms that may not consider themselves hard-core direct marketing companies, for example, all the direct door-to-door sales companies and cable TV firms.

Nontraditional direct marketers include all firms that use direct marketing methods, in combination with general advertising and nontraceable sales promotion techniques such as cents-off coupons, fulfillment offers, in-store price promotions, contests, refunds, sweepstakes, and the like to increase sales that are consummated either at retail or with the aid of a salesperson. This definition includes all retailers using classical direct marketing or database marketing methods to generate store traffic; all consumer products companies using targeted

FIGURE   32-1

A Framework for Understanding the Direct Marketing Industry

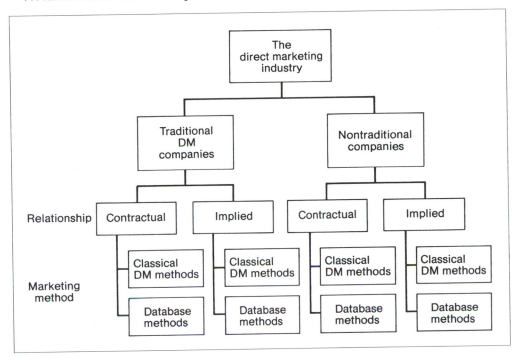

coupons or fulfillment offers to support retail sales; and all car manufacturers, telecommunications companies, computer manufacturers, and office equipment dealers. The list goes on and on, and includes any organization using direct marketing as just one of a number of advertising, promotion, and marketing options.

IMPLIED VERSUS CONTRACTUAL RELATIONSHIPS

Traditional direct marketing organizations may, in turn, be divided into two groups: those that have contractual obligations with their customers or members and those whose relationships are only, at best, implied. As you'll see, organizations with contractual relationships have been among the slowest to employ database marketing techniques—even though these firms are at the heart of the direct marketing business. In fact, as we'll see later in this chapter and throughout this book, it has been the nontraditional direct marketing companies that have made the greatest contribution to database marketing.

Contractual relationships exist in all subscription programs, clubs, and continuities. A contractual obligation, as executed by a signed coupon or telephone call, means that both the customer and the company understand what is expected of the other. Subscribers expect to receive a year's worth of magazines and then to be renewed (even though there's no contractual obligation to be renewed or to renew); club members expect to receive offers every three or four weeks; continuity members expect to receive a shipment every four, six, or eight weeks; and so on. Contractual relationships also exist within nontraditional direct marketing companies. For example, customers who sign on with a frequent flyer (or any other frequent purchaser or user) program understand what is expected of them and what is expected from the organization sponsoring the program.

On the other hand, an implied relationship is one in which there is no obligation on either party's part to do anything in the future. For example, in a catalog situation, after the initial response on the part of a consumer to a cold solicitation, there is no obligation on the consumer's part to purchase again or even on the cataloger's part to mail another catalog. However, most consumers will not be surprised when they receive another catalog in the mail. Some implied relationships are less obvious. For example, the flood of financial service offers that follow the establishment of a banking relationship, though not a complete shock to the knowledgeable consumer, might come as a surprise to the average person.

The extent to which relationships are contractual or implied is directly related to the decision-making discretion available to the direct marketer. In contractual obligations, there is less discretion, thus less obvious need for sophisticated decision-making tools. Conversely, when there is no contractual obligation, much more care needs to go into the decision of to whom to mail, what to mail, and how often to mail. Thus, don't be surprised to discover, later in this chapter, that database-driven decision making, or database marketing, is more likely in the absence of a contractual relationship or even a strong implied relationship.

CLASSICAL DIRECT MARKETING VERSUS DATABASE MARKETING

Having defined traditional and nontraditional direct marketing companies, we can begin to discuss in more detail how each of these types employs both classical direct marketing and database marketing methods. The principal difference between the two methods is that for all intents and purposes, classical direct marketing does not really deal with information about individuals; and database marketing, if it does nothing else, attempts to deal with information about individuals. Now that's a fairly broad generalization that requires some elaboration.

When we say that classical direct marketing does not really deal with individuals, what we mean is that the classical direct marketing methods used in traditional direct marketing companies focus attention on the behavior of groups of individuals. Traditional direct marketing companies include:

- Mail-order companies selling individual products or services
- Negative option book or record clubs
- Continuity programs
- Catalog companies
- Financial services, sold primarily through direct response media
- Magazines, newsletters, and other subscription services
- Fund-raisers

Anyone who has ever worked in a traditional direct marketing company knows that nearly all the analysis work is directed at groups of customers: all of the customers recruited from a particular list or a segment of a list, from a particular print ad, or from a particular TV spot. Even in firms using techniques generally associated with database marketing, such as *Prizm* clusters, the emphasis is on how well all the customers or the average customer from a particular cluster performs.

The way this is done, for those readers not familiar with the mechanics of the direct marketing business, is that each promotion vehicle, be it a rented list or ad in a magazine, is assigned a source code or key code (terminology changes from company to company) and all new customers acquired from that list or print ad are forever associated with that original source code.

The analysis task is then reduced to evaluating the cost of the promotion compared with the profit generated from the new customers acquired from the promotion. If the profit is sufficiently greater than the costs, then, all other things being equal, the direct marketer will probably decide to use that promotion vehicle, that is, that list or magazine, again in the future. We'll spend a lot of time on the mechanics of this decision-making process, but the basic point we want to stress is this focus on average or group behavior and how this information is used for decision-making purposes.

Later on we'll see that even within traditional direct marketing companies, more and more analysis work is being done at the individual level, thus affecting the way marketing decisions are made. In other words, classical direct marketers, too, are becoming database marketers.

So, classical direct marketing deals with groups or averages, and database marketing, in ways yet to be discussed, deals with individuals. That's only the beginning. Classical direct marketing tends to search for the perfect average solution to a variety of direct marketing business problems; database marketing searches for the perfect individual solution to the same set of problems. Both methods do a lot of compromising.

THE SEARCH FOR THE PERFECT CONTROL

A good example of the difference between classical direct marketing and database marketing is the way in which each method searches for the perfect new-customer acquisition strategy. Emotionally, the classical direct marketer would like to find one direct mail package that could be mailed to all prospects on all rented lists, regardless of the mix of lists that make up the total mailing and the composition of individuals within each list. The reasons for this are obvious and are perfectly valid. It's cheaper to create, produce, and mail one package to everybody than it is to create, develop, and mail multiple packages to different groups of individuals.

The database marketer, on the other hand, while understanding the economic impossibility of mailing a different package to each individual, intuitively prefers to move in this direction. Emotionally, the database marketer understands that there must be more than one market segment in a mailing going to a few million individuals. So, the database marketer reasons, doesn't it make economic sense to attempt to segment individuals on a mailing list or on a combination of mailing lists into at least a handful of different market segments and to create unique mailing packages that address the individual needs of the individual segments? Maybe, maybe not. Later, we'll see that the answer depends on the ability to implement a cost-effective segmentation strategy.

ONCE THE CUSTOMER IS ON THE FILE

New-customer acquisition is not the only area in which classical direct marketing differs from database marketing. In fact, new-customer acquisition is probably the one area in which classical direct marketers have moved closest to database marketing, without the aid of a marketing database. Once the direct marketing process moves beyond the new-customer acquisition phase, that is, after the new customer is acquired and is included on the customer file, there are even stronger reasons for treating all new customers in the same way.

Think about a book club or a continuity program or even a catalog operation for a moment. All these traditional direct marketing businesses are supported by computer systems (fulfillment systems, inventory systems, accounts receivable systems) that are infinitely easier to operate if all customers are treated in exactly the same way after they become part of the file. Remember, most computer support systems were originally designed to operate in only one way, and they have been fine-tuned over the years to handle larger and larger volumes with increasing efficiency.

Let's concentrate our attention again on the negative option book club, a business most readers will be familiar with as users or at least as readers of the *New York Times* Book Review section. It's obviously easier, and therefore, from a data processing perspective, more cost-efficient, to treat all new members the same way:

- Send the new member the four books the member chose within 48 hours.
- Place the new member on the member file and send every member the same advance announcement every four weeks.
- Give every member 10 days to return or not return the same negative option refusal form.
- Send every member who does not return the form within 10 days the same "Featured Selection."
- Provide every member with the same credit limits, and so on.

Compare this procedure with a process that attempts to place members into even as few as three or four segments based on this information about the individual members:

- The books they selected when they joined
- The books they purchased as members
- Their buying and paying patterns
- Individual-household-level demographics
- Lifestyle data obtained from internal research or overlays, and so on

Obviously, even if the data processing department could do it, implementation of a customized fulfillment system would cost considerably more, take more time, and so forth. Is it worth it? The answer depends on how much better individual members would respond to a more customized service.

The same argument, albeit to a lesser degree, applies to catalog marketers. You could argue that it's easier and therefore less expensive to send the same catalog to every catalog customer, with equal frequency, than it is to design special catalogs for individual market segments and to design customized mailing programs for customers based on individual performance data. And that's true—it is easier and less expensive. But catalog mailers, given their implied and therefore discretionary relationships with their customers, realized long before database marketing became fashionable that they could increase their profits by segmenting their file on three simple measures: recency of purchase, frequency of purchase, and some measure of the dollar volume of purchase. The shorthand for this methodology is *RFM*, which stands for recency, frequency, and monetary value. Based on relatively simple treatments of these three measures, catalogers determined whom to mail to and how often to mail. However, as we'll see shortly, one contribution of database marketing to this name selection process has been the introduction of more sophisticated analytical tools that introduce a broader set of predictive variables and make even better use of RFM data.

SOME ASSUMPTIONS ABOUT THE ECONOMICS
OF MULTIDIVISIONAL DATABASES

A common occurrence among multidivisional firms is the attempt to combine data from a variety of business units into a single marketing database. For example, companies such as Sears and J C Penney not only run retail stores and catalog businesses, but also have financial services operations as well. Many insurance companies sell multiple forms of insurance: life, health, disability, homeowners, automobile, and so on. Institutions such as the Smithsonian operate a number of different business units, from the magazine, to travel, to the museums. Companies such as Time-Warner and Reader's Digest operate magazines, clubs, and continuity programs. As often as not, each business unit has its own operations systems and its own customer file or database.

In these situations cross promotions across business lines are common, and each business unit is likely to have a model, or at least a strategy, for marketing to customers on each of the other business unit files.

The intuitive strategy is to develop a common marketing database by merging all the individual business files, combining information at the person or household level, or both. When we do this we are implicitly making two fundamental assumptions:

1. That there is considerable duplication among files—otherwise there is no reason for a common database.
2. That decision making will improve because we will be able to develop models based on a more complete understanding of our relationship with our customer.

The first assumption is easy enough to prove—use merge/purge technology to see what the true duplication rate is. If it's significant, continue with the project; if the duplication rate is very small, discontinue the project.

The second assumption is a bit more difficult to prove, but it can and should be tested before or during the early stages of a database development project by building models to actual mailings based on all the information that would be contained in the combined marketing database, and then comparing the results of these models against models built on just the information contained in the files of the individual business units.

For example, the term insurance department of a very large bank may have one model to be used against the bank's checking customers, another model to be used against customers that maintain savings accounts, a third model to be used against customers with auto loans, and additional models to be used against other business units within the bank. If these business units pooled their data into a common marketing database, would the term insurance division and the other divisions within the bank be able to build more effective models and mailing systems than those already in place? Would these systems be so much more efficient that they could cost-justify the investment in the common marketing database? These are the questions that need to be answered—it cannot just be assumed that a common database would be more effective and cost-efficient. These questions should be raised and answered during the early stages of a database development project.

Back to Basics: The Economics of Classical Direct Marketing

This chapter deals entirely with the economics of traditional direct marketing.[1] We will begin with a review of the major business issues associated with these business forms:

- Solo promotions
- Multistep promotions
- Catalogs
- Continuities
- Clubs
- Newsletters
- Magazines

This review initially focuses on the economic trade-offs that direct marketers deal with daily. After a general discussion of each business form, we will analyze each business in terms of the relationship between acquiring new customers, which direct marketers refer to as *front-end analysis*, and the profitability that results from transactions that occur after the customer is acquired, called *back-end analysis*.

Long before databases were fashionable, direct marketers understood that long-term growth and profitability depended primarily on the direct marketer's ability to manage the equation that balances expenditures on new-customer acquisition with the flow of sales and profits that come back over the economic life of the acquired customer. Of course, it's a lot simpler to measure the immediate costs of acquiring a new customer than it is to measure the value of an acquired customer, particularly when that value may take years to fully materialize. And as we'll see shortly, in an increasing number of direct marketing situations, the long-term value of an acquired customer is not simply a value waiting to be discovered; the long-term value of a customer is directly related to the way in which the customer is served by the direct marketing company. So we have a kind of chicken-and-egg problem that we'll try to solve after we've established some of the basic economic ground rules.

---

1. Portions of the following section first appeared in David Shepard, *Direct Marketing Handbook* (New York: McGraw-Hill, 1984).

The simplest form of direct marketing is the solo, or single-shot, promotion. Assume for the moment that the marketer has no other use for the name of the customer acquired. The only economic reason for the promotion is to make an immediate profit on this one mailing. In this situation, the marketer must design, produce, and mail promotion pieces to enough potential buyers to generate a response that will cover the cost of the promotion and yield an acceptable level of profit.

SOLO PROMOTIONS

Single-shot promotions are relatively simple, but the seller must still answer many questions in the course of the promotion process. Should the promotion piece be a classical, direct response package, including an outer envelope, letter, brochure, business reply card, and return envelope? Or should the seller use a less expensive mailing piece? If the classical full-mailing package is used, should the letter be two pages or four pages, and should the flier be black and white or in full color? Should the seller offer credit or require cash with the order? Should credit cards be used? Should the seller offer an inexpensive premium to hype sales or as a reward for cash with order? Should the mailing use third-class postage, or would the extra cost of first-class postage somehow result in extra sales and thereby pay for itself? Should an 800 telephone number be used? How strong should the guarantee be? Should the outer envelope contain copy and an illustration of the product, or just inviting copy, or no copy at all?

The list of legitimate questions that can be raised about even the simplest form of direct marketing is extensive, and answers to these questions affect the economics of the promotion. Many of these questions have to do with economic trade-offs. Does it pay to spend more on the promotion piece, to offer a premium, to offer credit, to mail first class, and so on? These questions with regard to a solo promotion apply to all types of direct response businesses and will be raised again and again throughout this chapter.

MULTISTEP PROMOTIONS LEADING TO A SALE

Frequently, it is possible to identify the potential market for a product in terms of the circulation of one or more magazines, while at the same time it is not profitable or legally possible to sell the product "off the page" in those magazines regardless of the unit of space employed. In some situations, the price of the product is exceptionally high, and closing the sale requires the power of a more expensive direct mail package with full-color illustrations and sufficient copy to define all the features and benefits of the product. Or in the case of financial services, it may be neither economically feasible nor legally possible to attempt to directly consummate a sale. In these instances, magazine space often is used to generate leads or inquiries, which are followed up by one or a series of direct mail pieces. In some cases, the initial leads are followed up by a combination of mail and phone. Products sold in this fashion include, in addition to financial services, encyclopedias, expensive exercise equipment, office equipment, and many business-to-business services. The "bingo cards" found in trade magazines and airline magazines are prime examples of this kind of direct response marketing.

The economics of multistep marketing differs from the economics of single-shot promotions in that the total costs of both the initial effort and all of the follow-up efforts must be tracked carefully and balanced against the sales and gross margin resulting from the total effort.

CATALOG SALES

A catalog may be thought of as a very expensive solo mailing, selling anywhere from a few dozen to hundreds or even thousands of products. It is also possible, as in the case of the solo mailing, to compare the total gross margin resulting from a catalog mailing with the total costs of the mailing, but the analogy between a catalog business and a business based on solo mailings cannot be taken much further.

The success of a catalog business is related directly to a catalog manager's ability to efficiently develop and manage a company's database of past buyers, or its *house list*, as it is still referred to by many in the industry. In very general terms, the response of an outside rented list to a catalog mailing may range anywhere from .5 percent to 2 or 3 percent, depending on the quality of the rented names and their predisposition to the products being offered in the catalog. By way of comparison, the response of past buyers to another catalog offering may range from 5 to 20 percent or even higher.

Naturally, a new catalog company cannot open its door with a list of past buyers. However, catalog operators have developed a number of techniques for developing house lists. One technique is to develop a relatively inexpensive "prospecting" catalog that can be mailed to names that have been rented from outside list owners. Respondents to these prospect mailings then are entered on the catalog company's prospect list. Of course, it is possible to mail a company's complete catalog to an outside rented list, and the limiting or deciding factor in this decision often is the catalog company's willingness and ability to sustain a large negative cash position while building its house file. Large companies wishing to enter the direct marketing business often are in a position to finance this development period, provided that they are convinced the eventual returns will justify the initial cash investment.

Smaller entrepreneurs generally attempt to exhaust all the other more conservative ways of building prospecting lists that can be converted eventually into buyers lists. Other techniques for building house lists include advertising the catalog free or for a token price in targeted-space media, using the same space to sell the most popular items in the catalog, and sending out solo mailings of individual popular products to names on rented lists. In general, regardless of the techniques used, it is common for a catalog operation to be in a net loss position with regard to new names added to the house list. As the mix between new names that result from cold prospect mailings, space advertising, and catalog buyer names changes in favor of the buyers, the profitability of the catalog operation increases.

However, even after the initial start-up period is behind the cataloger, this issue of allocating the amount spent on new-customer acquisition versus the amount spent on mailing catalogs to customers remains. In fact, this decision is one of the most crucial decisions a cataloger must make.

Ironically, advances in database marketing techniques have made this decision even more difficult. In pre-database days, most catalogers had a limited number of catalogs, which were mailed to all the customers on their buyers file. In many cases, the entire customer mailing strategy could be summed up in a sentence: "We mail four general catalogs a year to all customers on our file who have made a purchase within the last two years."

Now, given the ability to segment a file not only in terms of how frequently different customer segments should be mailed, but also in terms of which customers might respond better to specialized as opposed to general catalogs, the decision-making process has become infinitely more complex. Because of the importance of this subject, not only to catalogers but to all direct marketers that have implied as opposed to contractual relationships with their customers, let's spend some more time on the issue.

To the extent that a cataloger spends promotion dollars on acquiring new customers, the potential size of the business will grow. However, as we have seen, the response rate on new-customer acquisition mailings is significantly less than the response rate to mailings to the customer file. So in any one year, a dollar spent on new-customer acquisition, as opposed to customer mailings, will reduce both sales and profits. On the other hand, if year after year decreasing amounts are spent on new-customer acquisition, the potential of the business will diminish and eventually the actual size of the business will shrink as the customer file fatigues. Therefore, there has to be a strategy for managing both potential growth and annual profits.

In the simpler times referred to above, a cataloger could estimate the sales and profits expected from mailing a single catalog to the house file, say, three or four times a year. After allowing for overheads and desired profits, the cataloger could calculate the amount available for new-customer acquisition, and that would be that. The first complication was the discovery that not all customers need be or should be mailed the same number of catalogs each year. Relatively simple recency, frequency, monetary value (RFM) models were developed by catalogers that allowed them to segment a file into dozens of segments or cells based on recency of purchase, frequency of purchase, and the various measures of the dollar value of past purchases. The basic conclusion drawn from RFM cell segmentation was that individuals within the highest-performing cells should be mailed more frequently than individuals within the poorest-performing cells. So even if a cataloger still only produced four general catalogs a year, the best-performing customers might receive those four catalogs eight to twelve times a year (perhaps with a cover change), the poorest-performing customers might receive only one catalog a year, and some customers would in fact be dropped from the file of active buyers.

The introduction of more sophisticated forms of predictive modeling (regression, logistic, discriminant analyses) did nothing to change the basic finding that some customers should be mailed more frequently than others. However, the introduction of these techniques and the introduction of models that predict falloff from mailing to mailing have improved the efficiency of the modeling process.

What made a fundamental difference for some catalogers was the not-surprising discovery that not all buyers bought the same mix of products, and that segmentation techniques could be extended to include the kinds of products purchased as well as the quantity of products purchased. Now the decision-making process also had to be extended to include consideration of the creation and distribution of specialty catalogs. It is obviously a more difficult problem to decide who gets what mix of catalogs with what frequency than it is to simply decide how many general catalogs any one individual should receive.

Unfortunately, although predictive models are good at scoring customers in terms of their probability of responding to a promotion similar to one received in the past, the complications we just discussed do not lend themselves easily to statistical modeling solutions of the regression variety. To answer these kinds of economic trade-off questions we must rely on computer models that simulate an entire business structure and that are capable of answering "what-if" questions. The good news is that such models are relatively easy to build using spreadsheet programs such as Lotus 1-2-3 or Excel, or even more sophisticated simulation packages that provide a range of outcomes given different assumptions about the probability of key events taking place; the bad news is that the output of the models is only as good as the input assumptions. The model will tell you, for example, what the fiscal impact will be if you create a specialty catalog that will increase response for 30 percent of the file by 20 percent, but only old-fashioned direct marketing testing will tell you if the 20 percent number is correct.

Finally, no discussion of the catalog business would be complete without mention of the extraordinary problems of inventory control and fulfillment that are inherent in the catalog business. Success in mail order requires almost immediate fulfillment of orders as they are received, and the costs of carrying excess inventory can be as disastrous as the cost of being out of stock. Again, the ability of the catalog manager to perform advanced statistical analyses comes into play. Not only must catalog managers be able to forecast the expected level of overall response to a catalog mailing, but also they must be able to forecast the mix of products purchased so as to be in a position to manage inventories correctly.

CONTINUITY SALES

Continuity programs represent an important segment of the traditional direct marketing business. The continuity formula involves the periodic delivery of a product or service against periodic payments from the customer. The Time-Life Books series, the various Cooking Card programs, and the books and collectibles sold by the Franklin Mint are prime examples of products marketed this way. Because of the contractual nature of continuity programs, the management of a continuity operation is in many ways much less complicated than the management of a catalog operation. Given the product, such as a series of books, cards, or coins, the marketing problem is relatively straightforward. Options are severely limited relative to our catalog example.

New members or subscribers are acquired through the classical direct marketing channels: direct mail, magazine advertisements, newspaper preprints, broadcast (generally spot TV), and package inserts. In most cases, the first item in the continuity program is offered free or at a substantial discount. The subscriber then receives periodic shipments of the remaining items in the program until all the items have been shipped or until the subscriber notifies the seller to stop shipping the product.

From the subscriber's point of view, continuity programs are simple and easy to understand. From the seller's viewpoint, a number of key questions must be answered before the program can become operational. How should the items in the series be priced? Should the items be priced relatively high and therefore targeted against the upper end of the potential market, or should a lower-price/higher-volume strategy be attempted? How generous should the initial offer be? Should the first item in the series be given away free, or for $1, or at no discount at all? Should the interval between shipments be four weeks, six weeks, or eight weeks? How much open credit should be granted? Does it make sense to ship the third item in a series if payment has not been received for the first item? How does the credit decision depend on the interval between shipments? Should the program be open-ended with no limit on the number of items in the series, or should the series be limited to a fixed number of items, and if so, what is that number?

Clearly, the answers to these questions will have an important impact on the economics of the continuity program. Again, we are faced with a question of trade-offs. The more generous the offer and credit policy, the larger the program in terms of subscribers and sales volume. But what will be the effect on returns, bad debts, and profits?

Finally, let us briefly discuss the concept of a continuity load-up. The continuity programs we have described rely on periodic shipment of a product until cancellation or completion of the program. In continuity load-ups, the subscriber is informed that after he or she receives three or four single shipments, the balance of the items in the program will be shipped in a single load-up shipment. The load-up plan is an effective device for increasing the total number of items shipped to the average subscriber, but, again, there are economic trade-offs to consider. Federal trade regulations require that the load-up provision be defined clearly in all promotional messages, and this can reduce the total number of respondents to any given promotion. Second, most load-up programs follow a policy of reminding subscribers that the load-up shipment is about to be mailed unless the subscriber notifies the company not to proceed with the shipment and to cancel membership in the program. This reminder will cause some subscribers to cancel their membership faster than they might have done in an open-ended continuity program. Finally, there is the problem of credit collections. A load-up program is based on the assumption that after the subscriber receives the full load-up shipment, he or she will pay for the shipment on a monthly or bimonthly basis. Of course, some percentage of the load-up shipment will not be paid for and eventually will have to be written off as bad debts.

On balance, only testing the load-up concept against the open-ended, or "till forbid," continuity plan will determine which plan is best for any given product.

NEGATIVE OPTION CLUBS

We have discussed negative option clubs before, and they are indeed efficient vehicles for the distribution of books and records. The Book-of-the-Month Club, the Doubleday Book Clubs, and the Columbia House and BMG Music Clubs are all well-known examples of this type of direct marketing business. There are some similarities between continuity operations and negative option clubs. Most importantly, both employ contractual relationships with their members, thereby limiting service options. Both vehicles often are used as a means of distributing books, and both use the same media and direct marketing techniques for acquiring new members. But after the new member is acquired, the similarity from an operations or fulfillment point of view ends.

Negative option clubs constantly must ask their subscribers whether they wish to receive the coming selection, receive an alternative selection, or receive no product at all from the current catalog offering. If the member fails to respond, the shipment of the month is sent automatically. The fulfillment systems needed to handle a negative option club are much more complicated than those needed for a continuity program. In addition, the Federal Trade Commission has placed stringent restrictions on negative option clubs to ensure that members have sufficient time to return the negative option card should they not wish to receive the automatic shipment of the month.

Despite the differences in operating characteristics between negative option clubs and continuity programs, the economics of both types of businesses are remarkably similar. In both operations, new members are always acquired at a loss. The $1.00 or even the $4.95 that is often charged for the introductory shipment (the first book in a continuity series or the four books chosen from a book club's lead list) is never enough to cover the costs of promotion plus the cost of the introductory shipment. Therefore, continuity programs and negative option clubs are always in an investment position. The return on investment stems from future sales to the continuity subscriber or club member. In the case of continuity programs, future sales are simply a function of the price of the items in the program and the number of periods a subscriber chooses to stay in it. In a negative option club, the member need not buy from every catalog offering, and therefore sales are more dependent on the perceived quality of the merchandise offered and the effectiveness of the ongoing marketing effort. In both continuity and negative option, the final measure of profitability is the relationship between the cost of acquiring new members and the sales and payments those members yield over their economic life in the club or program. Later in this chapter we will develop the techniques used to measure and forecast these statistics.

As mentioned previously, up until quite recently, nearly all negative option clubs operated on the principle that all members would receive the same set of promotional materials. The notable exception was the music clubs, which have always asked their members to place themselves within listening preference segments. But within the book clubs, equality of treatment among all members was the general rule. Recently, the larger clubs have begun experimenting with customizing the negative option book selection to individuals based o the demonstrated reading preferences of the individuals. And clearly in a major book club that offers a wide range of both fiction and nonfiction, it makes sense to do so. This is particularly true in data processing environments in which this kind of decision making can be handled efficiently. Of course, there are production costs to pay for not treating all members the same, but these costs are offset by higher acceptance and lower returns of the negative option selection, increased purchase of alternative selections, and a longer member life as club members receive more and more selections that match their reading preferences.

NEWSLETTERS

Newsletters can be very profitable vehicles for distributing information to highly targeted markets. The most profitable newsletters often are aimed at small professional or business markets. Newsletters that are editorially able to provide critically needed information to a business audience that has both the need to know and the ability to pay (often referred to as "company money") have the greatest chance for success. This does not mean that more broadly based, lower-priced, mass-market newsletters can't be profitable, as witnessed by the continued success of the *Kiplinger Washington Newsletter* and the popularity of a number of consumer health newsletters such as the *Harvard Medical Letter* and the *Mayo Clinic Letter*, to name just two.

The economics of newsletters center on four key variables: pricing, new-order acquisition, conversion or pay rates, and renewal rates. Pricing is the most controllable of all the variables and perhaps the most important. Newsletters targeted at business markets can be priced anywhere from $9.95 to $495 or more. Generally, it is not difficult to determine whether the value of the information is worth closer to $10 than to $500, but it is often next to impossible to tell without testing whether a given newsletter should be priced at $37, $49, or even $97.

Clearly, pricing can make an enormous difference in profitability. Price testing is therefore almost always a necessity when one starts out in the newsletter business, particularly if the newsletter has little or no perceived competition.

Newsletters are almost always marketed solely by direct mail; therefore, it is critical that, before starting out in the newsletter business, the publisher be assured of continued access to the target market. If access to the market depends on the cooperation of a trade association, provisions should be made with the association to guarantee a continuous supply of names.

Properly priced newsletters can be successful with a relatively small response to initial new-subscriber promotions. Profits can be achieved with initial response rates as low as 5 to 10 orders per thousand names mailed because renewal rates are usually high.

However, before a newsletter can be considered a proven success, it must demonstrate the merits of its editorial material. The first test of the quality of the editorial material is the pay rate or conversion rate on new orders. Most newsletter promotions allow for payment (and cancellation) after one or more issues have been sampled by the reader. A high pay rate (over 70 percent) will be indicative of a high future renewal rate. Products that demonstrate a high cancellation rate should not count on a high renewal rate to ensure the profits of the newsletter venture.

MAGAZINES

Magazines are, of course, much like newsletters in that they depend on direct mail for much of their new-subscriber marketing and are highly sensitive to fluctuations in pay rates and renewal rates. The obvious differences between newsletters and magazines are that magazines are much more costly to produce and have two additional revenue streams: newsstand sales and advertising revenues. But even in the subscription circulation area, where one finds the greatest similarity to newsletters, there are important differences.

Magazine subscriptions are sold in many more ways than newsletter subscriptions. There are door-to-door sales, telephone sales, and sweepstakes-sold subscriptions from companies such as Publishers Clearing House. In addition, a magazine company's direct mail efforts may be dependent on preview or premium offers to an extent not often found in newsletter circulation. Each of these promotional channels and devices runs the risk of producing subscriptions with relatively low pay and renewal rates. Therefore, the evaluation and management of a magazine's circulation list is considerably more complicated and subject to greater risk than the evaluation and management of a newsletter.

PERFORMANCE MEASUREMENT

Front-End versus Back-End Performance

Front-end performance and *front-end analysis* are terms used by direct marketers to describe the process of measuring the initial costs of and response to a direct marketing promotion. The economic analysis of the process that takes place after an initial response is received is referred to as *back-end analysis* or *back-end performance*.

The first step in the process of measuring front-end performance is measuring the total expense attributable to a promotion. The only difficulty associated with this task is deciding which expenses will be included in the analysis and which expenses, if any, will be excluded.

Later we shall see how direct marketers generally approach this problem, but for now, let's assume we agree that it costs exactly $19,000 to mail 50,000 pieces of direct mail. The first statistic to be calculated is cost per thousand pieces mailed, more simply referred to as *cost per thousand (CPM)*:

$$\text{CPM} = \frac{\text{Total promotion expense} \times 1{,}000}{\text{Number of pieces mailed}}$$

In our example:

$$\text{CPM} = \frac{\$19{,}000 \times 1{,}000}{50{,}000}$$

$$\text{CPM} = \$380$$

The CPM concept applies to space advertising as well as to direct mail. In space advertising, CPM is calculated by dividing total media costs plus the costs of printing any special insert material by the circulation of the magazine:

$$\text{Space CPM} = \frac{\text{Media costs} + \text{insert costs} \times 1{,}000}{\text{Circulation}}$$

For example, consider a magazine with a circulation of 1 million and ad or media costs of $40,000 running an insert card that cost $20 per thousand to print:

$$\text{Space CPM} = \frac{\$40{,}000 + (20 \times 1{,}000) \times 1{,}000}{1{,}000{,}000}$$

$$\text{Space CPM} = \$60$$

In both direct mail and space advertising, the question always arises whether the fixed creative fees paid to an agency or a freelancer and the fixed mechanical preparation and art expenses should be included in the calculation of CPM. Opinion is divided on this subject. Some direct response marketers insist on including all costs in the calculation of CPM to ensure that profitability analyses consider all costs associated with the promotion. Other direct marketers argue that creative material and mechanicals are intended for use in multiple promotions. These marketers either allocate a portion of the fixed creative expenses to each use of the material or maintain separate budgets and controls for creative expenses. They do not include fixed nonrecurring costs in the analysis of promotion results. This latter approach, which is more oriented to decision making, is favored by most large mailers who are concerned more with the decision to remail a promotion or repeat a space insertion than with the recording of historical costs. For decision-making purposes, the direct marketer wants to know the incremental costs of repeating a promotion that has been used in the past, regardless of such costs.

Calculating CPM for Different Direct Response Media

Direct Mail
Direct marketers use three major types of direct mail promotion pieces, excluding catalogs, to generate new orders or new leads: the full-package solo mailing, the less expensive self-mailer, and the insert piece.

Full-Package Solo Mailings   Table 33–1 shows the components of a standard direct mail package, including a four-page letter and color brochure. The CPM of the full package is shown at three mailing quantities: 50,000, 100,000, and 300,000. Printing costs per thousand are shown to vary with the quantity printed, as the fixed printing preparation expenses (which must be incurred at each print run) are amortized over the number of pieces to be mailed. These fixed printing preparation expenses should not be confused with creative fees, art and production expenses, and other fixed fees such as agency or consultant's fees, which are truly one-time costs and do not vary with the quantity mailed or the size of the printing.

The example shown in Table 33–1 is typical of a consumer mailing of the kind used by book and record clubs, continuity programs, and magazines. These situations generally require a color brochure to display the product fully and almost always employ third-class postage.

On the other end of the direct response spectrum, marketers for a high-priced newsletter aimed at top corporate management may decide against a full-color brochure but may mail first class to create a more businesslike impression, and, it is hoped, avoid the secretary's wastebasket. In this case, the cost of the promotion will be reduced because the flier has been removed, but will be increased because first-class postage was used.

Therefore, there is no hard and fast rule to determine the correct cost of direct mail promotion. Costs are a function of the components of the mailing

T A B L E   33–1

Calculating CPM for a Typical Direct Mail Promotion at Three Mailing Quantities

Quantity	50,000		100,000		300,000	
Printing costs						
Package element	CPM	%	CPM	%	CPM	%
Outer envelope	$18	4	$16	4	$15	3
Four-page letter	33	7	23	5	22	5
Four-color brochure	28	6	25	6	21	5
Reply card	23	5	19	4	18	4
Return envelope	17	4	15	3	14	3
Total printing costs	119	26	98	22	90	21
Mailing costs						
Mailing lists	95	21	95	22	95	22
Letter shop	25	5	25	6	25	6
Computer processing	25	5	25	6	25	6
Postage	198	43	198	45	198	46
Total mailing costs	343	74	343	78	343	79
Total CPM	462	100	441	100	433	100
Dollar costs						
Total variable costs	23,100		44,100		129,900	
Creative	5,000		5,000		5,000	
Art and production	7,000		7,000		7,000	
Contingency	5,000		5,000		5,000	
Total costs	40,100		61,100		146,900	
Total CPM	802		611		490	

package. Direct mail package costs can vary from $300 to $1,000 per thousand. The real question is what mailing package will be most profitable for the product or service being offered.

Self-Mailers   One sure way to reduce mailing costs is to use a self-mailer, which is a promotion piece that does not contain multiple loose components. The self-mailer is a perforated form, one portion of which is a business reply card, and the respondent is instructed to tear off this card and return it to the mailer. The most common format is the two- or three-panel 8 by 11-inch card stock format. A self-mailer eliminates the need for an outer envelope, reduces lettershop expense, and combines the selling message of the letter and the brochure in one format. There is also no need for a separate business reply card and business reply envelope. With the use of a self-mailer, promotion costs can be reduced significantly, but again the question arises about what will happen to response. Will the self-mailer turn out to be more or less profitable than a full mailing package? By the way, the above should not be interpreted to imply that a self-mailer will pull less than a full mailing package; very often the reverse is the case. Nor should it be assumed that an inexpensive self-mailer will pull less than an expensive self-mailer.[2] As usual in direct response, only testing can provide the answer.

Inserts or Enclosures   Another very inexpensive but cost-effective mailing format is the insert piece or enclosure promotion. An insert or enclosure is any promotion piece mailed at no additional postage expense inside an invoice, statement, merchandise shipment, or other primary mailing piece. Insert pieces mailed along with first-class mailings such as bills or statements must be small so that they do not increase postage expenses. Enclosures in merchandise shipments are not weight-restricted.

In general, insert pieces pull a much lower response than direct mail packages or self-mailers. However, because of the lower cost, which can be as low as $20 per thousand, response does not have to be very great to generate a profit.

Space Advertising

The cost per thousand for space advertising is considerably lower than the CPM for direct mail. A typical magazine page may cost from $5 to $200 per thousand circulation, as compared with direct mail, which ranges between $300 and $1,000 per thousand pieces mailed. Of course, the response to a space advertisement will be less than the response to a direct mail promotion. In direct mail, a 3 percent response (30 orders per thousand) to a promotion costing $600 per thousand will result in a cost per response of $20, and is not atypical. In space advertising, a $20 cost per response is likely to be the result of a response rate of 1 percent in a medium with a CPM of $20.

As small as these numbers seem, they nevertheless result in very significant absolute numbers. For example, consider a mass-market magazine with a circulation of 3 million. The cost of a single black-and-white page is likely to be around

---

2. The first promotion piece for our two-day seminar based on the second edition of this book was a very expensive self-mailer. It won all sorts of praise. It was destroyed by a very inexpensive self-mailer. Why? Who knows? But we heard from course attendees, who received both over a period of time, that the second smaller piece could be faxed; the big piece couldn't go through most fax machines. As they say in New York, "go figure." As they also say in New York, go test.

$24,000 for a CPM of $8. If an ad in that magazine pulls at a rate of just .05 percent, or a rate of .5 order per thousand circulation, the ad will generate 1,500 responses at an average cost of $16 per response. (See Table 33–2.)

The actual CPM for an ad in any magazine will vary greatly, depending on a number of factors. For example, cover positions cost more than inside-the-book positions, color costs more than black and white, advertising in the direct mail section frequently costs less than advertising in the general editorial section, and discounts are available for multiple usage. Regional editions may be purchased, generally increasing the CPM but lowering the total dollar expenditure, and so on. The point is that buying space advertising is not simply a matter of placing an ad in a magazine. As always, the key decision is whether the more expensive ad format will result in a significantly greater response and increased profitability or, conversely, whether the less expensive format will result in fewer responses and lower profits.

Broadcast

Broadcast is an increasingly important direct response vehicle, and the emergence of cable TV with its highly targeted audiences has increased the significance of this medium.

TV broadcast advertising generally is purchased in one of two ways. In the first instance, an advertiser purchases a certain amount of time from a local station or national network at an agreed-on price. The exact times the commercial is to be aired and the number of spots or showings are agreed to in advance. This procedure is similar to placing an ad in a magazine. Before the ad is run or the commercial shown, the total investment in the medium is known. The cost per response will depend on the number of responses in the form of telephone calls to the local station or to an 800 number or on the number of responses received in the mail.

The second method of purchase is per inquiry (PI), also referred to as per order (PO). Very often, a broadcast station will agree with an advertiser to run a given commercial at times chosen by the station. In exchange for this airtime, the advertiser will pay the station an amount based on the number of responses received. In these situations, the initial response usually is directed to the local station and sent from there to the advertiser. PI or PO arrangements also are frequently available in space advertising.

When broadcast is used either to consummate a final sale or to generate leads, the key economic considerations are the length and frequency of the spot. Traditionally, direct response spots ran for 90 or 120 seconds, the argument for

TABLE 33–2

Calculating Front-End Space Results

Total circulation	3,000,000
Cost per single black-and-white page	$24,000
Total response	1,500
CPM	$8
Percent response: (1,500/3 million) × 100	0.05%
Orders per thousand circulation (OPM): (1,500/3,000)	0.5
Cost per response (CPR): CPM/OPM = $8.00/.50	$16.00

this length being the 20 seconds or so necessary for the tag line and the time it takes to establish the product and the offer in the viewer's mind. From the very outset, buying a 2-minute spot on network TV was expensive and very often not available. Thus, direct marketers turned to local spot TV with its larger inventory of late-night or non-prime-time spots. The advent of cable TV opened up a whole new inventory of available times, and the cable networks were more than happy to sell 90-second and 2-minute spots to direct response advertisers. However, as cable's popularity grew, the inventory of 2-minute spots decreased, and direct marketers are once again trying to make 30- and 60-second spots pay for themselves.

Closely aligned with the issue of the length of a direct response ad is the issue of frequency. How frequently should the spot appear in any one station? In any one market? Conceptually, there is a buildup period, a time in which response may be low but building, and then there is the falloff period after response has peaked. Obviously, the profits of a successful flight can be erased if airtime is purchased in significant quantity after the spot has peaked.

Thus, the economics of broadcast TV depend heavily on the marketer's ability to forecast response patterns and to tightly control spending decisions. Of course, this is particularly true in the case of the 30-minute infomercial.

A second important use of broadcast is in support of a major direct mail, newspaper insert, or magazine promotion. It is intuitive that broadcast spots urging the viewer to look in the paper, mailbox, or TV guide will increase response, but the economic question is how much airtime is enough and how much is too much? Up to a certain point or media weight, the broadcast advertising will not be able to make a significant impact and the support money will be wasted; on the other hand, too many spots can be equally unproductive. The answer, of course, is testing to determine the appropriate mix of broadcast support.

Finally, on the subject of broadcast, TV is not the only broadcast medium; we shouldn't forget radio. Radio, particularly drive-time radio with its upscale commuting audience, has always been a great captive market. But until the advent of the cellular car phone it has not been a great direct response medium. Of course, all that is changing rapidly as car phones move from luxury to necessity status among the most desirable market segments. So we see a great future for direct response radio, and when that happens, the same issues of time and frequency that affect broadcast TV will have to be addressed for radio.

Telemarketing

Outbound telemarketing is apparently here to stay, certainly for magazine renewals as well as for cold solicitations offering a one-issue trial examination. The phone also is used with great success in business-to-business direct response, in which the goal is to generate a lead or qualify a lead generated from a space ad or a direct mail offer.

Independent telephone operations currently sell their services at rates of approximately $30 to $50 per hour. Within this time period, a qualified phone operator can make between 6 and 20 contacts. The contact rate will vary depending on what time of the day it is, what day of the week it is, and whether the call is to a consumer at home or to a business executive or professional at the place of work. Because of its ability to generate low-cost trial subscriptions or leads, the telephone must be used with care. A low conversion rate can transform a very low cost per lead into a very high cost per order, as we'll see a little later on in this chapter.

The Internet

The Internet offers the possibility of acquiring customers at very low costs, and of course the costs of sending back e-mail solicitations are negligible compared with the costs of direct mail. The big unknown is the costs of attracting new customers to your site and the value of these customers over time. Will e-mail be the exception to the rule that there's no free lunch? Probably not, but we'll have to wait and see just what the economics of Internet and e-mail marketing turn out to be.

MEASURING RESPONSE

One-Step Promotions

The response to a direct mail promotion is expressed as a percentage of the quantity mailed or stated in terms of the number of responses per thousand pieces mailed (RPM). If the response is an order, the term *orders per thousand* (OPM) is used.

$$\text{Percentage response} = \frac{\text{Total response}}{\text{Quantity mailed}} \times 100$$

$$\text{RPM} = \frac{\text{Total response}}{\text{Quantity mailed}/1,000}$$

$$\text{OPM} = \frac{\text{Total orders}}{\text{Quantity mailed}/1,000}$$

Because the response to a direct mail promotion often is less than 1 percent, many direct marketers prefer to use the RPM or OPM terminology rather than express results in terms of a fraction of a percent. This is particularly true with regard to space advertising, in which a response of one order per thousand or even less is not uncommon.

Two-Step Promotions

As discussed above, not all direct response promotions are one-step promotions. Often the initial response to a direct response promotion is only the first step in a two-step or even a multistep promotion process. A magazine promoted by direct mail, using an offer that allows the potential subscriber to cancel after previewing one issue, is an example of a two-step promotion.

Consider a direct mail promotion of a magazine through a preview offer. Assume that 500,000 pieces are mailed and that 10,000 responses are received. The initial RPM is equal to:

$$\text{RPM} = \frac{10,000}{500,000/1,000} = 20$$

If only 40 percent of the respondents to the preview offer convert to paid subscriptions, the final paid orders per thousand pieces mailed (OPM) will be equal to:

$$20 \text{ RPM} \times 40\% = 8$$

CALCULATING COST PER RESPONSE

One-Step Promotions

In a one-step promotion the cost per response can be calculated by dividing the total number of responses into the total cost of the promotion. A quicker way preferred by many direct marketers is to divide the cost per thousand of the promotion by the number of responses per thousand to arrive at the cost per response (CPR):

$$CPR = \frac{CPM}{RPM}$$

Referring to our magazine example, assume that the cost of the mailing was $350 per thousand. The initial cost per response would be:

$$\frac{\$350}{20} = \$17.50$$

In two-step promotions, the promotion portion of the total cost per order is equal to the promotion cost per response divided by the conversion rate. In our magazine example, the cost per response is $17.50 and the conversion rate is 40 percent. Therefore, the promotion cost per order is equal to:

$$CPR = \frac{\text{Initial CPR}}{\text{Conversion rate}} = \frac{\$17.50}{.40} = \$43.75$$

However, dividing the promotion cost per response by the conversion rate understates the cost of acquiring a new magazine subscriber.

Assume that in the process of converting preview subscribers into paid subscribers, those potential subscribers who eventually will cancel will receive three issues of the magazine and five invoices. Let's also assume that those who decide to subscribe will receive an average of three invoices before paying. The costs of this conversion process can be added legitimately to the cost of acquiring the average paid subscription.

The calculations would be as follows. If the cost of one issue of the magazine on an incremental basis is $.75, and the cost of one invoice, including first-class postage, computer expense, and printing, is $.55, the amount spent on each eventual nonsubscriber or "cancel" is equal to:

$$
\begin{array}{lll}
3 \text{ issues} \times \$.75 \text{ per issue} & = & \$2.25 \\
+ \ 5 \text{ invoices} \times \$.55 \text{ per invoice} & = & \$2.75 \\
\text{Total cost per cancel} & = & \$5.00
\end{array}
$$

Because only 40 percent of the initial respondents will subscribe, the cost of attempting to convert the eventual cancels or nonsubscribers must be allocated over those who do subscribe. The equation for this calculation is as follows:

$$\frac{\text{Conversion expense per subscriber}}{\text{because of cancellations}} = \frac{\text{Cost per cancel} \times (1 - \text{pay rate})}{\text{Pay rate}}$$

Conversion expense per subscriber = [$5.00 × (1 − .40)]/.40

Cost expense per subscriber = $7.50

In addition, the cost of billing the respondents who eventually will pay will be equal to 3 × $.55, or $1.65. Therefore, the total conversion expense is equal to $7.50 plus $1.65, or $9.15 per paid order.

The total cost per new subscriber, including both promotion expense and conversion expense, is equal to the total new-subscriber acquisition expense:

Promotion expense + Conversion expense = Total acquisition expense
$43.75   + $9.15   = $52.90

The lesson to be remembered from this example is that the initial CPR may be only a small part of the total cost per final order in a multistep promotion. The costs of converting initial responses or leads can be particularly expensive when the conversion process requires expensive sales literature or requires a sales call.

TRACKING BACK-END PERFORMANCE

In the section on front-end performance, we discussed the techniques used to measure the costs of acquiring leads, buyers, or subscribers. In each case, costs were expressed not in terms of the total dollars spent but rather in terms of the amount spent to acquire the average customer from a particular media investment. By defining costs in terms of the average cost per customer, it is possible for us to compare alternative media without regard to their size.

We will follow this same approach in discussing back-end performance. In general, *back-end performance* refers to the purchase behavior of a group of respondents from the time their names are entered on the customer file. More specifically, we shall define back-end performance as the sales, contribution, and profits resulting from a group of respondents acquired from a particular advertising medium.

To measure, or track, back-end performance, it is necessary to maintain a system in which each customer is identified as coming from a specific advertising medium: a list, a space insertion, or a broadcast spot. When this is done, it is possible to accumulate the behavior of all customers from the same initial source medium and calculate average sales, contribution, or profits.

For this reason, direct marketing advertisers include a key code on every coupon in every space ad and print a key code on the return card or label of every direct mail promotion. The key code identifies the advertising medium and becomes a permanent part of the responding customer's record, along with name, address, and purchase history.

Direct marketers have proved over and over that for a given offer, back-end performance will vary significantly from one advertising medium to another. In general, direct marketers have discovered that buyers acquired from direct mail behave better than buyers acquired from space or magazine advertisements and that buyers acquired from direct mail or space will perform better than buyers acquired from broadcast promotions. However, there are wide variations in performance within the same media category. The best customers acquired from space media will perform better than the worst customers acquired from direct mail, and so on.

The critical concept to remember is that back-end performance varies from medium to medium and that the only way to operate a profitable direct response business is to be able to track the performance of customers in terms of the original source group so that the decision to reinvest promotion dollars can be made on the basis of proven performance.

At this point, it pays to remind you that we are describing classical direct marketing theory. Its concern is with the performance of the average customer, and what is being measured and about to be evaluated is the relationship between back-end performance and front-end or acquisition expense.

Back-end performance in this classical approach is assumed to be the same for every individual acquired from a given source code. In practice, when direct marketers set out to influence back-end performance, they do so using a natural extension of the source group concept. For example, if a classical direct marketer thought that it might be better in a continuity situation to ship books every six weeks instead of using the usual four-week shipment cycle, the procedure most likely to be followed would be to run an A/B split in one or more important media sources disclosing the six-week shipment cycle to the A group and a four-week shipment cycle to the B group. The marketer could then measure if there was any immediate difference in up-front response and wait to see if back-end performance was better or worse for either group. More on influencing back-end response, through classical as well as database methods, later. First, let's finish the discussion of how back-end performance is measured.

Measuring Back-End Performance

Single-Shot Mailing

The measurement of back-end performance for a solo, or single-shot, mailing is simply the statement of profit or loss for the promotion. Table 33–3 lists the assumptions that would be typical of a solo mailing of a product with a sales price

TABLE 33–3

Assumptions for a Single-Shot Promotion

Selling price	$65
Shipping and handling charge	$3.00
Return rate (percent of gross sales)	10.0%
Percentage of returns reusable	90.0%
Cost of product per unit	$15.00
Order processing:	
Reply postage per gross response	$0.32
Order processing and setup per gross response	$2.00
Percentage of gross orders using:	
Credit cards	85.0%
Checks	15.0%
Credit card expense	3.0%
Percentage of charge orders with bad checks	5.0%
Shipping and handling per gross response	$3.00
Return processing:	
Return postage per return	$1.50
Handling per gross return	$0.50
Refurbishing costs per usable return	$2.00
Premium expense per gross response	$6.00
Promotion CPM	$400
Quantity mailed	100,000
Percent response	2.0%
Overhead factor as a percent of net sales	10.0%

of \$60. The profit and loss statement in Table 33–4 is based on the assumptions defined in Table 33–3.

Clubs and Continuity Programs

In clubs and continuity programs, the statistic that measures back-end performance is the contribution to promotion, overhead, and profit. If this contribution for a group of new orders or starters is greater than the cost of acquiring the starting group, the investment in the starting group can be considered to be at least marginally profitable.

This contribution statistic sometimes is referred to as the *order margin*, the *allowable*, or the *break-even*. Each term implies a comparison to the cost per order expended to bring the starters into the business.

The contribution statistic excludes consideration of all fixed costs and overhead. Contribution is calculated by subtracting all direct expenses from the net sales of a group of starters and then dividing the result by the number of starters in the group.

In a club or continuity program, sales accumulate over the economic life of the starting group, and that life often can extend over a number of years. There-

TABLE 33–4

Profit & Loss Statement for a Single-Shot Promotion

	Units	Amount	Percent
Gross sales		$130,000	
Shipping and handling	2,000	6,000	
Total revenue	2,000	136,000	111.11%
Returns	200	13,600	11.11%
Net sales	1,800	122,400	100.00%
Cost of sales:			
Product			
Net shipments	1,800	$27,000	22.1%
Nonreusable units	20	300	0.2%
Order processing:			
Reply postage	2,000	640	0.5%
Setup costs	2,000	4,000	3.3%
Credit card costs	1,700	3,468	2.8%
Bad check expense	15	1,020	0.8%
Shipping and handling:	2,000	6,000	4.9%
Return processing:			
Postage	200	300	0.2%
Handling	200	100	0.1%
Refurbishing	180	360	0.3%
Premium	2,000	12,000	9.8%
Total cost of sales		$55,188	45.1%
Operating gross margin		$67,212	54.9%
Promotion expense		40,000	32.7%
Contribution to overhead and profit		$27,212	22.2%
Overhead allocation		12,240	10.0%
Profit		$14,972	12.2%

fore, in clubs or programs with an exceptionally long member life, the contribution from each monthly cycle should be discounted by some amount, generally the seller's cost of capital or opportunity cost, to take the time value of money into consideration. Appendix I, found at the end of this chapter, explains the concept of net present value in some detail.

The ability to forecast final sales and payments from individual starting groups on the basis of early performance data is critical in clubs and continuity programs. In these businesses, as in most direct response businesses, the key marketing decision is the decision to reinvest in media that have already been tested. Because of the long economic life of a club or continuity member, the decision to reinvest must be made on the basis of forecasted behavior. For example, if a new list is mailed in the winter and pulls as well as most other lists used by the club, the marketer may wish to remail the same names or test a larger segment of the list universe in the summer or fall campaign. However, by that time only a few cycles of actual data will be available for analysis. The decision, therefore, must be made on the basis of expected final contribution per starter. The forecast itself is based on the actual data accumulated to date.

In both clubs and continuity programs, one of the most important forecasting variables is the *attrition rate*. This is the term used to measure the rate at which members in a club or program either cancel their memberships or are canceled because of failure to pay for previously shipped items.

In negative option clubs, the attrition pattern measures the percentage of original starters eligible to receive the periodic advance announcements that advertise the negative option selection of the cycle and the alternative selections. In addition to being able to forecast the attrition pattern, it is also necessary to be able to forecast the acceptance rate of the featured negative option selection and the acceptance of the alternative selections as well as the average price of each category of sale.

Table 33–5 shows a simplified negative option club model that forecasts and accumulates average gross sales per starting member. As we mentioned before, in an actual club operation, the forecast would include separate estimates for the negative option selection and the alternative selections.

According to the model shown in Table 33–5, the average sale per starter will be $52.81. Assuming that direct costs, excluding all promotion and premium costs, are equal to 35 percent of gross sales, the contribution to promotion, overhead, and profit from this group of starters would be $34.32. It is this number minus premium costs that would be compared with promotion costs to determine the profitability of the starting group.

In continuity programs, there are two attrition patterns to be concerned with. The first pattern measures the percentage of starters who initially receive each shipment level at the earliest possible date. This attrition pattern reflects the payment behavior of starters who pay for each shipment on time and continue in the program. The second pattern represents the percentage of original starters who eventually receive each shipment level by the end of the economic life of the starting group. The difference in the two patterns is due to starters who fall behind in their payments and are suspended temporarily from receiving further shipments. As these starters eventually pay, the percentage of starters receiving each shipment level gradually increases.

To forecast sales properly, it is necessary to be able to forecast both attrition patterns. A forecast using only the first attrition pattern understates eventual sales. A forecast using just the second pattern forecasts final sales correctly but is un-

T A B L E   33–5

Average Sales Accumulated over Time in a Negative Option Club

Cycle	Still Active	Buying Product	Average Price	Incremental	Cumulative
Actual Data					
1	97.0%	51%	$12	$5.94	$5.94
2	95.0	47.0	12	$5.36	$11.30
3	83.0	42.0	12	$4.18	$15.48
4	75.0	38.0	12	$3.42	$18.90
5	70.0	33.0	12	$2.77	$21.67
Forecast Data					
6	65.1	32.0	12	$2.50	$24.17
7	60.5	31.0	12	$2.25	$26.42
8	56.3	31.0	12	$2.09	$28.52
9	52.4	30.0	12	$1.89	$30.40
10	48.7	30.0	12	$1.75	$32.16
11	45.3	30.0	12	$1.63	$33.79
12	42.1	30.0	12	$1.52	$35.30
13	39.2	30.0	12	$1.41	$36.72
14	36.4	30.0	12	$1.31	$38.03
15	33.9	30.0	12	$1.22	$39.25
16	31.5	30.0	12	$1.13	$40.38
17	29.3	30.0	12	$1.05	$41.43
18	27.3	30.0	12	$0.98	$42.42
19	25.3	30.0	12	$0.91	$43.33
20	23.6	30.0	12	$0.85	$44.18
21	21.9	30.0	12	$0.79	$44.97
22	20.4	30.0	12	$0.73	$45.70
23	19	30.0	12	$0.68	$46.38
24	17.6	30.0	12	$0.63	$47.02
25	16.4	30.0	12	$0.59	$47.61
26	15.2	30.0	12	$0.55	$48.16
27	14.2	30.0	12	$0.51	$48.67
28	13.2	30.0	12	$0.48	$49.14
29	12.3	30.0	12	$0.44	$49.59
30	11.4	30.0	12	$0.41	$50.00
31	10.6	30.0	12	$0.38	$50.38
32	9.9	30.0	12	$0.36	$50.73
33	9.2	30.0	12	$0.33	$51.06
34	8.5	30.0	12	$0.31	$51.37
35	7.9	30.0	12	$0.28	$51.66
36	7.4	30.0	12	$0.27	$51.92
37	6.9	30.0	12	$0.25	$52.17
38	6.4	30.0	12	$0.23	$52.40
39	5.9	30.0	12	$0.21	$52.61
40	5.5	30.0	12	$0.20	$52.81

able to forecast when those sales will occur. Table 33–6 provides an example of continuity attrition and the growth of the average number of units shipped over time to a group of starters in a continuity program in which one item is shipped per month.

T A B L E   33-6

Attrition Patterns in a Continuity Program

Shipment Number	Start Percent	End Percent	By End of Cycle	Average Units Shipped	By End of Week	Average Units Shipped
1	100	100	1	1.00	40	5.09
2	92	92	2	1.00	41	5.23
3	85	85	3	1.00	42	5.25
4	50	60	4	1.00	43	5.26
5	35	45	5	1.92	44	5.27
6	30	40	6	1.92	45	5.39
7	20	28	7	1.92	46	5.40
8	18	25	8	1.92	47	5.41
9	16	23	9	2.77	48	5.42
10	15	20	10	2.77	49	5.54
11	13	18	11	2.77	50	5.55
12	12	17	12	2.77	51	5.56
13	11	15	13	3.29	52	5.56
14	10	13	14	3.30	53	5.67
15	9	12	15	3.32	54	5.68
Total	5.16	5.93	16	3.34	55	5.69
			17	3.70	56	5.69
			18	3.74	57	5.79
			19	3.75	58	5.80
			20	3.77	59	5.80
			21	4.10	60	5.81
			22	4.14	61	5.83
			23	4.17	62	5.83
			24	4.19	63	5.84
			25	4.40	64	5.85
			26	4.43	65	5.86
			27	4.45	66	5.86
			28	4.46	67	5.87
			29	4.65	68	5.88
			30	4.67	69	5.88
			31	4.69	70	5.89
			32	4.70	71	5.89
			33	4.88	72	5.90
			34	4.89	73	5.91
			35	4.90	74	5.91
			36	4.91	75	5.92
			37	5.00	76	5.92
			38	5.07	77	5.93
			39	5.08	78	5.94

Newsletters and Magazines

The key economic variables that determine the profitability of a newsletter are (1) price, (2) the initial pay or conversion rate, (3) renewal rats, and (4) the response rate to direct mail promotions at different levels of promotion expense.

As we mentioned earlier in this chapter, many newsletters and magazines are successful in attracting trial subscribers through preview offers that allow the

CHAPTER 33   Back to Basics: The Economics of Classical Direct Marketing

potential subscriber to cancel without paying after examining one or a few sample issues. In these situations, the initial pay rate or conversion rate is the single most important variable affecting the ultimate success of the venture. However, even a relatively high initial pay rate can be offset by a poor renewal rate. Only after both conversion rates and renewal rates have been tested can we be sure of the potential profits of a newsletter. Table 33–7 shows the range of profits after two years from a direct mail investment of $3,000 that resulted in 200 gross subscriptions. The price of the subscription in this example is $37. In this situation the $3,000 investment is recovered at an initial conversion rate of a little more

TABLE 33–7

The Economics of Newsletter Direct Mail Marketing

Event	Unit Rate/Cost	Total Units/Dollars
Quantity mailed		10,000
Response rate	2.00%	
Pay rate	70.00%	
Gross subscribers		200
Paid subscribers		140
Canceled subscribers		60
Price	$37.00	
Year One revenue		$5,180.00
Year One costs		
Fulfillment and renewal costs		
Costs of fulfilling a paid subscriber	$8.00	$840.00
Costs of fulfilling a canceling subscriber	$2.25	$135.00
Costs of renewing a subscriber per starting subscriber	$1.25	$175.00
Total Year One costs		$1,150.00
Total Year One contribution		$4,030.00
Promotion costs		$3,000.00
Year One profits		$1,030.00
Year Two		
Renewal rate and number of renewals	70.00%	98
Nonrenewal rate and number of nonrenewals	30.00%	42
Revenue from renewals	$37.00	$3,628.00
Costs of fulfilling renewals	$6.00	$588.00
Costs of renewing a subscriber	$1.25	$122.50
Costs of fulfilling nonrenewals	$2.50	$105.00
Total Year Two costs		$815.50
Total Year Two contribution		$2,810.50
Cumulative Year Two profits		$3,840.50

Decision Table—Cumulative Second Year profits if Price = $37

Renewal Rates	Initial Pay or Conversion Rates 30.00%	40.00%	50.00%	60.00%	70.00%
40.00%	$906	$58	$790	$1,636	$2,486
50.00	713	200	1,113	2,025	2,938
60.00	519	458	1,435	2,412	3,389
70.00	326	716	1,758	2,799	3,841

than 40 percent coupled with a renewal rate of 40 percent; or the initial conversion rate could be as low as 40 percent if the renewal rate were to go to about 45 percent.

The profits that can be generated from a newsletter are related directly to the price charged for the newsletter, since editorial costs and printing costs are not affected by the price of the service. Thus, it is very important that price testing be employed at the outset to determine the best and most profitable price for the service. Tables 33–8 and 33–9 show the effect of a $10 increase or decrease in price on the newsletter described in Table 33–7.

The economics of magazines are similar to the economics of newsletters but with a number of critical differences. First, magazines rely heavily on newsstand sales and advertising to supplement the revenue stream provided by subscription income. Second, because of competition and because magazines are targeted to reach circulation levels measured in the hundreds of thousands rather than just thousands, as is the case with most newsletters, magazines have much less price-setting flexibility. However, just as in newsletters, the response rate to direct mail, the conversion rate, and the renewal rates are the key economic variables that eventually determine the success or lack of success of the magazine venture.

Catalogs

The term *back-end analysis* in a catalog operation can have multiple meanings. We may use the term with regard to the analysis of past media selections in much the same way as we analyze media performance in a club or continuity situation. Or we may be concerned with the profitability of an individual catalog mailing,

TABLE 33–8

Decision Table — Cumulative Second Year Profits If Price Is Reduced to $27

Renewal Rates	30 Percent	40 Percent	50 Percent	60 Percent	70 Percent
40%	(1,746)	(1,178)	610	42	$526
50	(1,613)	(1,000)	388	225	838
60	(1,479)	822	165	492	1,149
70	(1,346)	644	58	759	1,460

TABLE 33–9

Decision Table — Cumulative Second Year Profits If Price Is Increased to $47

Renewal Rates	30 Percent	40 Percent	50 Percent	60 Percent	70 Percent
40%	66	$1,062	$2,190	$3,318	$4,446
50	188	1,400	2,613	3,825	5,038
60	441	1,738	3,035	4,332	5,629
70	695	2,076	3,458	4,839	6,221

that is, whether the catalog made a profit, which items sold well, which didn't, and so on. Or we may be referring to the decision-making process in which we attempt to decide which customers should be mailed which catalogs and with what frequency in the future.

The first decision deals with evaluating individual media sources, and we act as if all customers acquired behave in exactly the same way by looking at the average performance of all customers acquired from the media source. Again, this is the classical direct marketing approach, as opposed to the database approach, which focuses its attention on the performance of individual customers across media sources. The reason we need two approaches is that two different decisions are involved. When evaluating a media source, we are asking, "Is the media source profitable?" and "Should we invest in it again?" What counts is the total or the average performance of all customers expected to be acquired from a future investment when compared with the cost of the investment. And we use past performance as a guide to future performance.

In a noncontractual relationship, after a customer is acquired from any media source, the decision to promote that customer is an independent decision. This decision should be based on the expected future performance of the individual, regardless of the source from which he or she was acquired, even though the original media source may be, as we'll see later, an important variable in making a prediction of future performance.

The mechanics of media source evaluation in a catalog or in any noncontractual relationship require computer systems that track performance by original source code. Again, as always, the key question is, "Will the eventual contribution from the customers acquired be greater than the cost of acquiring those customers, and if so, by how much?"

In practice, the same media source will have been used many times in the past, and an evaluation of each use reveals that profitability varies from use to use. Not only will the prediction of eventual contribution vary, but also the cost of acquiring new customers, as measured by the cost per order, will vary from promotion to promotion. Therefore, the prediction of future performance, both front-end CPO and back-end contribution, must be based on a forecasting procedure that takes this variability into account. Time-series analysis, taking such factors as trend and seasonality into account, may be employed if the data is suitable, or the analyst may use simpler averaging techniques giving greater weight to more recent occurrences. In practice, this becomes much more of an art than a science, and to imply that there are highly reliable standard procedures for this process would be misleading.

Financial Services

The direct marketer of financial services is, in theory, in a nearly identical position to the traditional catalog marketer with respect to the noncontractual nature of the relationship between the company and the customer. However, in practice, we've found financial service providers to be more concerned with individual-level database marketing decisions than with the classical direct marketing issue of relating back-end performance to initial cost per acquired customer. There are a variety of reasons for this, and although none of them completely justify current practices, they go a long way toward explaining why things are the way they are.

To begin with, many financial services providers using direct marketing methods are not traditional, closed-loop, direct marketing companies whose only contact with the customer is through direct marketing media. Therefore, because it is difficult if not impossible to attribute a new customer to a single ad or direct mail promotion, little attempt is made to do so. More significant, we suspect, is the fact that many direct marketing operations within financial services firms today were developed in an ad hoc manner. At some point a decision was made to use direct marketing methods and to support the direct marketing business by using the existing computer support systems. These systems were not designed for direct marketing purposes but were, in all likelihood, designed to support a sales force network.

In an information or database environment, where decision making is based on knowledge about the individual customer, one might argue that knowledge about the average behavior of all customers acquired from the same media source is unimportant. This argument, although it seems reasonable, is wrong for two reasons. First, the original media source is an important piece of individual information, and second, this approach confuses the need to make decisions about customers with the need to make decisions about where to prospect for customers. Again and again, direct marketers must make trade-off decisions about how much to spend on current-customer marketing and how much to spend on new-customer marketing. This is true for any company using direct marketing methods, be it a traditional direct marketing firm or one of the newer nontraditional users of direct marketing.

Attributing and Measuring Lifetime Value in a Financial Services Environment

Finally, with regard to financial services, the most difficult problem, much more difficult than not being able to trace customers to their source, a problem that can be dealt with adequately through attribution rules,[3] is the problem of first defining and then measuring lifetime value. Frequently, a customer will have multiple relationships with an institution, the initial relationship starting with the opening of one account. Intuitively we understand that the value of that customer must take all of his or her accounts into consideration, but how do you do that? To keep things simple, let's assume that the initial account was acquired through some traceable media, say a direct mail offer to open a mutual fund account. Over the course of that customer's life that customer will move money in and out of that fund and in and out of funds that may be opened at a later date, maybe even take all of his or her funds totally out of the institution and come back later. What is the lifetime value of that customer? How do you measure it? What if other members of the initial customer's family, living at the same address and having the same last name, therefore easily part of the same household, open their own accounts? Should their accounts be included in the definition of the household's lifetime value?

The more liberal, the more inclusive, your decision rules, the greater the imputed lifetime value, the greater the calculated return on the initial investment, the more the company will be likely to spend on acquiring customers from the initial source. Carried to an extreme, one might conclude that the rate of return of customers, acquired from, say, the *Wall Street Journal*, might be close to infinite!

---

3. By matching new-customer files with promotion files, a decision can be made that any new customer who was promoted within some time period, say the last three months, will be attributed to the promotion code found on the promotion file. The promotion code will identify the list source, offer code, campaign code, and other information related to the promotion.

What's more, all of the above assumes that systems exist to calculate lifetime value based on multiple relationships, and our experience is that, in many more cases than not, this is not true. So, what should a financial services company do? How should the lifetime value of a customer be defined? How much effort should go into building systems to measure this value?

In theory there's no good reason why if you were building a direct marketing application from the very beginning, and funding and time were not issues, that you would not want to be able to trace all of your current customers back to their initial transaction and therefore to their initial source. But this wouldn't be an easy task, even given appropriate funding. Therefore, as a practical matter we recommend an approach that would have the following achievable objectives:

- Build a rule-based decision system that will allow you to attribute non-key-coded inquiries and subsequent orders to previous promotions. There's no perfect system—some new customers will be missed, and others will be attributed to direct mail promotions that they never opened, but just by coincidence they became new customers within the attribution period. Since this can't be helped, don't spend too much time worrying about it and wind up not building anything because what you can build is not perfect.

- Commission a research study to define and measure the lifetime value of customers acquired from a couple of major media sources: direct mail, financial publications, broadcast, etc. An important objective of this study will be to clarify the different options available with regard to the scope of the lifetime value measurement and to identify the information sources required to complete the calculations. The other study deliverable will be the actual estimates of lifetime value by source.

- If the study confirms the feasibility of the exercise—*in some cases the data simply cannot be gotten at a reasonable cost*—the process can be extended to include other major media sources and then extended even further to other specific media: the *Wall Street Journal*, CNBC, *Barron's* Subscribers, etc.

- In addition, once the concept is proved, procedures should be established to keep these estimates up to date, so that at any point a company could provide an updated estimate of the lifetime value of a new customer acquired from each media source.

- We would not recommend attempting to build systems that produced projections for every single use of a particular medium, as the club and continuity companies do.[4] In those businesses, knowing the lifetime value of each use of a promotion medium is a natural by-product of their operating systems. What's more, clubs and continuities are relatively immune to changes in business conditions, and this is certainly not true of financial services companies.

- A system that results in average estimates of lifetime value by promotion source, estimates that could be used to compare against historical and current estimates of cost per new customer, would be more than sufficient for most financial services firms. And we suspect that a system that

---

4. The notion of lifetime value originated, we think, within the closed-loop club and continuity businesses, but that doesn't mean other businesses should duplicate their exact systems and procedures in order to reap the strategic benefits of the concept.

attempts to predict the present lifetime value of each new customer group, at the source code level, would not result in better acquisition decisions.

The Return of the Chicken-or-the Egg Problem

By now, the reader who has been paying close attention should have realized that we're back to the chicken-or-the-egg problem raised earlier in this chapter. The argument goes as follows. We wish to compare the lifetime performance or behavior of customers acquired from a media source with the cost of acquiring those customers. However, their performance will be a function of what we send them and how often we promote them. If our promotion decisions are faulty, if we mail too often or too infrequently, or if we mail the wrong products, the contribution of the group of customers will be less than it would have been if our decisions had been better. Fortunately, the only practical way to treat this problem is to ignore it—and that's OK if all media source groups have been treated in the same way, however good or bad that way was, and if all we're trying to do is rank media sources in terms of relative performance in order to decide how to allocate future media acquisition dollars. On the other hand, we always have to guard against self-fulfilling prophecies. If, for example, customers from a particular media source are always mailed less frequently because their performance is expected to be less than average, then we shouldn't be surprised to find that indeed sales from these customers always turn out to be less than sales from customers acquired from other sources. The solution to this problem, if the problem is thought to exist, is to create and track test groups across all media sources that are always treated in the same fashion.

We'll come back to the subject of how individuals should be evaluated for inclusion in future mailings in Chapter 34, where we discuss modeling and the relationship between modeling and RFM analyses. For now, let's assume that we can agree on an acceptable way to estimate the lifetime performance of customers acquired from individual media sources and that we can even agree on the expected CPO and the expected lifetime contribution of customers to be acquired in the future. How do we use this information in decision making?

MEASURING PROFITABILITY: COMBINING FRONT-END AND BACK-END MEASUREMENTS

The previous discussion implied that if the contribution to promotion, overhead, and profit for a given media investment was greater than the cost per order, the investment could be considered to be at least marginally profitable. We shall now continue to develop the relationship between front-end and back-end statistics.

Many direct marketers, particularly those engaged in club and continuity programs, prefer to use the concept of return on promotion to measure the relationship between front-end and back-end performance. Return on promotion (ROP) is defined as the ratio of the contribution to promotion, overhead, and profit minus the cost per order divided by the cost per order:

$$ROP = \frac{[Contribution - cost\ per\ order]}{Cost\ per\ order} \times 100$$

Conceptually, the ROP approach treats the decision to run a space ad or mail a list as an investment against which some financial return is expected. The return is measured by the difference between the contribution that results from all the purchases that occur after the order enters the house and the cost of acquiring the order.

For example, in the discussion on clubs and continuities, we showed how a group of starters with average sales of $52.81 might generate a contribution per starter of $34.21. Let's assume that the cost of acquiring this group of starters was $20 per starter. In this case, the ROP would be:

$$\text{ROP} = \frac{[\$34.32 - \$20.00]}{\$20.00} \times 100 = 71.6\%$$

The ROP statistic can be used in a variety of ways by direct marketers. One important use of this statistic is to evaluate alternative offers. The decision rule to be followed is that if the media investment required to implement both offers is the same, the offer with the highest ROP is the best offer.

Consider the example described in Table 33–10. In this example, the decision concerns whether to use a premium costing $6 per starter or a premium costing $9 per starter. The assumption is made that the average sales resulting from the use of either premium offer will be the same and will be equal to $70 per starter.

Naturally, increasing premium expense will reduce profits unless the premium offer results in an increased response. Thus, the question is, "What increase in response is necessary to justify the use of a $9 premium?" One way to answer this question is to assume a response rate to the $6 premium offer and

T A B L E   33–10

Using Incremental ROP to Evaluate New Offers (from 20 to 25 OPM)
But with No Increase in Advertising (Investment) Expense

	Case 1	Case 2	Incremental Results
Assumptions			
Quantity mailed	50,000	50,000	
Orders per thousand	20	25	
Average revenue per starter	$70.00	$70.00	
Direct costs excluding premium expense	$30.00	$30.00	
Contribution	$40.00	$40.00	
Adverting CPM	$350.00	$350.00	
Advertising expense	$17,500.00	$17,500.00	
Advertising CPO	$17.50	$14.00	
Premium expense	$6.00	$9.00	
Results			
Orders	1,000	1,250	250
Sales	$70,000	$87,500	17500
Costs	$30,000	$37,500	7500
Contributions	$40,000	$50,000	10000
Advertising	$17,500	$17,500	0
Premium	$6,000	$11,250	5250
Total contribution to overhead and profit	$16,500	$21,250	4750
Per starter	$16.50	$17.00	0.5
ROP	94.3%	121.4%	ERR

then search by trial and error for a response rate to the $9 offer that would result in the same profit and loss as the profit and loss resulting from the $6 offer.

Under the "Results" column for Case 1 in Table 33–10, we see the profit and loss resulting from the $6 premium if a response rate of 20 OPM is assumed. For Case 2, at a response rate of 25 OPM, which is assumed to result from the use of the $9 premium, contribution to overhead and profit would be increased by a total of $4,750. The ROP for each case is shown at the bottom of Table 33–10. The ROP for Case 2 is 121.4 percent, which is greater than the ROP of 94.3 percent for Case 1. As long as the media investment is the same — in this case, the $17,500 required to mail 50,000 pieces at a CPM of $350 — the alternative with the higher ROP will be the most profitable.

Therefore, it is possible to use the ROP equation directly to determine the response rate that would cause the ROP on the $9 premium offer to equal the ROP on the $6 premium offer:

$$\text{ROP} = \frac{\text{Contribution} - \text{premium} - \text{CPO}}{\text{CPO}}$$

$$\text{Old ROP} = .943 = \frac{\$40 - \$6 - \$17.50}{\$17.50}$$

$$\text{New ROP} = .943 = \frac{\$40 - \$9 - \text{new CPO}}{\text{New CPO}}$$

$$\text{New CPO} = \$15.95$$

$$\text{New OPM} = \frac{\text{CPM}}{\text{New CPO}} = \frac{\$350}{\$15.95} = \$21.94$$

The required new response rate is 21.94 orders per thousand.

When the initial media investment is not the same, the ROP analysis must be applied to the incremental investment in order to reach the correct decision. In this situation, if the incremental ROP is greater than zero, there will be an increase in the contribution to overhead and profit.

Refer to Table 33–11. In this example, the decision is whether to increase the quality of the mailing package in order to increase response. Costs are expected to increase from $350 per thousand to $400 per thousand, and the response rate is expected to increase from 20 OPM to 22 OPM. In Table 33–11, we see that if the more expensive mailing package were chosen, the average ROP would decline from 100 to 92.5 percent, but the incremental ROP would be 40 percent and total dollar contribution would increase by $1,000.

However, if the response rate increased to only 21 OPM, as shown in Table 33–12, the incremental ROP would be negative, and contribution would decline.

The decision to invest funds up to the point at which the incremental ROP is zero is a management decision. Generally, the cutoff rate is substantially higher, around 30 percent, to reflect other factors such as risk, the company's cost of capital, and opportunity costs resulting from competing uses of funds from other investments.

Another important use of the return on promotion statistic is to rank alternative investment opportunities for budget allocations. We have already seen that if the size of the investment is held constant, the investment alternative with the highest ROP is the most profitable.

In planning annual media budgets, a good first step is to begin by calculating the expected ROP for each independent media opportunity and then to rank

TABLE 33-11

Using Incremental ROP to Evaluate New Offers (from 20 to 22 OPM)
with an Increase in Advertising Expense

	Case 1	Case 2	Incremental Results
Assumptions			
Quantity mailed	50,000	50,000	
Orders per thousand	20	22	
Average revenue per starter	$70.00	$70.00	
Direct costs excluding premium expense	$30.00	$30.00	
Contribution	$40.00	$40.00	
Adverting CPM	$350.00	$400.00	
Advertising expense	$17,500.00	$17,500.00	
Advertising CPO	$17.50	$14.00	
Premium expense	$5.00	$5.00	
Results			
Orders	1,000	1,100	100
Sales	$70,000	$77,000	7000
Costs	$30,000	$33,000	3000
Contributions	$40,000	$44,000	4000
Advertising	$17,500	$20,000	2500
Premium	$5,000	$5,500	500
Total contribution to overhead and profit	$17,500	$18,500	1000
Per starter	$17.50	$16.82	($0.68)
ROP	100.0%	92.5%	40.00%

TABLE 33-12

Using Incremental ROP to Evaluate New Offers (from 20 to 21 OPM)
with an Increase in Advertising Expense

	Case 1	Case 2	Incremental Results
Assumptions			
Quantity mailed	50,000	50,000	
Orders per thousand	20	21	
Average revenue per starter	$70.00	$70.00	
Direct costs excluding premium expense	$30.00	$30.00	
Contribution	$40.00	$40.00	
Adverting CPM	$350.00	$400.00	
Advertising expense	$17,500.00	$17,500.00	
Advertising CPO	$17.50	$14.00	
Premium expense	$5.00	$5.00	
Results			
Orders	1,000	1,050	50
Sales	$70,000	$73,500	3500
Costs	$30,000	$31,500	1500
Contributions	$40,000	$42,000	2000
Advertising	$17,500	$20,000	2500
Premium	$5,000	$5,250	250
Total contribution to overhead and profit	$17,500	$16,750	−750
Per starter	$17.50	$15.95	($1.55)
ROP	100.0%	83.8%	−30.00%

all such opportunities in terms of descending order of ROP. Conceptually, as the size of the media budget increases, the average ROP generated by the budget decreases, but for any given budget total, a media budget constructed in such a fashion always yields the highest possible ROP.

One caution in the use of ROP in budget planning: the ROP statistic is an economic measure and does not take fiscal-year profit and loss considerations into account. An investment with a 50 percent ROP and a first-of-the-year expense date is considered to be the same in an ROP ranking scheme as an investment with a 50 percent ROP with an end-of-the-fiscal-year expense date. From a financial accounting point of view, the investment made on the first of the year will result in sales from new members in that same fiscal year. The investment made at the end of the fiscal year will result only in expense; the corresponding sales will come in the next fiscal year.

This problem is alleviated to some extent by accounting procedures that allow new-member acquisition expense to be amortized over the economic life of the acquired new members or subscribers. For example, assuming an economic life of 12 months, only one-twelfth of the expense of a promotion that was released in the last fiscal month would be charged to the current fiscal year.

ROP AND THE INFAMOUS 2 PERCENT RESPONSE RATE

It is customary for direct marketers to be accused of settling for low response rates. The implicit assumption is that through better targeting, response rates will increase to a rate higher than 2 percent—2 percent in this case being used as a kind of shorthand for a break-even level of response. Of course, adoption of the ROP principle suggests that direct marketers should, if funds are available and fiscal budget restraints are not an issue, always continue investing promotion dollars until the marginal rate of return on promotion approaches the cost of capital, and if that happens at a 2 percent response level, so be it. The goal of targeting should therefore not be to increase the marginal cutoff rate from 2 percent to some higher number; the goal of targeting should be to find more names that can be mailed with a response rate of 2 percent (that is, the break-even level) or better, and in this way to increase the size of one's business. Of course, if promotion funds are limited, then the effect of targeting will be to increase the average response rate over its current level, in turn increasing the average return on promotion.

The Present Value Concept

In this chapter we have argued that investment decisions should be evaluated using the return on promotion concept, which means that the contribution from a group of customers should be compared with the cost of acquiring those customers. However, in many direct marketing businesses the cash flow resulting from a steam of many transactions will take place over a number of years and somehow this time factor has to be taken into consideration.

In Exhibit 33–1 we show the results of an acquisition mailing to 1 million prospects. The promotion piece cost $660/m and the mailing pulls 33 orders per thousand; therefore the cost per new order is $20. The example we are using assumes that the 33,000 customers will attrit at the rate of 3 percent per month (each month 97 percent of the prior month's customers will still be active). At this rate it will take over 200 months for all of the customers to leave the program. We've also assumed that each month 25 percent of the active customer base will make a $10 purchase and the margin on this purchase will be 37.34 percent. The total contribution from this group of starters will be $1,025,057, or $31.06 per starter— $11.06 more than the CPO of $20. If we calculated ROP using the formula in this chapter, we would conclude that this promotion generated an ROP of 55.31 percent.

But clearly there's something wrong, because you really can't ignore the fact that the investment lasted close to 18 years! You would gladly give someone $20.00 if they would give you back $31.06 tomorrow, but I'm not sure that you would like to wait 200 months to collect all of your money. Why not? Because if you invested $20.00 today in, say, a CD that earned 5 percent, it would be worth $46.00 in 200 months, and if you could earn 10 percent on your money, it would grow to $105 in 200 months.

So the first thing you have to do when you decide to take the time value of money into account is decide on an interest rate or a discount rate, a rate by which future cash flows will be discounted to take the time value of money into account. Usually companies, to discount future cash flows to some present value, use discount rates of between 20 and 30 percent. A rate of 20 to 30 percent is well above the rate you could receive by putting your money in a CD or some other risk-free investment, and that is the point. Since all new-customer acquisition decisions entail some degree of risk, the higher discount, or "hurdle rate" as it is sometimes called, is meant to take that risk into consideration. Another way to think of the discount rate is that it represents an opportunity cost; in effect the

EXHIBIT 33-1

Discount Rate>	0.00%

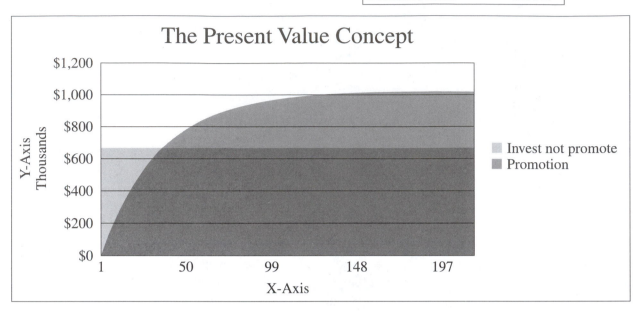

The Present Value Concept

Mailed	1,000	cpm	$660,000	<investment			
Response	33	$660	$20.00	<cpo			
Orders	33,000			ROP	Discount Rate>	0.00%	
Attrition	97.00%	Lifetime Value		55.31%			
Buy Rate	25.00%	Per Str	Per Str		Cash Flow from		
Margin	37.33520%	$31.06	$31.06		Invest at Dis Rte	PV>	$365,057
Price	$10.00	$1,025,057	$1,025,057	$0	$660,000	$1,025,057	$1,025,057
Col (1)	Col (2)	Col (3)	Col (4)	Col (5)	Col (6)	Col (7)	Col (8)
Months	Customers	Contrib	Cum PM		$660,000	$0	
1	33,000	$30,802	$30,802	$30,802	$660,000	$30,802	$30,802
2	32,010	$29,877	$60,679	$29,877	$660,000	$60,679	$29,877
3	31,050	$28,981	$89,660	$28,981	$660,000	$89,660	$28,981
4	30,118	$28,112	$117,772	$28,112	$660,000	$117,772	$28,112
5	29,215	$27,268	$145,040	$27,268	$660,000	$145,040	$27,268
6	28,338	$26,450	$171,491	$26,450	$660,000	$171,491	$26,450
7	27,488	$25,657	$197,147	$25,657	$660,000	$197,147	$25,657
8	26,663	$24,887	$222,035	$24,887	$660,000	$222,035	$24,887
9	25,864	$24,141	$246,175	$24,141	$660,000	$246,175	$24,141
10	25,088	$23,416	$269,591	$23,416	$660,000	$269,591	$23,416
11	24,335	$22,714	$292,305	$22,714	$660,000	$292,305	$22,714
12	23,605	$22,032	$314,338	$22,032	$660,000	$314,338	$22,032
13	22,897	$21,371	$335,709	$21,371	$660,000	$335,709	$21,371
14	22,210	$20,730	$356,439	$20,730	$660,000	$356,439	$20,730
15	21,544	$20,108	$376,548	$20,108	$660,000	$376,548	$20,108
16	20,897	$19,505	$396,053	$19,505	$660,000	$396,053	$19,505
17	20,270	$18,920	$414,973	$18,920	$660,000	$414,973	$18,920
18	19,662	$18,352	$433,325	$18,352	$660,000	$433,325	$18,352
19	19,072	$17,802	$451,127	$17,802	$660,000	$451,127	$17,802
20	18,500	$17,268	$468,395	$17,268	$660,000	$468,395	$17,268
21	17,945	$16,750	$485,144	$16,750	$660,000	$485,144	$16,750
22	17,407	$16,247	$501,391	$16,247	$660,000	$501,391	$16,247
23	16,885	$15,760	$517,151	$15,760	$660,000	$517,151	$15,760
24	16,378	$15,287	$532,438	$15,287	$660,000	$532,438	$15,287

EXHIBIT 33-1 (continued)

Mailed	1,000	cpm	$660,000 <investment				
Response	33	$660	$20.00 <cpo				
Orders	33,000		ROP	Discount Rate>		0.00%	
Attrition	97.00%	Lifetime Value	55.31%	Cash Flow from			
Buy Rate	25.00%	Per Str	Per Str		Invest at Dis Rte	PV>	$365,057
Margin	37.33520%	$31.06	$31.06				
Price	$10.00	$1,025,057	$1,025,057	$0	$660,000	$1,025,057	$1,025,057
Col (1)	Col (2)	Col (3)	Col (4)	Col (5)	Col (6)	Col (7)	Col (8)
Months	Customers	Contrib	Cum PM		$660,000	$0	
25	15,887	$14,828	$547,267	$14,828	$660,000	$547,267	$14,828
26	15,410	$14,384	$561,650	$14,384	$660,000	$561,650	$14,384
27	14,948	$13,952	$575,602	$13,952	$660,000	$575,602	$13,952
28	14,499	$13,533	$589,136	$13,533	$660,000	$589,136	$13,533
29	14,064	$13,127	$602,263	$13,127	$660,000	$602,263	$13,127
30	13,643	$12,734	$614,997	$12,734	$660,000	$614,997	$12,734
31	13,233	$12,352	$627,348	$12,352	$660,000	$627,348	$12,352
32	12,836	$11,981	$639,330	$11,981	$660,000	$639,330	$11,981
33	12,451	$11,622	$650,951	$11,622	$660,000	$650,951	$11,622
34	12,078	$11,273	$662,224	$11,273	$660,000	$662,224	$11,273
35	11,715	$10,935	$673,159	$10,935	$660,000	$673,159	$10,935
36	11,364	$10,607	$683,766	$10,607	$660,000	$683,766	$10,607
37	11,023	$10,289	$694,054	$10,289	$660,000	$694,054	$10,289
38	10,692	$9,980	$704,034	$9,980	$660,000	$704,034	$9,980
39	10,371	$9,681	$713,715	$9,681	$660,000	$713,715	$9,681
40	10,060	$9,390	$723,105	$9,390	$660,000	$723,105	$9,390
41	9,759	$9,108	$732,213	$9,108	$660,000	$732,213	$9,108
42	9,466	$8,835	$741,048	$8,835	$660,000	$741,048	$8,835
43	9,182	$8,570	$749,618	$8,570	$660,000	$749,618	$8,570
44	8,906	$8,313	$757,931	$8,313	$660,000	$757,931	$8,313
45	8,639	$8,064	$765,995	$8,064	$660,000	$765,995	$8,064
46	8,380	$7,822	$773,817	$7,822	$660,000	$773,817	$7,822
47	8,129	$7,587	$781,404	$7,587	$660,000	$781,404	$7,587
48	7,885	$7,359	$788,763	$7,359	$660,000	$788,763	$7,359
49	7,648	$7,139	$795,902	$7,139	$660,000	$795,902	$7,139
50	7,419	$6,924	$802,826	$6,924	$660,000	$802,826	$6,924
51	7,196	$6,717	$809,543	$6,717	$660,000	$809,543	$6,717
52	6,980	$6,515	$816,058	$6,515	$660,000	$816,058	$6,515
53	6,771	$6,320	$822,378	$6,320	$660,000	$822,378	$6,320
54	6,568	$6,130	$828,508	$6,130	$660,000	$828,508	$6,130
55	6,371	$5,946	$834,455	$5,946	$660,000	$834,455	$5,946
56	6,180	$5,768	$840,223	$5,768	$660,000	$840,223	$5,768
57	5,994	$5,595	$845,817	$5,595	$660,000	$845,817	$5,595
58	5,814	$5,427	$851,244	$5,427	$660,000	$851,244	$5,427
59	5,640	$5,264	$856,509	$5,264	$660,000	$856,509	$5,264
60	5,471	$5,106	$861,615	$5,106	$660,000	$861,615	$5,106
61	5,307	$4,953	$866,568	$4,953	$660,000	$866,568	$4,953
62	5,147	$4,805	$871,372	$4,805	$660,000	$871,372	$4,805
63	4,993	$4,660	$876,033	$4,660	$660,000	$876,033	$4,660
64	4,843	$4,521	$880,553	$4,521	$660,000	$880,553	$4,521
65	4,698	$4,385	$884,938	$4,385	$660,000	$884,938	$4,385
66	4,557	$4,253	$889,192	$4,253	$660,000	$889,192	$4,253
67	4,420	$4,126	$893,318	$4,126	$660,000	$893,318	$4,126
68	4,288	$4,002	$897,320	$4,002	$660,000	$897,320	$4,002
69	4,159	$3,882	$901,201	$3,882	$660,000	$901,201	$3,882

EXHIBIT 33-1 *(continued)*

Mailed	1,000	cpm	$660,000 <investment				
Response	33	$660	$20.00 <cpo				
Orders	33,000			ROP	Discount Rate>	0.00%	
Attrition	97.00%	Lifetime Value		55.31%			
Buy Rate	25.00%	Per Str	Per Str		Cash Flow from		
Margin	37.33520%	$31.06	$31.06		Invest at Dis Rte	PV>	$365,057
Price	$10.00	$1,025,057	$1,025,057	$0	$660,000	$1,025,057	$1,025,057
Col (1)	Col (2)	Col (3)	Col (4)	Col (5)	Col (6)	Col (7)	Col (8)
Months	Customers	Contrib	Cum PM		$660,000	$0	
70	4,034	$3,765	$904,967	$3,765	$660,000	$904,967	$3,765
71	3,913	$3,653	$908,620	$3,653	$660,000	$908,620	$3,653
72	3,796	$3,543	$912,162	$3,543	$660,000	$912,162	$3,543
73	3,682	$3,437	$915,599	$3,437	$660,000	$915,599	$3,437
74	3,571	$3,334	$918,933	$3,334	$660,000	$918,933	$3,334
75	3,464	$3,234	$922,166	$3,234	$660,000	$922,166	$3,234
76	3,360	$3,137	$925,303	$3,137	$660,000	$925,303	$3,137
77	3,260	$3,042	$928,345	$3,042	$660,000	$928,345	$3,042
78	3,162	$2,951	$931,296	$2,951	$660,000	$931,296	$2,951
79	3,067	$2,863	$934,159	$2,863	$660,000	$934,159	$2,863
80	2,975	$2,777	$936,936	$2,777	$660,000	$936,936	$2,777
81	2,886	$2,693	$939,629	$2,693	$660,000	$939,629	$2,693
82	2,799	$2,613	$942,242	$2,613	$660,000	$942,242	$2,613
83	2,715	$2,534	$944,776	$2,534	$660,000	$944,776	$2,534
84	2,634	$2,458	$947,235	$2,458	$660,000	$947,235	$2,458
85	2,555	$2,385	$949,619	$2,385	$660,000	$949,619	$2,385
86	2,478	$2,313	$951,932	$2,313	$660,000	$951,932	$2,313
87	2,404	$2,244	$954,176	$2,244	$660,000	$954,176	$2,244
88	2,332	$2,176	$956,352	$2,176	$660,000	$956,352	$2,176
89	2,262	$2,111	$958,463	$2,111	$660,000	$958,463	$2,111
90	2,194	$2,048	$960,510	$2,048	$660,000	$960,510	$2,048
91	2,128	$1,986	$962,497	$1,986	$660,000	$962,497	$1,986
92	2,064	$1,927	$964,423	$1,927	$660,000	$964,423	$1,927
93	2,002	$1,869	$966,292	$1,869	$660,000	$966,292	$1,869
94	1,942	$1,813	$968,105	$1,813	$660,000	$968,105	$1,813
95	1,884	$1,758	$969,863	$1,758	$660,000	$969,863	$1,758
96	1,827	$1,706	$971,569	$1,706	$660,000	$971,569	$1,706
97	1,773	$1,654	$973,223	$1,654	$660,000	$973,223	$1,654
98	1,719	$1,605	$974,828	$1,605	$660,000	$974,828	$1,605
99	1,668	$1,557	$976,385	$1,557	$660,000	$976,385	$1,557
100	1,618	$1,510	$977,895	$1,510	$660,000	$977,895	$1,510
101	1,569	$1,465	$979,360	$1,465	$660,000	$979,360	$1,465
102	1,522	$1,421	$980,780	$1,421	$660,000	$980,780	$1,421
103	1,476	$1,378	$982,159	$1,378	$660,000	$982,159	$1,378
104	1,432	$1,337	$983,495	$1,337	$660,000	$983,495	$1,337
105	1,389	$1,297	$984,792	$1,297	$660,000	$984,792	$1,297
106	1,348	$1,258	$986,050	$1,258	$660,000	$986,050	$1,258
107	1,307	$1,220	$987,270	$1,220	$660,000	$987,270	$1,220
108	1,268	$1,183	$988,453	$1,183	$660,000	$988,453	$1,183
109	1,230	$1,148	$989,601	$1,148	$660,000	$989,601	$1,148
110	1,193	$1,114	$990,715	$1,114	$660,000	$990,715	$1,114
111	1,157	$1,080	$991,795	$1,080	$660,000	$991,795	$1,080
112	1,122	$1,048	$992,843	$1,048	$660,000	$992,843	$1,048
113	1,089	$1,016	$993,859	$1,016	$660,000	$993,859	$1,016
114	1,056	$986	$994,845	$986	$660,000	$994,845	$986

EXHIBIT 33-1 (continued)

Mailed	1,000	cpm	$660,000 <investment				
Response	33	$660	$20.00 <cpo				
Orders	33,000			ROP	Discount Rate>	0.00%	
Attrition	97.00%	Lifetime Value		55.31%			
Buy Rate	25.00%	Per Str	Per Str		Cash Flow from		
Margin	37.33520%	$31.06	$31.06		Invest at Dis Rte	PV>	$365,057
Price	$10.00	$1,025,057	$1,025,057	$0	$660,000	$1,025,057	$1,025,057
Col (1)	Col (2)	Col (3)	Col (4)	Col (5)	Col (6)	Col (7)	Col (8)
Months	Customers	Contrib	Cum PM		$660,000	$0	
115	1,024	$956	$995,801	$956	$660,000	$995,801	$956
116	994	$928	$996,728	$928	$660,000	$996,728	$928
117	964	$900	$997,628	$900	$660,000	$997,628	$900
118	935	$873	$998,501	$873	$660,000	$998,501	$873
119	907	$847	$999,347	$847	$660,000	$999,347	$847
120	880	$821	$1,000,168	$821	$660,000	$1,000,168	$821
121	853	$796	$1,000,965	$796	$660,000	$1,000,965	$796
122	828	$773	$1,001,737	$773	$660,000	$1,001,737	$773
123	803	$749	$1,002,487	$749	$660,000	$1,002,487	$749
124	779	$727	$1,003,214	$727	$660,000	$1,003,214	$727
125	755	$705	$1,003,919	$705	$660,000	$1,003,919	$705
126	733	$684	$1,004,603	$684	$660,000	$1,004,603	$684
127	711	$663	$1,005,266	$663	$660,000	$1,005,266	$663
128	689	$644	$1,005,910	$644	$660,000	$1,005,910	$644
129	669	$624	$1,006,534	$624	$660,000	$1,006,534	$624
130	649	$606	$1,007,140	$606	$660,000	$1,007,140	$606
131	629	$587	$1,007,727	$587	$660,000	$1,007,727	$587
132	610	$570	$1,008,297	$570	$660,000	$1,008,297	$570
133	592	$553	$1,008,849	$553	$660,000	$1,008,849	$553
134	574	$536	$1,009,385	$536	$660,000	$1,009,385	$536
135	557	$520	$1,009,905	$520	$660,000	$1,009,905	$520
136	540	$504	$1,010,410	$504	$660,000	$1,010,410	$504
137	524	$489	$1,010,899	$489	$660,000	$1,010,899	$489
138	508	$475	$1,011,374	$475	$660,000	$1,011,374	$475
139	493	$460	$1,011,834	$460	$660,000	$1,011,834	$460
140	478	$447	$1,012,280	$447	$660,000	$1,012,280	$447
141	464	$433	$1,012,714	$433	$660,000	$1,012,714	$433
142	450	$420	$1,013,134	$420	$660,000	$1,013,134	$420
143	437	$408	$1,013,541	$408	$660,000	$1,013,541	$408
144	424	$395	$1,013,937	$395	$660,000	$1,013,937	$395
145	411	$383	$1,014,320	$383	$660,000	$1,014,320	$383
146	398	$372	$1,014,692	$372	$660,000	$1,014,692	$372
147	387	$361	$1,015,053	$361	$660,000	$1,015,053	$361
148	375	$350	$1,015,403	$350	$660,000	$1,015,403	$350
149	364	$339	$1,015,742	$339	$660,000	$1,015,742	$339
150	353	$329	$1,016,071	$329	$660,000	$1,016,071	$329
151	342	$319	$1,016,391	$319	$660,000	$1,016,391	$319
152	332	$310	$1,016,701	$310	$660,000	$1,016,701	$310
153	322	$301	$1,017,001	$301	$660,000	$1,017,001	$301
154	312	$292	$1,017,293	$292	$660,000	$1,017,293	$292
155	303	$283	$1,017,575	$283	$660,000	$1,017,575	$283
156	294	$274	$1,017,850	$274	$660,000	$1,017,850	$274
157	285	$266	$1,018,116	$266	$660,000	$1,018,116	$266
158	276	$258	$1,018,374	$258	$660,000	$1,018,374	$258
159	268	$250	$1,018,624	$250	$660,000	$1,018,624	$250

EXHIBIT 33–1 *(continued)*

Mailed	1,000	cpm	$660,000 <investment				
Response	33	$660	$20.00 <cpo				
Orders	33,000			ROP	Discount Rate>	0.00%	
Attrition	97.00%	Lifetime Value		55.31%			
Buy Rate	25.00%	Per Str	Per Str		Cash Flow from		
Margin	37.33520%	$31.06	$31.06		Invest at Dis Rte	PV>	$365,057
Price	$10.00	$1,025,057	$1,025,057	$0	$660,000	$1,025,057	$1,025,057
Col (1)	Col (2)	Col (3)	Col (4)	Col (5)	Col (6)	Col (7)	Col (8)
Months	Customers	Contrib	Cum PM		$660,000	$0	
160	260	$243	$1,018,867	$243	$660,000	$1,018,867	$243
161	252	$236	$1,019,102	$236	$660,000	$1,019,102	$236
162	245	$228	$1,019,331	$228	$660,000	$1,019,331	$228
163	237	$222	$1,019,553	$222	$660,000	$1,019,553	$222
164	230	$215	$1,019,768	$215	$660,000	$1,019,768	$215
165	223	$209	$1,019,976	$209	$660,000	$1,019,976	$209
166	217	$202	$1,020,178	$202	$660,000	$1,020,178	$202
167	210	$196	$1,020,374	$196	$660,000	$1,020,374	$196
168	204	$190	$1,020,565	$190	$660,000	$1,020,565	$190
169	198	$185	$1,020,749	$185	$660,000	$1,020,749	$185
170	192	$179	$1,020,928	$179	$660,000	$1,020,928	$179
171	186	$174	$1,021,102	$174	$660,000	$1,021,102	$174
172	181	$168	$1,021,271	$168	$660,000	$1,021,271	$168
173	175	$163	$1,021,434	$163	$660,000	$1,021,434	$163
174	170	$159	$1,021,593	$159	$660,000	$1,021,593	$159
175	165	$154	$1,021,746	$154	$660,000	$1,021,746	$154
176	160	$149	$1,021,895	$149	$660,000	$1,021,895	$149
177	155	$145	$1,022,040	$145	$660,000	$1,022,040	$145
178	150	$140	$1,022,180	$140	$660,000	$1,022,180	$140
179	146	$136	$1,022,317	$136	$660,000	$1,022,317	$136
180	141	$132	$1,022,449	$132	$660,000	$1,022,449	$132
181	137	$128	$1,022,577	$128	$660,000	$1,022,577	$128
182	133	$124	$1,022,701	$124	$660,000	$1,022,701	$124
183	129	$121	$1,022,821	$121	$660,000	$1,022,821	$121
184	125	$117	$1,022,938	$117	$660,000	$1,022,938	$117
185	121	$113	$1,023,052	$113	$660,000	$1,023,052	$113
186	118	$110	$1,023,162	$110	$660,000	$1,023,162	$110
187	114	$107	$1,023,268	$107	$660,000	$1,023,268	$107
188	111	$103	$1,023,372	$103	$660,000	$1,023,372	$103
189	108	$100	$1,023,472	$100	$660,000	$1,023,472	$100
190	104	$97	$1,023,570	$97	$660,000	$1,023,570	$97
191	101	$94	$1,023,664	$94	$660,000	$1,023,664	$94
192	98	$92	$1,023,756	$92	$660,000	$1,023,756	$92
193	95	$89	$1,023,845	$89	$660,000	$1,023,845	$89
194	92	$86	$1,023,931	$86	$660,000	$1,023,931	$86
195	90	$84	$1,024,014	$84	$660,000	$1,024,014	$84
196	87	$81	$1,024,096	$81	$660,000	$1,024,096	$81
197	84	$79	$1,024,174	$79	$660,000	$1,024,174	$79
198	82	$76	$1,024,251	$76	$660,000	$1,024,251	$76
199	79	$74	$1,024,325	$74	$660,000	$1,024,325	$74
200	77	$72	$1,024,396	$72	$660,000	$1,024,396	$72
201	75	$70	$1,024,466	$70	$660,000	$1,024,466	$70
202	72	$68	$1,024,534	$68	$660,000	$1,024,534	$68
203	70	$66	$1,024,599	$66	$660,000	$1,024,599	$66
204	68	$64	$1,024,663	$64	$660,000	$1,024,663	$64

EXHIBIT 33–1 *(continued)*

Mailed	1,000	cpm	$660,000	<investment			
Response	33	$660	$20.00	<cpo			
Orders	33,000			ROP	Discount Rate>	0.00%	
Attrition	97.00%	Lifetime Value		55.31%			
Buy Rate	25.00%	Per Str	Per Str		Cash Flow from		
Margin	37.33520%	$31.06	$31.06		Invest at Dis Rte	PV>	$365,057
Price	$10.00	$1,025,057	$1,025,057	$0	$660,000	$1,025,057	$1,025,057
Col (1)	Col (2)	Col (3)	Col (4)	Col (5)	Col (6)	Col (7)	Col (8)
Months	Customers	Contrib	Cum PM		$660,000	$0	
205	66	$62	$1,024,724	$62	$660,000	$1,024,724	$62
206	64	$60	$1,024,784	$60	$660,000	$1,024,784	$60
207	62	$58	$1,024,842	$58	$660,000	$1,024,842	$58
208	60	$56	$1,024,898	$56	$660,000	$1,024,898	$56
209	58	$55	$1,024,953	$55	$660,000	$1,024,953	$55
210	57	$53	$1,025,006	$53	$660,000	$1,025,006	$53
211	55	$51	$1,025,057	$51	$660,000	$1,025,057	$51

corporation is saying that it can earn 20 percent or 30 percent in some other investment of similar risk, so it won't fund your project unless you can at least earn a rate of return comparable to other investments with similar levels of risk.

To better understand the mechanics of this discounting operation, let's walk through the columns shown in Exhibit 33–1. Column 1 represents the number of months from the date the customers come on the file. We will assume that they all come on at the same time. Column 2 shows the number of customers still active at the end of any period. Column 3 shows the contribution the active customers generate in each month. Column 4 shows the cumulative present value of all contributions to date, based on the discount rate used in the example. In this first example, the discount rate has been set at 0 percent. In other words, future contributions are considered to be just as valuable as contributions received today. Under that assumption, the present value of the investment is equal to the sum of the nondiscounted contributions, $1,025,057. Column 5 shows the present value of the contributions received each month. Again since the discount rate is 0 percent, these numbers are identical to the numbers in Column 3. Column 6 shows the future value of the amount spent on acquisition if instead of making the acquisition, the funds were invested at the discount rate. Because the discount rate is 0 percent, this number never increases. Column 7 shows the value of the investment at any point in time assuming that all funds (contribution) received were invested at the discount rate used in the example. Column 8 shows the future value of each month's contribution, assuming funds were invested at the discount rate for the remainder of the economic life of this investment (the example runs for 212 months.)

Now let's turn to Exhibit 33–2. In this exhibit we use a discount rate of 10 percent. This means that all funds received in the future will be discounted at an annual rate of 10 percent [a monthly rate of 0.83 percent (10 percent/12)]. It also means that all funds received will, we assume, be reinvested in other projects that earn a 10 percent return (this is called the *reinvestment assumption*).

We now see that the present value of the investment is no longer $1,025,057, but rather $803,293, because all funds received beyond the end of the first period

EXHIBIT 33-2

Discount Rate>	10.00%

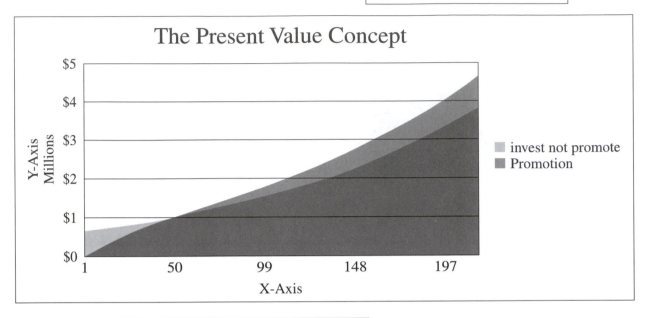

The Present Value Concept

Mailed	1,000	cpm	$660,000	<investment			
Response	33	$660	$20.00	<cpo			
Orders	33,000		ROP	Discount Rate>	10.00%		
Attrition	97.00%	Lifetime Value	21.71%				
Buy Rate	25.00%	Per Str	Per Str	Cash Flow from			
Margin	37.33520%	$31.06	$24.34	Invest at Dis Rte		PV>	$143,293
Price	$10.00	$1,025,057	$803,293	$221,764	$3,833,701	$4,666,038	$4,666,038
Col (1)	Col (2)	Col (3)	Col (4)	Col (5)	Col (6)	Col (7)	Col (8)
Months	Customers	Contrib	Cum PM		$660,000	$0	
1	33,000	$30,802	$30,547	$30,547	$665,500	$30,802	$177,436
2	32,010	$29,877	$59,933	$29,386	$671,046	$60,936	$170,691
3	31,050	$28,981	$88,201	$28,269	$676,638	$90,425	$164,202
4	30,118	$28,112	$115,395	$27,194	$682,277	$119,290	$157,959
5	29,215	$27,268	$141,555	$26,160	$687,962	$147,552	$151,954
6	28,338	$26,450	$166,721	$25,166	$693,695	$175,232	$146,178
7	27,488	$25,657	$190,930	$24,209	$699,476	$202,349	$140,620
8	26,663	$24,887	$214,218	$23,289	$705,305	$228,923	$135,274
9	25,864	$24,141	$236,621	$22,403	$711,182	$254,971	$130,132
10	25,088	$23,416	$258,173	$21,551	$717,109	$280,512	$125,185
11	24,335	$22,714	$278,905	$20,732	$723,085	$305,563	$120,426
12	23,605	$22,032	$298,849	$19,944	$729,111	$330,142	$115,847
13	22,897	$21,371	$318,035	$19,186	$735,187	$354,265	$111,443
14	22,210	$20,730	$336,491	$18,456	$741,313	$377,947	$107,207
15	21,544	$20,108	$354,246	$17,755	$747,491	$401,205	$103,131
16	20,897	$19,505	$371,326	$17,080	$753,720	$424,054	$99,210
17	20,270	$18,920	$387,756	$16,430	$760,001	$446,507	$95,439
18	19,662	$18,352	$403,562	$15,806	$766,334	$468,581	$91,810
19	19,072	$17,802	$418,767	$15,205	$772,720	$490,287	$88,320
20	18,500	$17,268	$433,394	$14,627	$779,160	$511,641	$84,962
21	17,945	$16,750	$447,465	$14,071	$785,653	$532,654	$81,733
22	17,407	$16,247	$461,001	$13,536	$792,200	$553,340	$78,625
23	16,885	$15,760	$474,022	$13,021	$798,801	$573,711	$75,636
24	16,378	$15,287	$486,548	$12,526	$805,458	$593,779	$72,761

EXHIBIT 33-2 (continued)

Mailed	1,000	cpm	$660,000	<investment			
Response	33	$660	$20.00	<cpo			
Orders	33,000		ROP		Discount Rate>	10.00%	
Attrition	97.00%	Lifetime Value	21.71%				
Buy Rate	25.00%	Per Str	Per Str		Cash Flow from		
Margin	37.33520%	$31.06	$24.34		Invest at Dis Rte	PV>	$143,293
Price	$10.00	$1,025,057	$803,293	$221,764	$3,833,701	$4,666,038	$4,666,038
Col (1)	Col (2)	Col (3)	Col (4)	Col (5)	Col (6)	Col (7)	Col (8)
Months	Customers	Contrib	Cum PM		$660,000	$0	
25	15,887	$14,828	$498,598	$12,050	$812,170	$613,556	$69,995
26	15,410	$14,384	$510,190	$11,592	$818,938	$633,052	$67,334
27	14,948	$13,952	$521,342	$11,151	$825,763	$652,280	$64,774
28	14,499	$13,533	$532,069	$10,727	$832,644	$671,249	$62,311
29	14,064	$13,127	$542,389	$10,320	$839,583	$689,970	$59,943
30	13,643	$12,734	$552,316	$9,927	$846,579	$708,453	$57,664
31	13,233	$12,352	$561,866	$9,550	$853,634	$726,709	$55,472
32	12,836	$11,981	$571,052	$9,187	$860,748	$744,746	$53,363
33	12,451	$11,622	$579,890	$8,838	$867,921	$762,574	$51,334
34	12,078	$11,273	$588,392	$8,502	$875,153	$780,201	$49,383
35	11,715	$10,935	$596,570	$8,178	$882,446	$797,638	$47,505
36	11,364	$10,607	$604,437	$7,867	$889,800	$814,892	$45,699
37	11,023	$10,289	$612,006	$7,568	$897,215	$831,971	$43,962
38	10,692	$9,980	$619,286	$7,281	$904,692	$848,884	$42,291
39	10,371	$9,681	$626,290	$7,004	$912,231	$865,638	$40,683
40	10,060	$9,390	$633,028	$6,738	$919,833	$882,242	$39,136
41	9,759	$9,108	$639,509	$6,481	$927,498	$898,703	$37,648
42	9,466	$8,835	$645,744	$6,235	$935,227	$915,027	$36,217
43	9,182	$8,570	$651,742	$5,998	$943,021	$931,222	$34,840
44	8,906	$8,313	$657,512	$5,770	$950,879	$947,295	$33,516
45	8,639	$8,064	$663,063	$5,551	$958,803	$963,253	$32,242
46	8,380	$7,822	$668,403	$5,340	$966,793	$979,102	$31,016
47	8,129	$7,587	$673,539	$5,137	$974,850	$994,848	$29,837
48	7,885	$7,359	$678,481	$4,941	$982,974	$1,010,498	$28,703
49	7,648	$7,139	$683,234	$4,754	$991,165	$1,026,057	$27,611
50	7,419	$6,924	$687,807	$4,573	$999,425	$1,041,532	$26,562
51	7,196	$6,717	$692,206	$4,399	$1,007,753	$1,056,929	$25,552
52	6,980	$6,515	$696,438	$4,232	$1,016,151	$1,072,252	$24,581
53	6,771	$6,320	$700,508	$4,071	$1,024,619	$1,087,507	$23,646
54	6,568	$6,130	$704,425	$3,916	$1,033,158	$1,102,700	$22,747
55	6,371	$5,946	$708,192	$3,767	$1,041,767	$1,117,835	$21,882
56	6,180	$5,768	$711,816	$3,624	$1,050,449	$1,132,918	$21,050
57	5,994	$5,595	$715,302	$3,486	$1,059,203	$1,147,954	$20,250
58	5,814	$5,427	$718,656	$3,354	$1,068,029	$1,162,947	$19,480
59	5,640	$5,264	$721,882	$3,226	$1,076,929	$1,177,903	$18,740
60	5,471	$5,106	$724,985	$3,104	$1,085,904	$1,192,825	$18,027
61	5,307	$4,953	$727,971	$2,986	$1,094,953	$1,207,718	$17,342
62	5,147	$4,805	$730,843	$2,872	$1,104,078	$1,222,587	$16,683
63	4,993	$4,660	$733,606	$2,763	$1,113,278	$1,237,436	$16,049
64	4,843	$4,521	$736,264	$2,658	$1,122,556	$1,252,268	$15,438
65	4,698	$4,385	$738,820	$2,557	$1,131,910	$1,267,089	$14,851
66	4,557	$4,253	$741,280	$2,460	$1,141,343	$1,281,901	$14,287
67	4,420	$4,126	$743,646	$2,366	$1,150,854	$1,296,709	$13,744
68	4,288	$4,002	$745,922	$2,276	$1,160,445	$1,311,517	$13,221
69	4,159	$3,882	$748,112	$2,190	$1,170,115	$1,326,329	$12,719

E X H I B I T 33–2 *(continued)*

Mailed	1,000	cpm	$660,000 <investment				
Response	33	$660	$20.00 <cpo				
Orders	33,000			ROP	Discount Rate>	10.00%	
Attrition	97.00%	Lifetime Value		21.71%			
Buy Rate	25.00%	Per Str	Per Str		Cash Flow from		
Margin	37.33520%	$31.06	$24.34		Invest at Dis Rte	PV>	$143,293
Price	$10.00	$1,025,057	$803,293	$221,764	$3,833,701	$4,666,038	$4,666,038
Col (1)	Col (2)	Col (3)	Col (4)	Col (5)	Col (6)	Col (7)	Col (8)
Months	Customers	Contrib	Cum PM		$660,000	$0	
70	4,034	$3,765	$750,218	$2,106	$1,179,866	$1,341,147	$12,235
71	3,913	$3,653	$752,245	$2,026	$1,189,698	$1,355,976	$11,770
72	3,796	$3,543	$754,194	$1,949	$1,199,612	$1,370,818	$11,323
73	3,682	$3,437	$756,069	$1,875	$1,209,609	$1,385,679	$10,892
74	3,571	$3,334	$757,873	$1,804	$1,219,689	$1,400,559	$10,478
75	3,464	$3,234	$759,608	$1,735	$1,229,853	$1,415,464	$10,080
76	3,360	$3,137	$761,277	$1,669	$1,240,102	$1,430,396	$9,696
77	3,260	$3,042	$762,883	$1,606	$1,250,436	$1,445,359	$9,328
78	3,162	$2,951	$764,428	$1,545	$1,260,856	$1,460,355	$8,973
79	3,067	$2,863	$765,914	$1,486	$1,271,364	$1,475,387	$8,632
80	2,975	$2,777	$767,344	$1,430	$1,281,958	$1,490,459	$8,304
81	2,886	$2,693	$768,719	$1,375	$1,292,641	$1,505,573	$7,988
82	2,799	$2,613	$770,042	$1,323	$1,303,413	$1,520,732	$7,685
83	2,715	$2,534	$771,315	$1,273	$1,314,275	$1,535,939	$7,392
84	2,634	$2,458	$772,539	$1,224	$1,325,227	$1,551,196	$7,111
85	2,555	$2,385	$773,717	$1,178	$1,336,271	$1,566,508	$6,841
86	2,478	$2,313	$774,850	$1,133	$1,347,406	$1,581,875	$6,581
87	2,404	$2,244	$775,939	$1,090	$1,358,635	$1,597,301	$6,331
88	2,332	$2,176	$776,988	$1,048	$1,369,957	$1,612,788	$6,090
89	2,262	$2,111	$777,997	$1,009	$1,381,373	$1,628,339	$5,859
90	2,194	$2,048	$778,967	$970	$1,392,885	$1,643,956	$5,636
91	2,128	$1,986	$779,900	$933	$1,404,492	$1,659,642	$5,422
92	2,064	$1,927	$780,798	$898	$1,416,196	$1,675,399	$5,215
93	2,002	$1,869	$781,662	$864	$1,427,998	$1,691,229	$5,017
94	1,942	$1,813	$782,493	$831	$1,439,898	$1,707,135	$4,826
95	1,884	$1,758	$783,292	$799	$1,451,897	$1,723,120	$4,643
96	1,827	$1,706	$784,061	$769	$1,463,996	$1,739,185	$4,466
97	1,773	$1,654	$784,801	$740	$1,476,196	$1,755,333	$4,297
98	1,719	$1,605	$785,512	$712	$1,488,498	$1,771,565	$4,133
99	1,668	$1,557	$786,197	$685	$1,500,902	$1,787,885	$3,976
100	1,618	$1,510	$786,855	$659	$1,513,409	$1,804,294	$3,825
101	1,569	$1,465	$787,489	$633	$1,526,021	$1,820,794	$3,680
102	1,522	$1,421	$788,098	$609	$1,538,738	$1,837,388	$3,540
103	1,476	$1,378	$788,684	$586	$1,551,561	$1,854,078	$3,405
104	1,432	$1,337	$789,248	$564	$1,564,490	$1,870,866	$3,276
105	1,389	$1,297	$789,791	$543	$1,577,528	$1,887,753	$3,151
106	1,348	$1,258	$790,313	$522	$1,590,674	$1,904,742	$3,031
107	1,307	$1,220	$790,815	$502	$1,603,929	$1,921,835	$2,916
108	1,268	$1,183	$791,298	$483	$1,617,295	$1,939,034	$2,805
109	1,230	$1,148	$791,762	$465	$1,630,773	$1,958,340	$2,699
110	1,193	$1,114	$792,209	$447	$1,644,363	$1,973,756	$2,596
111	1,157	$1,080	$792,639	$430	$1,658,066	$1,991,284	$2,497
112	1,122	$1,048	$793,053	$414	$1,671,883	$2,008,926	$2,402
113	1,089	$1,016	$793,451	$398	$1,685,815	$2,026,684	$2,311
114	1,056	$986	$793,833	$383	$1,699,864	$2,044,558	$2,223

E X H I B I T   33–2 *(continued)*

Mailed	1,000	cpm	$660,000 <investment				
Response	33	$660	$20.00 <cpo				
Orders	33,000			ROP	Discount Rate>	10.00%	
Attrition	97.00%	Lifetime Value		21.71%			
Buy Rate	25.00%	Per Str	Per Str		Cash Flow from		
Margin	37.33520%	$31.06	$24.34		Invest at Dis Rte	PV>	$143,293
Price	$10.00	$1,025,057	$803,293	$221,764	$3,833,701	$4,666,038	$4,666,038
Col (1)	Col (2)	Col (3)	Col (4)	Col (5)	Col (6)	Col (7)	Col (8)
Months	Customers	Contrib	Cum PM		$660,000	$0	
115	1,024	$956	$794,202	$368	$1,714,029	$2,062,553	$2,139
116	994	$928	$794,556	$354	$1,728,313	$2,080,668	$2,057
117	964	$900	$794,896	$341	$1,742,715	$2,098,907	$1,979
118	935	$873	$795,224	$328	$1,757,238	$2,117,270	$1,904
119	907	$847	$795,540	$315	$1,771,882	$2,135,761	$1,832
120	880	$821	$795,843	$303	$1,786,647	$2,154,380	$1,762
121	853	$796	$796,135	$292	$1,801,536	$2,173,129	$1,695
122	828	$773	$796,415	$281	$1,816,549	$2,192,011	$1,631
123	803	$749	$796,685	$270	$1,831,687	$2,211,028	$1,569
124	779	$727	$796,945	$260	$1,846,951	$2,230,180	$1,509
125	755	$705	$797,195	$250	$1,862,342	$2,249,470	$1,452
126	733	$684	$797,435	$240	$1,877,862	$2,268,899	$1,396
127	711	$663	$797,667	$231	$1,893,510	$2,288,470	$1,343
128	689	$644	$797,889	$222	$1,909,290	$2,308,184	$1,292
129	669	$624	$798,103	$214	$1,925,201	$2,328,043	$1,243
130	649	$606	$798,309	$206	$1,941,244	$2,348,049	$1,196
131	629	$587	$798,507	$198	$1,957,421	$2,368,204	$1,150
132	610	$570	$798,698	$191	$1,973,733	$2,388,509	$1,107
133	592	$553	$798,881	$183	$1,990,180	$2,408,965	$1,065
134	574	$536	$799,057	$176	$2,006,765	$2,429,576	$1,024
135	557	$520	$799,227	$170	$2,023,488	$2,450,343	$985
136	540	$504	$799,390	$163	$2,040,351	$2,471,267	$948
137	524	$489	$799,547	$157	$2,057,354	$2,492,350	$912
138	508	$475	$799,698	$151	$2,074,498	$2,513,594	$877
139	493	$460	$799,843	$145	$2,091,786	$2,535,001	$844
140	478	$447	$799,983	$140	$2,109,217	$2,556,572	$812
141	464	$433	$800,117	$134	$2,126,794	$2,578,310	$781
142	450	$420	$800,247	$129	$2,144,517	$2,600,216	$751
143	437	$408	$800,371	$124	$2,162,388	$2,622,292	$723
144	424	$395	$800,491	$120	$2,180,408	$2,644,540	$695
145	411	$383	$800,606	$115	$2,198,578	$2,666,961	$669
146	398	$372	$800,716	$111	$2,216,900	$2,689,558	$643
147	387	$361	$800,823	$107	$2,235,374	$2,712,332	$619
148	375	$350	$800,925	$102	$2,254,002	$2,735,284	$595
149	364	$339	$801,024	$99	$2,272,786	$2,758,418	$573
150	353	$329	$801,119	$95	$2,291,725	$2,781,734	$551
151	342	$319	$801,210	$91	$2,310,823	$2,805,234	$530
152	332	$310	$801,298	$88	$2,330,080	$2,828,921	$510
153	322	$301	$801,382	$84	$2,349,497	$2,852,796	$490
154	312	$292	$801,463	$81	$2,369,076	$2,876,861	$472
155	303	$283	$801,542	$78	$2,388,819	$2,901,117	$454
156	294	$274	$801,617	$75	$2,408,726	$2,925,568	$437
157	285	$266	$801,689	$72	$2,428,798	$2,950,214	$420
158	276	$258	$801,759	$70	$2,449,038	$2,975,057	$404
159	268	$250	$801,825	$67	$2,469,447	$3,000,099	$389

EXHIBIT 33–2 (continued)

Mailed	1,000	cpm	$660,000 <investment				
Response	33	$660	$20.00 <cpo				
Orders	33,000			ROP	Discount Rate>	10.00%	
Attrition	97.00%	Lifetime Value		21.71%			
Buy Rate	25.00%	Per Str	Per Str		Cash Flow from		
Margin	37.33520%	$31.06	$24.34		Invest at Dis Rte	PV>	$143,293
Price	$10.00	$1,025,057	$803,293	$221,764	$3,833,701	$4,666,038	$4,666,038
Col (1)	Col (2)	Col (3)	Col (4)	Col (5)	Col (6)	Col (7)	Col (8)
Months	Customers	Contrib	Cum PM		$660,000	$0	
160	260	$243	$801,890	$64	$2,490,026	$3,025,343	$374
161	252	$236	$801,952	$62	$2,510,776	$3,050,790	$360
162	245	$228	$802,011	$60	$2,531,699	$3,076,441	$346
163	237	$222	$802,069	$57	$2,552,796	$3,102,300	$333
164	230	$215	$802,124	$55	$2,574,070	$3,128,367	$320
165	223	$209	$802,177	$53	$2,595,520	$3,154,646	$308
166	217	$202	$802,228	$51	$2,617,150	$3,181,137	$296
167	210	$196	$802,277	$49	$2,638,959	$3,207,842	$285
168	204	$190	$802,324	$47	$2,660,951	$3,234,765	$274
169	198	$185	$802,369	$45	$2,683,125	$3,261,906	$264
170	192	$179	$802,413	$44	$2,705,485	$3,289,267	$254
171	186	$174	$802,455	$42	$2,728,030	$3,316,851	$244
172	181	$168	$802,496	$40	$2,750,764	$3,344,660	$235
173	175	$163	$802,534	$39	$2,773,687	$3,372,696	$226
174	170	$159	$802,572	$37	$2,796,801	$3,400,960	$217
175	165	$154	$802,608	$36	$2,820,108	$3,429,455	$209
176	160	$149	$802,642	$35	$2,843,609	$3,458,183	$201
177	155	$145	$802,676	$33	$2,867,305	$3,487,146	$193
178	150	$140	$802,708	$32	$2,891,199	$3,516,346	$186
179	146	$136	$802,739	$31	$2,915,293	$3,545,785	$179
180	141	$132	$802,768	$30	$2,939,587	$3,575,465	$172
181	137	$128	$802,797	$29	$2,964,083	$3,605,389	$166
182	133	$124	$802,824	$27	$2,988,784	$3,635,558	$159
183	129	$121	$802,851	$26	$3,013,691	$3,665,975	$153
184	125	$117	$802,876	$25	$3,038,805	$3,696,642	$147
185	121	$113	$802,900	$24	$3,064,128	$3,727,560	$142
186	118	$110	$802,924	$23	$3,089,663	$3,758,733	$136
187	114	$107	$802,947	$23	$3,115,410	$3,790,163	$131
188	111	$103	$802,968	$22	$3,141,371	$3,821,851	$126
189	108	$100	$802,989	$21	$3,167,550	$3,853,800	$121
190	104	$97	$803,009	$20	$3,193,946	$3,886,012	$117
191	101	$94	$803,029	$19	$3,220,562	$3,918,490	$112
192	98	$92	$803,047	$19	$3,247,400	$3,951,236	$108
193	95	$89	$803,065	$18	$3,274,462	$3,984,252	$104
194	92	$86	$803,082	$17	$3,301,749	$4,017,540	$100
195	90	$84	$803,099	$17	$3,329,263	$4,051,103	$96
196	87	$81	$803,115	$16	$3,357,007	$4,084,944	$93
197	84	$79	$803,130	$15	$3,384,982	$4,119,063	$89
198	82	$76	$803,145	$15	$3,413,191	$4,153,465	$86
199	79	$74	$803,159	$14	$3,441,634	$4,188,151	$82
200	77	$72	$803,173	$14	$3,470,314	$4,223,125	$79
201	75	$70	$803,186	$13	$3,499,233	$4,258,387	$76
202	72	$68	$803,199	$13	$3,528,394	$4,293,941	$73
203	70	$66	$803,211	$12	$3,557,797	$4,329,789	$71
204	68	$64	$803,223	$12	$3,587,445	$4,365,935	$68

EXHIBIT 33-2 *(continued)*

Mailed	1,000	cpm	$660,000 <investment				
Response	33	$660	$20.00 <cpo				
Orders	33,000			ROP	Discount Rate>	10.00%	
Attrition	97.00%	Lifetime Value		21.71%			
Buy Rate	25.00%	Per Str	Per Str		Cash Flow from		
Margin	37.33520%	$31.06	$24.34		Invest at Dis Rte	PV>	$143,293
Price	$10.00	$1,025,057	$803,293	$221,764	$3,833,701	$4,666,038	$4,666,038
Col (1)	Col (2)	Col (3)	Col (4)	Col (5)	Col (6)	Col (7)	Col (8)
Months	Customers	Contrib	Cum PM		$660,000	$0	
205	66	$62	$803,234	$11	$3,617,341	$4,402,379	$65
206	64	$60	$803,245	$11	$3,647,485	$4,439,125	$63
207	62	$58	$803,255	$10	$3,677,881	$4,476,176	$60
208	60	$56	$803,265	$10	$3,708,530	$4,513,534	$58
209	58	$55	$803,275	$10	$3,739,434	$4,551,201	$56
210	57	$53	$803,284	$9	$3,770,596	$4,589,181	$54
211	55	$51	$803,293	$9	$3,802,018	$4,627,475	$52

have been discounted at the 10 percent rate. The present value of future contributions per starter is $24.34, greater than the $20.00 acquisition cost. Column 6 indicates that if the initial investment of $660,000 were invested at 10 percent, it would grow to $3,833,701 in 212 months, but the acquisition investment would produce $4,666,038 by the end of 212 months, again making the assumption that the funds would be reinvested at the discount rate as they are received.

Another way to describe this investment is to say that the present value of the contributions generated by the investment, $803,293, exceeds the cost of the investment, $660,000, by $143,293, using a 10 percent discount rate. Because the net present value of the investment is positive at 10 percent, we know that the "real" rate of return (called the *internal rate of return*), the rate of return that would discount the future cash flows back to the value of the investment, must be greater than 10 percent.

Now let's look at Exhibit 33-3. Exhibit 33-3 uses a discount rate of 30 percent. The present value of the future contributions is $560,023, less than the cost of the initial investment, $660,000. Not surprisingly, therefore, the present value per starter is less than $20.00; it is $16.97. Finally, Columns 6 and 7 show that if the initial investment were invested at an interest rate of 30 percent, it would grow to $123,880,628 in 212 months, whereas the investment in new customers would grow to only $105,115,163 at the end of the same period, again assuming that all contributions could be reinvested in projects that earn 30 percent. All of the preceding indicates that the true rate of return must be less than 30 percent but greater than 10 percent.

Finally, let's look at Exhibit 33-4. Exhibit 33-4 employs a discount rate of 20 percent. At this discount rate the present value of future contributions exactly equals the value of the investment; the present value of future contributions per starter equals $20; and if the initial $660,000 were invested at 20 percent, its value at the end of 212 months would be exactly equal to the value of the investment in new customers, at the end of the same time period. In other words, the rate of return on this investment is 20 percent.

OK, now let's relate the present value concept to ROP. If in order to take the time value of money into account we first select a discount rate and then calculate

EXHIBIT 33-3

Discount Rate>	30.00%

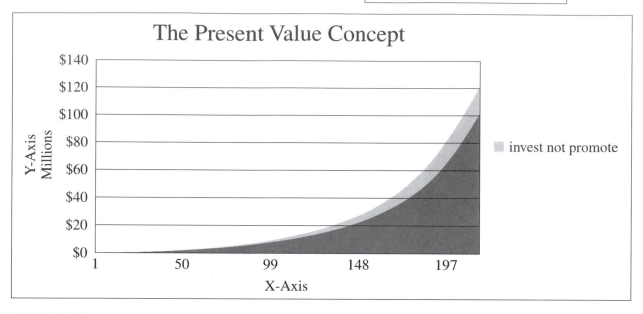

The Present Value Concept

Y-Axis Millions — X-Axis

■ invest not promote

Mailed	1,000	cpm	$660,000	<investment			
Response	33	$660	$20.00	<cpo			
Orders	33,000			ROP	Discount Rate>	30.00%	
Attrition	97.00%	Lifetime Value		−15.15%			
Buy Rate	25.00%	Per Str	Per Str		Cash Flow from		
Margin	37.33520%	$31.06	$16.97		Invest at Dis Rte	PV>	($99,977)
Price	$10.00	$1,025,057	$560,023	$465,034	$123,880,628	$105,115,163	$105,115,163
Col (1)	Col (2)	Col (3)	Col (4)	Col (5)	Col (6)	Col (7)	Col (8)
Months	Customers	Contrib	Cum PM		$660,000	$0	
1	33,000	$30,802	$30,050	$30,050	$676,500	$30,802	$5,640,376
2	32,010	$29,877	$58,488	$28,438	$693,413	$61,449	$5,337,721
3	31,050	$28,981	$85,400	$26,912	$710,748	$91,966	$5,051,307
4	30,118	$28,112	$110,868	$25,468	$728,517	$122,377	$4,780,261
5	29,215	$27,268	$134,969	$24,101	$746,729	$152,705	$4,523,759
6	28,338	$26,450	$157,777	$22,808	$765,398	$182,973	$4,281,021
7	27,488	$25,657	$179,361	$21,584	$784,533	$213,204	$4,051,308
8	26,663	$24,887	$199,787	$20,426	$804,146	$243,422	$3,833,921
9	25,864	$24,141	$219,117	$19,330	$824,250	$273,648	$3,628,198
10	25,088	$23,416	$237,410	$18,293	$844,856	$303,905	$3,433,514
11	24,335	$22,714	$254,721	$17,311	$865,977	$334,216	$3,249,277
12	23,605	$22,032	$271,104	$16,382	$887,627	$364,604	$3,074,925
13	22,897	$21,371	$286,607	$15,503	$909,817	$395,091	$2,909,929
14	22,210	$20,730	$301,278	$14,671	$932,563	$425,698	$2,753,787
15	21,544	$20,108	$315,162	$13,884	$955,877	$456,449	$2,606,023
16	20,897	$19,505	$328,302	$13,139	$979,774	$487,365	$2,466,187
17	20,270	$18,920	$340,736	$12,434	$1,004,268	$518,470	$2,333,855
18	19,662	$18,352	$352,503	$11,767	$1,029,375	$549,784	$2,208,624
19	19,072	$17,802	$363,638	$11,136	$1,055,109	$581,330	$2,090,113
20	18,500	$17,268	$374,176	$10,538	$1,081,487	$613,131	$1,977,960
21	17,945	$16,750	$384,149	$9,973	$1,108,524	$645,209	$1,871,826
22	17,407	$16,247	$393,586	$9,437	$1,136,237	$677,586	$1,771,386
23	16,885	$15,760	$402,517	$8,931	$1,164,643	$710,286	$1,676,336
24	16,378	$15,287	$410,969	$8,452	$1,193,759	$743,330	$1,586,387

EXHIBIT 33–3 (continued)

Mailed	1,000	cpm	$660,000 <investment				
Response	33	$660	$20.00 <cpo				
Orders	33,000			ROP	Discount Rate>		30.00%
Attrition	97.00%	Lifetime Value		−15.15%			
Buy Rate	25.00%	Per Str	Per Str		Cash Flow from		
Margin	37.33520%	$31.06	$16.97		Invest at Dis Rte	PV>	($99,977)
Price	$10.00	$1,025,057	$560,023	$465,034	$123,880,628	$105,115,163	$105,115,163
Col (1)	Col (2)	Col (3)	Col (4)	Col (5)	Col (6)	Col (7)	Col (8)
Months	Customers	Contrib	Cum PM		$660,000	$0	
25	15,887	$14,828	$418,967	$7,998	$1,223,603	$776,742	$1,501,263
26	15,410	$14,384	$426,536	$7,569	$1,254,193	$810,544	$1,420,708
27	14,948	$13,952	$433,699	$7,163	$1,285,548	$844,759	$1,344,475
28	14,499	$13,533	$440,478	$6,779	$1,317,687	$879,412	$1,272,332
29	14,064	$13,127	$446,893	$6,415	$1,350,629	$914,525	$1,204,061
30	13,643	$12,734	$452,963	$6,071	$1,384,395	$950,121	$1,139,453
31	13,233	$12,352	$458,708	$5,745	$1,419,004	$986,226	$1,078,311
32	12,836	$11,981	$464,145	$5,437	$1,454,480	$1,022,863	$1,020,451
33	12,451	$11,622	$469,290	$5,145	$1,490,842	$1,060,056	$965,695
34	12,078	$11,273	$474,159	$4,869	$1,528,113	$1,097,830	$913,877
35	11,715	$10,935	$478,766	$4,608	$1,566,315	$1,136,211	$864,840
36	11,364	$10,607	$483,127	$4,360	$1,605,473	$1,175,223	$818,434
37	11,023	$10,289	$487,253	$4,126	$1,645,610	$1,214,892	$774,518
38	10,692	$9,980	$491,158	$3,905	$1,686,750	$1,255,244	$732,958
39	10,371	$9,681	$494,854	$3,695	$1,728,919	$1,296,306	$693,629
40	10,060	$9,390	$498,351	$3,497	$1,772,142	$1,338,104	$656,410
41	9,759	$9,108	$501,660	$3,310	$1,816,446	$1,380,665	$621,188
42	9,466	$8,835	$504,792	$3,132	$1,861,857	$1,424,017	$587,856
43	9,182	$8,570	$507,756	$2,964	$1,908,403	$1,468,187	$556,312
44	8,906	$8,313	$510,561	$2,805	$1,956,113	$1,513,205	$526,461
45	8,639	$8,064	$513,215	$2,654	$2,005,016	$1,559,098	$498,212
46	8,380	$7,822	$515,727	$2,512	$2,055,142	$1,605,898	$471,479
47	8,129	$7,587	$518,104	$2,377	$2,106,520	$1,653,632	$446,180
48	7,885	$7,359	$520,354	$2,250	$2,159,183	$1,702,332	$422,239
49	7,648	$7,139	$522,483	$2,129	$2,213,163	$1,752,029	$399,582
50	7,419	$6,924	$524,497	$2,015	$2,268,492	$1,802,754	$378,141
51	7,196	$6,717	$526,404	$1,907	$2,325,204	$1,854,540	$357,850
52	6,980	$6,515	$528,208	$1,804	$2,383,334	$1,907,419	$338,649
53	6,771	$6,320	$529,916	$1,707	$2,442,918	$1,961,424	$320,477
54	6,568	$6,130	$531,531	$1,616	$2,503,990	$2,016,590	$303,281
55	6,371	$5,946	$533,060	$1,529	$2,566,590	$2,072,951	$287,007
56	6,180	$5,768	$534,507	$1,447	$2,630,755	$2,130,543	$271,607
57	5,994	$5,595	$535,877	$1,369	$2,696,524	$2,189,401	$257,033
58	5,814	$5,427	$537,173	$1,296	$2,763,937	$2,249,563	$243,241
59	5,640	$5,264	$538,399	$1,226	$2,833,035	$2,311,066	$230,189
60	5,471	$5,106	$539,560	$1,161	$2,903,861	$2,373,949	$217,837
61	5,307	$4,953	$540,658	$1,098	$2,976,458	$2,438,251	$206,148
62	5,147	$4,805	$541,697	$1,039	$3,050,869	$2,504,012	$195,087
63	4,993	$4,660	$542,681	$984	$3,127,141	$2,571,272	$184,619
64	4,843	$4,521	$543,612	$931	$3,205,319	$2,640,075	$174,712
65	4,698	$4,385	$544,493	$881	$3,285,452	$2,710,462	$165,338
66	4,557	$4,253	$545,326	$834	$3,367,589	$2,782,477	$156,466
67	4,420	$4,126	$546,115	$789	$3,451,778	$2,856,164	$148,070
68	4,288	$4,002	$546,862	$747	$3,538,073	$2,931,570	$140,125
69	4,159	$3,882	$547,568	$706	$3,626,525	$3,008,742	$132,606

EXHIBIT 33-3 *(continued)*

Mailed	1,000	cpm	$660,000 <investment				
Response	33	$660	$20.00 <cpo				
Orders	33,000			ROP	Discount Rate>	30.00%	
Attrition	97.00%	Lifetime Value		−15.15%			
Buy Rate	25.00%	Per Str	Per Str		Cash Flow from		
Margin	37.33520%	$31.06	$16.97		Invest at Dis Rte	PV>	($99,977)
Price	$10.00	$1,025,057	$560,023	$465,034	$123,880,628	$105,115,163	$105,115,163
Col (1)	Col (2)	Col (3)	Col (4)	Col (5)	Col (6)	Col (7)	Col (8)
Months	Customers	Contrib	Cum PM		$660,000	$0	
70	4,034	$3,765	$548,237	$669	$3,717,188	$3,087,726	$125,491
71	3,913	$3,653	$548,869	$633	$3,810,118	$3,168,571	$118,757
72	3,796	$3,543	$549,468	$599	$3,905,371	$3,251,329	$112,385
73	3,682	$3,437	$550,035	$567	$4,003,005	$3,336,048	$106,354
74	3,571	$3,334	$550,571	$536	$4,103,080	$3,422,783	$100,647
75	3,464	$3,234	$551,078	$507	$4,205,657	$3,511,586	$95,247
76	3,360	$3,137	$551,559	$480	$4,310,798	$3,602,513	$90,136
77	3,260	$3,042	$552,013	$454	$4,418,568	$3,695,618	$85,299
78	3,162	$2,951	$552,443	$430	$4,529,032	$3,790,959	$80,722
79	3,067	$2,863	$552,850	$407	$4,642,258	$3,888,596	$76,391
80	2,975	$2,777	$553,235	$385	$4,758,315	$3,988,588	$72,292
81	2,886	$2,693	$553,600	$364	$4,877,273	$4,090,996	$68,413
82	2,799	$2,613	$553,945	$345	$4,999,204	$4,195,883	$64,742
83	2,715	$2,534	$554,271	$326	$5,124,185	$4,303,315	$61,268
84	2,634	$2,458	$554,580	$309	$5,252,289	$4,413,356	$57,980
85	2,555	$2,385	$554,872	$292	$5,383,596	$4,526,074	$54,869
86	2,478	$2,313	$555,149	$277	$5,518,186	$4,641,539	$51,925
87	2,404	$2,244	$555,411	$262	$5,656,141	$4,759,821	$49,139
88	2,332	$2,176	$555,659	$248	$5,797,544	$4,880,993	$46,502
89	2,262	$2,111	$555,893	$234	$5,942,483	$5,005,129	$44,007
90	2,194	$2,048	$556,115	$222	$6,091,045	$5,132,305	$41,646
91	2,128	$1,986	$556,325	$210	$6,243,321	$5,262,599	$39,411
92	2,064	$1,927	$556,524	$199	$6,399,404	$5,396,090	$37,296
93	2,002	$1,869	$556,712	$188	$6,559,389	$5,532,861	$35,295
94	1,942	$1,813	$556,890	$178	$6,723,374	$5,672,996	$33,401
95	1,884	$1,758	$557,058	$168	$6,891,459	$5,816,579	$31,609
96	1,827	$1,706	$557,217	$159	$7,063,745	$5,963,699	$29,913
97	1,773	$1,654	$557,368	$151	$7,240,339	$6,114,446	$28,308
98	1,719	$1,605	$557,511	$143	$7,421,347	$6,268,912	$26,789
99	1,668	$1,557	$557,646	$135	$7,606,881	$6,427,191	$25,351
100	1,618	$1,510	$557,774	$128	$7,797,053	$6,589,381	$23,991
101	1,569	$1,465	$557,895	$121	$7,991,979	$6,755,580	$22,704
102	1,522	$1,421	$558,009	$114	$8,191,779	$6,925,891	$21,485
103	1,476	$1,378	$558,118	$108	$8,396,573	$7,100,416	$20,332
104	1,432	$1,337	$558,220	$103	$8,606,487	$7,279,263	$19,241
105	1,389	$1,297	$558,317	$97	$8,821,650	$7,462,542	$18,209
106	1,348	$1,258	$558,409	$92	$9,042,191	$7,650,363	$17,232
107	1,307	$1,220	$558,496	$87	$9,268,246	$7,842,842	$16,307
108	1,268	$1,183	$558,578	$82	$9,499,952	$8,040,096	$15,432
109	1,230	$1,148	$558,656	$78	$9,737,451	$8,242,247	$14,604
110	1,193	$1,114	$558,729	$74	$9,980,887	$8,449,416	$13,821
111	1,157	$1,080	$558,799	$70	$10,230,409	$8,661,732	$13,079
112	1,122	$1,048	$558,865	$66	$10,486,169	$8,879,323	$12,377
113	1,089	$1,016	$558,927	$62	$10,748,323	$9,102,322	$11,713
114	1,056	$986	$558,986	$59	$11,017,031	$9,330,866	$11,085

E X H I B I T   33-3 *(continued)*

Mailed	1,000	cpm	$660,000 <investment				
Response	33	$660	$20.00 <cpo				
Orders	33,000			ROP	Discount Rate>	30.00%	
Attrition	97.00%	Lifetime Value		−15.15%			
Buy Rate	25.00%	Per Str	Per Str		Cash Flow from		
Margin	37.33520%	$31.06	$16.97		Invest at Dis Rte	PV>	($99,977)
Price	$10.00	$1,025,057	$560,023	$465,034	$123,880,628	$105,115,163	$105,115,163
Col (1)	Col (2)	Col (3)	Col (4)	Col (5)	Col (6)	Col (7)	Col (8)
Months	Customers	Contrib	Cum PM		$660,000	$0	
115	1,024	$956	$559,042	$56	$11,292,457	$9,565,094	$10,490
116	994	$928	$559,095	$53	$11,574,769	$9,805,149	$9,927
117	964	$900	$559,145	$50	$11,864,138	$10,051,177	$9,394
118	935	$873	$559,193	$47	$12,160,741	$10,303,329	$8,890
119	907	$847	$559,237	$45	$12,464,760	$10,561,759	$8,413
120	880	$821	$559,280	$42	$12,776,379	$10,826,624	$7,962
121	853	$796	$559,320	$40	$13,095,788	$11,098,086	$7,534
122	828	$773	$559,358	$38	$13,423,183	$11,376,311	$7,130
123	803	$749	$559,394	$36	$13,758,763	$11,661,468	$6,748
124	779	$727	$559,428	$34	$14,102,732	$11,953,732	$6,386
125	755	$705	$559,460	$32	$14,455,300	$12,253,280	$6,043
126	733	$684	$559,491	$30	$14,816,683	$12,560,296	$5,719
127	711	$663	$559,520	$29	$15,187,100	$12,874,967	$5,412
128	689	$644	$559,547	$27	$15,566,777	$13,197,485	$5,121
129	669	$624	$559,573	$26	$15,955,946	$13,528,046	$4,847
130	649	$606	$559,597	$24	$16,354,845	$13,866,853	$4,587
131	629	$587	$559,620	$23	$16,763,716	$14,214,112	$4,340
132	610	$570	$559,642	$22	$17,182,809	$14,570,034	$4,108
133	592	$553	$559,663	$21	$17,612,379	$14,934,838	$3,887
134	574	$536	$559,682	$20	$18,052,689	$15,308,745	$3,679
135	557	$520	$559,701	$19	$18,504,006	$15,691,983	$3,481
136	540	$504	$559,718	$18	$18,966,606	$16,084,787	$3,294
137	524	$489	$559,735	$17	$19,440,771	$16,487,396	$3,118
138	508	$475	$559,751	$16	$19,926,791	$16,900,056	$2,950
139	493	$460	$559,766	$15	$20,424,960	$17,323,017	$2,792
140	478	$447	$559,780	$14	$20,935,584	$17,756,539	$2,642
141	464	$433	$559,793	$13	$21,458,974	$18,200,886	$2,500
142	450	$420	$559,806	$13	$21,995,448	$18,656,328	$2,366
143	437	$408	$559,818	$12	$22,545,335	$19,123,144	$2,239
144	424	$395	$559,829	$11	$23,108,968	$19,601,618	$2,119
145	411	$383	$559,840	$11	$23,686,692	$20,092,042	$2,005
146	398	$372	$559,850	$10	$24,278,860	$20,594,715	$1,898
147	387	$361	$559,859	$10	$24,885,831	$21,109,943	$1,796
148	375	$350	$559,868	$9	$25,507,977	$21,638,042	$1,700
149	364	$339	$559,877	$9	$26,145,676	$22,179,333	$1,608
150	353	$329	$559,885	$8	$26,799,318	$22,734,145	$1,522
151	342	$319	$559,893	$8	$27,469,301	$23,302,818	$1,440
152	332	$310	$559,900	$7	$28,156,034	$23,885,698	$1,363
153	322	$301	$559,907	$7	$28,859,934	$24,483,141	$1,290
154	312	$292	$559,913	$7	$29,581,433	$25,095,511	$1,221
155	303	$283	$559,919	$6	$30,320,969	$25,723,182	$1,155
156	294	$274	$559,925	$6	$31,078,993	$26,366,536	$1,093
157	285	$266	$559,931	$6	$31,855,968	$27,025,965	$1,035
158	276	$258	$559,936	$5	$32,652,367	$27,701,872	$979
159	268	$250	$559,941	$5	$33,468,676	$28,394,670	$927

EXHIBIT 33-3 *(continued)*

Mailed	1,000	cpm	$660,000 <investment				
Response	33	$660	$20.00 <cpo				
Orders	33,000			ROP	Discount Rate>	30.00%	
Attrition	97.00%	Lifetime Value		−15.15%			
Buy Rate	25.00%	Per Str	Per Str		Cash Flow from		
Margin	37.33520%	$31.06	$16.97		Invest at Dis Rte	PV>	($99,977)
Price	$10.00	$1,025,057	$560,023	$465,034	$123,880,628	$105,115,163	$105,115,163
Col (1)	Col (2)	Col (3)	Col (4)	Col (5)	Col (6)	Col (7)	Col (8)
Months	Customers	Contrib	Cum PM		$660,000	$0	
160	260	$243	$559,946	$5	$34,305,393	$29,104,779	$877
161	252	$236	$559,950	$4	$35,163,028	$29,832,634	$830
162	245	$228	$559,954	$4	$36,042,103	$30,578,678	$785
163	237	$222	$559,958	$4	$36,943,158	$31,343,367	$743
164	230	$215	$559,962	$4	$37,866,735	$32,127,166	$703
165	223	$209	$559,965	$4	$38,813,403	$32,930,554	$666
166	217	$202	$559,969	$3	$39,783,738	$33,754,020	$630
167	210	$196	$559,972	$3	$40,778,332	$34,598,067	$596
168	204	$190	$559,975	$3	$41,797,790	$35,463,209	$564
169	198	$185	$559,978	$3	$42,842,735	$36,349,973	$534
170	192	$179	$559,981	$3	$43,913,803	$37,258,902	$505
171	186	$174	$559,983	$3	$45,011,648	$38,190,548	$478
172	181	$168	$559,985	$2	$46,136,940	$39,145,480	$452
173	175	$163	$559,988	$2	$47,290,363	$40,124,281	$428
174	170	$159	$559,990	$2	$48,472,622	$41,127,546	$405
175	165	$154	$559,992	$2	$49,684,438	$42,155,889	$383
176	160	$149	$559,994	$2	$50,926,549	$43,209,935	$363
177	155	$145	$559,996	$2	$52,199,712	$44,290,328	$343
178	150	$140	$559,997	$2	$53,504,705	$45,397,727	$325
179	146	$136	$559,999	$2	$54,842,323	$46,532,806	$307
180	141	$132	$560,001	$2	$56,213,381	$47,696,258	$291
181	137	$128	$560,002	$1	$57,618,715	$48,888,793	$275
182	133	$124	$560,004	$1	$59,059,183	$50,111,137	$261
183	129	$121	$560,005	$1	$60,535,663	$51,364,036	$247
184	125	$117	$560,006	$1	$62,049,054	$52,648,253	$233
185	121	$113	$560,007	$1	$63,600,281	$53,964,573	$221
186	118	$110	$560,008	$1	$65,190,288	$55,313,797	$209
187	114	$107	$560,009	$1	$66,820,045	$56,696,749	$198
188	111	$103	$560,010	$1	$68,490,546	$58,114,271	$187
189	108	$100	$560,011	$1	$70,202,810	$59,567,228	$177
190	104	$97	$560,012	$1	$71,957,880	$61,056,506	$168
191	101	$94	$560,013	$1	$73,756,827	$62,583,014	$159
192	98	$92	$560,014	$1	$75,600,748	$64,147,680	$150
193	95	$89	$560,015	$1	$77,490,766	$65,751,461	$142
194	92	$86	$560,015	$1	$79,428,036	$67,395,334	$134
195	90	$84	$560,016	$1	$81,413,736	$69,080,301	$127
196	87	$81	$560,017	$1	$83,449,080	$70,807,390	$120
197	84	$79	$560,017	$1	$85,535,307	$72,577,653	$114
198	82	$76	$560,018	$1	$87,673,690	$74,392,171	$108
199	79	$74	$560,018	$1	$89,865,532	$76,252,049	$102
200	77	$72	$560,019	$1	$92,112,170	$78,158,422	$97
201	75	$70	$560,019	$0	$94,414,974	$80,112,452	$91
202	72	$68	$560,020	$0	$96,775,349	$82,115,331	$86
203	70	$66	$560,020	$0	$99,194,732	$84,168,280	$82
204	68	$64	$560,021	$0	$101,674,601	$86,272,551	$77

EXHIBIT 33–3 *(continued)*

Mailed	1,000	cpm	$660,000 <investment				
Response	33	$660	$20.00 <cpo				
Orders	33,000			ROP	Discount Rate>	30.00%	
Attrition	97.00%	Lifetime Value		−15.15%			
Buy Rate	25.00%	Per Str	Per Str		Cash Flow from		
Margin	37.33520%	$31.06	$16.97		Invest at Dis Rte	PV>	($99,977)
Price	$10.00	$1,025,057	$560,023	$465,034	$123,880,628	$105,115,163	$105,115,163
Col (1)	Col (2)	Col (3)	Col (4)	Col (5)	Col (6)	Col (7)	Col (8)
Months	Customers	Contrib	Cum PM			$660,000	$0
205	66	$62	$560,021	$0	$104,216,466	$88,429,426	$73
206	64	$60	$560,021	$0	$106,821,877	$90,640,221	$69
207	62	$58	$560,022	$0	$109,492,424	$92,906,285	$66
208	60	$56	$560,022	$0	$112,229,735	$95,228,998	$62
209	58	$55	$560,022	$0	$115,035,478	$97,609,778	$59
210	57	$53	$560,023	$0	$117,911,365	$100,050,075	$56
211	55	$51	$560,023	$0	$120,859,149	$102,551,379	$53

the present value per starter, we can compare this number with the cost per starter. If the present value per starter is equal to the cost per starter, the ROP equation would show at a rate of return of 0 percent. For example, if using a discount rate of 20 percent we determine that the present value per starter is $20 and the cost per order is also $20, then the ROP would be ($20 − $20)/$20 = 0/$20 = 0. So how can the ROP equal 0 percent when the rate of return that discounts future flows back to the cost of the investment is 20 percent? The answer is that while both concepts use similar words, the concepts are related but different.

We'll use Table 33–13 to help explain the differences.

The four investments shown in Table 33–13 are identical. In each case, an investment of $30,000 results in a cash flow of $12,000 received in each of the following 10 years. The nondiscounted net cash flow is therefore equal to $90,000 ($12,000*10 − $30,000). The internal rate of return, the discount rate which when applied to the cash inflows would yield a present value of $30,000, is 38.45 percent. The nondiscounted ROP is 300 percent [(12,0000 − 30,000)/30,000]. So far so good. Now if you wanted to evaluate these investments taking the time value of money into account, and you didn't want to use the IRR measure because of its unrealistic reinvestment characteristic, you would have to decide on an appropriate discount rate. As you can see from Table 33–13, the higher the discount rate you select, the lower the present value of the future cash inflows. By the same token, if you wanted to use the ROP equation, the higher the discount rate, the lower the ROP measure: a discount rate of 20 percent produces an ROP measure of 67.70 percent, whereas a discount rate of 40 percent yields an ROP measure of −3.46 percent. Alternatively you may choose to use the ratio of the present value of the cash inflows to the value of the investment as your measure of performance, to avoid confusion between the discount rate used and the resulting ROP percentage. Still confused? How can four investments that you know are identical be judged as different? The answer lies in the reinvestment assumption, which is reflected in the choice of the discount rate used in the calculation of the present value of the expected cash flow. If

EXHIBIT 33-4

Discount Rate>	20.00%

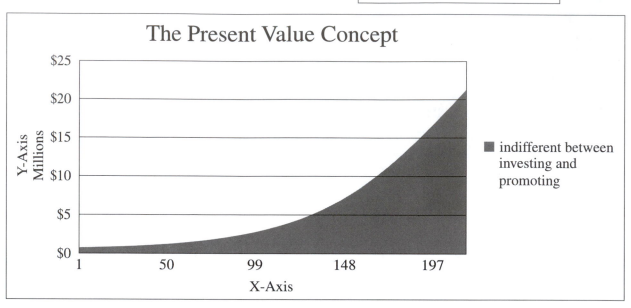

The Present Value Concept

Mailed	1,000	cpm	$660,000 <investment				
Response	33	$660	$20.00 <cpo				
Orders	33,000			ROP	Discount Rate>	20.00%	
Attrition	97.00%	Lifetime Value		0.00%			
Buy Rate	25.00%	Per Str	Per Str		Cash Flow from		
Margin	37.33520%	$31.06	$20.00		Invest at Dis Rte	PV>	$0
Price	$10.00	$1,025,057	$660,000	$365,057	$21,948,451	$21,948,463	$21,948,463
Col (1)	Col (2)	Col (3)	Col (4)	Col (5)	Col (6)	Col (7)	Col (8)
Months	Customers	Contrib	Cum PM		$660,000	$0	
1	33,000	$30,802	$30,297	$30,297	$671,000	$30,802	$1,007,520
2	32,010	$29,877	$59,203	$28,906	$682,183	$61,192	$961,273
3	31,050	$28,981	$86,782	$27,579	$693,553	$91,193	$917,149
4	30,118	$28,112	$113,095	$26,313	$705,112	$120,825	$875,051
5	29,215	$27,268	$138,200	$25,105	$716,864	$150,107	$834,884
6	28,338	$26,450	$162,153	$23,953	$728,812	$179,059	$796,562
7	27,488	$25,657	$185,007	$22,854	$740,959	$207,700	$759,998
8	26,663	$24,887	$206,811	$21,804	$753,308	$236,049	$725,113
9	25,864	$24,141	$227,615	$20,804	$765,863	$264,124	$691,829
10	25,088	$23,416	$247,463	$19,849	$778,628	$291,942	$660,073
11	24,335	$22,714	$266,401	$18,938	$791,605	$319,522	$629,775
12	23,605	$22,032	$284,469	$18,068	$804,798	$346,880	$600,867
13	22,897	$21,371	$301,708	$17,239	$818,211	$374,032	$573,286
14	22,210	$20,730	$318,156	$16,448	$831,848	$400,996	$546,972
15	21,544	$20,108	$333,849	$15,693	$845,712	$427,788	$521,865
16	20,897	$19,505	$348,821	$14,972	$859,808	$454,423	$497,910
17	20,270	$18,920	$363,106	$14,285	$874,138	$480,917	$475,055
18	19,662	$18,352	$376,736	$13,629	$888,707	$507,284	$453,249
19	19,072	$17,802	$389,740	$13,004	$903,518	$533,541	$432,445
20	18,500	$17,268	$402,146	$12,407	$918,577	$559,701	$412,595
21	17,945	$16,750	$413,984	$11,837	$933,887	$585,779	$393,656
22	17,407	$16,247	$425,278	$11,294	$949,452	$611,789	$375,586
23	16,885	$15,760	$436,054	$10,776	$965,276	$637,745	$358,346
24	16,378	$15,287	$446,335	$10,281	$981,364	$663,661	$341,898

EXHIBIT 33–4 (continued)

Mailed	1,000	cpm	$660,000 <investment				
Response	33	$660	$20.00 <cpo				
Orders	33,000			ROP	Discount Rate>	20.00%	
Attrition	97.00%	Lifetime Value		0.00%			
Buy Rate	25.00%	Per Str	Per Str		Cash Flow from		
Margin	37.33520%	$31.06	$20.00		Invest at Dis Rte	PV>	$0
Price	$10.00	$1,025,057	$660,000	$365,057	$21,948,451	$21,948,463	$21,948,463
Col (1)	Col (2)	Col (3)	Col (4)	Col (5)	Col (6)	Col (7)	Col (8)
Months	Customers	Contrib	Cum PM		$660,000	$0	
25	15,887	$14,828	$456,144	$9,809	$997,720	$689,551	$326,204
26	15,410	$14,384	$465,503	$9,359	$1,014,348	$715,427	$311,231
27	14,948	$13,952	$474,432	$8,929	$1,031,254	$741,303	$296,945
28	14,499	$13,533	$482,951	$8,519	$1,048,442	$767,191	$283,315
29	14,064	$13,127	$491,080	$8,128	$1,065,916	$793,105	$270,310
30	13,643	$12,734	$498,835	$7,755	$1,083,681	$819,057	$257,902
31	13,233	$12,352	$506,234	$7,399	$1,101,742	$845,060	$246,064
32	12,836	$11,981	$513,294	$7,060	$1,120,105	$871,125	$234,769
33	12,451	$11,622	$520,029	$6,736	$1,138,773	$897,266	$223,993
34	12,078	$11,273	$526,456	$6,426	$1,157,753	$923,493	$213,711
35	11,715	$10,935	$532,587	$6,131	$1,177,049	$949,820	$203,902
36	11,364	$10,607	$538,437	$5,850	$1,196,666	$976,257	$194,542
37	11,023	$10,289	$544,019	$5,581	$1,216,611	$1,002,816	$185,612
38	10,692	$9,980	$549,344	$5,325	$1,236,887	$1,029,510	$177,093
39	10,371	$9,681	$554,425	$5,081	$1,257,502	$1,056,349	$168,964
40	10,060	$9,390	$559,272	$4,848	$1,278,461	$1,083,345	$161,208
41	9,759	$9,108	$563,897	$4,625	$1,299,768	$1,110,509	$153,808
42	9,466	$8,835	$568,310	$4,413	$1,321,431	$1,137,852	$146,748
43	9,182	$8,570	$572,520	$4,210	$1,343,455	$1,165,387	$140,012
44	8,906	$8,313	$576,537	$4,017	$1,365,846	$1,193,123	$133,585
45	8,639	$8,064	$580,370	$3,833	$1,388,610	$1,221,072	$127,454
46	8,380	$7,822	$584,027	$3,657	$1,411,753	$1,249,245	$121,603
47	8,129	$7,587	$587,515	$3,489	$1,435,283	$1,277,652	$116,022
48	7,885	$7,359	$590,844	$3,329	$1,459,204	$1,306,306	$110,696
49	7,648	$7,139	$594,020	$3,176	$1,483,524	$1,335,216	$105,615
50	7,419	$6,924	$597,050	$3,030	$1,508,249	$1,364,394	$100,767
51	7,196	$6,717	$599,941	$2,891	$1,533,387	$1,393,851	$96,142
52	6,980	$6,515	$602,699	$2,758	$1,558,943	$1,423,597	$91,729
53	6,771	$6,320	$605,331	$2,632	$1,584,926	$1,453,644	$87,518
54	6,568	$6,130	$607,842	$2,511	$1,611,341	$1,484,001	$83,501
55	6,371	$5,946	$610,238	$2,396	$1,638,197	$1,514,681	$79,668
56	6,180	$5,768	$612,523	$2,286	$1,665,500	$1,545,693	$76,011
57	5,994	$5,595	$614,704	$2,181	$1,693,258	$1,577,050	$72,522
58	5,814	$5,427	$616,785	$2,081	$1,721,479	$1,608,761	$69,193
59	5,640	$5,264	$618,770	$1,985	$1,750,171	$1,640,838	$66,017
60	5,471	$5,106	$620,664	$1,894	$1,779,340	$1,673,292	$62,987
61	5,307	$4,953	$622,471	$1,807	$1,808,996	$1,706,133	$60,096
62	5,147	$4,805	$624,195	$1,724	$1,839,146	$1,739,373	$57,337
63	4,993	$4,660	$625,840	$1,645	$1,869,798	$1,773,023	$54,705
64	4,843	$4,521	$627,410	$1,570	$1,900,962	$1,807,094	$52,194
65	4,698	$4,385	$628,907	$1,497	$1,932,644	$1,841,597	$49,798
66	4,557	$4,253	$630,336	$1,429	$1,964,855	$1,876,544	$47,513
67	4,420	$4,126	$631,699	$1,363	$1,997,603	$1,911,945	$45,332
68	4,288	$4,002	$633,000	$1,301	$2,030,896	$1,947,813	$43,251
69	4,159	$3,882	$634,241	$1,241	$2,064,744	$1,984,158	$41,266

EXHIBIT 33–4 *(continued)*

Mailed	1,000	cpm	$660,000 <investment				
Response	33	$660	$20.00 <cpo				
Orders	33,000			ROP	Discount Rate>	20.00%	
Attrition	97.00%	Lifetime Value		0.00%			
Buy Rate	25.00%	Per Str	Per Str		Cash Flow from		
Margin	37.33520%	$31.06	$20.00		Invest at Dis Rte	PV>	$0
Price	$10.00	$1,025,057	$660,000	$365,057	$21,948,451	$21,948,463	$21,948,463
Col (1)	Col (2)	Col (3)	Col (4)	Col (5)	Col (6)	Col (7)	Col (8)
Months	Customers	Contrib	Cum PM		$660,000	$0	
70	4,034	$3,765	$635,424	$1,184	$2,099,157	$2,020,993	$39,371
71	3,913	$3,653	$636,554	$1,130	$2,134,143	$2,058,329	$37,564
72	3,796	$3,543	$637,632	$1,078	$2,169,712	$2,096,177	$35,840
73	3,682	$3,437	$638,660	$1,028	$2,205,874	$2,134,550	$34,195
74	3,571	$3,334	$639,641	$981	$2,242,638	$2,173,460	$32,625
75	3,464	$3,234	$640,577	$936	$2,280,015	$2,212,918	$31,128
76	3,360	$3,137	$641,470	$893	$2,318,016	$2,252,936	$29,699
77	3,260	$3,042	$642,322	$852	$2,356,649	$2,293,527	$28,336
78	3,162	$2,951	$643,135	$813	$2,395,927	$2,334,704	$27,035
79	3,067	$2,863	$643,911	$776	$2,435,859	$2,376,479	$25,794
80	2,975	$2,777	$644,651	$740	$2,476,457	$2,418,863	$24,610
81	2,886	$2,693	$645,357	$706	$2,517,731	$2,461,871	$23,480
82	2,799	$2,613	$646,031	$674	$2,559,693	$2,505,515	$22,403
83	2,715	$2,534	$646,673	$643	$2,602,355	$2,549,808	$21,374
84	2,634	$2,458	$647,287	$613	$2,645,727	$2,594,763	$20,393
85	2,555	$2,385	$647,872	$585	$2,689,823	$2,640,393	$19,457
86	2,478	$2,313	$648,430	$558	$2,734,653	$2,686,713	$18,564
87	2,404	$2,244	$648,962	$533	$2,780,230	$2,733,735	$17,712
88	2,332	$2,176	$649,471	$508	$2,826,568	$2,781,474	$16,899
89	2,262	$2,111	$649,955	$485	$2,873,677	$2,829,942	$16,123
90	2,194	$2,048	$650,418	$463	$2,921,572	$2,879,156	$15,383
91	2,128	$1,986	$650,859	$441	$2,970,265	$2,929,128	$14,677
92	2,064	$1,927	$651,280	$421	$3,019,769	$2,979,873	$14,003
93	2,002	$1,869	$651,682	$402	$3,070,098	$3,031,407	$13,361
94	1,942	$1,813	$652,066	$383	$3,121,267	$3,083,743	$12,747
95	1,884	$1,758	$652,431	$366	$3,173,288	$3,136,897	$12,162
96	1,827	$1,706	$652,780	$349	$3,226,176	$3,190,884	$11,604
97	1,773	$1,654	$653,113	$333	$3,279,946	$3,245,720	$11,071
98	1,719	$1,605	$653,431	$318	$3,334,611	$3,301,420	$10,563
99	1,668	$1,557	$653,734	$303	$3,390,188	$3,358,001	$10,078
100	1,618	$1,510	$654,023	$289	$3,446,691	$3,415,477	$9,616
101	1,569	$1,465	$654,299	$276	$3,504,136	$3,473,867	$9,174
102	1,522	$1,421	$654,562	$263	$3,562,539	$3,533,185	$8,753
103	1,476	$1,378	$654,813	$251	$3,621,914	$3,593,450	$8,351
104	1,432	$1,337	$655,053	$240	$3,682,279	$3,654,678	$7,968
105	1,389	$1,297	$655,281	$229	$3,743,651	$3,716,885	$7,602
106	1,348	$1,258	$655,499	$218	$3,806,045	$3,780,091	$7,253
107	1,307	$1,220	$655,708	$208	$3,869,479	$3,844,313	$6,920
108	1,268	$1,183	$655,906	$199	$3,933,970	$3,909,568	$6,603
109	1,230	$1,148	$656,096	$189	$3,999,536	$3,975,876	$6,300
110	1,193	$1,114	$656,276	$181	$4,066,195	$4,043,254	$6,010
111	1,157	$1,080	$656,449	$172	$4,133,965	$4,111,721	$5,735
112	1,122	$1,048	$656,613	$165	$4,202,865	$4,181,298	$5,471
113	1,089	$1,016	$656,770	$157	$4,272,912	$4,252,002	$5,220
114	1,056	$986	$656,920	$150	$4,344,128	$4,323,855	$4,981

E X H I B I T   33–4 (continued)

Mailed	1,000	cpm	$660,000	<investment			
Response	33	$660	$20.00	<cpo			
Orders	33,000			ROP	Discount Rate>	20.00%	
Attrition	97.00%	Lifetime Value		0.00%			
Buy Rate	25.00%	Per Str	Per Str		Cash Flow from		
Margin	37.33520%	$31.06	$20.00		Invest at Dis Rte	PV>	$0
Price	$10.00	$1,025,057	$660,000	$365,057	$21,948,451	$21,948,463	$21,948,463
Col (1)	Col (2)	Col (3)	Col (4)	Col (5)	Col (6)	Col (7)	Col (8)
Months	Customers	Contrib	Cum PM		$660,000	$0	
115	1,024	$956	$657,063	$143	$4,416,530	$4,396,875	$4,752
116	994	$928	$657,199	$136	$4,490,139	$4,471,084	$4,534
117	964	$900	$657,329	$130	$4,564,974	$4,546,502	$4,326
118	935	$873	$657,453	$124	$4,641,057	$4,623,150	$4,127
119	907	$847	$657,572	$118	$4,718,408	$4,701,049	$3,938
120	880	$821	$657,685	$113	$4,797,048	$4,780,220	$3,757
121	853	$796	$657,793	$108	$4,876,999	$4,860,687	$3,585
122	828	$773	$657,895	$103	$4,958,282	$4,942,471	$3,420
123	803	$749	$657,994	$98	$5,040,920	$5,025,595	$3,263
124	779	$727	$658,087	$94	$5,124,936	$5,110,082	$3,113
125	755	$705	$658,176	$89	$5,210,351	$5,195,955	$2,970
126	733	$684	$658,262	$85	$5,297,191	$5,283,239	$2,834
127	711	$663	$658,343	$81	$5,385,477	$5,371,956	$2,704
128	689	$644	$658,421	$78	$5,475,235	$5,462,132	$2,580
129	669	$624	$658,495	$74	$5,566,489	$5,553,792	$2,461
130	649	$606	$658,565	$71	$5,659,264	$5,646,961	$2,348
131	629	$587	$658,633	$67	$5,753,585	$5,741,664	$2,241
132	610	$570	$658,697	$64	$5,849,478	$5,837,928	$2,138
133	592	$553	$658,758	$61	$5,946,969	$5,935,780	$2,040
134	574	$536	$658,817	$59	$6,046,085	$6,035,245	$1,946
135	557	$520	$658,873	$56	$6,146,853	$6,136,353	$1,857
136	540	$504	$658,926	$53	$6,249,301	$6,239,130	$1,771
137	524	$489	$658,977	$51	$6,353,456	$6,343,604	$1,690
138	508	$475	$659,025	$48	$6,459,347	$6,449,806	$1,613
139	493	$460	$659,071	$46	$6,567,003	$6,557,763	$1,539
140	478	$447	$659,115	$44	$6,676,453	$6,667,505	$1,468
141	464	$433	$659,158	$42	$6,787,727	$6,779,064	$1,401
142	450	$420	$659,198	$40	$6,900,856	$6,892,468	$1,336
143	437	$408	$659,236	$38	$7,015,870	$7,007,750	$1,275
144	424	$395	$659,273	$37	$7,132,801	$7,124,941	$1,216
145	411	$383	$659,308	$35	$7,251,681	$7,244,074	$1,161
146	398	$372	$659,341	$33	$7,372,543	$7,365,180	$1,107
147	387	$361	$659,373	$32	$7,495,418	$7,488,294	$1,056
148	375	$350	$659,403	$30	$7,620,342	$7,613,449	$1,008
149	364	$339	$659,432	$29	$7,747,348	$7,740,679	$962
150	353	$329	$659,459	$28	$7,876,470	$7,870,020	$918
151	342	$319	$659,486	$26	$8,007,745	$8,001,506	$875
152	332	$310	$659,511	$25	$8,141,207	$8,135,174	$835
153	322	$301	$659,535	$24	$8,276,894	$8,271,061	$797
154	312	$292	$659,558	$23	$8,414,842	$8,409,204	$760
155	303	$283	$659,580	$22	$8,555,089	$8,549,640	$725
156	294	$274	$659,600	$21	$8,697,674	$8,692,408	$692
157	285	$266	$659,620	$20	$8,842,635	$8,837,548	$660
158	276	$258	$659,639	$19	$8,990,013	$8,985,098	$630
159	268	$250	$659,657	$18	$9,139,846	$9,135,100	$601

E X H I B I T   33–4 *(continued)*

Mailed	1,000	cpm	$660,000 <investment				
Response	33	$660	$20.00 <cpo				
Orders	33,000			ROP	Discount Rate>	20.00%	
Attrition	97.00%	Lifetime Value		0.00%			
Buy Rate	25.00%	Per Str	Per Str		Cash Flow from		
Margin	37.33520%	$31.06	$20.00		Invest at Dis Rte	PV>	$0
Price	$10.00	$1,025,057	$660,000	$365,057	$21,948,451	$21,948,463	$21,948,463
Col (1)	Col (2)	Col (3)	Col (4)	Col (5)	Col (6)	Col (7)	Col (8)
Months	Customers	Contrib	Cum PM		$660,000	$0	
160	260	$243	$659,675	$17	$9,292,177	$9,287,595	$574
161	252	$236	$659,691	$16	$9,447,047	$9,442,623	$547
162	245	$228	$659,707	$16	$9,604,497	$9,600,229	$522
163	237	$222	$659,722	$15	$9,764,572	$9,760,454	$498
164	230	$215	$659,736	$14	$9,927,315	$9,923,343	$475
165	223	$209	$659,750	$14	$10,092,771	$10,088,941	$453
166	217	$202	$659,763	$13	$10,260,983	$10,257,292	$433
167	210	$196	$659,775	$12	$10,432,000	$10,428,443	$413
168	204	$190	$659,787	$12	$10,605,866	$10,602,441	$394
169	198	$185	$659,798	$11	$10,782,631	$10,779,333	$376
170	192	$179	$659,809	$11	$10,962,341	$10,959,168	$359
171	186	$174	$659,819	$10	$11,145,047	$11,141,994	$342
172	181	$168	$659,829	$10	$11,330,798	$11,327,862	$326
173	175	$163	$659,838	$9	$11,519,644	$11,516,824	$311
174	170	$159	$659,847	$9	$11,711,639	$11,708,929	$297
175	165	$154	$659,856	$9	$11,906,833	$11,904,232	$283
176	160	$149	$659,864	$8	$12,105,280	$12,102,785	$270
177	155	$145	$659,872	$8	$12,307,034	$12,304,643	$258
178	150	$140	$659,879	$7	$12,512,152	$12,509,860	$246
179	146	$136	$659,886	$7	$12,720,688	$12,718,494	$235
180	141	$132	$659,893	$7	$12,932,699	$12,930,601	$224
181	137	$128	$659,899	$6	$13,148,244	$13,146,239	$214
182	133	$124	$659,905	$6	$13,367,381	$13,365,467	$204
183	129	$121	$659,911	$6	$13,590,171	$13,588,346	$195
184	125	$117	$659,917	$6	$13,816,674	$13,814,935	$186
185	121	$113	$659,922	$5	$14,046,952	$14,045,297	$177
186	118	$110	$659,927	$5	$14,281,068	$14,279,496	$169
187	114	$107	$659,932	$5	$14,519,085	$14,517,594	$161
188	111	$103	$659,937	$5	$14,761,070	$14,759,657	$154
189	108	$100	$659,941	$4	$15,007,088	$15,005,752	$147
190	104	$97	$659,945	$4	$15,257,206	$15,255,945	$140
191	101	$94	$659,949	$4	$15,511,493	$15,510,305	$134
192	98	$92	$659,953	$4	$15,770,018	$15,768,902	$128
193	95	$89	$659,957	$4	$16,032,851	$16,031,806	$122
194	92	$86	$659,960	$3	$16,300,066	$16,299,089	$116
195	90	$84	$659,964	$3	$16,571,733	$16,570,824	$111
196	87	$81	$659,967	$3	$16,847,929	$16,847,085	$106
197	84	$79	$659,970	$3	$17,128,728	$17,127,949	$101
198	82	$76	$659,973	$3	$17,414,207	$17,413,491	$96
199	79	$74	$659,976	$3	$17,704,443	$17,703,790	$92
200	77	$72	$659,978	$3	$17,999,517	$17,998,925	$88
201	75	$70	$659,981	$3	$18,299,509	$18,298,977	$84
202	72	$68	$659,983	$2	$18,604,501	$18,604,027	$80
203	70	$66	$659,985	$2	$18,914,576	$18,914,160	$76
204	68	$64	$659,988	$2	$19,229,819	$19,229,459	$73

EXHIBIT 33-3 *(continued)*

Mailed	1,000	cpm		$660,000 <investment			
Response	33	$660		$20.00 <cpo			
Orders	33,000			ROP	Discount Rate>	20.00%	
Attrition	97.00%	Lifetime Value		0.00%			
Buy Rate	25.00%	Per Str	Per Str		Cash Flow from		
Margin	37.33520%	$31.06	$20.00		Invest at Dis Rte	PV>	$0
Price	$10.00	$1,025,057	$660,000	$365,057	$21,948,451	$21,948,463	$21,948,463
Col (1)	Col (2)	Col (3)	Col (4)	Col (5)	Col (6)	Col (7)	Col (8)
Months	Customers	Contrib	Cum PM		$660,000	$0	
205	66	$62	$659,990	$2	$19,550,316	$19,550,012	$69
206	64	$60	$659,992	$2	$19,876,155	$19,875,905	$66
207	62	$58	$659,994	$2	$20,207,424	$20,207,228	$63
208	60	$56	$659,995	$2	$20,544,214	$20,544,072	$60
209	58	$55	$659,997	$2	$20,886,618	$20,886,528	$57
210	57	$53	$659,999	$2	$21,234,728	$21,234,689	$55
211	55	$51	$660,000	$2	$21,588,640	$21,588,652	$52

your company can really earn 40 percent on its money, then an investment whose internal rate of return is 38.45 percent will be judged unprofitable. On the other hand, if your company earns 20 percent on other investments, then a return of 38.45 percent will appear to be very attractive.

The bottom line—if your investments result in cash flows that come in over a long period of time, more than two or three years, and if you think that alternative strategies may result in different economic lives, then you should adjust your performance measure to take the time value of money into account. Table 33–14 shows how four investments all with the same nondiscounted measures of performance appear to be equal (same investment, same total contribution), but when

TABLE 33-13

The Difference between ROP, PV, NPV, and IRR

	1	2	3	4
Investment	$30,000	$30,000	$30,000	$30,000
Discount rate	20.00%	25.00%	30.00%	40.00%
Years	10	10	10	10
Annual cash flow	$12,000	$12,000	$12,000	$12,000
Undiscounted net cash flow	$90,000	$90,000	$90,000	$90,000
Present value CF	$50,310	$42,846	$37,098	$28,963
Net PV cash flow	$20,310	$12,846	$7,098	($1,037)
IRR	38.45%	38.45%	38.45%	38.45%
ROP undiscounted	300.00%	300.00%	300.00%	300.00%
ROP discounted	67.70%	42.82%	23.66%	−3.46%
ROP Index	167.70	142.82	123.66	96.54

TABLE 33-14

Four Investments: Same Nondiscounted ROP, But Not the Same Profitability

	1	2	3	4
Investment	$30,000	$30,000	$30,000	$30,000
Discount rate	20.00%	20.00%	20.00%	20.00%
Years	10	9	8	7
Annual cash flow	$12,000	$13,333	$15,000	$17,143
Undiscounted net cash flow	$90,000	$90,000	$90,000	$90,000
Present value CF	$50,310	$53,746	$57,557	$61,793
Net PV cash flow	$20,310	$23,746	$27,557	$31,793
IRR	38.45%	42.62%	47.80%	54.41%
ROP undiscounted	300.00%	300.00%	300.00%	300.00%
ROP discounted	67.70%	79.15%	91.86%	105.98%
ROP Index	167.70	179.15	191.86	205.98

the time value of money is taken into account, it can be seen that the fourth investment is more profitable than the other three opportunities because the total contribution is received within seven years, whereas the other investments take eight to ten years to generate the same absolute contribution.

CHAPTER 34

The Role of Modeling in the New Direct Marketing

By the time this book gets to print, close to 5,000 direct marketing professionals will have attended the Direct Marketing Association's (DMA's) course in statistics and modeling. In an industry whose annual convention draws between 12,000 and 15,000 delegates, this number reflects a tremendous interest in the subject. The high level of interest in statistics is due directly to rising promotion costs and declining response rates. In light of shrinking margins many direct marketers can no longer rely on relatively simple recency, frequency, monetary value (RFM) methods to manage their house files. Nor can direct marketers afford to make their new-customer acquisition decisions based solely on the limited name selection criteria that list owners have historically made available to them.

In this chapter we focus on the role of modeling in managing a database-driven direct marketing company. We will emphasize the application and implementation of models, not the statistical techniques used to build them. We hope you have found all you care to know about statistics in the previous chapters. Some readers may choose to start with this section and bypass all or some of the statistical theory found in earlier chapters. To accommodate them we necessarily have to repeat some points made earlier in the book.

The topics covered in this chapter will include:

- The difference between forecasts, predictions, and segmentation.
- How to implement scoring models.
- The relationship between RFM models and regression models.
- The relationship between CHAID models and both RFM and regression models.
- How to use principal components analysis to model buying patterns.
- Typical modeling results.
- How to tell if you have too many or too few variables in your model.
- ZIP code models and how to evaluate them against household-level models.
- How modeling can be used in a lead conversion situation.
- The role of enhancement data in the model-building and profiling process. How to organize your marketing department around unique customer or prospect segments or both and model each segment.

THE DIFFERENCE BETWEEN SCORING MODELS AND FORECASTS

In earlier chapters of this book we focused on the regression techniques used to build scoring models. A number of critical points bear repeating:

1. These scoring models are sometimes referred to as *predictive models*, and the word *predictive* is used essentially to distinguish these models from segmentation models.

2. In segmentation models the objective is to divide persons or geographic areas into groups or clusters so the persons or areas within one cluster are similar to each other and different from persons or areas in other clusters. A characteristic of a segmentation model is the absence of a specific dependent variable—no response rate, no average order, no conversion rate, and so on. On the other hand, the presence of such a dependent variable is an essential characteristic of a predictive model.

3. The problem with the term *predictive model* is that it reasonably implies that the owner of such a model has the ability to predict some future event, such as the response rate to an upcoming mailing. Unfortunately, predictive models, at least as the term is used in direct marketing circles, do not yield this kind of forecast. The modeling techniques that you would use to forecast the average response rate to an upcoming mailing are different from the techniques you use to score your entire file in terms of each individual's expected response. Sounds confusing? It is. But this is a critical point, and it's necessary to clearly understand the difference between the predictive scoring models that are used to obtain estimates of individual response and the forecasting techniques that are used for estimating the overall response rate to an upcoming mailing. In the former case we are saying that we think the probability of, say, Bill Smith responding is 4.5 percent; in the latter case we are saying that if we mail to all of our 2 million customers, we think the average response rate will be 2 percent.

4. Another key concept to remember is that when you are building a predictive model, say a response model, you will build it on the basis of some promotion that took place in the past. That promotion had some average response rate—let's say 2 percent. That 2 percent response rate was, in turn, a function of a host of factors that will never occur in exactly the same way again: seasonality, economic conditions, delivery conditions, competitive promotions, and the like. Therefore, it stands to reason that if you build a predictive model based on a mailing that pulled 2 percent, each individual's probability of response is in some way pegged or indexed to that average 2 percent response rate.

So if Bill Smith's 4.5 percent probability of response stems from a mailing that pulled 2 percent, you would expect his probability of response to be higher than 4.5 percent when the overall response is expected to be higher than 2 percent and vice versa. Because of the importance of this distinction between overall response rates and individual predictions of response, we discuss in some detail in this chapter the techniques that you need to use when you apply a single response model to multiple mailings, all of which are expected to have different response rates.

Obtaining Forecasts of Response

As we said before, estimating the response rate to one or more future mailings is an exercise in forecasting. To make such estimates, planners resort to techniques such as time-series analysis, econometric forecasting models, expert opinion, and crystal ball gazing, anything but the kinds of models we have been discussing in this book. This is not to downplay the need for this kind of forecasting ability. In fact, the need to be able to forecast absolute levels of response is equally as important as, if not more important than, the need to be able to rank individuals in terms of their relative response rate. Not only is forecasting the absolute response level more important, but also a good estimate of total response—what would happen if the whole file or large segments of the file were mailed—is the first step in applying scoring models.

Applying Scoring Models to Forecasts

To illustrate this point, let's consider the following situation. A company has a total customer file of 2 million names. Using a simple RFM scheme, the company decides that only about 1 million names are worth mailing. In the most recent summer mailing the average response rate among these million names was 2.0 percent. The company decides to build a model based on this mailing.

Since the variable being modeled is a yes/no response variable, the proper modeling technique is logistic regression. The model is built, and each of the 1 million persons mailed is now scored such that individual estimated response rates range from 18 to 0.4 percent and the average predicted response is, as it should be, 2 percent. Now the company wants to use the model to plan its fall holiday mailing. The company would like to mail more than 1 million names, but it insists on mailing only to individuals whose predicted response rate is 1 percent or more.

To use the model in this situation the analyst would first have to obtain an independent estimate of what the response rate would be if all of the 1 million names included in the summer mailing were mailed again in the fall holiday season. Because the mailing season in question is the company's best season, we would expect the average response rate to be above 2 percent. But how much above? Nothing in the modeling done to date answers this question.

Let's assume that management supplies a forecast of 2.5 percent. That helps, but more questions still have to be answered before the file can be scored for this mailing. What about the fact of seasonality itself? Can a model based on a mailing that took place in the slow summer months be applied to a fall holiday mailing? Does this make sense? Are there customers on the file that only buy in the holiday season, which means that they would probably score low on a model built on a summer mailing? Nothing in the modeling done to date answers this question.

Let's also assume for the purpose of this exercise that we agree that the model can be used, but to be sure that we don't make any serious errors we agree to mail to anyone who purchased in the last holiday season.

Incidentally, there's nothing wrong in mixing commonsense database selections with selections based on name-scoring models. On the contrary, this process is to be encouraged. In building mailing plans, database-driven selections should be made first, and then mailings should be supplemented on the basis of scoring models, not the other way around.

The next issue to be addressed is what to do about the other million names that were not included in the model-building process. The assumption here is that these names would have done appreciably worse than 2.0 percent had they been mailed in the summer, and that they will do appreciably worse than 2.5 percent if mailed in the fall.

To use the second million names we have to ask at least two questions:

- What does management think the response rate would be if the second half of the file were sent the fall holiday mailing?
- Do the variables in the model suggest that the scoring equation would apply to names on the second half of the file as well as to names on the first half of the file?

We also have to make a couple of assumptions. Let's assume that the answer to the second question is a qualified yes, and that the expected response rate to a holiday mailing among the second half of the file is 1 percent compared with the 2.5 percent response rate expected among the first half of the file.

Table 34–1 illustrates these assumptions.

The decile analysis of the summer mailing demonstrates our ability to divide the first half of the file into 10 segments of equal size so the best 10 percent of the file has an expected response rate of 5 percent and the worst 10 percent of the file has an expected response rate of .75 percent. The first critical assumption we must make is that these relative rankings will hold up in a fall holiday mailing, which will average 2.50 percent, if the entire top half of the file is mailed. In this case the top 10 percent would now respond at the rate of 6.27 percent and the bottom 10 percent would respond at a rate of .94 percent. The requirement that names should not be mailed unless their expected response rate is greater than 1 percent means that at least some portion of the names in the tenth decile would not be mailed in the fall.

Now working on the assumption that names in the second half of the file

T A B L E 34–1

Using Models to Score Files

| Decile | First Half of File | | | Second Half of File |
	Summer Model	Index	Fall Mailing	
1	5.00%	250	6.27%	2.50%
2	3.50	175	4.39	1.75
3	2.20	110	2.76	1.10
4	1.70	85	2.13	0.85
5	1.60	80	2.01	0.80
6	1.50	75	1.88	0.75
7	1.40	70	1.75	0.70
8	1.30	65	1.63	0.65
9	1.00	50	1.25	0.50
10	0.75	38	0.94	0.38
Average	2.00	100	2.50	1.00

The model and the index is based on the summer mailing. The index is applied to the fall mailing and to the second half of the file.

can be legitimately scored with the model built on names from the top of the file, we see that about 30 percent of the names in the bottom half of the file (according to management's old selection criteria) are expected to have response rates above 1 percent. Therefore, this analysis suggests that we mail 90 percent of the originally defined top of the file and 30 percent of the originally defined bottom of the file, or a total of 1.2 million names, all of which meet the expectation of a response rate in excess of 1 percent.[1]

From this exercise it should be clear that building a response model is only one part of the final name selection process. To summarize, nearly all models are built on mailings neither to the entire file nor to random samples from the file. Therefore, the issue arises of how to score segments of the file that were not included in the model-building process. Then, as noted earlier, there is the issue of adjusting expected response rates for seasonality. A model built on a mailing that averaged a 3 percent response will yield individual probabilities of response that average 3 percent. If the mailing in question is expected to average some other rate of response, then the individual expected response rates must be adjusted to reflect this new average—if the individual estimates of response are to be used for decision-making purposes. On the other hand, if all that the model is being used for is relative ranking, then this amount of care need not be taken. In this situation the marketer will have decided in advance how many names to mail, and the only issue is to make sure that the most responsive names are selected.

Implementing Scoring Models at the Individual Level

To produce Table 34–1 all we did was use a spreadsheet to apply the results of a model we built in the past to an estimate of the expected response rate from two files. In doing so we were able to see how deeply we could mail into each file. The next question is how to use this insight to actually score individual customers. There are a couple of ways to do this. One way is to score the entire file with the response model, sort the scored file in descending order of expected response, and then divide the entire file into 10 deciles. Knowing the expected performance of each decile to the average, and having obtained a separate estimate of the overall response rate, if the entire file were to be mailed, it's easy to obtain an estimate for each person in each decile. For example, if we think the entire file, if mailed, would pull 3 percent, then each person in Decile 1, based on the index shown in Table 34–1, would have an expected response rate of 2.5 times 3 percent or 7.5 percent. To obtain finer results, instead of creating the index at the decile level, you could divide the sorted file into 20 groups or into 100 groups— the principle and the process would be the same. Another possibility is to calculate each person's score and divide that number by the average score, creating an individual-level index and applying the index to the expected average. All these methods will produce essentially the same results, and your data processing people will tell you which approach they prefer. Again, the key point to remember is not to assume that the score will be the best estimate of response for any particular promotion; the scores have to be adjusted for current conditions.

---

1. At this point you may question why any names defined by management as being in the second half of the file should be mailed before any name included in the top of the file. The assumption is that management's ability to rank names is based on some model or set of rules that is less efficient than the model we are building—that management's judgment regarding relative ranking is generally but not totally correct.

RESPONSE MODELING: RFM VERSUS REGRESSION

Up to now we've referred to RFM models and implied that we believe that regression models will do at least as well as RFM models and that they have the potential to do considerably better. It's time to devote more attention to this issue and to spell out the advantages of regression models over RFM models.

Let's assume that we are managing a catalog company with 2 million customers that have been acquired and marketed to continuously over a five-year period. Our customer file contains the following information about each of our customers:

- Date the customer first came on the file.
- Original source code—at both the detail and major media level (direct mail, print, broadcast, etc.).
- Dates of all customer purchases.
- Dollar value of each purchase associated with each purchase date.
- Total number of purchases made.
- Total dollar value of purchases.
- Major product areas in which at least one purchase was made—assume there are a dozen possible product areas.
- Total dollars spent in each product area.
- Number of times the customer has been mailed.

Suppose we wished to mail the next catalog to only 1 million customers, rather than to the entire file of 2 million. Let's further assume that the last catalog mailing went to the entire file of 2 million and that we kept a copy of the file at the time of the mailing and have since updated that file with results from the mailing. What analysis could be done—with and without statistical modeling?

The experienced direct marketer will immediately recognize all the necessary ingredients for a traditional RFM (recency, frequency, monetary value) analysis, plus the data needed to extend RFM to include product information. So for starters, we could do an RFM model. Suppose we decided to create five recency periods:

1. *Period 1.* Includes all customers whose last purchase was within 6 months of the mailing date
2. *Period 2.* Includes all customers whose last purchase was within 7 to 12 months of the mailing date
3. *Period 3.* Includes all customers whose last purchase was within 13 to 24 months of the mailing date
4. *Period 4.* Includes all customers whose last purchase was within 25 to 36 months of the mailing date
5. *Period 5.* Includes all customers whose last purchase was more than 37 months ago

Now our 2 million names would be divided into five groups, and undoubtedly we would find that the response rate to the promotion being studied would be highest among those that purchased most recently.

The next step in the RFM process is to decide how to treat frequency of purchase. The more times customers have purchased in the past, the more likely they are to purchase again. Therefore it would make sense to divide each of the five recency cells into two or more new cells, which would now reflect recency and frequency behavior. Let's arbitrarily decide that frequency should be represented by four categories:

1. One lifetime purchase
2. Two or three lifetime purchases
3. Four or five lifetime purchases
4. Six or more lifetime purchases

Note that not only is our choice of four categories arbitrary, but also the definition of each category is arbitrary. And not only are these decisions arbitrary—and therefore not necessarily optimal in any sense—but also they fail to consider such important factors related to frequency as length of time on the file or number of times mailed.

Leaving these considerations aside for the moment, let's go on with the RFM analysis. We now have 20 cells to work with (5 recency cells times 4 frequency cells). What about monetary value? It's intuitive that someone who purchased three times within any time period and whose total purchases equaled $300 is a better prospect for our next mailing than someone who also purchased three times within the same time period but whose purchases totaled only $30.

Therefore, to complete this simple RFM model (yes, RFM can be called a model) we need to decide on rules for dividing each of the 20 cells by some measure of monetary value. Assume we can agree that each cell should be split three ways, depending on the total dollars spent to date—again this rule is arbitrary. We would arrive at a final model with 60 cells, each cell of different size but averaging 33,333 customers.

Even a cursory review of the above procedure makes clear the totally arbitrary nature of RFM analysis. Why choose only five recency periods and why those five? What's more, it's clear on further reflection that a tremendous amount of data is lost in the RFM process. As mentioned above, times mailed never had a chance to enter the picture, nor did purchases per times mailed, or even the dollar value of purchases made within any time frame other than the customer's total economic life with the company. What's more, we haven't included any way to take into account the types of product(s) purchased. We could, of course, have continued dividing cells by other variables, but doing so would quickly result in a very large number of very small, difficult to manage, and statistically unusable cells.

Eliminating Arbitrary Decisions from RFM

The problems associated with the arbitrary characteristics of traditional RFM analyses can be overcome by using a technique popularized by Arthur Hughes. Hughes suggests that you rank-order the customer file three different ways, first by recency, then by frequency, and then by some measure of monetary value. In each case you divide the rank-ordered file into five groups and tag each customer with the appropriate number. At the end of the process you will have 125 segments numbered from 111 to 555. A person tagged 111 is in the top 20 percent of each ranking, a person tagged 555 is in the bottom 20 percent of each ranking, and so on. While this process is certainly not arbitrary, it still results in a lot of cells and may not provide an optimal ranking.

Tree Analyses Compared with RFM Analyses

For all these reasons, direct marketers have adopted models or techniques other than RFM. One such technique is often referred to as a *tree analysis*. Technically, tree analyses are either AID, CHAID, or CART analyses. AID stands for automatic interaction detector, and the CH in CHAID stands for the chi-square test for statistical significance. CART stands for classification and regression trees. Both AID and CHAID analyses produce trees that physically resemble the treelike structure found in a graphic presentation of an RFM model. A number of products are now available to direct marketers that wish to use these tools. SPSS offers a suite of tools in its Answer Tree product, Angoss Software has a product called Knowledge Seeker, and Statistical Innovations has a product called SI-CHAID. These products were discussed in detail in the preceding chapters that dealt with the process of model building. In this chapter we treat AID and CHAID analyses more generally.

Essentially CHAID products start off by trying to find the one independent variable that does the best job of splitting an entire mailing population and its average response rate into two or more cells or market segments so the difference between response rates is as large as possible and is statistically significant according to the chi-square test of statistical significance. This best independent variable may be a recency, frequency, or monetary value variable, or it may be any other independent variable available for analysis.

After this first split is made, the program treats each resulting cell as a brand-new analysis, and the program attempts to split each cell derived from the first split into two or more cells. Again, the program searches all the available independent variables and finds the best variable to cause a split at this point. This process continues until no more splits are possible, given the condition that each split must meet the chi-square test of statistical significance. The analyst running the program can make the significance test more or less stringent by changing confidence levels.

Many direct marketers may find a CHAID program to be a perfectly acceptable replacement for an arbitrarily defined RFM methodology, and they may stop there. Others may choose to use the insights gained from such an analysis to improve their regression models and to use the output of the tree analysis as a benchmark to measure the success of their regression models. In the next section we first discuss trees as an aid to regression, and then as benchmarks against which to measure the results of a regression model.

A Quick Review of Interaction Variables

Previously, we discussed using a tree analysis to discover interactions among independent variables. Essentially, interactions occur when two variables combine to produce an effect that is significantly greater than the sum of the effects produced by each variable acting by itself. For example, we may know that all our customers both are highly educated and have high incomes. What's more, persons with high incomes but low levels of education are not our customers, and vice versa. A regression model that contained only income and education as independent variables would not capture this interaction effect. To capture it the analyst must create a third variable, an interaction variable, which is usually done by multiplying both independent variables together to create this third variable. For example, a model that includes only income and education would look like this:

$$Y = a + b1 \text{¥ Income} + b2 \text{¥ Education}$$

A model that includes both income and education plus their interaction, on the other hand, would look like this:

$$Y = a + b1 \text{¥ Income} + b2 \text{¥ Education} + b3 \text{¥ Income ¥ Education}$$

If interaction were truly present, the latter model would be much more powerful than the model that excluded the interaction effect (a higher R^2, a better fit, etc.).

An experienced analyst looking at a tree diagram would note when certain cells appear to have exceptionally high response rates or exceptionally high sales values. When these observations are made, the analyst will test to determine whether an interaction variable should be created and possibly be included in a regression model. Users or marketers commissioning models from outside vendors should remember that the ordinary and logistic regression programs their statisticians use do not automatically look for or create interaction variables. They have to be discovered by an analyst and "manually" entered into the set of variables to be processed through the regression programs.

Trees as a Benchmark against Regression Results

In previous chapters we have argued for models that contain fewer rather than more independent variables. We certainly want to examine as many potential variables as possible, but we want our models to contain only those variables that strongly influence the variable being predicted or modeled. Most importantly, we want the model to "hold up" for as long as possible, and it's been our experience that models with a small number of relatively strong variables will hold up better than models with a larger number of relatively weak variables.

A tree analysis, particularly one in which the confidence level is reduced from the usual 95 percent to 90 percent or lower (a statistician would say the alpha level is raised from 5 percent to 10 percent or more), will produce a large number of cells or breaks and will include a relatively large number of independent variables. Some of the cells will be very small and may only contain a few individuals, all of whom can be described by some unique combination of independent variables and all or nearly all of whom have responded to the offer being measured. We can think of such a tree as an analysis that has "beaten the data to death," or, in less dramatic prose, an analysis that has taken full advantage of chance. In a sense, what such an analysis is saying is that given all the independent variables we have to work with, no finer subdivision of the data is possible at the significance level we have chosen.

Now, and this is the point of this section, if a regression model can be created that uses only a few of the variables contained in the tree, and if the regression model does nearly as well as the tree in modeling the variable under consideration, then we would feel much more confident in using the regression model than we would in using the tree analysis. In other words, we feel more confident in using a model with relatively few independent variables than we do in using a regression model with as many variables as contained in the tree or in using the tree analysis itself.

Table 34–2 shows the results of a tree analysis compared with a regression model that was created with only four independent variables. The tree contained

TABLE 34–2

Tree Analysis Compared to a Regression Model Used to Benchmark Regression Results

Seg	Number / MLD	Cum / # Mld	Cum % / MLG	Number / Rsp	Cum / # Rsp	Cum % / Rsp	Rsp / Rate	Regression Model / Cum % Rsp
46	2	2	0%	2	2	0%	100.00%	
49	2	4	0%	2	4	0%	100.00%	
1	270	274	0%	74	78	3%	27.42%	
41	52	326	0%	12	90	3%	22.93%	
3	273	599	0%	56	146	5%	20.48%	
53	72	671	0%	13	159	6%	18.04%	
16	132	803	0%	20	179	7%	15.11%	
24	88	891	0%	13	192	7%	14.79%	
35	182	1073	0%	14	206	8%	7.67%	
42	318	1391	0%	20	226	8%	6.29%	
13	230	1621	1%	13	239	9%	5.64%	
19	1256	2877	1%	66	305	11%	5.26%	
9	82	2959	1%	4	309	12%	4.89%	
38	634	3593	1%	29	338	13%	4.57%	
2	5598	9191	3%	239	577	22%	4.27%	
15	624	9815	3%	21	598	22%	3.36%	
28	2536	12351	4%	85	683	26%	3.35%	
4	1799	14150	5%	52	735	28%	2.89%	
5	5260	19410	6%	145	880	33%	2.76%	
8	803	20213	6%	18	898	34%	2.24%	
18	2834	23047	7%	63	961	36%	2.22%	
47	428	23475	8%	9	970	36%	2.10%	
31	1246	24721	8%	25	995	37%	2.01%	
29	840	25561	8%	16	1011	38%	1.91%	
43	1249	26810	9%	20	1031	39%	1.60%	
27	1940	28750	9%	26	1057	40%	1.34%	34%
17	7510	36260	12%	89	1146	43%	1.19%	
39	5325	41585	13%	58	1204	45%	1.09%	
14	6079	47664	15%	65	1269	48%	1.07%	
44	1352	49016	16%	14	1283	48%	1.04%	
26	7331	56347	18%	72	1355	51%	0.98%	
7	7573	63920	20%	72	1427	54%	0.95%	48%
10	10097	74017	24%	94	1521	57%	0.93%	
12	17457	91474	29%	154	1675	63%	0.88%	58%
21	10722	102196	33%	91	1766	66%	0.85%	
51	4714	106910	34%	36	1802	68%	0.76%	
22	12917	119827	38%	96	1897	71%	0.74%	67%
32	21321	141148	45%	128	2025	76%	0.60%	
36	15107	156255	50%	86	2111	79%	0.57%	
23	8801	165056	53%	45	2156	81%	0.51%	
6	16917	181973	58%	78	2234	84%	0.46%	
34	11185	193158	62%	51	2285	86%	0.46%	
25	4538	197696	63%	21	2306	87%	0.46%	
11	9531	207227	66%	39	2345	88%	0.41%	
20	8237	215464	69%	34	2379	89%	0.41%	
30	16447	231911	74%	66	2445	92%	0.40%	
50	11338	243249	78%	45	2490	94%	0.40%	

TABLE 34-2

Concluded

Seg	Number MLD	Cum # Mld	Cum % MLG	Number Rsp	Cum # Rsp	Cum % Rsp	Rsp Rate	Regression Model Cum % Rsp
33	10444	253693	81%	36	2526	95%	0.34%	
37	4428	258121	83%	13	2539	95%	0.29%	
52	9939	268060	86%	26	2565	96%	0.26%	
45	36722	304782	98%	81	2645	99%	0.22%	
48	7055	311837	100%	14	2659	100%	0.20%	
54	202	312039	100%	0	2659	100%	0.00%	
40	81	312120	100%	0	2659	100%	0.00%	

twice as many variables as the regression model. Each row in Table 34–2 represents a segment produced by the tree analysis. The table shows that the first 32 segments defined by the tree accounted for 20 percent of the names mailed and 54 percent of the total responses. The last column of this table shows the percentage of responses accounted for by a regression model run on the same data, at approximately the same depth. The 48 percent figure in the last column represents the percentage of responses accounted for by the top two deciles according to the regression model. In other words, according to the regression model 20 percent of the names mailed produced 48 percent of the responses. It could be argued that the tree did better, but our judgment is that the results are close and the regression model will hold up much better over time.

CHAID, the Great Equalizer

Perhaps the most important use of CHAID, from the perspective of the marketer who is responsible for the commission or supervision of a model, is as a quality control tool—a use that the marketer can understand as well as any statistician. One of the most critical, if not the most critical, parts of a modeling project is getting the data right. How can a marketer tell if the process of selecting samples from a mailing and appending data to those samples was done correctly? If there was an error in the process, and as often as not there is, then it doesn't matter what follows. It's the old computer processing rule: garbage in–garbage out. Here's where CHAID can save the day for a marketer.

All that's required is to ask the analyst to produce a set of univariate CHAIDs. What does that mean? It means performing a CHAID analysis on each variable in order to see the relationship between the values of the variable and the thing that you are trying to measure.

The CHAID analysis below shows the results of a univariate CHAID analysis. The mailing went to 28,261 persons. The response rate was 2.7 percent. The independent variable being analyzed was product category. The CHAID shows that among previous buyers of Product Category 1, the response rate was 4.4 percent; among buyers selected from Product Category 2, the response rate was 3.5 percent; among buyers of Product Category 3, the response rate was 2.5 percent; and so on.

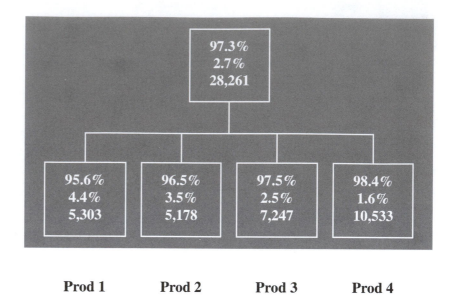

Prod 1   Prod 2   Prod 3   Prod 4

Now suppose we were to tell you that the mailing in question was for Product Category 1. The CHAID would confirm your belief, assuming that it is your belief, that prior buyers within the category are more likely to buy than buyers who have never purchased from the category before. But what if the CHAID showed the reverse, that previous buyers had the lowest response rate? How could that result be interpreted? Here are the choices: (1) Your knowledge of the business is wrong and has been for a long time. (2) Whoever did the CHAID either was given the wrong information or made a mistake. Your reaction, until proved otherwise, should be that an error was made. It's possible that you will be proved wrong, but the odds are overwhelmingly in favor of an error having been committed.

USING PRINCIPAL COMPONENTS TO MODEL PRODUCT USAGE PATTERNS

One of the most important tools available to direct marketers is principal components analysis. This tool was discussed in the modeling chapters, and the examples of its use had to do with modeling census data. Another important application is the modeling of product purchase data. Imagine for the moment that you are running a department store that has three dozen major departments and within each department there are another dozen product lines. Now imagine that you know how much each of your customers has spent on each product line, within some time period you specify. You can visualize this data residing in a big spreadsheet, the rows representing the customers and the columns representing the product lines. There would be one such sheet for each department and one summary sheet. In the summary sheet there would be 36 columns representing the amount spent (dollars or units) in each department.

Table 34–3 is an example of what one such sheet would look like. In this case the figures in the cells represent units. If we were to conduct a PCA on each sheet, the result would be a series of scores for each individual based on the relationship between each person's purchase pattern and the average purchase pattern. Again, let's assume that the first department we will look at comprises 12 product lines. The PCA algorithm will initially produce 12 new variables called

TABLE 34–3

Modeling Product Purchase Data

Customer	P-1	P-2	P-3	P-4	P-5	P-6	P-7	P-8	P-9	P-10	P-11	P-12	1st PC	2nd PC	3rd PC
	Number of Units Purchased Within Department X — Within Last X Months												*First 3 Principal Components*		
1	4	11	7	3	28	37	19	43	47	26	27	25	50	67	68
2	5	2	7	14	35	43	13	3	51	69	21	19	45	59	65
3	5	6	15	1	4	43	5	67	3	51	63	38	40	51	62
4	4	7	9	4	18	34	14	47	8	61	35	32	35	43	59
5	1	12	13	15	29	34	19	5	38	12	26	39	30	35	56
6	7	2	6	12	38	37	47	64	15	1	37	48	25	27	53
7	6	5	7	9	36	29	33	30	33	25	40	54	20	19	50
8	6	13	4	17	19	13	42	37	20	51	17	64	15	11	47
9	7	9	5	25	21	31	28	48	23	46	5	30	10	3	44
10	7	0	7	27	1	38	29	16	0	54	13	10	5	−5	41
11	4	12	3	11	28	21	5	21	57	49	28	46	0	−13	38
12	4	11	8	11	29	34	40	69	36	32	20	45	−5	−21	35
13	8	5	2	23	15	14	16	9	3	41	23	39	−10	−29	32
14	1	1	10	25	32	22	38	51	35	30	42	64	−15	−37	29
15	2	2	10	21	0	17	6	29	41	41	65	33	−20	−45	26
16	7	0	19	2	30	22	52	28	34	14	37	13	−25	−53	23
17	4	10	7	4	3	47	17	11	24	48	63	29	−30	−61	20
18	6	15	15	22	27	7	3	53	40	62	27	51	−35	−69	17
19	1	0	11	9	3	6	22	31	14	47	27	53	−40	−77	14
n	4	15	15	24	16	25	17	54	23	66	25	44	−45	−85	11

Because there are 12 Product lines within the department, the PCA procedure will produce 12 scores for each individual. Only a few of the scores (PCs) will be considered for inclusion in a subsequent model. Usually, but not always, three or four of the PCs will contain 70% or more of the information in the data set. The numbers in the PC Columns are not actual PC values. They are presented just to show that the principal components are continuous variables that can easily be used in regression analyses.

principal components (PCs). But not all of these scores (PCs) will be of equal importance. In most cases two or three of the PCs will contain most of the "information" in the entire data set.

These two or three PCs will then be used later in the model-building process as potential variables in a final regression model. In the example we made up, there were three dozen departments. If my estimates are correct, we would be considering about 72 to 108 PCs (36*2 or 36*3) to represent product purchase patterns within the individual departments and another 2 or 3 PCs representing the PCA analysis we would have done on the summary table. What's more, based on our experience, and depending upon what we were modeling, our final regression model would probably only contain a handful of PCs. Probably one PC would represent the purchase pattern across departments, and maybe three of four PCs would represent the purchase patterns within a few key (predictive) departments. Sounds confusing, but it's really not. Nor is it hard to do, if you're a trained statistician. The key point for marketers is to remember to have your statisticians use this procedure when you are faced with this kind of data. The alternative, creating dummy variables to represent the purchase of each product, or purchase within a category, won't, in our opinion, work nearly as well as this procedure, which will give the stable results.

REGRESSION MODELS

Regression modeling begins at the exact same place as RFM modeling—with the available data. In regression modeling, the first decision is the selection of the dependent variable—what do we want to model or predict? In this example, we, of course, want to predict response, and we will be in a position to predict response if the things we know about our customers, more formally referred to as the *independent variables*, are themselves good predictors of response.

The question is whether we believe that knowing past performance data, the same kinds of data that go into an RFM model, can help us predict who will and will not be likely to respond to a future mailing. Of course, because we know that RFM works, the real question is whether using all the information available to us in combination with the regression tool will produce a better result than using the same information in RFM analysis.

Let's review the list at the beginning of this chapter of the data we have to work with for each customer. Each element can be used to create a set of independent variables that will be considered for inclusion in a regression model. Generally, the data needs to be massaged before it can become useful for modeling. For example, the data types in the list could be turned into the set of independent variables in Table 34–4.

This list of independent variables that could be created from the data set is extensive, and it indicates the power of the modeling technique. It should be said immediately that the final model will contain only a few of the many possible variables. In fact, as we have repeatedly said, a sign of a good model is the presence of relatively few variables. The converse is also true; a model with a dozen or so variables is probably, despite its impressive appearance, a relatively poor model. (More about this subject is contained in Chapters 25 through 31 of this book.)

Now let's assume you build a regression model based on the data from the recent mailing to the entire file. What will it look like, and what will it do for you? For simplicity of presentation and interpretation, let's agree to use ordinary least-squares multiple regression as our modeling tool, even though in practice we would use logistic regression in a response model. Also, remember that we will be building the model on only half the names mailed, the calibration sample,

TABLE 34–4

Relating Original Data to Model Variables

VAR 1	=	Number of months on the file.
VAR 2	=	Number of months since last purchase.
VAR 3	=	Total dollars.
VAR 4	=	Total dollars divided by months on file.
VAR 5	=	Total dollars divided by number of times mailed.
VAR 6	=	Total dollars divided by number of purchases.
VAR 7	=	Number of times mailed.
VAR 8	=	Number of purchases.
VAR 9 . . . n	=	Number of purchases within last (3, 6, 9, 12 . . .) months.
VAR 10	=	Number of purchases divided by times mailed.
VAR 11	=	Number of purchases divided by months on file.
VAR 12 . . . n	=	Dollars per purchase within each product category.
VAR 13	=	Number of product categories with purchases.

and we will be validating the model on the other half of the names mailed, the validation sample.

What will the regression model look like? Which of the many possible independent variables will finally wind up in the model? To answer the second question first, the analyst using the statistical tools discussed in the earlier chapters will determine which independent variables are important in predicting response. Let's assume the following variables are important:

Variable Name		Variable Description
VAR 2	=	Number of months since last purchase
VAR 10	=	Number of purchases divided by times mailed
VAR 6	=	Total dollars divided by number of purchases

In addition to identifying those variables that are significant predictors of response, the model will assign weights to each variable, so the final regression equation or model might look something like this:

Expected response $= 2.3 - .4 ¥ (\text{VAR } 2) + .8 ¥ (\text{VAR } 10) + .0012 ¥ (\text{VAR } 6)$

Each customer on the file will be scored according to the above equation. For example, assume a customer with the following values for each of the performance variables:

VAR 2 = 6   Six months have elapsed since last purchase.
VAR 10 =   .10   Customer buys once out of every 10 times mailed.
VAR 6 = 55.33   Average purchase equals $55.33.

The equation, or the model (the model is simply the equation), makes intuitive sense. Each customer will start off with a score of 2.3 (the model provides this number, which could be positive or negative—in this case, it's positive). The weight of the variable VAR 2, number of months since last purchase, is negative and equal to $-.4$, so -2.4 ($-.4 ¥ 6$) will be added to the score. Since adding a negative number decreases the score, the longer the time since the last purchase, the smaller the score, which makes sense. The higher the score, the greater the propensity to respond, and we know from experience that the likelihood of responding is greater among persons who have purchased from us in the recent past.

The second variable, VAR 10, represents the individual's average response to all prior in-house mailings; the larger this number, the higher the score. In this case, we will add .08 ($.8 ¥ .10$) to the customer's score. The third variable, VAR 6, represents the individual's average sale from all prior purchases, and again we would expect a person's score to increase as this number increases. The value of the variable, its coefficient, is .0012; therefore, the person's score is increased by .0664 ($.0012 ¥ 55.33$).

Adding up all of the above, we determine that this person's score is equal to .0464 (obtained from the equation $2.3 - 2.4 + .08 + .0664$). This same procedure would be repeated for every customer on the validation file. Continuing our example, each customer would be scored and then all customers would be sorted or ranked, in descending sequence, in terms of their score. The last step in the procedure, for presentation purposes only, is to divide the entire validation file into 10 groups of equal size, called deciles. The persons in the top decile will have the highest scores and are expected to perform the best in an upcoming mailing.

Reminder about Ordinary versus Logistic Regression Models

In practice, as we said before, we would use the logistic regression model rather than the ordinary least-squares model for response models. One consequence of this difference would be that the scores assigned to each customer could be converted into probabilities of response, and the probabilities would range between 0 and 1.[2]

In the ordinary regression model, scores of less than 0 and greater than 1 are possible. This result may be acceptable if all you want to do is rank your customers in terms of their relative probability of responding, but it is not sufficient if you require an accurate measure of probability, as would be the case if you intended to stop mailing below some expected response rate.

How to Determine the Right Number of Variables to Include in Your Model

A big practical problem for direct marketers is making sure that their models hold up on rollouts. As explained elsewhere in this book, models are generally built on a sample of the available data and evaluated on another sample of the data called the *validation sample* or the *holdout sample*. If the model does not validate well, if the gains chart or the decile analysis is flat, the model will not be used. The problem we're concerned with in this section is the problem of using a model that validated well, but fails when used in a rollout mailing. One possible explanation, and this happens enough to be concerned with the issue, is that the model "overfit" the data. When this happens, the expected results will not materialize when the model is used in a similar but not identical situation, which is, of course, always the case in direct marketing. The best way to protect yourself from this situation is to make sure that your models do not contain more variables than are necessary to produce the best results.

The way to do this is to examine the statistics that accompany the output of regression models. In ordinary least-squares regression models the statistic that describes the significance of each variable in the model is the t statistic; in logistic regression models the corresponding statistic in the chi-square statistic. What you want to be on the lookout for is large differences in values. In the following table we show the results of eight models on the same validation sample. The top of the chart shows the statistics associated with the model in general (R-squared and the F statistic); the t statistic for each variable is shown below. On the bottom of the chart we show the decile analysis corresponding to the solution.

A model with eight variables was chosen as our starting point because each of the variables in the model had t statistics greater than 2. (The sign doesn't matter, and we rounded off the values, so 1.70 counts as a 2.) As you can see, the differences are very large; the t values associated with the recency, activity, and monetary variables are much greater than the t values associated with product line and source of order. To determine the best solution, we drop from consideration the variable with the smallest t value, create a new model with only the seven remaining variables, and redo the validation run. As you can see, the seven-variable model produces a decile analysis that is at least as good as, if not better than, the

---

2. When logistic regression models are used, the scores produced by the logistic equation are logits. The logits in turn can be transformed into probabilities.

eight-variable model. We then continue the process of dropping the variable with the smallest t value, rerunning the model, and rerunning the decile analysis. An inspection of all eight solutions clearly indicates that a model with fewer variables is better than a model with all the "significant" variables included. For example, the four-variable model has the best spread from the point of view that the results in the bottom two deciles are the lowest among all the choices and there are no "bumps" (results decrease from one decile to another) in the decile analysis.

TYPICAL RESPONSE MODEL RESULTS

The next question we have to ask ourselves is how response rates will vary among deciles. It's very important for anyone working with models to have some rules of thumb in mind. Most good models built on performance data show that the top two deciles behave much better than the bottom two deciles, and the six deciles in the middle are somewhat flat, though below the top two and above the bottom two deciles. For example, if our mailing to our house file of 2 million names pulled 8 percent on average, it would be reasonable, given the quality of the data discussed above, to expect the decile result shown in Table 34–5.

Each of the first four examples shown in Table 34–5 is based on a real case involving modeling response to a house file mailing. In each case, the independent variables were performance variables: when, what, and how much customers purchased in the past; how often were they promoted; and so on.

As the examples in the table show, models based on this kind of data allow users to divide a single house file into 10 distinct groups, each with its own expected response rate. We would describe Model 1 as a very powerful model. The best 10 percent of the file pulled 26.0 percent compared with the bottom decile, which pulled only 1.9 percent. Another way to look at the results is to compare the response rate of the top two deciles or the top eight deciles with the average. Again, referring to Model 1, the top two deciles (20 percent) did 2.3 times better than average [(26% + 11.2%)/2 = 17.1% and 17.1%/8% = 2.3]; the sum of the top eight deciles did 1.16 times better than average.

Performance Models 2, 3, and 4 are not as powerful as Model 1, but they are still strong models, each capable of creating groups that perform significantly better or significantly worse than average.

It's important to understand just what you can expect from modeling for a variety of reasons, not the least of which is the fact that knowing what to expect can save you considerable time and money.

For example, suppose you are responsible for mailings at a financial services company. The market has turned down drastically, and your house list, which used to pull 5 percent, now only pulls 2 percent, and you need to pull 3 percent to break even. Can modeling help? Let's apply the indexes from Table 34–5 to a 2 percent average response rate and see what conclusions we can draw. The results are shown in Table 34–6.

As you can see from Table 34–6, any of the four models will allow you to mail the first decile and achieve a response rate well above 3 percent. All the models will also allow you to mail the second decile and receive a response rate close to 3 percent. But if your goal was to mail 50 percent of your file, modeling can't do that for you—at least the four models shown here can't.

What if you were pulling not 2 percent but only one-half of 1 percent? Table 34–7 shows that modeling can't help you, and you should look elsewhere for relief.

TABLE 34-5

Typical Regression Modeling Results

| | Modeling Internal Performance Data | | | | | | | | Modeling Census Data at the ZIP Code Level | | | | | |
| | Example 1 | | Example 2 | | Example 3 | | Example 4 | | Example 1 | | Example 2 | | Example 3 | |
Decile	Percent Response	Index	Percent Response	Index	Percent Response	Index	Percent Response	Index	Percent Response	Index	Percent Response	Index	Percent Response	Index
1	26.0%	326	23.8%	298	18.3%	229	19.3%	241	3.2%	162	2.7%	137	2.3%	113
2	11.2	140	13.3	167	12.9	161	11.4	142	2.8	138	2.5	125	2.2	109
3	8.4	105	9.5	119	10.7	134	8.6	108	2.5	125	2.3	113	2.1	106
4	7.4	93	7.1	89	9.4	118	8.0	100	2.2	110	2.2	110	2.1	106
5	7.0	87	6.7	83	7.7	96	7.4	92	2.2	108	2.0	98	2.0	102
6	5.6	70	5.5	69	6.5	81	6.3	78	1.8	92	1.8	90	2.0	102
7	4.7	58	4.1	51	5.0	62	5.6	70	1.7	85	1.8	92	1.9	96
8	4.2	52	3.8	48	3.9	49	5.3	66	1.5	77	1.7	86	1.8	92
9	3.7	47	3.3	42	3.2	40	4.2	53	1.2	62	1.6	82	1.7	87
10	1.9	23	2.9	36	2.4	30	3.9	49	0.9	46	1.4	72	1.7	87
Average	8.0%	100	8.0%	100	8.0%	100	8.0%	100	2.0%	100	2.0%	100	2.0%	100
Best to worst	1400.0%		833.3%		767.1%		492.5%		350.0%		189.6%		130.4%	
Best 20 percent to average	232.6%		232.1%		195.0%		191.8%		150.0%		130.8%		111.3%	
Best 80 percent to average	116.3%		115.5%		116.3%		112.3%		112.1%		106.4%		103.3%	

TABLE 34–6

Regression Modeling against a 2 Percent Response Rate

| | Modeling Internal Performance Data | | | | | | | |
| | Example 1 | | Example 2 | | Example 3 | | Example 4 | |
Decile	Percent Response	Index	Percent Response	Index	Percent Response	Index	Percent Response	Index
1	6.5%	326	6.0%	298	4.6%	229	4.8%	241
2	2.8	140	3.3	167	3.2	161	2.8	142
3	2.1	105	2.4	119	2.7	134	2.2	108
4	1.9	93	1.8	89	2.4	118	2.0	100
5	1.7	87	1.7	83	1.9	96	1.8	92
6	1.4	70	1.4	69	1.6	81	1.6	78
7	1.2	58	1.0	51	1.2	62	1.4	70
8	1.0	52	1.0	48	1.0	49	1.3	66
9	.9	47	.8	42	.8	40	1.1	53
10	.5	23	.7	36	.6	30	1.0	49
Average	2.0%	100	2.0%	100	2.0%	100	2.0%	100

ZIP CODE MODELS

The last section referred to models based on internal performance data. What about response models that are based on mailings to outside rented lists? In this situation, there is no "hard" performance data. Generally, all you have to work with is ZIP code–based census data. There are a number of issues to consider,

TABLE 34–7

Regression Modeling against a 0.5 Percent Response Rate

| | Modeling Internal Performance Data | | | | | | | |
| | Example 1 | | Example 2 | | Example 3 | | Example 4 | |
Decile	Percent Response	Index	Percent Response	Index	Percent Response	Index	Percent Response	Index
1	1.6%	326	1.5%	298	1.1%	229	1.2%	241
2	.7	140	.8	167	.8	161	.7	142
3	.5	105	.6	119	.7	134	.5	108
4	.5	93	.4	89	.6	118	.5	100
5	.4	87	.4	83	.5	96	.5	92
6	.3	70	.3	69	.4	81	.4	78
7	.3	58	.3	51	.3	62	.3	70
8	.3	52	.2	48	.2	49	.3	66
9	.2	47	.2	42	.2	40	.3	53
10	.1	23	.2	36	.1	30	.2	49
Average	.5%	100	.5%	100	.5%	100	.5%	100

but first let's take a look at some typical ZIP code–based census models. Looking back to Table 34–5, you'll see, not surprisingly, that the ZIP code-based census models are not nearly as strong as the models built on internal performance data. In the best case shown, Model 1, the best decile does only 3.5 times better than the worst decile, and mailing to 80 percent of the universe of names corresponding to this model will lift response by only 12 percent. The results are still less impressive for Models 2 and 3.

Despite the fact that ZIP code response models based on census data are not as strong as internal performance models, they may still be worthwhile. For example, suppose you were doing a mailing to 3 million outside names and were expecting a 2 percent response, or 60,000 orders. A 10 percent improvement would mean another 6,000 orders, and if each order were worth $30, this would mean another $180,000 in contribution. Of course, the larger the universe, the larger the potential profits.

Response models based on census data are complicated and involve a number of issues. First of all, a model of a mailing to a million or more names means that we will be mailing to a large number of individual lists, and much fewer but still a significant number of list categories. One of the underlying assumptions of ZIP code modeling is that the impact of the demographic characteristics associated with each ZIP code will work across all list categories and across all lists within a category. The report that accompanies a good ZIP code model shows you exactly how well the model does across categories and by list within a category.

It is not unusual to find that the model performs better within some list categories than others. In Table 34–8, the general model is represented by the row labeled "Total"; we see that the response rate in the best decile is about 3.2 percent and the response rate in the poorest-performing decile is about 1.1 percent. Further, response rates decline as expected from Decile 1 through Decile 10. However, on closer inspection of the model's performance, among the four major list

TABLE 34–8

ZIP Code Regression Modeling

Category	Decile									
	1	2	3	4	5	6	7	8	9	10
Percent Response within Decile										
1	5.00%	3.90%	2.80%	2.60%	2.60%	1.60%	1.50%	1.10%	.40%	.01%
2	3.30	3.30	3.30	3.30	3.20	2.80	2.80	2.70	2.60	2.75
3	.50	.60	.70	.80	.90	1.10	1.20	1.30	1.40	1.50
4	3.80	3.20	3.00	2.20	2.20	1.70	1.50	1.00	.50	.00
Total	3.2%	2.8%	2.5%	2.2%	2.2%	1.8%	1.8%	1.5%	1.2%	1.1%
Indexed Response										
1	232	181	130	121	121	74	70	51	19	0
2	110	110	110	110	106	93	93	90	87	92
3	50	60	70	80	90	110	120	130	140	150
4	199	168	157	115	115	89	79	52	26	0
Total	156	136	121	110	110	89	87	76	61	53

categories that make up the total universe of names mailed we see that the model works very well for Categories 1 and 4; the model doesn't work well for Category 2; and Category 3 behaves contrary to the model predictions. What should the user and the modeler do at this point?

One option is to eliminate Categories 2 and 3 from the analysis and build a new model based solely on the results of lists within Categories 1 and 4. This would be a perfectly good solution if the mailing were very large and enough names were mailed in each list category. Generally, we try to build models in situations with 2,000 or more responders, using 1,000 responders and a representative sampling of nonresponders to build the model and validating the model by applying the results of the model to the remaining 1,000 responders and a corresponding sample of nonresponders.

However, suppose the mailing in question went to only 100,000 names and had a 2 percent response rate producing just 2,000 orders. Assuming that each category was equally represented would mean that a model built on just two list categories would include a total of only 1,000 responders. That would leave only 500 responders on which to build the model and 500 responders on which to validate the model. We could attempt to build a model on only 500 responders, but the odds of achieving a significant response model decrease as the number of responders decreases. Of course, there's no harm in trying, and the statistics that accompany the output of the model will tell the analyst whether the model is or is not significant.[3] What's more, if you are able to identify significant variables when the sample is small, the model you construct using these variables will also be strong.

Let's assume that a model based on List Categories 2 and 3 proves not to be statistically significant. What's the alternative, and how could we use the model shown in Table 34–8? We could certainly employ the model when using lists in Categories 1 and 4. We would not use the model against lists selected from Category 3, and we would probably consider using the model to select ZIP codes from lists in Category 2.

Another consideration in ZIP code models is the selection of the independent variables. As we discussed in Chapter 4, each ZIP code is associated with a string of census demographics. And although it is true that each ZIP code may therefore be described in terms of hundreds of census variables, it's also true that many of these variables are highly correlated with each other. Simply put, affluent people have high incomes, live in expensive homes, are better educated, have professional or managerial jobs, and so on. Therefore, a model that includes each, or many, of these variables is likely to suffer from multicolinearity. (See Chapters 25 through 30 for more details about multicolinearity.)

Analysts experienced with census data will be sure not to include variables that are highly correlated with each other, or they will perform a factor analysis prior to beginning a regression analysis to avoid this problem. In this case, factor analysis would combine the many variables that measure affluence into a single affluence factor that would be used as just one independent variable in a regression analysis. Another factor may measure the degree to which the ZIP code is an urban ZIP code, a third factor may be a measure of ethnicity, and so on.

---

3. It is interesting to note that models that do work—i.e., they pass all the tests for statistical significance—and that are based on a relatively small number of responders are probably particularly good models because their strength could be judged significant based on a small sample.

Adjusting for ZIP Code Size

A third issue in ZIP code modeling is the small mailing quantity and the correspondingly small number of responses achieved within any one ZIP code. For example, even a mailing of 1 million pieces and 20,000 responses averages only 36 pieces per ZIP code and less than 1 response per ZIP code (based on 28,000 residential ZIP codes). To adjust for this condition, analysts experiment with different weighting schemes so the response rates from ZIP codes that receive relatively large numbers of pieces count for more in the regression model than ZIP codes that receive only a few pieces and whose response rates would distort the model if the number of pieces mailed were not taken into consideration.

Table 34–9 presents an example in which 2 percent and 4 percent response rates are achieved in mailings into ZIP codes of different sizes. Intuitively, the ZIP code receiving 10,240 pieces and producing 205 orders should receive more consideration or weight than the ZIP code into which only 80 pieces were mailed and only two responses were generated, even though the response rate (2 percent) is the same.

Adjusting for ZIP code is accomplished by using a technique called weighted least-squares regression. In this procedure each ZIP code receives a weight equal to the ZIP code's response rate (P) times 1 minus the response rate (Q) times the number of mailings (N) or ($N ¥ P ¥ Q$). In our example, the ZIP code that received the larger mailing would receive a weight of 200.7 and the ZIP code that received only 80 pieces would receive a weight of 1.6.

You will notice that the $N ¥ P ¥ Q$ formula also assigns more weight to ZIP codes with higher response rates when the quantity mailed into each ZIP code is the same. Therefore, a ZIP code that received 10,240 pieces and produced a 2 percent response receives about half the weight of a ZIP code of similar size with a response rate of 4 percent.

Modeling Variables Other Than Response

The census data available for ZIP codes is also available for smaller geographic areas. Census data has always been available for block groups and census tracts, and it is now available at the ZIP+4 or nine-digit ZIP+4 code level.

Naturally, models built at the block group or the ZIP+4 level should outperform models built with data associated with larger ZIP codes. For example, according to Equifax National Decision Systems, the composition of ZIP code 07712 is as follows:

Percent of Households in Each MicroVision Cluster*

Lap of Luxury	7.9%
Home Sweet Home	9.1
Great Beginnings	21.4
A Good Step Forward	11.3
Struggling Minority Mix	11.8
Difficult Times	10.9

*For a complete description of MicroVision and other segmentation or clustering products, please refer to Appendix B at the end of this book.

Clearly the census data that describes this ZIP code represents a fairly meaningless set of averages, and models based on block group or ZIP+4 data

T A B L E   34–9

ZIP Code Models — Adjusting for the Quantity Mailed and Response Rates

	2% Response			4% Response	
Quantity Mailed	Response Rate	Weight	Quantity Mailed	Response Rate	Weight
10	2.0%	0.2	10	4.0%	0.4
20	2.0	0.4	20	4.0	0.8
40	2.0	0.8	40	4.0	1.5
80	2.0	1.6	80	4.0	3.1
160	2.0	3.1	160	4.0	6.1
320	2.0	6.3	320	4.0	12.3
640	2.0	12.5	640	4.0	24.6
1,280	2.0	25.1	1,280	4.0	49.2
2,560	2.0	50.2	2,560	4.0	98.3
5,120	2.0	100.4	5,120	4.0	196.6
10,240	2.0	200.7	10,240	4.0	393.2

would deal better with persons living in this area and similar areas in which the ZIP code does not represent anything close to a homogeneous neighborhood.

Our experience working with block group data suggests that models can be developed that could spread a 2 percent response rate as indicated in Table 34–10.

As always, before deciding to model at the block group or ZIP+4 level, a decision has to be made regarding the extra costs associated with implementing the model at this level of detail as opposed to implementing the model at the simpler and always available ZIP code level. If block group codes or ZIP+4 codes are not readily available, your files will have to be geo-coded before the models can be applied.

T A B L E   34–10

Model Results Built on Block Group Data

	Response		Cumulative
Decile	Rate	Index	Lift
1	4.16%	208	208
2	3.16	158	183
3	3.05	153	173
4	2.58	129	162
5	2.42	121	154
6	1.58	79	141
7	1.47	74	132
8	0.95	47	121
9	0.47	24	110
10	0.16	8	100
Average	2.00%		100

Finally, there's no reason to think of modeling as being limited to response modeling. Performance models are similar to response models in the sense that the independent variables, the things we know about the customer or prospect, may be the same as those used in a response model. This may be area-related census data if we are modeling performance against outside lists, or internal performance behavior, overlay data, or other research data if we are modeling existing customers.

COMBINING MODELS MODELING PROFIT

Long before modeling was a factor in direct marketing, direct marketers knew that response could be increased by softening or increasing the value of the offer. This is especially true for name acquisition models—mailings to rented lists. The rule of thumb is simple: increase the value of the offer, increase response—and watch out for poorer back-end performance. The same effect could be accomplished by extending payment terms, adding a trial offer, and so on. Direct marketers are good at increasing response, but they have always understood there is no such thing as a free lunch and would therefore expect back-end performance to be poorer.

The earlier ZIP code response modeling efforts sometimes missed this point, so models were built to identify those ZIP codes most likely to respond rather than those most likely to respond and produce profits. (We'll focus on ZIP code models in this section, but the same effect could be true for models dealing with persons.) Today, modelers understand that in situations in which the back-end is as important as the response itself—which is almost always the case unless you are selling a fixed-price product for cash with order—you must build two models, a response model and a performance model, and then combine the two models into a profit model.[4]

The response model provides you with an expected response rate or a probability of response, and the performance model provides you with a measure of expected lifetime profits. The product of expected response times expected profits is equal to expected profits per name mailed.

For example, a ZIP code with an expected response rate of 5 percent and an expected back-end profit of $15 has an overall expected value of $.75 ($15 ¥ .05 = $.75); a ZIP code with a lower expected response rate of 3 percent but a higher expected back-end profit of $50 has an expected value of $1.50. Clearly, you would be better off mailing to the latter ZIP code with the lower expected response rate but the significantly higher expected back-end performance.

For ZIP code modeling we recommend the following procedure:

1. For each ZIP code determine the response rate, the number of pieces mailed, and some measure of back-end performance per starter or responder.
2. Append ZIP code-level demographics to each ZIP code record.
3. Divide the total mailing file into two parts, a calibration sample and a validation sample. Do this by placing half of the ZIP codes in the calibration sample and the other half in the validation sample. Check to

---

4. Sometimes it is possible to model a single performance variable such as payments per name mailed, a variable which takes performance (sales, payments, profits, etc.) into account as well as response rates. However, we prefer to model back-end performance and front-end response separately, because we believe that more insights are gained into the causal effects of the independent variables by using this two-step procedure.

make sure that both samples contain close to an equal number of mailings and responses.

4. From the calibration sample build a response model. For technical reasons having to do with the uneven distribution of response rates, we recommend converting ZIP code response rates into logits and using weighted least-squares regression as the modeling tool, the weights being assigned by the $N \yen P \yen Q$ formula defined above.

5. Apply the response model, the regression equation, to the ZIP codes on the validation sample.

6. Sort the validation file by predicted response score and create a decile analysis. When creating the decile analysis, each ZIP code should be represented by the quantity mailed into that ZIP code. In other words, each ZIP code does not always count as one unit.

7. Empirically determine the actual response rate within each decile. Check to see if the model spreads response rates as expected, and check to see if the predicted response rates are close to the actual response rates.

8. If the model is satisfactory, apply the model equation to each of the 28,000 residential ZIP codes.

9. Each ZIP code, after it is scored, will then be assigned to a decile. This can be accomplished by sorting after the ZIP codes are scored or by using a table that relates ZIP code scores to decile levels.

10. Repeat the procedure, this time changing the dependent variable from a response rate to some measure of back-end performance, such as sales or payments.

11. Among the ZIP codes on the calibration sample, build a back-end performance model.

12. Apply the performance model to the validation sample.

13. Repeat Steps 6 through 9 to score all 28,000 ZIP codes and to assign each ZIP code to a performance decile.

14. For each ZIP code on the validation file, multiply the expected ZIP code response rate by the expected back-end performance measure. The result is expected performance per name mailed (expected sales per name mailed or expected payments per name mailed depending on the back-end measure selected).

15. Sort the file in terms of expected performance per name mailed.

16. Check to see if the actual performance per name mailed is consistent with the predictions of the model.

17. If the cross-multiplication process works for the ZIPs in the validation sample, apply the same procedures to all 28,000 residential ZIPs — multiply each ZIP's expected response rate by its expected performance measure. Then sort all 28,000 ZIPs in deciles based on each ZIP's expected performance per name mailed score.

18. Now create one or more ZIP code tapes that will contain the ZIP code number and three decile rankings: a response decile, a performance decile, and a combined profit decile.

19. You can now use the ZIP code tapes when ordering outside lists. You may request only names from the best deciles, or you may use the ZIP code tape as a suppression file and not accept names selected from the lower deciles.

A Word of Caution Regarding Combined Models

Before leaving this subject, we have a word of caution about combining front-end and back-end models. It is theoretically possible, and every once in a while it actually happens, that when you combine a front-end model with a back-end model, the resulting combined model will be flat. An example of how this might happen is shown in Table 34–11.

As you can see, when the front-end and back-end models are nearly mirror images of each other, the models tend to cancel each other out. When this happens, the alternatives are to attempt to build a model that uses contribution per name mailed as the dependent variable, but in practice this doesn't work well with demographic models. The better solution may be to use the response model against lists that have a relatively strong back-end—eliminating the poorest performing areas from these lists. Though more tedious than simply using a combined model, this procedure has worked well in practice.

TABLE 34–11

Combining Front-End and Back-End Models

Typical Results: Combining Models Results in a Usable Combined Model

Decile	Expected Response	Expected Contribution	Expected Contribution per Name Mailed	Response Index	Contribution Index	Combined Index
1	5.00%	$35.00	$1.75	187	63	133
2	4.25	38.50	1.64	159	69	124
3	3.61	42.35	1.53	135	76	116
4	3.07	46.59	1.43	115	84	109
5	2.61	51.24	1.34	97	92	102
6	2.22	56.37	1.25	83	101	95
7	1.89	62.00	1.17	70	111	89
8	1.60	68.21	1.09	60	122	83
9	1.36	75.03	1.02	51	135	78
10	1.16	82.53	0.96	43	148	73
Average	2.68%	$55.78	$1.32	100	100	100

Possible Results: Front-End and Back-End Models "Wash Out" Combined Effect

Decile	Expected Response	Expected Contribution	Expected Contribution per Name Mailed	Response Index	Contribution Index	Combined Index
1	5.00%	$24.29%	$1.21	187	44	101
2	4.25	28.40	1.21	159	51	100
3	3.61	33.28	1.20	135	60	100
4	3.07	39.08	1.20	115	70	100
5	2.61	45.94	1.20	97	82	99
6	2.22	54.09	1.20	83	97	100
7	1.89	63.75	1.20	70	114	100
8	1.60	75.21	1.21	60	135	100
9	1.36	88.80	1.21	51	159	100
10	1.16	104.91	1.21	43	188	101
Average	2.68%	$55.77	$1.21	100	100	100

Lead-Conversion Models

One of the frequently used applications of response models is in lead-generation and fulfillment situations. Many companies generate leads through print advertising or broadcast advertising and attempt to convert the leads into sales through a series of direct mailings.

If we consider the conversion rate as being similar to a response rate in a response model, it's clear that it's possible to model conversions. In fact, it's sometimes easier to model conversion than simple response, particularly if in the process of getting the lead one is able to capture additional information either on the coupon or in a telephone conversation.

In a conversion model, the objective is to divide all leads into deciles or some other scheme and assign a probability of conversion to each decile. The deciles with the highest probability of conversion should justify more follow-up mailings than the deciles in which the response rate is lower.

Table 34–12 shows a typical conversion sequence resulting in an overall conversion rate of 9.24 percent. The example describes a situation in which all leads receive a four-part follow-up series. The response rate for the first effort is 3.68 percent, the response rate for the second effort is 2.52 percent, and so on.

Table 34–12 also shows the effect of a regression analysis that results in a model with a 10 percent response rate among those in the top decile (Effort 1) and a 1.57 percent response rate among those in the last decile.

Table 34–12 is completed using the assumption of a 25 percent falloff rate among the top five deciles and a 50 percent falloff rate among the bottom five deciles. Continuing with these assumptions, the fourth effort to the top decile results in a 4.22 percent response, while the fourth effort to the bottom decile results in a conversion rate of only .20 percent. Clearly, it would appear that the money spent mailing the fourth effort to the bottom decile would have been better spent mailing a fifth effort to the persons in the top decile.

Table 34–13 completes this argument. Assuming that each person, regardless of decile assignment, must receive two efforts and further assuming that the total number of pieces mailed cannot be increased, Table 34–12 shows that it makes the most sense to send members of the top five deciles six efforts and members of the lower deciles only the two required mailings.

By following this strategy, the overall conversion rate is increased from 9.24 to 12.47 percent. Table 34–13 shows the economic impact of this.

From Table 34–14, we see that this company received 500,000 leads a year. Traditionally, each lead was mailed four efforts, or a total of 2 million pieces. (In practice, converters from early efforts would not be promoted again for the same offer.) Using the database marketing approach, which in this case evaluates an individual customer on the basis of a regression model score, the same number of total pieces are mailed but more mailings are directed at higher potential prospects, increasing the overall response rate to 12.47 percent and increasing the total number of converted prospects by 16,165. In our example, each converted prospect is worth $200, so this exercise is worth an additional $3,233,046 per year. Of course, if the margin were less, the overall increase in profits would be correspondingly reduced.

The example above assumed that the falloff between mailings was a constant 25 percent for the top deciles and a constant 50 percent for the bottom five deciles. Fortunately, there is a better way to estimate falloff rates between mailings that are equally spaced. In the Summer 1988 edition of the *Journal of Direct*

T A B L E 34–12

Results of Traditional Four-Part Follow-Up Conversion Efforts

Falloff for deciles 1 to 5: 75 percent
Falloff for deciles 6 to 10: 50 percent

Decile	Percent Falloff	Effort 1	Effort 2	Effort 3	Effort 4
1		10.00%	7.50%	5.63%	4.22%
2	69.5%	6.95	5.21	3.91	2.93
3	43.8	4.38	3.28	2.46	1.85
4	34.6	3.46	2.60	1.95	1.46
5	24.9	2.49	1.86	1.40	1.05
6	21.0	2.10	1.05	.53	.26
7	19.8	1.98	.99	.50	.25
8	19.8	1.98	.99	.50	.25
9	18.6	1.86	.93	.47	.23
10	15.7	1.57	.78	.39	.20
Conversion rate		3.68%	2.52%	1.77%	1.27%
Cumulative rate			6.20%	7.97%	9.24%

Decile	Percent Falloff	Effort 1	Effort 2	Effort 3	Effort 4
1		5,000	3,750	2,813	2,109
2	69.5%	3,476	2,607	1,955	1,467
3	43.8	2,189	1,642	1,232	924
4	34.6	1,731	1,298	974	730
5	24.9	1,243	932	699	524
6	21.0	1,050	525	263	131
7	19.8	991	496	248	124
8	19.8	991	496	248	124
9	18.6	932	466	233	116
10	15.7	784	392	196	98
Conversions		18,388	12,604	8,859	6,348
Cumulative			30,991	39,850	46,198
Conversion rate		3.68%	2.52%	1.77%	1.27%
Cumulative rate			6.20%	7.97%	9.24%

Marketing, Professors Bruce Buchanan and Donald G. Morrison presented a model for estimating the falloff rates for a third, fourth, fifth, or higher-level mailing based on the response rates to the first and second mailings, assuming a constant period between mailings.[5] This is nearly the perfect situation for a lead-generation model. Table 34–15 presents a simple Lotus 1-2-3 model that was published along with the article itself to estimate falloff. The Lotus model can be easily recreated by any spreadsheet user.

---

5. B. Buchanan and D. G. Morrison, "A Stochastic Model of List Falloff with Implications for Repeat Mailings," *Journal of Direct Marketing,* Summer 1988.

Results of Six-Part Database Conversion Effort

Falloff for deciles 1 to 5: 75 percent
Falloff for deciles 6 to 10: 50 percent

Decile	Percent Falloff	Effort 1	Effort 2	Effort 3	Effort 4	Effort 5	Effort 6
1		12.00%	9.00%	6.75%	5.06%	3.80%	2.85%
2	69.5%	8.34	6.26	4.69	3.52	2.64	1.98
3	43.8	5.25	3.94	2.96	2.22	1.66	1.25
4	34.6	4.15	3.12	2.34	1.75	1.31	.99
5	24.9	2.98	2.24	1.68	1.26	.94	.71
6	21.0	2.52	1.26			.00	.00
7	19.8	2.38	1.19			.00	.00
8	19.8	2.38	1.19			.00	.00
9	18.6	2.24	1.12			.00	.00
10	15.7	1.88	.94			.00	.00
Average		4.41%	3.02%	2.30%	2.76%	2.35%	2.02%

Decile	Percent Falloff	Effort 1	Effort 2	Effort 3	Effort 4	Effort 5	Effort 6
1		6,000	4,500	3,375	2,531	1,898	1,424
2	69.5%	4,172	3,129	2,347	1,760	1,320	990
3	43.8	2,627	1,970	1,478	1,108	831	623
4	34.6	2,077	1,558	1,168	876	657	493
5	24.9	1,491	1,118	839	629	472	354
6	21.0	1,260	630	0	0	0	0
7	19.8	1,189	595	0	0	0	0
8	19.8	1,189	595	0	0	0	0
9	18.6	1,118	559	0	0	0	0
10	15.7	941	470	0	0	0	0
Conversions		22,065	15,124	9,206	6,905	5,179	3,884
Cumulative average			37,189	46,396	53,300	58,479	62,363
Conversion rate	4.41%		3.02%	2.30%	2.76%	2.59%	2.59%
Cumulative rate			7.44%	9.28%	10.66%	11.70%	12.47%

	Traditional Marketing	Database Marketing	Difference
Annual number of leads	500,000	500,000	
Number of mailing efforts	4	4	
Total pieces mailed	2,000,000	2,000,000	
Overall response rate	9.24%	12.47%	
Number of conversions	46,198	62,363	16,165
Value of a customer	$200	$200	$0
Contribution to marketing and profits	$9,239,553	$12,472,598	$3,233,046
Mailing CPM	$450	$450	$0
Mailing costs	$900,000	$900,000	$0
Contribution to profits	$8,339,552	$11,572,598	$3,233,046
Decile	50,000		

TABLE 34-15

A Method for Estimating Falloff

A1: [W31] 'DESCRIPTIONS				*READY*
	A	**B**	**C**	**D**
1	DESCRIPTIONS		LOTUS 1-2-3 EQUATIONS	
2	Input: response to 1st mailing	5.00%	b2	
3	Input: response to 2nd mailing	3.00%	b3	
4	Calculate: fall off factor	0.4000	$1 - (b3/b2)$	
5	Input: unit margin	$80.00		
6	Input: cost per M Pieces Mailed	$1,000		
7	Calculate: BE response rate	1.25%	b6/b5/1000	
8	General Equation		$1 - ((1 + b4*(i - 2)/(1 + b4*(j - 2)))$	
9	Fall off between 2nd & 3rd	28.57%	$1 - ((1 + b4*(2 - 2)/(1 + b4*(3 - 2)))$	
10	Fall off between 3rd & 4th	22.22%	$1 - ((1 + b4*(3 - 2)/((1 + b4*(4 - 2)))$	
11	Fall off between 4th & 5th	18.18%	$1 - ((1 + b4*(4 - 2))/(1 + b4*(5 - 2)))$	
12	Fall off between 5th & 6th	15.38%	$1 - ((1 + b4*(5 - 2))/(1 + b4*(6 - 2)))$	
13	3rd response	2.14%	$b3*(1 - b9)$	
14	4th response	1.67%	$b13*(1 - b10)$	
15	5th response	1.36%	$b14*(1 - b11)$	
16	6th response	1.15%	$b15*(1 - b12)$	
17	Cost per order on 3rd mlg	$46.67	b$6(b13*1000)	
18	Cost per order on 4th mlg	$60.00	b$6(b14*1000)	
19	Cost per order on 5th mlg	$73.33	b$6(b15*1000)	
20	Cost per order on 6th mlg	$86.67	b$6(b16*1000)	

Attrition Models

An increasingly popular modeling application is predicting attrition. Credit card companies want to know which customers are likely not to renew their credit cards, banks would like to know when customers are about to close their checking accounts, long distance telephone companies would like to know which customers are likely to switch and when, cable companies want to know about disconnects, and the list goes on and on.

Some situations don't require models. Basically, new customers are much more likely to leave than established customers, so all companies that use a "try it and see if you like it" approach should certainly have retention programs in place that are targeted at all new customers. But in other situations, such as bank card cancellations, not all customers need be, or should be, subjects of a retention program, because it's possible to build models that will accurately predict those customers who are likely to stay and those who are likely to cancel or not renew their credit card.

Table 34-16 shows the kind of results you could expect if you used a logistic regression model to predict cancels four months prior to the fee billing month, in time, it is hoped, to execute an effective retention or anti-attrition program.

Of course, before a credit card company decides to target potentially high cancel rate cardholders, the company has to decide whether someone with a very high probability of canceling is worth saving. This means estimating the expected

TABLE   34–16

Modeling Attrition

	Response		Cumulative	
Decile	Rate		Index	Lift
1	39.7%		307	307
2	25.7		199	253
3	19.6		152	219
4	12.7		98	189
5	8.1		63	164
6	6.1		47	144
7	5.9		46	130
8	4.3		33	118
9	4.0		31	108
10	3.2		25	100
Average	12.9%			100

profits that would result from saving customers with a high probability of canceling. In the case represented by the model shown in Table 34–16 the company decided that Decile 1 cardholders would not be targeted by the retention program, but rather the program should be targeted against cardholders predicted to fall into Deciles 2 through 7. Cardholders in Deciles 8 through 10 were excluded from the program given their low probability of canceling.

ADDING HOUSEHOLD-LEVEL OVERLAY DATA TO PROSPECT MODELS

In earlier chapters we paid a great deal of attention to the sources and uses of enhancement data. In this chapter we will focus on the economics of enhancement data. As before, we first have to define whether we are concerned with new-customer acquisition through the use of rented lists or whether we are considering enhancing our customer database.

In the preceding sections of this chapter we discussed the procedures to follow in building a ZIP code or smaller-area model. However, geographic models are not the only option for prospect promotions. It's theoretically possible to build stronger demographic-lifestyle models based on individual- or household-level data. The argument for considering this alternative is based on the fact that individual-level data is more accurate than small-area data (when measuring the same variable) and that data is available at the individual level that is not available at the ZIP code or lower level. Car ownership is one example.

Two potential problems are associated with this method:

1. To apply the method, a significantly larger number of names has to be ordered than mailed.
2. All names ordered have to be overlaid with data and scored so that only the better (to be defined) names are mailed.

Let's look at the first problem, that is, ordering more names than the number eventually mailed. How many more? Maybe 50 to 100 percent more, depending on the effectiveness of the model. Ordering more names than necessary is not the problem; the problem is getting the list owner's permission and paying for the right to screen the scored names and decide on just how many you wish to mail.

If a list owner insists on being paid the full rate for names not mailed, it will take an unusually good model to make the economics of this transaction pay for itself. If, on the other hand, the list owner is reasonable, understands what you are trying to accomplish, understands that this may be the only way you can use the lists, and finally is willing to accept some reduced rate on names ordered but not mailed, the first hurdle can be overcome.

The second issue is that all names ordered will have to be overlaid with data and scored. If only half the names are mailed, then the effective cost of the data overlay in terms of the names mailed is doubled. This too may be acceptable provided the model is sufficiently strong. And again, the data owner, understanding what you are trying to accomplish, may very well provide you with a favorable rate for data.

So these are the two key issues—the need to examine names that will not be mailed and the need to overlay all names with data so that scoring can take place. As you can see, both issues get down to a question of costs. Is all this trouble and expense justified? Shouldn't we just continue doing business as usual or maybe just use a simple ZIP code model? And again, it all depends, as we shall see, on the strength of the model.

However, before getting to the economics of the model, there are other difficulties associated with this method that should be addressed. The first is that this process obviously takes time and effort on the part of a number of persons and departments. The cost of starting the mailing analysis sooner (all of the work discussed must occur after the merge but before the actual mailing) and the cost of the data processing work involved may be hard to quantify, but these costs are nevertheless real and must be evaluated as part of the decision to go ahead with the process.

Another issue is the fact that not all names will match against the overlay source. As we explained in Chapter 4, you can generally count on somewhere between 45 and 65 percent of your names matching against a national database such as Infobase, Polk, Donnelley, or Metromail. The exact match rate depends on the source and the quality of the names supplied to the outside party. Names that do not match also have to be scored, usually on the basis of block group or carrier route averages provided by the outside vendor.

Having said all this, let's get to the model itself and the decision making involved.

Table 34–17 presents the output of a model of a 1-million-name mailing. The mailing is assumed to have a CPM of $400, and each order is worth $30. In the absence of modeling, the mailer is assumed to have selected the best lists, so the mailing is expected to pull 3.21 percent. The profit from this mailing would be $563,031.

Table 34–18 defines the mailer's list universe of 2 million names and shows all the calculations leading to the $563,031 profit. For simplicity, we have put individual lists together in groups of 100,000. The best-responding lists are shown to have an average response rate of 4.0 percent, the next best a response rate of 3.80 percent, and so on to the poorest-performing lists, whose average response rate is 1.51 percent. The traditional direct marketing procedure, if the objective were to mail 1 million names, would be to stop after the tenth list grouping. That group's response rate is estimated to be 2.52 percent, and the average expected response rate from the top 10 groups is shown to be 3.2 percent.

T A B L E 34–17

The Economics of Predictive Modeling

CPM	$400
Profit per order	$30.00
Cost of data	$50.00
Cost of unused lists	$30.00
Extra lists	1,000,000
Pieces mailed	1,000,000
Average	3.21%

Ratio of Response by Decile

Decile	Individual Segmentation	ZIP	1 Million Piece Mailing	
1	240	150		
2	170	135	Contribution with individual segmentation	$770,084
3	138	125	Cost of data enhancement	100,000
4	112	120	Extra list rental costs	30,000
5	93	105	Profit with individual segmentation	$640,084
6	61	95		
7	55	89	Profit with ZIP code segmentation	$643,144
8	50	80	Difference	($3,060)
9	43	52	Profit without ZIP segmentation	$563,031
10	40	50	Difference	$80,113
Top/bottom	9.6	3.0		
Index	98	100		
Average response	3.91%	3.48%		

Now let's assume that a ZIP code model is available to the mailer, based on a prior mailing of the same offer to the same lists.

Table 34–17 shows the model under the heading "ZIP." As you can see, this model shows the top decile performing at 150 percent of average and the bottom decile performing at 50 percent of average. This is an example of a typical three-to-one ZIP code model.

Table 34–19 shows how the mailer would apply the ZIP code model to the list universe of 2 million names.

The first assumption is that the model would work equally well across all list segments. Thus, we would expect 10 percent of the best list segment, the segment that averages 4 percent, to pull at 150 percent of 4 percent, or at 6 percent. Similarly, the bottom 10 percent of this list segment should pull 2 percent, that is, 50 percent of average.

Table 34–19 therefore creates a 20-by-10 matrix. Each of the 20 list segments is broken up into 10 smaller segments based on the model. Using the traditional method for selecting lists, we find that no list in the eleventh segment (the segment that averages 2.4 percent) would have been mailed, whereas all names in the top 10 segments have been mailed. However, it's obvious that the top decile of lists in the eleventh segment (it pulls 3.6 percent) perform better than the bottom decile of the first segment (it pulls 2 percent).

In theory, what the mailer would like to do is obvious. The mailer would like to sort all of the 200 cells in descending order of expected response and mail

TABLE 34–18

Traditional List Selection Methods

List	Cumulative Quantity	Percent Response	Cumulative Percent Response	Orders	Profit	Cumulative Profit
100,000	100,000	4.00%	4.0%	4,000	$80,000	$80,000
100,000	200,000	3.80	3.9	3,800	74,000	154,000
100,000	300,000	3.61	3.8	3,610	68,300	222,300
100,000	400,000	3.43	3.7	3,430	62885	285,185
100,000	500,000	3.26	3.6	3,258	57,741	342,926
100,000	600,000	3.10	3.5	3,095	52,854	395,779
100,000	700,000	2.94	3.4	2,940	48,221	443,990
100,000	800,000	2.79	3.4	2,793	43,800	487,791
100,000	900,000	2.65	3.3	2,654	39,610	527,401
100,000	1,000,000	2.52	3.2	2,521	35,630	563,031
100,000	1,100,000	2.39	3.1	2,395	31,848	594,880
100,000	1,200,000	2.28	3.1	2,275	28,256	623,136
100,000	1,300,000	2.16	3.0	2,161	24,843	647,979
100,000	1,400,000	2.05	2.9	2,053	21,601	669,580
100,000	1,500,000	1.95	2.9	1,951	18,521	688,101
100,000	1,600,000	1.85	2.8	1,853	15,595	703,696
100,000	1,700,000	1.76	2.7	1,761	12,815	716,511
100,000	1,800,000	1.67	2.7	1,672	10,174	726,686
100,000	1,900,000	1.59	2.6	1,589	7,666	734,351
100,000	2,000,000	1.51	2.6	1,509	5,282	739,634

TABLE 34–19

The ZIP Code Model (List Segments Split on the Basis of the ZIP Code Model)

Quantity	List	D1	D2	D3	D4	D5	D6	D7	D8	D9	D10
100,000	4.0%	6.0%	5.4%	5.0%	4.8%	4.2%	3.8%	3.6%	3.2%	2.1%	2.0%
100,000	3.8	5.7	5.1	4.8	4.6	4.0	3.6	3.4	3.0	2.0	1.9
100,000	3.6	5.4	4.9	4.5	4.3	3.8	3.4	3.2	2.9	1.9	1.8
100,000	3.4	5.1	4.6	4.3	4.1	3.6	3.3	3.1	2.7	1.8	1.7
100,000	3.3	4.9	4.4	4.1	3.9	3.4	3.1	2.9	2.6	1.7	1.6
100,000	3.1	4.6	4.2	3.9	3.7	3.2	2.9	2.8	2.5	1.6	1.5
100,000	2.9	4.4	4.0	3.7	3.5	3.1	2.8	2.6	2.4	1.5	1.5
100,000	2.8	4.2	3.8	3.5	3.4	2.9	2.7	2.5	2.2	1.5	1.4
100,000	2.7	4.0	3.6	3.3	3.2	2.8	2.5	2.4	2.1	1.4	1.3
100,000	2.5	3.8	3.4	3.2	3.0	2.6	2.4	2.2	2.0	1.3	1.3
100,000	2.4	3.6	3.2	3.0	2.9	2.5	2.3	2.1	1.9	1.2	1.2
100,000	2.3	3.4	3.1	2.8	2.7	2.4	2.2	2.0	1.8	1.2	1.1
100,000	2.2	3.2	2.9	2.7	2.6	2.3	2.1	1.9	1.7	1.1	1.1
100,000	2.1	3.1	2.8	2.6	2.5	2.2	2.0	1.8	1.6	1.1	1.0
100,000	2.0	2.9	2.6	2.4	2.3	2.0	1.9	1.7	1.6	1.0	1.0
100,000	1.9	2.8	2.5	2.3	2.2	1.9	1.8	1.6	1.5	1.0	.9
100,000	1.8	2.6	2.4	2.2	2.1	1.8	1.7	1.6	1.4	.9	.9
100,000	1.7	2.5	2.3	2.1	2.0	1.8	1.6	1.5	1.3	.9	.8
100,000	1.6	2.4	2.1	2.0	1.9	1.7	1.5	1.4	1.3	.8	.8
100,000	1.5	2.3	2.0	1.9	1.8	1.6	1.4	1.3	1.2	.8	.8
2,000,000											

only those segments that make up the top 1 million names. In practice, the mailer will not be able to perform with this degree of precision, and he or she will approximate this procedure. For example, the mailer may mail all ZIPs where the expected average rate is above 3.5 percent, suppress the ZIPs represented by the bottom four deciles among lists expected to pull between 3 and 3.5 percent, suppress ZIPs from the bottom four deciles among lists expected to pull between 2 and 3 percent, and finally order only names from the top two deciles from among lists expected to pull between 1.5 and 1.99 percent.

Returning to Table 34–17, we see that the use of the ZIP code model would result in the average response rate going from 3.21 to 3.48 percent and profits going from $563,031 to $643,144, an increase of $80,113, or 14.2 percent.

Now let's consider the question of whether the mailer should attempt to build a more sophisticated model, built not on ZIP code census data but instead on individual specific-level data. These are the questions to ask:

- How good will this model be?
- What will it cost to overlay all of my 2 million names with data?
- What will I have to pay for names that are examined but not mailed?
- How will I model names that do not match the national household file?

The answer to the first question—how good will the model be—is shown in Table 34–17 under the heading "Individual Segmentation." As you can see, the household model is much stronger than the ZIP code model. In statistical shorthand, it's a six-to-one model, whereas the ZIP code model was a three-to-one model. Further, the model assumes that overlay data and model scoring will cost $50 per thousand, and list owners have agreed to accept $30 per thousand for names not mailed. We've also made the assumption that names that could not be matched would be subject to a ZIP code model and merged into the final name selection process.

If everything were to work as planned and the model could be applied with great precision across all lists, in theory response rates would increase to 3.91 percent, and contribution to profits would increase to $770,084 before data and extra list rental expense and would equal $640,084 after these expenses were taken into consideration. Table 34–20 shows how the decile segmentation would work in theory, and Table 34–21 details how the individual cells would be sorted and how the 1-million-piece mailing would be constructed.

This is a better statistical but less profitable model than the simpler and less expensive ZIP code model. Does this example mean that we should never try to use individual-level data to build customer acquisition models? Not at all; it just means that the models have to be significantly stronger to warrant their costs. Table 34–22 shows what would happen if the individual-level model were not a 6-to-1 model but rather a 10-to-1 model. In this case, the additional profits after list and data expense would exceed the results of the ZIP code model by $60,535.

Is $60,535 enough extra profit to cover the additional costs not explicitly defined in the model? That's a difficult question to answer, and different companies will answer it differently. However, the purpose of this exercise is primarily to provide mailers with a framework for evaluating model proposals. Armed with a framework in which to measure the likelihood of a model performing as promised, and knowing what cost questions to ask, mailers can make their own decisions about the value of new-customer acquisition modeling.

TABLE 34-20

The Household Model (List Segments Split on the Basis of Household Data)

Quantity	List	D1	D2	D3	D4	D5	D6	D7	D8	D9	D10
100,000	4.0%	9.6%	6.8%	5.5%	4.5%	3.7%	2.4%	2.2%	2.0%	1.7%	1.6%
100,000	3.8	9.1	6.4	5.2	4.2	3.5	2.3	2.1	1.9	1.6	1.5
100,000	3.6	8.6	6.1	5.0	4.0	3.4	2.2	2.0	1.8	1.5	1.4
100,000	3.4	8.2	5.8	4.7	3.8	3.2	2.1	1.9	1.7	1.5	1.4
100,000	3.3	7.8	5.5	4.5	3.6	3.0	2.0	1.8	1.6	1.4	1.3
100,000	3.1	7.4	5.3	4.3	3.5	2.9	1.9	1.7	1.5	1.3	1.2
100,000	2.9	7.0	5.0	4.0	3.3	2.7	1.8	1.6	1.5	1.3	1.2
100,000	2.8	6.7	4.7	3.8	3.1	2.6	1.7	1.5	1.4	1.2	1.1
100,000	2.7	6.4	4.5	3.7	3.0	2.5	1.6	1.5	1.3	1.1	1.1
100,000	2.5	6.0	4.3	3.5	2.8	2.3	1.5	1.4	1.3	1.1	1.0
100,000	2.4	5.7	4.1	3.3	2.7	2.2	1.5	1.3	1.2	1.0	1.0
100,000	2.3	5.4	3.9	3.1	2.5	2.1	1.4	1.2	1.1	1.0	0.9
100,000	2.2	5.2	3.7	3.0	2.4	2.0	1.3	1.2	1.1	0.9	0.9
100,000	2.1	4.9	3.5	2.8	2.3	1.9	1.3	1.1	1.0	0.9	0.8
100,000	2.0	4.7	3.3	2.7	2.2	1.8	1.2	1.1	1.0	0.8	0.8
100,000	1.9	4.4	3.1	2.6	2.1	1.7	1.1	1.0	0.9	0.8	0.7
100,000	1.8	4.2	3.0	2.4	2.0	1.6	1.1	1.0	0.9	0.8	0.7
100,000	1.7	4.0	2.8	2.3	1.9	1.6	1.0	0.9	0.8	0.7	0.7
100,000	1.6	3.8	2.7	2.2	1.8	1.5	1.0	0.9	0.8	0.7	0.6
100,000	1.5	3.6	2.6	2.1	1.7	1.4	0.9	0.8	0.8	0.6	0.6

TABLE 34-21

Contribution by Sorted List Segments

Segment Quantity	Cumulative Quantity	List Segment Ranked	Average	Orders	Before Enhancement Costs	
					Contribution	Cumulative
10,000	10,000	9.58%	9.58%	958	24,743	24,743
10,000	20,000	9.10	9.34	910	23,305	48,048
10,000	30,000	8.65	9.11	865	21,940	69,988
10,000	40,000	8.21	8.89	821	20,643	90,631
10,000	50,000	7.80	8.67	780	19,411	110,042
10,000	60,000	7.41	8.46	741	18,240	128,283
10,000	70,000	7.04	8.26	704	17,128	145,411
10,000	80,000	6.79	8.07	679	16,359	161,770
10,000	90,000	6.69	7.92	669	16,072	177,842
10,000	100,000	6.45	7.77	645	15,341	193,183
10,000	110,000	6.36	7.64	636	15,068	208,252
10,000	120,000	6.12	7.52	612	14,374	222,626
10,000	130,000	6.04	7.40	604	14,115	236,741
10,000	140,000	5.82	7.29	582	13,456	250,197
10,000	150,000	5.74	7.19	574	13,209	263,406
10,000	160,000	5.53	7.08	553	12,583	275,989
10,000	170,000	5.51	6.99	551	12,527	288,515
10,000	180,000	5.45	6.90	545	12,349	300,864
10,000	190,000	5.25	6.82	525	11,754	312,618
10,000	200,000	5.23	6.74	523	11,701	324,318
10,000	210,000	5.18	6.66	518	11,531	335,850
10,000	220,000	4.99	6.59	499	10,966	346,816

T A B L E 34–21

Contribution by Sorted List Segments

Segment Quantity	Cumulative Quantity	List Segment Ranked	Average	Orders	Before Enhancement Costs	
					Contribution	Cumulative
10,000	230,000	4.97%	6.52	497%	10,916	357,731
10,000	240,000	4.92	6.45	492	10,755	368,486
10,000	250,000	4.74	6.38	474	10,218	378,704
10,000	260,000	4.72	6.32	472	10,170	388,873
10,000	270,000	4.67	6.26	467	10,017	398,890
10,000	280,000	4.50	6.20	450	9,507	408,397
10,000	290,000	4.49	6.14	449	9,461	417,859
10,000	300,000	4.47	6.08	447	9,413	427,272
10,000	310,000	4.44	6.03	444	9,316	436,588
10,000	320,000	4.28	5.97	428	8,831	445,419
10,000	330,000	4.26	5.92	426	8,788	454,208
10,000	340,000	4.25	5.87	425	8,743	462,950
10,000	350,000	4.22	5.82	422	8,650	471,600
10,000	360,000	4.06	5.78	406	8,190	479,790
10,000	370,000	4.05	5.73	405	8,149	487,939
10,000	380,000	4.04	5.68	404	8,105	496,044
10,000	390,000	4.01	5.64	401	8,018	504,062
10,000	400,000	3.86	5.60	386	7,580	511,643
10,000	410,000	3.85	5.55	385	7,541	519,184
10,000	420,000	3.83	5.51	383	7,500	526,684
10,000	430,000	3.81	5.47	381	7,417	534,101
10,000	440,000	3.71	5.43	371	7,138	541,239
10,000	450,000	3.67	5.39	367	7,001	548,240
10,000	460,000	3.65	5.36	365	6,964	555,204
10,000	470,000	3.64	5.32	364	6,925	562,130
10,000	480,000	3.62	5.28	362	6,846	568,976
10,000	490,000	3.53	5.25	353	6,581	575,557
10,000	500,000	3.48	5.21	348	6,451	582,008
10,000	510,000	3.47	5.18	347	6,416	588,424
10,000	520,000	3.46	5.15	346	6,379	594,803
10,000	530,000	3.35	5.11	335	6,052	600,855
10,000	540,000	3.31	5.08	331	5,929	606,783
10,000	550,000	3.30	5.05	330	5,895	612,679
10,000	560,000	3.29	5.02	329	5,860	618,538
10,000	570,000	3.18	4.98	318	5,549	624,088
10,000	580,000	3.14	4.95	314	5,432	629,520
10,000	590,000	3.13	4.92	313	5,401	634,920
10,000	600,000	3.12	4.89	312	5,367	640,287
10,000	610,000	3.02	4.86	302	5,072	645,359
10,000	620,000	2.99	4.83	299	4,961	650,320
10,000	630,000	2.98	4.80	298	4,931	655,250
10,000	640,000	2.97	4.77	297	4,899	660,149
10,000	650,000	2.87	4.74	287	4,618	664,767
10,000	660,000	2.84	4.71	284	4,513	669,280
10,000	670,000	2.83	4.69	283	4,484	673,764
10,000	680,000	2.82	4.66	282	4,454	678,217
10,000	690,000	2.73	4.63	273	4,187	682,405
10,000	700,000	2.70	4.60	270	4,087	686,492
10,000	710,000	2.69	4.58	269	4,060	690,551
10,000	720,000	2.68	4.55	268	4,031	694,582

TABLE 34–21

Continued

Segment Quantity	Cumulative Quantity	List Segment Ranked	Average	Orders	Before Enhancement Costs	
					Contribution	Cumulative
10,000	730,000	2.59%	4.52%	259%	3,778	698,360
10,000	740,000	2.56	4.50	256	3,683	702,043
10,000	750,000	2.55	4.47	255	3,657	705,700
10,000	760,000	2.54	4.44	254	3,629	709,329
10,000	770,000	2.46	4.42	246	3,389	712,718
10,000	780,000	2.44	4.39	244	3,305	716,023
10,000	790,000	2.42	4.37	242	3,274	719,297
10,000	800,000	2.42	4.34	242	3,248	722,545
10,000	810,000	2.34	4.32	234	3,020	725,565
10,000	820,000	2.31	4.29	231	2,940	728,505
10,000	830,000	2.30	4.27	230	2,910	731,415
10,000	840,000	2.30	4.25	230	2,886	734,301
10,000	850,000	2.22	4.22	222	2,669	736,969
10,000	860,000	2.20	4.20	220	2,593	739,562
10,000	870,000	2.20	4.18	220	2,587	742,149
10,000	880,000	2.19	4.15	219	2,565	744,714
10,000	890,000	2.18	4.13	218	2,541	747,255
10,000	900,000	2.11	4.11	211	2,335	749,590
10,000	910,000	2.09	4.09	209	2,263	751,854
10,000	920,000	2.09	4.07	209	2,257	754,111
10,000	930,000	2.08	4.04	208	2,237	756,348
10,000	940,000	2.07	4.02	207	2,214	758,562
10,000	950,000	2.01	4.00	201	2,018	760,580
10,000	960,000	2.00	3.98	200	1,988	762,568
10,000	970,000	1.98	3.96	198	1,950	764,519
10,000	980,000	1.98	3.94	198	1,945	766,463
10,000	990,000	1.97	3.92	197	1,903	768,367
10,000	1,000,000	1.91	3.90	191	1,717	770,084
10,000	1,010,000	1.90	3.88	190	1,689	771,773
10,000	1,020,000	1.88	3.86	188	1,653	773,426
10,000	1,030,000	1.88	3.84	188	1,647	775,073
10,000	1,040,000	1.87	3.82	187	1,608	776,681
10,000	1,050,000	1.81	3.80	181	1,432	778,113
10,000	1,060,000	1.80	3.78	180	1,404	779,517
10,000	1,070,000	1.79	3.77	179	1,370	780,887
10,000	1,080,000	1.79	3.75	179	1,365	782,252
10,000	1,090,000	1.78	3.73	178	1,328	783,580
10,000	1,100,000	1.72	3.71	172	1,160	784,740
10,000	1,110,000	1.72	3.69	172	1,150	785,890
10,000	1,120,000	1.71	3.68	171	1,134	787,024
10,000	1,130,000	1.70	3.66	170	1,102	788,126
10,000	1,140,000	1.70	3.64	170	1,097	789,222
10,000	1,150,000	1.69	3.62	169	1,062	790,284
10,000	1,160,000	1.63	3.61	163	902	791,186
10,000	1,170,000	1.63	3.59	163	892	792,078
10,000	1,180,000	1.63	3.57	163	877	792,955
10,000	1,190,000	1.62	3.56	162	847	793,802
10,000	1,200,000	1.61	3.54	161	842	794,644
10,000	1,210,000	1.60	3.52	160	790	795,434
10,000	1,220,000	1.55	3.51	155	657	796,091

Continued

Segment Quantity	Cumulative Quantity	List Segment Ranked	Average	Orders	Before Enhancement Costs	
					Contribution	Cumulative
10,000	1,230,000	1.55%	3.49%	155	648	796,739
10,000	1,240,000	1.54	3.48	154	633	797,372
10,000	1,250,000	1.53	3.46	153	604	797,976
10,000	1,260,000	1.53	3.45	153	600	798,576
10,000	1,270,000	1.52	3.43	152	551	799,127
10,000	1,280,000	1.47	3.42	147	424	799,551
10,000	1,290,000	1.47	3.40	147	415	799,966
10,000	1,300,000	1.47	3.39	147	402	800,368
10,000	1,310,000	1.46	3.37	146	374	800,742
10,000	1,320,000	1.46	3.36	146	370	801,112
10,000	1,330,000	1.44	3.34	144	323	801,435
10,000	1,340,000	1.40	3.33	140	203	801,638
10,000	1,350,000	1.40	3.31	140	194	801,833
10,000	1,360,000	1.39	3.30	139	182	802,014
10,000	1,370,000	1.39	3.29	139	155	802,170
10,000	1,380,000	1.38	3.27	138	151	802,321
10,000	1,390,000	1.37	3.26	137	107	802,428
10,000	1,400,000	1.33	3.24	133	(15)	802,413
10,000	1,410,000	1.32	3.23	132	(27)	802,385
10,000	1,420,000	1.32	3.22	132	(52)	802,333
10,000	1,430,000	1.31	3.20	131	(56)	802,277
10,000	1,440,000	1.30	3.19	130	(98)	802,179
10,000	1,450,000	1.26	3.18	126	(214)	801,964
10,000	1,460,000	1.26	3.16	126	(226)	801,738
10,000	1,470,000	1.25	3.15	125	(250)	801,488
10,000	1,480,000	1.25	3.14	125	(253)	801,235
10,000	1,490,000	1.24	3.13	124	(293)	800,942
10,000	1,500,000	1.20	3.11	120	(404)	800,538
10,000	1,510,000	1.20	3.10	120	(415)	800,123
10,000	1,520,000	1.19	3.09	119	(437)	799,686
10,000	1,530,000	1.19	3.07	119	(441)	799,245
10,000	1,540,000	1.17	3.06	117	(479)	798,766
10,000	1,550,000	1.14	3.05	114	(584)	798,183
10,000	1,560,000	1.14	3.04	114	(594)	797,589
10,000	1,570,000	1.13	3.03	113	(615)	796,973
10,000	1,580,000	1.13	3.01	113	(619)	796,355
10,000	1,590,000	1.12	3.00	112	(655)	795,700
10,000	1,600,000	1.08	2.99	108	(754)	794,945
10,000	1,610,000	1.08	2.98	108	(764)	794,181
10,000	1,620,000	1.07	2.97	107	(785)	793,396
10,000	1,630,000	1.07	2.95	107	(788)	792,609
10,000	1,640,000	1.06	2.94	106	(822)	791,787
10,000	1,650,000	1.03	2.93	103	(917)	790,870
10,000	1,660,000	1.02	2.92	102	(926)	789,944
10,000	1,670,000	1.02	2.91	102	(945)	788,999
10,000	1,680,000	1.02	2.90	102	(948)	788,050
10,000	1,690,000	1.01	2.89	101	(981)	787,069
10,000	1,700,000	0.98	2.87	98	(1,071)	785,998
10,000	1,710,000	0.97	2.86	97	(1,080)	784,919
10,000	1,720,000	0.97	2.85	97	(1,098)	783,820

TABLE 34–21

Concluded

Segment Quantity	Cumulative Quantity	List Segment Ranked	Average	Orders	Before Enhancement Costs	
					Contribution	Cumulative
10,000	1,730,000	0.97%	2.84%	97	(1,101)	782,719
10,000	1,740,000	0.96	2.83	96	(1,132)	781,588
10,000	1,750,000	0.93	2.82	93	(1,217)	780,370
10,000	1,760,000	0.92	2.81	92	(1,226)	779,145
10,000	1,770,000	0.92	2.80	92	(1,243)	777,901
10,000	1,780,000	0.92	2.79	92	(1,246)	776,655
10,000	1,790,000	0.91	2.78	91	(1,275)	775,380
10,000	1,800,000	0.88	2.77	88	(1,356)	774,024
10,000	1,810,000	0.88	2.76	88	(1,365)	772,659
10,000	1,820,000	0.87	2.75	87	(1,384)	771,276
10,000	1,830,000	0.86	2.74	86	(1,411)	769,864
10,000	1,840,000	0.84	2.73	84	(1,489)	768,376
10,000	1,850,000	0.83	2.72	83	(1,496)	766,879
10,000	1,860,000	0.83	2.70	83	(1,514)	765,365
10,000	1,870,000	0.82	2.69	82	(1,541)	763,824
10,000	1,880,000	0.80	2.68	80	(1,614)	762,210
10,000	1,890,000	0.79	2.67	79	(1,621)	760,588
10,000	1,900,000	0.78	2.66	78	(1,664)	758,924
10,000	1,910,000	0.76	2.65	76	(1,733)	757,191
10,000	1,920,000	0.75	2.64	75	(1,740)	755,451
10,000	1,930,000	0.74	2.64	74	(1,781)	753,670
10,000	1,940,000	0.72	2.63	72	(1,847)	751,823
10,000	1,950,000	0.70	2.62	70	(1,892)	749,932
10,000	1,960,000	0.68	2.61	68	(1,954)	747,977
10,000	1,970,000	0.67	2.60	67	(1,997)	745,980
10,000	1,980,000	0.65	2.59	65	(2,057)	743,923
10,000	1,990,000	0.63	2.58	63	(2,097)	741,826
10,000	2,000,000	0.60	2.57	60	(2,192)	739,634

ADDING HOUSEHOLD-LEVEL OVERLAY DATA TO INTERNAL CUSTOMER MODELS

Although new-customer acquisition models are totally dependent on ZIP code-level data or individual-level data appended from external sources, internal models of customer performance don't necessarily need to include enhancement data. In fact, the recommended procedure for building internal predictive models is to start with internal data and proceed to build the best model possible. Then, add external enhancement data to the set of independent data and see if the external data will enable you to build a more powerful model.

What are you likely to find? It depends on your business. If you are in the financial services business, selling expensive products or age-dependent products (and age and income are not normally captured internal variables on your prospect file), then there is a good likelihood that adding this kind of information will result in more powerful models. On the other hand, if the kinds of external demographic data, psychographic data, or both available to you are not as criti-

T A B L E 34–22

The Economics of Predictive Modeling

CPM	$400.00
Profit per order	$30.00
Cost of data	$50.00
Cost of unused lists	$30.00
Extra lists	1,000,000
Pieces mailed	1,000,000
Average	3.21%

Ratio of Response by Decile

Decile	Individual Segmentation	ZIP	One Million Piece Mailing	
1	250	150		
2	200	135	Contribution with individual segmentation	$833,679
3	150	125	Cost of data enhancement	100,000
4	110	120	Extra list rental costs	30,000
5	80	105	Profit with individual segmentation	$703,679
6	61	95		
7	50	89	Profit with ZIP code segmentation	$643,144
8	40	80	Difference	$60,535
9	33	52	Profit without segmentation	$563,031
10	25	50	Difference	$80,113
Top/bottom	10.0	3.0		
Index	100	100		
Average response	4.11%	3.48%		

cal to the sale of your product or service, then the chances are less likely that the addition of external data will make a difference in your ability to develop predictive models.

So the answer is that you have to experiment and see if external data makes a difference. There are really two questions that need to be answered:

- First, will external data produce a better model in a statistical sense? That is, have the external variables entered the model, and are they statistically significant?

- Second, will the model account for more variation (have a higher R^2)? And most importantly, will the validation study assign more customers to the top deciles than was the case based on the models that excluded external data?

If the answers to these questions are yes, the model is better from a statistical standpoint. The second issue is then one of costs. How much did it cost to overlay your entire file, and are the extra costs worth the added power they brought to your model? This kind of question can be answered quickly with a simple Lotus 1-2-3 model like the one shown in Table 34–23.

The example shown in Table 34–23 is that of a mailer with 2 million names on the customer database. Let's assume that the mailer has built a model based just on internal performance data, and that the model predicts that the response

TABLE 34–23

The Value of Enhancement Data to Predictive Customer Models

	Assumptions	Results
Total customer database	2,000,000	
Percent of customers to be mailed	50.00%	
Number of names to be mailed		1,000,000
Internal data model		
Expected response rate using internal data only model	8.00%	
Expected number of responses		80,000
Value of an order	$20.00	
Value of all orders		$1,600,000
Internal plus enhancement data model		
Expected response rate using enhanced data model	8.80%	
Expected number of responses		88,000
Value of an order	$20.00	
Value of all orders		$1,760,000
Incremental results		
Incremental responses		8,000
Incremental value from enhanced model before data costs		$160,000
Cost of enhancement data M	$50.00	
Total cost of enhancement data		$100,000
Incremental value from enhanced model after data costs		$60,000

rate to the next mailing among the top half of the file will be 8 percent and will produce $1.6 million in profits.

Would this mailer have been better if the entire file had been overlaid with external data and a model that included both internal and external variables had been built? Let's assume that to build and implement such a model, the mailer would have had to overlay the entire file with data and that data costs $50 per thousand names, or $100,000. If a model built on this data could result in a 10 percent improvement in response (from 8 to 8.8 percent), profits before enhancement data from just this one mailing alone will increase by $160,000. Profits after enhancement data costs would be up by $60,000. So in this case, enhancing the file would have made sense. And it's important to point out that an enhanced file can support many mailings and many models, so there is no need for enhanced data to pay for itself on the basis of just one mailing application.

Of course, if the mailer wished to mail less than 50 percent of the file, if the enhanced model were less powerful, or if data costs were more than $50 per thousand, the results would have been different. For example, Table 34–24 shows that if the mailing quantity were reduced to only 20 percent of the customer database, the result of this exercise would be $36,000 in reduced profits.

The point of this exercise is that each mailer will have to decide the likely benefits of enhancing the file. Of course, predictive modeling may not be the only

T A B L E   34–24

The Value of Enhancement Data to Predictive Customer Models

	Assumptions	Results
Total customer database	2,000,000	
Percent of customers to be mailed	20.00%	
Number of names to be mailed		400,000
Internal data model		
Expected response rate using internal data only model	8.00%	
Expected number of responses		32,000
Value of an order	$20.00	
Value of all orders		$640,000
Internal plus enhancement data model		
Expected response rate using enhanced data model	8.80%	
Expected number of responses		35,200
Value of an order	$20.00	
Value of all orders		$704,000
Incremental results		
Incremental responses		3,200
Incremental value from enhanced model before data costs		$64,000
Cost of enhancement data M	$50.00	
Total cost of enhancement data		$100,000
Incremental value from enhanced model after data costs		$(36,000)

reason to enhance a database with overlay information. It may not even be the best reason.

Let's assume for the moment that enhancement does not result in better, more cost-effective predictive models, but that an examination of the customer file based on enhanced data shows that those customers in the best-performing deciles have a different demographic profile than those customers in the poorer-performing deciles have. Let's assume that age and sex are the demographic variables in question, that younger males are performing better than older males, and that both male groups are performing worse than females of any age. Wouldn't it make sense either to develop different creative strategies for each market segment or to attempt to develop different products for males? It's important to remember that predictive modeling only forecasts what is likely to happen if you repeat the same offer to the same population. Predictive modeling won't necessarily tell you anything about the characteristics of your buyers and your nonbuyers. Profiling will, and profiling generally requires overlay data.

ENHANCING YOUR DATABASE WITH INTERNAL SURVEY DATA

Up to now we have dealt with only two kinds of data—internal performance data and external demographic or lifestyle overlay data. We expect that the next major source of data will be individual-level research data based on internal customer surveys.

One of the interesting things about predictive models is that despite their ability to identify the best- and poorest-responding customers or prospects, even the best models, particularly response models, generally account for less than 5 or 10 percent of the variation we see in response. What's missing from our models is better, more relevant data. It's obvious that persons living within the same ZIP code, or even within the same block group, differ dramatically with regard to their product and service needs, and even individuals with identical demographic characteristics will differ significantly in their response to our promotions. So we need to know much more about the individual needs and wants of our customers and prospects, and this can only happen by creating a dialogue with the customer.

As mentioned in Chapter 1, Lester Wunderman observed that a customer has to be (1) able, (2) willing, and (3) ready to buy before a direct sale can be consummated. Overlay data is helpful in determining if a prospect has the economic ability to buy from us, but overlay data provides little or no information about the prospect's willingness or readiness to buy. So we have to ask.

The alternative to asking is to continue as usual, sending mailing pieces to lists and geographic areas within lists that work for our product or service. The problem with asking is that it is perceived to be difficult and expensive. Like everything else in this book, we eventually get back to the question of economic trade-offs.

Fortunately, we at least know how to ask questions if costs are of no concern. As we first mentioned in Chapter 2, for years market researchers have performed in-depth segmentation studies for traditional and nontraditional direct marketing companies. The process involves both survey design skills and statistical skills, and it goes as follows:

1. Select a random sample of from 500 to a few thousand customers or prospects.
2. Design an in-depth questionnaire. The total questionnaire may contain 100 or more questions. Frequently, the questionnaire is divided into three sections:
   a. *Behavior information.* Do you belong to a book club? Do you subscribe to magazines? Do you buy financial services through the mail? Do you have a stockbroker?
   b. *Attitudes about the category.* Do you read to relax or for information? Would you describe yourself as an intellectual? How important is it to you to be aware of best-sellers? Would you describe yourself as a financial risk taker? Do you rely on others for financial advice? Do you think banks provide good investment advice?
   c. *Demographic questions.* The usual age, income, education, occupation, and family-size questions.
3. Perform a factor and a cluster analysis on the results (see Chapter 29). If you are successful, you will probably discover that there are three to six different market segments within your prospect or customer file.

Staying with our book club and financial services examples, the book club might discover that one segment of its market is composed of people who consider books absolutely critical to their existence—to these people, books are the key to knowledge and information and without books they could not function.

Conversely, the club is likely to find that there is another segment that reads a lot but entirely for escape. A third segment may consist of infrequent readers who feel guilty about not reading more, and so on.

On the financial services side there may be a segment of independent risk takers. These people do their own research, make up their own minds, and aren't afraid to invest by mail. On the other end of the spectrum may be the very conservative, who need the comfort of a personal representative to close a transaction. Nevertheless, this segment responds to mailings that promise financial rewards — they're great leads but very difficult to convert into customers.

The information and the insights that this kind of segmentation analysis provides are clearly invaluable to direct marketers. If we knew to which segment an individual belonged, we could tailor our creative strategy and offers accordingly. However, the problem for direct marketers has been an inability to translate research results into actionable marketing information. Obviously, you can't send a 100-question survey to all your customers, much less to all your prospects.

Database marketers committed to making this process work are experimenting with two solutions.

The first solution involves building a model in which the dependent variable is segment membership, and the independent variables are all those performance and overlay variables we know about the customer or prospect. This model scores each customer on the likelihood of belonging to any one segment according to values on the variables that were statistically determined to be linked with segment membership. In this case, each customer will have a probability of belonging to any of the market segments discovered by the survey.

If the model is successful, then every customer on the database can be scored and the database will maintain a record of each customer's probability of belonging to each market segment. The direct marketer will then be able to develop a targeted appeal to members of each segment and mail only to members whose probability of belonging to the particular segment exceeds some chosen level. Of course, it's possible that modeling will not be able to reliably link segment membership with the known performance and demographic variables.

In that case, there is a second method that can be tested. This method starts by using statistical methods to identify the smallest number of questions that can reliably define segment membership. The hope is that the analysis will discover a handful of questions that can be asked of everyone and that this information can economically be added to the database. This method offers particular promise to those companies that maintain large prospect files consisting of leads who have failed to respond to prior efforts but who may respond to more targeted appeals.

Table 34–25 provides a framework for examining the economics of this methodology. Table 34–25 begins by assuming a prospect file of 500,000 names to which a cumulative 14.32 percent response would be achieved if each person received up to six mailings. However, as shown, the response rates to the fourth, fifth, and sixth mailings are unprofitable. Therefore, this company would make only three mailings to the entire file.

What if, instead of mailing everyone on the file three times, we began by mailing everyone on the file a short questionnaire designed to determine if the prospect wished to receive more offers from the company, and, if so, to have the respondent supply us with the answers to a few attitude and demographic ques-

TABLE 34-25

The Economics of Questionnaire Research

Mailing Effort	Percent Response	Mailed	Cost	Orders	Cost/ Order	Profit/ Order	Cumulative			
							Orders	Costs	Profits	Csts/Ord
1	5.00%	500,000	$300,000	25,000	$12.00	$18.00	25,000	$300,000	$450,000	$12.00
2	3.00	500,000	300,000	15,000	20.00	10.00	40,000	600,000	600,000	15.00
3	2.14	475,000	285,000	10,165	28.04	1.96	50,165	885,000	619,950	17.64
4	1.67	460,750	276,540	7,695	35.93	(5.93)	57,860	1,161,450	574,336	20.07
5	1.36	450,890	270,534	6,132	44.12	(14.12)	63,992	1,431,984	487,765	22.38
6	1.15	443,360	266,016	5,099	52.17	(22.17)	69,090	1,698,000	374,708	24.58

Cumulative   14.32%

Assumptions

Cost Per Piece	$.60
Profit Per Order	$30.00
Mailing Universe	500,000

Percent of universe answering questionnaire	30.00%	Questionnaire costs	
Number answering questionnaire	150,000	Mailing costs per questionnaire	$0.50
Percent wishing to be dropped	10.00%	Total mailing costs	$250,000
Number wishing to be dropped	15,000	Costs of processing completed questionnaires	$1.00
Number receiving six mailings	135,000	Total processing costs	$135,000
Number of mailings	810,000	Costs of taking persons off file	$0.50
Costs of promotion mailings	$486,000	Total costs of taking persons off file	$7,500
Percent of total orders received	80.00%	Total questionnaire related costs	$392,500
Number of orders received	55,272	Contribution after questionnaire costs	$779,666
Contribution from orders	$1,658,166		
Contribution to profits before		Increased profits from questionnaire strategy	
questionnaire costs	$1,172,166	Normal profits	$619,950
		Questionnaire strategy	$779,666
		Increase	$159,716

tions so that we could better serve his or her needs. We'll use this information to place the respondent in the correct market segment and send members of each segment the most appropriate mailing packages.

Can this process possibly pay for itself? As usual, the answer depends on the validity of some set of assumptions. Let's assume that 30 percent of the names receiving the questionnaire respond but that these 30 percent include 80 percent of the orders that would have resulted from a six-part mailing. Let's further assume that it costs $.50 to mail out the questionnaires to everyone, an additional $1 to process the respondents that complete the questionnaire and wish to receive more mailings, and $.50 to take a customer off the file, with 10 percent of the respondents asking to be taken off the file.

This means that a total of $392,500 will be spent before the first promotional mailing is made. Then, all of the respondents who wish to receive more information will stay on the database and receive six mailings at a cost of $.60 per mailing. The nonrespondents will not receive additional mailings.

The result of this work will be an additional $159,716 in bottom-line profits, after questionnaire costs.

How repeatable are these numbers? Again, it's very hard to say, and the results will vary from company to company. Once more, our primary objective is not to produce a set of rules but rather to provide a framework for thinking about the economics of database marketing.

IMPLEMENTING MODELS

The tendency among marketers new to modeling is to focus their attention on the statistical aspects of modeling—whether we should use logistic or ordinary regression, and so on. In fact, the more difficult problems have to do with the accuracy of the data available for modeling and the problems associated with integrating models into existing business systems.

For these reasons it is imperative to bring in data processing and operations personnel at the start of the modeling process. From the beginning they should be thinking about the systems that will have to be put in place if the modeling shows the results everyone is hoping for. In turn, the modeling effort should be tempered by the realities of the data that will be available for modeling on an ongoing basis.

For example, one common problem is that historical trend data is frequently useful in certain types of modeling applications, especially attrition models. Changes in behavior often signal an impending cancellation. But the problem is that historical data is frequently unavailable because files are updated each month with new data and cumulative fields recalculated. The need for historical information should be considered in advance—either existing systems will have to be changed if the models warrant this kind of expense, or the modeling will have to make do without historical data, as valuable as it might be.

The time to make all these decisions is at the start of the project. Before modeling begins, everyone involved should know what the consequences of a successful modeling project will be on existing operations.

MODELING, MANAGING, AND MARKETING TO UNIQUE CUSTOMER SEGMENTS

To a large extent this chapter has dealt with the issue of selecting customers or prospects for a single mailing or a series of mailings. The underlying premise has been that some mailing universe is about to become the target of a single mailing or mailing campaign; however, all available names will not be mailed either for budget or for profitability reasons.

In the first instance the budget is not sufficient to mail all the names available, so a mechanism is needed to identify and mail to the most profitable segments within the mailing universe. In the second instance the budget may be sufficient, but not all names can be mailed profitably. That is, if everyone were mailed, the response rate would fall below the break-even point, and so a process or a model is needed to identify segments of the mailing universe whose expected response rate is above break-even, or some agreed-upon rate of return.

This scenario is useful for teaching purposes because it is simple and we can focus our attention on the statistical issues involved in building reliable models. But the real world is more complicated. Not all customers or prospects should necessarily be placed into the same mailing universe to which we will apply a single selection model.

For example, we all know of companies that produce only one monthly or one quarterly catalog. All customers selected for mailing receive the same promotion. In some cases the same promotion vehicle, especially if it is a catalog, is sent to prospects as well as to customers. (In this context prospects are defined as unconverted leads or inquirers, i.e., names on the database that have not yet made their first purchase, as opposed to rented names or compiled names.)

By now, everyone has figured out some strategy for deciding who gets mailed and how often. This contact strategy may be based on common sense, on simple or complex RFM models, or on regression models. For example, a company may choose to mail unconverted leads twice a year, and "model" the customer file so that one-third of the file receives 12 catalogs a year, another third of the file receives eight catalogs a year, and the bottom third of the file receives only four catalogs a year.

Although this approach to managing contact strategy is a step in the right direction, the problem is that the only marketing element that changes is frequency of contact. Anyone and everyone who is mailed is mailed the same thing. That's the problem we want to address in this section.

The hypothesis to be tested and, it is hoped, proved is that not all leads and not all customers should receive the same promotion. To throw all customers and prospects into the same pool, develop a frequency strategy for individual groups, and then mail them all the same promotion is easy to do and efficient from a cost perspective, but not necessarily the right thing to do.

One way to approach this problem is to first divide the potential mailing universe into customer or prospect groups or both to whom you would intuitively do different things. Some of the more obvious groups are these:

1. One-time inquiries or leads from cold catalog mailings or print or broadcast ads
2. Leads that have responded more than once to your mailings or advertising but have never purchased
3. Customers who have made only one purchase
4. Customers who have made multiple purchases but from only one product line
5. Customers who have purchased from multiple product lines

To test the hypothesis that profitability can be increased by treating different customer segments differently, you need to establish specific objectives and to develop different promotion strategies to test against your current control strategy. For example:

1. For one-time inquirers you might be looking for more information before attempting to close your first sale. Depending upon the characteristics of your product or service, different strategies for converting leads into buyers may be required. In the financial services area it is more cost-effective in some situations to use a two-step questionnaire and conversion strategy to reactivate dormant leads than it is to attempt to sell the leads directly.
2. For multiple inquiries or prospects who have responded to your request for more information your objective must be to close that first sale. A

very targeted low-risk (to the customer) offer may be the way to achieve this objective.

3. For one-time purchasers you need to develop the buying habit, to turn a one-time sale into an ongoing relationship. One-time buyers are a major problem (or opportunity) for many mail-order and catalog companies. All too often one-time buyers do not think of themselves as your customers—you just happened to be there at the right time with that right offer for a particular product that the customer needed right away.

4. For customers who have purchased in only one category you need to move them into the "other sections of your store." This phenomenon is common to all businesses but especially men's and women's clothing. "I like their shirts, but I buy my ties elsewhere" is the kind of comment frequently heard in focus groups. Why not just send a tie to your best shirt customers, or at least a coupon with a substantial discount for trying a tie?

5. For customers who have purchased from multiple categories your objective should be to understand the most common product affinities and then develop customized promotions that take advantage of these affinities. The concept is simple: if most people who buy Product X also buy Products A, B, and C, find people who have purchased A, B, and C but not X and offer them Product X.

In situations where the number of customers, prospects, or both within each target group is large, it often makes sense to organize marketing responsibility around each of the target groups. For example, one person may be assigned the responsibility for converting one-time buyers into repeat purchasers and another person the responsibility for reactivating dormant leads. Both are difficult but critical tasks.

Assigning specific management responsibility for individual customer or prospect segments ensures that each segment receives the attention it deserves. This approach of organizing around the customer prevents management from focusing its attention on easier and often more interesting things to do, such as generating more new leads from advertising.

Companies that fail to make this commitment may find that they are building a large database of unconverted leads or that their one-time buyers never make the commitment to become steady repeat customers.

CHAPTER 35

Applications of the New Direct Marketing

ABOUT THIS CHAPTER

In this chapter we will identify a number of the major marketing applications that characterize the new direct marketing and distinguish it from the "old" or traditional direct marketing. In particular, we will focus our attention on applications the are model-driven. By no means is this list exhaustive, but we believe it to be representative of the ways in which database technology, modeling, and marketing come together.

MOVING FROM THE OLD TO THE NEW DIRECT MARKETING

Perhaps the best way to appreciate the new direct marketing is to understand how it differs from the old or traditional direct marketing, and how both the *old* and the *new* direct marketing relate to a host of other expressions, such as *database marketing, one-to-one marketing, relationship marketing, frequency marketing, information-based marketing, integrated marketing, interactive marketing*, and on and on.

Essentially, the old direct marketing was about marketing to groups of people, not to individuals. In direct marketing shorthand, It was source/key code–based and CPO-driven. Prior to the introduction of the IBM 360 system in the mid-1960s direct marketers kept careful records about how much they spent on individual promotions and the number of leads, inquiries, or customers those promotions produced. The summary measure of this activity was cost per order, or CPO, and direct marketers became experts at manipulating this number up or down by increasing the value of their offer or softening the terms of the commitments they would require from their prospects, or both. For example, going from a four-books-for-a-dollar offer with a commitment to buy four more books within one year to a five-books-for-a-dollar offer with just a four-book commitment over the life of a membership is a classic way to soften an offer and produce more customers. In the magazine subscription business, the preview offer replaced the "harder" pro rata refund offer, even though conversion and renewal rates were lower. For many magazines the increase in up-front response more than made up for the deterioration of back-end performance. In the insurance business, the "bonus offer" that offered three months free insurance before billing began became the control offer for many companies, and so on.

Intuitively, direct marketers knew that the quality of the incremental customers they would attract by softening the offer would be less than the quality of the customers attracted by the "harder" offer. Testing was used extensively to measure the effect on both front-end response (CPO) and back-end performance—what we now call *lifetime value*, but was called the *order margin* or the *allowable* in fifties and sixties.

Technically, while different companies referred to measures of back-end performance with different names, the working definition was pretty much the same everywhere. The measure of back-end performance was *contribution to advertising and promotion, overhead, and profits*. In some companies this contribution was adjusted for the time value of money, so that contribution was really the *present value* of the cash flow generated by customers over their economic life in the program or club into which they were recruited.

Given measures of up-front response and back-end performance, promotion decisions were made on the basis of return on promotion, a subject discussed in detail in Chapter 33. The essence of this method of marketing was the never-ending search for the best offer and the best fulfillment strategy for each group of definable prospects.

For example, book and music clubs would test endlessly to determine the right number of fulfillment cycles per year, the time between shipment of the advanced catalog that would announce the "month's" negative option selection and shipment of the selection. At one time all of these "of-the-month" clubs shipped 12 times a year, actually 13 times a year if you counted four weeks as a month. Today the typical cycle is closer to 20 times a year. In the continuity business, the key question was the number of weeks between the automatic shipment of one package and the next. Should it be four weeks or should it be six weeks? And because of the limitations of the fulfillment systems in place in the sixties and seventies, it had to be one or the other. The same thinking applied to credit. How long could a program ship product without receiving payment—one month, two months, three months? You had to pick one, because the supporting systems required that all customers be treated the same way.

The notion of treating individual prospects or individual customers differently simply wasn't part of the direct marketing methodology. There were a couple of reasons for this strategy, not all of them bad. First, as we said above, the technology that was available to direct marketers as recently as the early eighties didn't cost-effectively allow for customized fulfillment strategies. Second, treating all customers the same way is obviously less expensive than treating individual customers differently. And, finally, with regard to new customer acquisition, it wasn't until after the acceptance of ZIP code modeling that direct marketers could suppress or select names from individual promotion lists.

Gradually, as internal fulfillment and reporting systems improved, direct marketers learned that it was not necessarily a good idea to treat all customers the same way. In some areas this awareness came sooner than in others. Catalogers, for example, using just simple RFM models, realized that they could increase profits by mailing customers according to their probability of response. Not everyone needed to receive four or six catalogs a year, nor was it necessary for everyone to receive the same catalog.

This notion that all customers should *not* be treated the same way took hold in most if not all traditional, closed-loop, direct marketing companies. Based on a combination of models and decision rules, customers began to be treated as individuals, not as identical members of a common acquisition group. Nevertheless, even though efforts were now directed toward improving the performance of individual customers, it was, and still is, just as necessary as it always has been to measure the lifetime value of groups of customers defined by their common source of key code. Why hold on to this relic of the old direct marketing? Because new-customer acquisition decisions still have to be made based on the relationship between lifetime value of the average customer and the cost of acquiring that customer.

Outside of the traditional direct marketing arena even stronger forces were shaping the course of direct marketing. Nontraditional direct marketing companies were learning that they could affect customer behavior through direct communications without abandoning their existing channels of distribution and, most importantly, without becoming "mail-order" companies.[1] Concurrent with this realization were a number of external phenomena often given credit for the widespread adoption of direct marketing methods. They include (1) the credit card, (2) the 800 number, (3) the increase in working women, and (4) the decline of service at retail.

But perhaps the most important single event to impact the adoption of direct marketing methods was the introduction of American Airlines' Frequent Flyer Program. The success of this program spurred the growth of similar programs, first among competing airlines and then among the related travel industry players—the car rental companies and the hotels. The rest, as they say, is history. The notion that customer performance could be affected by direct marketing communications—in particular, loyalty and frequency-reward-driven programs—is taken as a given today by many direct marketers, both traditional and nontraditional. Unfortunately, it's not necessarily true that all loyalty and all frequency reward programs are cost-effective. But more on this subject later in this chapter.

GENERAL APPLICATIONS OF THE NEW DIRECT MARKETING

While there are numerous specific applications of the new direct marketing, and we will go through them one at a time in the next section, it's useful to step back and generalize about what it is that direct marketers can and cannot do, given the state of the art today. To that end we have identified four general applications. We can and do:

1. Respond to events
2. Create market segments—one customer at a time
3. Predict customer/prospect behavior
4. Create, test, and evaluate marketing strategies

Let's go through these four processes one at a time.

---

1. Early efforts to bring packaged goods companies into the direct marketing arena focused on the creation of mail-order businesses. The best example of this phenomenon is General Food's launching of a series of businesses under the umbrella name of Creative Village. These early efforts failed not because of the inherent profitability of these businesses, because their size was of little interest to these giant companies. Attempts to grow these businesses beyond their potential caused these businesses to eventually become unprofitable.

Respond to Events

Conceptually there are two kinds of events direct marketers respond to: (1) events that are about to happen and (2) events that have happened in the recent past. Sometimes you know an event will happen and you know to whom it will happen, for example, a birthday or a policy anniversary date. In these cases, sometimes referred to as "magic moments," your database could generate a promotion scheduled to arrive at the optimal time. In other cases you know that the next update of the marketing database will identify customers that have taken some action that should, based on judgment or testing, generate a response—for example, a change of address, or a particular purchase, or a cancellation request. In each of these cases the marketing database could be directed to respond with an appropriate response. The extent to which the response will or will not be cost-effective depends on the creativity (for lack of a better expression) of the response. For example, a simple repetitive "thank you for purchasing letter" will quickly become tired and not effective, but a response that changes from purchase to purchase may result in increased sales. Naturally, the shorter the time period between the event and the response, the more likely the response will turn out to be cost-effective. This fact will impact the decision of how frequently the marketing database should be updated. On the other hand, if the response to a customer-driven event can be generated by some other more frequently updated system, such as customer service, then that may be a perfectly good solution. In that case the marketing database would be updated after the fact, which is certainly acceptable, assuming that the customer service system maintained a record of the promotion. Companies that are on the very leading edge of database-driven relationship marketing are striving toward the goal of real time across the enterprise information. In this environment all customer actions are known to all systems that come into contact with the customer, if not in real time, as close to real time as possible. For a fuller discussion of this process, please refer to Chapter 5 on relationship marketing.

Create Market Segments— One Customer at a Time

In the age of one-to-one marketing why should it be necessary to create segments of more than one? The answer is that in some cases it's not, and one-to-one marketing is exactly what you want to do. In the section above, we discussed responding to events. That's one-to-one marketing. Direct marketers are doing more and more with surveys and specifically responding to the information those surveys provide, and that's one-to-one marketing. In fact, Don Peppers and Martha Rogers have written at least two books chock-full of examples of one-to-one marketing, but direct marketers do much more than respond to events surveys. We proactively generate promotions for our products or services, and when we do so, we need to think about the markets we're addressing and what, if anything, we want to say differently to different market segments. Clearly, we may want to address young singles differently from the way we address older empty nest couples; or we may want to communicate with small business owners differently from the way we communicate with large corporate purchasing agents. So, given these differences, we may identify a handful or even a couple of dozen different market segments, but certainly not hundreds or thousands of segments. How many segments should a business have? Of course, there's no one answer that's right for everyone. One way to approach this question is to start with the data you have for segmentation. Let's assume that all you have is demographic data, and you choose not to use any mathematical methods for creating your segments. Then the answer is easy. Choose the demographic variables most important to your business from a communications perspective. These variables may include age, or marital status, or presence of children, or income. Let's assume for the moment that you want to use all of these variables and these are the breaks you consider to be important within each variable:

Age
1. Under 21
2. 21–35
3. 36–54
4. 55–64
5. 65+

Marital Status
1. Married
2. Single
3. Divorced
4. Widow

Children Living at Home
1. None
2. Under 5
3. 6–12
4. 13–18
5. 19+

Income
1. Low
2. Medium
3. High

This arbitrary segmentation scheme would produce (5*4*5*3), or 300, segments—a lot more than you want to deal with. So you would first eliminate all segments with little if any membership. Say, you arrive at 15 meaningful segments, just with regard to size. The next step is to ask yourself if you really have a different strategy or creative execution for each possible segment. If the answer is no, which it will be more often than not, you can start combining segments until you reach a number that corresponds to the number of different strategies (tone and manner of presentation, offer selection, frequency of contact, etc.) you envision implementing.

The fact that we arrived at this solution without the aid of any mathematical modeling is beside the point. We could just as easily have used a combination of factor and cluster algorithms and arrived at a similar conclusion with regard to the number of segments we wished to maintain. The only difference is that the mathematical process would have created the segments differently. But the final mathematical solution, the number of segments the process would have defined as being different, would still produce more segments than you could create strategies for, and you would still need to trim back the number of segments to match the number of strategies you planned to implement.

Later on in this chapter and in other chapters we will argue that while direct marketers do a pretty good job in creating segments, they don't do a terribly good job in designing strategies that improve the performance of the segments, over and above what that performance would be if everyone were treated as members of the same segment. We think that this weakness can be overcome by a strategy of placing customers into segments along three separate dimensions: behavior, attitudes, and demographics. The result is a set of segments, the members of which have commonalties along all three dimensions.

Predict Customer/Prospect Behavior

If "new" direct marketers are good at segmentation, they're even better at prediction. In fact you could say that they've just about beaten this subject to death. A large part of this book is devoted to the myriad of techniques that exist to either (1) calculate the probability of a prospect or a customer taking any particular action: respond, purchase, attrit, convert, pay, return, etc., or (2) estimate the value of some event or transaction such as an expected sale amount or lifetime value. To this end, we've mastered the techniques of ordinary and logistic regression and have even become somewhat knowledgeable with regard to the nuances of neural nets and genetic algorithms, and we argue endlessly about which techniques are the most appropriate. However, regardless of the techniques we employ, it's very important to understand what direct marketers mean and don't mean by their ability to predict response or behavior. What we're very good at is predicting how well a particular individual will do *relative* to the average. In other words, if you tell a new direct marketer that if he or she mails 1 million pieces next month and that the overall response rate is expected to be, say, 2 percent, the new direct marketer will be able to identify individuals expected to do much better or much worse than the 2 percent average, and we can quantify our estimates for each individual. That's what we're good at, predicting relative performance. What we're not exceptionally good at, or for that matter exceptionally bad at, is predicting what the average will be. With regard to that kind of "forecasting," our ability varies from company to company, just as in any other industry.

Given these quantitative skills, the most advanced companies build their marketing strategies around their ability to predict the behavior of customers, or prospects, within relatively homogeneous marketing segments. In short, if you know what segment your customer belongs to (based upon past behavior, demographics, and attitude toward your company's products and/or services) and if you can predict near-term behavior, you should be able to figure out an intelligent strategy for marketing to that customer. And that brings us to the last generalization about what it is that new direct marketers do.

Create, Test, and Evaluate Marketing Strategies

Regardless of how far we've come, both in our database management skills and in our mathematical skills, we still come down to the question of what to do, given all this information. How frequently should a customer or prospect be promoted, through which channels, in which sequence, with which products, and with which creative strategy? To some extent, questions regarding frequency of contact can be addressed through optimization models that incorporate the results of other models that predict response to alternative products, fatigue factors, margin considerations, and so on. But the need to conceive alternative strategies and to then test them never really goes away. Thus the "new" direct marketers of the nineties must still employ the basic testing procedures that were the hallmark of the "old" direct marketers that preceded them.

SPECIFIC DIRECT MARKETING APPLICATIONS

What follows are 18 specific new direct marketing applications that we've observed over the last few years. Again, the list is certainly not exhaustive, but should provide you with a pretty good idea of what others are doing—and, it is hoped, give you some ideas about things you might want to try, if you're not already doing them.

Marketing to Current Customers

1. Modeling Existing Customer Files to Predict Response, Sales, Payments, Attrition, etc.

We start with this general application not only because modeling individual and group behavior is so pervasive, but also because we want to remind the reader that modeling does not require the building of a new marketing database. All that's needed to get started is access to data, and very often that data can be easily found in the company's master file, which almost always contains important summary data including measures of recency, frequency, and monetary value.

2. Building Marketing Databases That Combine Data from both Operations and Promotion Files

A simple working definition of a marketing database is that a marketing database is a collection of data that combines customer information from a variety of sources: master files, transaction files, promotion files, overlay files, and research files.

This definition says nothing about the structure of the collection of data. It could be a large flat file or a collection of linked tables as is the case in relational or relational-like databases. The key point here is that the database allows the marketer to gather all available customer information in one place so that better marketing decisions can be made. Having said that, it should be quickly added that the structure of the database is critically important with regard to the ultimate usability of the database, but that is the subject of other sections of this book.

The key observation we want to make in this section is that the data that goes into the database should be useful for marketing purposes. Clearly, certain levels of summary data are important and some level of transaction data is also important, but how much data, at what level of detail, and for how long is the subject of endless discussion during the database-building process. Our philosophy is that if you can't imagine how you would use it, don't keep it on-line. You won't "figure it out someday," and despite the ever-decreasing costs of data storage—a reason frequently cited for keeping as much data as possible—our experience is that the more you keep, the more complicated the maintenance and update process. In any event, with the database tools available today, you can always change your mind. If you keep what you're not using on tape, you can restore the data you missed on the first pass.

Finally, a note on promotion data. If you're a telemarketer, keeping disposition data is absolutely critical. If you only use direct mail, you may be surprised how difficult it is to measure the effect of repeated mailings. We're not saying to not keep the data. It's just that, in more cases than not, knowing more than, say, the last six months of detailed promotion history, plus some summary promotion data, is hard to justify.

3. Building Models to Predict Attrition and Targeting Retention Programs against High-Probability Cancels

The goal of the next application is to drive home the point that if you believe that you have a retention problem and you want to reduce it, you should first build a model to predict who's most likely to attrit and who's most likely to stay with you. Retention programs directed at the entire population can't be cost-justified, because the vast majority (80 to 90 percent) will stay with you, and the costs of marketing to them would have to be recovered by the improvement realized by the customers you manage to save.

The chart below shows the results of a model built to predict customers who will stop using their credit cards. The average attrition rate was 11.2 percent, but clearly 60 percent of the customer base was not leaving and the retention program was directed at only those customers in Deciles 1 to 4 who in addition to having

EXHIBIT 35–1

Modeling to Predict Attrition

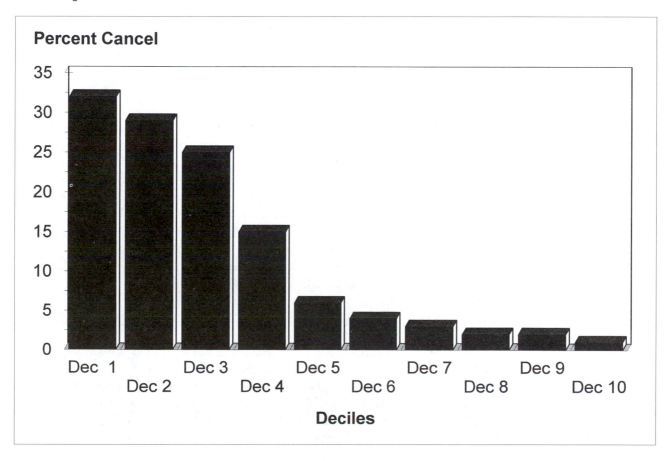

high expected cancel rates were judged to be worth saving. The table below shows that the cost of a saved customer could be reduced by more than 50 percent if the retention program were directed at just those customers with high expected cancellation rates. Of course, if your anti-attrition program results in customers who were not about to stop buying more from you, then this factor has to be added to the evaluation of the program. In summary, you have to be clear about the goals of the program and how you intend to measure its success or failure.

Retention Economics

Number of customers	100,000
Expected cancel rate among Deciles 1–4	25.00%
Expected cancel rate among Deciles 5–10	2.00%
Total expected cancel rate	11.20%
Number of expected cancels in Deciles 1–4	10,000
Number of expected cancels in Deciles 5–10	1,200
Total number of cancels	11,200
Percent of contacted saved	20.00%
Number saved from Deciles 1–4	2,000
Number saved from Deciles 5–10	240
Total saved if all contacted	2,240
New number of cancels	8,960
New cancel rate	8.96%
Program costs per customer	$5.00
Total costs if all customers are included	$500,000
Cost per saved customer	$223.21
Costs if program directed to top 40%	$200,000
Cost per saved customer	$100.00

4. Building Frequency and Loyalty Programs to Increase Lifetime Value

Want to increase the lifetime value of your existing and expected new customers? Of course you do. How do you do it? You need to understand why they are buying from you, figure out where else they satisfy their needs for the same service or products you are supplying to them, determine what share of their requirements you are providing, and set out to increase your share of their requirements—without going broke in the process. Increasing the lifetime value of your customers—the value of your customers to you—may mean decreasing your price, or it may mean increasing your price, depending upon the price elasticity of demand. It may mean increasing or decreasing your level of service, depending upon the needs and expectations of your customers—you may need to provide service at a level Nordstrom's would be proud of, or you may be better off trimming away all the frills as Southwest Airlines did. What works for one company need not work for you.

So, what does this have to do with loyalty and frequency reward programs? Same thing. Just because they *seem* to work for travel and leisure companies doesn't mean they'll necessarily work for you. And even though they *seem* to be working for your direct competition, it doesn't necessarily mean that they'll work for you, or that the money invested in them couldn't be better spent in other places. At the time of this writing, an article has just appeared in the *Harvard*

Business Review[2] suggesting that consumers have just about had it with companies that are trying to develop *relationships* with them when all they want is good service, low prices, and to be left alone—no more phone calls, no more cards to carry. Of course, any direct marketer that reads this article and rushes out to kill his or her program would be overreacting, to say the least. The point is that not all loyalty and reward programs work, or work the same for each segment of your market. If you have a good segmentation scheme, and an across-the-board reward program, the odds are pretty good that some segments of your market will love your program and other segments won't even know it exists.

The bottom line is that we are neither recommending nor not recommending that you develop a loyalty or reward program that goes beyond your current service levels. We are just recommending caution against the development of "me-too" programs.

Finally, we've taken the liberty to reprint in this section an abbreviated version of Craig Underwood's 10 rules for developing a loyalty program. Craig is the president of Loyalty Management in Canada and has developed Air Canada's very successful Loyalty Program.

1. *A winning strategy*: A great loyalty program will not compensate for a noncompetitive price, inconvenience, inferior quality, and bad service.
2. *Aspirational awards*: The award must be valuable enough and meaningful enough to motivate behavior, e.g., concentrated spending with one supplier, referrals, advocacy.
3. *Attainable rewards*: The reward should be reachable in a reasonable length of time.
4. *Affordable rewards*: The economics must work!
5. *Commitment*: Consumer awareness requires long-term commitment, care and feeding across all channels and media.
6. *Ease*: The program must be simple, convenient, and easy for customers to collect and redeem.
7. *Measureable results*: Enough said.
8. *New customer acquisition*: To be truly successful the program must help capture new customers in addition to rewarding current customers.
9. *Sustainable competitive advantage*: The power of any program will be significantly diminished if it can be copied by competitors.
10. *Experienced, dedicated team*: A program cannot be anybody's extracurricular activity; without committed resources and accountability it won't succeed.

5. Modeling Category or Product Usage among Customers and Promoting According to the Probability of Response

This application sometimes comes under the heading of "look-alike models," a terrible name because it is so often confused with simple and not very useful profiling.

Look-alike models are used when a model is desired but there's been no promotion to base the model upon. For example, suppose you are a direct marketer at a bank with 1.5 million customers and a budget to mail a home equity

---

2. "Preventing the Premature Death of Direct Marketing," *Harvard Business Review*, January–February 1998.

loan offer to 300,000 customers. You've never mailed this offer before, but 5 percent of your customers have this product. How could a look-alike model help you?[3] One strategy would be to build a look-alike model with the dependent variable being product ownership.

Assuming the model works, we would be able to identify customers with a significantly higher probability of having a home equity loan than the average bank customer. For example, it's likely that we could build such a model and identify 20 percent of the file where the actual ownership rate would be between 15 and 20 percent. We could then mail to just customers in those deciles, excluding, of course, those customers that already owned the product. A better strategy would be to mail very heavily into the top two deciles, say 250,000 names selected from these two top deciles, and then mail 50,000 names selected from Deciles 3 through 7. If we structured the mailing this way, we could then build a "true" response model that would apply to 70 percent of the file, after the mailing based on the "look-alike" model was made.

The graphs below show the results achieved in building look-alike models for a packaged goods company and for a mutual funds company. In each case the objective was to decide whom to promote in the absence of a test mailing. In the packaged goods case the objective was to find customers likely to respond to a

EXHIBIT 35–2

A Packaged Goods Example Using "A Look-Alike" Model to Predict Ownership of Health Foods

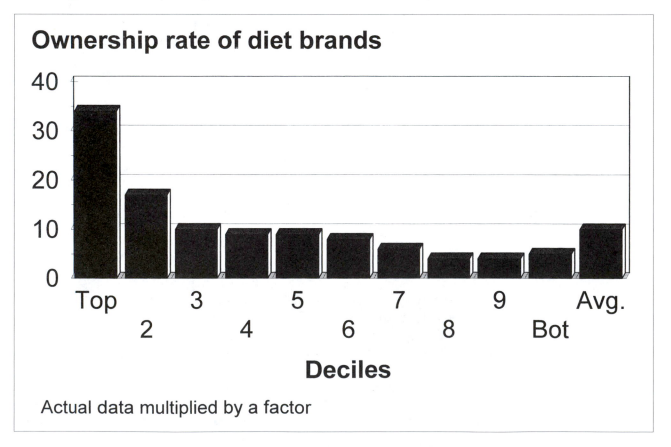

Ownership rate of diet brands

Deciles

Actual data multiplied by a factor

---

3. My thanks to the direct marketer who called me with this question, just as I was writing this chapter.

EXHIBIT 35–3

A Mutual Funds Example Using "A Look-Alike" Model to Predict Ownership of a Particular Fund

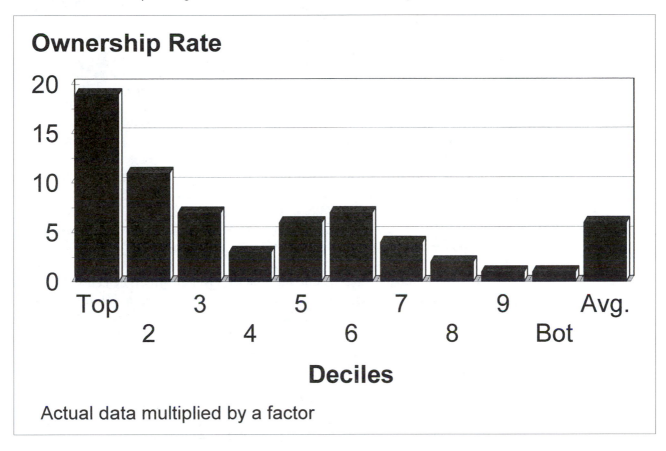

Ownership Rate

Deciles

Actual data multiplied by a factor

health food offer. The dependent variable was prior purchases of health food products. The independent variables included demographic, lifestyle, and other product-purchased data. In the mutual funds example, the objective was to find customers suitable for a particular kind of fund. The dependent variable was ownership of a similar fund. The independent variables included everything else the fund knew about its customers.

In the mutual funds example you will notice the uneven distribution of ownership rates in the middle deciles. This indicates a relatively weak model; nevertheless the model was good enough to identify 10 percent of the file with exceptionally high ownership rates.

6. Using the Database to Identify Customers That Appear on Multiple Input Files and Using This Information to Increase Modeling Performance

Because a marketing database is by definition a combination of business and promotion files, the database will contain different amounts of information about each customer. A customer that does a lot of business with your company may appear on many files. A customer that does less business with you may appear on only a few files or perhaps only one file.

Suppose you did a mailing to a sample of the customers on your database for some particular product or service and then set out to build a model to predict the response to this mailing. Because some customers selected will have data about them gathered from a number of files and others from only one or two files, to the modeler this would appear as a missing value problem; i.e., we have different data about different customers—a serious problem for the modeler. If he or she uses only data fields that are populated for all customers, the value of the additional information is lost.

The solution is to divide the modeling data set into groups, as shown in Exhibit 35–4. All customers that appear on all four (we just made this example up) input files are in Group 1. Customers that appear on only the base file, the file that everyone was on in this example, were placed in Group 8. And other combinations populated the other groups.

The final step is to build eight separate models, one for each group. Generally the more files a customer is on, all other things being equal, the higher the expected response rate for another product or service from your company. However, regardless of this condition, if the modeling technique used is logistic regression, the scores each individual will receive are probabilities of response, and the scores can be commingled.

The result of using this methodology in a real-life database situation is shown in Exhibit 35–5. The difference in gain is dramatic. When customers were scored based on models that used only base file information, information available for everyone mailed, the customers in the top decile did two times average. By using this new modeling method, taking advantage of all the database information available, the gain in the top decile was four times average—a very significant improvement.

7. Mapping All Points of Customer Contact and Making Contact Information Available throughout the Organization

The typical marketing database, defined as a collection of information from multiple sources, is almost always batch updated, i.e., not updated in real time, and certainly does not contain every bit of information theoretically known to the organization. Not surprisingly, therefore, this deficiency has been identified by some as an important strategic weakness, and some consultants argue that the

EXHIBIT 35–4

Modeling a Marketing Database

	Base	**File 1**	**File 2**	**File 3**
Group 1	YES	YES	YES	YES
Group 2	YES	YES	YES	NO
Group 3	YES	YES	NO	YES
Group 4	YES	NO	YES	YES
Group 5	YES	YES	NO	NO
Group 6	YES	NO	YES	NO
Group 7	YES	NO	NO	YES
Group 8	YES	NO	NO	NO

EXHIBIT 35-5

Comparing Modeling Results

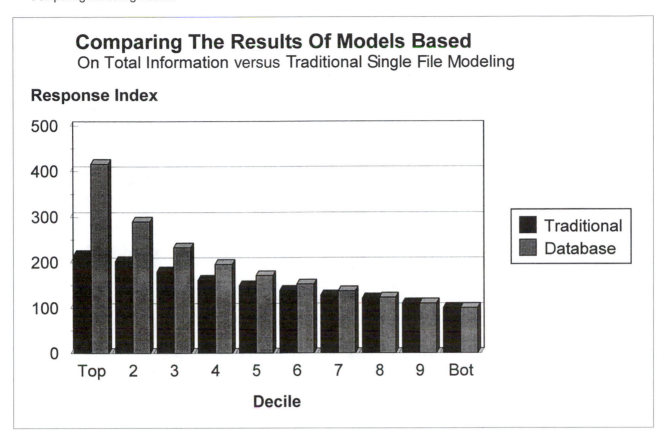

Comparing The Results Of Models Based
On Total Information versus Traditional Single File Modeling

next major step in the database management process is to define all points of customer contact and to integrate all of this information such that it is available to anyone in the organization that deals with the customer. Obviously, this strategy implies much larger databases and much more sophisticated systems than the systems we currently employ. This process sometimes goes under the name of Enterprise Contact Management; sometimes it just appears within a definition of true integrated marketing.

8. Using Overlay Data to Profile Defined Segments and Customizing Future Promotions

It's not unusual for companies to send their entire customer file to one of a number of computer service bureaus to have their files overlayed with demographic data, at either the individual household level or the ZIP code or block group level or both. If the files are large, their customer profile will tend to match the state or national average and the marketer may turn out to be disappointed because no clear course of action results from the exercise. Or even if the profile of the typical customer is different from the national or state average, the profile may only confirm the differences the marketer already expected.

To avoid this scenario we suggest using overlay data to either (1) increase the power of your internal house file models or (2) profile the differences between members of high, low, and average deciles. Overlay data may or may not result in stronger internal models. By stronger we mean increasing the spread between the top and bottom deciles, or smoothing out bumps in the model, or decreasing the difference between actual and expected results. Regardless of whether this happens or not, overlay data should be used to profile and, it is hoped, to understand the differences between members of different deciles. In the best of all worlds the differences will be obvious: Deciles 1 and 2 consist of upper-income, older males; Deciles 9 and 10 consist of lower-income, younger females. Of course, such obvious differences are never found, but you may discover differences that are, though not so pronounced, nevertheless actionable.

Finally, on this subject, it's certainly not necessary to overlay your entire database to discover if some overlay variables will help you build a better model or profile differences. All that's necessary is to overlay the sample data sets that will be used to build and validate your models. On the other hand, if one or more overlay variables turn out to be significant and added to your models, then those variables will have to be purchased for the entire file.

9. Building Databases That Contain Survey, as Well as Transaction and Overlay Data to Better Understand and Predict Consumer Behavior and to Nurture Long-Term Relationships

Survey data can be used in a variety of ways, from collecting limited amounts of data on all or practically all of your customers, to small surveys that provide insight and direction, to surveys that result in segmentation schemes (see below), to surveys that are designed to elicit a response that will become part of an ongoing dialog. At one end of the spectrum the objective is to gain a limited amount of information about all of your customers, information that will be used directly, or used in models as predictive variables. At the other end of the spectrum the objective is to be begin an ongoing, two-way communications program. Going beyond the first two or three communications is the challenge. It's easy enough to ask your customers to provide you with some information and then to respond to them using their answers and the answers of others as part of the response, it's keeping the follow-up conversations interesting and meaningful that determines the difference between a program that builds lifetime value and a program that just increases costs without impacting lifetime at all. And, admittedly your success, or lack of, will depend in large measure upon the product or service you are providing and the communication vehicle you use. For this technique to work it's possible to use regular mail, but it's a lot more convenient, less expensive, and more intuitive to use e-mail or the Internet. What's more, these relationship-building communications can, in some cases, become profit centers in their own right. For example, if you were running a securities company, how much would your customers pay you to have their portfolio presented (e-mailed or faxed) to them at the end of each trading day, showing comparisons to yesterday, last month, year to date, etc., with comparisons to all the major indices and to your company's buy-sell-or-hold recommendation? And, of course, this information would be coupled with customer-friendly trading features. If you're a retailer, shouldn't you be e-mailing your best customers with information about new arrivals? If you're an airline or a hotel chain, should you wait for your best customers to come to your Web site, or should you be e-mailing them special weekend offers? The list of things one could do is practically endless. Just think about the things you would like to tell your customers every day, every week, or even just periodically, when you had something important to say. You would have to decide how to go about doing it, what it would cost, whether some of the costs could be recovered, and what the increase in long-term value would have to be to justify the cost of the operation, and then you would have to make a decision. Of course, if your competitors are already doing what you're just thinking about doing, the decision may be easier.

10. Using Classical Research Techniques to Identify Attitudinal and Behavior-Based Clusters and Modeling Cluster Membership Using Regression Techniques

Increasingly, direct marketers are trying to better understand the needs, wants, and requirements of their customers and prospects. And increasingly, they are turning to the traditional tools of market research. The usual procedure is to select a random sample of a few thousand customers and try to get them to complete a rather long questionnaire that deals with their behavior and their attitudes with regard to the general business area in question, specific competitors, and of course perceptions about the sponsoring company. For example, a mutual funds company might sponsor a survey about savings and investments, probing for their customers' attitudes toward them, the competition, and the topic in general. For instance, the survey might ask how the customers make decisions, what their goals are, what levels of risk they can tolerate, whom do they consider to be the most respected players, and, of course, where do they stand with respect to the competition—and so on.

Typically, the survey will be completed by 40 to 70 percent of the selected sample. The results will be processed, and invariably the survey will result in the identification of three to six or more segments that differ among themselves across a number of important attitudinal and behavioral dimensions: actual investment behavior, risk tolerance, decision-making methods, media read or watched, and so on.

So far, so good. The problem for direct marketers is that they now know that they are not serving one market, with one common set of goals and concerns; they are serving at least three of four different markets. And if they could have everyone on their database complete the survey, they could place everyone into the most appropriate segment, but that's not feasible.

Once more, statistical modeling can, in some cases, come to the rescue. In this instance the challenge for the modeler is to place each survey respondent into the right segment, based not on the answers to the survey, but on all of the other known database variables. If this can be done, then the model that worked for the survey responders can be applied to the entire database. The tool to perform this function is either a multiway logistic or discriminant analysis.

Exhibit 35–6 shows how well this modeling can be expected to perform. Within the entire database the incidence of Segment 1 members, our client's best prospects, was 37 percent, and another 27 percent fell into the second best segment. Based upon our model of segment membership, and based upon the results of the top two deciles, of those most likely to belong to Segment 1, 54 percent actually belonged to Segment 1 and another 25 percent belonged to Segment 2. Looked at another way, 64 percent of mailings to a random sample of the database would go to the best two segments; based on the model, and only going 20

EXHIBIT 35-6

Using Models to Predict Segment Membership

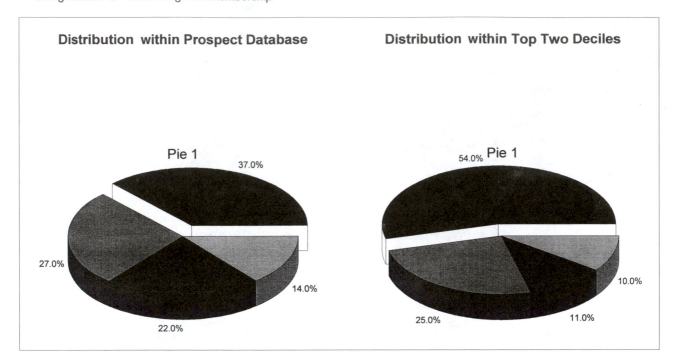

percent deep, 79 percent of our mailings would go to prospects in our best two segments. We would not characterize these results as great, but they are typical of what you can expect when you try to model the results of a segmentation study, so that the results can be applied back to the entire database.

Before leaving this topic, it should be noted that while segmentation studies generally involve dozens if not hundreds of questions, the results of the study with regard to segment membership can usually be replicated based on just the answers to a handful of questions. For example, in the study referred to above, knowing just the answers to eight questions allowed us to be 80–85 percent accurate with regard to placement. This finding led to the insight that we might be able to ask all of our prospects to complete a short questionnaire as part of the ongoing dialogue we were attempting to develop with them in any case. The strategy worked, and short questionnaires were incorporated into our client's marketing program.

11. Placing New Customers into Segments Based on Expected Performance and Testing Alternative Marketing Strategies against Each Cluster

As mentioned at the beginning of this chapter, the hallmark of the old direct marketing was that by and large all new customers were treated equally after the acquisition process was completed. All customers would be contacted the same number of times with the same promotion materials; all might be granted the same credit levels, at least until their creditworthiness was proved; etc. Conversely, the hallmark of the new direct marketing is the ability to treat each customer individually in order to increase the lifetime value of the average customer, thereby increasing overall return on promotion expenditures.

In this particular application the objective is to be able to determine the expected value of new customers at the earliest possible date: at the time the customers request membership in a club or program, take out their first insurance policy, make their first catalog purchase, open their first mutual fund, etc. The need to make decisions about new customers is particularly important for clubs and continuities. These businesses are characterized by offers of a relatively expensive gift upon enrollment and their granting of open credit. Not surprisingly, a large number of new enrollees accept their gift and never make another purchase, and more than a few don't even pay for their heavily discounted new enrollment offer. Therefore, an important objective for these businesses is to be able to predict who these potentially unprofitable customers are, prior to their acceptance in the club or continuity. Exhibit 35–7 shows the results of modeling new-member behavior prior to the time of enrollment. At this time a book or music club or continuity will know a fair amount about the potential enrollee:

- The address will provide a large amount of census data and historical information regarding others recruited from the same ZIP code, sectional center, or commercial cluster (Prism, MicroVision, etc.).
- The key code will indicate the source of the order, and there should be a lot of history at the source code level.
- The selection of product (if it's a choice offer) will tell a lot about potential behavior.

As Exhibit 35–7 shows, the model of new-customer behavior—and these results are typical—indicates that potential enrollees expected to perform among the bottom 10 percent of all new enrollees can be expected to perform at a level equal to about 20 percent of the average for all new enrollees. On the other hand, new enrollees expected to perform among the top 10 percent of all enrollees perform at a rate equal to about 160 percent of average.

The questions for the marketer are these: (1) Should customers in the bottom decile, or the two bottom deciles, be enrolled or rejected? (2) Is it possible, knowing what's likely to happen, to create marketing programs that will increase the profitability of these potentially unprofitable, or at best marginally profitable, prospects? (3) Conversely, is it possible to create marketing programs to make the best customers even better?

Very frequently, direct marketers discover that the contribution from just a few good customers can more than cover the costs of enrolling bad customers. In other words, if your model indicates that in the bottom decile, 20 percent of the potential new enrollees will turn out to be profitable, even though 80 percent will be unprofitable, as predicted by the model, it may still pay to enroll everyone. In this situation companies have had success in purchasing additional information about all of the potentially bad customers, and building models to identify the few good customers within these groups.

Of course, modeling expected customer performance need not stop at the time of enrollment. Incremental performance can be predicted at any time. Exhibit 35–8 shows the result of predicting incremental lifetime value after just three months of membership. Again, the same question arises: if you know what's likely to happen in the future, under existing marketing strategies, can this behavior be modified through programs that take full advantage of what you know about your customer?

EXHIBIT 35-7

Modeling the Expected Behavior of New Customers

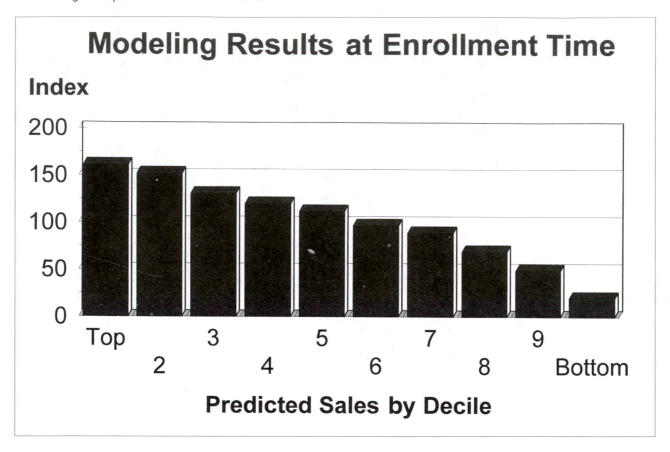

Modeling Results at Enrollment Time

12. Using Campaign Management Tools to Build Rule-Based Marketing Programs to Manage Contacts, Especially to New Customers

Database management tools exist not only to select customers for promotions but also to manage their subsequent contacts. For example, let's assume you are working with a prospect database. Based on selection models or on ad hoc selection criteria, you can select a group of prospects to be contacted. It's then possible, using relatively simple rule-based systems, to predetermine how responders among this group will be treated after their responses are processed. In addition, not all responders have to be treated the same way, as demonstrated in the prior application. New customers can be scored and placed into alternative strategies. And within this context, alternative strategies for each segment of new customers can be planned and tested. The use of a campaign management tool automates this process.

Generally, after an initial period of between six months and one year, all new customers are reevaluated through the use of models that will predict their expected incremental lifetime value, and based on the outcome of these models future promotion decisions are made. More on this process in the next section.

Modeling Expected Incremental Behavior Based on Early Performance Data

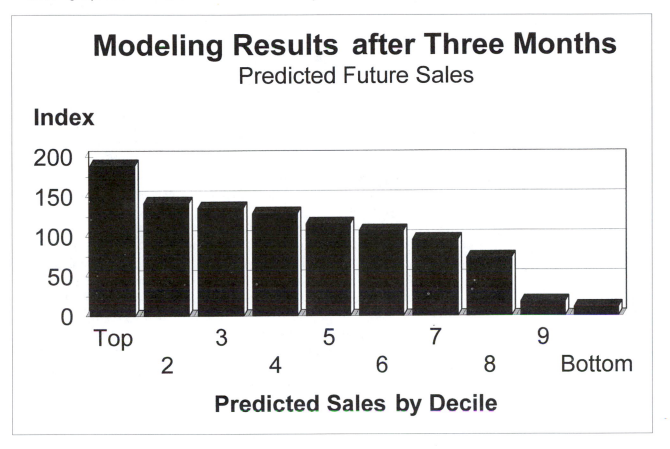

13. Building Optimization Models to Maximize Return on Marketing Expenditures over a Promotion Season

Models have obviously helped direct marketers market smarter, but at the same time they have caused their own set of problems. In short, a reliance on predictive models may result in overmailing your best customers and underpromoting average or marginal customers. It's easy to see how this happens. After an initial period during which new customers are exposed to a number of promotions, models are used to help determine subsequent marketing strategy. Most models rely heavily on RFM data elements, even though other variables are certainly included in many of our better models. But the fact of the matter is that customers that score high for one product tend to score high for other products as well. So if this month you're promoting Product A, customers with high RFM values will score high and be promoted. The next month you may be promoting Product B and the same customers that scored high for Product A may well score high for Product B, be promoted, and so on. Over a long period of time this process will reduce overall response rates among your best customers, especially if your product offerings are not particularly compelling. To protect against this possibility, most companies have placed simple limitations on how frequently a customer can be promoted, either by telephone or through the mail, for any one product, or for any product at all.

An alternative to this scenario is to develop a system that attempts *not* to maximize the response to any single promotion, but rather to maximize response or even better—contribution to overhead and profits over some longer planning period; usually somewhere between three to six months is about right.

Conceptually the notion is straightforward and fairly simple. For example, consider the table below that shows the response rates we could expect from promoting to either Customer 1 or Customer 2 over a three-month period. For simplicity, assume that we only have one product to promote, no seasonality to consider, no corporate restrictions, and only the effect of fatigue and model scores to consider.

Table 35–1 shows that if Customer 1, whose initial expected response rate is 5 percent, were mailed the same promotion three times, given the fatigue factors built into the model, he or she would have an average expected response rate of 3.93 percent over the three promotion efforts. If, on the other hand, Customer 1 were promoted in Months 1 and 3, and Customer 2, whose initial expected response rate is 4 percent, were promoted in Month 2, the average expected response rate could be increased to 4.50 percent [(5 + 4.5 + 4)/3].

Of course, to implement such a model requires the ability to estimate response rates and margins for each customer for all possible combinations of product and frequency; and then after budget, product availability, fulfillment limitations, and other restrictions have been added to the system, an algorithm can be executed that will maximize some objective, such as overall response, sales, margin, or return on total promotion expenditures. Of course, because customer information changes from cycle to cycle, as customers buy, return, or attrit, the system has to be updated each cycle.

Admittedly this is much easier said than done, primarily because good estimates of response under multiple scenarios are hard to come by, but reasonable estimates based on some level of testing should produce useful results. If nothing else they should produce some interesting insights into the possible effects of oversaturating your best customers.

TABLE 35–1

Customer	Jan.	Feb.	Mar.	Average
1	5.00%			5.00%
1		5.00%		5.00%
1			5.00%	5.00%
1	5.00%	4.00%		4.50%
1	5.00%		4.50%	4.75%
1		5.00%	4.00%	4.50%
1	5.00%	4.00%	2.80%	3.93%
	Jan.	**Feb.**	**Mar.**	**Average**
2	4.00%			4.00%
2		4.00%		4.00%
2			4.00%	4.00%
2	4.00%	3.20%		3.60%
2	4.00%		3.60%	3.80%
2		4.00%	3.20%	3.60%
2	4.00%	3.20%	2.24%	3.15%

New-Customer Acquisition

14. Building Models Based on Census Data—Modeling ZIP Code or Lower Level Data—Balancing Front-End Response with Back-End Performance

Just as direct marketers have learned that they don't have to treat all of their customers the same way, they have also learned that they don't have to treat all customers from a particular list as if they have the same potential. Depending upon the information known about the list source and the information about the area the prospect lives within, a decision can be made to include or exclude the prospect from promotion. The implication is that a prospect from an otherwise poor-performing area, ZIP code, or census block group may be included in a promotion if his or her list source is particularly strong, or conversely, a prospect from an otherwise strong-performing area may be excluded if the list source performs well below average. More about this subject can be found in the chapter on the role of modeling in this book. However, one word of caution bears repeating. Marketers have discovered, not surprisingly, that the characteristics of a ZIP code that are correlated positively with front-end response tend to be correlated negatively with measures of back-end performance. For example, the lower the area's income, the higher the response to an offer with a gift or expensive offer associated with it; and conversely, the lower the area's income, the lower expected sales or payments will be. Therefore, marketers need to build models that consider both response and performance separately and then combine the results of both models before making a final decision to include or exclude a particular area from consideration, given the source of the name.[4]

15. Using Principal Components In ZIP Models to Model Census Data

In other chapters of this book we have discussed the benefits of using principal components analysis to capture complicated product purchase behavior patterns. This technique can also be used in ZIP code modeling. The two ZIP codes in Exhibit 35–9 couldn't be more different with regard to income. In one ZIP code, 60 percent of the households earn more than $40,000; in the other, 65 percent earns less than $40,000. But in both cases, exactly 25 percent earn between $20,000 and $40,000. A model that included the single variable *percent of households earning between $20,000 and $40,000* would treat these two households identically with regard to this component of the score, and would obviously be giving an incorrect indication. To overcome this difficulty, which is always encountered when using census variables, we recommend not just modeling the individual rows of the frequency distributions that make up census data, but rather modeling the entire distribution. The technique that is applicable to this task is principal components analysis.

16. Building Proprietary Databases

Increasingly, marketers are finding themselves going through essentially the same list selection and merge/purge process season after season, sometimes month

---

4. In some situations it may be possible to create and model a single dependent variable that captures the effect of both front-end response and back-end performance, for example, sales per thousand pieces mailed. As a practical matter, the best procedure is to try both approaches. For more information on this subject, see the chapter on the role of modeling in this book.

EXHIBIT 35-9

Using Principal Components in ZIP Code Models

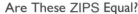

Are These ZIPS Equal?

11746   10032

Income < $20m = 15%	Income < $20m = 40%
Income < $40m = 25%	**Income < $40m = 25%**
Income < $75m = 30%	Income < $75m = 15%
Income > $75m = 30%	Income > $75m = 20%

after month. When this is the case, users are turning to the creation of proprietary databases. Essentially the process entails identifying lists that are used time and again and negotiating with the list owners for unlimited usage.

All such lists are placed into a common database, usually overlaid with individual household data where possible and with census data derived at the ZIP or block group level. In addition, the database may be appended with commercial cluster codes such as Prism or MicroVision codes. These databases are heavily modeled, and frequency of usage is carefully monitored. The net result is usually an increase in response rates and/or reduced name selection costs.

17. Building Custom Models for Individual Users

Very often list users will notice that they can make a small segment of a list work, but they can't use large segments of the list. For example, they may be able to make hotline names work, but they can't make the active file work. When this happens, a custom model may be appropriate. The usual procedure is to match your file against the list owner's file and determine the match rate. If the rate is significant (anything more than 2 percent is probably OK, but the larger the match rate, the more likely the probability of success), the next step is to determine if the data on the list owner's file (RFM data, product-purchased data, original source code, etc.) can be used to predict the match rate. If the model is a success, the next step is to test-mail the match-rate model. Again, you would mail more names from the top deciles, but enough from the lower deciles that a response model could be built from the test mailing. Of course, starting with a match-rate model is not a requirement. You could just test-mail a random sample of the list and build a response model. But building a match-rate model first reduces the risk of the test mailing, which can be expensive if the response to a random mailing is low and the list owner's data does not produce a usable model.

While we have approached this application from the perspective of the list user, in reality, more often than not, it's the list owners that are taking the initiative and identifying list users that could benefit from custom models. The table below shows the magnitude of the incremental income such modeling can produce and explains why this application has become so popular among owners of large lists.

List size	1,000,000	5,000,000
Percent of list made usable by modeling	20.00%	10.00%
Number of names	200,000	500,000
Number of uses per year	4	2
Total names rented	800,000	1,000,000
List rental per 1,000 names	$100	$100
List rental from one user	$80,000	$100,000
Number of users	10	15
Annual increase in gross list rental	$800,000	$1,500,000

18. Participating in Co-Op or Commercial Databases

Another growing trend is the move toward cooperative or commercial databases. In this scenario, companies from a common industry or companies that frequently rent or exchange lists (catalogs, books, fund-raisers, etc.), agree to place all of their names in a common database, which is managed by a third party. (Abacus, Acxiom, Direct Tech, and Metromail all maintain cooperative databases.) Again, these databases are overlayed with additional information, and models are built for the particpating companies by the third-party service suppliers. Only contributors to the database can select names from the database, and the number of names any one company can use is related to the number of names contributed to the database. As with the proprietary databases discussed above, the idea is that the costs of name selection can be reduced and the response rates to promotions increased through this process.

19. Reorganizing the Marketing Function around the Customer

Finally, the last application we'll discuss in this chapter is the trend to reorganize around customers, as opposed to an organization centered on product. Companies with large customer files and a significant number of products frequently seem out of control from the perspective of the customer. Usually, in these organizations there is no real control on the sequence of offers a customer receives as each product manager fights for his or her access to the customer database. Particularly frustrating, from the customer's perspective, are offers that fail to recognize that the customer is already a customer. To counter this problem, companies with customer databases are doing the only sensible thing to do after investing in a customer database—they are creating customer segment managers. These customer segment managers are responsible for all direct contacts with the customer. This generally means all direct mail and all outbound phone contacts. In this scenario, product managers are still responsible for product development and general advertising, but they have to convince the segment managers that their products are appropriate for the segment managers' customers. Again, as with many of the applications discussed in this chapter, this application is easier said than done. At least most mathematical applications aren't political!

CHAPTER 36

Financial Models

In this last chapter, we will attempt to tie together everything we've been talking about with the aid of financial business planning models. To begin this last section, in Chapter 33 we examined the way traditional direct marketers practiced the art of classical direct marketing—marketing that focuses on groups of people linked together because they come from the same list or the same print media ad. We said that the emphasis in classical direct marketing is on the new-customer acquisition decision. To decide whether to use a particular medium again, or with what frequency, it is necessary to know how customers recruited from that medium behave—thus the emphasis on measuring and evaluating group performance. Then we switched gears and discussed the impact of customer-focused database marketing, the movement toward measuring and improving the performance of the individual, and we associated this development with the development of database marketing. The source from which an individual is recruited is only one of many pieces of data that will influence our decision to promote or not to promote, and what to promote to the individual.

In both models—the traditional group behavior model and the individual database marketing model—we acted as if financial time constraints didn't exist. Maximizing lifetime profits and return on promotion were the tools on which economic decision making was based. But the reality is that direct marketing operations exist within companies that are required to report on their financial performance on at least an annual, if not a quarterly, basis. So our decision-making apparatus must include provisions for the realities of the financial world. Investments cannot be made just because they make economic sense in the long run. Investments have to be funded, and their effect on current-period profits has to be taken into account.

We also stated in the beginning of this section that one of the most critical decisions a direct marketing manager has to make is the decision regarding how much to invest in new-customer acquisition promotion and how much to invest in current-customer promotions. Spending more on current customers tends to increase short-term profits at the expense of long-term customer growth, and vice versa.

The decision-making tool that allows direct marketers to make this decision in a business environment that focuses on reported results is the financial planning model. The financial planning model lets the marketer experiment with the option of investing more or less in new-customer promotions, and it allows the marketer to see the effect of new-customer decisions on long-term fiscal profits immediately. What's more, the financial planning model starts with a model of lifetime value.

We will present the inputs and outputs of a simple spreadsheet model and then show and discuss the effect on annual profits stemming from changing just a few critical assumptions. We'll begin with the inputs to a five-year book club model.

Table 36–1 assesses the lifetime value of the average customer. For simplicity, we will assume that all customers behave the same regardless of their source. In practice, we would create different models for each class of customer and then add all the models together to arrive at a model for the total club.

The key assumptions in a book club model regarding lifetime value are these:

- *Attrition rate.* In this example, we assume that 2.5 percent of the starting group drops out or is canceled each cycle. (This model assumes 13 shipping cycles a year and runs for five years. Only the first three years are shown in detail to save space.)

- *Negative option acceptance, return, and bad debt rates.* The rates shown are for the remaining members at each point in time, not the averages for the starting group. Here, we have assumed that the negative option rate will decline over time as members become accustomed to the negative option procedure. Returns and bad debt rates are also shown to decline as members become more familiar with the operations of the club and dissatisfied members cancel or are dropped from the club because of excessive returns or bad debts.[1]

- *Similar acceptance, return, and bad debt assumptions for alternative selections.* All alternatives are treated as a group.

- *Average price of the negative option and alternative selections.* Adjustments for inflation are handled separately by an inflation multiplier so that the analyst can think in terms of constant dollars.

Combining all these assumptions together with other assumptions regarding product and fulfillment costs results in a fifth-year margin per starter of $73.48. (See Year 5 in Table 36–7.)

Tables 36–2 and 36–3 provide the other assumptions to the model. Table 36–2 provides the input assumptions regarding direct mail advertising. The key assumption, which we will change shortly, is a response rate of 35 OPM (3.5 percent), which in this first pass of the model is not shown to change even though the quantity mailed increases from 200,000 pieces in the test year to 10 million in Year 5. Table 36–3 provides the details of our print or space advertising plan. According to this first pass of the model, print orders will cost $20 per customer and will stay at that rate over five years as print media budgets go from $25,000 in the first year to $2 million in the fifth year.

Tables 36–4a, 36–4b, and 36–4c provide the balance of the assumptions needed to complete the model:

- Direct mail cost per thousand
- New-member premium expense
- Provision for package insert orders

---

1. Chapter 33 discusses the nature of negative option clubs and programs, so we won't repeat that material in this chapter.

TABLE 36–1

Lifetime Value Assumptions

Retention Rate	97.5%
Average Customer Life	32.28

		Negative Option				Other Selections			
Cycle	Retention	Accept Rate	Return Rate	Bad Debt Rate	Avg Price	Accept Rate	Return Rate	Bad Debt Rate	Avg Price
01	100	29%	20.0%	20.0%	$25.00	5.0%	15.0%	3.0%	$17.50
02	98	28%	19.5%	15.0%	$26.00	6.0%	14.0%	3.0%	$17.50
03	95	27%	19.0%	12.0%	$27.00	7.0%	13.0%	3.0%	$17.50
04	93	26%	18.5%	10.0%	$28.00	8.0%	12.0%	3.0%	$17.50
05	90	25%	18.0%	6.0%	$29.00	9.0%	11.0%	3.0%	$17.50
06	88	24%	17.5%	6.0%	$30.00	10.0%	10.0%	3.0%	$17.50
07	86	23%	17.0%	6.0%	$25.00	11.0%	10.0%	3.0%	$17.50
08	84	22%	16.5%	6.0%	$25.00	12.0%	10.0%	3.0%	$17.50
09	82	21%	16.0%	6.0%	$25.00	13.0%	10.0%	3.0%	$17.50
10	80	20%	15.5%	6.0%	$25.00	13.0%	10.0%	3.0%	$17.50
11	78	19%	15.0%	6.0%	$25.00	13.0%	10.0%	3.0%	$17.50
12	76	18%	14.5%	6.0%	$25.00	13.0%	10.0%	3.0%	$17.50
13	74	17%	14.0%	6.0%	$25.00	13.0%	10.0%	3.0%	$17.50
YEAR 2	72	16%	13.5%	6.0%	$25.00	13.0%	10.0%	3.0%	$17.50
02	70	15%	13.0%	6.0%	$25.00	13.0%	10.0%	3.0%	$17.50
03	68	14%	12.5%	6.0%	$25.00	13.0%	10.0%	3.0%	$17.50
04	67	13%	12.0%	6.0%	$25.00	13.0%	10.0%	3.0%	$17.50
05	65	13%	11.5%	6.0%	$25.00	13.0%	10.0%	3.0%	$17.50
06	63	13%	11.0%	6.0%	$25.00	13.0%	10.0%	3.0%	$17.50
07	62	13%	10.5%	6.0%	$25.00	13.0%	10.0%	3.0%	$17.50
08	60	13%	10.0%	6.0%	$25.00	13.0%	10.0%	3.0%	$17.50
09	59	13%	10.0%	6.0%	$25.00	13.0%	10.0%	3.0%	$17.50
10	57	13%	10.0%	6.0%	$25.00	13.0%	10.0%	3.0%	$17.50
11	56	13%	10.0%	6.0%	$25.00	13.0%	10.0%	3.0%	$17.50
12	54	13%	10.0%	6.0%	$25.00	13.0%	10.0%	3.0%	$17.50
13	53	13%	10.0%	6.0%	$25.00	13.0%	10.0%	3.0%	$17.50
YEAR 3	52	13%	10.0%	6.0%	$25.00	13.0%	10.0%	3.0%	$17.50
02	50	13%	10.0%	6.0%	$25.00	13.0%	10.0%	3.0%	$17.50
03	49	13%	10.0%	6.0%	$25.00	13.0%	10.0%	3.0%	$17.50
04	48	13%	10.0%	6.0%	$25.00	13.0%	10.0%	3.0%	$17.50
05	47	13%	10.0%	6.0%	$25.00	13.0%	10.0%	3.0%	$17.50
06	46	13%	10.0%	6.0%	$25.00	13.0%	10.0%	3.0%	$17.50
07	44	13%	10.0%	6.0%	$25.00	13.0%	10.0%	3.0%	$17.50
08	43	13%	10.0%	6.0%	$25.00	13.0%	10.0%	3.0%	$17.50
09	42	13%	10.0%	6.0%	$25.00	13.0%	10.0%	3.0%	$17.50
10	41	13%	10.0%	6.0%	$25.00	13.0%	10.0%	3.0%	$17.50
11	40	13%	10.0%	6.0%	$25.00	13.0%	10.0%	3.0%	$17.50
12	39	13%	10.0%	6.0%	$25.00	13.0%	10.0%	3.0%	$17.50
13	38	13%	10.0%	6.0%	$25.00	13.0%	10.0%	3.0%	$17.50
YEAR 4	37	13%	10.0%	6.0%	$25.00	13.0%	10.0%	3.0%	$17.50
02	36	13%	10.0%	6.0%	$25.00	13.0%	10.0%	3.0%	$17.50
03	35	13%	10.0%	6.0%	$25.00	13.0%	10.0%	3.0%	$17.50
04	35	13%	10.0%	6.0%	$25.00	13.0%	10.0%	3.0%	$17.50
05	34	13%	10.0%	6.0%	$25.00	13.0%	10.0%	3.0%	$17.50

TABLE 36−1

continued

Retention Rate	97.5%
Average Customer Life	32.28

		Negative Option				Other Selections			
Cycle	Retention	Accept Rate	Return Rate	Bad Debt Rate	Avg Price	Accept Rate	Return Rate	Bad Debt Rate	Avg Price
06	33	13%	10.0%	6.0%	$25.00	13.0%	10.0%	3.0%	$17.50
07	32	13%	10.0%	6.0%	$25.00	13.0%	10.0%	3.0%	$17.50
08	31	13%	10.0%	6.0%	$25.00	13.0%	10.0%	3.0%	$17.50
09	30	13%	10.0%	6.0%	$25.00	13.0%	10.0%	3.0%	$17.50
10	30	13%	10.0%	6.0%	$25.00	13.0%	10.0%	3.0%	$17.50
11	29	13%	10.0%	6.0%	$25.00	13.0%	10.0%	3.0%	$17.50
12	28	13%	10.0%	6.0%	$25.00	13.0%	10.0%	3.0%	$17.50
13	27	13%	10.0%	6.0%	$25.00	13.0%	10.0%	3.0%	$17.50
YEAR 5	27	13%	10.0%	6.0%	$25.00	13.0%	10.0%	3.0%	$17.50
02	26	13%	10.0%	6.0%	$25.00	13.0%	10.0%	3.0%	$17.50
03	25	13%	10.0%	6.0%	$25.00	13.0%	10.0%	3.0%	$17.50
04	25	13%	10.0%	6.0%	$25.00	13.0%	10.0%	3.0%	$17.50
05	24	13%	10.0%	6.0%	$25.00	13.0%	10.0%	3.0%	$17.50
06	24	13%	10.0%	6.0%	$25.00	13.0%	10.0%	3.0%	$17.50
07	23	13%	10.0%	6.0%	$25.00	13.0%	10.0%	3.0%	$17.50
08	22	13%	10.0%	6.0%	$25.00	13.0%	10.0%	3.0%	$17.50
09	22	13%	10.0%	6.0%	$25.00	13.0%	10.0%	3.0%	$17.50
10	21	13%	10.0%	6.0%	$25.00	13.0%	10.0%	3.0%	$17.50
11	21	13%	10.0%	6.0%	$25.00	13.0%	10.0%	3.0%	$17.50
12	20	13%	10.0%	6.0%	$25.00	13.0%	10.0%	3.0%	$17.50
13	20	13%	10.0%	6.0%	$25.00	13.0%	10.0%	3.0%	$17.50

- Product costs and revenue associated with new orders
- Cost of the periodic catalog (advance announcement, or AA) that announces the featured negative option selection and the alternative selections
- Provision for preparation expense defined as a percentage of the total promotion budget
- Product cost of sales rates
- Bad debt and return rates for new customers
- Fulfillment, warehousing, and customer service costs measured as a percentage of net sales
- Summary provision for fixed overheads (which would be supported by detailed schedules and budgets)
- Response patterns and cash flows from collections
- A vehicle for adjusting the model for inflation

Table 36−5 shows the five-year profit and loss statement (P&L) resulting from combining all the assumptions. As you can see from inspecting the last two lines in Table 36−5, the assumptions provided have resulted in a very profitable

TABLE 36-2

Key Assumptions Direct Mail Advertising

Base Year Response Rate in OPM's			35.0		
Response Rates In following Years indexed to Year 1					
		Year 2	100.00%		
		Year 3	100.00%		
		Year 4	100.00%		
		Year 5	100.00%		
		Year 6	100.00%		

Quantity Mailed Year 1		Quantity Mailed In Thousands		Years 2-5	
CYCLE 1	0	YEAR 2	2,000	CYCLE 1	50.00%
CYCLE 2	0	YEAR 3	6,000	CYCLE 2	0.00%
CYCLE 3	0	YEAR 4	8,000	CYCLE 3	0.00%
CYCLE 4	0	YEAR 5	10,000	CYCLE 4	0.00%
CYCLE 5	0	YEAR 6	0	CYCLE 5	0.00%
CYCLE 6	0			CYCLE 6	0.00%
CYCLE 7	0			CYCLE 7	0.00%
CYCLE 8	0			CYCLE 8	0.00%
CYCLE 9	200			CYCLE 9	50.00%
CYCLE 10	0			CYCLE 10	0.00%
CYCLE 11	0			CYCLE 11	0.00%
CYCLE 12	0			CYCLE 12	0.00%
CYCLE 13	0			CYCLE 13	0.00%
				TOTAL	100.00%

business. Profit as a percentage of sales in Year 5 is 17.5 percent, the business breaks even on an annual basis in Year 3, and it breaks even on a cumulative basis in Year 4. Tables 36–6, 36–7, and 36–8 present the additional diagnostics a direct marketer in this business would want to examine for consistency and reasonableness.

Some skeptics might refer to this as a typically rosy consultant's projection. So let's change it—that's what models are for. Let's see what effect a less optimistic set of assumptions would have on projected profits.

We can begin with a key assumption regarding lifetime value. Whereas the initial model assumed that customers would leave the club at the rate of 2.5 percent per cycle, let's make that 3.5 percent per cycle. This seemingly small change has the effect of reducing profits over five years from $13,146,000 to $9,375,000. (See Table 36–9.) But it's not a small change. It's a 40 percent change in the cycle attrition rate, and in fact profits dropped by 40 percent.

A couple of points need to be made about the retention assumption. By changing the rate of decile from 2.5 percent per cycle to 3.5 percent per cycle, we've reduced the average member life from 32.28 cycles to 25.75 cycles. Again, the point is that a seemingly small change in attrition rates will have a major impact on profits, so accurate estimates of customer life are critical to the accuracy of a model. The bad news is that it is very hard to predict what effect changes in marketing strategy will have on retention and therefore lifetime value. The even

T A B L E   36–3

Key Assumptions Print (Space) Advertising
Base Response Rate Measured in Cost per Order $20.00

Print Media Budget		Cost per Order in Following Years Indexed to Year One	
YEAR 2	$65,000	YEAR 2	100.00%
YEAR 3	$1,000,000	YEAR 3	100.00%
YEAR 4	$1,250,000	YEAR 4	100.00%
YEAR 5	$2,000,000	YEAR 5	100.00%
YEAR 6		YEAR 6	100.00%
		OTHER ORDERS PER CYCLE	50
Year One		**Distribution of Expenditures Year 2-5**	
CYCLE 1	$0	CYCLE 1	7.69%
CYCLE 2	$0	CYCLE 2	7.69%
CYCLE 3	$0	CYCLE 3	7.69%
CYCLE 4	$0	CYCLE 4	7.69%
CYCLE 5	$0	CYCLE 5	7.69%
CYCLE 6	$0	CYCLE 6	7.69%
CYCLE 7	$0	CYCLE 7	7.69%
CYCLE 8	$0	CYCLE 8	7.69%
CYCLE 9	$5,000	CYCLE 9	7.69%
CYCLE 10	$5,000	CYCLE 10	7.69%
CYCLE 11	$5,000	CYCLE 11	7.69%
CYCLE 12	$5,000	CYCLE 12	7.69%
CYCLE 13	$5,000	CYCLE 13	7.69%
		TOTAL	100.00%

T A B L E   36–4

Marketing Assumptions — Not Adjusted for Inflation

New Member Marketing	Year 1	Year 2	Year 3	Year 4	Year 5
Direct Mail Average CPM	$600	$600	$600	$600	$600
Premium Expense	$5.00	$5.00	$5.00	$5.00	$5.00
Insert CPO	$5.00	$5.00	$5.00	$5.00	$5.00
Prep Exp as A % of VAR Promo	5.0%	5.0%	5.0%	5.0%	5.0%
New Order Product Costs Including S&H					
Space or Print Advertising	$9.00	$9.00	$9.00	$9.00	$9.00
Direct Mail Package Inserts	$9.00	$9.00	$9.00	$9.00	$9.00
New Order Revenue					
Space or Print Advertising	$9.98	$9.98	$9.98	$9.98	$9.98
Direct Mail Package Inserts	$9.98	$9.98	$9.98	$9.98	$9.98
Bad Debts on New Orders	5.0%	5.0%	5.0%	5.0%	5.0%
Current Member Marketing					
Fixed Cycle Expense	$2,000	$2,000	$2,000	$2,000	$2,000
AA Expense per MBR Serviced	$0.50	$0.50	$0.50	$0.50	$0.50

TABLE 36-4B

Cost of Sales and Other Expenses

Cost of Sales	Year 1	Year 2	Year 3	Year 4	Year 5
Negative Option Selection	71.0%	40.0%	28.0%	28.0%	28.0%
Alternate Selections	71.0%	40.0%	28.0%	28.0%	28.0%
Inventory W/O % Net Sales	3.0%	3.0%	3.0%	3.0%	3.0%
Returns and Delivery					
Percent of Returns Reusable	20.00%	20.00%	20.00%	20.00%	20.00%
Cost of Returns	$1.00	$1.00	$1.00	$1.00	$1.00
New Order Return Percent	5.00%	5.00%	5.00%	5.00%	5.00%
Net DEL EXP/GRS Shipment	$0.00	$0.00	$0.00	$0.00	$0.00
Distribution and Customer Service					
Fulfillment	15.0%	14.0%	12.0%	9.0%	9.0%
Warehousing	4.0%	3.0%	2.0%	2.0%	2.0%
Customer Service	6.0%	5.0%	4.0%	4.0%	4.0%
Overhead and Inflation					
Overhead Expense	$100,000	$100,000	$100,000	$100,000	$100,000
Revenue Inflators	100.0%	100.0%	100.0%	100.0%	100.0%
Costs/Expense Inflators	100.0%	100.0%	100.0%	100.0%	100.0%

TABLE 36-4C

Other Assumptions by Cycle — Timing of Cash Receipts and Order Flows

	Timing of PMTS	Flow of Orders Dir Mail	Space
MONTH 1	0.00%	50.00%	60.00%
MONTH 2	20.00%	30.00%	30.00%
MONTH 3	30.00%	20.00%	10.00%
MONTH 4	30.00%		
MONTH 5	10.00%		
MONTH 6	10.00%		
	100.0%	100.0%	100.0%

Promotion Amortized over 12 Months

worse news is that changes in marketing strategy sometimes have the effect of only accelerating or postponing sales, so what might appear to be an increase or decrease in customer life might not be reflected in customer lifetime value. For example, sales promotion activities often accelerate sales, but have little if any long-term effect on lifetime value. The bottom line on this subject is that you have to be very careful about measuring the effect that changes in marketing strategy have on both customer life and customer lifetime value.

Now let's examine the assumption that direct mail and print response rates will not change over time, despite rising expenditures. We agree that this set of assumptions is not realistic, so let's decrease direct mail OPMs and increase print cost per orders (CPOs) by 5 percent per year. The result is that the direct mail

T A B L E   36–5

	Year 1	Year 2	Year 3	Year 4	Year 5	TOTAL
Five Year P&L Statement						
Gross Sales						
Negative option	$260	$3,988	$15,286	$28,204	$41,504	$89,242
Other	43	1,037	4,515	10,275	16,674	32,544
Total Gross Sales	$303	$5,025	$19,802	$38,480	$58,177	$121,786
Returns						
Negative Option	50	711	2,640	4,570	6,443	14,414
Other	6	115	491	1,082	1,738	3,432
Total Returns	55	826	3,131	5,652	8,181	17,845
Net Sales	$248	$4,199	$16,671	$32,828	$49,996	$103,941
Cost of Sales						
Product costs	176	1,680	4,668	9,192	13,999	29,714
Inventory W/O	7	126	500	985	1,500	3,118
Delivery						
Return Processing	0	7	27	49	71	155
Total Cost of Sales	$184	$1,813	$5,195	$10,226	$15,570	$32,987
Gross Margin	$64	$2,386	$11,476	$22,602	$34,426	$70,955
Operations Costs						
Customer Service	15	210	667	1,313	2,000	4,205
Fullfillment/EDP	37	588	2,000	2,955	4,500	10,080
Warehousing	10	126	333	657	1,000	2,126
Operations Bad Debt	36	442	1,646	2,798	4,033	8,955
New Order Bad Debt	4	37	129	171	224	566
Total Operations Costs	$103	$1,402	$4,776	$7,893	$11,756	$25,931
Operating Margin	($39)	$984	$6,700	$14,709	$22,669	$45,024
Marketing						
Amortized						
Promotion/Acquisition	$77	$1,303	$4,648	$7,449	$9,754	$23,231
New Order Revenue	88	738	2,583	3,420	4,483	11,311
New Order returns	4	37	129	171	224	566
New Order Cost of Sales	79	665	2,330	3,084	4,043	10,201
Current Member Expense	18	316	1,301	2,694	4,233	8,562
Fixed AA Expense	26	26	26	26	26	130
Total Marketing	$117	$1,609	$5,850	$10,004	$13,798	$31,377
CONTRIBUTION TO						
OVERHEAD & PROFIT	($155)	($625)	$850	$4,705	$8,872	$13,646
OVERHEAD	100	100	100	100	100	500
CNTRBTN TO PRFT	($255)	($725)	$750	$4,605	$8,772	$13,146
% NET SALES	−103.1%	−17.3%	4.5%	14.0%	17.5%	
CUMULATIVE	($255)	($980)	($230)	$4,375	$13,146	

TABLE 36–6

Shipment Statistics

	Year 1	Year 2	Year 3	Year 4	Year 5
Books shipped					
Negative Option	10	160	611	1,128	1,660
Alternates	2	59	258	587	953
Total Books Shipped	13	219	869	1,715	2,613
Books Returned					
Negative Option	2	28	106	183	258
Alternates	0	7	28	62	99
Total Books Returned	2	35	134	245	357
AA's Mailed to Members					
Members	36	632	2,601	5,388	8,467
Year End Membership	8,077	67,675	266,805	480,108	723,734
Average Membership	2,770	48,590	200,088	414,443	651,299
Net Books per Member Serviced	0.29	0.29	0.28	0.27	0.27
Net Books/Year	3.80	3.78	3.68	3.55	3.20

change reduced five-year profits by $2,943,000, and the print changes reduced five-year profits by another $605,000.

What's more, this model does not treat new-member acquisition expenditures as an expense taken in the month incurred. New-customer expenditures are written off over a 12-month period. However, if new-member expenses were written off over the full life of the member, the effect on profits would be reduced. On the other hand, if the company followed a practice of immediately writing off acquisition expenditures, the effect on annual profits would be significantly worse. The point is that accounting practices and the effect of new-member expenditures on reported profits must be carefully watched; direct marketing decisions cannot be made solely on the basis of long-term lifetime value and ROP considerations.

Now let's look at what would happen if we reduced the sales rate from 26 to 24 percent per cycle for all members that stayed past three years. The effect on five-year profits would be a decrease of less than $208,000, because, first, the change itself was small and, second, not many members stay for more than three years, so the effect on total sales is therefore relatively small.

The point of the above "sensitivity" exercise is to demonstrate the usefulness (really the necessity) of a financial model in measuring the effect on profits based on changes in key variables.

Finally, before leaving this negative option club example, let's use the model to evaluate the decision to allocate marketing resources between new-customer acquisition and current-customer marketing. The model we are examining at this point in the process assumes that we will spend $.50 per customer per cycle on current-member promotions. What if we were to increase that amount by 20 percent to $.60 (an increase of about *$1,500,000* over five years assuming

T A B L E   36-7

Promotion and Starter Statistics

	Year 1	Year 2	Year 3	Year 4	Year 5
Total New Orders	9	74	261	343	451
Total CPO	$16.66	$17.16	$17.66	$17.64	$17.76
					0
Pieces Mailed	200	2,000	6,000	8,000	10,000
DM Orders	7	70	210	280	350
OPM	35	35	35	35	35
Promotion Expense					
Direct Mail	120,000	1,200,000	3,600,000	4,800,000	6,000,000
Print	25,000	65,000	1,000,000	1,250,000	2,000,000
Inserts	3,250	3,250	3,250	3,250	3,250
Total Promotion	$148,250	$1,268,250	$4,603,250	$6,053,250	$8,003,250
Cost Per Order					
Direct Mail	$17.14	$17.14	$17.14	$17.14	$17.14
Print	20	20	20	20	20
Inserts	5	5	5	5	5
Total Promotion	$16.66	$17.16	$17.66	$17.64	$17.76
Subscriber Statistics					
Start of Year	50	8,077	67,675	266,805	480,108
Added	8,775	73,900	258,852	342,669	449,208
End of Year	8,077	67,675	266,805	480,108	723,734
Lost	748	14,302	59,722	129,366	205,581
% Ave Lost	4.60%	9.44%	8.93%	8.66%	8.54%
Per Starter Statistics					
Gross Sales	$206.00	$206.00	$206.00	$206.00	$206.00
Returns	$26.29	$26.29	$26.29	$26.29	$26.29
Net Sales	$179.71	$179.71	$179.71	$179.71	$179.71
Prod Costs	$127.59	$71.88	$50.32	$50.32	$50.32
Variable costs	$61.51	$54.93	$48.05	$42.91	$43.24
Bad Debts	$12.67	$12.67	$12.67	$12.67	$12.67
Margin	($22.06)	$40.22	$68.67	$73.81	$73.48
Contribution					
Gift Revenue	$8.98	$8.98	$8.98	$8.98	$8.98
New Order Expense	$9.00	$9.00	$9.00	$9.00	$9.00
Premium Expense	$5.00	$5.00	$5.00	$5.00	$5.00
Net gift Expense	$5.02	$5.02	$5.02	$5.02	$5.02
Contribution to:					
OH, Promo & Profit	($27.08)	$35.20	$63.65	$68.79	$68.46
OH & Profit	($43.74)	$18.04	$45.99	$51.15	$50.70
ROP	−202.34%	163.60%	317.23%	346.86%	342.01%
Average Member Life		32.28			
Number of AAs per Year	13	13	13	13	13
Percent Response					
to Advance Announcements	33.23%	26.46%	26.00%	26.00%	26.00%

TABLE 36-8

| | Percent of Net Sales | | | | |
	Year 1	Year 2	Year 3	Year 4	Year 5
Gross Sales					
Negative Option	85.7%	79.4%	77.2%	73.3%	71.3%
Other	14.3%	20.6%	22.8%	26.7%	28.7%
Total gross Sales	100.0%	100.0%	100.0%	100.0%	100.0%
Returns					
Negative Option	19.1%	17.8%	17.3%	16.2%	15.5%
Other	12.9%	11.1%	10.9%	10.5%	10.4%
Total Returns	18.2%	16.4%	15.8%	14.7%	14.1%
Net Sales	100.0%	100.0%	100.0%	100.0%	100.0%
Cost of Sales					
Product Costs	71.0%	40.0%	28.0%	28.0%	28.0%
Inventory	3.0%	3.0%	3.0%	3.0%	3.0%
Operations Delivery	0.0%	0.0%	0.0%	0.0%	0.0%
Return Processing	0.2%	0.2%	0.2%	0.1%	0.1%
Total Cost of Sales	74.2%	43.2%	31.2%	31.1%	31.1%
Gross Margin	25.8%	56.8%	68.8%	68.9%	68.9%
Operations					
Customer Service	6.0%	5.0%	4.0%	4.0%	4.0%
Fulfillment/EDP	15.0%	14.0%	12.0%	9.0%	9.0%
Warehousing	4.0%	3.0%	2.0%	2.0%	2.0%
Operations Bad Debt	14.7%	10.5%	9.9%	8.5%	8.1%
New Order Bad Debt	1.8%	0.9%	0.8%	0.5%	0.4%
Total Operations	41.4%	33.4%	28.7%	24.0%	23.5%
Operating Margin	−15.6%	23.4%	40.2%	44.8%	45.3%
Marketing					
Amortized					
Promotion/Acquisition	31.0%	31.0%	27.9%	22.7%	19.5%
New Order revenue	35.4%	17.6%	15.5%	10.4%	9.0%
New Order Returns	1.8%	0.9%	0.8%	0.5%	0.4%
New Order Cost of Sales	31.9%	15.8%	14.0%	9.4%	8.1%
Current Member Expense	7.3%	7.5%	7.8%	8.2%	8.5%
Fixed AA Expense	10.5%	0.6%	0.2%	0.1%	0.1%
Total Marketing	47.1%	38.3%	35.1%	30.5%	27.6%
Overhead Expense	40.4%	2.4%	0.6%	0.3%	0.2%
Contribution OH/Profit	−103.1%	−17.3%	4.5%	14.0%	17.5%

no change in member life)? The immediate effect on the model is to reduce cumulative profits to $4,274,000. What if we try to recover some of this decrease by reducing acquisition expense? Let's start with a $750,000 reduction in Years 4 and 5. Table 36−9 shows that this change will have no appreciable effect on profits because of the sales that will be lost from the reduction in spending by new customers. But we haven't taken advantage of the gains we can expect from the 20 percent increase in customer spending. What if this increase reduces attrition from 3.5 to 3.0 percent per cycle? Again referring to Table 36−9, we see that

TABLE 36-9

The Effect of Changing Assumptions

Base case

Net Sales	$248	$4,199	$16,671	$32,828	$49,996	$103,941
Contribution to Profit	($255)	($725)	$750	$4,605	$8,772	$13,146
Percent of Net Sales	−103.1%	−17.3%	4.5%	14.0%	17.5%	12.6%
Cumulative Profits	($255)	($980)	($230)	$4,375	$13,146	
Number of Members EOY	8,077	67,675	266,805	480,108	723,734	

The effect of increasing attrition from 2.5% per month to 3.5% per month

Net Sales	$243	$3,997	$15,626	$29,876	$44,304	$94,046
Contribution to Profit	($254)	($765)	$374	$3,457	$6,564	$9,375
Percent of Net Sales	−104.8%	−19.1%	2.4%	11.6%	14.8%	10.0%
Cumulative Profits	($254)	($1,020)	($646)	$2,811	$9,375	
Number of Members EOY	7,812	62,633	243,384	422,453	619,601	

The effect of decreasing direct mail response rates by 5% per year

Net Sales	$243	$3,830	$14,489	$26,953	$38,828	$84,343
Contribution to Profit	($254)	($781)	$77	$2,557	$4,832	$6,432
Percent of Net Sales	−104.8%	−20.4%	0.5%	9.5%	12.4%	7.6%
Cumulative Profits	($254)	($1,035)	($958)	$1,600	$6,432	
Number of Members EOY	7,812	59,906	225,702	380,211	542,435	

The effect of increase print costs by 5% per year

Net Sales	$243	$3,824	$14,301	$26,387	$37,588	$82,342
Contribution to Profit	($254)	($781)	$30	$2,385	$4,447	$5,827
Percent of Net Sales	−104.8%	−20.4%	0.2%	9.0%	11.8%	7.1%
Cumulative Profits	($254)	($1,036)	($1,005)	$1,380	$5,827	
Number of Members EOY	7,812	59,784	221,951	371,015	522,436	

The effect of decreasing cycle sales from 26% to 24% in years three to five

Net Sales	$243	$3,824	$14,295	$26,300	$37,252	$81,914
Contribution to Profit	($254)	($781)	$28	$2,343	$4,284	$5,619
Percent of Net Sales	−104.8%	−20.4%	0.2%	8.9%	11.5%	6.9%
Cumulative Profits	($254)	($1,036)	($1,008)	$1,335	$5,619	
Number of Members EOY	7,812	59,784	221,951	362,490	500,561	

The effect of increasing current member marketing expenses from
$0.50 to $0.60 per cycle—no immediate improvement in lifetime value

Net Sales	$243	$3,824	$14,295	$26,300	$37,252	$81,914
Contribution to Profit	($258)	($838)	($194)	$1,912	$3,653	$4,274
Percent of Net Sales	−106.2%	−21.9%	−1.4%	7.3%	9.8%	5.2%
Cumulative Profits	($258)	($1,096)	($1,291)	$622	$4,274	
Number of Members EOY	7,812	59,784	221,951	371,015	522,436	

The effect of reducing new customer spending by $750,000 to offset
the increase in current customer spending

Net Sales	$243	$3,824	$14,295	$25,879	$35,914	$80,156
Contribution to Profit	($258)	($838)	($194)	$1,954	$3,682	$4,345
Percent of Net Sales	−106.2%	−21.9%	−1.4%	7.5%	10.3%	5.4%
Cumulative Profits	($258)	($1,096)	($1,291)	$663	$4,345	
Number of Members EOY	7,812	59,784	221,951	362,490	500,561	

The effect of reducing attrition from 3.5% to 3.0% per sales cycle—due to increased
customer spending and reduced acquisition

Net Sales	$243	$3,824	$14,295	$25,879	$35,914	$80,156
Contribution to Profit	($254)	($781)	$28	$2,378	$4,292	$5,662
Percent of Net Sales	−104.8%	−20.4%	0.2%	9.2%	11.9%	7.1%
Cumulative Profits	($254)	($1,036)	($1,008)	$1,370	$5,662	
Number of Members EOY	7,943	62,143	232,412	386,922	542,192	

this improvement restores both sales and profit to the level they were before the change. In fact, because the number of members at the end of Year 5 on this plan has increased from 500,561 to 542,192, after all assumed changes have been accounted for, we could say that this is a better plan.

So what's the non–book club marketer to learn from this model? A couple of things. The direct marketing business is about trade-offs. A seemingly small change in one assumption can have an enormous effect on the bottom line. To really understand the dynamics of your business you need a model similar to, if not much better than, the model presented above, so that you can simulate changes in strategy and see their possible effects on near- and long-term profits. Of course, every business is different, but the need to be able to identify the important leverage points in one's business is critical.

Before leaving this chapter we will take a brief look at one other direct marketing business, the catalog business, and take a peek at the kinds of models that catalogers employ. We won't go into as much detail, but simply focus on the importance of understanding and influencing repeat purchase among groups of new customers.

EXHIBIT 36-1

Annual and Cumulative Profits Negative Option Club

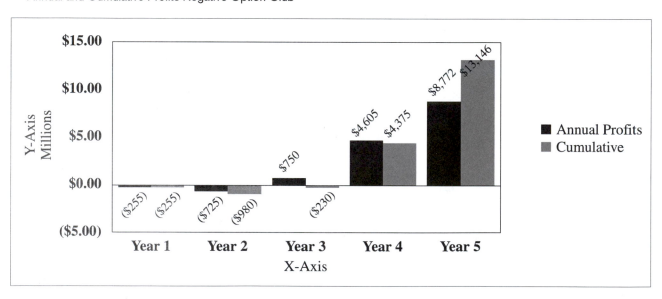

	Annual Profits	Cumulative
Year 1	($255,243)	($255,243)
Year 2	($724,979)	($980,222)
Year 3	$749,765	($230,457)
Year 4	$4,605,014	$4,374,557
Year 5	$8,771,774	$13,146,332
Year 1	($255)	($255)
Year 2	($725)	($980)
Year 3	$750	($230)
Year 4	$4,605	$4,375
Year 5	$8,772	$13,146

BUILDING CATALOG MODELS

At the beginning of this section, we discussed the differences between traditional direct marketing companies that had contractual relationships and those that had implied relationships, and we said that book clubs were good examples of the former and catalogs were good examples of the latter.

In the five-year planning model discussed above, you will notice that the book club had relatively little discretion in terms of the number of times each customer would be sent a promotional catalog (advance announcement). On the coupon that the member returned when he or she joined the club, the club defined the number of announcements the customer would receive in a 12-month period. In a catalog operation, the choices are more interesting because no contractual amount need be spent on current-customer marketing. As we said before, it's up to the cataloger to decide how much to spend on each.

Tables 36–10 and 36–11 present an example of the way in which a catalog marketer might allow customer segments to "develop naturally" over a period of six catalog mailings and then, based on the purchase patterns that evolve, create segments and choose to market differently to members of each segment.

The customer behavior model shows (Table 36–10) that, on the first catalog mailing (after the new-customer acquisition mailing that acquired the customers), 15 percent of the base purchased again. In the following period, 25 percent of the customers that responded to the first catalog mailing responded to the second mailing. Among those that didn't respond to the first mailing, 10 percent responded to the second mailing. This means that the original starting group now consists of four subgroups: (1) those that responded to both mailings (3.75 percent of the total); (2) those that responded to the first but not the second (11.25 percent); (3) those that responded to the second but not the first (8.5 percent); and (4) those that responded to neither (76.5 percent).

This analysis is carried out, in this case, over the first six catalog mailings. The graph within Table 36–10 shows period and cumulative sales over the first 24 mailings, assuming a falloff rate of 85 percent, from period to period. The bottom portion of Table 36–10 shows that after five catalog mailings 3.59 percent of the original starting group account for 21.49 percent of all sales; another 9.90 percent account for an additional 36.90 percent; and a third group (those that have made only one purchase)—22.3 percent of the total—account for the balance of the sales. Unfortunately, a full 64 percent of the starting customers have not yet made another sale.

Table 36–11 shows the same statistics, but the assumption is made that 25 percent of the starters make a repeat purchase at the first opportunity to do so. The impact on total sales is huge, but at the end of the fifth cycle, even under this set of assumptions, 56 percent of the original starting group has yet to make a repeat purchase—which is, of course, a real problem for many catalog merchandisers.

At this point in the customer life cycle, the cataloger needs to decide how he or she will treat the individual starting groups. Will a special effort be made to reward the very heavy buyers? What should be done to the large majority of the starting group that has yet to make a purchase?

We hope this last chapter on financial modeling has given you a better understanding of how all the elements of the economics of traditional direct marketing fit together. Front-end, back-end, lifetime value, and return on promotion all come together in the financial model. When this type of financial planning and analysis is combined with the database marketing methods discussed in the prior chapters of this book, the result is what we have called *the new direct marketing*.

Lifetime Value of a Starter Group in a Catalog Environment

Number of Starters   10,000   15.00% Buy on First Customer Mailing

1st Promotion	Segment	Pop Dist At Start	% Response On 1st		Time	Orders	Cum Orders	Percent of Prior
		100.00%			1	1,500	1,500	
					2	1,225	2,725	81.67%
2st Promotion	**Segments**	**Pop Dist Aft 1st**	**% Response On 2nd**		3	1,101	3,826	89.86%
					4	839	4,665	76.26%
Percent Response (Y)		15.00%	25.00%		5	699	5,365	83.32%
Percent nonresponse (N)		85.00%	10.00%		6	504	5,868	72.05%
Total		100.00%	12.25%		7	363	6,231	85.00%
					8	262	6,493	85.00%
3nd Promotion	**Segments**	**Pop Dist Aft 2st**	**% Response On 3nd**		9	188	6,681	85.00%
					10	136	6,817	85.00%
YY		3.75%	25.00%		11	98	6,915	85.00%
YN		11.25%	20.00%		12	70	6,986	85.00%
NY		8.50%	20.00%		13	51	7,036	85.00%
NN		76.50%	8.00%		14	37	7,073	85.00%
TOTAL		100.00%	11.01%		15	26	7,099	85.00%
					16	19	7,118	85.00%
4rd Promotion	**Segments**	**Pop Dist Aft 3rd**	**% Response On 4th**		17	14	7,132	85.00%
					18	10	7,142	85.00%
YYY	1	0.94%	25.00%		19	7	7,149	85.00%
YYN	2	2.81%	20.00%		20	5	7,154	85.00%
YNY	3	2.25%	20.00%		21	4	7,158	85.00%
YNN	4	9.00%	15.00%		22	3	7,160	85.00%
NYY	5	1.70%	20.00%		23	2	7,162	85.00%
NYN	6	6.80%	15.00%		24	1	7,164	85.00%
NNY	7	6.12%	15.00%					
NNN	8	70.38%	5.00%					
TOTAL	9	100.00%	8.39%					

5th Promotion	Segments	Pop Dist Aft 4th	% Response On 5th
YYYY	1	0.23%	25.00%
YYYN	2	0.70%	25.00%
YYNY	3	0.56%	25.00%
YYNN	4	2.25%	15.00%
YNYY	5	0.45%	15.00%
YNYN	6	1.80%	15.00%
YNNY	7	1.35%	15.00%
YNNN	8	7.65%	10.00%
NYYY	9	0.34%	20.00%
NYYN	10	1.36%	15.00%
NYNY	11	1.02%	15.00%
NYNN	12	5.78%	15.00%
NNYY	13	0.92%	15.00%
NNYN	14	5.20%	10.00%
NNNY	15	3.52%	10.00%
NNNN	16	66.86%	4.00%
TOTAL		100.00%	6.99%

Lifetime Value of a Starting Group
Monthly and Cumulative Sales

R-square = 0.914   # pts = 24
$y = 2.17e+003 + 1.78e+003(\ln x)$

T A B L E 36–10

continued

Number of Starters   10,000   15.00% Buy on First Customer Mailing

6th Promotion	Segments	Pop Dist Aft 5th	% Response On 6th	Customer Segments Formed after the Fifth Mailing					
				Segment	Units	%	% Customer	Units	% Orders
YYYYY	1	0.06%	27.50%	YYYYY	5	0.06%	0.06%	29	
YYYNY	2	0.18%	27.50%	YYYYN	4	0.18%	0.23%	70	
YYNYY	3	0.14%	27.50%	NYYYY	4	0.07%	0.30%	27	
YYNNY	4	0.34%	16.50%	YYYNY	4	0.18%	0.48%	70	
YNYYY	5	0.07%	16.50%	YNYYY	4	0.07%	0.55%	27	
YNYNY	6	0.27%	16.50%	YYNYY	4	0.14%	0.69%	56	
YNNYY	7	0.20%	16.50%	YYYNN	3	0.53%	1.21%	158	
YNNNY	8	0.77%	11.00%	NNYYY	3	0.14%	1.35%	41	
NYYYY	9	0.07%	22.00%	YYNYN	3	0.42%	1.77%	127	
NYYNY	10	0.20%	16.50%	NYYYN	3	0.27%	2.05%	82	
NYNYY	11	0.15%	16.50%	NYYNY	3	0.20%	2.25%	61	
NYNNY	12	0.87%	16.50%	NYNYY	3	0.15%	2.40%	46	
NNYYY	13	0.14%	16.50%	YNYYN	3	0.38%	2.78%	115	
NNYNY	14	0.52%	11.00%	YNNYY	3	0.20%	2.99%	61	
NNNYY	15	0.35%	11.00%	YNYNY	3	0.27%	3.26%	81	
NNNNY	16	2.67%	4.40%	YYNNY	3	0.34%	3.59%	101	
YYYYN	17	0.18%	20.00%	**subtotal**		**3.59%**		**1,153**	**21.49%**
YYYNN	18	0.53%	20.00%	NYYNN	2	1.16%	4.75%	231	
YYNYN	19	0.42%	20.00%	YNNYN	2	1.15%	5.90%	230	
YYNNN	20	1.91%	12.00%	NYNYN	2	0.87%	6.77%	173	
YNYYN	21	0.38%	12.00%	YNYNN	2	1.53%	8.30%	306	
YNYNN	22	1.53%	12.00%	NNYNY	2	0.52%	8.82%	104	
YNNYN	23	1.15%	12.00%	YYNNN	2	1.91%	10.73%	383	
YNNNN	24	6.89%	8.00%	NNNYY	2	0.35%	11.08%	70	
NYYYN	25	0.27%	16.00%	NNYYN	2	0.78%	11.86%	156	
NYYNN	26	1.16%	12.00%	NYNNY	2	0.87%	12.73%	173	
NYNYN	27	0.87%	12.00%	YNNNY	2	0.77%	13.49%	153	
NYNNN	28	4.91%	12.00%	**subtotal**		**9.90%**		**1,979**	**36.90%**
NNYYN	29	0.78%	12.00%	NNNYN	1	3.17%	16.66%	317	
NNYNN	30	4.68%	8.00%	NNYNN	1	4.68%	21.34%	468	
NNNYN	31	3.17%	8.00%	NNNNY	1	2.67%	24.02%	267	
NNNNN	32	64.19%	2.00%	NYNNN	1	4.91%	28.93%	491	
TOTAL		100.00%	5.04%	YNNNN	1	6.89%	35.81%	689	
				subtotal		**22.32%**		**2,232**	**41.61%**
				NNNNN	0	64.19%	100.00%	0	
				Total	0	100.0%		5,365	100.0%

Lifetime Value of a Starter Group in a Catalog Environment

Number of Starters   10,000   25.00% Buy on First Customer Mailing

1st Promotion		Pop Dist At Start	% Response On 1st		Time	Orders	Cum Orders	Percent of Prior
		100.00%			1	2,500	2,500	
					2	1,375	3,875	55.00%
		Pop Dist	**% Response**		3	1,221	5,096	88.82%
2st Promotion	**Segments**	**Aft 1st**	**On 2nd**		4	944	6,041	77.32%
Percent Response (Y)		25.00%	25.00%		5	775	6,816	82.11%
Percent nonresponse (N)		75.00%	10.00%		6	578	7,394	74.59%
Total		100.00%	13.75%		7	431	7,826	85.00%
					8	322	8,147	85.00%
		Pop Dist	**% Response**		9	240	8,387	85.00%
3nd Promotion Segments		**Aft 2st**	**On 3nd**		10	179	8,566	85.00%
YY		6.25%	25.00%		11	134	8,700	85.00%
YN		18.75%	20.00%		12	100	8,799	85.00%
NY		7.50%	20.00%		13	74	8,874	85.00%
NN		67.50%	8.00%		14	55	8,929	85.00%
TOTAL		100.00%	12.21%		15	41	8,970	85.00%
					16	31	9,001	85.00%
		Pop Dist	**% Response**		17	23	9,024	85.00%
4rd Promotion	**Segments**	**Aft 3rd**	**On 4th**		18	17	9,041	85.00%
YYY	1	1.56%	25.00%		19	13	9,054	85.00%
YYN	2	4.69%	20.00%		20	10	9,064	85.00%
YNY	3	3.75%	20.00%		21	7	9,071	85.00%
YNN	4	15.00%	15.00%		22	5	9,076	85.00%
NYY	5	1.50%	20.00%		23	4	9,080	85.00%
NYN	6	6.00%	15.00%		24	3	9,083	85.00%
NNY	7	5.40%	15.00%					
NNN	8	62.10%	5.00%					
TOTAL	9	100.00%	9.44%					

5th Promotion	Segments	Pop Dist Aft 4th	% Response On 5th
YYYY	1	0.39%	25.00%
YYYN	2	1.17%	25.00%
YYNY	3	0.94%	25.00%
YYNN	4	3.75%	15.00%
YNYY	5	0.75%	15.00%
YNYN	6	3.00%	15.00%
YNNY	7	2.25%	15.00%
YNNN	8	12.75%	10.00%
NYYY	9	0.30%	20.00%
NYYN	10	1.20%	15.00%
NYNY	11	0.90%	15.00%
NYNN	12	5.10%	15.00%
NNYY	13	0.81%	15.00%
NNYN	14	4.59%	10.00%
NNNY	15	3.11%	10.00%
NNNN	16	59.00%	4.00%
TOTAL		100.00%	7.75%

Lifetime Value of a Starting Group
Monthly and Cumulative Sales

■ Orders
♦ Cum Orders

R-square = 0.93   # pts = 24
y = 3.13e+003 + 2.1e+003(lnx)

T A B L E   36–11

continued

Number of Starters   10,000   25.00% Buy on First Customer Mailing

6th Promotion	Segments	Pop Dist Aft 5th	% Response On 6th	Customer Segments Formed after the Fifth Mailing					
				Segments	Units	%	% Customer	Units	% Orders
YYYYY	1	0.10%	27.50%	YYYYY	5	0.10%	0.10%	49	
YYYNY	2	0.29%	27.50%	YYYYN	4	0.29%	0.39%	117	
YYNYY	3	0.23%	27.50%	NYYYY	4	0.06%	0.45%	24	
YYNNY	4	0.56%	16.50%	YYYNY	4	0.29%	0.74%	117	
YNYYY	5	0.11%	16.50%	YNYYY	4	0.11%	0.86%	45	
YNYNY	6	0.45%	16.50%	YYNYY	4	0.23%	1.09%	94	
YNNYY	7	0.34%	16.50%	YYYNN	3	0.88%	1.97%	264	
YNNNY	8	1.28%	11.00%	NNYYY	3	0.12%	2.09%	36	
NYYYY	9	0.06%	22.00%	YYNYN	3	0.70%	2.79%	211	
NYYNY	10	0.18%	16.50%	NYYYN	3	0.24%	3.03%	72	
NYNYY	11	0.14%	16.50%	NYYNY	3	0.18%	3.21%	54	
NYNNY	12	0.77%	16.50%	NYNYY	3	0.14%	3.35%	41	
NNYYY	13	0.12%	16.50%	YNYYN	3	0.64%	3.99%	191	
NNYNY	14	0.46%	11.00%	YNNYY	3	0.34%	4.32%	101	
NNNYY	15	0.31%	11.00%	YNYNY	3	0.45%	4.77%	135	
NNNNY	16	2.36%	4.40%	YYNNY	3	0.56%	5.34%	169	
YYYYN	17	0.29%	20.00%	**subtotal**		**5.34%**		**1,720**	**25.23%**
YYYNN	18	0.88%	20.00%	NYYNN	2	1.02%	6.36%	204	
YYNYN	19	0.70%	20.00%	YNNYN	2	1.91%	8.27%	383	
YYNNN	20	3.19%	12.00%	NYNYN	2	0.77%	9.03%	153	
YNYYN	21	0.64%	12.00%	YNYNN	2	2.55%	11.58%	510	
YNYNN	22	2.55%	12.00%	NNYNY	2	0.46%	12.04%	92	
YNNYN	23	1.91%	12.00%	YYNNN	2	3.19%	15.23%	638	
YNNNN	24	11.48%	8.00%	NNNYY	2	0.31%	15.54%	62	
NYYYN	25	0.24%	16.00%	NNYYN	2	0.69%	16.23%	138	
NYYNN	26	1.02%	12.00%	NYNNY	2	0.77%	16.99%	153	
NYNYN	27	0.77%	12.00%	YNNNY	2	1.28%	18.27%	255	
NYNNN	28	4.34%	12.00%	**subtotal**		**12.93%**		**2,587**	**37.95%**
NNYYN	29	0.69%	12.00%	NNNYN	1	2.79%	21.06%	279	
NNYNN	30	4.13%	8.00%	NNYNN	1	4.13%	25.20%	413	
NNNYN	31	2.79%	8.00%	NNNNY	1	2.36%	27.55%	236	
NNNNN	32	56.64%	2.00%	NYNNN	1	4.34%	31.89%	434	
TOTAL		100.00%	5.78%	YNNNN	1	11.48%	43.36%	1148	
				subtotal		**25.10%**		**2,510**	**36.82%**
				NNNNN	0	56.64%	100.00%	0	
				Total	**0**	**100.0%**		**6,816**	**100.00%**

Appendixes

SITUATION 1: Create a Confidence Interval (CI)

YOU HAVE COMPLETED A TEST MAILING AND OBTAINED A RESPONSE RATE. HOW CONFIDENT CAN YOU BE OF THIS RATE—WHAT IS THE CONFIDENCE INTERVAL?

TEST MAILING			
PERCENT RESPONSE			2.00%
CONFIDENCE LEVEL: 80%, 85%, 90% OR 95%			95.00%
SAMPLE SIZE			10,000

THIS IS A TWO-SIDED TEST

THE EXPECTED RESPONSE RANGE IS BETWEEN	1.7256%	AND	2.2744%

WORK AREA

PERCENT RESPONSE	$P =$	2.00%	
SAMPLE SIZE =	$N =$	10,000	
STANDARD ERROR = SE = sqrt{P*(1–P)/N} =	$SE =$	0.14%	
CONFIDENCE LEVELS:	$=$	80.00%	1.282
TWO SIDED TEST		85.00%	1.440
		90.00%	1.645
		95.00%	1.960
LEVEL USED =	$a =$	1.96	
CONFIDENCE INTERVAL = P+/– a*SE;	$a*SE=$	0.27%	
P+a*SE =		2.27%	
P–a*SE =		1.73%	

```
C1:  [W40] 'SITUATION 1: Create A Confidence Interval (CI)
C2:  [W40] 'YOU HAVE COMPLETED A TEST MAILING AND OBTAINED A RESPONSE RATE.
C3:  [W40] 'HOW CONFIDENT CAN YOU BE OF THIS RATE, WHAT IS THE CONFIDENCE
C4:  [W40] 'INTERVAL?
C6:  [W40] 'TEST MAILING
C7:  [W40] 'PERCENT RESPONSE
F7:  (P2) [W13] 0.02
C8:  [W40] 'CONFIDENCE LEVEL: 80%, 85%, 90% OR 95%
F8:  (P2) [W13] 0.95
C9:  [W40] 'SAMPLE SIZE
F9:  (,0) [W13] 10000
C11 [W40] 'THIS IS A TWO SIDED TEST
C12: [W40] 'THE EXPECTED RESPONSE RANGE IS BETWEEN
D12: (P3) [W7] +E31
E12: (P3) [W7] "AND
F12: (P3) [W13] +E30
C17: [W40] 'WORK AREA
C19: [W40] "PERCENT RESPONSE
D19: [W7] "P =
E19: (P2) [W7] +F7
C20: [W40] "SAMPLE SIZE=
D20: [W7] "N=
E20: (,0) [W7] +F9
C22: [W40] "STANDARD ERROR = SE = sqrt{P*(1-P)/N} =
D22: [W7] "SE =
E22: (P2) [W7] @SQRT (F7*(1-F7)/E20)
C23: [W40]
C24: [W40] "CONFIDENCE LEVELS:
D24: [W7] "=
E24: (P2) [W7] 0.8
F24: (F3) [W13] 1.282
C25: [W40] "TWO SIDED TEST
E25: (P2) [W7] 0.85
F25: (F3) [W13] 1.44
E26: (P2) [W7] 0.9
F26: (F3) [W13] 1.645
E27: (P2) [W7] 0.95
F27: (F3) [W13] 1.96
C28: [W40] "LEVEL USED =
D28: [W7] "a =
E28: [W7] @VLOOKUP (F8,E24..F27,1)
C29: [W40] "CONFIDENCE INTERVAL = P +/- a*SE;
D29: [W7] "a*SE =
E29: (P2) [W7] (E22*E28)
C30: [W40] "P+a*SE =
E30: (P2) [W7] +E19+E29
C31: [W40] "P-a*SE=
E31: (P2) [W7] +E19-E29
```

SITUATION 2: Solve for *N*–Two-Sided Test

YOU HAVE AN ESTIMATED RESPONSE RATE FOR AN UPCOMING MAILING.

HOW MANY PIECES SHOULD YOU MAIL GIVEN THAT YOU

WANT TO DEVELOP A CONFIDENCE INTERVAL OF PLUS OR MINUS SOME

PERCENT AROUND THAT EXPECTED RESPONSE RATE?

PERCENT RESPONSE	2.00%		
CONFIDENCE LEVEL: 80%, 85%, 90%, OR 95%	95.00%		
ALLOWABLE PERCENTAGE ERROR	0.2744%		
CONFIDENCE INTERVAL	1.73%	TO	2.2744%

THIS IS A TWO-SIDED TEST

ANSWER: THE QUANTITY MAILED SHOULD BE:	10,000

WORK AREA

PERCENT RESPONSE	P =	2.00%	
DESIRED PRECISION	D =	0.27%	
CONFIDENCE LEVELS:		80.00%	1.282
		85.00%	1.440
		90.00%	1.645
		95.00%	1.96
CONFIDENCE LEVEL USED	a =	1.96	
DESIRED PRECISION D=	(a*SE)	0.2744%	
If D = a*SE then D/a = SE =		0.140000%	
SE(SQUARED)= SE*SE =		0.0000020	

If SE = sqrt{(P*(1–P))/N}

Then SE (squared) = P*(1–P)/N =

And (P*(1–P+) =		0.0196	
SAMPLE SIZE = N = [P*(1–P)]/SE*SE	N =	10,000	

```
H1:  [W37] 'SITUATION 2: Solve For N - Two Sided Test
H3:  [W37] 'YOU HAVE AN ESTIMATED RESPONSE RATE FOR AN UPCOMING MAILING.
H4:  [W37] 'HOW MANY PIECES SHOULD YOU MAIL GIVEN THAT YOU
H5;  [W37] 'WANT TO DEVELOP A CONFIDENCE INTERVAL OF PLUS OR MINUS SOME
H6:  [W37] 'PERCENT AROUND THAT EXPECTED RESPONSE RATE?
H8:  [W37] 'PERCENT RESPONSE
J8:  (P2) [W10] 0.02
H9:  [W37] 'CONFIDENCE LEVEL: 80%, 85%, 90% OR 95%
J9:  (P2) [W10] 0.95
H10: [W37] 'ALLOWABLE PERCENTAGE ERROR
J10: (P4) [W10] 0.002744
H11: [W37] 'CONFIDENCE INTERVAL
J11: (P3) [W10] +J8-J10
K11: (P2) [W6] ^TO
L11: (P3) [W7] +J8+J10
H13: [W37] 'THIS IS A TWO SIDED TEST
H14: [W37] 'ANSWER: THE QUANTITY MAILED SHOULD BE:
J14: (,0) [W10] +J32
H17: [W37] 'WORK AREA
H19: [W37] "PERCENT RESPONSE
I19: [W7] 'P =
J19: (P2) [W10] +J8
H20: [W37] "DESIRED PRECISION
I20: [W7] 'D =
J20: (P2) [W10] +J10
H21: [W37] "CONFIDENCE LEVELS:
J21: (P2) [W10] 0.8
L21: (F3) [W7] 1.282
J22: (P2) [W10] 0.85
L22: (F3) [W7] 1.44
J23: (P2) [W10] 0.9
L23: (F3) [W7] 1.645
J24: (P2) [W10] 0.95
L24: (F3) [W7] 1.96
H25: [W37] "CONFIDENCE LEVEL USED
I25: [W7] 'a =
J25: [W10] @VLOOKUP (J9, J21 .. L24, 2)
H26: [W37] "DESIRED PRECISION D=
I26: [W7] ' (a*SE)
J26: (P4) [W10] +J20
H27: [W37] "If D = a*SE then D/a = SE =
J27: (P6) [W10] +J26/J25
H28: [W37] "SE(SQUARED) = SE*SE =
J28: (F7) [W10] +J27*J27
H29: [W37] 'If SE =sqrt{(P*(1-P))/N}
H30: [W37] 'Then SE (squared) = P*(1-P)/N =
H31: [W37] "And (P*(1-P+) =
J31: [W10] (J19)*(1-J19)
H32: [W37] 'SAMPLE SIZE = N = [P*(1-P)]/SE*SE
I32: [W7] 'N =
J32: (,0) [W10] +J31/J28
```

SITUATION 3: Solve for *N*–One-Sided Test

YOU HAVE AN ESTABLISHED CONTROL OR BREAK-EVEN RESPONSE RATE. YOU WON'T CHANGE THE CONTROL UNLESS YOU ARE SURE THAT THE NEW PACKAGE IS REALLY BETTER THAN THE CONTROL. HOW MANY PIECES SHOULD YOU MAIL OF THE NEW TEST PACKAGE?

(assumes certainty of control response, i.e., no sampling error on control side)	CONTROL RESPONSE	TEST PACKAGE
BREAK-EVEN RESPONSE RATE	2.00%	
CONFIDENCE LEVEL: 80%, 85%, 90% OR 95%	95.00%	
REQUIRED IMPROVEMENT IN RESPONSE		13.72%
THE NEW RESPONSE RATE MUST BE AT LEAST		2.2744%
ONE-SIDED TEST		
SAMPLE SIZE		7,988

WORK AREA

HISTORICAL CONTROL (BE) RESPONSE	P =	2.00%	
PERCENT RESPONSE FROM TEST	T =	2.27%	
DIFFERENCE	d =	0.27%	
CONFIDENCE LEVELS	CI =	80.00%	0.842
ONE-SIDED TEST		85.00%	1.036
		90.00%	1.282
		95.00%	1.645
SIGNIFICANCE LEVEL USED =	a =	1.645	
ANSWER		7,988	

LOGIC

If $T - a*SE$(of T) Must Be $> P$

$T - P = d$ Must Be $> a*SE$(of T)

d Must BE $> a*sqrt[T*(1-T)/N]$

SQUARING BOTH SIDES

$d*d > a*a\{T*(1-T)/N\}$

$n > [a*a\{T*(1-T)\}]/d*d$

Exercise: Use Situation 1 to find CI for N = 7,988 and P = 2.2774%

```
N1:  [W34] 'SITUATION 3: Solve For N - One Sided Test
N3:  [W34] 'YOU HAVE AN ESTABLISHED CONTROL OR BREAKEVEN RESPONSE RATE. YOU
N4:  [W34] 'WON'T CHANGE THE CONTROL UNLESS YOU ARE SURE THAT THE NEW PACKAGE
N5:  [W34] 'IS REALLY BETTER THAN THE CONTROL. HOW MANY PIECES SHOULD
N6:  [W34] 'YOU MAIL OF THE NEW TEST PACKAGE?
N8:  [W34] '(assumes certainty of control response,
P8:  [W12] "CONTROL
Q8:  [W12] "TEST
N9:  [W34] 'i.e. no sampling error on control side)
P9:  [W12] "RESPONSE
Q9:  [W12] "PACKAGE
N10: [W34] 'BREAKEVEN RESPONSE RATE
P10: (P2) [W12] 0.02
N11: [W34] 'CONFIDENCE LEVEL: 80%, 85%, 90% OR 95%
P11: (P2) [W12] 0.95
N12: [W34] 'REQUIRED IMPROVEMENT IN RESPONSE
Q12: (P2) [W12] (0.022744/0.02) -1
N13: [W34] 'THE NEW RESPONSE RATE MUST BE AT LEAST
Q13: (P4) [W12] +P10*(1+Q12)
N15: [W34] 'ONE SIDED TEST
N16: [W34] 'SAMPLE SIZE
P16: (,0) [W12] '
Q16: (,0) [W12] +P28
N19: [W34] 'WORK AREA
N20: [W34] "HISTORICAL CONTROL (BE) RESPONSE
O20: "P =
P20: (P2) [W12] +$P$10
N21: [W34] "PERCENT RESPONSE FROM TEST
O21: "T =
P21: (P2) [W12] +Q$13
N22: [W34] "DIFFERENCE
O22: "d =
P22: (P2) [W12] +P$21-P$20
N23: [W34] "CONFIDENCE LEVELS
O23: "CI =
P23: (P2) [W12] 0.8
Q23: [W12] 0.842
N24: [W34] "ONE SIDED TEST
P24: (P2) [W12] 0.85
Q24: (F3) [W12] 1.036
P25: (P2) [W12] 0.9
Q25: [W12] 1.282
P26: (P2) [W12] 0.95
Q26: [W12] 1.645
N27: [W34] "SIGNIFICANCE LEVEL USED =
O27: "a =
P27: [W12] @VLOOKUP(P$11,P$23..Q$26,1)
N28: [W34] "ANSWER
P28: (,0) [W12] (P$27*P$27)*(P$21*(1-P$21))/(P22*P22)
N29: [W34] "
P30: [W12] '
N31: [W34] "LOGIC
N32: [W34] "If T -a*SE (of T) Must Be > P
N33: [W34] "T - P = d Must Be > a*SE(of T)
N34: [W34] "d Must BE > a*sqrt[T*(1-T)/N]
N35: [W34] "SQUARING BOTH SIDES
N36: [W34] "d*d > a*a{T*(1-T)/N}
N37: [W34] "n > [a*a{T*(1-T)}]/d*d
N38: [W34] 'Exercise: Use Situation 1 to find CI for N = 7,988 and P = 2.277
```

SITUATION 4: Test for Significant Differences

IS THE RESPONSE TO THE TEST PACKAGE STATISTICALLY BETTER
(OR WORSE) THAN THE RESPONSE TO THE CONTROL PACKAGE?

(Better or worse implies a one-sided test.)

	CONTROL PACKAGE	TEST PACKAGE
(When both test and control sides are mailed, sampling error applies to both mailings)		
	2.00%	2.274%
CONFIDENCE LEVEL: 80%, 85%, 90% OR 95%	95.00%	
SAMPLE SIZE	15,000	15,000

ANSWER: IMPROVEMENT IN RESPONSE RATE IS . . . . . . **NOT SIGNIFICANT**

WORK AREA

CONTROL PROPORTION =	P	2.00%	
TEST PROPORTION =	T	2.27%	
ABSOLUTE DIFFERENCE =	d	0.27%	
CONFIDENCE LEVEL		80.00%	0.842
THIS IS A ONE-SIDED TEST		85.00%	1.036
		90.00%	1.282
		95.00%	1.645
LEVEL USED =	a =	1.645	
SAMPLE SIZE CONTROL =	N1 =	15,000	
SAMPLE SIZE TEST =	N2 =	15,000	
EST OF POPULATION VALUE OF % RSP =	p* =	0.02137	

$[\{N1*P\}+\{N2*T\}]/[N1+N2]$

ESTIMATED STANDARD ERROR OF THE
DIFFERENCE BETWEEN TWO SAMPLE
PERCENTAGES–ESTIMATED FROM THE
SAMPLES THEMSELVES: USING   SE(of p*) =   0.001670
$sqrt[\{p*(1-p*)*(N1+N2)\}/(N1*N2)]$

DECISION PARAMETER

          (P–T)/SE(of p*) =   dp =   1.6431731783

DECISION RULE:

    if @ABS(dp)>a then diff is significant   0

                                         TABLE =   0 NOT SIGNIFICANT
                                                                          1 SIGNIFICANT

                              ANSWER =   NOT SIGNIFICANT

```
S1: [W34] 'SITUATION 4: Test for Significant Differences
S3: [W34] 'IS THE RESPONSE TO THE TEST PACKAGE STATISTICALLY BETTER (OR
S4: [W34] 'WORSE) THAN THE RESPONSE TO THE CONTROL PACKAGE?
S5: [W34] '(Better or worse implies a one-sided test.)
S7: [w34] '(When both test & control sides are mailed,
U7: [W12] "CONTROL
V7: [W16] "TEST
S8: [W34] 'sampling error applies to both mailings)
U8: [W12] "PACKAGE
V8: [W16] "PACKAGE
U9: (P2) [W12] 0.02
V9: (P3) [W16] 0.022744
S10: [W34] 'CONFIDENCE LEVEL: 80%, 85%, 90% OR 95%
U10: (P2) [W12] 0.95
S11: [W34] 'SAMPLE SIZE
U11: (,0) [W12] 15000
V11: (,0) [W16] 15000
S13: [W34] 'ANSWER: IMPROVEMENT IN RESPONSE RATE IS.........
U13: [W12] +U40
S15: [W34] 'WORK AREA
S16: [W34] "CONTROL PROPORTION =
T16: [W9] "P
U16: (P2) [W12] +U9
S17: [W34] "TEST PROPORTION =
T17: [W9] "T
U17: (P2) [W12] +V9
S18: [W34] "ABSOLUTE DIFFERENCE =
T18: [W9] "d
U18: (P2) [W12] +U17-U16
S19: [W34] 'CONFIDENCE LEVEL
U19: (P2) [W12] 0.8
V19: [W16] 0.842
S20: [W34] 'THIS IS A ONE SIDED TEST
U20: (P2) [W12] 0.85
V20: (F3) [W16] 1.036
U21: (P2) [W12] 0.9
V21: [W16] 1.282
U22: (P2) [W12] 0.95
V22: [W16] 1.645
S23: [W34] "LEVEL USED =
T23: [W9] "a =
U23: [W12] @VLOOKUP(U10,U19..V22,1)
S24: [W34] "SAMPLE SIZE CONTROL =
T24: [W9] "N1 =
U24: (,0) [W12] +U11
S25: [W34] "SAMPLE SIZE TEST =
T25: [W9] "N2 =
U25: (,0) [W12] +V11
S26: [W34] "EST OF POPULATION VALUE OF % RSP =
T26: [W9] "p* =
U26: (F5) [W12] ((U16*U24)+(U17*U25))/(U24+U25)
V26: [W16] '
S27: [W34] '[{N1*P}+{N2*T}]/[N1+N2]
S29: [W34] 'ESTIMATED STANDARD ERROR OF THE
S30: [W34] 'DIFFERENCE BETWEN TWO SAMPLE
```

```
S31: [W34] 'PERCENTAGES—ESTIMATED FROM THE
S32: [W34] 'SAMPLES THEMSELVES: USING
T32: [W9] "SE(of p*)=
U32: (F6) [W12] @SQRT(U26*(1-U26)*(U24+U25)/(U24*U25))
S33: [W34] 'sqrt[{p*(1-p*)*(N1+N2)}/(N1*N2)]
S34: [W34] 'DECISION PARAMETER
S35: [W34] "(P-T)/SE(of p*) =
T35: [W9] "dp =
U35: [W12] +U18/U32
S36: [W34] 'DECISION RULE:
S37: [W34] "if @ABS(dp)>a then diff is significant
U37: [W12] @IF(@ABS(U35)>=U23,1,0)
S38: [W34] "TABLE =
U38: [W12] 0
V38: [W16] 'NOT SIGNIFICANT
U39: [W12] 1
V39: [W16] 'SIGNIFICANT
S40: [W34] "ANSWER =
U40: [W12] @VLOOKUP(U37,U38..V39,1)
```

Appendix B
Vendors of Data

Direct marketers interested in enhancing their customer and prospect files with individual household-level data; with census data gathered at the block group, census tract, or ZIP code level; or with geography-based cluster codes can do so by obtaining such data from a number of data sources.

Some of the more popular sources are listed below, and selected samples of their promotional literature have been reproduced on the pages that follow.

The sources listed are by no means a directory of all available data sources, nor is the material presented for any of the listed sources meant to be a complete presentation of the data and services that these companies provide. For a complete listing of data sources and computer service bureaus, contact

The Direct Marketing Association
6 East 43rd Street
New York, NY 10017
Telephone: 212-768-7277

In addition we have provided information regarding the database management system developed by one of this book's authors, Dr. Dhiraj Sharma, which is available through David Shepard Associates, Inc., and MegaPlex, Inc.

TABLE OF CONTENTS FOR EXHIBITS

PRIZM
Cluster Narratives

CLARITAS

PRIZM—The Third Generation

Recent demographic changes and new methods of data analysis challenge marketers to make sure their data and tools are up to date. The new generation of PRIZM reflects the demographic changes that have swept across the U.S. It incorporates many data-collection innovations instituted by the Bureau of the Census, as well as new analytical measures developed by Claritas statisticians.

The revised 1990 Census offered marketers an unprecedented opportunity to analyze U.S. consumers using fresh data. Innovations include the release of new demographic details, data at smaller levels of geography, detailed "TIGER" electronic street mapping files, and uniform geographic units for the entire U.S.

For a company in the lifestyle segmentation business, these changes mandated that any existing model be *completely* re-constructed using the new data. This is exactly what Claritas has done with its third generation of PRIZM.

This booklet contains brief "thumbnail" descriptions for each of the 62 PRIZM clusters. These descriptions are organized by social group to form a handy reference to the demographics and lifestyle of each cluster.

PRIZM Is Precision Marketing

PRIZM is a versatile marketing tool that classifies every U.S. neighborhood into one of 62 distinct types or "clusters." Marketers use PRIZM to segment their customers into groups to better understand their lifestyles and behavior, and then target their best prospects.

The first step in putting PRIZM to work is to use the system to identify which clusters perform at above or below average rates for your product or service. By identifying the types of neighborhoods where you find your existing customers, you can accurately predict the types of neighborhoods where you will find customers in the future. You can then develop target marketing plans that focus on these areas. The best source of data for PRIZM profiling is your own customer data. Almost any data with an address, or at least a ZIP Code, can be PRIZM-coded and profiled. If customer data is unavailable, syndicated studies from MRI, Simmons, and others can be used to create an appropriate PRIZM profile of your target audience.

Maps and reports can be created at various levels of geography to help you find your best prospects. Nationally, television markets can be compared to specific PRIZM profiles and to each other to isolate markets representing the best opportunities from a national, "big picture" perspective. At the local level, specific ZIP Codes, census tracts, or block groups can be identified as having the best opportunity relative to the PRIZM profile and to each other. This is vital information for site location, outdoor advertising, and other "site-based" marketing activities.

A reliable tool for developing an effective media strategy, PRIZM provides target rankings for markets and media—television programs, magazines, cable systems, and radio. Nearly all mass-compiled direct marketing lists are PRIZM coded, as are many vertical lists. This allows you to select names (or telephone numbers) by PRIZM cluster. Your direct marketing program can be implemented at the ZIP Code, Carrier Route, or ZIP+4 level. Target marketing maps can help you select the right cable systems for local cable advertising and place your outdoor and Yellow Page directory advertising.

PRIZM provides a sound basis for effective decision making in every aspect of consumer marketing: strategic marketing, retail targeting, media strategy, direct mail, and site location.

Standard PRIZM Social Groups

All of the 62 clusters are grouped into 15 broader social groups, as shown in the grid on the right. The "width" of the grid across the bottom indicates the degree of urbanization—from the rural countryside to urban high-rises. The "height" of the grid along the side indicates the degree of affluence or socioeconomic status (i.e., income, education, home value, occupation, etc.) spanning the lower, middle, and upscale markets. For instance, at the top of the affluence and density scale are the "U1" big-city urban clusters: "Urban Gold Coast," "Money & Brains," "Young Literati," "Bohemian Mix," and "American Dreams." At the bottom of the affluence and density scale is the "R3" rural group: "Blue Highways," "Rustic Elders," "Back Country Folks," "Scrub Pine Flats," and "Hard Scrabble."

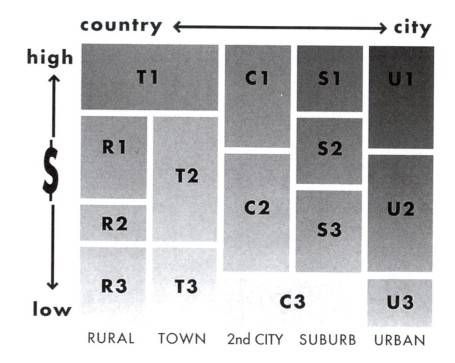

How PRIZM Is Created And Annually Updated

PRIZM cluster analysis begins with the 1990 U.S. Census database, which contains thousands of demographic data items from small neighborhood areas across the country. The primary geographic unit for our demographic analysis is the census block group—the smallest neighborhood geographic unit that provides statistical stability and the full range of demographic details from the census. (A block group contains an average of about 340 households.) In addition, the limited but important block-level data from the census is used to create finer resolution for small neighborhoods and as a statistical "anchor," in conjunction with ZIP+4 level data, to create unique cluster assignments for each of the over 20 million residential ZIP+4s.

Factor analysis of census data reveals that several dozen demographic and lifestyle variables in six broader categories explain most of the variance between different neighborhood types. These six categories are:

- Social rank (income, education, etc.)
- Household composition (age, size, etc.)
- Mobility (length of residence, etc.)
- Ethnicity (race, foreign birth, etc.)
- Urbanization
  (population/housing density)
- Housing (owner/renter, home value, etc.)

Cluster analysis of these factors produced 62 basic neighborhood types which provide the optimal predictive power and ease-of-use for the system. The clusters have been tested and refined using hundreds of millions of actual consumer purchase data records from multiple sources.

Claritas annually updates each PRIZM neighborhood cluster assignment using its proprietary demographic update process, which taps a comprehensive network of more than 1,600 local, state, and federal demographic data sources.

The resulting PRIZM system provides a flexible framework for decision-making that's consistent from one level of geography to another. For instance, the PRIZM assignments for census block groups which are ideal for customer profiling can be accurately translated into PRIZM assignments for census tracts (well-suited for mapping and site location), or postal ZIP Codes and ZIP+4s for direct marketing. This ability to "upshift" or "downshift" from one level of geography to another— with total consistency—is a feature that is unique to PRIZM.

Building PRIZM Clusters

Census Demographics & Claritas Updates

Social Rank	HH Composition	Housing
Ethnicity	Urbanization	Mobility

Neighborhood Geography

Tracts	Block Groups	ZIP Codes
ZIP+4s	Carrier Routes	Blocks

Data Analysis

Consumer Behavior Data

Automotive	Magazines	Direct Marketing
Real Estate	Credit	Expenditures

PRIZM Lifestyle Clusters

APPENDIX B   Vendors of Data

S1 - Elite Suburbs

The five clusters of group S1, the nation's most affluent social group, rank in the first and second deciles of Claritas' education and affluence scale. Group S1 is concentrated in major metro areas, with over 90% of total households in the top 25 TV markets. The S1 clusters share high income, education, investment, and spending levels. Despite low incidence levels, groups 1 and 2 share high index concentrations of wealthy Asian and Arabic immigrants. Beyond these shared patterns, there are marked differences.

01 Blue Blood Estates   *Elite Super-Rich Families*

America's wealthiest suburbs are populated by established executives, professionals, and heirs to "old money." They are accustomed to privilege and live in luxury, often supported by servants. A tenth of this group is a multi-millionaire. The next affluence level is a sharp drop from this pinnacle.

Elite (1)   Age Groups: 35-44, 45-54, 55-64   Dominant White, High Asian

---

02 Winner's Circle   *Executive Suburban Families*

As its name implies, cluster 2 is second in American affluence. Typified by "new money," they live in expensive new mansions in the suburbs of major metros. They are well-educated, mobile executives and professionals with teen-aged families. They are prolific spenders who enjoy global travel.

Wealthy (2)   Age Groups: 35-44, 45-54, 55-64   Dominant White, High Asian

---

03 Executive Suites   *Upscale White-Collar Couples*

Cluster 3 describes yesterday's "Young Influentials," who are enroute to becoming tomorrow's "Winner's Circle." Many have married, and moved into condos or starter homes. Unique for S1, this cluster is above average in pre-school kids. Although they rank well below "Winner's Circle" in affluence, they are as well-educated, ambitious, and competent; they're just ten years younger.

Affluent (8)   Age Groups: 25-34, 35-44   Dominant White, High Asian

---

04 Pools & Patios   *Established Empty Nesters*

Older, established couples in executive, professional, sales, and communication fields make up cluster 4. Since many have reached their "golden" post-child years, there is a high index for dual incomes which in turn support a rich, busy life of travel, leisure activities, and entertainment.

Affluent (9)   Age Groups: 45-54, 55-64, 65+   Dominant White, High Asian

---

05 Kids & Cul-de-Sacs   *Upscale Suburban Families*

Close to "Executive Suites" and "Pools and Patios" on all affluence measures, cluster 5 is ranked first of all 62 PRIZM clusters in married couples with children, and large, 4+ person families. Since "family" governs its lives and activities, "Kids and Cul-de-Sacs" is a noisy mix of bikes, dogs, carpools, and sports.

Affluent (10)   Age Groups: 35-44, 45-54   Dominant White, High Asian

---

U1 - Urban Uptown

With three of its five clusters in the first affluence decile plus two in the third decile, group U1 is ranked as the nation's second most affluent social group. Major market concentrations are high, with over 94% of total households in the top 10 TV markets. Consistent for over two decades, these clusters show high concentrations of executives and professionals in business, finance, entertainment, and education. More recently, they have absorbed a wave of upscale immigrants from Eastern Europe, Asia, and the Middle East.

06 Urban Gold Coast

Elite Urban Singles & Couples

Cluster 6 is unique. It is the most densely populated per square mile, with the highest per-capita income, the greatest concentration of singles in multi-unit, high-rise buildings, the lowest incidence of auto ownership, and the fewest children. Cluster 6 is tops in urbania, and over half of its population lives in New York City.

Affluent (3)   Age Groups: Mixed   Dominant White, High Asian

07 Money & Brains

Sophisticated Townhouse Couples

Although cluster 7 closely trails "Urban Gold Coast" in affluence measurement, it's very different. Upscale homes and condos on the urban fringe are owned by older, married couples who have few children. Since many enjoy dual incomes, they are sophisticated consumers of adult luxuries, travel, and entertainment.

Affluent (5)   Age Groups: 44-54, 55-64, 65+   Dominant White, High Asian

08 Young Literati

Upscale Urban Singles & Couples

Although cluster 8 is below "Money & Brains" in affluence, it leads in education. A younger mix of executives, professionals, and students live in multi-unit apartments, condos, and townhouses near private urban universities. Having few children, these bons vivants are free to pursue their interests in art, fitness, and travel.

Upper Middle (6)   Age Groups: 25-34, 35-44   Dominant White, High Asian

09 American Dreams

Established Urban Immigrant Families

Cluster 9 typifies the "American Dream." Immigrants and descendants of multi-ancestries populate these multi-racial, multi-lingual neighborhoods. Cluster 9 tends to have big families, which is unique to group U1. Multiple incomes from trades and public service have raised them to the second affluence level.

Upper Middle (14)   Age Groups: 35-44, 45-54   Ethnically Diverse

10 Bohemian Mix

Bohemian Singles & Couples

Although it's a short trip from the "Upper East Side" to the "Village," the lifestyle and perspective shifts dramatically. Cluster 10 is America's "Bohemia," a truly integrated mixture of executives, students, actors, and writers living in multi-unit buildings. This multi-racial, educated group is dominated by singles, and has the nation's second lowest index for children.

Middle (17)   Age Groups: Under 24, 25-34   Ethnically Diverse

C1 - 2nd City Society

The three clusters of social group C1 comprise the upper deck in hundreds of America's "second" and "satellite" cities. As a group, they share high educations and incomes, with one cluster in the second and two in the third affluence deciles. They also share high home ownership, employment as executives and professionals in essential local industries, such as business, finance, health, law, communications, and wholesale. They are far more conservative than their upscale S1 peers in the suburbs of major metros.

11 Second City Elite   *Upscale Executive Families*

Cluster 11 describes the "movers and shakers" of our second cities that are found coast to coast, with its typical example in the wealthy enclaves of Huntsville, Alabama. Primarily married with teenage children, they give first attention to their families, homes, and clubs, then steal away to play in Europe.

Affluent (7)   Age Groups: 45-54, 55-64   Dominant White

12 Upward Bound   *Young Upscale White-Collar Families*

Young, college-educated, computer-literate, dual-income, frequent-flying executives and professionals describe those in "Upward Bound." Most of this group is married, with pre- and school-aged children, and live in new, owner-occupied single family homes. They are found in over 100 TV markets that cover 75% of the total U.S. population.

Upper Middle (13)   Age Groups: 25-34, 35-44   Dominant White, High Asian

---

13 Gray Power   *Affluent Retirees in Sunbelt Cities*

Cluster 13 represents over two million senior citizens who have pulled up stakes and moved to the country or the Sunbelt to retire among their peers. While these neighborhoods are found nationwide, almost half are concentrated in 13 retirement areas. They are health and golf fanatics who maintain fat investment portfolios.

Middle (16)   Age Groups: 55-64, 65+   Dominant White

T1 - Landed Gentry

The four clusters of social group T1 are found in 180 of 212 TV markets, covering a vast amount of American geography. With one cluster in the first, one in the second, and two in the third affluence deciles, T1 is the fourth most affluent group. As a group, they all show large, multi-income families of school-aged kids, headed by well-educated executives, professionals, and "techies." Above all, they share serenity, for T1 neighborhoods tend to lie far outside the metro beltways in the nation's most spectacular coastal areas and uplands.

14 Country Squires   *Elite Exurban Families*

A private island off the coast of Maine; an elegant restored colonial village in the Berkshires; lush fenced-in horse farms in Leesburg, VA; or manicured gardens in Carmel by the Sea. . . The wealthy have escaped urban stress to live in rustic luxury in Country Squires neighborhoods. Fourth in affluence, this group has "big bucks in the boondocks."

Wealthy (4)   Age Groups: 35-44, 45-54   Dominant White

15 God's Country   *Executive Exurban Families*

Many educated, upscale married executives and professionals are raising their large families in the remote exurbs of major metros, the outskirts of second cities, and scenic towns. Multiple incomes support their affluence and life centers around family and outdoor activities. This is cluster 15, in the second affluence decile.

Affluent (11)   Age Groups: 35-44, 45-54   Dominant White

16 Big Fish Small Pond   *Small Town Executive Families*

Similar to cluster 15 in size and national distribution, but seven rungs down the affluence ladder is "Big Fish Small Pond." Though every bit as married and family-oriented, these neighborhoods are older and far more conservative. Best described as captains of local industry, they invest in their homes and clubs, and vacation by car in the U.S.

Upper Middle (18)   Age Groups: 35-44, 45-54   Dominant White

17 Greenbelt Families   *Young, Middle-Class Town Families*

A rung below "Big Fish, Small Pond" in affluence, cluster 17 is smaller and more concentrated in our smaller second cities and uplands. This heavily mortgaged group are young marrieds with lots of children. Their energies are devoted to family entertainment and outdoor sports.

Upper Middle (19)   Age Groups: 25-34, 35-44   Dominant White

S2 - The Affluentials

The five clusters of social group S2 represent the upper-middle income suburbs of major metros. Almost 77% of its total households are concentrated in the top 25 TV markets, with 90% in the top 50. With one cluster each in the second and third, two in the fourth, and one in the fifth affluence deciles, S2 is our fifth most affluent group. As a group, these clusters share above-average incomes and rentals, an eclectic mix of homes, condos, and apartments, a broad spectrum of business, technical, and public service jobs, daily commuting. . and very little else.

18 Young Influentials   *Upwardly Mobile Singles & Couples*

Cluster 18 was hot in the eighties. Dubbed the "Young Urban Professionals," these were the educated, high-tech, metropolitan sophisticates, the "swingles" and childless live-in couples, whose double incomes bought the good life in Boomtown U.S.A. Then they married, and reduced cluster 18 to half its former size. Here's what's left: The Last of the Yuppies.

Upper Middle (12)   Age Groups: Under 24, 25-34, 35-44   Dominant White, High Asian

19 New Empty Nests   *Upscale Suburban Fringe Couples*

Only three rungs down the affluence ladder, cluster 19 is much more conservative than "Young Influentials," and skewed to the northeast. Cluster 19 achieved its affluence through education and career accomplishments in numerous professions and industries. Most of them are married, in their post-child years, and have dual incomes.

Upper Middle (15)   Age Groups: 45-54, 55-64, 65+   Dominant White

20 Boomers & Babies   *Young White-Collar Suburban Families*

Cluster 20 ranks second of all PRIZM clusters for married couples with children, and first for total households with children, many of whom are pre-schoolers. Skewed to the West, cluster 20 is composed of executives and "techies" working in varied fields. Their relative youth and early careers place them at the bottom of the third affluence decile.

Upper Middle (21)   Age Groups: 25-34, 35-44   Dominant White, High Asian

21 Suburban Sprawl   *Young Midscale Suburban Couples & Singles*

Multi-racial, multi-lingual neighborhoods are typically found in the centers of major metros. Cluster 21 is the exception, showing above average concentrations of native and foreign-born ethnics who have used education to become executives, administrators, and technicians. They have moved to the suburbs and the fourth affluence decile.

Middle (24)   Age Groups: Under 24, 35-34   Ethnically Diverse

22 Blue-Chip Blues   *Upscale Blue-Collar Families*

For twenty years, cluster 22 was one of the largest PRIZM clusters. Dual income, high school-educated parents headed large suburban families, and topped the blue-collar ladder. During these two decades, their kids grew up and left, and blue-collar employment declined sharply. A smaller core remains, centered in the Great Lakes region.

Middle (30)   Age Groups: 35-54   Dominant White

S3 - Inner Suburbs

The four clusters of social group S3 comprise the middle income suburbs of major metros, concentrated 59% in the top 25, 84% in the top 50, and 95% in the top 75 TV markets. With two clusters at the bottom of the fifth and two at the top of the seventh affluence decile, S3 straddles the U.S. average. Otherwise, they are markedly different, two having more college-educated white collars, two with more high-school-educated blue collars, two young, one old, one mixed, and all showing distinct, variant patterns of employment, lifestyle, and regional concentration.

23 Upstarts & Seniors

Middle Income Empty Nesters

Cluster 23 shows that youths and seniors are very similar if they're employable, single, and childless. In cluster 23, they share average educations and incomes in business, finance, retail, health, and public service. Preferring to live in condos and apartments, cluster 23 folks like the Sunbelt and the West.

Middle (28)   Age Groups: Under 34, 65+   Dominant White

24 New Beginnings

Young Mobile City Singles

Concentrated in the boomtowns of the Southeast, the Southwest, and the Pacific coast, cluster 24 is a magnet for fresh starts. Populated by well-educated youths, many are minorities. Some are divorced, while many others are solo parents. The majority live in multi-unit rentals, and work in a variety of low-level, white-collar jobs.

Middle (29)   Age Groups: Under 24, 25-34   Ethnically Diverse

---

25 Mobility Blues

Young Blue-Collar/Service Families

In most of the same markets, but two deciles down in affluence, cluster 25 is the blue-collar equivalent of "New Beginnings:" young, ethnically mixed, and highly mobile. Conversely, this cluster shows high indices for Hispanics and large families with children. The military, industry, transportation, and public service are the primary employers of these breadwinners.

Middle (41)   Age Groups: Under 24, 25-34   Mixed, High Hispanic

---

26 Gray Collars

Aging Couples in Inner Suburbs

For almost two decades, we read about the decline of the Great Lakes industrial "Rust Belt." Decimated by foreign takeovers in the steel and automobile industries, the area lost a million jobs. Although most of the kids left, their highly skilled parents stayed, and are now benefiting from a major U.S. industrial resurgence.

Middle (42)   Age Groups: 55-64, 65+   Ethnically Diverse

U2 - Urban Midscale

The five clusters of social group U2 comprise the middle income, urban-fringe neighborhoods of America's major metros. As with group U1, group U2 is highly concentrated, with 75% of total households in the top five TV markets, and 96% in the top 25. With one cluster in the fourth, two in the sixth, and two in the seventh affluence deciles, group U2 averages below the mean. As a group, the U2 clusters share high population densities, ethnic diversity, public transportation, and all the perks and risks of urban life, yet are otherwise unique.

27 Urban Achievers   *Mid-Level White-Collar Urban Couples*

Due to its rank in the third decile of college education, cluster 27 is the most affluent of the U2 clusters. Often found near urban, public universities, these neighborhoods are ethnically diverse with a bi-modal, young/old age profile. Single students mix with older professionals in business, finance, and public service.

Middle (22)   Age Groups: 25-34, 65+   Dominant White, High Asian & Hispanic

28 Big City Blend   *Middle-Income Immigrant Families*

High indices for Asians, Hispanics, and other foreign-born immigrants make cluster 28 the most ethnically diverse in the U2 group. Skewed to the West, its affluence level drops two deciles from "Urban Achievers." They have big families, are employed in an even mix of white- and blue-collar jobs, and live in old, stable, high density, urban rowhouse areas.

Middle (32)   Age Groups: 25-34, 35-44   Dominant Hispanic, High Asian

29 Old Yankee Rows   *Empty-Nest, Middle-Class Families*

"Magnet" neighborhoods for recent Asian and Latin American immigrants and centered in the Northeast, cluster 29 is the most multi-lingual cluster in U2. Although it's five affluence rungs below "Big City Blend," cluster 29 has the same white/blue-collar job mix, and tends toward singles living in multi-unit rentals.

Middle (37)   Age Groups: 25-34, 65+   Ethnically Diverse

30 Mid-City Mix   *African-American Singles & Families*

Cluster 30 is in the seventh affluence decile, geographically centered in the Northeast and Great Lakes regions. Similar to all U2's, cluster 30 shows above-average ethnic diversity and a mix of white- and blue-collar employment. These rowhouse neighborhoods on the urban fringe are two-thirds black and have a high incidence of college enrollment.

Middle (46)   Age Groups: Under 24, 25-34, 35-44   Dominant Black

31 Latino America   *Hispanic Middle-Class Families*

Dominated by Latin Americans, with the nation's highest index for foreign-born immigrants, cluster 31 is a giant step in achievement. They are concentrated in New York, Miami, Chicago and the Southwest. in large young families with lots of children. Although they live in rented homes and have blue-collar jobs, they are moving up, and are college bound.

Middle (44)   Age Groups: Under 24, 25-34   Dominant Hispanic

C2 - 2nd City Centers

The five clusters of social group C2 describe the midscale, middle-density, "satellite" cities surrounding major metros, as well as many smaller second-tier cities, and cover all but 10 minor TV markets in the U.S. With one cluster in the fourth, two in the fifth, and one each in the sixth and seventh affluence deciles, and with a lower cost of living, the C2 clusters are generally more prosperous than their peers in group U2. With minor exceptions, they are predominantly white. Otherwise, they are fundamentally different in age, marriage, education, occupations, and lifestyle.

32 Middleburg Managers   *Mid-Level White-Collar Couples*

They keep the wheels rolling in our second cities: the business executives, bankers, doctors, lawyers, retailers, and city-hall officials. Half are older, married, post-child; half are younger, single, pre-child. Above-average incomes in all dollar brackets allow active leisure pursuits of clubs and sports.

Middle (20)   Age Groups: 55-64, 65+   Dominant White

33 Boomtown Singles   *Middle Income Young Singles*

Cluster 33 plays host to the youth of a hundred, fast-growing second cities in the Southern, Mid-West, and West. They are young professionals and "techies" in public and private service industries who live in multi-unit rentals, like music, and enjoy vacationing in the Caribbean.

Middle (27)   Age Groups: Under 24, 25-34   Dominant White

34 Starter Families   *Young Middle-Class Families*

Bucking recent trends, "Starter Families" opted for early marriage and parenthood. Here we see a higher index for blue-collar jobs, large families, and solo parents with young children. Many are living in natural beauty with a skew to the Pacific coast, the Rockies, and the northwestern Canadian borderlands.

Middle (36)   Age Groups: Under 24, 25-34   Mixed Ethnicity, High Hispanic

35 Sunset City Blues   *Empty Nests in Aging Industrial Cities*

Equal to "Starter Families" in affluence, cluster 35 describes older, skilled blue-collars, policemen, firemen, and technicians who have reached the end of their careers. Some retire to the mountains or "St. Pete," but most stay home to rock on their porches near the Great Lakes and Mohawk Valley.

Lower Middle (39)   Age Groups: 55-64, 65+   Dominant White

36 Towns & Gowns   *College Town Singles*

Many college towns and university campus neighborhoods are typically mixed with half locals ("Towns") and half students ("Gowns"). Cluster 36 is composed of thousands of 18-to-24 year-olds on limited budgets and highly educated but perhaps underpaid professionals, all with a penchant for prestige products that are beyond their evident means.

Lower Middle (31)   Age Groups: Under 24, 25-34   Dominant White, High Asian

T2 - Exurban Blues

Since the four clusters of social group T2 cover the midscale, low-density towns lying at the outskirts of all major metros and second cities alike, the group is represented in all but three small TV markets. With one cluster each in the fourth and fifth, two in the sixth, and one in the seventh affluence deciles, group T2 is comparable to groups S3, U2, and C2. Three of these clusters are predominantly white, show an even age distribution, own homes, marry, and raise kids. The fourth defines lifestyles in military group quarters, and is unique.

37 New Homesteaders   *Young Middle-Class Families*

Cluster 37 is the only T2 cluster that shows above average college educations. Executives and professionals work in local service fields such as administration, communications, health, and retail. Most are married; the young have children, the elders do not. Life is homespun with a focus on crafts, camping, and sports.

Middle (26)   Age Groups: 35-44, 45-54   Dominant White

38 Middle America   *Midscale Families in Midsize Towns*

Sitting atop the sixth affluence decile of the U.S. median income, cluster 38 is aptly named. These are family neighborhoods with a high index for married couples with children. They are busy with kids and dogs, and enjoy fast food, sports, fishing, camping, and watching TV. In approximate balance with the U.S. population, they are found coast to coast.

Middle (33)   Age Groups: 25-34, 35-54   Dominant White

39 Red, White & Blues   *Small Town Blue-Collar Families*

Just below "Middle America" in affluence, cluster 39 is far more industrial and blue-collar, with skilled workers primarily employed in mining, milling, manufacturing, and construction. Geo-centered in the Appalachians, Great Lakes industrial region, and Western highlands, these folks love the outdoors.

Middle (35)   Age Groups: 35-54, 55-64   Dominant White

40 Military Quarters   *GIs & Surrounding Off-Base Families*

Since cluster 40 depicts military life with personnel living in group quarters, its demographics are wholly atypical. Located on/or near military bases, cluster 40 skews toward our principal harbors and defense perimeters. Fully integrated, and with the highest index for adults under 35, "Military Quarters" likes fast cars, bars, and action sports.

Lower Middle (40)   Age Groups: Under 24, 25-34   Ethnically Diverse

R1 - Country Families

The four clusters of social group R1 confirm a continuing trend to strong economic growth in rural America. With two clusters in the fourth, one in the sixth, and one in the eighth affluence deciles, group R1 now rivals groups S3, U2, C2 and T2 in midscale affluence and, with far lower living costs, suffer less poverty. From hundreds of small towns and remote exurbs, the group covers all but a few TV markets. They are largely composed of white, married couples, many with children, in industrial and agrarian occupations, living in owned houses and mobile homes.

41 Big Sky Families   *Midscale Couples, Kids & Farmland*

With an average incidence for college educations, cluster 41 has income levels well above the U.S. median. They are well-paid skilled craftsmen, machinists, and builders who live in scenic locales from New England to the Tidewater, in the Great Lakes region, and the Rockies. Family-centered lifestyles are devoted to hobbies, hunting, and boating.

Upper Middle (23)   Age Groups: 35-44, 45-54   Dominant White

42 New Eco-topia   *Rural White/Blue-Collar/Farm Families*

Found in the Northern Pacific, the Rockies, and northern New England, cluster 42 is the only R1 cluster with above-average college educations. "New Eco-topia" has an even mix of white/blue-collar jobs. A high index for personal computers reflects several new, high-tech industries in these pristine areas.

Middle (25)   Age Groups: 35-44, 45-54, 55-64, 65+   Dominant White

43 River City, USA   *Middle-Class Rural Families*

Cluster 43 sweeps across New England and the Mohawk Valley, through the corn, grain, and dairy belts, to the Pacific orchards. Solid blue-collar citizens, in towns like Utica, NY; Zanesville, OH; and Butte, MT are raising sturdy, Tom Sawyer-ish children in modest front-porch houses. Yes, July 4th parades are still a big event in cluster 43.

Middle (34)   Age Groups: 35-44, 45-54   Dominant White

44 Shotguns & Pickups   *Rural Blue-Collar Workers & Families*

In the 8th decile, cluster 44, the least affluent of the R1 clusters, is found in the Northeast, the Southeast, and in the Great Lakes and Piedmont industrial regions. They lead the group in blue-collar jobs; most are married with school-age kids. They are church-goers who also enjoy bowling, hunting, sewing, and attending car races.

Middle (43)   Age Groups: 35-44, 45-54   Dominant White

U3 - Urban Cores

The three clusters of social group U3 are highly concentrated, with over 60% of total households in the top 25 TV markets and over 99% in the top 50. With one cluster in the ninth, and two in the tenth affluence deciles, and with the nation's lowest incomes and highest poverty ratios, U3 is the least affluent group. These clusters share multi-racial, multi-lingual communities of dense, rented row- and high-rise apartments, show high indices for singles, solo parents with pre-school children, and perennial unemployment.

45 Single City Blues   *Ethnically-Mixed Urban Singles*

Cluster 45 is found in most Eastern megacities, in the new West, and is third in the most singles in America. Often found near urban universities, cluster 45 hosts a fair number of students. With very few children, it's a mixture of races, transients, and night trades, and is best described as a "poor man's Bohemia."

Lower Middle (51)   Age Groups: < 24, 25-34, & 65+   Mixed, High Asian

46 Hispanic Mix   *Urban Hispanic Singles & Families*

Cluster 46 is composed of the nation's bi-lingual, Hispanic barrios, which are chiefly concentrated in the Atlantic metro corridor, Chicago, Miami, Texas, Los Angeles, and the Southwest. These neighborhoods are populated by large families with many small children. They rank second in percent foreign-born, and are first in transient immigration.

Poor (60)   Age Groups: Under 24, 25-34   Dominant Hispanic

47 Inner Cities   *Inner City, Solo-Parent Families*

Concentrated in large Eastern cities and among America's poorest neighborhoods, cluster 47 has twice the nation's unemployment; many residents are receiving public assistance. Eight out of ten households are African American and seven in ten households with children are single-parent families.

Poor (61)   Age Groups: Under 24, 25-34, 35-44   Dominant Black

11

C3 - 2nd City Blues

The four clusters of social group C3 cover the downtown neighborhoods of hundreds of second cities and edge cities on the fringes of major metros. With one cluster in the eighth, one in the ninth, and two in the tenth affluence deciles, and with lower costs of living, these clusters are better off than their big-city cousins in group U3. Coupled with pockets of unemployment, broken homes, and solo parents, we also see a wide range of occupations, including clerical, retail, labor, transportation, agrarian, public and private services.

48 Smalltown Downtown   *Older Renters & Young Families*

Highly skewed west of the Mississippi, cluster 48 has gained a flood of Eastern immigrants who are mostly young and single. Often found near city colleges, cluster 48 is populated with students and those looking for fresh starts and first jobs. They are employed as lower-echelon white-collar salespeople, clerks, and technicians.

Lower Middle (49)   Age Groups: < 24, 25-34, 65+   Dominant White, Some Hispanic

49 Hometown Retired   *Low-Income, Older Singles & Couples*

Cluster 49 is three rungs down from "Smalltown Downtown" at opposite ends of the age range and geography. Except for some hot spots in the West, cluster 49 lies mostly in the Appalachians and central Florida. It ranks third in singles, second in ages over 65, and first in retirement. These folks take bus tours, collect stamps, and play cards and chess.

Lower Middle (52)   Age Groups: 55-64, 65+   Dominant White

50 Family Scramble   *Low-Income Hispanic Families*

Although cluster 50 is found in many markets, it is centered across the Southwest and Pacific. It ranks third in Hispanic population, with an overlay of Native Americans. Ranked last in higher educations, cluster 50 shows all the scars of poverty, but many are staying ahead with employment in transport, labor, and service jobs.

Lower Middle (59)   Age Groups: Under 24, 25-34   Dominant Hispanic

51 Southside City   *African-American Service Workers*

Cluster 51 is almost entirely concentrated in the Southeast in the smaller cities of the Mississippi delta and the Gulf and Atlantic states. Over 70% of its households are black. Ranking 61st in median household incomes, cluster 51 is very poor, but low living costs and a mix of labor and service jobs keep it afloat.

Poor (62)   Age Groups: Under 24, 65+   Dominant Black

T3 - Working Towns

The four clusters of social group T3 comprise thousands of remote exurbs and satellite towns, lying well outside our major metros and second cities, and in all but four TV markets. With one cluster in the sixth, one in the eighth, and two in the ninth affluence deciles, T3 is considerably better off than groups U3 and C3. As a group, these clusters share lower educations and incomes, with predominant blue-collar occupations, an equal mix of owned and rented single-unit houses, religion, home crafts, and a lot of awesome scenery. Otherwise, they are distinctly different.

52 Golden Ponds   *Retirement Town Seniors*

Found coast to coast, cluster 52 is a myriad of rustic towns and villages in scenic coastal, mountain, lake and valley areas, where seniors living in cottages retire among their country neighbors. Not as old, urban, or affluent as other retirees, a few play golf, but most prefer to adopt local customs.

Lower Middle (38)   Age Groups: 55-64, 65+   Dominant White

53 Rural Industria   *Low-Income, Blue-Collar Families*

Cluster 53 is the most industrial of the T3 clusters. Once dependent on railroads and major markets, "18-wheelers" freed light industry to go farther afield to seek low-cost, non-union labor. It's found in cluster 53 which is comprised of hundreds of blue-collar mill towns on America's rural backroads.

Lower Middle (50)   Age Groups: < 24, 25-34   Dominant White, High Hispanic

54 Norma Rae-ville   *Young Families, Bi-Racial Mill Towns*

Cluster 54 is geographically centered in the South, in the Mississippi delta, and in the Gulf coast and Atlantic states, which have become the center for our non-durable industries, such as clothing and home furnishings. With minimal educations, a black/white population mix, and unskilled labor, cluster 54 falls in the ninth affluence decile.

Poor (54)   Age Groups: Under 24, 65+   Dominant Black

55 Mines & Mills   *Older Families, Mine & Mill Towns*

Although equal to "Norma Rae-ville" in income, cluster 55 is very different. Down the Appalachians, across the Ozarks to Arizona, and up the Missouri to the coal fields of Montana, cluster 55 is exactly as its name implies. This older, mostly single population with few children lives in the midst of scenic splendor.

Poor (56)   Age Groups: 55-64, 65+   Dominant White

R2 - Heartlanders

The two clusters of social group R2 describe the nation's agrarian heartland, broadly geo-centered in the Great Plains, South Central, Mountains, and Pacific, with a few pockets in the East. With one cluster each in the eighth and tenth affluence deciles, the group is hardly the jet set. Since they are comparatively self-sufficient with a low cost of living, they are not deprived. As a group, they share large, multi-generation families, long residential tenure in low-density houses and mobile homes, a mix of Hispanics and Native Americans, and a fierce independence.

56 Agri-Business   *Rural Farm-Town & Ranch Families*

In census parlance, this title covers farming, forestry, fishing, ranching, mining, and other rural occupations. Consequently, cluster 56 is more affluent and more skewed to the greater northwest from Lake Michigan to the Pacific. It is famous for very large families with lots of kids, countless animals, apple pie, and going fishing.

Middle (45)   Age Groups: 45-54, 55-64, 65+   Dominant White

57 Grain Belt   *Farm Owners & Tenants*

Feeding America and sometimes the world, cluster 57 is our breadbasket. Centered in the Great Plains and South Central regions, this cluster shows a high index of Latino migrant workers. Life here is tied to the land, and ruled by the weather. Mostly self-sufficient, family- and home-centered, these families are poor only in money.

Lower Middle (57)   Age Groups: 65+, 55-64   Dominant White, Some Hispanic

---

R3 - Rustic Living

The five clusters of social group R3 describe thousands of remote country towns, villages, hamlets, and reservations scattered across the U.S. With two clusters in the eighth, two in the ninth, and one in the tenth affluence deciles, they are neither affluent nor destitute. In fact, since the five R3 clusters have lower-middle incomes and their cost of living is minimal, they are a promising market. As a group, they tend to be older, married mobile home-dwellers who work in labor-related occupations.

58 Blue Highways
Moderate Blue-Collar/Farm Families

On most maps, the interstates are red and the old highways are blue. Cluster 58 follows these remote roads through our mountains and deserts, and along the coasts and lake shores. These are R3's youngest neighborhoods, with its largest families, and the most children. They hunt and fish, love country music, camping, and attending "tractor pulls."

Lower Middle (47)   Age Groups: 35-44, 45-54   Dominant White

59 Rustic Elders
Low-Income, Older, Rural Couples

Cluster 59 is the third most elderly cluster in America, with the lowest incidence of children in group R3. It covers the nation, but is concentrated in the Great Plains and along the West coast. Although the lifestyle is pure country, the high indices for country clubs, power boats, sailboats, volleyball, and health walks are surprising.

Lower Middle (48)   Age Groups: 65+, 55-64   Dominant White

60 Back Country Folks
Remote Rural/Town Families

Cluster 60 is centered in the Eastern uplands along a wide path from the Pennsylvania Poconos to the Arkansas Ozarks. Anyone who visits their playgrounds in Branson, MO or Gatlinburg, TN can attest that these are the most blue-collar neighborhoods in America. Centered in the "Bible Belt," many "Back Country Folks" are hooked on Christian and country music.

Lower Middle (53)   Age Groups: 55-64, 65+   Dominant White

61 Scrub Pine Flats
Older African-American Farm Families

Cluster 61, the most geo-centric of all the clusters, is found mainly in the coastal flatlands of the Atlantic and Gulf states from the James to the Mississippi rivers. These humid, sleepy rural communities, with a mix of blacks and whites, live in a seemingly timeless, agrarian rhythm.

Poor (55)   Age Groups: 65+, 55-64   Dominant Black

62 Hard Scrabble
Older Families in Poor Isolated Areas

"Hard scrabble" means to scratch a living from hard soil. Cluster 62 describes our poorest rural areas that reach from Appalachia to the Colorado Rockies, and from the Texas border to the Dakota badlands. The highest indices for Native Americans, mining occupations, and chewing tobacco are in "Hard Scrabble."

Poor (58)   Age Groups: 55-64, 65+   Dominant White

PRIZM is recognized as the industry standard for lifestyle segmentation. From *Money & Brains* to *Mines & Mills*, PRIZM classifies all U.S. households into one of 62 unique neighborhood types, or "clusters." Marketers use PRIZM clusters to segment their customers into groups in order to identify, locate and target their best prospects.

PRIZM has been used by Fortune 500 companies since the mid-1970s, when it was launched by Claritas as the nation's first neighborhood clustering system. Find out what the Fortune 500s already know, and get better results from your marketing efforts— use PRIZM.

Claritas, in Arlington, Virginia, has been the leader in precision marketing for over 20 years. The firm provides America's leading marketers with information, expertise and data delivery systems to assist them in making more effective marketing decisions.

VNU Marketing Information Services provides micromarketing information and solutions to agencies, advertisers and media through the combined resources of: Claritas, CMR, IMS, MRP, PERQ Research, Scarborough, Spectra and Trade Dimensions.

INFO-ADD

for today's competitive business environment

THE DATABASE

AMERICA FAMILY

OF BUSINESS

AND CONSUMER

ENHANCEMENT

SERVICES

100 PARAGON DRIVE
MONTVALE, NJ 07645-0416
1 800 223 7777
FAX 201 476 2405

INFO-ADD

*The Database America Family of Business
and Consumer Enhancement Services*

Database America offers a comprehensive family of sophisticated List Enhancement Services for both Consumer and Business mailers. The variety of options and services allow you to customize a program to suit your specific needs and budget.

The Data

The DBA databases are compiled by drawing on a number of different sources. These multiple sources contribute a total of 61 different categories of information about consumers and 13 types of data about businesses. These data items can be used to target specific file segments for list rentals, or to enhance the value of your own files.

Enhancement Match Rates

Nearly 3 decades of experience in name/address matching go into the INFO-ADD matching process. Accurate parsing of name and address components insure the highest degree of accuracy.

Households and Individuals

The majority of the consumer data on INFO-ADD describes entire households, rather than specific individuals. However, many of the household records include data on up to four individuals within the household. This data is available for enhancement on an individual-name basis. The first individual listed on our file is considered to be the head of the household. Remaining individuals (2 - 4) are listed in order by age, eldest to youngest.

Turnaround

We provide 24-hour service on INFO-ADD enhancements of consumer files, and 48 hour service on enhancements of business data. We provide next day service on TELE-MAX PLUS telephone number appending, and three-day service on reverse phone appending.

Service times assume that we receive files on magnetic tape (or cartridge) in one of the formats listed in Database America's general guidelines for tapes, and that the file does not need to be converted or sorted prior to processing. Files with more than 5 million records may require additional processing time.

Pricing

Prices shown are for the data only, and are applied against the number of hits to your file. In addition, a processing charge of $1/M is applied against the input quantity for the job (minimum processing charge of $500). Total price is the processing charge plus the charge for data.

Special Pricing For Data Packages

Special pricing is available when two or more data elements are specified and processed at one time as a single "data package" to enhance one input file. Please call for a quote.

Ordering Information

Consumer data is grouped by category, and data items are identified by an alpha-numeric code. Please refer to this code when ordering.

THE DATABASES

THE DATABASE AMERICA CONSUMER FILE

- **Data Sources:** Created by blending over 300 million records from over 20 different sources. Offers reliable marketing information on nearly every household and individual in America.

- **Data Accuracy:** File is updated four times a year with new information. National Change of Address (NCOA) processing is part of every update.

- **Data Quality:** A data-rich source of consumer information. Recognized by *American Demographics* magazine as a top source of business information. Criteria for this distinction includes demographic content, geographic scope of information, general availability of information, experience of the company and level of customer service.

- **File Size:** Contains names, addresses and information on over 95 million households and over 165 million individuals.

THE DATABASE AMERICA BUSINESS FILE

- **Data Sources:** Compiled from over 15 different sources, including Standard & Poor's data.

- **Coverage:** File is the largest and most accurate of its kind. If you need complete coverage or if you need to go beyond the information in the phone book, this file is the clear choice.

- **Data Accuracy:** Updated quarterly. Includes NCOA processing. Approved by BPA International as having met the criteria for accuracy for a general business database.

- **File Size:** Over 11 million American businesses and 9 million business executives and professionals.

LISTS FOR PROSPECTING

Compiled databases are playing a major role in prospecting mail plans of today's savvy mailers. The reason? Compiled names, enriched by demographic and geographic data, allow mailers to improve the bottom line in six ways:

1. Lower List Costs. Names from our databases cost 20%-50% less than names from traditional response lists. And the power added by data can result in response that is comparable to responder lists.

2. Lower Break-Even. As in-the-mail costs go down, the revenue required to reach break-even drops; it takes less to become profitable.

3. Abundant Data. The multitude of data elements give you more opportunities to identify and select the most desirable file segments.

4. Data Analysis. We offer a range of state-of-the-art analysis techniques that will identify segments of our database that will be most responsive to your offer. At the same time, you get to know more about who your customers and prospects actually are.

5. Fresh Prospects. Wide market coverage from our compiled names will allow you to uncover prospective buyers that you haven't been able to reach before.

6. "Rest" Tired Response Lists. By tapping into a major new list source, you avoid over-working standard response lists, and you don't have to search for new ways to revive lists you've exhausted.

DATABASE AMERICA TELEPHONE NUMBER APPENDING

TELE-MAX PLUS

TELE-MAX PLUS is the largest database of telephone numbers available today. It combines multiple sources of names and phone numbers – including the Database America Consumer File – into one powerful appending source. Proven matching logic maximizes the number of accurate telephone numbers that are appended to your records. If you already have the telephone numbers, but lack the names and addresses, we can provide those to you through our "reverse" appending process.

PRICING:

To Append Phone Numbers

Minimum Order:	$500.00
Input under 1,000,000	$20.00/M
1,000,000 - 1,999,999	$18.00/M
2,000,000 - 3,999,999	$16.00/M
4,000,000 - 4,999,999	$14.00/M
5,000,000 and over	$12.00/M
To Confirm Phone Numbers	$ 5.00/M
"Reverse" Phone Matching	$25.00/M matches
Minimum charge of $1,000	

DATABASE AMERICA BUSINESS FILE – DATA FOR ENHANCEMENTS

B1 Individual (Executive) Name, Gender & Title $20/M

B2 Professional SIC $20/M

B3 SIC – 8-Digit Code $20/M

B4 Description of SIC Code $5/M
(Available only with B03 SIC Code)

B5 Number of Employees $20/M

1 - 4	100 - 249
5 - 9	250 - 499
10 - 19	500 - 999
20 - 49	1,000 Plus
50 - 99	

B6 Sales Volume $20/M

Under $1 Million
$1MM - 4.9MM
$5MM - 9.9MM
$10MM - 24.9MM
$25MM - 74.9MM
$75MM - 199.9MM
$200MM - 499.9MM
$500MM - 999.9MM
$1 Billion Plus

B7 Location Type (Headquarters/Branch) $20/M

B8 Year Started $10/M

B9 Telephonically Confirmed $10/M

B10 Import/Export $20/M

B11 Stock Exchange Code $20/M
New York Stock Exchange, American Stock Exchange, or Over The Counter Exchange

B12 Fortune 1000 .... $20/M
Listed by first 500 companies, then next 500

B13 Advertising Code $20/M
Type of Yellow Pages Listing:
Regular, Bold Face, In-Column, or Display Ad

B14 Business In Motion $20/M
New Listing in Most Recent Quarter
New Listing in 2nd Most Recent Quarter
New Listing in 3rd Most Recent Quarter
New Listing in 4th Most Recent Quarter

B15 County Code $5/M

B16 MSA Code $5/M

B17 Population Code $5/M
Population of the Town/City in which business is located, 1990 Census figures.

1 - 4,999	100,000 - 249,999
5,000 - 9,999	250,000 - 499,999
10,000 - 24,999	500,000 - 999,999
25,000 - 49,999	1 Million Plus
50,000 - 99,999	

B18 Telephone Number Append $20/M

B19 Telephone Number Verify $10/M

B20 Reverse Telephone Match $25/M

B30 SIC Penetration Analysis $5/M
with a Minimum Charge of $500

THE DATABASE AMERICA CONSUMER FILE – Info-Add Data Element Prices

DESCRIPTION	PRICE
DATA AVAILABLE at the INDIVIDUAL LEVEL	

Three options are available:

1. Data on the head of the household only
   (person listed as Individual #1 on our file);
2. Data on the individual name that appears in the input record
   (requires a match on first name, so the hit rate may be low);
3. Data on any or all individuals (up to 4) within the household.

The following data items are available for each Individual:

Personal Data

Includes Title, First Name, Middle Initial, Seniority Suffix, Gender, and a code to indicate when marital status is "single"
Title codes are:

1 = Mr.	6 = Rev.
2 = Initial (no title)	7 = (no title)
3 = Miss	8 = Military (no title)
4 = Mrs.	9 = Ms.
5 = Dr.	

Date of Birth

Expressed as Year and Month (YYMM)

Age

In 1-year intervals from ages 18 through 79
(from ages 80-94+, two year ranges available)

10-Year Age Range

For Household Head, age is specific (actual data) or inferred (modeled or inferred from other data). For others, age is specific. Age ranges are:

18 - 24 years
25 - 34 years
35 - 44 years
45 - 54 years
55 - 64 years
65 - 74 years
75 + years

Presence of Credit Cards

Indicates the types of credit cards that the individual holds.
Bank Card, Premium Bank Card, Retail Card, Upscale Retail Card, and/or Finance Card

Occupation

Business Owner, Professional, Upper Management/Executive, Middle Management, White Collar, Blue Collar, Health Services, Secretarial/Clerical, Homemaker, Retired, Military, Teacher, Nurse, Data Processing, Civil Service, Part Time, Student, Volunteer, Disabled

Deceased

Available for Input Name only. Y = individual on the input record is deceased.

DATA ITEMS at the INDIVIDUAL LEVEL

Head of the Household (person listed as Individual #1)

	PRICE
P1 Household Head – Personal Data	$3/M
P2 Household Head – Date of Birth	$15/M
P3 Household Head – Age	$10/M
P4 Household Head – 10 Year Age Range	$8/M
P5 Household Head – Credit Cards	$20/M
P6 Household Head – Occupation	$8/M

Individual Listed on the Input Record

	PRICE
P7 Input Name – Personal Data	$3/M
P8 Input Name – Date of Birth	$15/M
P9 Input Name – Age	$10/M
P10 Input Name – 10-Year Age Range	$8/M
P11 Input Name – Credit Card	$20/M
P12 Input Name – Occupation	$8/M
P37 Input Name – Deceased	$75/M

Any or All Individuals (up to 4) Within Household

	PRICE
P13 Individual #1 – Personal Data	$3/M
P14 Individual #1 – Date of Birth	$15/M
P15 Individual #1 – Age	$10/M
P16 Individual #1 – 10-Year Age Range	$8/M
P17 Individual #1 – Credit Card	$20/M
P18 Individual #1 – Occupation	$8/M
P19 Individual #2 – Personal Data	$3/M
P20 Individual #2 – Date of Birth	$15/M
P21 Individual #2 – Age	$10/M
P22 Individual #2 – 10-Year Age Range	$8/M
P23 Individual #2 – Credit Card	$20/M
P24 Individual #2 – Occupation	$8/M
P25 Individual #3 – Personal Data	$3/M
P26 Individual #3 – Date of Birth	$15/M
P27 Individual #3 – Age	$10/M
P28 Individual #3 – 10-Year Age Range	$8/M
P29 Individual #3 – Credit Card	$20/M
P30 Individual #3 – Occupation	$8/M
P31 Individual #4 – Personal Data	$3/M
P32 Individual #4 – Date of Birth	$15/M
P33 Individual #4 – Age	$10/M
P34 Individual #4 – 10-Year Age Range	$8/M
P35 Individual #4 – Credit Card	$20/M
P36 Individual #4 – Occupation	$8/M

THE DATABASE AMERICA CONSUMER FILE – Info-Add Data Element Prices

DESCRIPTION	PRICE

HOUSEHOLD DEMOGRAPHICS

H1 Number Persons in Household $3/M

   1 = one or two persons, 2 = three or more

H2 Number of Adults $3/M

   From 0 to 5, where 5 = 5 or more

H3 Age – 10-Year Range $8/M

H4 Age of Head of Household $10/M

24 or less	55 - 59
25 - 29	60 - 64
30 - 34	65 or more
35 - 39	65 - 69
40 - 44	70 - 75
45 - 49	75 or more
50 - 54	

H5 Presence of Children (y = yes) $3/M

H6 Number of Children $5/M

   From 0 to 5, where 5 = 5 or more

H7 Presence Child by Year of Birth (y = yes) $8/M

   Birth years for females, for males, and for unknown gender
   under 18 years of age

H8 Age Range of Children. $6/M

   0 - 5
   0 - 11
   0 - 17
   6 - 11
   12 - 17 female
   12 - 17 male
   12 - 17 unknown

H9 Length of Residence $3/M

   1 = 1st year on list
   2 = 2nd year on list, etc.

H10 New Mover (y = yes). $5/M

H11 Owner/Renter $3/M

   1 = renter
   2 = home owner
   0 = unknown

H12 Marital Status. $4/M

   1 = single
   2 = married
   0 = unknown

H13 Estimated Household Income $8/M

under $5,000	$50,001 - $55,000	$100,001 - $105,000
$5,001 - $10,000	$55,001 - $60,000	$105,001 - $110,000
$10,001 - $15,000	$60,001 - $65,000	$110,001 - $115,000
$15,001 - $20,000	$65,001 - $70,000	$115,001 - $120,000
$20,001 - $25,000	$70,001 - $75,000	$120,001 - $125,000
$25,001 - $30,000	$75,001 - $80,000	$125,001 - $130,000
$30,001 - $35,000	$80,001 - $85,000	$130,001 - $135,000
$35,001 - $40,000	$85,001 - $90,000	$135,001 - $140,000
$40,001 - $45,000	$90,001 - $95,000	$140,001 - $145,000
$45,001 - $50,000	$95,001 - $100,000	$145,001 and up

DESCRIPTION	PRICE

H14 Credit Card (any type) in HH (y = yes) $20/M

H15 Bank Credit Card in Household (y = yes). $20/M

H16 New Credit Issue (y = yes) $20/M

H17 Ethnic. $20/M

Arabic	Hungarian	Polish
Armenian	Icelandic	Portuguese
Bangladesh	Indian	Russian
British	Indonesian	Scandinavian
Bulgarian	Irish	Scottish
Burmese	Italian	Serbo Croatian
Cambodian	Japanese	Singapore
Chinese	Jewish	Spanish
Czech	Korean	Lankan
Danish	Laotian	Swedish
Dutch	Latvian	Swiss
Estonian	Lithuanian	Telegu
Ethiopian	Malaysian	Thai
Finnish	Manx	Turkish
French	Mid East	Ukrainian
German	Norwegian	Vietnamese
Greek	Pakistani	Welsh
Hebrew	Persian	Yugoslavian
Hindu	Philippine	

H18 Hispanic Surname (y = yes) $20/M

H19 Student Resident (y = yes) $8/M

H20 Deceased Household Member $75/M

   Y = A household member is included on deceased list

PLACE of RESIDENCE

R1 Apartment Number $2/M

R2 SFDU/MFDU $5/M

   S = SFDU
   M = MFDU

R3 Dwelling Size $3/M

   Number of families/surnames at this address:

    1 = 1
    2 = 2
    3 = 3
    4 = 4
    5 = 5
    6 = 6
    7 = 7
    8 = 8
    9 = 9
    10 = from 10 to 19
    20 = from 20 to 29
    30 = from 30 to 39
    40 = from 40 to 49
    50 = from 50 to 99
    99 = 100 or more

R4 Year Listed $3/M

   From 62 (1962) to 99 (1999)

THE DATABASE AMERICA CONSUMER FILE – Info-Add Data Element Prices

DESCRIPTION	PRICE
R5 Estimated Home Value	**$20/M**

up to $24,999	$275,000 - $299,999
$25,000 - $49,999	$300,000 - $349,999
$50,000 - $74,999	$350,000 - $399,999
$75,000 - $99,999	$400,000 - $449,999
$100,000 - $124,999	$450,000 - $499,999
$125,000 - $149,999	$500,000 - $599,999
$150,000 - $174,999	$600,000 - $699,999
$175,000 - $199,999	$700,000 - $799,999
$200,000 - $224,999	$800,000 - $899,999
$225,000 - $249,999	$900,000 - $999,999
$250,000 - $274,999	$1,000,000 and over

MAJOR EXPENDITURES

E1 Mortgage Present (y = yes) **$10/M**

E2 Mortgage 1 Type, Date, & Amount **$25/M**
(pertaining to most recent mortgage)

MORTGAGE TYPE

Converted Real Estate Mortgage	Real Estate Mortgage
FHA Loan	Real Estate Loan, equity
FHA Home Improvement	Secured Loan
FHA Real Estate Mortgage	Secured Home Improvement
Home Equity Loan	Second Mortgage
Home Improvement Loan	VA Loan
Real Estate	VA Real Estate Mortgage
Real Estate, junior liens	(blank) = no known loan

MORTGAGE DATE: Indicates the year and the month for 2 dates (YYMMYYMM). The first YYMM indicate the year and month that the mortgage was opened. If the mortgage has been paid off, the next second YYMM will indicate the year and month the mortgage was closed out. When this information is lacking for a mortgage, a code of 0000 is returned.

MORTGAGE AMOUNT:
   under $25,000
   $25,000 - $49,999
   $50,000 - $74,999
   $75,000 - $99,999
   $100,000 - $149,999
   $150,000 - $199,999
   $200,000 - $249,999
   $250,000 - $499,999
   $500,000 - $999,999
   $1,000,000+

E5 Mortgage 2 Type, Date & Amount **$25/M**
For Households carrying more than one mortgage, information pertaining to the older mortgage. Same coding as Mortgage 1

E8 Auto Loan/Lease Amount **$8/M**
   $1 - $5,000
   $10,001 - $15,000
   $15,001 - $20,000
   $20,001 - $30,000
   $30,001 - $40,000
   $40,001 - $50,000
   $50,001 - $100,000
   $100,001+

DESCRIPTION	PRICE
E9 Student Loan	**$8/M**

   $1 - $499
   $500 - $999
   $1,000 - $2,999
   $3,000 - $4,999
   $5,000 - $6,999
   $7,000 - $9,999
   $10,000 - $14,999
   $15,000 - $19,999
   $20,000 and over

E10 Number of Trades **$20/M**
Indicates the number of credit transactions (mortgage, personal loan, car loan, student loan, etc). With few exceptions, these are credit lines that were open and active within the most recent six month period.

LEISURE AND LIFESTYLE

L1 Photography (interest in) (y = yes) **$20/M**

L2 Stamps/Coins (interest in) (y = yes) **$20/M**

L3 Sports Cards/Collectibles (y = yes) **$20/M**

L4 Pet Owner (dog or cat) (y = yes) **$20/M**

L5 Computer/PC Owner (y = yes) **$20/M**

L6 Sweepstakes/Gambling (interest in) (y = yes) **$20/M**

L7 Mail Order Buyer/Responder (y = yes) **$20/M**

L8 Mail Order Buyer (y = yes) **$20/M**

L9 Mail Order Buyer by Category (y = yes) **$30/M**
Finance/Investments, Electronics, Computer Software, Health/Fitness, Outdoor/Recreational, Entertainment/Travel, Food/Wine, Books/Music, Magazines, Apparel/Jewelry, Crafts/Sewing, Horticulture/Housekeeping, Children's Items, Collectibles, Miscellaneous Merchandise, Sweepstakes/Contests, Value Hunter, High Ticket, Catalog Buyer, Continuity/Membership Clubs

L10 Cause-Related Donor **$20/M**

L11 Donor by Category **$30/M**
Environmental Contributors
Health Contributors
Religious Contributors
Political Contributors
Misc Contributors

THE DATABASE AMERICA CONSUMER FILE – Info-Add Data Element Prices

DESCRIPTION	PRICE

VEHICLE DATA

V1 Number of Vehicles in Household **$8/M**

> from 1 to 6, where 6 = 6 or more

V2 Price Class **$10/M**

> CM = Compact
> LO = Low
> ME = Medium
> HI = High
> LX = Luxury
> FR = Foreign
> FL = Foreign Luxury
> UK = Unknown

V3 Body Style of Newest Vehilcle......................... **$10/M**

> Hatchback, Convertible, Two door, Four door, Hard top, Four door hard top, Sedan, Four door sedan, Station wagon, Jeep, Pickup, Van, Motor home, Mini van, Mini station wagon, Unknown

V4 Highest Vehicle Value **$12/M**

> In increments of $500, to a max of $99,500

V5 Combined Vehicle Value **$12/M**

> In increments of $500, to a max of $99,500

V6 Purchased in Model Year (Y = YES).................... **$10/M**

V7 Truck (y = yes) **$10/M**

NEIGHBORHOOD CHARACTERISTICS

G1 Geo Data **$2/M**

Nielsen County Rank

> A = in one of 21 largest metro areas
> B = in metro area over 85,000 pop., not included in A above
> C = in metro area over 20,000 pop., but less than 85,000
> D = in metro area under 20,000

ADI (Area of Dominant Influence)

Census

> Census State Code
> Census County Code
> Census Tract
> Census Block Group

G2 Socio-Economic Status............................. **$10/M**

> Values from 01 to 99 (The higher the number, the higher the neighborhood quality)

G4 Census Demographics.............................. **$4/M**

Demographic Level

> B = data at the Block group level
> C = data at the County level
> T = data at the Tract level
> Z = data at the ZIP code level
> N = No information found

DESCRIPTION	PRICE

G4 Census Demographics (continued)

Census '90 Data

AGE AND FAMILY COMPOSITION
> % HH with children
> % HH no person age 65+
> Ratio children 0-5 yrs per 100 HH
> Median age of adult population
> % HH with 3 or more persons
> % HH with married couple
> % single householders w/child

INCOME
> % HH with income under $25,000
> % HH with income $50,000+
> % HH with income $150,000+
> Median HH income
> % persons below poverty level
> % occupied units with 2 autos

EDUCATION
> % age 25+ who are college grads
> Mean yrs school, person's age 25+

HOUSING
> % with single units in structure
> Median value owner-occupied housing
> % Owner-occupied units valued $300K+
> % Owner-occupied units valued under $75K
> Median gross rent as % of HH income
> Median owner cost as % of HH income
> % Urban persons
> % Owner occupied units

OCCUPATION
> % Professional/Managerial
> % White Collar
> % Blue Collar
> % Persons age 16+ unemployed

RACE/ETHNIC
> % Black HH
> % Asian HH
> % Hispanic HH

A1 Posicode.. **$1/M**

> Indicates a match made to household record on Info-Add database

BUSINESS AND CONSUMER ENHANCEMENT SERVICES • COMPUTER SERVICES • LEAD GENERATION • STATISTICAL MODELING

LISTS FOR DIRECT MAIL, TELEMARKETING AND MARKET RESEARCH • BUSINESS AND CONSUMER INFORMATION DATABASES

DOMESTIC AND INTERNATIONAL DATA AND POSTAL PROCESSING • ELECTRONIC MEDIA AND INTERNET SERVICES

DATABASE CREATION AND MAINTENANCE

100 PARAGON DRIVE • MONTVALE, NJ 07645-0416 • 1 800 223 7777 • FAX 201 476 2405
E-MAIL reception@databaseamerica.com • WEB SITE http://www.databaseamerica.com

Products And Services

THE MARKETING Information Company

EQUIFAX NATIONAL DECISION SYSTEMS

Table Of Contents

Your decisions are only as good as the tools you use to make them.

What Can You Expect From Our Marketing Tools?

The most current consumer and business data available. Software options that address your national, regional and local market analysis needs. A segmentation system to profile today's consumers. Business segmentation, targeting and forecasting systems that portray the current and future business market. Geocoding that turns standard addresses into meaningful information. Database marketing strategies that lead you to more customers. And experienced applications experts who know how to handle your custom projects.

If these are the qualities you expect, then the company to rely on is **Equifax National Decision Systems.**

Software Delivery Systems

Powerful Market Analysis Systems For Your Desktop

Equifax National Decision Systems offers a number of sophisticated, yet easy-to-use, information analysis tools. Whether you need to evaluate markets on a national, regional or local basis, these tools can help you make the best decisions possible.

INFOMARK

As the nation's most widely used desktop marketing system, Infomark® provides immediate access to more than 65 national databases, as well as sophisticated analysis, reporting and mapping capabilities. This extraordinary decision support tool enables you to evaluate the entire U.S. on a macro-to-micro level, and offers many powerful applications, including site evaluation, market analysis, customer profiling, target marketing, competitive analysis and business-to-business marketing.

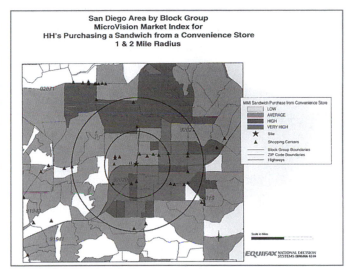

Comprehensive Marketing Databases — Infomark gives you unlimited access to demographic, consumer, product, business, customer segmentation, industry-specific and geographic data. To maximize the value of your system, you select only the databases you need. Databases are updated quarterly, semi-annually or annually to ensure you are using the most accurate, up-to-date information available.

Infomark's mapping module produces full color presentation quality maps for easy analysis of complex data. This map highlights where target customers live in relation to a potential site.

Marketing Applications Expertise — Every Infomark customer benefits from Equifax National Decision Systems' experienced, industry-specific support teams. These applications experts help you fully leverage Infomark's powerful features in the quickest and most efficient ways possible. Infomark is the answer when you need to address a full range of applications, including:

• Selecting the best site for a new branch or retail location

• Determining the best merchandise mix for a market

Software Delivery Systems
-------- --------------------------------

• Exploring market potential for future expansion

• Identifying and targeting your best customers

• Allocating resources based on household distributions

• Defining sales territories based on actual market potential

• Measuring market penetration and conducting gap analysis

• And much more

Advanced Technology — Proprietary data compression technology allows information from more than 20 sources to be compressed onto a single CD per region, for fast data retrieval. The user-friendly Quick Reports™ Wizard® enables anyone within an organization to quickly produce the most popular reports — and custom reports, as well. In addition, Infomark can be networked throughout your organization, allowing users to share information and work concurrently on time-critical projects.

Customization and Flexibility —   Each Infomark installation is customized to meet your specific needs. You select the databases, software modules and geographic coverages that best address your unique challenges. The advanced input and output technologies allow you to customize your analysis and maximize your productivity. Third-party and proprietary data can be imported easily into Infomark using Open Database Connectivity™ (ODBC) technology, supported through the Windows™ operating system. Exporting options allow you to transport Infomark data to GIS, database management and spreadsheet software, as well as ASCII formats, for further analyses.

With Infomark's Custom Report Editor you can create the exact reports you need using any of our 65+ databases or your own information.

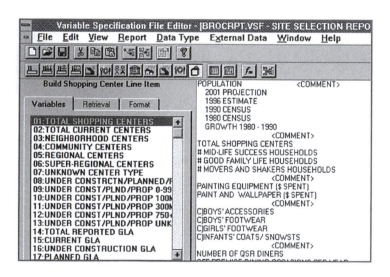

Unmatched Customer Support — Customer support and satisfaction have always been a vital part of the total Infomark package. When you become an Infomark user, you get immediate access to on-site training, unlimited toll-free telephone support, industry-specific support teams, user group seminars, workshops, thorough documentation, and an Annual Users Conference. This strong line of customer support ensures that you maximize the return on your Infomark investment.

One Complete System For Success — With Infomark you have the advantage of working with one completely integrated mapping and analysis system. Market analysis software, comprehensive data, applications technology and customer support — all included with one powerful system.

--- INFOMARK EXPRESS ---

When your analysis needs are targeted to a specific metropolitan area or region, Infomark Express is the system for you. This economical, easy-to-use software and data package allows you to generate an unlimited number of demographic, lifestyle and retail trade potential reports, for one low price. This valuable information gives you the ability to select the most profitable site within any metropolitan area in the nation.

Producing reports is easy with Infomark Express. You simply identify the area you wish to analyze, select the reports, and then process your request to print.

Simple Operation — With Infomark Express you simply select an area to analyze using circles, custom polygons or standard geographies (e.g., counties, ZIP Codes or Census tracts). Then choose and print your choice of demographic, lifestyle and retail trade potential reports. To help you visualize your analysis, Infomark Express provides an on-screen map of your market that can include roads, highways, shopping centers, ZIP Codes and Census tract boundaries.

Popular Reports — Infomark Express contains the most widely used reports for small area analysis.

- *Pop-Facts®: Full Data Report* — A seven-page report containing more than 250 demographic characteristics, including 1990 Census data, as well as current-year estimates and five-year projections for key variables.

- *Pop-Facts: Summary Report* — A concise, one-page summary of key demographic characteristics, including 1990 Census data, as well as current-year estimates and five-year projections.

- *Pop-Facts: Demographic Trend Report* — Tracks key demographic changes by comparing 1990 Census data, current-year estimates and five-year projections.

4

Software Delivery Systems

• *MicroVision® Area Profile Report* — A lifestyle report that identifies the number, percentage and concentration of households in all 50 MicroVision segments within an area. (See page 6 for a description of MicroVision.)

• *MicroVision: Custom Group Report* — A one-page report that provides data on the distribution of nine MicroVision groups within an area.

• *Component Geography Report* — Identifies every selected subgeography (e.g., Census tract) and percentage of each subgeography within a selected radius or trade area.

• *Retail Trade Potential™ Report* — Provides retail trade potential for 12 store-type categories and a total retail category.

Mapping Capability — To help you visually present your data, you can add the Infomark Express mapping option. With this option, full-color maps can be generated displaying key characteristics such as population, income or retail trade potential. Full-color thematic maps enable you to compare and contrast market data and geographic size relationships, without needing to read and interpret detailed statistical reports.

QUICKCODE

Translating an address to a spatial point has never been easier than with QuickCode™. This convenient, geocoding software package has the power to turn your customer, business and competitive address files into data that can be used for insightful mapping and target marketing applications. By appending geographic and MicroVision lifestyle segment codes to your customer files, QuickCode gives you the ability to map the locations of your customers and prospects in relation to your stores or branches, as well as determine the interests, buying behaviors and media habits of your customers.

Now, with QuickCode you can handle complex geocoding projects on your own PC. To improve your cost-efficiencies, you only pay for the amount of address information you generate.

Using single addresses or your entire customer file, the QuickCode Lookup Module can find and append the correct geographic and lifestyle data to your address records.

5

Once the software appends this key information to your database, the file can be output in a wide range of formats, including ASCII, ArcView™, MapInfo®, dBase™, Access™ and Excel®. Multiple file formats also are accepted as input files. These include ASCII, Access, Excel and dBase. This flexibility allows you to easily integrate QuickCode into your total information system.

MicroVision Analysis Software

Knowing the interests, purchasing behaviors, media preferences, and product and service needs of your target customers is vital to the success of any marketing campaign. MicroVision Analysis Software (MVAS) improves your success rate by helping you understand your clients and prospects.

MicroVision is a micro-geographic consumer targeting system that classifies every household in the United States into one of 50 unique market segments. It's built at the ZIP+4 level of geography by using both Census data and aggregated consumer economic information from Equifax.

With MVAS you can profile your own customer database, as well as generate unique reports and graphs that allow you to easily identify, quantify, locate and target your best customers and prospects. You can find the relationship between a customer's behavior and demographic characteristics, analyze average product usage tendencies to estimate demand, identify cross-sell opportunities, choose the best media for reaching key customers, plus much more.

A variety of market-level data can be accessed in the MVAS system, including syndicated national survey data from well-respected research companies and studies such as Mediamark Research, Inc. (MRI), Simmons Market Research Bureau, The NPD Group, Consumer Forum, and many others. To best meet your needs, the analysis software is available for a variety of custom and industry-specific systems, such as MicroVision-Banking™, MicroVision-Insurance™, MicroVision-Daytime™ and MicroVision-XR™.

Database Marketing

Database Marketing

Find, Keep & Upsell Customers With Database Marketing

Equifax National Decision Systems offers a variety of innovative database marketing capabilities, from detailed data overlays and segmentation systems to sophisticated models, predictive forecasting tools and responsive mailing lists. By combining these resources with the power of your own customer database, you'll be on your way to finding, keeping and upselling more customers.

CONSUMER MARKETING

ACE-Indicators™ — If you want to target consumers based on actual financial behavior, then ACE-Indicators is for you. This powerful, one-of-a-kind database contains actual consumer economic information summarized at the ZIP+4 level of geography. Since ACE-Indicators is a strong gauge of financial status and purchasing behaviors, you can use it to:

• Build models that improve direct mail response

• Predict the likelihood of a consumer purchase

• Maximize the profitability of a campaign

MicroVision — When you want to know what appeals to your customers and then target others just like them, MicroVision is your answer. Every household in the U.S. is assigned to one of 50 MicroVision lifestyle segments, so the appropriate MicroVision code can be appended to each record on your customer address file. Once your file is coded, you can identify which segments are your best customers and determine their interests and buying behaviors, as well as evaluate their media habits. In addition, you can target other consumers just like them, since the nation's most respected mailing lists are MicroVision coded.

Data Overlays And Lists — Are you searching for lists to increase your response rates while reducing your acquisition costs? If so, you'll value our large selection of consumer lists and data overlays. By joining forces with the industry's top suppliers like Metromail, Infobase and R.L. Polk, we are able to provide you information on more than 98 million U.S. households and 250 million consumers.

7

Net Worth And Investable Assets Model Data — These models use actual consumer survey and aggregated economic data to project the estimated net worth and investable assets of a household. This information has proven to effectively predict consumer behavior in hundreds of custom models. By coding your customer file with this data, you can identify the most appropriate products and services to market to a household.

Modeling And Analytical Services — Our custom modeling services rely on a variety of analytical tools that deliver high-performance direct marketing models. When building models, we can incorporate performance history or any other data from your in-house files. To enhance the performance of our models, we also can leverage our proprietary data elements, such as ACE-Indicators. Our unique approach to profitability and conversion modeling incorporates MicroVision geodemographic information to maximize your response rates and ACE-Indicators to explain your profit potential. Using traditional, nonlinear and semi-parametric statistical techniques, our models maximize the volume of high value names while nearly eliminating unprofitable names.

8

--- **BUSINESS MARKETING** ---

Business-Facts® — When you want to know more about the businesses in the U.S., Business-Facts is your solution. Based primarily on data from American Business Information, Inc. (ABI), this database provides detailed information on more than 10 million U.S. businesses. Business-Facts is updated quarterly, covers all industries as well as markets, and incorporates geographic precision point coding for accurate location identification. With Business-Facts, you can enhance your business customer database by appending variables such as SIC Codes, sales, employee counts, business type (HQ/single/branch), mail deliverability flag and more.

MarketFocus™ — This unique business segmentation process enables you to identify the companies most likely to purchase your products and services, then allocate your marketing and sales resources accordingly. Because it is tailored to your own customer base and marketing needs, MarketFocus is extremely accurate. The MarketFocus process includes up to four steps: Customer Matching and Data Appending; Market Segmentation Analysis; Current Market Potential Analysis; and Future Market Potential Analysis.

ProphetPoint™ Growth Demand Forecasts — We developed this unique capability to enable you to identify growth rates by industry, then evaluate when, where and how they'll change over the next five years. Plus, you can forecast the demand for products and services by industry and geography to optimize your distribution networks and sales territories. You can append this valuable information to your business file and use it to strategically position your company for the future.

Modeling And Analytical Services — Our custom business-to-business modeling services have proven to be effective in a variety of industries. Sophisticated penetration analysis tools are used to identify high-profit-potential segments by SIC Code, employee size or other key organizational characteristics. Although penetration analysis often is the most cost-effective solution, larger and more extensive business-to-business mailers benefit from our custom scoring models for targeting purposes. Using a variety of statistical and mathematical techniques, along with extensive industry experience, we model business potential with sales, transaction, customer and profitability data. When you want to maximize the performance of your business-to-business marketing, you can rely on our custom modeling and analytical services.

Custom Projects

No Staff. No Time. No Problem!

When a business problem is complex or when resources are limited, we provide consultation and custom projects to meet your specific decision-making needs.

Through these services, you can tap into our extensive data and technological resources and benefit from the knowledge and experience of our industry specialists, statisticians, programmers, analysts and data experts. Our high performance modeling and analytical services cover consumer, locational, merchandising and business-to-business marketing research, as well as other custom projects. Our methods employ the most reliable techniques, including:

- Clustering Algorithms
- Logistic Regression
- Pattern Recognition/Artificial Intelligence
- Gravity Models
- Spatial Choice Models
- Analog Models
- Linear Programming
- Custom GIS Programming

CONSUMER RESEARCH

Through our extensive consumer research capabilities, we can accurately identify, quantify, locate and target your best customers and prospects. These valuable services will help you maximize your marketing dollars.

10

MicroVision Profiling — These projects provide an easy way to determine customer characteristics and consumption propensity by product or service. A MicroVision profile can be cross-correlated with thousands of behavioral, media, lifestyle and product profiles to create a portrait of a current customer or prospect. Marketing plans are optimized since behavior can be predicted and prospects can be located and targeted.

To meet your specialized needs, your MicroVision profiling project can be completed using any of our powerful systems, including:

• *MicroVision-Banking* — Targets consumers based on financial product and service usage.

• *MicroVision-Insurance* — Uses consumer demand and insurance product usage data to pinpoint consumers.

• *MicroVision-Daytime* — Targets consumers based on where they work and identifies the daytime demand for products and services.

• *MicroVision-XR* — Eliminates all race and ethnicity as a determinant factor in the targeting program.

• *MicroVision-Custom* — Incorporates your own data for the most precise level of targeting possible.

LOCATIONAL RESEARCH

Whether your goal is to maximize performance in an entire market or to locate a single new site, there is a proven location-based model for you.

Market Potential — Quickly and easily ranks markets by sales potential.

Market Screening — Uses multiple success criteria for specific product or concept forecasting. Identifies hot markets and prioritizes them for new market development.

Network Optimization — Provides a systematic approach to market expansion or consolidation by defining the optimal number and location of stores within a market.

Site Screening — Identifies key drivers of performance, generates a site quality score, and ranks potential sites within a market.

Site Evaluation — Provides a quality score and forecasts sales performance for a 12-month period.

Trade Area Analysis — Identifies the actual distance draw patterns of customers around a site or potential site. Determines actual trade area and drive distance for a given site.

MERCHANDISING RESEARCH

Designed to maximize sales opportunities by developing optimal merchandising strategies at the store level. These analyses can be performed by category or brand, for existing or new product categories.

Site Typing — Determines market demand for store or branch concepts. Evaluates the success factors for different investment strategies, such as full service, superstore or mini concept.

Merchandise Mix — Uses customer analysis to determine the actual product mix that will best satisfy demand and maximize sales performance.

BUSINESS-TO-BUSINESS RESEARCH

By leveraging our Business-Facts database and our advanced analytical techniques, you can identify, segment, profile and target your most profitable business customers and prospects.

MarketFocus Segmentation — Identifies and clusters your business customer database by size, SIC Code and other criteria, so you can better understand the quality and quantity of different customer types.

ProphetPoint Demand Forecasting — Uses business data to predict future demand for goods and services in any market area by industry or product type.

List Generation — Provides targeted direct mail lists from a database of more than 10 million business locations. You can enhance the response from these lists by incorporating our applied modeling services.

OTHER CUSTOM PROJECTS

In addition to our modeling and analytical capabilities, we also offer:

Custom Mapping Projects — For powerful presentations and visual analysis, we will display your data on a full-color thematic map. Depending upon the size of your market, your map will range in size from 8 1/2″ x 11″ to 32″ x 32″.

Geocoding Projects — To make your internal data more useful, we will append the following information to your address files: ZIP Codes, ZIP+4s, latitudes/longitudes, MicroVision lifestyle codes, block groups and Census tract assignments.

Specialized Data Sets — To provide you with the exact data you need, we will customize our data sets, integrate your own data and append our data to your files. Plus, we will contract with additional outside data sources on your behalf.

Marketing Information

A Multitude Of Databases

Your decisions are only as good as the information you use to make them. That's why we use the most proven methodologies to fully integrate more than 65 national databases into actionable, geography-based tools.

Our up-to-date data and lists provide information on all households and consumers in the U.S. Our business information gives detailed information on more than 10 million U.S. businesses, covering all industries as well as markets. We also provide industry-specific databases to help you make the right marketing decisions using the best information available. All of our data is available with Infomark, or you can get the information in report, color map and electronic formats by calling our toll-free number **1-800-866-6510.**

CONSUMER DATA

POP-FACTS DEMOGRAPHICS

More than 1,200 U.S. Census demographic, socioeconomic and housing variables, available down to the block group level of geography.

POP-FACTS DEMOGRAPHIC UPDATES AND PROJECTIONS

Current-year updates and five-year projections of key U.S. Census variables: population, households, income, sex-by-age, and ethnicity. Database incorporates migration, employment, economic conditions and time-series data.

POP-FACTS CANADIAN DEMOGRAPHICS

More than 500 variables from the 1991 Canadian Census, 300 from the 1986 Census and 175 from the 1981 Census.

POP-FACTS PUERTO RICAN DEMOGRAPHICS

Up to 900 STF1 and STF3 Census variables and boundary files for Puerto Rico.

AGE-BY-INCOME

Current-year estimates and five-year projections of households by age of the head-of-household and household income ranges. Counts and percentages are provided for seven age and seven income ranges.

ACE-INDICATORS

> Approximately 50 actual consumer economic, financial behavior and demographic variables, summarized at the ZIP+4 level of geography.

CONSUMER-FACTS™

> Current-year estimates and five-year projections of consumer spending on more than 400 products and services.

RETAIL TRADE POTENTIAL

> Current-year potential retail sales for 12 store types and a total retail sales category.

DAYTIME DINERS™

> Number of lunch diners and dining occasions per year for quick-service, mid-scale, casual, fine dining and off-premise dining categories.

HOME MORTGAGE DISCLOSURE ACT

> Applicant statistics on home purchases and improvements, refinance and multi-family loans; loan originations and denials by Census tract (HMDA I). Key demographics for Census tracts provide the same files used in compliance evaluation (HMDA II).

LIMRA'S MARKET MAP

> County, state and MSA level estimates of the number of life insurance policies sold, premium per policy, annualized premiums and number of agents; as well as age categories for whole, term, universal and variable life insurance purchasers.

MARKET METRICS

> Custom demand data for grocery store locations with greater than $2 million in revenue, and drug stores with 10 or more locations.

CAPCRIME™

> Provides scores indexed to the national average for any geographical area to the Census tract level for specific categories of crime, including homicide, robbery, burglary and motor vehicle theft.

14

Marketing Information

TRAFFIC COUNTS

Street traffic counts for the nation's most heavily populated metropolitan areas and highway volumes for all states.

CONSUMER LISTS

Direct mail and telemarketing lists, offering MicroVision and many other selects, for more than 98 million consumers. List sources include Metromail, Infobase and R.L. Polk.

BUSINESS DATA

BUSINESS-FACTS BASIC

Summary counts of total businesses for ZIP Codes, radii, polygons and other geographies. Data can be selected by SIC Code, employee size, sales and more.

BUSINESS-FACTS EMPLOYMENT

Employment counts aggregated by industry type.

BUSINESS-FACTS LISTS

Direct mail and telemarketing lists that include data on more than 10 million U.S. business locations with variables such as company name, address, phone number and executive name.

BUSINESS-FACTS LOCATION

Detailed data for more than 10 million business locations and 10 industry categories, including name, address, latitude/longitude, SIC Codes, number of employees, type and more.

BUSINESS-FACTS OCCUPATION

Data on 21 occupational categories that can be used to segment and target the work force.

SHOPPING CENTER

Name, location and square footage of more than 33,000 centers that are larger than 75,000 square feet.

SHOPPING CENTER AND TENANTS

Adds tenant information and screening variables to the standard Shopping Center database.

RESTAURANT-FACTS™

Name, location and type of more than 500,000 restaurants, including more than 2,000 chains classified into 54 categories.

15

FINANCIAL-FACTS™

> More than 88,000 individual bank and thrift branch locations with name, address, deposits, latitude/longitude, date established and more.

PROPHETPOINT FORECASTS

> Provides 11 years (1991-2001) of business forecasting information down to ZIP Code and industry levels.

PROPHETPOINT INDUSTRY DEMAND

> Provides 11 years (1991-2001) of data showing every industry's demand for goods and services from all other industries.

MARKET METRICS

> Location data for grocery stores with greater than $2 million in revenue and drug stores with 10 or more locations.

SEGMENTATION AND LIFESTYLE DATA

MICROVISION

> An advanced consumer segmentation and targeting system that classifies every U.S. household into one of 50 segments. Classifications are based on the demographic, lifestyle, socioeconomic, buying, media and behavior characteristics of households within every ZIP+4.

MICROVISION-DAYTIME

> A targeting system that classifies employees into segments to determine the demand for products and services during the daytime.

MICROVISION-BANKING

> A segmentation system tailored for bank and thrift marketers that integrates financial product and service usage information from our unique Financial Forum™ survey.

MICROVISION-INSURANCE

> A segmentation system tailored for insurance marketers that integrates insurance product and service usage information from the Financial Forum survey.

MicroVision-XR

A segmentation system based on a model that eliminates all race and ethnicity factors.

MicroVision-Custom

A segmentation system that incorporates your own customer, survey or syndicated data for a perfectly tailored targeting solution.

MicroVision Area Profiles

Provides the number and percentage of households within the MicroVision segments for any area in the U.S.

MicroVision Consumer Demand™ Profiles

MicroVision profiles and consumption propensities for more than 2,500 products and services in the following categories:

• *Consumer Products and Services* — Alcohol, apparel, automotive products and services, convenience stores, coupon usage, electronics, footwear, grocery and drug, grocery shopping, home furnishings, appliances, home improvements, jewelry, over-the-counter drug and diet, personal services, sporting goods, tobacco, toys, travel and more.

• *Banking & Finance Products and Services* — Checking and savings accounts, CDs, IRAs, loans, credit cards, stocks, bonds, mutual funds, insurance policies, annuities and more.

• *Insurance & Investments Products, Services and Attitudes* — Life, property, casualty and other insurance policy types, annuities, IRAs, mutual funds, stocks, bonds, partnerships, investments, and attitudes towards products and institutions.

• *Restaurant Dining Behavior* — Quick-service, mid-scale and upscale restaurants by time of week and day, eat-in, take-out, food type and more.

• *Utility Usage and Attitudes* — Consumer usage of utilities, appliances, home features and improvements, home lighting, energy conservation, demand and load control; as well as consumer satisfaction, attitudes and behaviors.

• *Telecommunications Usage and Attitudes* — Consumer usage of home office technologies, and local and long distance telephone services; as well as consumer satisfaction, attitudes and behaviors.

• *Cable Television Usage and Attitudes* — Consumer usage of cable services, pay-per-view, premium channels, VCRs and more; as well as consumer satisfaction with pricing, premium channels, programming and regulations.

• *Nonprofit Activities* — Participation of consumers in clubs, fundraising, volunteer work, recycling, politics, civic issues, writing to media, and contributions to PBS.

• *Media Usage* — Consumer usage of television, radio, magazines, cable TV, telephone Yellow Pages and overall media usage.

• *Leisure and Recreation Activities* — Consumer participation in aerobics, skiing, movies, biking, pet ownership, boating, bowling, camping, gambling, golf, dancing, fishing, jogging, tennis, photography, gardening, volleyball and more.

GEOGRAPHIC REFERENCE DATA

BOUNDARIES FOR MAPPING

BLOCK GROUP BOUNDARIES

Accurate boundaries for mapping more than 226,000 block groups.

BOUNDARYMAP - ZIP CODES

Accurate boundaries for all five-digit ZIP Codes within the U.S.

BOUNDARYMAP - CENSUS

Accurate boundaries for Census tracts, counties, states and MSAs.

YELLOW PAGES DIRECTORY BOUNDARIES

Distribution boundaries for more than 3,500 Yellow Pages directories.

DMA BOUNDARIES

Media boundaries for Nielsen markets.

CABLE BOUNDARIES

Boundaries for 10,000 U.S. cable systems and the data associated with those boundaries.

UTILITY SYSTEM BOUNDARIES

Boundaries for all 20 utility systems in the U.S.

BTA/MTA BOUNDARIES

> Boundaries for 487 Basic Trading Areas (BTAs) and 47 Major Trading Areas (MTAs). This data is the standard for cellular and PCS regulation, and is used by the FCC and telecommunications companies for market delineation and operator assignment.

ROADS AND HIGHWAYS FOR MAPPING

TIGEROADS™

> Provides 1990 Census highways and roads, as well as name labels, for small-area mapping applications.

TIGER™ HIGHWAYS

> Provides 1990 Census major highways with name labels for large-area mapping applications.

OTHER GEOGRAPHIC DATA

MICROVISION DIRECT MAIL CORRESPONDENCE

> Offers corresponding MicroVision segment codes for every postal carrier route number in the U.S.

MICROVISION ZIP+4 CORRESPONDENCE

> Corresponds the appropriate MicroVision segment code to every ZIP+4 in the nation.

ZIP+4 LAT/LON CORRESPONDENCE

> Specific latitude and longitude coordinates for all ZIP+4s.

ZIP+4 CENSUS GEOGRAPHY CORRESPONDENCE

> Corresponds the Census geography codes to all ZIP+4s in the country.

CARRIER ROUTE IDENTIFICATION

> Provides quick, easy access to postal carrier route data within any radius, polygon or ZIP Code.

GEOGRAPHY EQUIVALENCY/CROSS-REFERENCE

> Determines which sub-geographies are part of a parent geography (i.e., which ZIP Codes are in a county).

Delivery Options

Delivery Options To Meet Your Needs

Our distribution network includes a field sales force that will discuss your needs at your facility; an inside sales force that is ready to accept your toll-free calls; and a value-added reseller channel that enhances your own products and services.

Cost-effective market information is available on an *á la carte* basis by calling our Information Services department toll-free (**1-800-866-6510**). This option is ideal for companies with occasional or time-critical data needs.

Helpful Information Specialists — Information Services is staffed by data and applications experts skilled at assessing your needs and determining the best solution for you.

Multiple Format and Media Options — All of our data can be delivered in hard copy reports, color maps, lists and electronic formats (e.g., ASCII, dBase, Lotus® 1-2-3, Excel, ARC/INFO®, ArcView, MapInfo, Infomark Mapping, Tactician®, etc.).

Data On Demand — Many of our products can be delivered via FAX or on-line within three hours of placing your order. For convenience, overnight delivery is available.

Just A Phone Call Away — Representatives are ready to serve you, Monday through Friday, from 6:00 a.m. to 5:00 p.m., Pacific Time, **1-800-866-6510.**

A Company You Can Trust

Equifax National Decision Systems is dedicated to the marketing information and analysis needs of small to large organizations. Our respect for consumer privacy and client data confidentiality makes us a company you can trust. We are a subsidiary of Equifax Inc. (NYSE:EFX), a leading provider of information services to businesses around the world. For almost two decades, Equifax National Decision Systems has helped companies successfully analyze markets, select sites, target customers and promote products.

The More You Know, The More You Grow

To find out how our products and services can help you make better decisions, call us toll-free today.

1-800-250-7817

http://www.ends.com

Decisions

DECISIONS

decisions

EQUIFAX NATIONAL DECISION
SYSTEMS

Corporate Office: 5375 Mira Sorrento Place, Suite 400

San Diego, CA 92121

1-800-250-7817

FAX: 619-550-5800

http://www.ends.com

prodinfo@ends.com

Regional Offices: 8430 W. Bryn Mawr Ave., Suite 660

Chicago, IL 60631

773-693-0070

FAX: 773-693-1723

500 Fifth Avenue, 50th Floor

New York, NY 10110

212-840-2220

FAX: 212-764-4899

8300 Boone Blvd., Suite 740

Vienna, VA 22182

703-883-8900

FAX: 703-883-8910

1957 Lakeside Parkway, Suite 502

Tucker, GA 30084

770-492-0716

FAX: 770-492-0595

Form #023

InfoBase Data Products

TABLE OF CONTENTS

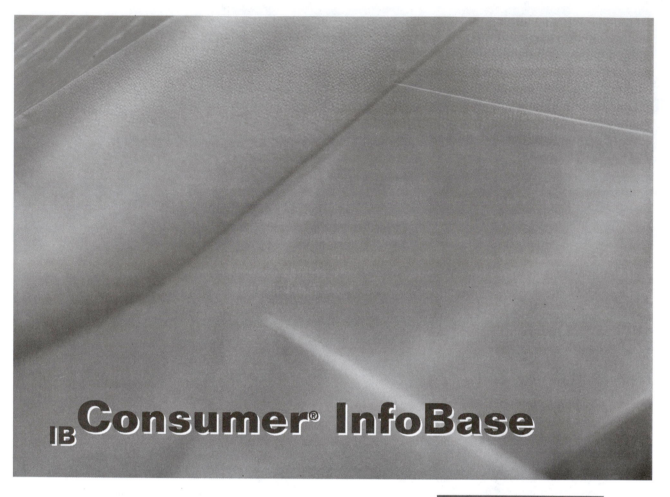

IBConsumer® InfoBase

IBConsumer InfoBase offers you the most sophisticated tool available to help you achieve increased profits and better response rates from your customer and prospect files.

This powerful tool can help you:

- **Define your customers.**
- **Effectively cross-sell existing customers.**
- **Target prospects who look most like your best customers.**
- **Raise response rates.**
- **Enhance the value of your list rental file.**
- **Design new products and services matched to your customer's buying preferences.**

InfoBase Premier

Premier elements are our multi-sourced demographic data elements. Our unique system architecture ensures you the highest quality and maximum coverage for each data element by comparing the information from multiple contributors and overlaying only the most accurate information to your customer files. Over 30 demographic variables are available in Premier, including age, income, real property data, children's data, and others.

2

₁ᵦPowerPak™

₁ᵦPowerPak offers you an exciting alternative to traditional data packages by incorporating the best InfoBase data, Trans Union SOLO Codes and a version of Claritas Affluence. With InfoBase's new ₁ᵦPowerPak, you get the most valuable and predictive data elements available in the industry. ₁ᵦPowerPak will help you plan effective marketing strategies to help you acquire new customers and retain the best customers for life.

Data Categories

- Personal
- Household
- Real Property
- Purchase Behavior
- Wealth Indicators
- Auto Data
- Address Data
- Telephone Data
- Lifestyle Data
- Lifestyle Dimensions
- Lifestyle Composites

Expertise

Our staff of statisticians and analysts can help you achieve better response rates and determine the long-term value of your customers. In addition to our analysts, we also have data consultants with specific industry expertise to assist you with meeting your business objectives.

All The Best Sources In One Database

₁ᵦConsumer InfoBase holds information on most all the households in the U.S., making it the largest database of its kind. It contains valuable data from the nation's acknowledged top data sources.

The integration of all this data into one national consumer database is unique in the industry and provides the maximum coverage and accuracy available. The graph below illustrates the additional coverage that multi-sourcing provides. ₁ᵦConsumer InfoBase gives you the most types of data along with the flexibility to select the most specific data available from any data provider you choose.

You can select demographic information such as age, income, occupation, marital status, and children's age ranges. You might choose socio-economic data such as car and home ownership, as well as lifestyle information on specific interests, hobbies, activities, and mail order purchase information. InfoBase data is put through rigorous screening to assure that you get the highest quality information available in the industry, and it is kept current through monthly updating.

InfoBase Premier™

Premier elements are our multi-sourced data elements. InfoBase Premier includes data from over 10 of the nation's top acknowl-

edged data sources to guarantee that the most recent, most specific, and most accurate data is selected for each Premier data element. In short, this sophisticated system architecture assures you the highest quality and maximum coverage for each data element. You simply select the Premier elements desired, or one of our bundled packages of data, and the system does the rest.

Data Experts To Help Maximize Results

An anlaytical staff is available with direct marketing experience. Our professionals can help you achieve better response rates, or determine the long-term value of your customers, using advanced segmentation techniques such as CHAID, Logit, and Regression Analysis. If you want a snapshot to gain more knowledge of your customers, Acxiom's research staff can prepare a Data Profile Analysis using key InfoBase data. In addition to our analysts, we also have data consultants aligned by industry. These consultants have industry specific expertise to assist you with meeting your business objectives. Together, our research and data consultant teams can give meaning to the numbers and statistics that you receive. Acxiom provides more than data. We provide solutions.

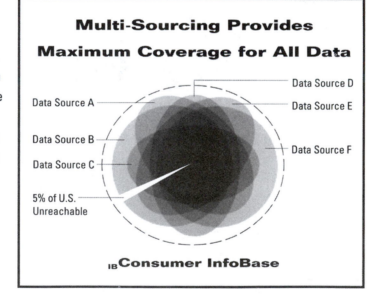

Multi-Sourcing Provides Maximum Coverage for All Data

Data Source A, Data Source B, Data Source C, 5% of U.S. Unreachable, Data Source D, Data Source E, Data Source F

₁ᵦConsumer InfoBase

New to InfoBase

Introducing _{IB}PowerPak – _{IB}Consumer InfoBase's Most Powerful Bundle Of Data Ever

With InfoBase's NEW _{IB}PowerPak, you get a comprehensive bundle of data which allows you to identify characteristics and buying patterns within specific households to create more accurate segments of your best prospects and customers.

_{IB}PowerPak contains the best InfoBase data, Trans Union's SOLO® Codes, and a version of Claritas Affluence. _{IB}PowerPak offers you an exciting alternative to traditional data packages.

The data elements of _{IB}PowerPak include:

- Home Market Value
- Age
- Presence of Children
- Marital Status
- Homeowner/Renter
- Income
- Affluence Code
- Home Equity
- DQ Decile Code
- Children's Ages
- SOLO
- Length of Residence
- Dwelling Size
- Credit Card Holder

With _{IB}PowerPak, you can plan marketing strategies to target the right individuals to increase response rates, lower acquisition costs and improve marketing efficiency. Plus, expand markets by targeting more individuals who fit your customer profile, regardless of where they live. _{IB}PowerPak can help you uncover a lot of potential customers that your previous programs overlooked.

Through _{IB}PowerPak you'll get fresher, better quality predictive data. And you get it quickly. _{IB}PowerPak is so powerful, we can turn a standard file for you in three days.

New to _{IB}Consumer InfoBase – InfoBase Response Data

The InfoBase Response Data is a new category of data supplied to InfoBase by a major compiler of retail response data. It consists of a series of files compiled from warranty card registrations and monthly accounts receivable files that are commonly used by organizations involved in the retail field. Information is also provided on individuals who:

- Are users of credit.
- Have received a new credit card recently.
- Have moved and provided a change of address.
- Have made a purchase at a retail store.

This data is not credit data, but is, by nature of the data, useful for predicting credit-like behavior. We will incorporate data on approximately 100 million consumers. Some of the elements that will be offered are:

- Categories of retail activity (i.e. upscale retail, specialty stores, finance company, etc.)
- Multi-buyer indicator.
- Date of last activity.
- New credit card issues, including the range of new lines of credit.

This data adds a unique dimension of actual purchase behavior data in addition to the wealth of consumer characteristics available on _{IB}Consumer InfoBase.

Data Packages

Bundled Premier™

Data Element No.	Description	Price per M Matches
165	**Truck/Motorcycle/RV Owners**	$10.00
194	**Aggregate Value of Vehicles Owned**	$12.00
	The total value of all vehicles registered in the household based on blue book value.	
600	**Adult Age Ranges Present in Household**	$10.00
	Includes an indication of male, female or unknown gender. • 18-24 • 35-44 • 55-64 • 75+ • 25-34 • 45-54 • 65-74	
601	**Children's Age Range**	$15.00
	Children's age including indication of male, female or unknown gender, reported as: • 0-2 • 6-10 • 16-17 • 21-22 • 3-5 • 11-15 • 18-20	
604	**Occupation–First Individual**	$10.00
	Expressed as: • Professional/Technical • Housewife • Administrative/Managerial • Retired • Sales/Service • Farmer • Clerical/White Collar • Military • Craftsman/Blue Collar • Religious • Student (Includes code indicating self-employed for any of the above.)	
605	**Occupation–Second Individual**	$10.00
	Expressed as: • Professional/Technical • Housewife • Administrative/Managerial • Retired • Sales/Service • Farmer • Clerical/White Collar • Military • Craftsman/Blue Collar • Religious • Student (Includes code indicating self-employed for any of the above.)	
606	**Homeowner/Renter**	$10.00
607	**Length of Residence Expressed in One-Year Increments from Less than One to 15+ Years**	$7.50
608	**Dwelling Size (Single or Multi-Family)**	$5.0
609	**Marital Status**	$3.00
	• Married • Inferred Married • Single • Inferred Single	
610	**First Individual–Name, Gender**	$3.00
612	**Second Individual–Name, Gender and Relationship to Head of Household**	$3.00
614	**Verification Date**	$5.00
	Year and quarter of most recent address verification.	
615	**Mail Order Buyer**	$12.00
616	**Age Range in Two-Year Increments–First Individual**	$14.00
	Categories extend from under 18 to 100 plus.	
617	**Age Range in Two-Year Increments–Second Individual**	$14.00
619	**Working Woman**	$5.00
	Working woman present in the household.	
620	**Mail Responders**	$8.00
621	**Credit Card Holder**	$15.00
	Indication of possession of one or more of the following types of credit cards. • Retail/Other • Premium (Gold Cards) • Bank Card • Upscale Dept. Stores • Travel and • Credit Card Holder Entertainment • (Unspecified Type)	
622	**Presence of Children**	$5.00
	Indicates the known presence/absence of children age 0-18 in the household.	

Data Element No.	Description	Price per M Matches
626	**Age Range in Two-Year Increments–Individual Name Appearing on Customer's File**	$14.00
628	**Number of Adults**	$8.00
	Counts the number of adults in the household up to six or more.	
639	**InfoBase Match**	$5.00
	Customer name and address exists on InfoBase database.	
641	**Estimated Income Code**	$10.00
	Reported as one of the following: • Less than $15,000 • $ 50,000 - $ 74,999 • $15,000 - $19,999 • $ 75,000 - $ 99,999 • $20,000 - $29,999 • $ 100,000 - $124,999 • $30,000 - $39,999 • $ 125,000 Plus • $40,000 - $49,999	
646	**New Car Buyer/Leased Car Indicator**	$12.00
	Indicates a history of new car buying and leasing.	
647	**Known Number of Vehicles Owned**	$12.00
648	**Dominant Vehicle Lifestyle Indicator**	$8.00
	This indicator distinguishes the classification of the primary vehicle registered to the household. • Personal Luxury Car, e.g. Corvette, Audi 100, Infiniti • Truck or Passenger Utility Vehicle, e.g. Jeep Cherokee, Toyota Previa, Lumina APV • Station Wagon, e.g. Buick Roadmaster, Taurus Station Wagon • Import (standard or economy car), e.g. Toyota Camry, Nissan Stanza, Volkswagen Passat • Regular (mid-size or luxury car), e.g. Dodge Spirit • Specialty (mid-size or luxury car), e.g. Grand Marquis, Eagle, Mustang, Accord, Corolla, Saab • Full Size (standard or luxury car), e.g. Taurus, LeBaron, Continental, Cadillac	
649	**Individual Name Appearing on Customer's File–Household Status Indicator**	$3.00
	Reported as: • First Individual • Second Individual	
659	**Apartment Number**	$2.00
635	**Bundled Premier Group Element**	$45.00
	Includes all InfoBase Premier Data Elements listed above. Volume discounts available.	

Additional Premier Data

(Not included in the Bundled Premier Package)

Data Element No.	Description	Price per M Matches
611	**Date of Birth–First Individual**	$20.00
	Day and month when available.	
618	**Date of Birth–Second Individual**	$20.00
	Day and month when available.	
623	**Date of Birth–Individual Name Appearing on Customer's File.**	$20.00
	Day and month when Available.	
624	**Date of Birth–Individual Name Appearing on Customer's File with Default to Head of Household.**	$20.00
	Day and month when available.	
627	**Age Range in Two-Year Increments of Individual Name Appearing on Customer's File, with Default to First Individual**	$14.00
632	**Homeowner Data Package**	$25.00
	Includes above elements: Home Market Value, Purchase Date, Year and Month. (642, 643, 644, and 645).	

6

Data Packages

Data Element No.	Description	Price per M Matches
633	**Element 632 Purchased in Conjunction with Bundled Premier for an additional $10.00/M overall Premier Matches**	
642	**Home Market Value**	$20.00

- $ 1,000 - $ 24,999
- $ 25,000 - $ 49,999
- $ 50,000 - $ 74,999
- $ 75,000 - $ 99,999
- $ 100,000 - $ 124,999
- $ 125,000 - $ 149,999
- $ 150,000 - $ 174,999
- $ 175,000 - $ 199,999
- $ 200,000 - $ 224,999
- $ 225,000 - $ 249,999
- $ 250,000 - $274,999
- $ 275,000 - $299,999
- $ 300,000 - $349,999
- $ 350,000 - $399,999
- $ 400,000 - $449,999
- $ 450,000 - $499,999
- $ 500,000 - $774,999
- $ 775,000 - $999,999
- $ 1,000,000 Plus

Data Element No.	Description	Price per M Matches
643	**Purchase Date of Home** Both year and month of purchase where available. Ranges from 1901 to present.	$10.00
644	**Year Home was Purchased** Ranges from 1901 to present.	$7.50
645	**Month Home was Purchased** Ranges from 01 to 12.	$5.00
660	**Third Individual–Name, Gender, and Relationship to First Individual**	$3.00
661	**Fourth Individual–Name, Gender, and Relationship to First Individual**	$3.00
662	**Fifth Individual–Name, Gender, and Relationship to First Individual**	$3.00
663	**Available Home Equity**	$20.00

- $ 1,000 - $ 4,999
- $ 5,000 - $ 9,999
- $ 10,000 - $ 19,999
- $ 20,000 - $ 29,999
- $ 30,000 - $ 49,999
- $ 50,000 - $ 74,999
- $ 75,000 - $ 99,999
- $ 100,000 - $149,999
- $ 150,000 - $ 199,999
- $ 200,000 - $ 249,999
- $ 250,000 - $ 499,999
- $ 500,000 - $ 749,999
- $ 750,000 - $ 999,999
- $ 1,000,000 - $1,999,999
- $ 2,000,000 Plus

IB PowerPak

Data Element No.	Description	Price per M Matches
119	**Children's Age Range in One Year Increments**	$20.00
463	**DQ Market Decile Code** Relative home market value indicator as compared to all homes located within the same county (top 10%, top 20%, etc.).	$20.00
600	**Adult Age Ranges Present in Household** Includes an indication of male, female or unknown gender.	$10.00

- 18-24
- 25-34
- 35-44
- 45-54
- 55-64
- 65-74
- 75+

601	**Children's Age Range** Children's age including indication of male, female or unknown gender, reported as:	$15.00

- 0-2
- 3-5
- 6-10
- 11-15
- 16-17
- 18-20
- 21-22

606	**Homeowner/Renter**	$10.00
607	**Length of Residence Expressed in One-Year Increments from Less than One to 15+ Years**	$7.50
608	**Dwelling Size (Single or Multi-Family)**	$5.00
609	**Marital Status**	$3.00

- Married
- Single
- Inferred Married
- Inferred Single

Data Element No.	Description	Price per M Matches
610	**First Individual–Name, Gender**	$3.00
612	**Second Individual–Name, Gender and Relationship to First Individual**	$3.00
614	**Verification Date** Year and quarter of most recent address verification.	$5.00
616	**Age Range in Two-Year Increments– First Individual** Categories extend from under 18 to 100 plus.	$14.00
617	**Age Range in Two-Year Increments– Second Individual**	$14.00
621	**Credit Card Indicator** Indication of possession of one or more of the following types of credit cards.	$15.00

- Retail/Other
- Bank Card
- Travel and Entertainment
- Premium (Gold Cards)
- Upscale Dept. Stores
- Credit Card Buyer
- (Unspecified Type)

622	**Presence of Children** Indicates the known presence/absence of children age 0-18 in the household.	$5.00
626	**Age Range in Two-Year Increments–Individual Name Appearing on Customer's File**	$14.00
639	**InfoBase Match** Customer name and address exists on InfoBase database.	$5.00
642	**Home Market Value**	$20.00

- $ 1,000 - $ 24,999
- $ 25,000 - $ 49,999
- $ 50,000 - $ 74,999
- $ 75,000 - $ 99,999
- $ 100,000 - $ 124,999
- $ 125,000 - $ 149,999
- $ 150,000 - $ 174,999
- $ 175,000 - $ 199,999
- $ 200,000 - $ 224,999
- $ 225,000 - $ 249,999
- $ 250,000 - $274,999
- $ 275,000 - $299,999
- $ 300,000 - $349,999
- $ 350,000 - $399,999
- $ 400,000 - $449,999
- $ 450,000 - $499,999
- $ 500,000 - $774,999
- $ 775,000 - $999,999
- $ 1,000,000 Plus

649	**Individual Name Appearing on Customer's File Household Status Indicator** Reported as:	$3.00

- First Individual
- Second Individual

663	**Available Home Equity**	$20.00

- $ 1,000 - $ 4,999
- $ 5,000 - $ 9,999
- $ 10,000 - $ 19,999
- $ 20,000 - $ 29,999
- $ 30,000 - $ 49,999
- $ 50,000 - $ 74,999
- $ 75,000 - $ 99,999
- $ 100,000 - $149,999
- $ 150,000 - $ 199,999
- $ 200,000 - $ 249,999
- $ 250,000 - $ 499,999
- $ 500,000 - $ 749,999
- $ 750,000 - $ 999,999
- $ 1,000,000 - $1,999,999
- $ 2,000,000 Plus

676	**Claritas Affluence Broad Range**	$20.00

Net Worth Broad Range Segment Code	IPA Broad Range Segment Code
$500,000+	$500,000 +
$250,000-500,000	$200,000 -500,000
$125,000-250,000	$ 75,000 -200,000
$ 50,000-125,000	$ 20,000 - 75,000
$ 0 - 50,000	$ 5,000 - 20,000
Less than $0	Less than $0 -$ 5,000

841	**Trans Union SOLO Codes** SOLO classifies individuals into 41 unique clusters, each defined by 10 socio-economic and demographic characteristics, such as age, income, length of residence, occupation, education, etc.	$60.00
638	**IB PowerPak Group Element** Includes a subset of InfoBase Premier data elements, DataQuick Market Value Decile Codes, TU Solo Codes, and the Broad Range Claritas Affluence Codes (including Net Worth and IPA).	$65.00

Data Categories

All 600 series elements are Premier Multi-Sourced Elements.

Personal Data

Data Element No.	Description	Price per M Matches
341	**Education–First Individual**	$14.00
	• Completed High School	
	• Completed College	
	• Completed Graduate School	
	• Attended Vocational/Technical School	
342	**Education–Second Individual**	$14.00
	• Completed High School	
	• Completed College	
	• Completed Graduate School	
	• Attended Vocation/Technical School	
527	**Race**	$25.00
	B = Black N = Japanese	
	W = White H = Hispanic	
	P = Portuguese O = Other	
	J = Jewish	
528	**Corrective Lenses**	$25.00
529	**Height**	$25.00
530	**Weight**	$25.00
531	**Voter/Party**	$20.00
	V = Voter/No Party D = Voter/Democrat	
	R = Voter/Republican I = Voter/Independent	
604	**Occupation–First Individual**	$10.00
	Expressed as:	
	• Professional/Technical • Housewife	
	• Administrative/Managerial • Retired	
	• Sales/Service • Farmer	
	• Clerical/White Collar • Military	
	• Craftsman/Blue Collar • Religious	
	• Student	
	(Includes code indicating self-employed for any of the above.)	
605	**Occupation–Second Individual**	$10.00
	Expressed as:	
	• Professional/Technical • Housewife	
	• Administrative/Managerial • Retired	
	• Sales/Service • Farmer	
	• Clerical/White Collar • Military	
	• Craftsman/Blue Collar • Religious	
	• Student	
	(Includes code indicating self-employed for any of the above.)	
610	**First Individual–Name, Gender**	$3.00
611	**Date of Birth–First Individual**	$20.00
	Day and month when available.	
612	**Second Individual–Name, Gender and Relationship to First Individual**	$3.00
616	**Age Range in Two-Year Increments– First Individual**	$14.00
	Categories extend from under 18 to 100 plus.	
617	**Age Range in Two-Year Increments– Second Individual**	$14.00
618	**Date of Birth–Second Individual**	$20.00
	Day and month when available.	
623	**Date of Birth–Individual Name Appearing on Customer's File**	20.00
	Day and month when available.	
624	**Date of Birth–Individual Name Appearing on Customer's File with Default to First Individual**	$20.00
	Day and month when available.	

Data Element No.	Description	Price per M Matches
626	**Age Range in Two-Year Increments–Individual Name Appearing on Customer's File**	$14.00
627	**Age Range in Two-Year Increments–Individual Name Appearing on Customer's File, with Default to First Individual**	$14.00
660	**Third Individual–Name, Gender, and Relationship to First Individual**	$3.00
661	**Fourth Individual–Name, Gender, and Relationship to First Individual**	$3.00
662	**Fifth Individual–Name, Gender, and Relationship to First Individual**	$3.00
890	**Two-Year Age–Third Individual**	$14.00
	Age represented in two-year increments starting at under eighteen and ending with 100 plus.	
891	**Date of Birth–Third Individual**	$20.00
	Year of birth and month when available.	
893	**Two-Year Age–Fourth Individual**	$14.00
	Age represented in two-year increments starting at under eighteen and ending with 100 plus.	
894	**Date of Birth–Fourth Individual**	$20.00
	Year of birth and month when available.	
896	**Two-Year Age–Fifth Individual**	$14.00
	Age represented in two-year increments starting at under eighteen and ending with 100 plus.	
897	**Date of Birth–Fifth Individual**	$20.00
	Year of birth and month when available.	

Household Data

Data Element No.	Description	Price per M Matches
119	**Children's Age Range in One-Year Increments**	$20.00
130	**Tertiary Tri-Cell-Code Comprised of Occupation, New Vehicle Buyer and Vehicle Type Information**	$16.00
131	**Secondary Tri-Cell-Code Comprised of Household Composition Information**	$16.00
132	**Primary Tri-Cell-Code Comprised of Income and Age Information**	$16.00
600	**Adult Age Ranges Present in Household**	$10.00
	Includes an indication of male, female or unknown gender.	
	• 18-24 • 35-44 • 55-64 • 75+	
	• 25-34 • 45-54 • 65-74	
601	**Children's Age Range**	$15.00
	Children's age including indication of male, female or unknown gender, reported as:	
	• 0-2 • 6-10 • 16-17 • 21-22	
	• 3-5 • 11-15 • 18-20	
602	**Number of Children**	$10.00
609	**Marital Status**	$3.00
	• Married • Inferred Married	
	• Single • Inferred Single	
619	**Working Woman**	$5.00
	Working woman present in the household.	

Data Categories

Data Element No.	Description	Pricer per M Matches
621	**Credit Card Indicator**	$15.00

Indication of possession of one or more of the following types of credit cards.

- Retail/Other
- Bank Card
- Travel and Entertainment
- Premium (Gold Cards)
- Upscale Dept. Stores
- Credit Card Holder
- (Unspecified Type)

622	**Presence of Children**	$5.00

Indicates the known presence/absence of children age 0-18 in the household.

628	**Number of Adults**	$8.00

Counts the number of adults in the household up to six or more.

629	**Household Size**	$6.00
639	**InfoBase Match**	$5.00

Customer name and address exists on InfoBase database.

640	**Number of Sources**	$10.00
641	**Estimated Income Code**	$10.00

Reported as one of the following:

- Less than $15,000
- $15,000 - $19,999
- $20,000 - $29,999
- $30,000 - $39,999
- $40,000 - $49,999
- $ 50,000 - $ 74,999
- $ 75,000 - $ 99,999
- $100,000 - $124,999
- $ 125,000 Plus

649	**Individual Name Appearing on Customer's File Household Status Indicator**	$3.00

Reported as:
- First Individual
- Second Individual

652	**Number of Generations**	$3.00
664	**DMA No Mail Solicitation Flag**	*No Charge
665	**DMA No Phone Solicitation Flag**	*No Charge
800	**CB Owner**	$10.00
802	**Veterans**	$10.00
882	**Ten-Year Adult Age Ranges**	$10.00

- 18-24
- 25-34
- 35-44
- 45-54
- 55-64
- 65-74
- 75+

962	**Ethnic Code**	$10.00

A = American
H = Hispanic
F = French
I = Italian
G = German
O = Oriental
S = Scottish/Irish
N = Northern European
J = Jewish
R = Arab

*Appended with all enhancement orders.

Real Property Data

Data Element No.	Description	Price per M Matches
138	**Structure Age (Year)**	$5.00

Year in which this structure (house number) first appeared on some source list.

162	**Dwelling Unit Size**	$5.00

Counts the number of known households at an address:

1 3 5 7 9   10-19   30-39   50-99
2 4 6 8   20-29   40-49   100+

Data Element No.	Description	Price per M Matches
581	**Property Type**	$5.00

- Single Family Dwelling
- Condo
- Cooperative
- 2-4 Unit
- Miscellaneous Residence
- Apartment
- Mobile Home
- Timeshare
- Other

584	**Loan-to-Value**	$20.00

LTV ratio based on modeling of current and historical mortgages compared to market value. Derived from public record sources; updated quarterly.
Available in the following ranges:

- Over 100%
- 95-99%
- 90-94%
- 85-89%
- 80-84%
- 75-79%
- 70-74%
- 60-69%
- 50-59%
- 01-49%
- 0% (no loans)

586	**Lendable Home Equity**	$20.00

Lendable equity is computed on 80% of market value less total loans. Derived from public record sources; updated quarterly.
Available in the following ranges:

- $ 0
- $ 1 - $ 4,999
- $ 5,000 - $ 9,999
- $ 10,000 - $ 19,999
- $ 20,000 - $ 29,999
- $ 30,000 - $ 49,999
- $ 50,000 - $ 74,999
- $ 75,000 - $ 99,999
- $100,000 - $149,999
- $150,000 - $199,999
- $ 200,000 - $ 249,999
- $ 250,000 - $ 299,999
- $ 300,000 - $ 349,999
- $ 350,000 - $ 399,999
- $ 400,000 - $ 499,999
- $ 500,000 - $ 749,999
- $ 750,000 - $ 999,999
- $1,000,000 - $1,999,999
- $2,000,000 Plus

588	**Home Size Range–Square Footage**	$7.50

Estimated size of home in square footage.

589	**Lot Size Range–Square Footage**	$7.50

Estimated size of lot in square footage.

590	**X-Date (Projected insurance expiration date)**	$15.00

Based on month of purchase and/or refinance. Derived from public record sources; updated quarterly.

591	**Presence of Pool**	$10.00

Swimming pool present within property.

592	**Year Built**	$7.50

Year that home was constructed.

596	**Packaged Element Consisting of Market Value, Loan-to-Value, Available Home Equity and Lendable Home Equity**	$30.00
606	**Homeowner/Renter**	$10.00
607	**Length of Residence Expressed in One-Year Increments from Less than One to 15+ Years**	$7.50
608	**Dwelling Size (Single or Multi-Family)**	$5.00
642	**Home Market Value**	$20.00

- $ 1,000 - $ 24,999
- $ 25,000 - $ 49,999
- $ 50,000 - $ 74,999
- $ 75,000 - $ 99,999
- $100,000 - $124,999
- $125,000 - $149,999
- $150,000 - $174,999
- $175,000 - $199,999
- $200,000 - $224,999
- $225,000 - $249,999
- $ 250,000 - $274,999
- $ 275,000 - $299,999
- $ 300,000 - $349,999
- $ 350,000 - $399,999
- $ 400,000 - $449,999
- $ 450,000 - $499,999
- $ 500,000 - $774,999
- $ 775,000 - $999,999
- $1,000,000 Plus

643	**Purchase Date of Home**	$10.00

Both year and month of purchase where available. Ranges from 1901 to 1996.

644	**Year Home was Purchased**	$7.50

Ranges from 1901 to 1996.

9

Data Categories

Data Element No.	Description	Price per M Matches
645	**Month Home was Purchased** Ranges from 01 to 12.	$5.00
663	**Available Home Equity**	$20.00

- $ 1,000 - $ 4,999
- $ 5,000 - $ 9,999
- $ 10,000 - $ 19,999
- $ 20,000 - $ 29,999
- $ 30,000 - $ 49,999
- $ 50,000 - $ 74,999
- $ 75,000 - $ 99,999
- $ 100,000 - $149,999
- $ 150,000 - $ 199,999
- $ 200,000 - $ 249,999
- $ 250,000 - $ 499,999
- $ 500,000 - $ 749,999
- $ 750,000 - $ 999,999
- $ 1,000,000 - $1,999,999
- $ 2,000,000 Plus

Data Element No.	Description	Price per M Matches
763	**Structure Age Range** Derived from building permit records supplemented with census block group statistics to achieve maximum coverage.	$5.00

- 1900-1940
- 1941-1950
- 1951-1960
- 1961-1970
- 1971-1980
- 1981-1986
- 1987-1989
- 1990 and after

Data Element No.	Description	Price per M Matches
776	**Substantial Minority Census Tract Flag** Flag indicating household is located in a census tract where over 50% of the households are non-white.	$5.00
778	**Community Reinvestment Act (CRA) Income Classification Code** Median family income of the census tract as compared to the MSA family median income. 0 = Unknown 1 = Low (<50% of MSA median) 2 = Moderate (50-80% of MSA median) 3 = Middle (80-120% of MSA median) 4 = High (>120% of MSA median)	$5.00

Purchase Behavior Data

Data Element No.	Description	Price per M Matches
109	**Credit Card User** Indicates active credit card purchases.	$15.00
177	**Direct Mail Donors**	$12.00
178	**Mail Order Buyer by Dollar Amount** • Low (less than $15) • High (greater than $50) • Medium ($15-$50)	$20.00
179	**Mail Order Responder by Dollar Amount** • Low (less than $15) • High (greater than $50) • Medium ($15-$50)	$20.00
180	**Mail Order Donor by Dollar Amount** • Low (less than $15) • High (greater than $50) • Medium ($15-$50)	$20.00
182	**Mail Order Responder by Type** • Catalog General Merchandise • Health/Fitness/Exercise • Magazines • Bargain Seekers • General Merchandise • Books/Music • Investments • Health Donor	$20.00
183	**Low Dollar Mail Order Buyer by Type** **(Less than $15)**	$20.00
184	**Medium Dollar Mail Order Buyer by Type** **($15 -$50)**	$20.00
185	**High Dollar Mail Order Buyer by Type** **(Greater than $50)**	$20.00

Data Element No.	Description	Price per M Matches
186	**Low Dollar Mail Order Donor by Type** **(Less Than $50)** • Religious • Health Causes • Environmental, Humanitarian, Educational • Political	$20.00
187	**Medium Dollar Mail Order Donor by Type** **($50 - $100)**	$20.00
188	**High Dollar Mail Order Donor by Type** **(Greater than $100)**	$20.00
615	**Mail Order Buyer**	$12.00
620	**Mail Responders**	$8.00
803	**Miscellaneous Electronic Buyer**	$10.00
804	**PC Products Buyer**	$10.00
805	**Photographic Equipment Buyer**	$10.00
808*	**New Bank Card** Indicates a recent bank card issue.	$17.00
815	**Presence of Bank Card** Indicates the presence of bank card.	$10.00
816	**Multi-Buyer Indicator** Indicates purchases at multiple categories of retail stores.	$5.00
836	**Range of New Credit** Indicates the range of new credit granted.	$20.00
837	**Types of Retail Activity** Indication of purchase at one or more of the following retail category(s): • Standard retail • Bank • Oil Company • Standard Specialty • Upscale Retail • Finance Company • Upscale Specialty • Miscellaneous	$15.00
838	**Subtypes of Retail Activity** Indications of purchase at one or more of the following retail subcategory(s): • Standard Retail • Main Street Retail • Travel/Personal Services • High Volume Low End Department Store • High End/Upscale Retail • Specialty • Specialty Apparel • Financial Services – Insurance • Financial Services – Banking • Financial Services – Installment credit • Computer/Electronics • Home/Office Supply • Furniture Buyers • Home Improvement • Membership Warehouse • TV/Mail Order • Oil Company • Sporting Goods • Grocery • Miscellaneous	$20.00
839	**Date of Last Activity** The most recent date of retail transaction.	$5.00

*Available December '97.

Data Categories

Wealth Indicators

Data Element No.	Description	Price per M Matches
337	**InfoBase Investor Model–Highly Likely Investors**	$15.00
	Names from the top 10% of the InfoBase file who are at least two and one-half times more likely to fit the profile of an investor.	
339	**InfoBase Investor Model–Highly Likely Investors**	$12.00
	Names from the next 10% of the InfoBase file who are at least two times more likely to fit the profile of an investor.	
463	**DQ Market Decile Code**	$20.00
	Relative home market value indicator as compared to all homes located within the same county (top 10%, top 20%,etc.)	
479	**InfoBase Networth Indicator**	$34.00
	The $_{IB}$Consumer InfoBase Net Worth Indicator is a summary of data that has been found to be predictive of net worth. Reported as:	

- Less than or equal to 0
- $ 1 - $ 4,999
- $ 5,000 - $ 9,999
- $ 10,000 - $ 24,999
- $ 25,000 - $ 49,999
- $ 50,000 - $ 99,999
- $100,000 - $ 249,999
- $250,000 - $ 499,999
- $500,000

587	**Real Estate Investor**	$20.00
675	**Claritas Affluence Narrow Range**	$35.00
676	**Claritas Affluence Broad Range**	$20.00

Net Worth Broad Range Segment Code	IPA Broad Range Segment Code
• $500,000+	• $500,000 +
• $250,000 -500,000	• $200,000 -500,000
• $125,000 -250,000	• $ 75,000 -200,000
• $ 50,000 -125,000	• $ 20,000 - 75,000
• $ 0 - 50,000	• $ 5,000 - 20,000
• Less than $0	• Less than $0 -$ 5,000

761	**Income Deciles**	$7.50
	Relative household income indicator as compared to all households located within the same county (top 10%, top 20%, etc.)	
772	**Household Income/Household Income Decile**	$20.00
	Ratio of household income to household income decile.	

Auto Data

Data Element No.	Description	Price per M Matches
164	**Registered Cars/Number of Cars Owned**	$8.00
165	**Truck/Motorcycle/RV Owners**	$10.00
	Many of these specialty vehicle owners display a greater-than-average interest in outdoors and do-it-yourself activities.	
175	**Registered Vehicle Model Years**	Call for Quote
	Up to three registered vehicles' model years.	

Data Element No.	Description	Price per M Matches
192	**Body Size of Newest Registered Car**	$12.00

- Standard, e.g. Buick Roadmaster, Caprice, Crown Victoria, Grand Marquis
- Luxury, e.g. Cadillac DeVille, Chrysler New Yorker
- Personal Luxury, e.g. Lincoln Continental, Corvette, Cadillac Seville, Dodge Viper
- Intermediate Regular, e.g. Oldsmobile Cutlass Ciera, Chrysler LeBaron Sedan, Chevrolet Lumina, Ford Taurus
- Intermediate Specialty, e.g. Cougar/XR7, Dodge 600 ES, Thunderbird
- Compact Regular, e.g. Dodge Spirit, Skylark, Tempo, Topaz
- Compact Specialty, e.g. Eagle, Grand Am, Mustang, Probe
- Subcompact Regular, e.g. Escort, Saturn SC/SL1/SL2, Sundance
- Subcompact Specialty, e.g. Eagle Talon, Plymouth Laser, Pontiac 2000
- Passenger Utility, e.g. Jeep Cherokee, GMC Suburban, Mazda MPV, Pontiac Trans Sport, Toyota Previa
- Economy Import, e.g. Geo Metro, Volkswagen Golf, Hyundai Excel, Nissan Sentra, Toyota Tercel
- Standard Size Import, e.g. Accord, Mazda 626, Mitsubishi Galant, Volkswagen Passat, Saab 900, Subaru Legacy
- Sporty Import, e.g. Audi 80/Quattro, Volkswagen Corrado, Jaguar XJS, Mazda Miata, Porsche
- Luxury Import, e.g. Bentley, Infinity, Lexus, Mercedes Benz, Rolls Royce

194	**Aggregate Value of Vehicles Owned**	$12.00
	The total value of all vehicles registered in the household based on blue book value.	
646	**New Car Buyer/Leased Car Indicator**	$12.00
	Indicates a history new car buying and leasing.	
647	**Known Number of Vehicles Owned**	$12.00
648	**Dominant Vehicle Lifestyle Indicator**	$8.00
	This indicator distinguishes the classification of the primary vehicle registered to the household.	

- Personal Luxury Car, e.g. Corvette, Audi 100, Infiniti
- Truck or Passenger Utility Vehicle, e.g. Jeep Cherokee, Toyota Previa, Lumina APV
- Station Wagon, e.g. Buick Roadmaster, Taurus Station Wagon
- Import (standard or economy car), e.g. Toyota Camry, Nissan Stanza, Volkswagen Passat
- Regular (mid-size or luxury car), e.g. Dodge Spirit
- Specialty (mid-size or luxury car), e.g. Grand Marquis, Eagle, Mustang, Accord, Corolla, Saab
- Full Size (standard or luxury car), e.g. Taurus, LeBaron, Continental, Cadillac

857	**Purchase Date of Auto 1**	$12.50
	Both year and month of purchase where available. Year ranges from 70 to 96.	
858	**Purchase Date of Auto 2**	$12.50
	Both year and month of purchase where available. Year ranges from 70 to 96.	
866	**Personal Luxury Vehicle**	$8.00
	Indicates the presence of a vehicle in a price range of $25,000 or more.	
867	**Vehicle Price Class**	$8.00
	Low priced/used car buyers, medium and high priced car buyers.	

Low = $ 500 - $ 9,999
Med = $ 10,000 - $ 19,999
High = $ 20,000 - $100,000

Data Categories

Address Data

Data Element No.	Description	Price per M Matches
614	**Verification Date** Year and quarter of most recent address verification.	$5.00
639	**InfoBase Match** Customer name and address exists on InfoBase database.	$5.00
659	**Apartment Number**	$2.00
819	**Move Date** Indicates the reported move date.	$5.00

Telephone Data

Data Element No.	Description	Price per M Matches
887	**Area Code, Telephone, Time Zone (₁ᵦTeleSource)** See ₁ᵦTeleSource on pages 14-17 for a complete listing of telephone data.	$60.00

Lifestyle Data

Individual Household Level	$7.00/M Matches
Neighborhood Level	$3.00/M Input

Data Element No.	Description	Data Element No.	Description
205	Art/Antiques	238	Needlework/Knitting
207	Automotive Work	239	Our Nation's Heritage
208	Book Reading	240	Personal/Home Computer
209	Bible/Devotional Reading	241	Photography
210	Bicycling	242	Physical Fitness/ Exercise
211	Boating/Sailing	244	Real Estate Investments
213	Cable TV Viewing	245	Recreational Vehicles
214	Camping/Hiking	246	Running/Jogging
216	Collectibles	247	Science Fiction
217	Community/Civic Activities	248	Science/New Technology
218	Crafts	249	Self-Improvement
220	Cultural/Arts Events	250	Sewing
221	Current Affairs/Politics	251	Snow Skiing
222	Electronics	252	Stamp/Coin Collecting
223	Fashion Clothing	253	Stereo/Records/ Tapes/CDs
224	Fishing	254	Stock/Bond Investments
225	Foreign Travel	255	Sweepstakes/Contests
226	Gardening	256	Tennis
227	Grandchildren	257	Watching Sports on TV
228	Golf	258	Video Games
229	Gourmet Cooking/ Fine Foods	259	VCR Recording/ Home Video
230	Health/Natural Food	260	Walking for Heatlh
231	Home Furnishings/ Decorating	261	Wildlife/Environmental
232	Home Workshop	262	Wines
233	Household Pets	308	Career Oriented Activities
234	House Plants	309	Casino Gambling
235	Hunting/Shooting	310	Dieting/Weight Control
236	Money Making Opportunities	311	Donate to Charities
		312	Military Veteran
237	Motorcycling	313	Mail Order

Data Element No.	Description	Data Element No.	Description
314	Buy Pre-Recorded Videos	318	Own a Dog
315	Power Boating	319	Sailing
316	Own a CD Player	336	Travel in USA
317	Own a Cat		

Lifestyle Dimensions

Individual Household Level	$7.00/M Matches
Neighborhood Level	$3.00/M Input

Data Element No.	Description
271	**Domestic** (Checked off three or more) • Crafts • Gourmet Cooking/Fine Foods • Home Workshop • Needlework/Knitting • Sewing • Gardening • House Plants • Book Reading
272	**Do-It-Yourself** (Checked off two or more with at least one being*) • Automotive Work* • Motorcycling • Recreational Vehicles • Electronics* • Home Workshop*
273	**Fitness** (Checked off two or more with at least one being*) • Bicycling • Running/Jogging • Health/Natural Foods • Self-Improvement • Physical Fitness/Exercise*
274	**Athletic** (Checked off two or more) • Bicycling • Running/Jogging • Golf • Snow Skiing • Tennis
275	**Outdoors** (Checked off three or more) • Boating/Sailing • Hunting/Shooting • Camping/Hiking • Motorcycling • Recreational Vehicles • Fishing
276	**Good Life** (Checked off three or more) • Cultural/Arts Events • Health/Natural Foods • Fashion Clothing • Home Furnishings/ Decorating • Gourmet Cooking/ Fine Foods • Wines • Foreign Travel
277	**Cultural** (Checked off two or more with at least one being *) • Collectibles/Collections • Crafts • Foreign Travel • Art/Antique Collecting* • Cultural/Art Events*
278	**Blue Chip** (Checked off two or more with at least one being *) • Real Estate Investments* • Community/Civic Activities • Self-Improvement • Stocks/Bonds Investments*
279	**Technology** (Checked off three or more) • Electronics • Stereo/Records/Tapes/CDs • Photography • Home Video Recording • Video Games • Science/New Technology • Home/Personal Computers

Data Categories

Lifestyle Composites

| Individual Household Level | $7.00/M Matches |
| Neighborhool Level | $3.00/M Input |

Data Element
No.   Description

263   Collector
(Checked off two or more)
- Art/Antique Collecting   • Collectibles/Collections
- Stamp/Coin Collecting

264   Handicrafts
(Checked off two or more)
- Crafts   • Sewing
- Needlework/Knitting

320   Club Sports
(Checked off two or more)
- Bicycling   • Snow Skiing
- Tennis

321   Traditionalist
(Checked off two or more)
- Bible/Devotional   • Sweepstakes/Contests
  Reading   • Health/Natural Foods
- Grandchildren   • Stamps/Coin Collecting
- Our Nation's Heritage

322   Professional
(Checked off two or more)
- Career-Oriented Activities   • Self-Improvement
- Money Making Opportunities

323   Investor
(Checked off two or more)
- Real Estate Investments
- Stock/Bond Investments
- Money Making Opportunities

324   Audio/Visual
(Checked off two or more)
- Cable TV Viewing   • Home Video Recording
- Stereo/Records/   • Own a CD Player
  Tapes/CDs   • Buy Pre-Recorded Videos
- Home Video Games   • Photography

325   Campgrounder
(Checked off two or more)
- Boating/Sailing   • Motorcycling
- Camping/Hiking   • Recreational Vehicles

326   Intelligentsia
(Checked off three or more)
- Cultural/Arts Events   • Art/Antique Collecting
- Book Reading   • Community/Civic
- Current Affairs/Politics   Activities
- Foreign Travel

327   Mechanic
(Checked off two or more)
- Electronics   • Automotive Work
- Home Workshop   • Motorcycling

329   Chiphead
(Checked off two or more)
- Electronics   • Personal/Home Computers
- Science/   • Home Video Games
  New Technology

330   Home & Garden
(Checked off two or more)
- Gardening   • Home Workshop
- Home Furnishings/   • Household Pets
- Decorating   • House Plants

331   Triathlete
(Checked off two or more)
- Bicycling   • Health/Natural Foods
- Physical Fitness/   • Running/Jogging
  Exercise   • Walking for Health

Data Element
No.   Description

332   Connoisseur
(Checked off two or more)
- Cultural/Arts Events   • Foreign Travel
- Gourmet Cooking/   • Wines
- Fine foods

333   Ecologist
(Checked off two or more)
- Our Nation's Heritage   • Science/
- Wildlife/   New Technology
  Environmental Issues

334   TV Guide
(Checked off two or more)
- Cable TV Viewing   • Buy Pre-recorded
- Golf   Videos
- Home Video Recording   • Watching Sports on TV

335   Field & Stream
(Checked off two or more)
- Boating/Sailing   • Fishing
- Hunting/Shooting

Price Structure for "Lifestyle Coding" Customer Files

Prices per thousand input records for individual household level and neighborhood level data. Lifestyle coding includes lifestyle data, lifestyle dimensions, lifestyle composites.

Input File Quantity	All Lifestyles	20 Selected Lifestyles	10 Selected Lifestyles
Under 1.0MM	$30.00/M	$20.00/M	$15.00/M
1.0MM-1.9MM	$25.00/M	$17.00/M	$13.00/M
2.0MM-3.9MM	$20.00/M	$15.00/M	$11.00/M
4.0MM-4.9MM	$17.00/M	$12.00/M	$9.00/M
5.0MM Plus	$15.00/M	$10.00/M	$7.00/M

Minimum order $1,500.00

*Additional $1.00/M input processing charge for neighborhood level data.

13

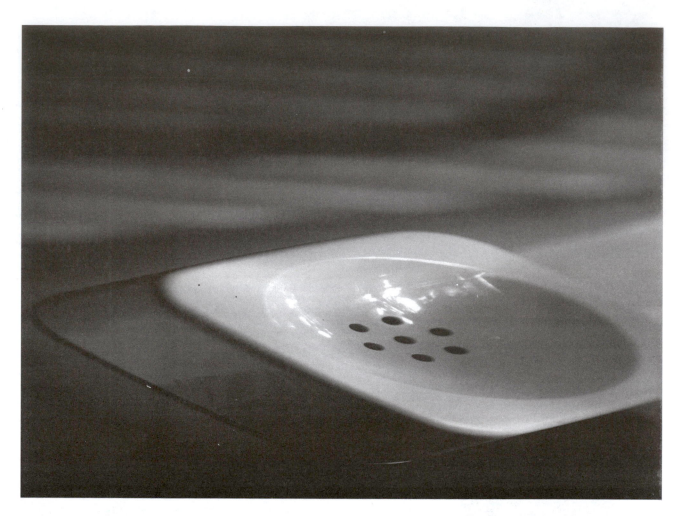

With nearly twice the phone numbers of our closest competitor (140+ million), IBTeleSource can help you reach more of the customers and prospects you have been looking for.

Accuracy and recency is maintained by bringing together five of the top data contributors in the industry through continual updates and verifications using a variety of proprietary technologies.

IBTeleSource has the solution whether you need telephone numbers instantly, same day, or overnight.

Data

- 130 Million Residences
- 14 Million Businesses
- Telephone White Pages
- Polk – Multilple Sources
- Targus – Most all Billable Telephone Numbers
- Area Code Changes

14

Features	Delivery	Applications
• Telephone Append • Telephone Confirmation • Reverse Append • Area Code Correction • Name Append • Private Flag • Time Zones • DMA, Florida, and Oregon Suppressions	• Batch – Processing in as little as 24 hours • Express – Automated same day service • On-Line – Interactive sub-second response • Tape-to-Tape, Modem, and Dedicated Access	• New numbers for telemarketing • Confirm customer telephone numbers • Create direct mail campaigns from customer and prospect telephone numbers • In-bound call center solutions

IB TeleSource

IB TeleSource Batch

Phone Append $60.00
Residential telephone number appending based on a name/
address match.
- Over 105 million telephone numbers
- Provides the DMA Telephone Preference Service and
  Mail Preference Service indicators, the Florida and
  Oregon do not call indicators, and Time Zone codes
- 24-Hour capability

Private Phone Indicator $100.00
Option to append private telephone indicator to eliminate
costly manual/EDA lookups.
- 24-Hour capability

Phone Append Plus $60.00
Residential telephone number appending based on a name/
address or address only match.
- Over 125 million telephone numbers
- Provides the DMA Telephone Preference Service and
  Mail Preference Service indicators, the Florida and
  Oregon do not call indicators, and Time Zone codes
- Option to append private telephone indicator to eliminate
  costly manual/EDA lookups
- 24-Hour capability

Confirmation $30.00
For files with residential telephone numbers IB TeleSource
will match on telephone and confirm that the telephone
number is current at the address.
- Over 125 million telephone numbers
- Area Code Correction applied to customer telephone
  numbers
- Confirmed telephone numbers are appended with the
  DMA Telephone Preference Service and Mail Preference
  Service indicators, the Florida and Oregon do not call
  indicators, Time Zone codes, and private telephone
  indicator
- Non-confirmed records are processed through Phone
  Append (see above)
- 24-Hour capability

Confirmation Plus $30.00
For files with residential telephone numbers IB TeleSource
will match on telephone and confirm that the telephone
number is current at the address.
- Over 125 million telephone numbers
- Area Code Correction applied to customer telephone
  numbers
- Confirmed telephone numbers are appended with the
  DMA Telephone Preference Service and Mail Preference
  Service indicators, the Florida and Oregon do not call
  indicators, Time Zone codes, and private phone indicator
- Non-confirmed records are processed through Phone
  Append Plus (see above)
- 24-Hour capability

Reverse Append $60.00
Residential name/address appending based on a 10 digit
telephone number match.
- Over 105 million telephone numbers
- Provides the DMA Telephone Preference Service and
  Mail Preference Service indicators, the Florida and
  Oregon do not call indicators, Time Zone codes, and
  private telephone indicator
- 24-Hour capability

Reverse Append Plus $60.00
Residential name/address and address only appending
based on a 10 digit telephone number match.
- Over 125 million telephone numbers
- Provides the DMA Telephone Preference Service and
  Mail Preference Service indicators, the Florida and
  Oregon do not call indicators, Time Zone codes, and
  private telephone indicator
- 24-Hour capability

TeleSource Name Append $60.00
Residential name appending based on an address match.
- Update old or incomplete files
- 24-Hour capability

Area Code Correction $1.50/M Input
                                              $250 for Area Correction File
Update Area Codes as splits occur across the country.
- 12 month history of splits maintained on the database

Business Append $60.00
Business telephone number appending based on a name/
address match.
- Over 15 million telephone numbers
- Provides business do not solicit indicators, FIPS codes,
  Census Tract and Block, and Time Zone codes
- 24-Hour Capability

Business Reverse Append $60.00
Business name/address appending based on a 10 digit
telephone number match.
- Over 15 million telephone numbers
- Provides business do not solicit indicators, FIPS codes,
  Census Tract and Block, and Time Zone codes
- 24-Hour Capability

> **Input Data Media**
> 9-Track tape 1600 – 6250 bpi
> 3480 IBM cartridge
> 3.5 diskette
> Modem transfer

ᴵᴮ**TeleSource**

ᴵᴮTeleSource Express

Description	Price per Match

ᴵᴮTeleSource Express Append   **$.13**
Residential telephone appending based on a name/address match.

- Over 105 million telephone numbers
- Files up to 100,000 records
- Provides the DMA Telephone Preference Service and Mail Preference Service indicators, the Florida and Oregon do not call indicators
- Automated same day capability

ᴵᴮTeleSource Express Reverse Append   **$.10**
Residential and business name/address and address only appending based on a 10 digit telephone number match.

- Over 125 million telephone numbers
- Files up to 100,000 records
- Provides the DMA Telephone Preference Service and Mail Preference Service indicators, the Florida and Oregon do not call indicators
- Automated same day capability

ᴵᴮTeleSource On-Line

Description	Price per Match

ᴵᴮTeleSource On-Line Phone Append   **$.22**
Residential phone appending based on a name/address match.

- Over 105 million telephone numbers
- Provides the DMA Telephone Preference Service and Mail Preference Service indicators, the Florida and Oregon do not call indicators
- Sub-second interactive processing

ᴵᴮTeleSource On-Line Reverse Append   **$.18**
Residential and business name/address and address only appending based on a 10 digit telephone number match.

- Over 125 million telephone numbers
- Provides the DMA Telephone Preference Service and Mail Preference Service indicators, the Florida and Oregon do not call indicators
- Sub-second interactive processing

Connectivity Options	
Protocols:	Networks:
TCP/IP	CompuServe
SNA/LU6.2	Advantis
SNA/LU2	AT&T
X.25	MCI

On-Line Services

| nfoBase's On-line services have a wide degree of applicability in multiple industries. Uses range from simple access to one service to more complex decision support systems that include multiple services. Customers use InfoBase's On-line services to support many applications including skiptracing, insurance underwriting, direct marketing, directory assistance, and fraud identification.

Benefits

The most comprehensive and current information available in the U.S.

- Sub-second access 24 hours a day, 7 days a week.
- Direct integration into your business systems.
- Flexible network communications for easy connectivity.

18

Facts

An extensive data warehouse containing 95 percent of all households in the U.S. offers complete coverage for your information needs.

- Find the information on the consumers you need.
- Prevent costly downstream processing errors in handling information about your customers by verifying information as it is captured.
- Reduce the possibility of a fraudulent transaction entering the system.

Connectivity Options

InfoBase's On-line Services are available through our Information Gateway providing the most flexible and reliable access anywhere.

- Connect with your current communication protocol.
- Connection sizing options assure required response times.
- Dual connections provide for maximum fault tolerance.

Express Processing

Access to most applications is also provided through a batch file processing front-end. This automated Express Batch service is designed to process files within hours.

- Files can be transmitted 24 hours a day.
- Processing begins as soon as a file is received.
- Customer is notified when the processing is complete.
- Performance reports are generated and returned with the output file.

On-Line Services

Products

Description	Price per Match

Reverse Phone Append On-line: $.18
Express: $.10

Appends name and address information to incoming telephone numbers. Acxiom's telephone number database contains over 120 million consumer, 12 million Canadian and over 15 million business telephone listings. Primary customers are large inbound call centers and information resellers.

Name and Address Matching On-line: $.22
Express: $.13

Appends telephone numbers and demographic information to incoming name and address records.

Change of Address On-line: $.07 per inquiry
Express: $.07 per inquiry

On-line access to a national change of address database compiled from magazine publishers, mail order firms, credit bureaus and others. This service is an on-line alternative to NCOA* which is restricted to batch use only.

DataQuick Property Search Call for Quote

Gateway access to DataQuick's national database of real property information. Search options include property address search, owner's name search, and property mailing address search.

Address Standardization/Geocoding Call for Quote

Interactive address standardization as well as the ability to append geocode information such as latitude, longitude, census track, block group, FIPS county code, and FIPS state code.

Description	Price

Trans Union Search Call for Quote

Gateway access to Trans Union's TRACE®, ReTRACE℠ and HAWK® Fraud Identification services.

Electronic Directory Assistance On-line: $.40 per inquiry
Express: $.40 per inquiry

Access to the directory assistance databases of all Regional Bell Operating Companies (RBOCs) and other large independent telephone companies. Most RBOCs allow searching on both name/address and telephone number. Included are:
• Ameritech
• Bell Atlantic
• Bell South
• Cincinnati Bell
• NYNEX
• Pacific Telesis
• Southern New England Telephone
• Southwestern Bell
• US West

Volume discounts are available.

*Acxiom is a non-exclusive licensee of the USPS.

On-Line Services

Connectivity and Access Methods

InfoBase's information gateway supports a variety of communication protocols including TCP/IP, SNA, X.25, and others.

Networking Options

- **Internet**
  Can be used in some instances where privacy of data is not an issue.

- **Leased Lines**
  All sizes of leased lines (typically from 56 KB to T1 sized lines) are supported.

- **Value Added Networks** (i.e., Advantis, CompuServe)

Monthly Minimums

Description	Price
On-line	
Reverse Telephone Append (only)	$5,000
Other Products	$7,500
2 or more products	$10,000
Express	
Up to 10 Files Per Month*	
Files processed Monday - Friday	
Minimum per month	$2,500
Up to 20 Files Per Month*	
Files processed Monday - Friday	
Minimum per month	$5,000
Unlimited Files Per Month	
Files processed Monday - Sunday	
Minimum per month	$7,500

*Additional Express files processed will be billed a minimum of $300 per run.

Total matches per month will be used to calculate the per match price.

Both options require an annual agreement.

Acxiom has a research department made up of experienced statisticians and analysts. Using advanced segmentation and modeling techniques, in combination with expertise in the direct marketing field, our professionals can help you understand your customers, or achieve better response rates. The products research offers include Data Profile Analysis, CHAID, and Regression Analysis.

Match Rate Report

Shows a customer how much data is available from the $_{IB}$Consumer InfoBase Database. A powerful program counts occurrences of data items to generate the Match Rate Report.

Analytical Products

Data Profile Analysis	CHAID	Regression
A special reference file can be provided by you, the customer, or one can be created from the $_{IB}$Consumer InfoBase Database using selected geographic and/ or demographic data.	CHAID Analysis examines a customer list, separates the file into groups most likely to respond, and describes the key characteristics of each group.	A predictive modeling technique that ranks customers or non-customers as to their likelihood of responding to a specific promotion.

Analytical Products

Match Rate Report

Data Element	
No.	Description

R1 **Match Rate Report**

Shows a customer how much data is available from the ₁ᵦConsumer InfoBase Database. A powerful program counts occurrences of data items to generate the Match Rate Report.

This is an inexpensive way to generate demographic reports without buying data. In most cases the fee for generating a Match Rate Report will be credited if data is later purchased. Send a name and address file to Acxiom for enhancement with demographic data from ₁ᵦConsumer InfoBase Database.

Summary Page	$150.00
Full Report	$500.00

Data Profile Analysis (DPA)

Data Element		
No.	Description	Price

Data Profile Analysis

Compares customers to prospects, or compares any two files, without purchasing data.

Excellent tool for getting a jump-start on targeting a model or for understanding customers better. The DPA is used by publishers to understand circulation base, catalogers to understand responders, telecommunications companies to understand high toll customers, and financial services companies to understand loyalty and multi-product use.

Send name and address files for customer and prospects, or any two files, to Acxiom for enhancement with demographic data. If a comparison file is not available, a reference file can be composed from ₁ᵦConsumer InfoBase Database.

R2 **Data Profile Analysis–** $2,800.00
National Reference File (includes Match Report) Compares customer file to the ₁ᵦConsumer InfoBase National Reference File.

R3 **Data Profile Analysis–** $3,300.00
Special Reference File (includes Match Report) Compares customer file to any special reference file other than the ₁ᵦConsumer InfoBase National Reference file (e.g. geographic area, other customer segments, etc.)

Analytical Products

CHAID Analysis

Data Element

No.	Description	Price

R4 **CHAID**   Call for quote
(Chi Square Automatic Interaction Detector)
Identifies market segments using a statistical technique
called CHAID. Combinations of demographic and
customer data are tested by CHAID to identify the
segmentation that "best" achieves the business
objective.

Segments are defined by a simple set of characteristics
that can be interpreted and also can be used to prioritize or select names for upcoming promotions. CHAID is
more sophisticated than a DPA because it considers
combinations of data items. Send mail and response
files, or any two files, to Acxiom to build the CHAID.
Demographic data from the $_{IB}$Consumer InfoBase
Database or data from the customer can be included in
the segmentation.

Scoring Analysis - Regression

Data Element

No.	Description	Price

R5 **Regression Analysis**   Call for quote
Enables a customer to prioritize and select names. By
converting data items into numbers, it is possible to
compare two or more prospects based on their
potential. Based on Regression Analysis techniques,
this tool is a highly sophisticated way to analyze
demographic and customer data.

Regression Models aren't as easy to interpret as the
CHAID, but generally it is the most powerful way to
identify the "best" prospects. Send mail and response
files, or any two files, to Acxiom to build a Regression
Model. Demographic data from $_{IB}$Consumer InfoBase
or data from the customer can be included in the
model.

Other Products And Services

Area Level Data

Data Element No.	Description		Price
P5	**GeoCodes Only**	$500 (min.)	$2.50/M input
	GeoPlus (GeoCodes and SMACS)		$3.50/M input

GeoPlus is a software system developed by Polk which will append the following census geo-data elements to a name and address record:

- FIPS State Code
- Census Tract Number
- Confidence Code
- FIPS MCD/CCD
- FIPS Place/CPD Code
- MSA Code
- Census MCD/CCD
- Census Place Code
- FIPS County Code
- Block Group Number
- Small Area Characteristics (SMACS)

If only selected items are desired, $1.00/M additional charge applies.

The GeoPlus System contains information for all of the U.S. but not its territories or possessions.

P7	**Carrier Route Marketing**	$750 (min.)	$3.50/M input
	Information (CRMI)		

Polk builds the CRMI file from over a billion data records each year. The TotaList file sources, plus ethnic and religious lists, are cross-referenced with the U.S. Census information to create this dynamic source.

P8	**The Neighborhood Selector**	$750 (min.)	$4.50/M input

The TNS file is a carrier route based file developed by Polk. This file describes the demographic and lifestyle characteristics of U.S. Postal Service Carrier Routes. The information used to create this file is generated from The Lifestyle Selector individual level data, which is then aggregated to the carrier route level.

Ethnic Codes

Data Element No.	Description		Price
962	**Ethnic Coding**	$300 (min.)	$10.00/M matches

An ascribed data element based on the surname of the individual.

A = American	O = Oriental
H = Hispanic	S = Scottish/Irish
F = French	N = Northern European
I = Italian	J = Jewish
G = German	R = Arab

Market Segmentation Services

Individual Level

Data Element No.	Description	Price
841	**SOLO®**	$60.00/M matches

SOLO is a unique segmentation system using Trans Union data. Individual level spending and payment data along with other socio-economic and demographic characteristics are used to group people into 40 distinct clusters. SOLO targets only those individuals most likely to respond to your offer.

Household Level

Data Element No.	Description	Price
459	**Lifestages Segmentation Codes with Purchase of Bundled Premier**	$10.00/M input
460	**Lifestages Segmentation Codes without Purchase of Bundled Premier**	$34.00/M input

An easy-to-use segmentation system using all the features and multi-source power of individual household level InfoBase Premier Data. 42 major life segments and 252 sub-segments. Based on the following six key data variables:

- Age
- Income
- Marital Status
- Number of Adults
- Presence of Children
- Work Status

Area Level

Data Element No.	Description		Price
365	**MicroVision**	$750 (min.)	$1.50/M input (licensee)
			$55.00/M input (non-licensee)

Classifies households into market segments based on demographic, socio-economic, and housing characteristics at the ZIP+4 level. (File must be ZIP+4 coded before MicroVision codes can be applied. See Element P10.)
*** Please contact your data consultant for license information**.

831	**PORTRAIT**	$40.00/M matches

PORTRAIT is Trans Union's newest market segmentation system that incorporates aggregated credit data with geodemographic information to help marketers target and define neighborhoods. PORTRAIT consists of 32 unique clusters, targeting diverse buying forces, that frame 7.5 million blocks of the United States. PORTRAIT can be used for a store site selection, target marketing, list segmentation, cross-sell opportunities and more. PORTRAIT is available to select names or to be overlaid onto a file.

P6	**PRIZM**	$750 (min.)	$1.50/M input (licensee)
			$45.00/M input (non-licensee)

Geo-demographic segmentation codes that classify all U.S. neighborhoods into 62 unique neighborhood types based on ZIP+4 information. Available at ZIP+4, ZIP, Census Tract, and Block group levels.
*** Please contact your data consultant for license information**.

P15	**PRIZM Social**	$750 (min.)	$1.50/M licensee
	Groups (Claritas)		$15.00/M non-licensee

Codes that classify all U.S. neighborhoods into 15 unique social groups based on ZIP+4 information. Groupings are based on affluence and urbanization.
*** Please contact your data consultant for license information**.

S4	**Hispanic Portraits**	$30.00/M matches

Hispanic Portraits is the first lifestyle segmentation product built specifically for micromarketers interested in the Hispanic consumer market in the United States. It features 18 lifestyle clusters and offers marketers the opportunity to define the Hispanic marketplace along ethnic lines.

S5	**ClusterPLUS 2000**	$10.00/M matches

ClusterPLUS 2000 classifies U.S. neighborhoods (blocks and block groups) and postal areas (ZIP Codes and ZIP+4s) into 60 unique lifestyles, and five urbanicity groups with a sixth group, Group Quarters.

Products and Services

List Cleaning

Data Element No.	Description		Price

P3   **NCOA Address** $750 (min.) $2.95/M input
Standardization and Forwarding Address
NCOA Nixie Matches $15.00/M matches
NCOA is the U.S. Postal Service's National Change of Address service. It represents a timely and cost-efficient way to increase the accuracy of a file and reduce undeliverables. NCOA contains records for all the permanent change of address records filed with the U.S. Postal Service in the last 36 months– giving you access to the most current consumer and business addresses available. Besides providing a forwarding address, the NCOA process also corrects five-digit ZIP Codes, standard- izes addresses and applies ZIP+4 Codes. The file is updated bi- monthly.

NCOA Nixie Matches indicate that a move has occurred or the address is no longer deliverable. A forwarding address is not included.

P16   **ChangePlus®** $750 (min.) $5.00/M input
The ChangePlus system is a combination of National Change of Address File (NCOA) and Polk's Address Change Service (PACS). These are change of address files that can be used by mailers to obtain forwarding address information on their customers.

P4   **AddressAbility®** $500 (min.) $2.00/M input
- Verifies and corrects five-digit ZIP Codes.
- Overlays the correct ZIP+4 and associated carrier route codes to each output record.
- Passes and standardizes addresses according to postal service specifications.
- Standardizes city names and state abbreviations.

P10   **ZIP+4 Coding** $300 (min.) $2.00/M input
Prepares your file to take advantage of postal presort discount and faster delivery.

P13   **Deceased Suppression** $300 (min.) $50/M matches
This service will flag names of deceased, or return your file with those names deleted.

P17   **Delivery Sequence File** $750 (min.) $2.95/M input
The DSF is provided by the U.S. Postal Service and contains valid addresses serviced by the Postal Service. This compre- hensive system eliminates undeliverable addresses, allows mailers to obtain walk sequence discounts, and provides valuable information about each matched delivery point on your files.

Geographical Data

We deliver the most complete source of geographical data for spatial applications from Geographic Data Technology (GDT). GDT is the leading supplier of geographical data for your Mapping, GIS and other spatial applications. These data allow you to spatially enable your database for a variety of marketing and business related applications. To maintain the quality of the data, continual National updates are performed quarterly.

G1   **Zip+6 Lat/Long** $10.00/M Matches

G2   **Zip+4 Lat/Long** $4.00/M Matches

G3   **Census Geocoding** $3.00/M Input
- Census Geographical Codes
- FIPS STATE
- FIPS COUNTY
- FIPS MCD
- PIPS PLACe
- Consolidated Metropolitan Statistical Area
- Metropolitan Statistical Area
- Census State
- Census County
- Census Tract
- Census Block Group
- Census Block
- Census Place
- Census MCD
- Match Level Indicator
- Point Geographical Centroid
- ZIP Centroid
- ZIP+2 Centroid
- ZIP+4 Centroid
- ZIP+6 Centroid (Housetop)

This data enables such spatial applications as:
- Geographical Information Systems
- Customer Mapping
- Territory Alignment
- Site Selection
- Trade Area Analysis
- Routing Regulatory Compliance
- Spatial Query and Selections

How To Order

To Place an Order by Mail

1. Fill out the order form completely. (If you have any questions regarding this form, please feel free to call (501) 336-3600 and ask to speak with one of our data consultants.)

2. List the data element numbers of all data elements desired. (For example if you wish to select "Estimated income data from InfoBase Premier," you would list #641.)

3. Make sure you fill out each section, so that we will have all the information we need to process your order.

4. Sign page 3 of the order form on the line titled Authorized Signature.

5. Be sure to also sign the "Data Use Agreement" that you will find on page 4 of the order form.

When you have completed the order form, send it with your record layout and printout of 100 sample records to:

Acxiom Corporation
Deliver to: Data Processing, Project: InfoBase
301 Industrial Boulevard
Conway, AR 72032

If your order is more complex or if you would like to discuss special processing options, please phone us between 9:00 a.m. and 5:00 p.m., Central Standard Time, at (501) 336-3600 and ask for one of our data consultants. We'll be glad to discuss your needs with you.

Scheduling

Standard ᵢᵦ**Consumer InfoBase** processing takes place nightly and will be shipped to you within three to four business days.

When ᵢᵦConsumer InfoBase is used in conjunction with research or other list services, additional time is required. Your data consultant can assist you in developing a schedule that meets your needs.

Standard ᵢᵦ**TeleSource** processing takes place nightly and will be shipped to you the following business day.

ACXIOM®
InfoBase

Acxiom Corporation
301 Industrial Boulevard
P.O. Box 2000
Conway, AR 72033-2000
1-888-3ACXIOM
1-888-322-9466
WWW:
http://www.acxiom.com
E-mail: info@acxiom.com

NEW YORK OFFICE:
441 Lexington Avenue, 18th
Floor
New York, New York 10017-
3910
212-983-0154

Fall 1997

Experian Information Services

Catalog of Consumer Lists and Processing Services

For next-day service, use our electronic delivery–it's fast and easy

Dear Friend,

Someone once said the only thing certain in life is change. For us, this old saying has never been more true -- starting with our recent acquisition of Direct Marketing Technology. Together we continue to blend our separate capabilities into a single, seamless operation that combines Experian's direct marketing business with Direct Tech's state-of-the-art processing technology. This acquisition is just one example of how we're changing to better serve our customers. As we move forward through 1997 and into '98, we will continue to build a stronger Experian through quality products and services dedicated to helping you, our valued customer.

Direct Tech Adds "Punch" to Our Processing

As I mentioned, the addition of Direct Tech to the Experian family has been a major change -- and it's producing major results. For example, our new List Rental Fulfillment capabilities are a direct result of our teaming Experian's marketing data on 90 million households with Direct Tech's advanced processing technology. Our combined strengths give us the the best "one-two punch" in the industry, and further demonstrate Experian's commitment to its customers and the direct marketing business.

List Rental Fulfillment Available to List Owners & Managers

You asked for it. Now you've got it. We've added a complete line of list rental fulfillment services. From enhancing your database to fulfilling the orders, we now have the data and processing capabilities to handle your job -- whatever its size. Ask your Experian Account Representative for more information about this new service.

Electronic Delivery

Thank goodness for modern technology! Now you can download your orders directly to your PC via our electronic bulletin board delivery service. It's fast and easy!

We're excited about the many changes taking place at Experian. We hope you are, too! As always, let us know how we're doing. You can call us at 1 800 527 3933.

Sincerely,

Raelyn Wade

Raelyn Wade, Director of Sales

Fall 1997

experían

Table of Contents

Experian Information Services – Fall 1997

Make Experian your preferred source for lists.

You have many choices when selecting a source for your list rentals. Take a closer look at how Experian brings both quality and quantity list selections to the discriminating marketer.

We Have the Names You Want

Experian's flexible list selections help you reach the targeted group you want. More than 160 million consumers are available on our Consumer Database, easily segmented by multiple selects.

Comprehensive data makes it easy for you to reach your desired market segment:

Families with children We have the most comprehensive children's data anywhere -- more than 25 million households with children or young adults from birth to 25 years old.

New Movers Reach the hottest buyers when their propensity to buy is strongest.

Homeowners Multiple selects, including purchase transactions, make it easy to select out of nearly 23 million homeowners, those most in need of your product or service.

Motor vehicle owners Get comprehensive data on 121 million vehicles. Select households by 20 specific vehicle characteristics.

Modeled vehicle data Replicate the predictive power of vehicle registration data in states that restrict the use of this data for marketing purposes.

Likely credit card responders Extend likely prospects an offer to apply for a new credit card.

Ethnic populations Reach consumers in specific ethnic groups with special offers of interest. Our Asian Database accurately targets Chinese, Japanese, Korean and Vietnamese consumers.

Lifestyle indicators Understand your customers better and find more just like them. Two distinctly different geodemographic classification systems - U.S. MOSAIC and Experian Smart Targeting Tools℠ - differentiate households by lifestyle, product preference and interests.

Financial lifestyle indicator Experian/P$YCLE Financial Markets uses socio-economic factors to identify patterns of consumer financial behavior.

Radius marketing Experian's sophisticated geographic segmentation identifies the best prospects surrounding your locale. You specify the business locations which will serve as a reference point and the distance around those locations you want to explore. Then we quickly and accurately locate prospects within that radius.

Experian PerformanceData℠ System

The Experian PerformanceData℠ System is the centerpiece of our consumer list services. It combines the best of compiled and response lists into a performance list. We offer you an up-to-date source of names with the size and concentration of a compiled list, coupled with the purchasing power characteristics of a response file.

How do we do that? We start with our foundation of public record files, consumer credit names and addresses, and demographic data, then we add fresh data from questionnaires, product registration cards, publications, direct mail, real estate deed recordings, birth records, tax assessor files, white pages, and the U.S. census.

We double-verify names at the individual level to ensure improved quality with maximum selectivity. Plus you can choose from 160 million consumers in approximately 90 million households.

DASD Platform

The Experian PerformanceData℠ System physically stores data on DASD – Direct Access Storage Device. This foundation allows for continual updates, giving you fresh data with improved currency.

Accurate Household Status Coding

The Experian household methodology is unique...and more precise than our competitors'. Using precise household coding, we determine family relationships based on tighter age and gender criteria. You can accurately target young adults living with their parents, elderly parents living with their children, and married couples with children.

America's Premier Age Database

Experian has the broadest, most accurate exact age information available. We have exact age on 122 million individuals. The Experian Inferred Age model provides a reliable predictor of age range when exact age is unknown. Our age model applies advanced statistical techniques along with census level demographics, age information on other household members, presence of children, and other variables.

Income Options

Experian offers you not only accurate household income estimations, but you can also select income by geographic percentile. Our Estimated Income model uses census demographics, individual demographic data, and aggregated household financial data to predict income. If you're trying to reach a certain income niche but don't know what specific income level to select for each area, our Geographic Income Percentile lets you select a level of affluence by percentile within a county or across the nation.

Broad Selectivity

The Experian PerformanceData℠ System provides a wide variety of demographic selects for maximum targeting. Customize your next list by selecting:

- Age (exact or inferred)
- Length of residence
- Gender
- Dwelling type
- Marital status
- Telephone numbers
- Household status
- Direct mail responders
- Presence of children
- Ethnicity
- Census data
- Homeowners
- Geographic (state, ZIP, SCF, etc.)
- Families with children by age and gender
- PC owners
- Home businesses
- Estimated household income
- Geographic income percentile
- U.S. MOSAIC clusters
- PRIZM® (Claritas) clusters
- Radius marketing

Fast Service -- When You Want It

Experian makes sure you get your list when you need it. For the fastest delivery available, try our electronic delivery service. Most list orders received by 5 PM CST will be available the next day for downloading from the Experian Bulletin Board. For standard shipping, most list orders received by 5 PM CST will be shipped the next day. Express service orders received by 10 AM CST are on their way to you the same day.

Fall 1997

A Commitment To Deliverability

A list is only as good as its address quality. We're committed to first-class deliverability and we do what's necessary to ensure your offer gets to the right mailbox.

To ensure maximum deliverability, Experian takes these steps:

■ Lists are updated monthly instead of quarterly.

■ Every new record added to the Experian PerformanceData℠ System is address standardized, ZIP corrected, and ZIP+4 coded.

■ Frequent address hygiene, including NCOA* and LACS processing, ensures Coding Accuracy Support System (CASS) certified address quality.

■ All names are verified at both the individual and household level by at least two sources.

■ Multiple suppression file processing eliminates deceased individuals, prison and jail addresses, and persons who do not wish to receive direct mail offers.

Enhancement and File Cleaning Services

In addition to comprehensive list offerings, Experian provides the quality enhancement and file cleaning services integral to every successful direct marketing campaign. Experian is equipped to process both low and high volume jobs. Our data center operates all day, every day of the year. Our round-the-clock operations and sophisticated hardware mean reliable, competitive turnaround for you.

We are licensed by the United States Postal Service (USPS) and are regularly audited by the USPS to verify that our processes meet standards and specifications. We presort your mailing using CASS certified software to qualify for postal discounts.

Count on us to deliver these services efficiently and accurately:

■ Address Cleaning

■ Enhancement Services

    ■ Demographic Data Overlay

    ■ Segmentation

    ■ Geo Coding

    ■ Telephone Number Append

■ NCOA, LACS, Nixie, and COA

■ Merge Purge

■ Postal Qualification

■ Experian Customer Link℠

Respect For Consumer Privacy

Experian endorses the Direct Marketing Association's Fair Information Practices guidelines. Experian policies and procedures meet or exceed each of the DMA's recommended practices. Experian makes standard use of its own in-house suppression files, the DMA Mail and Telephone Preference files, and other consumer-requested suppression files. We encourage the appropriate use of consumer disclosure and opt-out options.

P$YCLE® is a registered trademark of Claritas, Inc.
*Experian is a non-exclusive licensee of the USPS.

Experian Consumer Database

This file is composed of records on more than 160 million consumers in approximately 90 million households nationwide. You can demographically segment any portion of the list to reach the best prospects for your products or services.

Target people by exact age, gender, estimated household income, marital status, dwelling type, families with children, telephone numbers, household status, and a variety of other selections. The vast quantity of names on this database and its varied selection capabilities make this one of the largest and most flexible lists on the market today.

Information on this file is processed through National Change of Address[1] (NCOA) monthly and all names are ZIP+4 coded and reported by two or more sources.

Test these popular consumer market segments:

- *Young adults living at home*
- *Married with children*
- *Affluent households*
- *Homeowners*
- *Active seniors*
- *Hispanic households*

Demographic Selects   Price

All select charges apply in addition to the Base Price.

Exact age	$13/M
Combined exact and inferred age (ranges 18-35, 36-49, 50-64, 65+)	$7.75/M
Gender	$2.50/M
Telephone numbers	$8/M
Head of household	N/C
Household status (wife, elderly parent, young adult)	$2.50/M
Married	$2.50/M
Presence of children	$6.50/M
Families with children (by age and/or gender)	$7.50/M
Homeowners	$5/M
PC owners	$6/M
Home businesses	$12/M
Estimated HH income ($0-99K)	$5/M
Estimated HH income ($100K+)	$10/M
Geographic income percentile	$3.50/M
Length of residence	$2.50/M
Ethnicity	$10/M
Direct mail responders	$5/M
Dwelling type	N/C
1990 census data	$2/M
Geographic (state, ZIP, SCF, county, MSA, DMA, census tract/BG)	$2/M
Radius marketing	(call for custom quote)

Vital Statistics Selects   Price

Corrective lenses	$10/M
Height/Weight	$10/M

Neighborhood Selects   Price

U.S. MOSAIC	$10/M
PRIZM® (Claritas)	$10/M
Maximum list charge	$80/M

Total Count
161,235,677

Base Price
$25/M

Source
Public Records

Minimum Order
$250 net
Includes all select charges. Extra charge for unlimited usage, copies, tapes & freight

Updated Monthly
with CASS certified software

Delivery
Next day or same day. Electronic delivery available!

Call for on-line counts and quantity discounts

---

[1]Experian is a non-exclusive licensee of the United States Postal Service. Names and addresses owned by Experian are processed through the NCOA system. Matches to the NCOA file are included in the Experian Consumer Database.

Fall 1997

Experian Consumer Database

A fresh, accurate source of prospect names.

Experian believes the information concerning these names to be accurate, but cannot guarantee their accuracy or the outcome of the mailing. Information on this file is updated monthly and the counts for particular elements are subject to change.

Contact
Experian
701 Experian Parkway
Allen, Texas 75013-3714
800 527 3933
972 390 5000
FAX 972 390 5100

Commission Policy
Trade and volume discounts available to all qualified brokers.

Rental Policy
All names ordered/processed are for **one-time use**; for subsequent usage/unlimited usage, call for pricing. Tape for prior order suppression is $25 flat.

Format	Price
4-up Cheshire labels	N/C
4-up pressure sensitive labels	
Under 50M	$6/M
Over 50M	$5/M
1-up pressure sensitive labels	$10/M
3 x 5 cards (1-up)	$15/M
Mag tape 9T 1600/6250 or cartridge, non-refundable	$15 each
Diskette	$20 each
CD-ROM	$35 each
Electronic delivery (quantity limits apply)	$50 flat
Bar coding	$.50/M
Key coding	$1/M
Keying month/year of birth	$1/M
Resequence/breaks	$1/M
Splits	$.50/M
Running charge	$5/M
Carrier route code with bar code	$2.50/M
Prioritizing	$2/M

experian

Mature Consumers
Experian Consumer Database

Today's senior market is the fastest growing segment of our society. Millions of Baby Boomers are joining the senior ranks as their ages reach the half-century mark.

Seniors are great prospects for travel opportunities, health and vision care services, insurance, investment offers, and smaller niche marketers who offer specialized products or services.

An often hidden segment of the mature market is elderly parents living with their children. Caretakers of elderly parents comprise an expanded market segment for items targeting older Americans. Target higher income households with elderly parents for cooking, housecleaning, and lawncare services.

These active Americans often have the time and income to support humanitarian and fund-raising causes. Remember, too, that mature Americans with grandchildren are excellent prospects for children's products.

Information on this file is processed through National Change of Address[1] (NCOA) monthly and all names are ZIP+4 coded and reported by two or more sources.

Suggested Applications:
- ■ *Travel offers*   ■ *Clothing, toys for grandchildren*   ■ *Insurance promotions*
- ■ *Retirement community offers*   ■ *Health and vision care*

Family Selects	**Price**
Elderly parents living with their children	$2.50/M

Demographic Selects	**Price**

All select charges apply in addition to the Base Price.

Exact age	$13/M
Combined exact and inferred age (ranges 18-35, 36-49, 50-64, 65+)	$7.75/M
Gender	$2.50/M
Telephone numbers	$8/M
Head of household	N/C
Household status (wife, young adult)	$2.50/M
Married	$2.50/M
Presence of children	$6.50/M
Families with children (by age and/or gender)	$7.50/M
Homeowners	$5/M
PC owners	$6/M
Home businesses	$12/M
Estimated HH income ($0-99K))	$5/M
Estimated HH income ($100K+)	$10/M
Geographic income percentile	$3.50/M
Length of residence	$2.50/M
Ethnicity	$10/M

Direct mail responders	$5/M
Dwelling type	N/C
1990 census data	$2/M
Geographic (state, ZIP, SCF, county, MSA, DMA, census tract/BG)	$2/M
Radius marketing	(call for custom quote)

Vital Statistics Selects	**Price**
Corrective lenses	$10/M
Height/Weight	$10/M

Neighborhood Selects	**Price**
U.S. MOSAIC	$10/M
PRIZM® (Claritas)	$10/M
Maximum list charge	$80/M

Total Count
42,657,302

Base Price
$25/M

Source
Public Records

Minimum Order
$250 net
Includes all select charges. Extra charge for unlimited usage, copies, tapes & freight

Updated Monthly
with CASS certified software

Delivery
Next day or same day. Electronic delivery available!

Call for on-line counts and quantity discounts

[1]Experian is a non-exclusive licensee of the United States Postal Service. Names and addresses owned by Experian are processed through the NCOA system. Matches to the NCOA file are included in the Experian Consumer Database.

Fall 1997

Tap into the growing senior market.

Experian believes the information concerning these names to be accurate, but cannot guarantee their accuracy or the outcome of the mailing. Information on this file is updated monthly and the counts for particular elements are subject to change.

Mature Consumers

Experian Consumer Database

Contact
Experian
701 Experian Parkway
Allen, Texas 75013-3714
800 527 3933
972 390 5000
FAX 972 390 5100

Commission Policy
Trade and volume discounts available to all qualified brokers.

Rental Policy
All names ordered/processed are for **one-time use**; for subsequent usage/unlimited usage, call for pricing. Tape for prior order suppression is $25 flat.

Format	Price
4-up Cheshire labels	N/C
4-up pressure sensitive labels	
Under 50M	$6/M
Over 50M	$5/M
1-up pressure sensitive labels	$10/M
3 x 5 cards (1-up)	$15/M
Mag tape 9T 1600/6250 or cartridge, non-refundable	$15 each
Diskette	$20 each
CD-ROM	$35 each
Electronic delivery (quantity limits apply)	$50 flat
Bar coding	$.50/M
Key coding	$1/M
Keying month/year of birth	$1/M
Resequence/breaks	$1/M
Splits	$.50/M
Running charge	$5/M
Carrier route code with bar code	$2.50/M
Prioritizing	$2/M

Fall 1997

Families With Children
Experian Consumer Database

Children of all ages influence household spending decisions. Target more than 25 million families with children by age and/or gender from birth through 25 years.

Parents of young children are good prospects for learning products, baby items, daycare services, school supplies, athletic shoes and clothing.

Don't overlook the lucrative teen market segment. Today's teens are entrusted with family money to purchase household items, and they often have their own income as well.

Among single 19-25 year-olds, one half of the men and one third of the women live at home. Households with young adults at home have a higher ratio of earners to dependents and spend 9% more than households with younger children.

Information on this file is processed through National Change of Address[1] (NCOA) monthly and all names are ZIP+4 coded and reported by two or more sources.

Test these market segments:

■ *Households with preschoolers*
■ *Households with young adults living at home*
■ *Homeowners with children*

Prior to receiving list orders segmented by presence of children, mailers must submit mail pieces to Experian for approval.

Family Selects	Price
Families with children (age and/or gender)	$7.50/M
Young adults living with their parents	$2.50/M
Presence of children	$6.50/M

Demographic Selects   Price
All select charges apply in addition to the Base Price.

Exact age	$13/M
Combined exact and inferred age (ranges 18-35, 36-49, 50-64, 65+)	$7.75/M
Gender	$2.50/M
Telephone numbers	$8/M
Head of household	N/C
Household status (wife, elderly parent)	$2.50/M
Married	$2.50/M
Homeowners	$5/M
PC owners	$6/M
Home businesses	$12/M
Estimated HH income ($0-99K))	$5/M
Estimated HH income ($100K+)	$10/M
Geographic income percentile	$3.50/M
Length of residence	$2.50/M
Ethnicity	$10/M

Direct mail responders	$5/M
Dwelling type	N/C
1990 census data	$2/M
Geographic (state, ZIP, SCF, county, MSA, DMA, census tract/BG)	$2/M
Radius marketing	(call for custom quote)

Vital Statistics Selects   Price
Corrective lenses	$10/M
Height/Weight	$10/M

Neighborhood Selects   Price
U.S. MOSAIC	$10/M
PRIZM® (Claritas)	$10/M
Maximum list charge	$80/M

Total Count
25,555,603 Households

Base Price
$25/M

Source
Public Records

Minimum Order
$250 net
Includes all select charges. Extra charge for unlimited usage, copies, tapes & freight

Updated Monthly *with CASS certified software*

Delivery *Next day or same day. Electronic delivery available!*

Call for on-line counts and quantity discounts

[1]Experian is a non-exclusive licensee of the United States Postal Service. Names and addresses owned by Experian are processed through the NCOA system. Matches to the NCOA file are included in the Experian Consumer Database.

Fall 1997

Families With Children
Experian Consumer Database

Contact
Experian
701 Experian Parkway
Allen, Texas 75013-3714
800 527 3933
972 390 5000
FAX 972 390 5100

Commission Policy
Trade and volume discounts available to all
qualified brokers.

Rental Policy
All names ordered/processed are for **one-time use**;
for subsequent usage/unlimited usage, call for
pricing. Tape for prior order suppression is $25 flat.

Format	Price
4-up Cheshire labels	N/C
4-up pressure sensitive labels	
Under 50M	$6/M
Over 50M	$5/M
1-up pressure sensitive labels	$10/M
3 x 5 cards (1-up)	$15/M
Mag tape 9T 1600/6250 or cartridge,	
non-refundable	$15 each
Diskette	$20 each
CD-ROM	$35 each
Electronic delivery (quantity limits apply)	$50 flat
Bar coding	$.50/M
Key coding	$1/M
Keying month/year of birth	$1/M
Resequence/breaks	$1/M
Splits	$.50/M
Running charge	$5/M
Carrier route code with bar code	$2.50/M
Prioritizing	$2/M

Experian Asian Database

Asian-Americans represent more than $100 billion in purchasing power. The Experian Asian Database, created with leading Asian marketing company Kang & Lee, helps open the door to this important marketplace.

The Experian Asian Database analyzes first and last names for more accurate targeting of consumers of Chinese, Japanese, Korean and Vietnamese descent. If both first and last name are not confirmed as being from the same ethnic group, the name falls under the 'Asian' selection.

This unique resource is derived from ethnic directories, subscription and membership lists, public records and compiled data.

Information on this file is processed through National Change of Address[1] (NCOA) monthly and all names are ZIP+4 coded and reported by two or more sources.

Suggested applications:

- *Advertising*
- *Books, magazines, newspapers*
- *Event planning*
- *Foods*
- *Fashion items*
- *Education programs*
- *Specialty retailers*

Asian Selects	Price
Asian	N/C
Specific ethnicity (Chinese, Japanese, Korean, Vietnamese)	$10/M

Demographic Selects	Price

All select charges apply in addition to the Base Price.

Exact age	$13/M
Combined exact and inferred age (ranges 18-35, 36-49, 50-64, 65+)	$7.75/M
Gender	$2.50/M
Telephone numbers	$8/M
Head of household	N/C
Household status (wife, elderly parent, young adult)	$2.50/M
Married	$2.50/M
Presence of children	$6.50/M
Families with children (by age and/or gender)	$7.50/M
Homeowners	$5/M
PC owners	$6/M
Home businesses	$12/M
Estimated HH income ($0-99K))	$5/M
Estimated HH income ($100K+)	$10/M
Geographic income percentile	$3.50/M

Length of residence	$2.50/M
Direct mail responders	$5/M
Dwelling type	N/C
1990 census data	$2/M
Geographic (state, ZIP, SCF, county, MSA, DMA, census tract/BG)	$2/M
Radius marketing	(call for custom quote)

Vital Statistics Selects	Price
Corrective lenses	$10/M
Height/Weight	$10/M

Neighborhood Selects	Price
U.S. MOSAIC	$10/M
PRIZM® (Claritas)	$10/M
Maximum list charge	$100/M

Total Count
1,153,404

Base Price
$45/M

Source
Ethnic directories, subscription and membership lists, public records and compiled data.

Minimum Order
5,000 names
Extra charge for copies, tapes & freight

Updated Monthly
with CASS certified software

Delivery
Next day or same day. Electronic delivery available!

Call for on-line counts and quantity discounts

---

[1]Experian is a non-exclusive licensee of the United States Postal Service. Names and addresses owned by Experian are processed through the NCOA system. Matches to the NCOA file are included in the Experian Asian Database.

Fall 1997

Experian Asian Database

Contact
Experian
701 Experian Parkway
Allen, Texas 75013-3714
800 527 3933
972 390 5000
FAX 972 390 5100

Commission Policy
Trade and volume discounts available to all qualified brokers.

Rental Policy
All names ordered/processed are for **one-time use**; for subsequent usage/unlimited usage, call for pricing. Tape for prior order suppression is $25 flat.

Format

Format	Price
4-up Cheshire labels	N/C
4-up pressure sensitive labels	
Under 50M	$6/M
Over 50M	$5/M
1-up pressure sensitive labels	$10/M
3 x 5 cards (1-up)	$15/M
Mag tape 9T 1600/6250 or cartridge, non-refundable	$15 each
Diskette	$20 each
CD-ROM	$35 each
Electronic delivery (quantity limits apply)	$50 flat
Bar coding	$.50/M
Key coding	$1/M
Keying month/year of birth	$1/M
Resequence/breaks	$1/M
Splits	$.50/M
Running charge	$5/M
Carrier route code with bar code	$2.50/M
Prioritizing	$2/M

experían

Experian Credit Card Markets Database

Finding consumers who respond to credit card offers is becoming a challenge. Over-solicitation and traditional targeting methods have lead to serious list fatigue. Many consumers, however, would love to get a credit card offer, and Experian Credit Card Markets helps you find them.

Jointly developed with Austin Logistics Inc., this demographic option predicts the likelihood of a consumer establishing a credit card relationship. Unlike traditional prescreen services, no credit information is used, so you can use Experian Credit Card Markets to reach prospects with an offer to apply.

Experian Credit Card Markets uses over 62 demographic characteristics to predict the probability of a consumer acquiring a credit card. It's ideal for financial product marketers offering bankcard alternatives such as unsecured lines of credit. It also offers new options to change-of-lifestyle marketers or direct marketers trying to reach likely credit card holders.

Information on this file is processed through National Change of Address[1] (NCOA) monthly and all names are ZIP+4 coded and reported by two or more sources.

Suggested applications:

- *Bankcards*
- *Gasoline credit cards*
- *Change-of-lifestyle products*
- *Retail cards*
- *Lines of credit*

Demographic Selects	Price
All select charges apply in addition to the Base Price.	
Exact age	.$13/M
Combined exact and inferred age (ranges 18-35, 36-49, 50-64, 65+)	.$7.75/M
Gender	.$2.50/M
Telephone numbers	.$8/M
Head of household	.N/C
Household status (wife, elderly parent, young adult)	.$2.50/M
Married	.$2.50/M
Presence of children	.$6.50/M
Families with children (by age and/or gender)	$7.50/M
Homeowners	.$5/M
PC owners	.$6/M
Home businesses	.$12/M
Estimated HH income ($0-99K)	.$5/M
Estimated HH income ($100K+)	.$10/M
Geographic income percentile	.$3.50/M
Length of residence	.$2.50/M
Ethnicity	.$10/M
Direct mail responders	.$5/M
Dwelling type	.N/C
1990 census data	.$2/M

Geographic (state, ZIP, SCF, county, MSA, DMA, census tract/BG)	.$2/M
Radius marketing	(call for custom quote)

Vital Statistics Selects	Price
Corrective lenses	.$10/M
Height/Weight	.$10/M

Neighborhood Selects	Price
U.S. MOSAIC	.$10/M
PRIZM® (Claritas)	.$10/M
Maximum list charge	.$100/M

Total Count
158,886,647

Base Price
$60/M

Source
Statistically derived from demographic, census and Experian consumer data

Minimum Order
5,000 names
Extra charge for copies, tapes & freight

Updated Monthly
with CASS certified software

Delivery
Next day or same day. Electronic delivery available!

Call for on-line counts and quantity discounts

[1]Experian is a non-exclusive licensee of the United States Postal Service. Names and addresses owned by Experian are processed through the NCOA system. Matches to the NCOA file are included in the Experian Credit Card Markets Database.

Fall 1997

Experian Credit Card Markets Database

Contact

Experian
701 Experian Parkway
Allen, Texas 75013-3714
800 527 3933
972 390 5000
FAX 972 390 5100

Commission Policy

Trade and volume discounts available to all qualified brokers.

Rental Policy

All names ordered/processed are for **one-time use**; for subsequent usage/unlimited usage, call for pricing. Tape for prior order suppression is $25 flat.

Format	Price
4-up Cheshire labels	N/C
4-up pressure sensitive labels	
Under 50M	$6/M
Over 50M	$5/M
1-up pressure sensitive labels	$10/M
3 x 5 cards (1-up)	$15/M
Mag tape 9T 1600/6250 or cartridge, non-refundable	$15 each
Diskette	$20 each
CD-ROM	$35 each
Electronic delivery (quantity limits apply)	$50 flat
Bar coding	$.50/M
Key coding	$1/M
Keying month/year of birth	$1/M
Resequence/breaks	$1/M
Splits	$.50/M
Running charge	$5/M
Carrier route code with bar code	$2.50/M
Prioritizing	$2/M

Fall 1997

Experian New Mover Database

Every year, nearly one in five Americans changes residence. New movers are eager to establish relationships with a wide range of local businesses. Reach out to this diverse, yet highly responsive, market with the Experian New Mover Database.

The Experian 30-Day New Mover list is available each month with a fresh source of recently reported new movers. Or, take advantage of the Experian 14-Day New Mover list and reach prospects weeks ahead of your competition! Both options assure you deliverable names and broad, in-depth coverage.

New movers are excellent prospects for household furnishings and appliances, home improvement offers, phone service, garden and workshop tools, insurance, local retail stores, banks, credit card organizations, catalogers, fund-raising associations, and restaurants.

Target new movers by distance of move, whether the move was local or out-of-state, or by type of dwelling moved from and to. Refine your prospect universe further with Experian demographic selects like age, estimated income and presence of children to target the right households for your offer.

Suggested applications:

- *Home improvement, furnishings*
- *Lawn tools and services*
- *Retail, restaurant promotions*
- *Newspaper/magazine offers*

New Mover Selects	Price
Distance of move (0-50, 51-150, or 151+ miles)	$7.75/M
Intra/interstate move	$5/M
Dwelling (moved from/to)	$5/M

    SFDU/SFDU
    MFDU/SFDU
    SFDU/MFDU
    MFDU/MFDU

Demographic Selects	Price
All select charges apply in addition to the Base Price.	
Exact age	$13/M
Combined exact and inferred age (ranges 18-35, 36-49, 50-64, 65+)	$7.75/M
Gender	$2.50/M
Married	$2.50/M
Presence of children	$6.50/M
Number of children	$7.50/M
Estimated HH income ($0-99K)	$5/M
Estimated HH income ($100K+)	$10/M
Dwelling type	N/C
1990 census data	$2/M
Geographic (state, ZIP, SCF, county, MSA, census tract/BG)	$2/M
Radius marketing	(call for custom quote)
Maximum list charge	$110/M

30 Day Hot Line Count
950,000 Approx. New files available on the 10th of each month

Price $65/M

14 Day Hot Line Count
550,000 Approx. New movers available every 14 days

Price $75/M

Last 12 Months
11,406,804

Price $55/M

Source
Experian consumer data and public deed records

Minimum Order
5,000 names
Extra charge for copies, tapes & freight

Updated Twice Monthly *with CASS certified software*

Delivery *Next day. Electronic delivery available!*

Call for on-line counts and quantity discounts

Page 15

Fall 1997

Experian New Mover Database

Meet the new opportunity in your neighborhood.

Experian believes the information concerning these names to be accurate, but cannot guarantee their accuracy or the outcome of the mailing. Information on this file is updated twice monthly and the counts for particular elements are subject to change.

Contact

Experian
701 Experian Parkway
Allen, Texas 75013-3714
800 527 3933
972 390 5000
FAX 972 390 5100

Commission Policy

Trade and volume discounts available to all qualified brokers.

Rental Policy

All names ordered/processed are for **one-time use**; for subsequent usage/unlimited usage, call for pricing. Tape for prior order suppression is $25 flat.

Format

	Price
4-up Cheshire labels	N/C
4-up pressure sensitive labels	
Under 50M	$6/M
Over 50M	$5/M
1-up pressure sensitive labels	$10/M
3 x 5 cards (1-up)	$15/M
Mag tape 9T 1600/6250 or cartridge, non-refundable	$15 each
Diskette	$20 each
CD-ROM	$35 each
Electronic delivery (quantity limits apply)	$50 flat
Bar coding	$.50/M
Key coding	$1/M
Keying month/year of birth	$1/M
Resequence/breaks	$1/M
Splits	$.50/M
Running charge	$5/M
Carrier route code with bar code	$2.50/M
Prioritizing	$2/M

Experian Motor Vehicle Database

This Experian database of 121 million vehicles in 32 states offers you one of the largest, most selectable vehicle owner lists on the market.

The sheer size and broad selectivity of this file make it ideal for automotive marketers of all types. Combine the vehicle selects with Experian's demographic and lifestyle selects for more highly focused targeting. For example, households with teenage children and young drivers are good prospects for new and pre-owned vehicles and automotive accessories, credit cards, insurance, and service offers.

For most households, expenses related to motor vehicle ownership are exceeded by only one other expense—the cost of housing. Combine motor vehicle and homeownership selects for enhanced lifestyle targeting. This list will help you reach just about everyone—families with everyday practical interests, luxury lovers, recreational travelers, the outdoors-type, and the sporty fun seeker.

Information on this file is processed through National Change of Address[1] (NCOA) monthly and all names are ZIP+4 coded.

Suggested applications:

- *Car dealership promotions*
- *Service center programs*
- *Auto accessories*
- *Insurance offers*
- *Gasoline credit cards*
- *Recreational equipment*
- *Financial services*
- *Magazines*

Vehicle Selects   Price

Year, make, series, trim level	N/C
Body style (sedan, coupe, van, etc.)	$5/M
MSRP	$5/M
Current value	$5/M
Purchase type (new and used)	$5/M
Lease indicator	$5/M
Fuel type (gas, diesel, propane)	$5/M
Date of registration	$10/M
Title date	$10/M
Highest vehicle value in household	$5/M
Aggregate vehicle value in household	$5/M
Number of doors	$5/M
Country of origin	$5/M
Presence of RV, motorcycle, or boat	$10/M
Presence of special plate	$10/M
Price class (low, medium, high, luxury)	$5/M
Model class (budget, luxury, sporty)	$5/M

State Coverage

AK AZ CO DC DE FL IA ID IL
KY LA MA MD ME MI MN MO MS
MT NC ND NE NH NY OH OR SD
TN TX UT WI WV WY

Call for availability and state restrictions.

Demographic Selects   Price

All select charges apply in addition to the Base Price.

Exact age	$13/M
Combined exact and inferred age (ranges 18-35, 36-49, 50-64, 65+)	$7.75/M
Gender	$2.50/M
Telephone numbers	$8/M
Head of household	N/C
Household status (wife, elderly parent, young adult)	$2.50/M
Married	$2.50/M
Presence of children	$6.50/M
Families with children (by age and/or gender)	$7.50/M
Homeowners	$5/M
PC owners	$6/M
Home businesses	$12/M
Estimated HH income ($0-99K))	$5/M
Estimated HH income ($100K+)	$10/M
Geographic income percentile	$3.50/M
Length of residence	$2.50/M
Ethnicity	$10/M
Direct mail responders	$5/M

Selects Continued

Total Count
121,131,376

Base Price
$60/M

Source
Public Records

Minimum Order
5,000 names
Extra charge for copies, tapes & freight

Updated Monthly
with CASS certified software

Delivery
Next day. Electronic delivery available!

Call for on-line counts and quantity discounts

---

[1]Experian is a non-exclusive licensee of the United States Postal Service. Names and addresses owned by Experian are processed through the NCOA system. Matches to the NCOA file are included in the Experian Motor Vehicle Database.

Fall 1997

Experian Motor Vehicle Database

Recent vehicle buyers are more responsive.

Experian believes the information concerning these names to be accurate, but cannot guarantee their accuracy or the outcome of the mailing. Information on this file is updated monthly and the counts for particular elements are subject to change.

Contact
Experian
701 Experian Parkway
Allen, Texas 75013-3714
800 527 3933
972 390 5000
FAX 972 390 5100

Commission Policy
Trade and volume discounts available to all qualified brokers.

Rental Policy
All names ordered/processed are for **one-time use**; for subsequent usage/unlimited usage, call for pricing. Tape for prior order suppression is $25 flat.

Statement of Intended Use
A Statement of Intended Use is required with every order requesting motor vehicle data to assure compliance with specific state restrictions. Mailers must submit mail pieces to Experian for approval.

Demographic Selects...   Price

Dwelling type	.N/C
1990 census data	$2/M
Geographic (state, ZIP, SCF, county, MSA, DMA, census tract/BG)	$2/M
Radius marketing	(call for custom quote)

Vital Statistics Selects   Price

Corrective lenses	$10/M
Height/Weight	$10/M

Neighborhood Selects   Price

U.S. MOSAIC	$10/M
PRIZM® (Claritas)	$10/M
Maximum list charge	$120/M

Format   Price

4-up Cheshire labels	N/C
4-up pressure sensitive labels	
Under 50M	$6/M
Over 50M	$5/M
1-up pressure sensitive labels	$10/M
3 x 5 cards (1-up)	$15/M
Mag tape 9T 1600/6250 or cartridge, non-refundable	$15 each
Diskette	$20 each
CD-ROM	$35 each
Electronic delivery (quantity limits apply)	$50 flat
Bar coding	$.50/M
Key coding	$1/M
Keying month/year of birth	$1/M
Resequence/breaks	$1/M
Splits	$.50/M
Running charge	$5/M
Carrier route code with bar code	$2.50/M
Prioritizing	$2/M

Fall 1997

Experian Modeled Vehicle Owner Database

We've applied the advanced modeling technology of Pattern Associates, Inc. to Experian's Consumer Database to create the Experian Modeled Vehicle Owner Database. Use it to predict automobile ownership in states which prohibit the use of vehicle ownership information for marketing purposes and all across America.

Segment likely owners according to their vehicle's forecasted age, price class, country of origin, model class, body style, or purchase type. Reach multiple market segments with high propensities to own the type of vehicle you specify.

To provide up-to-date predictions, we forecast automobile ownership based on the latest demographic data in the Experian Consumer Database. We dynamically score households, i.e. predict ownership, when records are accessed.

Information on this file is processed through National Change of Address[1] (NCOA) monthly and updated monthly with CASS certified software. All names are ZIP+4 coded and reported by two or more sources.

Suggested applications:

- *Auto dealership promotions*
- *Service center programs*
- *Auto customization and accessories*
- *Insurance offers*
- *Gasoline credit cards*
- *Recreational equipment*

Modeled Vehicle Owner Selects

- Subcompact
- Compact
- Mid-size
- Full-size
- Premium
- Sporty
- Sport utility
- Minivan
- Full size van
- Pick-up truck
- Domestic
- Foreign
- Less than two years old
- Two to five years old
- More than five years old
- Luxury priced
- High priced
- Medium priced
- Low priced
- Purchased new

Choose one or a combination of Modeled Vehicle Owner selects for the base price of $45/M.

Demographic Selects   Price

All select charges apply in addition to the Base Price.

Exact age	$13/M
Combined exact and inferred age (ranges 18-35, 36-49, 50-64, 65+)	$7.75/M
Gender	$2.50/M
Telephone numbers	$8/M
Head of household	N/C

Household status (wife, elderly parent, young adult)	$2.50/M
Married	$2.50/M
Presence of children	$6.50/M
Families with children (by age and/or gender)	$7.50/M
Homeowners	$5/M
PC owners	$6/M
Home businesses	$12/M
Estimated HH income ($0-99K))	$5/M
Estimated HH income ($100K+)	$10/M
Geographic income percentile	$3.50/M
Length of residence	$2.50/M
Ethnicity	$10/M
Direct mail responder	$5/M
Dwelling type	N/C
1990 census data	$2/M
Geographic (state, ZIP, SCF, county, MSA, DMA, census tract/BG)	$2/M
Radius marketing	(call for custom quote)

Selects Continued

Total Count
90,121,333
Households

Base Price
$45/M

Source
Statistically derived using Experian consumer data and models developed by Pattern Associates, Inc.

Minimum Order
5,000 names
Extra charge for copies, tapes & freight

Delivery
Next day. Electronic delivery available!

Call for on-line counts and quantity discounts

---

[1]Experian is a non-exclusive licensee of the United States Postal Service. Names and addresses owned by Experian are processed through the NCOA system. Matches to the NCOA file are included in the Experian Modeled Vehicle Owner Database.

Fall 1997

Experian Modeled Vehicle Owner Database

A break-through in predictive modeling of vehicle ownership at the household level.

Experian believes the information concerning these names to be accurate, but cannot guarantee their accuracy or the outcome of the mailing. Information on this file is updated monthly and the counts for particular elements are subject to change.

Contact
Experian
701 Experian Parkway
Allen, Texas 75013-3714
800 527 3933
972 390 5000
FAX 972 390 5100

Commission Policy
Trade and volume discounts available to all qualified brokers.

Rental Policy
All names ordered/processed are for **one-time use**; for subsequent usage/unlimited usage, call for pricing. Tape for prior order suppression is $25 flat.

Vital Statistics Selects   Price
Corrective lenses $10/M
Height/Weight $10/M

Neighborhood Selects   Price
U.S. MOSAIC $10/M
PRIZM® (Claritas) $10/M

Maximum list charge $100/M

Format   Price
4-up Cheshire labels ....N/C
4-up pressure sensitive labels
   Under 50M $6/M
   Over 50M $5/M
1-up pressure sensitive labels $10/M
3 x 5 cards (1-up) $15/M
Mag tape 9T 1600/6250 or cartridge,
   non-refundable ....$15 each
Diskette ....$20 each
CD-ROM...........................$35 each
Electronic delivery (quantity limits apply) .....$50 flat
Bar coding...........................$.50/M
Key coding $1/M
Keying month/year of birth................$1/M
Resequence/breaks $1/M
Splits ....$.50/M
Running charge $5/M
Carrier route code with bar code $2.50/M
Prioritizing...........................$2/M

Fall 1997

Experian Vehicle Buyers Database

Vehicle ownership is an excellent indicator of lifestyle and future product usage. In addition to identifying vehicle buyers, the Experian Vehicle Buyers Database is ideal for targeting recent purchasers of high-ticket items and as a reliable source of Hotline names. This unique data source helps you target recent purchasers of cars and trucks.

The Experian Vehicle Buyers Database offers three key vehicle buyer segments:

- *New Vehicle Buyers*
- *Near-New Vehicle Buyers*
- *Previously-Owned Vehicle Buyers*

Each segment is designed to help you reach the right consumers for your offer. Each vehicle buyer select also offers a 30-Day Hotline. Call for current Hotline counts for Near-New and Previously Owned Buyers.

Information on this file is processed through National Change of Address[1] (NCOA) and all names are ZIP+4 coded.

Suggested applications:

▪ *Hotline source of names*	▪ *Parts and service programs*	▪ *Market research*
▪ *Insurance offers*	▪ *Aftermarket retail promotions*	▪ *Financial services*

Vehicle Buyer Selects   Price

New vehicle buyers ....N/C
Near-new vehicle buyers ....N/C
Previously-owned vehicle buyers ....N/C

Vehicle Selects   Price

Model year ....N/C
Make...............................N/C
Series ....N/C
Date of registration $10/M
Lease indicator $5/M

State Coverage

AK	AZ	CO	DC	DE	FL	IA	ID	KY
LA	MA	MD	ME	MI	MN	MO	MS	MT
NC	ND	NE	NH	NY	OH	OR	SD	TN
TX	UT	WI	WV	WY				

Call for availability and state restrictions.

Demographic Selects   Price

Exact age $13/M
Combined exact and inferred age
(ranges 18-35, 36-49, 50-64, 65+) $7.75/M
Gender $2.50/M

Telephone numbers $8/M
Head of household ....N/C
Household status
  (wife, elderly parent, young adult) $2.50/M
Married $2.50/M
Presence of children $6.50/M
Families with children (by age and/or gender) $7.50/M
Homeowners $5/M
Estimated HH income ($0-99K)) $5/M
Estimated HH income ($100K+) $10/M
Geographic income percentile $3.50/M
Length of residence $2.50/M
Ethnicity.............................$10/M
Direct mail responder $5/M
Dwelling type ....N/C
1990 census data $2/M
Geographic (state, ZIP, SCF, county,
  MSA, census tract/BG) $2/M
Radius marketing ....(call for custom quote)

Neighborhood Selects   Price

PRIZM® (Claritas) $10/M
Maximum list charge $120/M

---

30 Day New Vehicle Hot Line Count
600,000 Approximately

Base Price
$75/M

Last 12 Months Price
$65/M

Source
Public Records

Minimum Order
5,000 Names
Extra charge for unlimited usage, copies, tapes & freight

Updated Monthly
with CASS certified software

Delivery
48-hour turnaround on most orders

---

[1]Experian is a non-exclusive licensee of the United States Postal Service. Names and addresses owned by Experian are processed through the NCOA system. Matches to the NCOA file are included in the Experian Vehicle Buyers Database.

Page 21

Fall 1997

Experian Vehicle Buyers Database

Contact

Experian
701 Experian Parkway
Allen, Texas 75013-3714
800 527 3933
972 390 5000
FAX 972 390 5100

Commission Policy

Trade and volume discounts available to all qualified brokers.

Rental Policy

All names ordered/processed are for **one-time use**; for subsequent usage/unlimited usage, call for pricing. Tape for prior order suppression is $25 flat.

Statement of Intended Use

A Statement of Intended Use is required with every order requesting motor vehicle data to assure compliance with specific state restrictions. Mailers must submit mail pieces to Experian for approval.

Format	Price
4-up Cheshire labels	N/C
4-up pressure sensitive labels	
Under 50M	$6/M
Over 50M	$5/M
1-up pressure sensitive labels	$10/M
3 x 5 cards (1-up)	$15/M
Mag tape 9T 1600/6250 or cartridge, non-refundable	$15 each
Diskette	$20 each
CD-ROM	$35 each
Electronic delivery (quantity limits apply)	$50 flat
Bar coding	$.50/M
Key coding	$1/M
Keying month/year of birth	$1/M
Resequence/breaks	$1/M
Splits	$.50/M
Running charge	$5/M
Carrier route code with bar code	$2.50/M
Prioritizing	$2/M

Experian HomeownersPlus℠ Database

The Experian HomeownersPlus Database offers marketers a variety of real estate transaction selectivity. This powerful database is built from tax assessor files and recorded deed information.

Marketers use valuable information such as home sale price to determine consumer affluence, or loan-to-value ratio to identify homeowners with significant equity in their homes. The Experian HomeownersPlus℠ Database is updated with the latest county recorded deed and tax assessor information. Combine this with our demographic selects to find the right homeowner for your offer.

Information on this file is processed through National Change of Address[1] (NCOA) monthly and all names are ZIP+4 coded.

Test these popular consumer market segments:

- *Affluent homeowners*
- *Hispanic homeowners*
- *Expensive home buyers*
- *Insurance prospects*
- *New homeowners*

Purchase Transaction Selects   Price

Residing status (owner occupied) $10/M
Sale price (in ranges) $10/M
Recording date (year/month) $10/M
Purchase loan amount (in ranges) $10/M
Type of loan (fixed/variable) $10/M
Kind of loan (CONV/VA/FHA) $5/M
LTV ratio (at recording date) $10/M

Demographic Selects   Price

All select charges apply in addition to the Base Price.

Exact age $13/M
Combined exact and inferred age
  (ranges 18-35, 36-49, 50-64, 65+) $7.75/M
Gender $2.50/M
Telephone numbers $8/M
Head of household . . . . .N/C
Household status
(wife, elderly parent, young adult) $2.50/M
Married $2.50/M
Presence of children $6.50/M
Families with children (by age and/or gender) $7.50/M
PC owners $6/M
Home businesses $12/M
Estimated HH income ($0-99K)) $5/M

Estimated HH income ($100K+) $10/M
Geographic income percentile $3.50/M
Length of residence $2.50/M
Ethnicity $10/M
Direct mail responders $5/M
Dwelling type . . . . .N/C
1990 census data $2/M
Geographic (state, ZIP, SCF, county,
  MSA, DMA, census tract/BG) $2/M
Radius marketing . . . .(call for custom quote)

Neighborhood Selects   Price

U.S. MOSAIC $10/M
PRIZM® (Claritas) $10/M

Maximum list charge $100/M

Total Count
22,998,203

Base Price
$50/M

Source
Public deed
record, state tax
assessor files

Minimum Order
5,000 names
Extra charge
for copies, tapes
& freight

Updated Monthly
*with CASS
certified
software*

Delivery
*Next day or
same day.
Electronic
delivery
available!*

**Call for
on-line
counts and
quantity
discounts**

---

[1]Experian is a non-exclusive licensee of the United States Postal Service. Names and addresses owned by Experian are processed through the NCOA system. Matches to the NCOA file are included in the Experian HomeownersPlus℠ Database.

Fall 1997

Experian HomeownersPlus℠ Database

Contact
Experian
701 Experian Parkway
Allen, Texas 75013-3714
800 527 3933
972 390 5000
FAX 972 390 5100

Commission Policy
Trade and volume discounts available to all
qualified brokers.

Rental Policy
All names ordered/processed are for **one-time use**;
for subsequent usage/unlimited usage, call for
pricing. Tape for prior order suppression is $25 flat.

Format	Price
4-up Cheshire labels	N/C
4-up pressure sensitive labels	
Under 50M	$6/M
Over 50M	$5/M
1-up pressure sensitive labels	$10/M
3 x 5 cards (1-up)	$15/M
Mag tape 9T 1600/6250 or cartridge, non-refundable	$15 each
Diskette	$20 each
CD-ROM	$35 each
Electronic delivery (quantity limits apply)	$50 flat
Bar coding	$.50/M
Key coding	$1/M
Keying month/year of birth	$1/M
Resequence/breaks	$1/M
Splits	$.50/M
Running charge	$5/M
Carrier route code with bar code	$2.50/M
Prioritizing	$2/M

experian

Experian Smart Targeting Tools℠

Experian Smart Targeting Tools℠ lets you target consumers by lifestyle interest or product usage. This advanced segmentation system was built from the bottom up using Experian demographic data, census data, Simmons Market Research Bureau information, and Ruf proprietary models.

Use intuitive selections or do a comprehensive analysis of your customers. Choose the Smart solution which is best for you:

Experian Smart Targets℠
Select households with the propensity to buy from 56 general product categories

Experian Smart TargetsPlus℠
Reach households by 517 specific product and brand preferences

Experian Smart Consumer Clusters℠
Choose from these distinct lifestyle cluster options:

■ *50 Neighborhood clusters*   ■ *112 Household clusters*   ■ *3,600 Detailed household clusters*

Experian Smart Profile℠

Analyze your customer file to reveal lifestyle and product interests you never would have discovered intuitively.

Information in this file is processed through National Change of Address[1] (NCOA) monthly and all names are ZIP+4 coded and reported by two or more sources.

Demographic Selects   Price

All select charges apply in addition to the Base Price.

Exact age	$13/M
Combined exact and inferred age (ranges 18-35, 36-49, 50-64, 65+)	$7.75/M
Gender	$2.50/M
Telephone numbers	$8/M
Head of household	N/C
Household status (wife, elderly parent, young adult)	$2.50/M
Married	$2.50/M
Presence of children	$6.50/M
Families with children (by age and/or gender)	$7.50/M
Homeowners	$5/M
Estimated HH income ($0-99K))	$5/M
Estimated HH income ($100K+)	$10/M
Geographic income percentile	$3.50/M
Length of residence	$2.50/M
Ethnicity	$10/M
Direct mail responder	$5/M
Dwelling type	N/C
1990 census data	$2/M
Geographic (state, ZIP, SCF, county, MSA, DMA, census tract/BG)	$2/M
Radius marketing	(call for custom quote)
Maximum list charge	$100/M

Experian Smart Targets℠

Apparel
Men's
Women's

Autos/Automotive
Domestic
Economy
Foreign
Luxury
Rental or lease
Vans and trucks
Auto products/services
Tires
Motorcycles

Financial
Bank cards
Retail cards
Financial services
Investments
Loans
Savings

Food and Beverages
Beer
Wines
Distilled spirits
Low calorie drinks
Soft drinks
Home dining
Restaurant dining

High-Tech Electronics
Compact discs
Records/audio tapes
VCRs/videocassettes
Home PCs
Cameras

House and Home
Household appliances
Home furnishings
Home improvements
Microwaves
Tools
Pets

Insurance
Health insurance
Homeowner insurance
Life insurance

Mail Order
Financial
Leisure
General merchandise

Sports and Leisure
Leisure activities, hobbies
Games and toys
Travel
Sports
Magazines
Newspapers
Television
Radio
Public activities, contributions
Memberships

Total Count
85,734,368

Base Price
$30/M–Experian Neighborhood Clusters

$40/M–Experian Household Clusters

$40/M–Experian Smart Targets℠

$50/M– Experian Smart TargetsPlus℠

Source
Cooperatively developed by Experian and Ruf Strategic Solutions

Minimum Order
5,000 names
Extra charge for copies, tapes & freight

Updated Monthly
with CASS certified software

Delivery
Next day. Electronic delivery available!

Call for on-line counts and quantity discounts

[1]Experian is a non-exclusive licensee of the United States Postal Service. Names and addresses owned by Experian are processed through the NCOA system. Matches to the NCOA file are included in Experian Smart Targeting Tools℠.

Fall 1997

Experian Smart Targeting Tools℠

Contact

Experian
701 Experian Parkway
Allen, Texas 75013-3714
800 527 3933
972 390 5000
FAX 972 390 5100

Commission Policy

Trade and volume discounts available to all qualified brokers.

Rental Policy

All names ordered/processed are for **one-time use**; for subsequent usage/unlimited usage, call for pricing. Tape for prior order suppression is $25 flat.

Experian Smart TargetsPlus℠ (Example)

HIGH-TECH ELECTRONICS

Compact Discs
Own a compact disc player

Records and Audio Tapes
Bought $250+ of stereo equipment
Bought 1940s to 1960s pop records/tapes
Bought 1960s rock records/tapes
Bought Broadway/movie/ soundtrack records/tapes
Bought classical records/tapes
Bought comedy records/tapes
Bought disco/dance records/tapes
Bought gospel/sacred records/ tapes
Bought heavy rock records/tapes
Bought traditional/contem- porary/jazz records/tapes
Bought new wave records/tapes
Bought contemporary pop/rock records/tapes
Bought soul/R&B records/tapes
Recorded music/other entertainment

VCR and videocassettes
Bought blank video cassettes
Bought pre-recorded video cassettes
Own a VCR
Rented video cassettes

Home PCs
Have a personal computer
Spent $300+ on home computer peripherals
Use home PC/computer games
Use PC at home (not for games)

Cameras
35MM camera: total buyers/last year
Bought 126/110 camera
Cartridge camera: total buyers/last year
Instant development camera: total buyers/last year

Format	Price
4-up Cheshire labels	N/C
4-up pressure sensitive labels	
Under 50M	$6/M
Over 50M	$5/M
1-up pressure sensitive labels	$10/M
3 x 5 cards (1-up)	$15/M
Mag tape 9T 1600/6250 or cartridge, non-refundable	$15 each
Diskette	$20 each
CD-ROM	$35 each
Electronic delivery (quantity limits apply)	$50 flat
Bar coding	$.50/M
Key coding	$1/M
Keying month/year of birth	$1/M
Resequence/breaks	$1/M
Splits	$.50/M
Running charge	$5/M
Carrier route code with bar code	$2.50/M
Prioritizing	$2/M

experian

Experian/P$YCLE® Financial Markets

Experian/P$YCLE® Financial Markets is a proven household segmentation system which helps marketers accurately predict consumer financial behavior. The Experian/P$YCLE system reveals significantly different and consistent patterns of consumer behavior such as incidence, value, and profitability of deposit, credit and investment products.

The P$YCLE model is based on the socio-economic factors that have the greatest effect on consumer financial behavior. Our strategic partner, Claritas, Inc., surveys more than 80,000 households each year to update these factors.

Households are classified into eight major segments and 42 subsegments clearly differentiating household financial diversity. With that diversity comes diverse needs for products, services and delivery methods. The Experian/P$YCLE system helps you customize offerings for your customers.

Information in this file is processed through National Change of Address[1] (NCOA) monthly and all names are ZIP+4 coded and reported by two or more sources.

Suggested applications:
- *Profiling and targeting customers*
- *Market analysis and segmentation*

Experian/P$YCLE Financial Markets Selects

- Wealth market
- Mass market
- Upscale retired
- Midscale retired
- Upper affluent
- Lower market
- Lower affluent
- Downscale retired

You may choose one or a combination of Experian/P$YCLE® selects or its subsegments for the base price of $45/M.

Demographic Selects   Price

All select charges apply in addition to the Base Price.

Exact age $13/M
Combined exact and inferred age
  (ranges 18-35, 36-49, 50-64, 65+) $7.75/M
Gender $2.50/M
Telephone numbers $8/M
Head of household ....N/C
Household status
  (wife, elderly parent, young adult) $2.50/M

Married $2.50/M
Presence of children $6.50/M
Families with children (by age and/or gender) $7.50/M
Homeowners $5/M
PC owners $6/M
Home businesses $12/M
Estimated HH income ($0-99K)) $5/M
Estimated HH income ($100K+) $10/M
Geographic income percentile $3.50/M
Length of residence $2.50/M
Ethnicity $10/M
Direct mail responders $5/M
Dwelling type ....N/C
1990 census data $2/M
Geographic (state, ZIP, SCF, county,
  MSA, DMA, census tract/BG) $2/M
Radius marketing ....(call for custom quote)

Maximum list charge $100/M

Total Count
84,223,933
Households

Base Price
$45/M

Source
Cooperatively developed by Experian and Claritas, Inc.

Minimum Order
5,000 names
Extra charge for copies, tapes & freight

Updated Monthly
with CASS certified software

Delivery
Next day or same day. Electronic delivery available!

Call for on-line counts and quantity discounts

---

[1]Experian is a non-exclusive licensee of the United States Postal Service. Names and addresses owned by Experian are processed through the NCOA system. Matches to the NCOA file are included in Experian/P$YCLE® Financial Markets.

Page 27

Fall 1997

Experian/P$YCLE® Financial Markets

Contact

Experian
701 Experian Parkway
Allen, Texas 75013-3714
800 527 3933
972 390 5000
FAX 972 390 5100

Commission Policy

Trade and volume discounts available to all qualified brokers.

Rental Policy

All names ordered/processed are for **one-time use**; for subsequent usage/unlimited usage, call for pricing. Tape for prior order suppression is $25 flat.

Experian / P$YCLE®
Financial Markets (Example)

UPSCALE RETIRED

Affluent Retired
Retired households with more than $50,000 income per year and income producing assets of less than $1 million. Ages 65 and older. High users of fixed-interest accounts, investments products and annuities.

With high annual incomes despite their retired status, Affluent Retireds have planned and saved for their golden years. They hold sophisticated products and have many financial relationships. Their lifestyles are active and clearly upscale.

Comfortably Retired
Households with income between $35,000 and $49,999 with income producing assets of less than $1 million. Ages 65 and older.

While not as affluent as Affluent Retireds, the Comfortably Retired have saved well. They are less sophisticated in their use of investment products but still hold diversified portfolios.

UPPER AFFLUENT

High Asset Pre-retired Investors
Households with income higher than $75,000 and income producing assets between $100,000 and $1 million. Between ages of 55 and 64.

In their pre-retirement years with high income producing assets. Affluent Pre-retired Investors are doing well and planning for active affluent retirements. They use credit products, as well as investments. In particular, they use home equity credit.

High Asset Suburban Boomers
Households with income higher than $75,000 and income producing assets between $100,000 and $1 million. Between ages of 35 and 54. Live in metropolitan areas.

High-Asset Suburban Boomers are the best off of the Boomers, with high annual incomes, high assets, and homes in better metro suburbs. They dabble in unsophisticated investments but widely use mutual funds. Look for major credit needs in this segment.

Format

	Price
4-up Cheshire labels	N/C
4-up pressure sensitive labels	
Under 50M	$6/M
Over 50M	$5/M
1-up pressure sensitive labels	$10/M
3 x 5 cards (1-up)	$15/M
Mag tape 9T 1600/6250 or cartridge, non-refundable	$15 each
Diskette	$20 each
CD-ROM	$35 each
Electronic delivery (quantity limits apply)	$50 flat
Bar coding	$.50/M
Key coding	$1/M
Keying month/year of birth	$1/M
Resequence/breaks	$1/M
Splits	$.50/M
Running charge	$5/M
Carrier route code with bar code	$2.50/M
Prioritizing	$2/M

P$YCLE® is a registered trademark of Claritas, Inc.

Experian Customer Link℠

Connect with your customers

Experian Customer Link℠ turns customer identification data you routinely gather during purchase and telephone transactions into opportunities. Use data you already own to build your customer database, strengthen relationships with clients, and research your market.

Experian Customer Link matches your customers'

■ Telephone number

■ Driver's license number, or

■ Social Security number

to our national databases to provide you with their names and addresses.

Build your database

Replace the time-consuming, manual process of collecting, storing, preparing and keying your customers' names and addresses. Experian Customer Link is an easy, fast, and cost-efficient method to build and update your customer database. Save time by processing millions of records in days instead of weeks.

Strengthen relationships with customers

Experian Customer Link helps you make lasting connections with customers. Without disrupting or lengthening business transactions, Experian Customer Link gives you the means to contact your customers through direct mail. This new connection benefits you and your customer when you use it to:

■ Pre-announce sales or special promotions

■ Treat consumers as preferred customers

■ Thank customers for their interest or purchase

■ Encourage and reward customer loyalty

■ Provide improved customer service by quickly identifying recipients of rebates or product/service announcements

Research your market

Experian Customer Link gives you new ways to analyze your existing data. Use it in your market research to:

■ Track purchase behavior to identify your best customers and their locations

■ Correlate telephone area codes and exchanges with ZIP Codes to research or validate your customers' locations

■ Test new market segments by sending catalogs to customers who shop at your retail outlets

Respect for consumer privacy

Experian Customer Link helps you bring opportunity to your customers while respecting the choice of consumers who don't wish to receive direct mail. To exclude the names of consumers who wish to opt out of direct marketing programs, Experian applies suppression files (including the DMA Mail and Telephone Preference files) to its databases before matching them with your records.

Make the connection

Capitalize on the data you already own. Contact your local Experian representative or call 800 527 3933 to discuss how you can use Experian Customer Link to learn more about your market.

Page 29

Use data you already own to build your client files and create new marketing opportunities.

Experian Customer Link℠

Contact

Experian
701 Experian Parkway
Allen, Texas 75013-3714
800 527 3933
972 390 5000
FAX 972 390 5100

Commission Policy

Trade and volume discounts available to all qualified brokers.

Payment Policy

All orders are filled under the terms of the Experian Master Services Agreement. All orders due and payable 30 days after shipment of order.

Processing Turnaround & Output

Four business days.

Discuss output options with your Experian sales representative.

Processing Fees

Input $1.60/M
Match fee $45/M
Quantity discounts available.

Minimum: $350

Fall 1997

experian

INSOURCE℠ Enhancement Database

Make your files more productive

The INSOURCE Enhancement Database adds value and productivity to your customer file. Quality data enhancement lets you make sound, cost-effective marketing decisions so you can:

■ *Define the unique characteristics of your best and most profitable customers*
■ *Anticipate likely future behaviors and buying trends*
■ *Identify prospects most like your best customers for new growth opportunities*

The ultimate enhancement source

The INSOURCE Enhancement Database is the intelligent combination of the independent databases of two direct marketing leaders, Experian and Metromail. Together we have created a superior data enhancement product which offers marketers accuracy, reliability and coverage not available before.

The INSOURCE Enhancement Database provides coverage on 95% of U.S. households and offers more than 300 attributes for unequaled appending options. Every six weeks, synchronized updates to the INSOURCE database assure consistent delivery of the most recent and accurate information available.

Household Composition Data

Individual and Household Level Data

	Price
* Date of birth	$14.50/M
Inferred age ranges	$8/M
Estimated income (household)	$7/M
Given name/First initial	$1.50/M
Marital status	$3/M
Ethnic markets	$10/M
* Asian markets	$18/M
PC owners	$8/M
Individual household status	$1.50/M

Residence Data

Homeowners	$5/M
Length of residence	$3/M
Address type	$1/M

Children's Data

Presence of children	$5/M
Children by age range/gender	$12/M

Additional Household Members Data

* HH name, DOB and gender	$18/M
Number of adults in HH	$1/M

Aggregate Direct Response Data

Direct mail responder	$6/M
Magazine buyers	$12/M

Prime Data

	Price
* Telephone numbers	$15/M
Unlisted phone number indicator	$2/M
Home business indicator	$15/M
Business owner indicator	$15/M
Real estate data	varies by element
* Experian/P$YCLE	$70/M
* Experian Credit Card Markets	$45/M
Experian Smart Targeting Tools	Varies

* Quantity discounts available

Data bundles make ordering easy!

Instead of ordering each data element separately, simply order convenient pre-defined data packages.

Much more data available

This data sheet contains only a sampling of the more than three hundred data elements available on the INSOURCE database.

For full details on the INSOURCE Enhancement Database, ask your Experian representative or call 800 527 3933 to receive a free copy of the INSOURCE catalog.

Page 31

Fall 1997

The ultimate tool to maximize the potential of your customer database.

INSOURCE℠ Enhancement Database

Contact
Experian
701 Experian Parkway
Allen, Texas 75013-3714
800 527 3933
972 390 5000
FAX 972 390 5100

Processing Turnaround
Three business days (for quantities less than 10MM)

Commission Policy
Trade and volume discounts available to all qualified brokers.

Payment Policy
All Enhancement orders are filled under the terms of the Experian Master Services Agreement. All orders due and payable 30 days after shipment.

Input Quantity

	$/Thousand
0-1MM	$3/M
Larger quantities	Request quote
Minimum:	$1,500

Area Level Data

	Price
Geo codes	$1.50/M
DMA codes	$2/M
U.S. MOSAIC codes	$35/M

Motor Vehicle Data

	Price
Year	$12/M
Make	$10/M
Series	$15/M

Consumer Response Data

	Price

Household Lifestyle Interests

Camping/hiking	$8/M
Travelers, domestic & foreign	$8/M

Household Product Ownership

Audio	$8/M
Exercise equipment/health	$8/M
Home furnishings	$8/M
Outdoor recreation equipment	$8/M

Computer Owners Data

Personal computer	$8/M
Online service provider	$8/M

Investor Data

Bonds	$8/M
Mutual funds	$8/M

Pet Owners Data

Number of dogs	$8/M
Number of birds	$8/M

Mail Order Data

Book club, current	$8/M
Video club, current	$8/M

Education/Occupation Data

College degree	$8/M
White collar	$8/M

Which Experian product or service do you need?

Experian's list and processing services can be creatively combined to fine-tune your targeting, locate fresh prospects, and make your marketing dollars work harder. Use this chart for helpful suggestions about products or services that meet common needs. See the Table of Contents for complete information about consumer lists and processing services provided by Experian.

List Services

	"I need motor vehicle data, but some states restrict the use of this data. How can I mail to restricted states?"	*"I get my best results when working with hotlines. Which lists will work best for me?"*	*"How can I reach fresh prospects who demographically resemble my best customers?"*	*"I want to reach affluent consumers."*
Experian Consumer Database (p. 5)			✔	
Experian Asian Database & Ethnicity select (p. 11)			✔	
Experian Credit Card Markets Database (p. 13)			✔	
Experian New Mover Database (p. 15)		✔		
Experian Motor Vehicle Database (p. 17)				✔
Experian Modeled Vehicle Owners Database (p. 19)	✔			
Experian Vehicle Buyers Database (p. 21)		✔		
Experian Smart Targeting Tools℠ Database (p. 25)	✔		✔	✔
Experian/P$YCLE® Financial Markets (p. 27)				✔

Other Services

	"Tell me more about the customers I already have."	*"I want to test new market segments by sending catalogs to customers who shop at my store."*	*"I want to anticipate likely future behaviors and buying trends."*	*"I want to maximize the productivity of every piece I mail."*
Experian Customer Link (p. 29)	✔	✔		
INSOURCE Enhancement Database (p.31)	✔		✔	✔

FAST-COUNT*™* DBMS
David Shepard Associates, Inc.
and
MegaPlex Software, Inc.

OVERVIEW

What is Fast-Count DBMS?

Fast-Count™ DBMS is a very high-speed database management system that has been especially designed to support:

- Executive information systems.

- Decision support systems.

- Back-end data processing applications that involve data merging, matching, sorting, and other bulk data operations.

It offers state-of-the-art software technology on Unix platforms to build:

- Analysis and reporting applications.

- Batch data processing -- including data update, extraction, and transformation.

Benefits of Using Fast-Count DBMS

Potential benefits of using Fast-Count DBMS are:

- **Productivity Improvements:** Very high processing speeds boost productivity for decision makers and analysts alike.

- **Ease of Data Access:** Its point-and-click interface allows decision makers to easily access all the data.

- **Unlimited Variety of Data Exploration:** Unlike systems with precomputed results, all data is accessible for processing at all times. No restrictions, period!

- **Cost Savings:** Due to high processing speeds and data compression, Fast-Count DBMS can perform the same tasks on smaller, less-expensive computers.

Fast-Count is a trademark of MegaPlex Software, Inc. *Unix* is a trademark of AT&T.

POSSIBLE USES

Fast-Count DBMS can be used to efficiently perform the following tasks:

- Perform *ad-hoc* count queries using Boolean conditions of any complexity.

- Create *ad-hoc* reports consisting of one-, two-, and three-dimensional profiles of customers selected by a previous query.

- Create multi-column, customized reports involving elementary statistical operations.

- Reports can be exported to a variety of PC programs, including spreadsheets, graphics packages, word processors, and databases; for example, Lotus 123, Improv, Excel, Quattro, Harvard Graphics, Freelance, Word, Word Perfect, Paradox, and DBase.

- Segment Customer and Prospects Files using *ad-hoc* or custom procedures.

- Allocate marketing codes to segments.

- Incorporate response analysis data in the decision support databases.

- Perform elementary statistical analysis on groups of products, customers, prospects, and households.

- Extract selected samples from the decision support database to be exported for modelling purposes, and format them for the statistical analysis systems such as SAS, S, SYSTAT, Sigma-Stat, Knowledge-Seeker, and others.

- Implement a variety of scoring equations, which are created by statistical modelling.

- Export selected data to an operations system for incorporation in the fulfillment stream. This data is sorted and pre-formatted so that it can be imported into the operations system with minimal additional processing.

- Process operations data to create the decision support data through a combination of data extraction, linking, matching, consolidation, and summarization operations. Such processing could involve the following steps:

    a. Summarize Transactions File.

    b. Link Customers File with Transactions File.

    c. Link Prospects File with Customers File.

    d. Link Promotion History and Responses with Customers and Prospects Files.

□ Page 2 □

CAPABILITIES

Speed and Compression

Fast-Count DBMS achieves its high speed, usually 100's of times faster than the Relational DBMSs, through built-in data compression and efficient algorithms. Data compression of 2 to 4 times is achieved in most practical applications.

Since it does not use any type of indexing or pre-calculated results to achieve the high speed, it can be used to perform virtually limitless types of query, reporting, and processing functions. It can process household, person, and transaction level data with equal ease. Moreover, data can be quickly updated and refreshed because loading is not slowed down by creation of indexes or calculation of pre-stored results.

Operations that would otherwise take hours to complete can be done literally in minutes by Fast-Count DBMS. This not only boosts productivity, but also greatly shrinks the hardware costs by allowing the use of less expensive computer models and fewer disks. Alternatively, much more comprehensive analysis and reporting could be performed for the same hardware cost.

Ease-Of-Use

All the speed and power of this DBMS is brought out to the end-users through a user-interface that runs under Windows 3.1 in a client-servers architecture.

The user-interface program paints the screen, accepts user's point-and-click selections, and formulates the requests that are sent to the server. The server carries out the requests and sends the results back to the user-interface program which displays them in a window.

For presentation quality output, the results obtained from the DBMS can be imported into the popular PC programs, for example, Lotus 123, Improv, Excel, and FrameMaker, running under Windows 3.1.

Data Import and Export

Fast-Count DBMS can accept customer, transactions and any other data from the mainframe or mini-based operations support systems. It can also accept practically any kind of enhancement and overlay data from other data sources.

It has comprehensive data export capabilities to support a variety of formats required by the operations support systems or PC-based analysis systems.

Support of Statistical Modelling

In addition to performing simple statistical calculations, Fast-Count DBMS can be used to draw samples for statistical modelling. The samples could be downloaded to a modelling platform, e.g., SAS, where statistical models would be built. Fast-Count DBMS could then be used to score the full database and to validate the models on the Unix host.

SUCCESSFUL APPLICATIONS

Bench Mark Figures

In a Transactions table of 1 million rows, a relational DBMS running on Sun 4/490 took 30 minutes to count the number of customers who bought one product and not another. Fast-Count DBMS does the same task in under 5 seconds on a comparable hardware platform.

Timely Scoring of Customer Records

This application required scoring customers based upon their recent purchasing behavior using a scoring equation. All the customers had to be scored within a time interval of 2 days and results had to be uploaded to the mainframe fulfillment system for further processing. The Fast-Count DBMS was able to perform this task in under 3 hours, leaving ample time to schedule jobs on the fulfillment system. This task was not considered suitable for the mainframe due to a long expected run time and high expected cost of programming.

Attribution of Sales to Reps

This application required attributing sales dollars and number of units sold from 4 millions transactions to 10,000 reps. This task took over 10 hours on a large mainframe. It could be done in under 5 minutes on a desk-top Sun computer.

Assignment of Geo-Demographic Codes

This application required assigning geo-demographic codes to customers in a Customers table of 3 million rows. Some customers had 5 digit zip code while the others had 9 digit zip codes, and the cluster codes table has 16 million rows. This task was programmed in approximately 1 hour and took under 1 hour on a high-end IBM RS-6000 computer to run. It could have been done on the mainframe, but would have taken so long that it could not be allocated a processing window and would have required a couple of days of programming time.

A Report-Intensive Application

This application required reporting the number of current and dormant customers, number of units sold, and revenue for each product, for groups of products, and for all products. These reports also compare year-to-date figures of last and this year and percentage changes from last to this year.

This set of over 50 reports is done on a low-end Sun computer in under 4 hours by using the Fast-Count DBMS in batch mode. Before the introduction of Fast-Count DBMS, about 200 of these reports were done on an AS-400 in more than 8 days.

* * *

□ Page 4 □

FAST-COUNT™ DBMS
David Shepard Associates, Inc.
and
MegaPlex Software, Inc.

TECHNICAL DESCRIPTION

Ease-Of-Programming

Fast-Count DBMS is programmed in Fast-Count Language (FCL), a 4GL which is specially designed to support analysis, reporting, and batch applications. Its English-like syntax makes it easy to learn and use and thereby enhances programmer productivity and reduces application development costs.

FCL's capabilities include:

- A complete set of data definition, access, and manipulation facilities, including arbitrarily complex arithmetic expressions and logical conditions, creation of temporary, user-defined fields, and ability to handle transactions-level data.

- Comprehensive report generation facilities to generate a wide variety of reports, including built-in support for one-, two-, and three-dimensional profiles and crosstabs.

- Programming facilities that are suitable to build large, multi-module applications as well as small, *ad-hoc* applications.

By including the above capabilities in one systems, FCL provides one seemless environment to build complete applications -- large or small. This makes the design, creation, and maintenance of application easier and less costly than using multiple programming environments (which is the case in several popular DBMSs).

Flexible Data Storage

- Fast-Count DBMS can store a large number of tables with hundreds of fields each, limited by the available disk space.

- Data tables can be *linked* in a one-to-one, one-to-many, or many-to-many fashion.

- Records can have repeating fields. For example, in a database of households, children's names and ages would be repeating fields -- one household may have only 1 name and age, while another may have 2 or 3.

- Fields can be of the following types: *alpha*, *label*, *unsigned*, *signed*, *float*, and *date*.

- Several *data-systems* can be setup, each with its own tables.

  This facility can be used to keep multiple versions of the decision-support data wherein the current download can be processed to create the *new* version while the end-users continue using the *current* version. After a successful processing run, the *new* data would be made *current*.

- Several simultaneous users can access shared data for reading and their own private data for reading and writing.

- Data is stored in the standard Unix file systems -- the use of raw disk partitions is not required.

Speed

Fast-Count DBMS can perform most *ad-hoc* queries 100's of times faster than the conventional relational DBMSs.

For example, it would *count* the number of records that satisfy a single condition in a table at the rate of 16 million records per second for a one-field query on a computer equivalent to the Silicon Graphics Model 2000. This speed is independent of the number of fields in the table.

The *join* operation on sorted tables takes approximately twice as long as the above-described *count* operation, and *sort* proceeds at the rate of 1 million records per minute.

Data Analysis

Data analysis capabilities include, but are not limited to, the following:

- Identify records that satisfy any arbitrary Boolean expression. The Boolean expression could contain constants and fields both.

- Aggregation operations: sum, average, minimum, and maximum of a field over a selected set of records.

- Determine the distribution of records over a 1, 2, or 3 dimensional grid of fields. For example, number of customers by state by income range.

- Determine the distribution of aggregates (sum, average, minimum, and maximum) of a field over a 1, 2, or 3 dimensional grid of fields. For example, average age by state by income range.

- *Ad-hoc* RFM analyses.

- Draw contiguous batches or uniformly spaced samples of records.

- Calculate break-points in the distributions of records, e.g., deciles and quartiles.

Data Transformation

Data transformation capabilities include, but are not limited to, the following:

- Create number, date, and alpha fields using arbitrarily nested expressions involving other fields and constants.

- Create fields using conditional assignment of values drawn from other fields.

- Create and delete temporary tables and fields.

- Create label fields, that is, those with categorical values, such as income range.

- Convert fields from one type to another; for example, from *unsigned* to *alpha*.

- Sort a field in the order of another field.

- Remove duplicates in a field.

- Combine data from multiple tables using *join* and *group-join* operations. The latter can perform group counts, sums, averages, minimums, and maximums.

- Match data using a combination of *join* and *sort* operations.

Report Generation

- Reports are 2-dimensional grid of cells of sizes that are limited only by the available disk space. Report-related commands can be used to navigate in the grid and paste information in it.

- Cell values can be left aligned, right aligned, or centered.

- Distributions (of one, two, or three dimensions) can be pasted on the grid using crosstabs. For example, in a distribution of customers by state by income level, the state names would be placed along the rows on the left and income levels would be placed along the columns at the top.

- Row and column sums can be calculated from the distributions and placed on the report.

- Existing reports, fields from tables, and Unix files can also be pasted to make complex reports.

- Reports can be output in the ASCII form suitable for printing directly or in the quoted form suitable for importing into other programs such as Lotus 123.

Data Import and Export

Fast-Count DBMS accepts ASCII data in a variety of data formats including fixed or variable length records, with or without record terminator, with or with out repeating fields, etc. It also accepts binary data compatible with the Unix host.

It can export data in a variety of ASCII formats, including the database formats listed above and quoted and comma delimited formats.

In addition to ASCII data, Fast-Count DBMS can also import and export binary data compatible with the Unix host. This facility can be used to pass the required data to specialized processing algorithms outside the database and to import the results back into the database.

Programming Constructs

FCL provides the following programming constructs, which can be combined with other FCL commands to build complete applications or custom operations that can be invoked from the graphical user-interface.

- String macros.

- Global and local variables.

- If-then-else construct.

- While-do construct.

- Internal and external procedures, which are called in a stack-based execution environment.

- Access Shell variables.

- Invoke standard Unix utilities or other special-purpose programs.

* * *

□ Page 4 □

INDEX

About the Authors

David Shepard Associates has provided award-winning direct marketing and database consulting services to more than 100 direct marketing companies, advertisers, computer service bureaus, and *Fortune* 500 companies since 1976.

The company's client list has included such notable firms as Allstate Insurance, American Express, Ameritech, Caterpillar, Canadian Imperial Bank of Commerce, Dow Jones, Doubleday Direct, Gillette, Hallmark Cards, J.C. Penney Financial Services, Kraft General Foods, Newfield Publications, NOVUS, Pacific Care, Mercedes Benz North America, Service Merchandise, Scudder Stevens and Clark, SNET, Sotheby's, Time Insurance, and Vector Marketing.

Professionals with the firm are frequent speakers at direct mail conferences and other association functions in the United States, Europe, Asia, and Australia.